THE SOCIALIST REGISTER 1997

RUTHLESS CRITICISM OF ALL THAT EXISTS

SOCIALIST REGISTER 1997

Edited by LEO PANITCH

MERLIN PRESS LONDON
MONTHLY REVIEW PRESS NEW YORK
FERNWOOD PUBLISHING HALIFAX

First published in 1997
by The Merlin Press Ltd
2 Rendlesham Mews, Rendlesham
Nr. Woodbridge, Suffolk
IP12 2SZ

© The Merlin Press 1997

Published in the US by:
   Monthly Review Press
   122 West 27 Street
   New York
   NY 10001

Published in Canada by:
   Fernwood Publishing Co.
   P.O. Box 9409
   Station A
   Halifax
   Nova Scotia
   B3K 5S3

British Library Cataloguing in Publication Data

The Socialist Register. — 1997
   1. Socialism — 1997
   I. Panitch, Leo
   355'.005

ISBN 0-85036-466-3 (UK)
ISBN 0-85345-995-9 (US)

Typesetting by
Creative Print and Design, Harmondsworth, Middlesex

Printed in Finland by WSOY

TABLE OF CONTENTS

PREFACE

But if constructing the future and settling everything for all times are not our affair, it is all the more clear what we have to accomplish at present: I am referring to *ruthless criticism of all that exists*, ruthless both in the sense of not being afraid of the results it arrives at and in the sense of being just a little afraid of conflict with the powers that be . . .

This year's volume, the thirty-third, of *The Socialist Register* takes as its theme the phrase that Marx emphasized in the above quotation from a letter to his friend Arnold Ruge in 1843. The ideas expressed therein appear to us to be as relevant to socialists today as when they were first published in the Deutsch-Franzosiche Jahrbuche in 1844. (We rely on the translation offered in the Marx/Engels *Collected Works*, Volume 3, New York, International Publishers 1975, p. 142.) Perhaps they are even more relevant. We live in an era when capitalism stands astride the whole globe, the power of its ruling classes and the waste and inegalitarianism of its markets unregulated and unchallenged. Yet we also live in an era when, for the first time in well over a century, there are no significant political projects which articulate and campaign for a socialist alternative to capitalism. There is popular resistance, people continue to fight back, they hold on to values that assert our humanity in the face of global commodification. But one of the main contributions socialists can still make today, is to not shrink from a ruthless criticism of the limits of this resistance in so far as it is not socialist, even not yet fundamentally anti-capitalist; nor should we desist from criticising those socialists who still blithely imagine that every popular resistance has it in its genes to become socialist.

In the wake of the historic failure of Communism and the no less historic transformation of Social Democracy into a barely recognisable shadow of the ideas and movements that spawned it, and in the wake of the inability of the New Left to transform those parties or generate alternative socialist political formations of significant size and permanence, the very notion of a socialist future beyond capitalism has been pushed off the agenda. This is almost as much the case intellectually as it is politically. It has been hard for socialists to come to terms with the idea that

1

constructing the future is not their affair, in the sense of socialism not being something already present (that is, actually being constructed in Russia, or China, or Mozambique, or Nicaragua) or at least something imminent, a project we might actively embark on in our lifetimes. Socialists have often mixed up their own mortality with a timetable for, if not the realization of socialism, then at least the 'final conflict' with capitalism and the regimes of the old order. In this respect, the weight that was placed by some on electoral victories and welfare statist reforms as having laid the foundations for the construction of the future proved as delusionary as the weight placed on insurrection and vanguardism by others. Recognising these delusions has driven many erstwhile socialists into a stoic realism which not only accomodates itself to capitalism as a system but in the process ignores or covers over its immoralities, exploitations and contradictions. After all, what is the point of raising these, if constructing the future is not our affair?

If we can divest ourselves of the hubris of tying our own mortality to the construction of the future, however, the point becomes quite clear. The point is to continue to play a role in ensuring that, as the Communist Manifesto put it: '. . . man is at last compelled to face with sober senses his real conditions of life and his relations with his kind.' We need, more than ever, to draw on socialist values and analysis to undertake a ruthless criticism of what exists today, so the ground may be cleared to rebuild socialist projects tomorrow. The greatest tragedy of the failure of socialism in this century would be the loss of these values and this analysis at the very time when popular resistence from Korea to Canada refuses to go away, in spite of capitalism's greatest cultural, political and spatial reach. Ruthless criticism is, therefore, not a matter of striking a pose as mere 'critics'. On the contrary, it is to insist on the need for the most searching analysis, groping for understanding – critique in the proper sense – without fear of being thrown off by the charge that such analysis is invalid without an immediate answer to 'there is no alternative.' What we know now, more clearly than ever, is that what is on offer, by either neoliberalism or social democracy today, does not provide solutions to contemporary capitalism's problems and injustices, let alone acceptable alternatives in terms of socialist goals and values.

Last year's volume posed the sober question of 'Are There Alternatives?', rather than blithely asserting that there are alternatives, precisely because we are aware that genuine alternatives cannot be constructed out of thin air. A large part of our purpose in that volume was to show that what is presented by way of alternatives to neoliberalism in the present conjuncture are nothing of the sort precisely because they are captured within the very contradictions and dynamics that gave rise to neoliberalism. We extend that orientation in this volume. The essays in this volume undertake sober analysis and ruthless criticism of the dynamics, depredations and contradictions of today's global capitalism; of the abject accomodation to it by ertswhile Communists, Social Democrats and Liberals; of the failed socialist and 'new left' movements over the past century; and, not least, of the defeatist and confused 'post-' intellectuals of our time, who would leave us with no analytic capacity, let alone with no commitment, with which to contribute today to the eventual relaunching of socialist politics.

Among our contributors, Gregory Albo teaches political science at York University, Toronto. Elmar Altvater is Professor of Political Science at the Free University of Berlin. Larry Pratt teaches political science at the University of Alberta, in Edmonton, Canada and Wendy Montgomery is a graduate of that University. Gerard Greenfield is Research Co-ordinator of the Asia Monitor Resource Centre in Hong Kong and Apo Leong is the Director of that Centre. George Ross is the Morris Hillquit Professor in Labor and Social Thought at Brandeis University, Boston. Barbara Epstein teaches in the Department of History of Consciousness at the University of California, Santa Cruz; and Doug Henwood is the Editor of the *Left Business Observer*, New York. Joan Smith is Reader in the School of Social Sciences, Staffordshire University; and Paul Cammack teaches in the Department of Government, Manchester University. Vicente Navarro is Professor of Public Policy at Johns Hopkins University, Baltimore and of Political and Social Sciences at the Universitat Pompeu Fabra, Barcelona. Ananya Mukherjee-Reed teaches in the Department of Political Science at York University, Toronto; and Scott Forsyth is in the Film and Video Department of the Faculty of Fine Arts at that University. Scott McCracken teaches in the Department of English at the University of Salford in Salford, England; and Meera Nanda is in the Department of Science and Technology Studies at the Rensselaer Polytechnic Institute in Troy, New York. Aijaz Ahmad is Professorial Fellow at the Centre of Contemporary Studies, Nehru Memorial Museum and Library, New Dehli.

I want to express my appreciation to all the contributors for the effort they put into their essays for this volume. Thanks are also due to Nicholas C. F. Hubble of the Institute for German Studies at the University of Birmingham for the translation of Elmar Altvater's essay. This is the second volume of *The Socialist Register* to be produced with the help of the editorial collectives in Manchester and Toronto, and I want to express my gratitude to Greg Albo, Paul Cammack, Sam Gindin, Judy Hellman, John Saul, Reg Whitaker, Ellen Wood and, above all, to David Coates for the active role they played in making this volume possible. Nor would this volume have been possible without the commitment and help of my research assistant at York University, Alan Zuege, for which I am very grateful. As I also am to Julie Millard and Martin Eve at Merlin Press, who have, as always, have been unfailing in the support and energy they put into *The Socialist Register*.

It is our long-standing tradition to remind the readers that neither our contributors nor the editors necessarily agree with everything that appears in the volume. On this occasion I should also like to point out that the essay, 'How It All Began: A Footnote To History' by Marion Kozak in the 1995 *Socialist Register* requires some correction and qualification as regards comments made about Walter Greendale. This stauch industrial militant and committed socialist from Hull, England who became lay chairman (president) of the TGWU, and one of that union's representatives on the TUC General Council, was mistakenly referred to as 'Greenald', and did not attend the *New Reasoner and Universities and Left Review* Industrial Conference in Leeds in November 1958; nor was he ever a member of the Communist Party. This last was not stated in the essay, but might possibly be inferred from the context. Our apologies.

February 1997   *L.P.*

A WORLD MARKET OF OPPORTUNITIES?
CAPITALIST OBSTACLES AND LEFT
ECONOMIC POLICY

Gregory Albo

As Ralph Miliband observed in his last book, *Socialism for a Sceptical Age*, the socialist project for a radical social order of equality has rested on two central propositions: capitalism constitutes a massive obstacle to resolving a range of social evils and injustices; a socialist alternative makes possible a resolution of these offences and inequities.[1] The pessimism that infuses the Left at the end of the century is founded, in the first instance, in the reassessment of capitalist market processes as more efficient in meeting human needs than previously conceded and, moreover, capable of extensive institutional variation so as to allow egalitarian policy outcomes without confronting capitalist social power. Economic efficiency can be combined with social equity.

It is further argued that socialist economic policy is, in any case, no longer capable – if it ever was – of advancing solutions to the injustices of capitalist markets (let alone of offering a plausible alternative social order). This political qua policy impotence is due, in large measure, to the formation of a world economy that provides an overwhelming external constraint to policies that are inconsistent with the *irreversible* processes of globalisation. The crisis years after 1974 have ceded, moreover, to an era of *restabilized* capitalism, ascendant and embraced in all corners of the world. So even if there is a margin of manoeuverability for national economic policies, as Paul Hirst and Grahame Thompson assert (to cite a much noted recent example), this is merely a question of further building 'extra-market institutions' to manage the new conjuncture as capitalist markets have proven their greater inherent efficiency and dynamism.[2] If there are *injustices* still residing in capitalism, and even New Labour concedes there are, these are best resolved by measures that work with rather than against markets. Egalitarian policy measures should thus only seek to equalize market opportunities through widening the 'stakes' in capitalist enterprises via employee share ownership plans, self-employment initiatives, life-long training accounts, and the like.[3] To

5

uphold socialist propositions in the face of the prevailing political consensus is, as Miliband himself recognized of the predictable charge, 'to demonstrate a lamentable lack of realism.'[4]

In the advanced capitalist countries, this broad disillusionment with Left economic policy is deeply entwined with the last two decades of social democratic setback and retreat followed by further openings to the disciplines of neoliberalism and the world economy. The electorally most successful case of social democratic governance over this period, the example of Australian Labor, has only offered, in the brilliant analysis of John Wiseman, a 'kinder road to hell' of cutbacks and austerity in its efforts to recast itself as an 'East Asian capitalism.'[5] Labor's defeat at the polls in 1996 promises to veer Australia down the even more treacherous path of neoliberal austerity in a desperate effort to maintain a faltering external competitiveness. The postwar social democratic strongholds of Austria and Sweden have their governments extensively scaling back their welfare states, disposing state enterprises and adopting the neoliberal policy stance of economic openness and flexible labour markets. With the external sector bursting from capital outflows and unemployment at pan-European levels, it cannot seriously be maintained, as so many on the Left still attempted to do even during its 1980s breakup, that the Swedish model is still alive and prospering.[6] A similar story could be told of the Rhineland Model of Germany, which has all of Sweden's problems and others. Its 'concertation capitalism' has witnessed over the last year increasingly ferocious efforts by employers to scale back employee benefits and involvement. Ever alert to new opportunities to proclaim that the legacy of reform is being cast aside, New Labour's Tony Blair, on a visit to Wall Street in April 1996, drew the lessons from these experiences that a social democratic Britain 'must be competitive internationally to help attract international business investment. I am a passionate free trader and unashamed anti-protectionist.'[7]

The divergent economic trajectories after 1974 that first seemed to characterize social democratic governments like Sweden's and technologically-ascendant economies like Germany's now only seem to be alternate routes converging in neoliberalism. Indeed, the varied experiences of the 'previously existing socialisms' of Eastern Europe and the anti-imperialist nationalisms of the Third World also appear to represent no more than circuitous and calamitous routes to ending up on the same capitalist road. The world economy in the 1990s accommodates, it seems, only one model of development: export-oriented production based on flexible labour markets, lower real and social wages, less environmental regulation and freer trade. Neoliberal economic strategies are proposed for political and economic conditions as vastly different as those faced by the new ANC government in South Africa, the Forza Italia centre-Left coalition and transitional economies like the Czech Republic and Hungary.

These concessions to the imperatives of the law of value in the world market – 'we are powerless, there is no alternative' – has been met with a mixture of rejoicing and submission. The leading neoliberal periodical, *The Economist*, has exulted in the transformation so that today – without even a hint of reflexive irony – the central political 'challenge is to help the global capital market to become more effective in encouraging good behaviour [by governments].'[8] The 'shock therapy' strategy for integration into the world economy is simply, as its foremost strategist Jeffrey Sachs puts it, the most efficient means to gain the 'organizational methods and financial capital needed to overcome the dismal economic legacy of the past forty years.'[9]

The Left has met these developments with far more resignation but with the same sense of inevitability. A stalwart American liberal such as Robert Reich baldly concludes that 'as almost every factor of production ... moves effortlessly across borders, the very idea of an American economy is becoming meaningless.'[10] Fritz Scharpf, a leading strategist of the German SDP, voices what is often convention on the Left that 'unlike the situation of the first three postwar decades, there is now no economically plausible Keynesian strategy that would permit the full realisation of social democratic goals within a national context without violating the functional imperatives of a capitalist economy.'[11] Social democracy must rethink its traditional aspirations to accommodate the new imperatives of global capitalism to maintain, at least, 'socialism in one class.' The only egalitarian policy that it is possible to pursue in the context of internationally mobile capital – and Scharpf is more ambitious than most – is one that redistributes income and jobs among workers as 'growth rates are inadequate and because the distributive claims that capital is able to realize have increased.'[12]

Yet, to make any sense of these formulations, a further set of premises must be held. The present geographical expansion of accumulation must be seen, for instance, as an *irreversible* process that reflects economic dynamism and stability supplanting instability and crisis. It must be argued additionally that any specific *constraints* to economic *stability* can be overcome by policies that further expand global market opportunities.[13] Neoliberals argue for free trade and the deregulation of labour markets as the means to surpass the constraint of limited markets; social democrats opt for policies to train an insufficiently skilled workforce to overcome market constraints on labour adjustment. Within these confines economic policy disputes do indeed go 'beyond Left and Right,' as Anthony Giddens phrases it; they are limited to the issue of which specific constraint should be acted upon and the relative speed of flexible adjustment of market processes.[14] But no one disputes that flexible adjustment of markets will eventually occur to allow the harvest of globalisation to be reaped.

A final premise is that capitalist globalisation represents a historically *progressive* development such that traditional socialist economic objectives, on grounds of political necessity and economic soundness, must be rejected as hopelessly flawed. There is no political need for the Left to put forward policies that encroach upon capitalist social property relations beyond that of a 'stakeholders' capitalism.'[15] Indeed, the principal struggle for socialists today, as writers from as diverse methodological backgrounds as Andrew Gamble and John Roemer have advised, should be limited to the Pareto-optimal distribution of 'ownership rights' between workers and capitalists in internationally competitive enterprises.[16]

There is good reason, however, to at least qualify, perhaps even to reject, each of these premises about internationalisation. This essay will, first, briefly recall the instabilities that still reside at the centre of the world economy and the limitations of neoliberal adjustment measures. It will then question the claims made by social democratic economic policy advocates that only *specific constraints* need to be overcome to re-establish stability, concluding that Miliband's first proposition on the obstacles that capitalism poses *as a system* cannot be relinquished. Finally, an outline of emerging alternative principles for socialist economic policy to confront these obstacles and constraints will be presented. Rather than a world economy being a new opportunity, contemporary internationalisation of markets is a contradictory 'space of flows' between the 'spaces of places of production' that are constituted by the specific territorially-embedded conflictual social property relations of capitalism.[17] The economic programme of the Left cannot, following Miliband's second proposition, put to the side questions of market disengagement and the democratic organisational forms that will permit the *transition* to a more fundamentally egalitarian and co-operative economy.

I. Neoliberalism and Imbalances in the World Economy

The neoliberal claim that market exchanges always tend to arrive at equilibrium depends upon a number of highly abstract assumptions; it is embedded in deductive models which, however rigorous, are set outside of concrete time and space. The neoliberal position begins from the proposition that overcoming the constraint of *limited markets* is central to resolving unemployment and trade imbalances. Capitalism is an economic system best understood as a process of free individual exchange operating in competitive markets. According to individual behavioural preferences, *individual* economic agents save, innovate and form firms to purchase labour; others prefer leisure, consumption and sell to their labour. In accord with the famous law of Say, all demand is effective demand; and if prices are not constrained flexible adjustment in competitive markets will ensure that all needs are satisfied and all markets clear. Unemployment is the 'mutual' and 'voluntary' product of limitations of local labour market flexibility and the global competitiveness of firms. The role of trade in expanding market opportunities and reallocating resources on the basis of Ricardian comparative advantage – that is, specialization in production where relative cost advantage is highest produces shared output gains for trading nations – depends on free trade in commodities and financial liberalisation to ensure that 'savings are directed to the most productive investments without regard for national boundaries.'[18] Globalisation is, in other words, capitalism surpassing the limited market constraint on the division of labour: it is a market of expanding opportunities.

There are many angles from which to address strong objections to this idealised view of market processes always balancing. An unemployed worker willing to work for a lower real wage, for example, does not itself lead to a job offer – at least not without resistance from existing employees whose jobs he may take away or whose wages may be cut. From the firm's perspective, given the incompleteness of market information, a low wage offer often signals lower labour quality and hence a less employable candidate. Such lack of flexible prices in the real world raises, of course, the traditional Keynesian argument that decreasing real wages in rigid labour markets not only fails to increase employment, but it also takes demand out of the system causing a further increase in the jobless. This is not to say that wage-cutting does not occur as unemployment levels rise, but that quantity adjustments are as important as price movements so that market-clearing is unlikely to be smooth and instabilities may be compounded. The trends claimed to have caused the real wage rigidity of the 1970s – demographic bulge, welfare and unemployment insurance rates, trade unionization – have been reversed and inflation has fallen to some of its lowest levels in over half a century but OECD area unemployed reserves remain high and climbing. As David Gordon acidly noted, it is more accurate to speak of a 'rising natural rate of unemployment' with no acceptable neoliberal explanation, except the preposterous notion of an exogenous shift in the preference functions of individuals toward more unemployment.[19]

The existence of unemployment, whether from wage rigidities or information asymmetries, poses a serious problem for free trade policy. For comparative advantage to hold each country is *assumed* to have full employment and to be producing on their production possibility frontier, that factors of production are completely mobile internally and subject to perfect competition, that monetary fluctuations do not occur and trade is balanced. None of these, of course, are real world assumptions. Predictions from free trade theory, such as output and employment smoothly expanding in new export sectors, or no country consistently running surpluses or deficits, have only the most brittle historical foundation: they are only assertions that in the long run it will all work out.[20] The case for protectionism, or at least for the regulation of trade, is on stronger theoretical grounds purely in terms of employment considerations alone. Even granting all the assumptions necessary for static gains from trade, trade balance depends upon processes of adjustment occurring in actual societies and through history: workers everywhere must have the capacity to raise wages and rates of technical progress must equalise over time or else competitive advantage and trade surplus will become cumulative, raising structural trade imbalances and problems of employment in deficit countries. The deficit country with strong trade unions and high money wages will be forced to adjust, but not the surplus country with weak unions and low wages. It is always difficult to impose appreciation or expenditure increases on surplus countries, as the U.S.-Japan trade rivalry over the last decade indicates. There is instead a tendency for competing countries to match devaluation and austerity to avoid large losses. Indeed, this becomes an imperative as economies become more open. In other words, trade liberalisation, especially in a climate of uncertainty and unemployment, tends to reproduce the same effects as protection: everybody attempts to export unemployment but now through competitive austerity which limits domestic demand for imports and improves the price of exports.

While international exchanges have grown tremendously, vastly outstripping the growth of the real economy, the argument that global markets 'provide healthy discipline which in the long term will encourage better economic policies and performance'[21] cannot be sustained in the face of growing evidence of unevenness and instability rather than equalization and equilibration. Economic openness as measured by dependence on exports has increased from under 30 per cent in 1950 to almost 40 per cent by 1994 in the six largest OECD countries, with trade volumes in the U.S. alone doubling since the early 1970s. Structural trade imbalances have become a key feature of the world economy. The Third World debt crisis remains unresolved: total debt levels have continued to rise, and debt servicing in terms of GDP remains where it was when the debt crisis began in the early 1980s. As important for global imbalances, the structural current account deficit that the U.S. has been running since the early 1980s has made it the largest debtor in history. In contrast, Asia and Japan in particular have been running current surpluses. The clearest measure of the problem is that financial flows, in all forms increasing exponentially over and above trade volumes, have assumed ever greater salience in any calculation of global economic activity. International banking, for example, at the peak of the boom in the 1960s accounted at about 1 per cent of GDP of market economies while it now measures more than 20 per cent. Foreign exchange transactions are exceeding $1 trillion U.S. *daily* reflecting an explosion in speculation in global equity, bond and currency markets.

Financial movements of this order are completely out of any rational balance when trade volumes are only $3.5 trillion *yearly*. These trends certainly indicate a growth in interdependence of production zones through economic flows, but as much as a symptom of disarray, instability and stagnation as of dynamism.

As the economic crisis developed from the 1970s into the 1980s, the advanced capitalist countries turned to policies of disinflation.[22] International trade became a competitive battle for market share and unit labour costs in a futile effort to maintain domestic employment. The mounting trade deficits of many countries – which floating exchange rates were promised to stabilize but failed miserably – were added to fiscal deficits arising from slow growth. As Paul Sweezy has argued, the financing of these deficits meant that international credit markets boomed but increasingly apart, and often directly at odds, from developments in the real economy.[23] Yet rather than stabilize aggregate demand or the external sector, by the mid-80s all the advanced countries had begun to adopt supply-side polices of cutting wages and welfare, adding competitive capacity and financial liberalization. Third World countries went through a similar process of structural adjustment as import-substitution industrial-ization policies were abandoned for export ones to pay off credits. In other words, all countries were putting more resources into the external sector while cutting domestic demand. This could only increase volatility in the international market and the capacity of interdependent financial markets to transfer swiftly any economic instability across the world economy. In the 1990s most Latin American and African economies continue to be extremely depressed. All economies in Eastern Europe remain well below the pre-shock therapy output peaks of the 1980s. Stagnant growth and wage depression encompass all the advanced countries, including Northern Europe and Japan. Yet even more resources are being redeployed to the external sector at the same time as austerity policies dominate corporate wage-setting and government economic strategies.

We should be extremely careful to avoid attempting to explain every recent turn – from the collapse of state plans in India to unemployment protests in Paris to the defeat of a universal health plan in the U.S. – in terms of the forces of globalisation. It is difficult not to record, however, that a stable alternative for capitalist expansion is far from being achieved. Yet the imperatives of the world economy compel that this unstable process be kept going. Nobody is willing to break ranks first, which is under-standable in light of the sanctions that would be viciously meted out by global markets. But this is not warrant to engage in the pretence that imbal-ances are being overcome, that neoliberal policies are theoretically coherent, that globalisation is irreversible or that labour market adjustment is producing socially just outcomes.

II. Open-Economy Social Democracy

The problems associated with market adjustment to imbalances of trade or unemployment have a lot to do with the fact that economic processes occur in real historical time rather than the timeless space of neoliberal equilibrium models. In discussing the future of the international payments system after the war, Keynes charged that 'to suppose that there exists some smoothly functioning automatic mechanism of adjustment that preserves equilibrium if only we trust to methods of laissez-fare is a doctrinaire delusion which disregards the lessons of historical experience without having behind it the support of sound theory.'[24] In the real world, capitalist techniques and workers' wage demands do not alter instantly with excess labour supply; currency devaluation does not necessarily produce expenditure-switching to domestic industry or export demand: in the Keynesian view, relative price adjustments to restore equilibrium take time to work themselves out in a world of uncertainty.

According to social democratic economic policy, the temporal processes of adjustment signify that the market needs to be governed by managing the *specific* constraints impeding capitalism from reaching the full employment volumes of output that is to the benefit of all, capitalists and workers.[25] This is the central – and ultimately conservative – message of Keynes' *General Theory*: 'if effective demand is deficient, not only is the public scandal of wasted resources intolerable, but the individual enterpriser who seeks to bring these resources into action is operating with the odds loaded against him.'[26] In the postwar period this meant that capitalists had to support a 'national bargain' over taxes and investment, and workers had to endorse public consumption and to set nominal wages so as to control inflation to maintain external balance and a positive sum game of high profits, high employment and rising incomes.[27] Within the capitalist bloc, the Bretton Woods system emphasis on national adjustment helped, as did the low trade volumes and partial controls over capital mobility left over from the era of depression and war. Temporary import controls, wage restraint through incomes policies or realignment of pegged currencies was enough to restore adequate payments balance. It was thought – in perhaps the most egregious of bourgeois modernism's faith in progress through quantity – that with the release of the constraint on demand growth could be endless (and that planetary ecology could take care of itself). The distributional relations necessary for high employment, however, have not been so easily found since the 1970s. Slow growth and declining productivity has meant that capitalists have been less willing to accept the old Keynesian 'national bargain' between the social classes. In order to restore profits, high unemployment rather than incomes policy has kept wage claims in check. Internationalization of production, too, has strengthened the leverage of capitalists to bargain wage restraint and rollbacks with unions, especially as the various GATT rounds lowered trade tariffs, and low wage production zones such as Korea and Brazil gained technological capacity and foreign investment. All this added to the competitive export pressures already internal to the advanced capitalist bloc. The social democratic experience of Sweden is telling: although developing the foremost 'social market' and raising its relative competitive position, Sweden has had an 'employer offensive' for over a decade to lower real wages, cut taxes and allow unemployment to rise. Direct investment by Swedish capitalists abroad has increased from below 1 per cent of GDP in 1982 to above 6 per cent by 1990, and it continues to rise.[28] Andrew Glyn now notes that 'Sweden has joined the rush towards stabilisation and explicit anti-egalitarianism as the route to economic recovery.'[29] Nowhere does the old social democratic positive-sum national compromise within a constraint-freed capitalism still hold.

As a consequence, the social democratic 'rethink' of economic policy for an alternative to neoliberalism has had to address the three options that must confront all Left economic policy. First, an attempt could be made to counter internationalisation by controlling capital mobility, by protecting domestic producers and employment through controls over the traded sector and by building alternative planning mechanisms all the way from the local to the international spheres. Second, national stabilisation policies could try to maintain the welfare state, establish a competitive exchange rate to insulate domestic compromises and redistribute a more slowly growing output and income so as to keep unemployment down (although in consequence likely allowing national competitiveness to fall relative to less egalitarian countries willing to lower unit labour costs more directly). Finally, the challenge of the world market could be met head-on by attempting to raise national competitiveness relative to competitors through improving workplace productivity by involving highly-skilled workers, by adopting new production techniques and by developing new products for export.

The first option is closest to traditional socialist orientations (although it could vary tremendously in methods and ends) and would entail confronting the disembedded processes of the world market. It would, no doubt, alarm domestic and foreign capitalists, the consequences of which in a global market could be massively disruptive for individual states accepting the challenge. In the eyes of social democratic policy-makers (at least since the defeat of the Left inside social democratic parties in the early 1980s), this has never really been an option. Social democratic policy had already come to accept internationalisation of economic flows over the postwar period and this has been a parameter that social democratic leaders have not wanted to breach, above all because they know that capitalists would actively oppose it. The second strategy is closest to postwar social democracy, and it once was plausible for countries with large and solidaristic unions. But such 'shared austerity' is entirely defensive in posture and increasingly difficult to sustain as external pressures increase and relative economic decline takes hold. There is, in any respect, little fondness any longer amongst capitalists for such a strategy as it keeps in check their market power relative to workers and closes off the option of higher unemployment for external competitiveness. The third option of forming an 'open-economy social democracy' amounts to a more offensive strategy, which, through the promises of increased productivity and output, would possibly re-found the positive-sum compromise between the social classes.[30] This strategy has special appeal because it suggests that there is something 'activist' social democratic governments can do to protect the 'national interest.' If markets are imperfect historical processes, labour adjustment, trade flows and international specialization cannot be left to the working out of comparative advantage through free trade: states can and must help 'shape advantage' to improve labour market performance, trade balance and competitiveness.[31] Some workers and some capitalists might, under the right conditions, even favour this third strategy of launching a 'stakeholders' capitalism.'

The case for a social democratic economic policy of national competitiveness has, moreover, a basis in the theoretical critique being advanced against the pure Ricardian trade theory of neoliberalism. One aspect comes from within the confines of general equilibrium theory itself.[32] That is, if imperfect competition and economies of scale are introduced into international trade models, then 'extra profit' can be gained for exporting industries as price will exceed marginal cost. In these cases, it cannot be ruled out that state intervention into industry may improve national economic welfare and domestic output. In industries with technological spillovers to other sectors or that may earn technological rents by protecting their initial product development the case is even somewhat stronger. New industries, for example, often require protection before they can face import competition. Historical precedence and increasing returns to scale can 'lock-in' market share before rivals gain a chance to develop. In this way, the technically superior BETA recorders lost out in the capitalist marketplace to the less capable VHS in the early 1980s. The earlier QWERTY typewriter case and the massive aerospace complex around Seattle are other oft-cited examples. It is possible, in other words, to have a 'strategic trade policy' to get new products developed and into markets as quickly as possible to maximize the profit-shift between countries. Thus even within general equilibrium theory states can 'logically' adopt protective tariffs and industrial policies that depart from free markets and comparative advantage: the ideologically contentious question is whether or not they are politically successful in choosing indus-

trial winners.³³ For liberals, like Paul Krugman, the answer is no and the
case for free trade stands.³⁴ For social democrats, like Robert Kuttner, the
answer is yes and the German and East Asian experiences suggest an alternative approach.³⁵

The social democratic case for shaped advantage can be bolstered once
the general equilibrium model of individual agent market exchanges is let
go, and alliances of competing states and firms are explicitly allowed to
shape the 'path-dependency' of economic outcomes. That is, 'history
matters' to economics. If the income elasticities of various commodities
diverge through time, for example, as the early dependency theory critique
of Raul Prebisch argued for primary commodities relative to manufactured
goods, price divergence and growth polarisation may well occur.³⁶ For
countries locked into the production and trade of declining commodities,
initial competitive advantage becomes an obstacle to future competitive
viability. Shaped advantage can also be invoked to explain something about
more general processes of economic decline and ascendancy that has historically shifted the places of states in the world economic hierarchy. Countries
losing technological capacity, it is argued, can suffer the economic misfor-
tunes vividly depicted by Britain's fall in world standing. In this case, every
attempt at demand expansion by a 'weak' country to raise output 'to catch-
up' ends in an economic policy 'stop' to avert a looming balance of
payments crisis as high demand sucks in imports. A vicious cycle of stop-
go keeps investment in check over the historical long-run because sustained
high investment requires stable growth. But depreciation does not correct
the underlying productivity differences and thus the reason for the imbalances. As a result, competitiveness increasingly comes to depend upon low
cost production or continual competitive devaluations as new technical
capacity is blocked from being built. In contrast, technologically ascendant
competitors can continue to keep investment high in new techniques as this
only adds to output capacity thereby enhancing the payments position and
competitive advantage over the long-run.

This conception of 'cumulative causation', in which trade volumes and
export and import propensities impact upon aggregate demand,
unemployment and competitiveness, becomes more critical the more that
states have large open sectors.³⁷ Competitive performance holds the
potential for competitive advantage (or disadvantage) and higher levels of
employment (or unemployment). In a liberalised world trading system, the
competitive pressures to achieve advantage intensify as technical development and product specialization spread in a continual process of
imitation and innovation, of 'catching-up', 'forging-ahead' and 'falling
behind'. The implications of this point – so central to the programmatic
designs of national competitiveness and the project of 'stakeholders'
capitalism' – need to be underlined. In this view, trade occurs not based on

'differential endowments' of the factors of production, but rather on the basis of 'country-specific conditions of technological learning and accumulation.'[38] The conditions that define national (or regional) competitiveness can be summarised as the input efficiencies derived from product quality, workplace 'trust' between workers and employers, 'learning-by-doing' and research effort. As technological change is a continual process of building up technical skills capacity and entrepreneurship, a 'Schumpeterian technological dynamism' needs to be nourished as an overarching societal policy objective.[39] In open economies, therefore, economic growth and unemployment levels are increasingly dependent upon world market share and export capacity derived from relative competitive advantage in the world hierarchy of competing nations. The social democratic redistributional agenda of the 'mixed economy' is thus succeeded by the 'mixed enterprise economy' of 'stakeholders' capitalism' that is at the core of open-economy social democracy. It is also what lies behind the conclusion, stated here by the British centre-Left Institute for Public Policy Research but held across social democratic parties, that 'globalisation offers more opportunities than threats for British business, people and government.'[40]

There are several competing social democratic positions – though to some extent they complement each other – on how shaped advantage can be supplemented to meet also the internal balance of employment (while keeping unit labour costs competitive for external balance). The 'progressive competitiveness' strategy, most closely allied to the views of shaped advantage, emphasises the demand-side *external* constraint produced by internationalisation. Social democratic employment policy should, therefore, concern itself with the growth of productive capacities (or effective supply) so as to keep unit labour costs low by productivity gains rather than low wages. Productive capacities are, according to Wolfgang Streeck, productivity-enhancing collective goods such as training, research and development and workplace trust that encourage flexible adjustment of production and labour supply to externally set demand conditions.[41] The problem, however, is that the market fails to provide an adequate supply of these collective goods and creates needless conflicts over the need for joint governance between capital and labour in their production. Yet, in fact, they form the national basis of competitiveness in high-waged high value-added economies. Training policies should, therefore, be the central component of a jobs and welfare strategy, while relationships of 'trust' and co-operation should be fostered within enterprises through works councils and other forms of 'associative democracy.' A strategy of effective supply can contribute, Joel Rogers and Streeck insist, to the 'restoration of competitiveness in western capitalism ... [and] can establish a new bargain between equity and efficiency.'[42]

Another variant of the social democratic strategy is that of 'shared austerity.' It stresses that the *internal* constraint of distribution relations is critical. Incomes policy has a role to play in spreading work through wage restraint and keeping unit labour costs down for exports. For Andrea Boltho, the highly centralized collective bargaining institutions of the corporatist countries 'lead to a much greater responsiveness of real wages to unfavourable shocks ... [lessening] their destructive effect on unemployment.'[43] Thus the control of inflation for export position falls on corporatist labour market institutions. These institutions also provide the basis, according to Andrew Glyn, for the solidaristic income and tax policies that allow 'employment-spreading' of capitalist sector work and income and the financing of public sector employment. 'In a context of weak private demand and slow productivity growth, maintaining full employment required severe restraint on workers' pay and consumption to keep exports competitive, investment profitable and the budget under control. Where social democracy was capable of mobilizing such support, full employment was sustainable.' Glyn argues that in today's world the key issue is not economic openness, but rather the need to re-establish these mechanisms 'for regulating conflicting claims over distribution and control.'[44] But given that the key distributional compromise today excludes the capitalist class, high employment depends upon the collective capacity of trade unions (supported by social democratic parties) to impose restraint on their members – 'shared austerity in one class'.

A third position, the 'international Keynesian' perspective, maintains that removing the demand constraint of an open-economy simply requires the *political will* to re-establish expansionary policies at the supranational level where leakages to exports and capital outflows would be irrelevant and where competitive firms could realize the additional output through exports. This was the view some on the Labour Left arrived at in the aftermath of the Mitterand 'U-turn' in France in the early 1980s.[45] As bluntly stated recently by David Held: 'government economic policy must to a large degree be compatible with the regional and global movements of capital, unless a national government wishes to risk serious dislocation between its policy objectives and the flows of the wider international economy.'[46] International co-ordination of economic policy is, therefore, required to re-establish the basis for adequate effective demand conditions for higher growth and lower unemployment that are now beyond the capacity of any single state. A 'cosmopolitan democracy' imposed on global governance structures, of the kind favoured by Held, would be one means to legitimate the rules of international economic co-ordination.

All these views avoid the neoliberal illusions that free trade and deregulation of labour markets will resolve trade and employment balances. There is an understanding here of the processes of cumulative causation, of the interaction between internal and external imbalances, of actual contemporary trade patterns and the comparative cost advantage of various competitive capitals, the differentiation of development amongst regions, and of the variable means by which employment may be spread. Unfortunately (but all too common among progressive economists), as Leo Panitch has pointed out, there is little analysis of why social democratic governments have instead gone so far to accommodate neoliberalism.[47] The answer may lie, as he suggests, in the *inadequacy* of the strategy of shaped advantage. For the fact is that it fails to adequately account for the mechanisms behind the constraints on governments and thus the obstacles capitalism poses to stabilizing the imbalances resident in the world market.

First, let us consider the treatment of the growing reserve army of unemployed.[48] Unemployment is regarded as the result of the rate of accumulation generated by competitive capacity and demand conditions. Employment must then be a constant coefficient of average labour required per unit of output. Shaped advantage to improve competitive capacity, however, will lower this coefficient through labour-saving technological change (the basic form of technical change within capitalism). If work-hours and employment ratios are left constant despite technical advance, there must be an increase in total income and total employment hours demanded to compensate for the labour-saving per unit of output otherwise unemployment will increase. This 'knife-edge' balance was difficult to maintain in even the conditions of the 'golden age.'[49] But when the strategy must be implemented in our actual historical time and with the expectation that external trade will increase relative to domestic output, it becomes fanciful to imagine that this balance can be achieved.

Indeed, growth in trade will need to exceed the growth rate of output, which must itself exceed the combined growth rates of productivity and employment to absorb the many forms of the reserves of unemployed. Moreover, as technological change continues through time (notably in the traded goods sector whose advantage is being shaped), the growth of trade must continue at an accelerating rate to generate a given volume of employment and hours of work. In a stable world economy with a co-ordinated international macroeconomic policy it is extremely dubious that this would all work out; in a capitalism that generates differentiated competitive capacities and that is exhibiting the trade asymmetries and currency instability that exist today, it is quite impossible to envision. Shaped trade advantage to improve external competitiveness in the hope that trade growth will overcome internal obstacles to high employment is no substitute for national and local employment policies to constrain the capitalist market.[50]

Apart from the issue of unemployment, a second fundamental problem is an equally questionable presumption that shaped advantage offers a solution to the external imbalances that derive from the uneven development of competitive capacities within capitalism. Indeed, the reliance on market adjustment may well compound global external imbalances by the competitive imperatives of shaped advantage in the present world configuration. Let us further consider the obstacles capitalism presents just on the basis of developing the theme of uneven competitive capacities as it relates to individual country strategies. At the conceptual level, a trade surplus presupposes unit labour costs and hence export prices that are internationally competitive. Countries of successful export-led growth can sustain high investment without fear of a balance of payments crisis. The trade surplus is expected, moreover, to have positive effects on national income and employment. If the profit from full capacity utilization is reinvested in new technological capacity, and exchange rates do a poor job of equilibriating trade balance through appreciation, then economic growth and competitiveness will be maintained through decline in unit labour costs from productivity advance in surplus countries.[51] The point is, however, that *the opposite will be the case for deficit countries which will have listless investment and faltering technological capacity*. This seems to explain in good part the consistency of countries in structural current account deficit and declining competitive capacity such as Britain and the U.S., in relation to countries such as Germany and Japan that have been relatively in constant surplus. In other words, uneven development and trade imbalances can be expected to persist as one of the normal obstacles capitalism presents to alignment of market-friendly development trajectories.[52]

For individual technologically laggard countries, then, the problem is to rupture the vicious circle of stagnation before it perpetuates chronic relative decline or even the potential falling per capita incomes of absolute peripheralization. The strategy of shaped advantage proposes to convert the institutional structures and social relations that have fostered a particular model of development over time into a new development model of national (or regional) competitiveness. Strengthening competitive capacity will require, for example, a shift in existing resources out of present usage (and they may still be at maximum usage even if relatively uncompetitive) or mobilisation of unused resources if unemployment exists or plant is laying idle. This investment shift would, then, entail a 'collective' decision either to lower wages, to reduce public consumption or to tax the financial and productive sectors to raise capital. The investment in new capacity, moreover, would have to be planned and investment banks of considerable size and dynamism established to push through the industrial policy programme. All of this requires a great degree of non-market co-ordination and political mobilisation. This raises all the well-known problems of attempting to graft an economic model (or set of technologies) from one institutional context to another: the existing social relations and geographies of production provide an enormous obstacle to mobilization in new production sectors and work relations.[53]

This is what we can call the 'capitalist reformer's dilemma': market-led processes will tend to reinforce the existing patterns that are judged to be inadequate, but state-led projects will run up against embedded market power and institutionalised rules of co-ordination of economic policy yet require the co-operation of the actors that command these resources. There may thus be no co-operative political foundation for the project of shaped advantage from the capitalist classes internal to declining societies or within the capacities of the existing state apparatuses. The foundation may be as weak on the workers' side: it will involve union leaderships in taking on the corporatist agenda of external competitiveness at the expense of traditional collective bargaining and social demands. If the strategy is vigorously pursued to its final logic in national competitiveness, it is more likely to split than unite workers in rising sectors from those in declining sectors (over subsidies, adjustment policies, exchange rates) and those in the private from the public sector (over competitive tax rates, comparable pay levels, commodification).[54] There is, at the level of the structural logic of collective action, no 'common interest' in national competitiveness that does not have to confront the institutionally and geographically embedded social property relations of power. From the vantage point of the capitalist reformer's dilemma, shaped advantage is simply infeasible.

The relative decline in competitive capacity in existing plant will, therefore, tend to push these countries to put their wage structures into competition to lower unit labour costs to resolve trade imbalances. As the Anglo-American cases of the U.S., Britain and Canada have demonstrated over the last decade, it is quite possible to restore relative competitive capacity in certain sectors, or even across countries as a whole, on the basis of devaluing labour and intensifying work-hours, although the damage to the welfare of the working population may be enormous. Given the potential basis for competitiveness in devalued wages, the ruling bloc may quite logically – and quite consciously with Labour and Socialist Party Governments as in New Zealand and Spain – prefer the option of raising the rate of exploitation by undermining workers' rights and thus actively – and not merely passively – oppose moving in the direction of industrial planning. This strategy is not blind irrational logic which a better policy mix would change, as social democratic theorists often claim, but an accumulative logic within the system itself.

Putting wages into competition and opposing policies of shaped advantage may, moreover, be a quite logical response even in countries that would appear to have the foremost institutionalised conditions for opposing low wage strategies. Hypothetically, it is possible to envision

external competitiveness being shaped on the foundation of the 'high institutional prerequisites' of a stakeholders' capitalism of shaped advantage
(although quite clearly not all countries can do so in an unregulated world
market). This conceptualisation would posit a 'world indifference curve'
between the external competitiveness of diverse (national) economic
models differentially internalising environmental costs and involving
highly-skilled workers.[55] The 'competitiveness indifference curve' depicts
a static equivalence from the standpoint of capitalists between the
strategies of environmental dumping and cheap flexible labour versus
environmental cost internalization and expensive skilled workers. On a
static basis alone it is quite unclear why capitalists would choose the latter
model *except* for a minority of workers in key production positions when
undertaking the former involves fewer costs. Nor does the flexible labour
model prevent firms from undergoing continual innovation in product and
technique (as the 'drive system' of exploitative work-hours applied to
American software engineers proves all too well).

The only way to avoid this conclusion is to fall back on technologically
determinist claims that the flexible specialisation of new technologies (or
that of Japanization or Kalmarianism) uniquely leads to skills upgrading
across the labour force.[56] This is not an empirically or theoretically
plausible argument: capitalists in even technologically leading countries
are just as likely to forward policies for devaluing labour and limiting the
skills upgrading of workers to as narrow a stratum as feasible. The
foreclosure of the cheap labour option to competitiveness depends upon
strong and mobilized unions actively opposing – rather than co-operating
with – capitalists in the pursuit of national competitiveness. To accept
national competitiveness as the objective of economic policy as proposed
by the policy of shaped advantage is, in fact, to undermine the structural
capacity of workers to oppose cheap labour strategies when capitalists
propose this, as they inevitably do, on the very basis of national competitiveness. And it is to sacrifice the long-time egalitarian project of building
up workers' independent productive capabilities apart from the logic of the
capitalist enterprise. Capitalism provides a blockage to shaped advantage
producing egalitarian outcomes in technologically ascendant countries too.

Beyond the drawbacks at the level of individual countries, there are
even greater contradictions for social democratic economic policies of
shaped advantage at the level of the system as a whole. This third fundamental problem can be seen, first, by simply moving from one country to
a second trading partner whose only objective is maintaining payments
balance so as to avoid a deterioration in internal economic conditions. To
the extent that shaped advantage relies on export-led growth at the expense
of internal demand, trading partners must leave their economies open while
the country shaping advantage improves its competitive position. An

immediate problem arises: if the partner whose market is to be penetrated responds with austerity or protectionism (or even the potentially more disruptive shaped advantage policies of their own) to preserve their payments position, any trade and employment gains are wiped out.[57] There may be internal efficiency gains from industrial rationalisation, but how they affect employment and output will be determined by both countries' internal policies as the payments position will simply balance. Whatever output and employment gains occur if overall trade volumes increase, given payments in balance, depends upon an assessment of static gains from trade against the loss of macroeconomic control from opening the economy. The extent to which economies have gained from trade has always been a historical minefield (given that trade shares and output gains have a complex interaction and not a uniform correlation). The macroeconomic loss of control may be small initially but everyone except neoliberals would concede that it can cumulatively build so as to be damaging. Managed trade such as voluntary export restrictions provides a partial solution to the problems arising between two trading partners shaping advantage, although this is less generalisable to the international economy as a whole. But trade controls of even this sort lead to a broader range of planning than is implied by shaped advantage.

If the actions of a single trading partner encounters obstacles for shaped advantage, a world of many – if not all – countries seeking to shape advantage for national competitiveness poses enormous hurdles for social democratic economic policy. There is a basic compositional fallacy of aggregation underlying a strategy of shaping advantage for national competitiveness: all countries cannot be export-oriented to solve their individual employment imbalances. The world market as an opportunity to increase output and employment may work if virtually no one else follows. But the more countries that adopt a strategy of shaped advantage, the less likely this is to be the case – in other words, a positive game for some can become a negative-sum game for all. The reasoning is straightforward. For individual country strategies, there is every incentive for national competitiveness over unit labour costs to spread from productivity gains to austerity *even* in technologically leading countries as trade imbalances persist. Technological laggards must compete on lower wages to reduce unit costs or face a deteriorating trade deficit (especially as surplus countries may not increase aggregate demand). The sluggish conditions for the realisation of profits, while capacity to produce more output is increasing from productivity advance, makes it imperative that technological leaders eventually follow or lose their surpluses and employment. The pole of structural competitiveness will keep being pushed higher as economic openness increases so that all regions – from Johannesburg to Delhi to Manchester to Montreal – must keep up with the pace being set by productivity advance in Frankfurt and Tokyo and by low wage manufactures exporters in Shanghai and Nogales.

This is, more or less, the configuration that the world economy is now locked into.[58] The increased congruence and depth of business cycles since the economic clampdown and oil crisis of 1971-73, particularly the Volcker shock of 1981–82, the stock market deflation of 1987 and the 1991-2 U.S. Budget slowdown, illustrate the demand-side precariousness that is now embedded and successively leaving unemployment at higher levels over the cycle. Every time the U.S. moves to remedy its structural imbalances by deflating or devaluating (which blocks export strategies elsewhere), the rest of the capitalist countries must respond or face massive upset (of which Japan, in its own way, is now a victim). But then it becomes quite unclear – and no one has an answer to it – how the credit-money being advanced to the U.S. will be paid for by eventual U.S. payments surpluses. So the world economy moves sideways; and even the technologically advanced countries with an explicit policy of shaping advantage like Japan and Germany begin to feel the sting of 'competitive austerity' through spreading informalisation and increased exploitation.

In countries with a more egalitarian policy legacy such as Sweden, the 'shared austerity' strategy of using incomes policies to spread work and keep unit labour costs low will be increasingly invoked as traditional competitive devaluations are now ruled out by capital mobility, responses by trading partners and capitalists less willing to make national bargains over income distribution. This strategy, however, might well worsen the international demand problem too by reducing purchasing power and throwing more exports into a world market less capable of absorbing them. And this external impact will feed back through a neoliberal world to make more 'advanced' compromises on work conditions and wages consistent with external competitiveness difficult to sustain (especially as competitive devaluations become more difficult to undertake as increased openness favours currency stability and capital outflows). Internally, in a world hostile to alternate development models, employers will become increasingly opposed to centralised bargaining and more openly politicised to break with the 'egalitarian model.'[59] But 'shared austerity in one class' will also become politically unstable as it reaches the limit of the organisational capacity of unions to continually demand restraint for national competitiveness, especially in a context where the class distribution of income is becoming more unequal.[60]

The North American bloc of countries, in contrast, explicitly adopt a strategy of devaluing labour and informalisation so as to combine both high levels of productivity, intensive resource exploitation and relatively cheap labour. At the moment, they are rewarded by climbing the ranks of the world competitiveness charts, while peripheral economies that are severely indebted like Ghana, or that depend upon exploiting environmentally endangered resources like Newfoundland, eventually buckle and collapse from the exhaustion of a never-ending competitive spiral. Thus external competitiveness increasingly turns to those societies that combine cheap labour with improving technological capacity and externalisation of environmental costs. But even in Korea this does not appear to be enough. In justifying the passage of repressive trade union laws that weaken job security in secret session in the middle of the night, Korean President Kim Young-Sam responded: 'The stark reality facing us today is that without the labour reforms, workers will get neither the income nor jobs in the face of cut-throat global economic competition.'[61]

There is still a fourth fundamental obstacle to shaped advantage strategies if we add the real world condition of massive capital mobility. Here the problem is more indirect but equally damaging to the assumption that globalization is irreversible. Shaped advantage requires long-term planning horizons and thus what social democrats like to call 'patient capital'. Yet financial capital in a global market is increasingly driven by short-term demands for profit and liquidity against risk. In contrast to the wisdom of the financial press for investors, for borrowers international diversification of financial portfolios makes any degree of risk (which increases with the period of investment) and profit for a specific country less acceptable as there are more options to combine less risk and more profit. This will produce pressure toward a world interest rate the more that net capital flows grow relative to trade balances and thus a reference rate of return for capital advanced will be formed irrespective of specific conditions for accumulation.[62] In purely static terms, then, global financial markets pose an obstacle to industrial policy. If there is instability, this increases risk and creates dynamic uncertainties which means that financial capital will be even less willing to be tied to the long-term investments necessary to increase capacity in export industries. Moreover, speculative runs stemming from either systematic trade imbalances or alternative political projects, such as with Mexico at the end of 1994 or France in the early 1980s, can rapidly destabilize any industrial plans.

Capital mobility and floating exchange rates in a world economy thus raise to a new level the old Keynesian problem of the mismatch of time horizons of industrial and financial capital. The 'Tobin Tax' proposals 'to throw sand into the wheels of financial capital' by a levy on international capital transfers might slow some of these processes at the margin.[63] But it neither can prevent new speculative instruments from emerging nor address the source of the problem in the increasing autonomy of the circuits of credit money from the real economy. We face a situation where rentier interests increasingly determine national development models and can veto alternatives through the currency convertibility of capital flight.

The obstacles this poses to shaped advantage in fact makes the traditional socialist argument that democratising financial capital and 're-embedding' international financial flows are necessary conditions for political alternatives *more economically sound and politically necessary than ever*.

The international Keynesianism forwarded by some social democrats as the means to regulate the imbalances of a global economy do not resolve either the trade or capital mobility problems. To call for democratised structures of international governance simply begs the question: 'to do what?' At the national and regional levels, it is already known from postwar experience that capital allocation for industrial plans requires extensive constraints on capital mobility. More democratic international institutions of themselves only imply a greater political legitimacy to the global economic space formed by internationalized capital movements. Any other agenda pursued by these agencies would require a break from the consensus that globalization is irreversible and the capitalist market essentially efficient that forms the basis for the social democratic policy of shaped advantage.

Similarly, international Keynesianism must assume that world market imbalances only stem from a specific problem of adequate demand. Yet global demand stimulation to reduce unused capacity would likely only compound the trade imbalances already evident in a situation of differentiated competitive capacity. It will do nothing to clear these imbalances. Neither will it reverse unemployment in economically declining regions that lack industrial capacities (or who have lost an earlier advantage in natural resources, as with the competitive assault on the Atlantic fishery).[64] Nor will it reverse the cheap labour strategies adopted in, say, southern U.S. states like Alabama. Moreover, the capitalist market imperatives to compete prevent the co-operation necessary for international reflation. How do you compel co-operation when it is always possible to do better in terms of trade balance and employment by cheating, through import restraints, cheap currency or austerity, before your competitor does? The lack of symmetry in adjustment processes, uneven development and the export fallacy of shaped advantage all raise capitalist obstacles that only stronger forms of international co-ordination than mere international reflation, or vague calls for democratic international governance, could meet.

The key obstacles confronting the social democratic case for shaped advantage stem from the differentiating processes produced by competitive capitalists in a world market. The objective of equalisation of relative competitiveness and output levels lies behind the project of national competitiveness. But this objective runs up against the capitalist reformer's dilemma. It is not the state that guides economic enterprises (even ones with stakeholders' rights), allocates investment and, most plainly, controls balance of payments flows in a competitive world market. These all depend upon the actions of profit-seeking capitalists who may or may not identify their particular interest with the 'national interest' of a stakeholders' capitalism in external competitiveness. In any respect, the national interest is defined by the state in relationship to the structural attributes of the various blocks of capital resident in the national formation and their historical models of development. Canadian capitalists, for instance, have favoured large capital inflows to prop up their domestic investment levels and thus have typically not been preoccupied about the composition of exports or a chronic current account deficit. British capitalists have typically exported long-term capital and allowed a weak payments situation to be covered by short-term borrowing (a process only modestly shifted under Thatcherism). Each state has accommodated rather than challenged the relative competitive weakness and economic decline that these different processes have entailed. The balance of payments as a constraint of competitive capacity (as registered in the flow of accounts) is always relative to particular class strategies and the institutional arrangements and economic structures that are inscribed in these strategies. The embedded social relations stand in the way of all attempts by individual states to import models of national competitiveness developed through different historical processes and class relations.

The strategy of shaped advantage suggests all economic actors can adopt outward-oriented trade and industrial strategies while ignoring the contradictions that such actions pose for capitalism as a whole. Some advocates of shaped advantage, such as Robert Kuttner and Susan Strange, have argued for managed trade to maintain balance between states to avoid generating competitive austerity.[65] But trade management only makes the case that the capitalist obstacles which prompt a strategy of shaped advantage can not really be resolved by it: they require international regimes that plan trade and control capital mobility. What is altogether contestable, however, is an open-economy social democracy that begins from the premise that 'states are not like markets: they are communities of fate which tie together actors who share certain common interests in the success or failure of their national economies.'[66] Such tenuous arguments as Hirst and Thompson advance can hardly be said to constitute an adequate defence of the notion that the world market constitutes an opportunity for social development that is historically progressive so as to make socialist economic policies inappropriate and irrelevant. But even the strongest case for social democratic economic policy for national competitiveness must rest on indefensible assumptions that globalisation is irreversible, that market imperatives require the global economy be maintained as it is, and that, even if the planet is ravaged by endless economic growth, there is no other way to sustain employment.

III. Socialist Alternatives and Diversity of Development

Capitalist economic policy is usually narrowed to the choice-theoretic definition of the most efficient use of scarce resources as determined by self-interested individual agents. *Socialist economic policy may be defined as the development of democratic capacities for control of the transformation of economic structures towards egalitarian ecologically-sustainable reproduction.* In capitalist economies, this is primarily the issue of market disengagement and control strategies. In socialist economies, this is the issues of democratic planning and economic co-ordination. The internationalization of capitalist economies no doubt accentuates the imperatives of the market, placing limits on socialist economic policy. Yet the only thing that obliges us to conclude that there is no alternative to the pursuit of international competitiveness is the *a priori* (and unexamined) assumption that existing social property relations – and hence the structural political power sustained by these relations – are sacrosanct.[67] Even *The Economist* seems to concede the point. They admit that the 'powerless state' in the global economy is a 'myth' in that governments have 'about as many economic powers as they ever had.'[68] It is in this sense that the notion that the nation-state acted as an institutional container of social power and regulator of economic activity before globalisation, and that it is no longer capable of doing so today, is fundamentally misleading. The processes of world market formation together with the 'international constitutionalism of neoliberalism has taken place through the agency of states.'[69]

This does not mean that the imperatives of competition in a world market have not lessened the autonomous agency of individual capitalists or states. The NAFTA, Maastricht, and the WTO agreements all have restricted the capacity of nation-states (or regions) to follow their own national (or local) development models. It does mean, however, that the limits on state policy are to a significant extent self-imposed. The world market certainly places limits on state policy, but there is no obligation to accept these imperatives.[70] If we are prepared to question the social property and power relations of capitalism that impose world market imperatives – a proposition that should lie at the centre of socialist economic policy – the scope for state action and the range of alternatives increases.

Globalisation has to be considered not just as an economic regime but as a system of social relations, rooted in the specifically capitalist form of social power, which is concentrated in private capital and the nation-state.[71] Globalisation basically means that the market – now the world 'space of flows' or exchanges – has become increasingly universal as an economic regulator. As the scope of the market widens, the scope of democratic power narrows: whatever is controlled by the market is not subject to democratic accountability. The more universal the market becomes as an economic regulator, the more democracy is confined to certain purely 'formal' rights, at best the right to elect the political ruling class. And this right becomes less and less important, as the political disrepute of parliaments testifies, as the domain of political action is taken over by market imperatives. So the more internationalised capitalism becomes, the less possible it is for socialists just to tinker with economic policies to improve equity or firm-level competitiveness. The more internationalised the economy the less possible it is for socialist economic policy to avoid political contestation over the social property relations of capitalism.

An alternative to globalisation, then, is as much a question of democracy in opposition to the imperatives of the market as it is of alternate development models. The opposite to globalisation is democracy, not only in the crucial sense of civil liberties and the right to vote, but also in the no less crucial sense of the capacity to debate collectively as social equals about societal organisation and production, and to develop self-management capacities in workplaces and communities. Democracy in this sense is both a form of political organisation and an alternative to the market as an economic regulator.[72]

The geographic expansion of production prompts, then, challenging questions for socialists about the spaces and scales for both economic activity and democracy. (I say for socialists, but it is hard to conceive how anyone genuinely committed to democracy can seriously avoid these questions.) The alternative logic to the imperatives of a global capitalist market suggests a dual, and somewhat paradoxical, strategy: expanding the scale of democracy while reducing the scale of production.[73] Expanding the scale of democracy certainly entails changing the governance and policy structures of international agencies and fora, but also of extending the basis for democratic administration and self-management nationally and locally. Let us be clear here. Expanding the scale of democracy along these dimensions in any meaningful sense will entail a challenge to the social property relations of capitalism. To make collective decisions implies some democratic capacity, backed by the coercive sanctions of the state, to direct capital allocation and thus to establish control over the economic surplus. The point is to enhance, with material supports, the capacities of democratic movements (which will vary tremendously according to the class relations and struggles in specific places), at every level, from local organizations to communities up to the nation-state and beyond, to challenge the power of capital.

Reducing the scale of production means shifting towards more inward-oriented economic strategies, but also forming new economic relations of co-operation and control internationally. The logic of the capitalist market creates a need for large-scale production, an obsession with quantity and size, to which all other considerations – of quality, of social need, of bio-regionalism, of negative externalities, of local democracy – are subordinated. The general objective of socialist policy should be to devalue scale of production as the central economic objective by putting other social considerations before quantity and size. Of course, the massive material inequalities between nations mean that the general principle of reducing the scale of production will vary between developed and developing countries.[74] Certain major industrial sectors necessary to produce adequate levels of welfare will obviously need to be put in place. Scale economies will also be important in some sectors to achieve the most efficient plant size in terms of reducing inputs and environmentally damaging outputs. But the reduction of scale should remain the general guiding principle, in keeping with the socialist conviction that production should above all meet basic needs, foster self-management capacities and adopt more labour-intensive techniques when capital-intensive ones, like clear-cut foresting or chemicalized agriculture, have crippling environmental consequences. The desperate levels of economic insecurity, the volume of contamination and resource use, and degradation of local ecologies in the developed countries has surely made clear that economic growth cannot be equated with human welfare in any simple manner.[75]

There are two corollary propositions that would seem to follow from this strategic orientation for socialist economic policy. First, it implies taking a strong stand in favour of the institutional structures at the level of the world economy that sponsor alternative development models. There is a sound basis to this approach. The postwar period displayed a variety of models of economic development, in the diversity of Fordism in the North, import-substitution industrialization in the South, and the various 'socialist experiments'.[76] Even the attempt to impose a neoliberal homogeneity of development confirms this: there is now a diversity of disasters across the North, the East and the South. The concept of inward strategies is, to a degree, a notional orientation as all economic strategies will necessarily have a vibrant open component and in all cases the world configuration will need to be accounted for. But, as Ajit Singh has argued, openness is a multi-dimensional concept that can apply variously to trade, capital movements, migration and culture and between times and places. International economic relations should not be a uniform market compulsion, but always encompass a 'strategic degree of involvement' in external exchanges.[77] In this view, balance of payments is still an accounting measure of the 'space of flows' of money and commodities internationally (although necessarily disaggregated to account for the distributional interests of social classes) and a constraint indicative of productive capacities in specific 'spaces of production.' But payments balance also represents, however indirectly, the articulation between diverse economic models and thus the social relations of production between specific places of production. It is impossible for socialists to put forward alternatives unless it is insisted that there are variable ways of organizing economic and ecological relations, and of managing the external relations between diverse models. The objective of such a solidaristic international economic policy can be summed up like this: the maximization of the capacity of different national collectivities to choose democratically alternate development paths subject to the limitation that the chosen path does not impose externalities (such as environmental damage or structural payments surpluses or deficits) on other countries. This objective can only be realized through re-embedding financial capital and production relations in democratically organized national and local economic spaces sustained through international solidarity and fora of democratic co-operation.[78]

Second, full employment has come to mean a level of unemployment associated with stable prices even within social democratic employment policy. But this mixes up labour and product market performance and contains nothing of the traditional demands of the Left that employment be related to production for need and not for exchange. As Joan Robinson once noted, it would be 'preferable to take a simple-minded definition, and to say that there is "full employment" when no one is unemployed.'[79] Better still would be a definition that incorporated the measure of adequate labour market performance. Full employment might then be seen in relation to the maximization of voluntary participation of the adult population in socially-useful paid work at full-time hours for solidaristic wages.

This strategic orientation for a socialist economic policy for market disengagement allows us to put some order around a set of economic principles that have been emerging out of the Left and Green movements. These principles should be envisioned as transitional (they neither represent socialism nor even the model-building of recent years) in the sense of 'structural reforms' that initiate democratic modes of regulation against market imperatives.[80] For both substantive reasons, as well as to maximize support today for socialist economic policy, they should be conceived as a strategy to move in the direction of full employment through alternative development models which encompass aspects of the following ten principles.[81]

(1) Inward-oriented economic strategies will be necessary to allow a diversity of development paths and employment stability. Economic policies have been geared to cost-cutting, fostering capital mobility and common treatment without regard to the integration of national economies or local production. Governments have poured an inordinate amount of resources into the export sector, although these efforts have not dented

unemployment (and probably could not, even in the absence of stagnation). Yet, it is an absolute falsehood that freer trade will necessarily lead to an expansion of employment and income. There are all sorts of conditions, such as infant industries, mass unemployment or research market failures, that make the theoretical case for protective devices such as quotas and tariffs for positive industrial strategies.   There is an equally strong theoretical – not to speak of moral – case against free trade in goods produced in absolutely appalling labour conditions.

The Left debate about trade and protectionism has often been, therefore, specious and hopelessly contradictory. Free trade is recognized as a neoliberal project, but rejection of it is shied away from as an affront to internationalism. It is feared that protection of domestic workers will come at the expense of workers abroad. Yet, it should not be a question of being for or against trade: this is a conjunctural strategic issue related to stability and egalitarian outcome. World trade in its present form is massively imbalanced, unstable and coercive in its regulatory impact on national economies; the consequence is increased social polarisation of income and work. At stake, then, is a wider principle: the active pursuit of alternative development paths for full employment requires that the open sector not restrict domestic priorities, and that *the international system support rather than undermine these options*.[82] The export orientation of all economic strategies is neither sustainable nor desirable; it will have to be replaced by a strategy of inward development (which is essential to any egalitarian economic strategy). This is partly what the early Bretton Woods system permitted through temporary trade restrictions to allow full employment policies.

This casts a quite different light on what should be expected of trade. It means, for example, that trade would have to come under regulation to allow different orientations on local production, environmental standards, restrictions on child labour, and so on, without sanction from 'worst-practice' production models. In other words, divergent economic models imply a degree of tariff protection and control over the open sector. It has proven impossible, moreover, for surplus countries to inflate enough, or deficit countries to deflate enough, to restore payments balance without further job losses. A single global market, with no common labour or ecological standards, will inevitably bargain standards down in response to the fear of competitive losses in conditions of competitive austerity. Of course, if the use of tariffs and quotas in support of employment, or to resolve payments imbalances, is to be minimised a degree of international co-ordination and planning of trade is required. None of these measures imply closing the economy from trade as economies of scale, diversified consumption, and transfer of new products and processes remain important. However, they quite clearly imply planning the open sector in the national context with international regulation and co-ordination required for the clearing of balances and the reinforcement of long-term diverse development trajectories.

(2) Financial capital must be subjected to democratic controls on debt payment and capital mobility. It seems quite clear from the histories of the interwar period and the post-1974 experience that the external constraint on national economic policy less imposes itself from outside than grows out of the internal contradictions of domestic accumulation and the actions of the national state. A phase of material expansion, as Giovanni Arrighi and Elmar Altvater contend, ends in a phase of internationalization as products seek markets and capitalists seek higher returns in financial flows.[83] A series of problems arises: financial assets are increasingly oriented to short-term returns because of stagnant output; debts cannot be serviced; national economies are increasingly vulnerable to currency movements as central bank reserves are dwarfed by financial flows.

International debts, with virtually all countries becoming more indebted, pose a special difficulty. Settling them requires a net surplus of exports: everything goes into competitive and export capacity with the hope of paying debts plus interest. But other countries adopting the same approach of expanding exports and lessening import demands generates weaker employment conditions all around. Because of weaker demand, meeting debt and interest payments requires further squeezing of the public sector and workers' living standards. It is impossible, then, to redistribute work at solidaristic wages and to continue to transfer massive funds to financial interests. Finding an alternative way out of the debt crisis is essential to the expansion of employment and alternative development. The debt burden can only be alleviated by either a controlled inflation leading to negative or minimal real rates of interest or a rescheduling of payments that accomplishes the same thing. Anything else simply temporally displaces an inevitable default into the future while running down resources and capacities in the present. A hierarchy of credit and capital controls – a credit regime – also needs to be drawn up and implemented to constrain the power of financial capital over national development. Such measures might range from: micro-banks; more democratic control over national banks and credit allocation to enforce planning; short term taxes on speculative turnover in currency, bond and equity markets; quantitative capital controls; and restructured international agencies that regulate credit repayment and long term capital flows. Macroeconomic stability will be wishful thinking without financial controls.[84]

(3) Macroeconomic balance requires not only aggregate demand management, but also new forms of investment planning and collective

bargaining norms. It is one thing to say that there is a capitalist employment crisis and quite another to say that releasing the aggregate demand restraint to increase output will necessarily lead to employment expansion. This misses the point that capitalist development means increased output but with increased surplus labour (and an indeterminate effect on workers' incomes). An appalling dimension of capitalism, and neoliberal employment policy, is that the costs of the system's need for flexibility are born by workers while the benefits are reaped by capitalists. This is as unacceptable today as it has ever been. Macroeconomic stability should translate into employment stability through firm level job security but also a social guarantee of retraining and new job creation in local communities facing industrial restructuring. Such macroeconomic balance will have to entail new mechanisms of control over market forces: national and sectoral planning councils; planning agreements over investment flows and technology strategies; regional and local development boards; and public ownership of core sectors (including financial industries).

Macroeconomic balance means something quite beyond control of demand volatility of the Keynesian kind. There are distributional imbalances between the social classes, public and private goods, present consumption and future sustainability. On ecological, anti-globalisation and equity grounds a redistributional macroeconomic balance makes eminently more sense than one of unrestrained growth.

For effective demand to be restored, the break that has been put on productivity-sharing with workers to the end of cost-cutting needs to be revoked. But egalitarian employment also requires more than this. Increased production requires consumers for the output and the income for this should certainly go to workers. Yet output increases have to become more ecologically constrained. So reductions in work-time, which are the most effective means to increase employment historically, should be strongly pushed. A trade union bargaining norm of an *'annual free-time factor'* should, in solidarity with the unemployed, have precedence over an 'annual wage improvement' in sharing out productivity increases (allocated to favour additional employment and the poorest workers). Any decline in employment will also depend upon the form the expansion takes. Capitalist sector jobs are governed by the logic of profitability; non-capitalist sector jobs (in the state and collective organizations) are governed by the logic of redistribution. The decline in capitalist sector employment in the manufacturing sector is permanent. Employment growth should be tilted, therefore, toward sustainable community services which are more labour-intensive. The question really is not one of work to do: there is a serious lack of adequate public facilities from new classrooms to art galleries; there is a tremendous pent-up demand for affordable health care, housing and public transportation; and there is a great deal to be done in terms of environmental clean-up from the wreckage caused by industrialization and neoliberalism.

(4) Reducing unemployment will entail both less work and a redistribution of work. Postwar employment policies fought unemployment through faster growth of output and exports. Contemporary capitalist employment policies attempt, with little success, to do the same. If export-led strategies to increase employment in conditions of competitive austerity soon become a zero-sum (or negative) game of dumping job losses on other countries which will eventually respond in kind, national macroeconomic expansion will not be sufficient to lower unemployment. In the absence of measures to restrict population growth (and given the objective of not lowering the participation rate of adults in the economy), employment growth alone would require a significant level of expanded output. The increased capital-intensity of production suggests, moreover, that growth rates would have to consistently approach, or exceed, levels of the postwar boom to lower unemployment (at present average hours of work and labour force growth). This still would leave unaddressed unused labour stocks and productivity gains that even at modest levels would require significant growth. Yet levels of growth of the postwar period, with similar extensive growth bringing more land and resources into production, would be enormously costly to the natural environment. Growth-centred employment strategies must now be firmly rejected as both unviable in reducing unemployment and undesirable on ecological grounds.

An unexpected side-effect of globalisation has been an increase in work-time as part of competitive austerity (time reduction initially stalling with the crisis in 1974 and now getting longer and more polarised).[85] Hours of work and intensity of work have increased even as workers' purchasing power has been cut. The movement to lower hours has typically required an international movement to impose an alternate logic on capitalism's tendencies to increase work intensity and hours. In a static sense, it is quite obvious that work, like income, is unequally distributed. But unlike income redistribution work redistribution has the positive consequence of producing free-time. A variety of measures are equalising of work-time (especially if developed as universal standards): overtime limits and severe restrictions on 'double-dipping' by professionals; extending vacations and national holidays; and voluntary job-sharing plans by work-site. But to have a major impact on unemployment nothing will do except a sharp reduction in standard work-time with the clear objective of moving to an average annual volume of, say, 1500 hours of work with a 32 hour work-week (bringing the advanced industrial countries below current German levels). Existing plant might be worked harder (until fixed investment expands) through expanded shift work. But with slow output increases, the short term reduction in unemployment will require a shift in income (offset by productivity gain, less hours, lower unemployment claims and better public services) as well as work. So a strategy of less work must be implemented in as egalitarian a manner as possible (avoiding the folly of having only the public sector work shorter hours, which both ruins public goods and increases inequality). An expansion of output will then have the maximum impact on employment. A defensive struggle to spread work can form the basis of an offensive struggle for a different way of life.

(5) A 'politics of time' should extend beyond setting standard hours to consider the allocation of work-time and free-time. 'Work without end' has been the history of capitalism. Fordism added 'endless consumption' and the Keynesian conviction – check the old textbooks – that expanded output should always have precedence over reduced work-time for any labour time freed by productivity advance. Changing this orientation will raise questions of an existential order about work, employment and the self-management of time. This has a collective and a personal side. On the personal side, there is an obvious increase in discretion over free time. It is also possible to pursue more flexible patterns of work-time through flex-time, banked time, single seniority lists based on hours worked, and paid educational leaves that re-shape the control of time. There is an equally important collective side to lowering work-time. There is, for instance, more ample time, as both Andre Gorz and Ernest Mandel have argued, for collective decision-making in administrative and legislative activities.[86] The radical reduction in work-time, with greater worker control over the allocation of time, raises the concrete possibility of realizing the long-standing goal of the socialist movement for a 'democratically controlled economy.'

(6) Productivity gains in the labour process should be negotiated against the requalification of work. The economic crisis also relates to the supply-side crisis of production (which in turn structures labour demand). The new technologies further restructure the supply-side through changes to the labour process and work-time. Competitive austerity, however, is compelling work speedup and job fragmentation of a Taylorist kind, even though this often involves sacrificing productivity gains that might occur from increased worker input into production. A positive restructuring – which would depend upon altering the balance of class relations on the shopfloor and in society – would entail exploiting the capacity of the new technologies to involve workers in production and the planned elimination of boring, repetitive jobs. The fight against Taylorism extends into the kind of training that is premised on preserving and expanding workers' skills. This means long-term, broad skills rather than short-term, specific ones;

transferable skills over firm-specific skills; theoretical as well as practical knowledge; and skills that extend worker autonomy over the labour process. Thus formal qualifications, earned through institutional training or a mixture of formal training and on-the-job training, tend to allow workers more flexibility and control over their labour process. The requalification of work would extend broad skills of technical competency to all workers.

Employment and education have always been linked. Training plays a central role in industrial policy and thus aggregate and sectoral labour demand, in matching labour supply with skills demand, facilitating adjustment between jobs, and in improving skills in cyclical downturns. So training has to fit with other initiatives as it cannot create labour demand for imaginary jobs. But building workers' capacities and skills as a continual process has the positive benefit of providing an oversupply of high skills, which can make easier adjustment to demand and technology shifts. Increased worker participation in the labour process to increase productivity is undoubtedly a struggle waged on the terrain of the capitalists. Yet reuniting conception and execution and rebuilding workers' capacities advances materially the possibility of worker self-management which any democratic socialism must be premised upon. Life-time education rather than narrowly conceived 'training' should really be the goal.

(7) The requalification of work should be linked to quality production within a quality-intensive growth model. It is not possible any more to simply lay to one side the quality of the growth process, issues of work process and product design, or production for social need. The failure of social democratic Keynesianism was possibly greatest here, in that it never developed state, community or worker planning capacities or offered a 'different way of life.' Keynesianism above all attempted to alleviate the capitalist unemployment problem by growth in the quantity of consumption goods and thereby the quantity of employment hours demanded. Yet it is now more necessary than ever to connect the skills, resources and employment that go into the labour process to the ecological quality of the production process and the use-values which come out.

An alternative socialist policy might accentuate a number of positive trends that can be discerned. The requalification of work, for example, makes it feasible for unions to develop their own technology networks, popular plans for industry, and socially-useful products. As well, there is an element of the new technologies that does allow decentralized small-scale batch production or flexible specialization (although this cannot be generalized into an entire economic system as some wildly wrong theories did in the 1980s).[87] This allows for a whole range of customized instruments, clothing, housewares. Quality-intensive growth also speaks to the provision of public services. Here the problem is two-fold. The bureaucratic Fordist-style of the postwar public sector can also gain from diversified and quality production to overcome standardization and input-controlled production of public services. The quantitative restrictions of austerity have also seriously damaged the quality and range of public goods from such basics as clean streets to the variety of art available in public spaces. A socialist economic policy will foster, therefore, a quality-intensive growth model that encourages workers' skills and capacities, incorporates resource-saving and durable production techniques, and produces free time, collective services and quality products.

(8) The decline in work-time allows the administrative time for workplace democracy. An unexpected benefit from decreased work-time is that it allows for a democratic expansion of employment by freeing administrative and deliberative time for workplace and community planning of output and work. With work-time reduction and job security so central to an alternative, it is quite necessary and possible to put workplace planning agreements on the bargaining table. These include, most obviously, information on compensation, profits, trade and investment plans, but also should advance toward product design and long term workers' plans. Labour productivity gains not taken in increased output can be taken in increased time devoted to workers' control and environmental sustainability. Of course, capital will not yield such 'structural reforms' over democratic control without threat of capital strike. Capital would prefer to continue with Taylorism than risk worker self-management. But it is exactly this that makes the external regulation over capital flows so critical.

(9) Local planning capacities will be central to sustaining diverse development and full employment. Postwar Keynesianism concentrated on centralized aggregate demand management with little economic planning. It was recognized that employment planning and adjustment policies were a necessary supplement to demand management in tight labour markets. Yet this largely remained limited to forecasting occupational and labour force trends. It did not involve planning resource usage and never even extended to implementing the postwar idea of a 'public works shelf' of projects to be taken up in downturns. The local component of planning was labour exchanges which served largely as a location for job listings and counselling, but which never did much in the way of identifying local job or skill needs. In many countries, even these limited services provided by local employment centres have been allowed to run down under neoliberal policies. An alternative employment policy will, in contrast, have as a priority the development of local administrative capacities. There is a desperate need to formulate local labour plans accounting for the existing

labour stock and skills, but also that forecasts local labour force trends, skill shortages and job trends. This kind of knowledge cannot be found or developed centrally. Local labour market authorities, therefore, must become much more forward-looking and active planning units rather than the passive dispensers of dole payments or centres for the video display of job postings that they have become.

There is an added dimension to local planning. In the service sector, where most job growth will be, the challenge is not only to raise the quality of work and pay, but also to collectivize many service activities that are too expensively provided by private markets (daycare), or are not available at all because of underfunding (cleaner environment). It is impossible to envision these being done without planning of resource use and input from users and producers of the services. How does one go about providing library resources in a multi-cultural society from an office tower in Washington or Berlin? Decentralized popular planning should be central to a non-capitalist 'third sector,' that is, self-managed community services (either newly formed or partly devolved from traditional state administration) such as cultural production, environmental clean-up, education and leisure. These activities will have to be planned, through local labour market boards, to determine socially-useful activities, community needs, and local skills. This reinforces the linkages between the expansion of employment and the formation of democratic capacities.

(10) Socialist economic policy should encompass new forms of democratic administration. Employment policy, the central focus of this discussion, is typically administered though traditional hierarchical bureaucracies of central offices of control, planning and funding and decentralized employment exchanges.[88] The exchanges grew in prominence with war mobilization and the subsequent adoption of unemployment insurance schemes. The exchanges embodied, in many ways, the worst aspects of postwar bureaucratic administration: poorly planned and ill-focused at the centre and rigid and remote in local communities. Where could it have possibly been said that the local employment centre was the key location for discussing and planning work in the community? Yet, in a democratic society where most of us spend a large portion of our adult lives working (or seeking work), this is exactly what they could and should be. It would be quite possible to establish a statutory labour market system structured through local, democratically accountable bodies. This could be encompassed within a national employment policy, with the local boards allowed a decentralization of decision-making and thus local communities a more active role in establishing production, employment and training priorities. Such democratically elected boards could serve as a 'space for the alternative' on a broad range of local issues: where workers' plans are linked to

community economic development plans; where the improvement in the quality of jobs is actually taken on as a societal project; where workers and unions are specifically given resources and assistance to form employment plans; where community environmentalists and unions come together around health and safety and workplace pollution; and where communities are mandated to plan local needs and to provide socially-useful employment.

IV. Conclusion: Capitalist Obstacles, Socialist Imperatives

It is conventional wisdom that the internationalisation of capitalist economies at the end of the twentieth century has created historical conditions that have vitiated traditional socialist economic objectives and, indeed, their policy means as well. This accounts, in part, both for the boldness with which neoliberal policies are being pursued and the appalling servile character of the latest revisionist turn of social democracy. I have argued, in contrast, that the internationalisation of market processes has caused unmitigated disasters in many parts of the world as well as economic imbalances and social polarisations between and within countries that cannot be resolved by economic approaches that would intensify these processes. This is the case for both neoliberal and social democratic policies targetted at widening the economic space for internationalisation. Widening the space for international governance of the market to match its global expansion, as the advocates on the Left for a 'cosmopolitan democracy' and the formation of an 'international civil society' argue, begs far more questions than it answers and depends upon an untenable view of market processes (even when accompanied by the laudable goal of 'throwing sand into the wheels' of global financial capital). Capitalist social relations remain a massive obstacle to social justice.

There are eventually only two options facing individual countries in the hyper-competitive conditions of structurally imbalanced and unmanaged internationalised capitalist markets – protectionism or austerity. In the current conjuncture, the neoliberal 'Washington Consensus' of the IMF, World Bank and the GATT-WTO has ruled out protectionism – and thus the 'beggaring-thy-neighbour' process of exporting unemployment of the 1930s – by lowering tariff and non-tariff barriers. The Consensus's constraint on protectionism, however, does not resolve the underlying pressures but only shifts them elsewhere (particularly as the WTO is as much an investment pact for private investment flows as a trade agreement). Thus the entire burden of adjustment has to fall on a continual process of technical rationalisation (which is slow, costly and risky), intensification of work and environmental degradation. The demand-side effects of this defensive adjustment produces a spiral of 'competitive austerity' so that the pressures to rationalise and cut costs is ceaseless. Improving external balance and competitiveness in the 1990s takes the form of 'beggar-thy-working class' policies of expanding unemployment at home. Neither neoliberal free trade nor social democratic proposals of shaped advantage for national competitiveness provide an exit from this destructive form of capitalism. Nor would simply taming financial markets resolve it as this would only modify the temporal dimension of the asymmetries in the world economy and not their spatial underpinnings. These obstacles also apply to the misguided faith common amongst the new market socialists in the allocative efficiency of global markets in determining investment and research and development, as opposed to the allocative efficiency of democratic planning in determining where these expenditures might best meet social needs. This is an impossibly shallow view of consumer sovereignty and the sustainability of present distributional and consumption patterns.

These criticisms still leave, of course, the most difficult question: on what basis might a political challenge to these processes be mounted and socialist economic policies be forwarded? The social democratic proposals to forge a progressive competitiveness approach to internationalisation, often put in terms of creating a 'stakeholders' capitalism', has been the pole of attraction for most Left political parties and intellectuals. But as a result of the contradictions analysed here, nowhere is this strategy posed as a serious alternative to neoliberalism. It is the North American model of longer hours of work at income-splitting, insecure jobs and an impoverished public sector that is spreading. This is the case even in Sweden and Germany, which best combine the pre-conditions of strong labour movements brokering compromises with a national bourgeoisie traditionally committed to national competitiveness. Similarly the East Asian miracle economies, so commonly put forth as a progressive alternative to neoliberalism in even the usually most clear-headed socialist periodicals, only makes the case that state intervention to support national industry is not always a failure in raising output levels. They are neither generalisable models because of the external constraint nor desirable ones on the egalitarian, democratic or ecological grounds of socialist politics.

I have argued in this essay, again in opposition to most current thinking on the Left, that socialist economic policy still provides a vital alternative to resolving these problems. This is not to declare that ready-made blueprints can be offered: it is to search for viable sets of strategic orientations and principles around which struggles in specific times and places might advance. The calls made in this context for re-territorialisation of the 'spaces of production' and for constraints over the 'space of flows' of monetary and commodity exchanges at the world level should, then, hardly be controversial. To cite Miliband again: 'The fact of class struggle on an international scale inexorably points to the need for a socialist government to preserve as large a measure of independence as is possible ... socialists cannot accept a parallel political internationalization which, for the present and immediate future, is bound to place intolerable constraints on the purposes they seek to advance.'[89] The point of controversy more properly resides in two areas: at what political moment, to what extent and in what forms should sovereignties be sacrificed to democratised multi-national blocs and international agencies reinforcing the diverse autocentric, ecologically-sound development trajectories of their constituent members; and at what moments, to what extent and in what forms should democratic forums within states have priority to plan and control production and ecology? Working through these challenges requires political movements which are thoroughly international in their thinking, linkages and solidarities. But such movements can only arise if they are firmly rooted in their own local and national communities and ecologies in developing their democratic capacities and economic alternatives. The obstacle lies not in the impossibility of developing viable socialist economic policies for these movements to pursue as opportunities present themselves. Nor are the sentiments of a majority of the world's population North and South, who wish for a 'different way of life' from the competitive treadmill and despair of capitalism at the end of the century, inhospitable to such policies. The obstacle is a minority class that draws its power and wealth from a historically specific form of production. There is a route forward if the market basis of this power is seen for what it is: contingent, imbalanced, exploitative and replaceable.

NOTES

1. Ralph Miliband, *Socialism for a Sceptical Age* (Oxford, Polity Press, 1994), p. 1. A shorter version of this article previously appeared in *Monthly Review* in December 1996. I would like to thank Leo Panitch and Ellen Wood for their most helpful editorial advice.
2. P. Hirst and G. Thompson, *Globalization in Question* (Oxford, Polity Press, 1996). They put it: 'The opposite of a globalized economy is thus not a nationally inward-looking one, but an open world market based on trading nations and regulated to a greater or lesser degree both by the public policies of nation states and by supra-national agencies.' Their case is built around, inter alia, protection of investment flows, co-operative capitalists and faster growth. See: *Globalization*, p. 16.
3. See: David Miliband (ed.), *Reinventing the Left* (Oxford, Polity Press, 1994); and N. Thompson, 'Supply Side Socialism,' *New Left Review*, 216 (1996).
4. Ralph Miliband, *Socialism for a Sceptical Age*, p. 2.
5. J. Wiseman, 'A Kinder Road to Hell? Labor and the Politics of Progressive Competitiveness in Australia,' in L. Panitch (ed.), *Socialist Register 1996: Are There Alternatives?* (London, Merlin, 1996).
6. Just at the time many Marxists were coming to praise and advocate the Swedish model as the way of the future, one of its main architects was decrying its end. See: R. Meidner, 'Why Did the Swedish Model Fail?' in R. Miliband and L. Panitch (eds.), *Socialist*

Register 1993: Real Problems False Solutions (London, Merlin, 1993).

7. 'Labour Leader Seeks to Reassure NY Financiers,' *Financial Times*, 11 April 1996. After his new year interview with the *Financial Times*, 16 January 1997, it was reported that Blair 'really does believe the ideological battles over economics during the present century will be seen in the long sweep of history as an aberration.'

8. 'The World Economy,' *The Economist*, 7 October 1995, p. 5.

9. Quoted in P. Gowan, 'Neo-Liberal Theory and Practice for Eastern Europe,' *New Left Review*, 213 (1995), p. 9.

10. R. Reich, *The Work of Nations* (New York, Knopf, 1991), p. 9.

11. F. Scharpf, *Crisis and Choice in European Social Democracy* (Ithaca, Cornell University Press, 1991), p. 274.

12. *Ibid.* Scharpf invokes 'socialism in one class' positively, if gloomily, as the necessary strategy for the present period. In contrast, Leo Panitch, in *Social Democracy and Industrial Militancy* (Cambridge, Cambridge University Press, 1976), p. 244, first used the term to denote the loss of the objective of taking anything away from capital.

13. I follow here E. Wood's distinction in conceptualizing capitalism between the market as opportunity 'always conducive to growth and the improvement of productive forces,' and the market as imperative with 'its specific laws of motion which uniquely compel people to enter the market and compel producers to produce "efficiently" by raising labour productivity.' See: 'From Opportunity to Imperative: The History of the Market,' *Monthly Review*, 46:3 (1994).

14. A. Giddens, *Beyond Left and Right: The Future of Radical Politics* (Cambridge, Polity Press, 1994).

15. The idea of stakeholding refers to some notion of inclusiveness and partnership in private enterprises, but the rhetoric of partnerships is easily applied by social democrats to state policy as well. There may or may not be some participation or property rights attached to the term. It describes well the type of capitalism favoured by social democratic policies for national competiveness.

16. J. Roemer, *A Future for Socialism* (Cambridge, Ma., Harvard University Press, 1994); and A. Gamble and G. Kelly, 'The New Politics of Ownership,' *New Left Review*, 220 (1996). This view recalls Paul Samuelson's comment, in the midst of the 1950s 'end of ideology' phase, that as far as economic theory was concerned it was a matter of indifference if workers hired capitalists or capitalists hired workers. The mixed economy had made dispute over modes of production pointless. For the new market socialists, socialism is now a question of degrees of ownership mixes in a global marketplace.

17. 'The coherence, such as it is, arises out of the conversion of temporal patterns into spatial restraints to accumulation. Surplus value must be produced and realized within a certain timespan. If time is needed to overcome space, surplus value must also be produced and realized within a certain geographical domain . . . It is production in particular locales that is always the ultimate source of [capitalist] power.' See: D. Harvey, *The Limits to Capital* (Oxford, Basil Blackwell, 1982), pp. 416, 423.

18. 'The World Economy,' *The Economist*, 7 October 1995, p. 4. The Hecksher-Ohlin theorem adds that the basis of comparative advantage will be a country's relative abundance of factors of production. Floating exchange rates of currencies, moreover, will keep trade in balance by altering relative prices. Hence free trade is always to be preferred to national (or local) self-sufficiency. For accessible surveys of the relevant literature and its critique see: D. Irwin, *Against the Tide: An Intellectual History of Free Trade* (Princeton, Princeton University Press, 1996); and R. Heilbroner and W. Milberg, *The Crisis of Vision in Modern Economic Thought* (Cambridge, Cambridge University Press, 1995).

19. D. Gordon, 'Six-Percent Unemployment Ain't Natural,' *Social Research*, 54:2 (1987); and J. Michie and J. Grieve Smith (eds.), *Unemployment in Europe* (London, Academic Press, 1994).

20. The most interesting case being Ricardo's own example of Portugal: S. Sideri, *Trade and Power: Informal Colonialism in Anglo-Portugese Relations* (Rotterdam, Rotterdam University Press, 1970). See also the critiques in: J. Friedan, 'Exchange Rate Politics: Contemporary Lessons from American History,' *Review of International Political Economy*, 1:1 (1994); and M. Bienefeld, 'Capitalism and the Nation State in the Dog Days of the Twentieth Century,' in R. Miliband and L. Panitch (eds.), *Socialist Register 1994: Between Globalism and Nationalism* (London, Merlin, 1994).
21. 'The World Economy,' *The Economist*, 7 October 1995, pp. 4-5. *The Economist* goes so far as to argue that the outcomes of trade liberalization are efficient because they are the result of freer markets even when they 'give perverse signals.'
22. For a survey of the trends described here see: A. Glyn, et al., 'The Rise and Fall of the Golden Age,' in S. Marglin and J. Schor (eds.), *The Golden Age of Capitalism* (Oxford, Oxford University Press, 1990).
23. P. Sweezy, 'The Triumph of Financial Capital,' *Monthly Review*, 46:2 (June 1994).
24. J. M. Keynes, *The Collected Writings: Activities 1941-46, Shaping the Postwar World, Bretton Woods and Reparations* (Cambridge, Cambridge University Press, 1980), pp. 21-2.
25. By social democratic economic policy we mean the set of economic ideas and practices to compensate for specific market constraints and failures within capitalism. These policies are market controlling and not transitional strategies.
26. J. M. Keynes, *The General Theory of Employment, Interest and Money* (London, Macmillan, 1936), pp. 380-1.
27. This national compromise had its parallels in the import-substitution industrialisation strategies of the South and the command economies of Eastern Europe.
28. S. Wilks, 'Class Compromise and the International Economy: The Rise and Fall of Swedish Social Democracy,' *Capital and Class*, 58 (1996), p. 103.
29. 'Growth and Equality since 1945: The Role of the State in OECD Economies,' in C. Naastepad and S. Storm (eds.), *The State and the Economic Process* (Cheltenham, Edward Elgar, 1996), p. 96.
30. Ian Roxborough, for example, in looking at open-economy social democracy in Latin America, argues that 'there is no question of attempting a complete reversal of all neoliberal reforms.' See: 'Neoliberalism in Latin America: Limits and Alternatives,' *Third World Quarterly*, 13:3 (1992), p. 432.
31. R. Kuttner, *The End of Laissez-Faire* (Philadelphia, University of Pennsylvania Press, 1991).
32. The relevant essays are accessible in P. Krugman (ed.), *Strategic Trade Policy and the New International Economics* (Cambridge, MIT Press, 1986). For evaluations from Right and Left: M. Corden, 'Strategic Trade Policy,' in D. Greenaway, et al. (eds.), *A Guide to Modern Economics* (London, Routledge, 1996); and M. Humbert, 'Strategic Industrial Policies in a Global Industrial System,' *Review of International Political Economy*, 1:3 (1994). The new trade theory also explains empirical trade phenomena such as intra-industry trade and the extensive trade flows between developed economies, two facts poorly dealt with in the pure Ricardian case.
33. W. Ruigrok and R. van Tulder's *The Logic of International Restructuring* (London, Routledge, 1995), ch. 9, goes even further in arguing that virtually the entire Fortune 100 list of the world's largest non-financial corporations enjoyed key government support and trade protection. This is another example of just how ideological the theoretical defence of free trade is.
34. 'Is Free Trade Passe?' *Journal of Economic Perspectives*, 1 (1987); and 'Does the New Trade Theory Require a New Trade Policy,' *The World Economy*, 15 (1992).
35. *The End of Laissez-Faire*, ch. 4.
36. R. Prebisch, *The Economic Devlopment of Latin America and Its Principal Problems* (New York, UN Economic Commission for Latin America, 1950). The assumption of

THE SOCIALIST REGISTER 1997

shaped advantage is that the key issue is surplus trade in manufactured goods for high growth. But as students of Canada have long noted, there can be high growth with deficits in value-added trade. The real question becomes the form, quality and control of development, an assessment precluded by notions of national competitiveness. The classic argument remains: M. Watkins, 'A Staple Theory of Economic Growth,' *Canadian Journal of Economics and Political Science*, 29 (1963).

37. The cumulative causation argument builds on the work of Nicholas Kaldor and Joan Robinson. The implications of the arguments today, however, have become skewed away from the need to control the open sector, as the Cambridge Economic Policy Group and the British Alternate Economic Strategy argued in the late 1970s in its case for import controls, toward primarily export promotion in high technology industry as globalisation has blocked other options. There is some relation to the Marxian notion of absolute cost advantage as developed in different directions by dependency theory, especially in A. G. Frank, *Capitalism and Underdevelopment in Latin America* (1967) and S. Amin, *Unequal Development* (1976), and in value theory by G. Carchedi, *Frontiers of Political Economy* (1991) and A. Shaikh, 'Free Trade, Unemployment and Economic Policy,' in J. Eatwell (ed.), *Global Unemployment* (Armonk, M.E. Sharpe, 1996).

38. G. Dosi and L. Soete, 'Technical Change and International Trade,' in D. Dosi, et al. (eds.), *Technical Change and Economic Theory* (London, Pinter, 1988), p. 419. Also see: G. Dosi, K. Pavitt and L. Soete, *The Econnomics of Technical Change and International Trade* (Hemel Hempstead, Harvester, 1990); and C. Freeman and L. Soete, *Work for All or Mass Unemployment?* (London, Pinter, 1994).

39. Thus the social democratic case for shaped advantage has particularly strong advocates in the economically declining powers of Britain, Canada and the U.S., as with popular writers like Will Hutton, James Laxer, Lester Thurow and Robert Reich.

40. Commission on Public Policy and British Business, *Promoting Prosperity: A Business Agenda for Britain* (London, IPPR, 1997), quoted in M. Wolf, 'Labour of Prosperity,' *Financial Times*, 21 January 1997.

41. W. Streeck, *Social Instituions and Economic Performance* (London, Sage, 1992). For a wider assessment of these views see: G. Albo, 'Competitive Austerity and the Impasse of Capitalist Employment Policy,' R. Miliband and L. Panitch (eds.), *Socialist Register 1994: Between Globalism and Nationalism* (London, Merlin, 1994); and P. Burkett and M. Hart-Landsberg, 'The Use and Abuse of Japan as a Progressive Model,' in L. Panitch (ed.), *Socialist Register 1996: Are There Alternatives?* (London, Merlin, 1996).

42. J. Rogers and W. Streeck, 'Productive Solidarities: Economic Strategy and Left Politics,' in David Miliband, ed., *Reinventing the Left*, p. 143. See also the critique of these views developed by Ash Amin, 'Beyond Associative Democracy,' *New Political Economy*, 1:3 (1996).

43. 'Western Europe's Economic Stagnation,' *New Left Review*, 201 (1993), p. 73. Also see: R. Dore, R. Boyer and Z. Mars (eds.), *The Return to Incomes Policies* (London, Pinter, 1994); T. Notermans, 'Social Democracy and External Constraints' (University of Oslo, ARENA Working Paper #15-95, 1995); Scharpf, *Crisis and Choice*; and J. Pekkarinen, M. Puhojola and R. Rowthorn, (eds.), *Social Corporatism: A Superior Economic System?* (Oxford, Clarendon Press, 1992).

44. 'Social Democracy and Full Employment,' *New Left Review*, 211 (1995), pp. 54-5. This view, of course, is somewhat marginal to the actual policy orientation toward national competitiveness of social democratic parties today. In actual practice the solidarity is invoked by social democratic governments to impose real wage losses on workers via a consensus to lower unit labour costs and tax loads.

45. See, for instance, S. Holland (ed.), *Out of Crisis* (Nottingham, Spokesman, 1983).

46. D. Held, *Democracy and the Global Order: From the Modern State to Cosmopolitan Governance* (Stanford, Stanford University Press, 1995), p. 131.

47. 'Globalisation and the State,' in R. Miliband and L. Panitch (eds.), *Socialist Register*

1994: Between Globalism and Nationalism (London, Merlin Press, 1994).

48. See the arguments in J. Eatwell (ed.), *Global Unemployment* (Armonck, M.E. Sharpe, 1996).

49. Thus Canada exhibited what I have termed a 'limping golden age' to describe growth conditions that were more extensive than the intensive growth of other Fordisms and also that exhibited a secularly growing unemployment level since the 1940s. See: G. Albo, *The Impasse of Capitalist Employment Policy? Canada's Unemployment Experience, 1956-74* (Ottawa, Carleton University Ph.D. Thesis, 1994).

50. See R. Rowthorn and J. Wells, *De-industrialization and Foreign Trade* (Cambridge, Cambridge University Press, 1987), pp. 25-7.

51. Devaluation also loses some of its impact for deficit countries in that the increased complementarity of economies makes imports less price-sensitive. This is another consideration in terms of the need to control the open sector and to reduce import elasticities.

52. See: A. Singh, 'Openness and the Market-Friendly Approach to Development: Learning the Right Lessons from the Development Experience,' *World Development*, 22:12 (1994).

53. For a full development of this theme see the compelling arguments in: D. Coates, *The Question of UK Decline* (London, Harvester, 1994); J. Tomaney, 'A New Paradigm of Work Organization and Technology?' in A. Amin (ed.), *Post-Fordism* (Oxford, Blackwell, 1994); and J. Price, 'Lean Production at Suzuki and Toyota,' *Studies in Political Economy*, N.45 (1994).

54. This position has been best articulated by the most dynamic and successful union in North America: Canadian Auto Workers, *False Solutions, Growing Protests: Recapturing the Agenda* (Toronto, CAW, 1996).

55. This formulation is offered by A. Lipietz, moving somewhat away from his earlier views, but its antecedents also lie in the position of R. Boyer on offensive and defensive forms of flexibility strategies. They are, of course, arguing for the more egalitarian outcome and do not gloss over some of the contradictions as do advocates of flexible specialisation, diversified quality production and others. See: A. Lipietz, 'The New Core-Periphery Relations: The Contrasting Examples of Europe and America,' in C. Naastepad and S. Storm (eds.), *The State and the Economic Process* (Cheltenham, Edward Elgar, 1996); and R. Boyer and D. Drache (eds.), *States Against Markets: The Limits of Globalization* (London, Routledge, 1996).

56. See especially M. Piore and C. Sabel, *The Second Industrial Divide* (New York, Basic Books, 1984). For a critique see the excellent J. Peck, *Work*-Place: *The Social Regulation of Labour Markets* (New York, Guilford, 1996).

57. D. Laussel and C. Montet, 'Strategic Trade Policies,' in D. Greenaway and L. Winters (eds.), *Surveys in International Trade* (Oxford, Blackwell, 1994); and M. Kitson and J. Michie, 'Conflict, Co-operation and Change: The Political Economy of Trade and Trade Policy,' *Review of International Political Economy*, 2:4 (1995).

58. See: J. Robinson, 'The Need for a Reconsideration of the Theory of International Trade,' *Collected Economic Papers*, Vol. 4 (Oxford, Blackwell, 1973); and R. Guttman, *How Credit-Money Shapes the Economy* (Armonk, M.E. Sharpe, 1994), pp. 345-6.

59. R. Mahon, 'Swedish Unions in New Times.' (Paper presented at the Annual Meetings of the APSA, Chicago, 1995).

60. In other words, the rate of return to capital is set by world market forces and wages must adjust, with corporatist institutions providing the best means to do so. This recalls Marx's old warning that 'wages are the dependent and not the independent variable' in terms of capital accumulation.

61. 'Seoul Threatens to Expel Foreign Trade Union Groups,' *Financial Times*, 14 January 1997.

62. E. Altvater, *The Future of the Market* (London, Verso, 1993), pp. 83-4.

63. J. Tobin, 'A Proposal for International Monetary Reform,' *Eastern Economic Journal*, 4 (1978); and B. Eichengreen, J. Tobin and C. Wyplosz, 'Two Cases for Sand in the Wheels

of International Finance,' *The Economic Journal*, 105 (Jan. 1995).

64. Thus the regional differentiation of competitive capacities must be compensated by regional planning agencies of the multi-national authorities whose tasks are to do what other levels of government previously did, but with the loss of the main instruments to control development – currency control and import controls.

65. Kuttner, *End of Laissez-Faire*, chs. 6-8; J. Stopford and S. Strange (eds.), *Rival States, Rival Firms: Competition for World Market Shares* (Cambridge, Cambridge University Press, 1992); and R. Blecker (ed.), *U.S. Trade Policy and Global Growth* (Armonk, M.E. Sharpe, 1996).

66. Hirst and Thompson, *Globalisation in Question*, p. 146.

67. The point is that the 'capitalist reformer's dilemma' cannot be overcome within its own terms. As Mike Lebowitz argues, there is in fact a need for socialists to create a 'capitalists' dilemma': the penalty for refusing to compromise is a loss of control over financial and productive assets. See, for example, his 'Trade and Class: Labour Strategies in a World of Strong Capital,' *Studies in Political Economy*, 27 (1988).

68. 'The Myth of the Powerless State,' *The Economist* (7 October 1995), p. 16. They were, of course, warning of the dangers of state intervention.

69. Panitch, 'Globalisation and the State,' p. 87; and S. Gill, 'Globalisation, Market Civilisation and Disciplinary Neoliberalism,' *Millennium*, 24:3 (1995).

70. As Elmar Altvater puts it: 'Successful adaptation to exogenous conditions has relatively little to do with the functioning of markets; on the contrary, it depends on the extent to nations manage to control the operation of world market forces by political power.' See: *The Future of the Market*, p. 81.

71. See: N. Poulantzas, *Classes in Contemporary Capitalism* (London, Verso, 1974).

72. See: E. Wood, *Democracy Against Capitalism: Renewing Historical Materialism* (Cambridge, Cambridge University Press, 1995), conclusion.

73. This is, of course, a theme from the ecological Left going back to the 1970s, but also now among some Marxists, notably in the important journal *Capitalism, Nature, Socialism* under the editorship of Jim O'Connor. This should not be confused with an autarkic strategy, but control of the external sector internationally and nationally for reasons of democratic diversity, ecology and equality.

74. Economies of scale here means increased output for a given amount of inputs through long production runs. Increasing returns to scale are conceptually possible from other forms of organizing production by combining flexibility, external organizational economies and specialization. Robin Murray's varied writings have made this point most forcefully in attempting to find the rational kernel in current debates about production. See, for instance, 'Ownership, Control and the Market,' *New Left Review*, 164 (1987).

75. B. Sutcliffe, 'Development after Ecology,' in V. Bhaskar and A. Glyn (eds.), *The North, The South and the Environment: Ecological Constraints and the Global Economy* (New York, St. Martin's Press, 1995).

76. The variability of capitalist development has, if anything increased, now that the world configuration is no longer that of the classic age of imperialism. The flows of the world economy are no longer a one-sided necessity for capitalism in the North. How else can we account for the four tigers of Asia, the relative economic decline and trade problems of the U.S., and the mobilization of national capitalists in numerous countries against inward-oriented economic policies? The study of imperialism today is about the *particular mechanisms* which allow a centre economy to advantageously control the local resources of a periphery, rather than a search for uniform laws. This definition also encompasses relations of dependence between advanced capitalist states, as between Canada and the U.S. On the importance still of national models see: S. Berger and R. Dore (eds.), *National Diversity and Global Capitalism* (Ithaca, Cornell University Press, 1996); and J. Zysman, 'The Myth of a "Global Economy": Enduring National Foundations and Emerging Regional Realities,' *New Political Economy*, 1:2 (1996).

77. A. Singh, 'Industrial Policy in the Third World in the 1990s: Alternative Perspectives,' in K. Cowling and R. Sugden (eds.), *Current Issues in Industrial Economic Strategy* (Manchester, Manchester University Press, 1992). This is to say that differentiated competitive capacities do not always lead to cumulative competitive weakness; that external relations must be managed so as not to defeat other planning objectives; and that internal class struggles are crucial to embedding a process for more autonomous and integrated economies. These points are argued forcefully by C. Leys, *The Rise and Fall of Development Theory* (London, James Currey, 1996) and M. Bienefeld, 'The New World Order: Echoes of a New Imperialism,' *Third World Quarterly*, 15:1 (1994).

78. This would appear to be a strong version of Robert Cox's suggestion that 'the core institutions of a new multilateralism would have to reflect [civilisational] diversity . . . a weak centre in a fragmented whole.' See: 'Civilisations in a World Political Economy,' *New Political Economy*, 1:2 (1996), pp. 153-4.

79. *Collected Economic Papers*, Vol. 1. (New York, Augustus M. Kelley, 1951), p. 105.

80. A transitional socialist economic strategy 'between the demands of today's struggles and tomorrow's alternative society,' as John Palmer has pointed out, 'remains a seriously under-theorized subject among Marxists.' Important recent surveys, however, have helped clarify some of the issues at hand for socialist economies. See: J. Palmer, 'Municipal Enterprise and Popular Planning,' *New Left Review*, 159 (1986), pp. 117 and 122; D. Elson, 'Market Socialism or Socialization of the Market,' *New Left Review*, 172 (1988); and R. Blackburn, 'Fin de Siecle: Socialism after the Crash,' *New Left Review*, N.185 (1991).

81. This draws upon material published in G. Albo, 'Canadian Unemployment and Socialist Employment Policy,' in T. Dunk, S. McBride and R. Nelson (eds.), *Socialist Studies Annual 11: The Training Trap* (Halifax: Fernwood, 1996).

82. Recent valuable surveys have developed further ideas on alternate trade regimes: J. Michie and J. Grieve Smith (eds.), *Managing the Global Economy* (Oxford, Oxford University Press, 1995); M. Barratt Brown, *Models of Political Economy* (London, Penguin, 1995), chs. 17-19; and G. Epstein, J. Graham and J. Nembhard, eds., *Creating a New World Economy* (Philadelphia, Temple University Press, 1993).

83. G. Arrighi, *The Long Twentieth Century* (London, Verso, 1994), pp. 230-8; and E. Altvater, 'Financial Crises on the Threshold of the 21st Century,' in this volume.

84. For relevant surveys, with the first closer to the views here, see: J. Crotty and G. Epstein, 'In Defence of Capital Controls,' in L. Panitch (ed.), *Socialist Register 1996: Are There Alternatives?* (London, Merlin, 1996); and R. Pollin, 'Financial Structures and Egalitarian Economic Policy,' *New Left Review*, 214 (1995).

85. The views here follow A. Lipietz, *Towards a New Economic Order* (New York, Oxford, 1992); and G. Strange, 'Which Path to Paradise: Gorz and the Greens,' *Capital and Class*, N. 59 (1996).

86. E. Mandel, *Power and Money* (London, Verso, 1992), p. 202; and A. Gorz, *A Critique of Economic Reason* (London, Verso, 1989), p. 159.

87. See: C. Sabel, 'Flexible Specialization and the Re-emergence of Regional Economies,' in P. Hirst and J. Zeitlin, (eds.), *Reversing Industrial Decline* (Oxford, Berg, 1989). This is a point on which Wolfgang Streeck's work cited above has been most insightful, but also see R. Mahon, 'From Fordism to ?: New Technologies, Labour Markets and Unions,' *Economic and Industrial Democracy*, 8 (1987).

88. This approach to administration draws upon: G. Albo, D. Langille and L. Panitch (eds.), *A Different Kind of State? Popular Power and Democratic Administration* (Toronto, Oxford, 1993).

89. *Socialism for a Sceptical Age*, pp. 179-80.

FINANCIAL CRISES ON THE THRESHOLD OF THE 21ST CENTURY

Elmar Altvater

Introduction: the Value of Money

The fact that the 'wealth of nations' (Adam Smith) appears not only as a 'huge collection of commodities' (Marx) but also as a *monetary asset* has to do with the social form of money, which has developed so imaginatively through history. For money has a sensual effect which makes it, as a stimulus for innovation (from the cowrie shell through gold to cyber money), comparable at the very least to forms of transport from the horse-drawn carriage to the jumbo jet. The material form of money enables all qualities to be reduced to one: it makes apples and pears, pneumatic drills and nappies the same and so renders them comparable on the market. Once it has been reduced to this one quality of money, any quantitative variety is just a monetary characteristic. 'Having' triumphs over 'being'; the dynamics of accumulation are let loose. Money is differentiated in *time* merely by means of interest, and moneys (in the plural) become comparable in *space* by means of exchange rates.

So money has a price.[1] Interest expresses the fact that under conditions of developed capitalism money is potential capital, 'a means for the production of profit' (MEW 25: 351). Whoever makes use of this means must ensure that profit is produced. Thus money and its price, interest, exert a 'hard budgetary constraint' (Kornai), it functions as a material restraint. Keynes, as Marx before him, states that money is like 'the drink which stimulates the system to activity' (Keynes 1936: 173), the decisive difference being that Marx examined closely the social relations which establish the system of incentives and in doing so discovered money's *social form* which requires analysis in order to understand the *functions* and *institutions* of money. Because the process of globalisation has also caused the 'hard budgetary constraint', money's restraining function, to become globalised, it is now possible to talk of the existence of a 'ubiquitous money fetish' (see Altvater/Mahnkopf 1996).

The social form of money has in effect been understood, the 'money riddle solved' (Marx, MEW 23: 62), when the material form of commodities has been recognised as a social relation which requires an external appearance. Money makes societies uniform by allowing all substantial variety to be wrapped up in its formal quality as the common referent; money is so to speak a *socially constructed substanceless nothing*. Yet without this nothing no-one is worth anything:[2] money is the 'true common being' (Marx), the *moneytheistic* correlate to the *monotheism* of Judaism, Christianity and Islam:

> ... Everything can be had for 'cash', which itself as something external to the individual is to be catched (sic) by fraud, violence etc. Everything can thus be appropriated by all and what the individual can appropriate or not is dependent on chance, for it is dependent on the money in his possession. Thus, the individual per se is established as the master of everything. There are no absolute values for value as such is relative to money. Nothing is unsaleable as everything can be sold for money. There is nothing higher, holy etc. as everything can be appropriated with money. The 'res sacrae' and 'religiosae', ... absolved from the 'commercio hominum', do not exist before money–, as before God, all are equal. It was splendid how the Roman Church was the main propagandist of money in the Middle Ages (Marx 1953: 723).

Yet at the same time money also splits societies, for money always has a double purpose: a claim (monetary asset) on the one hand, and a corresponding obligation (debt) on the other. Thus, a social relationship between creditor and debtor is established which can become an entrenched one-sided conflict. When the relationship is global, so is the conflict between creditors and debtors. This is one of the main theses of this essay.

Because money constitutes a social relationship for which it is the referent, it is not surprising that substantial money (above all metal money, gold) has freed itself from its substantial form during the course of its history. This is particularly clear in the example of the development of computer money ('cyber money'). It no longer exists as gold, not even as paper, but merely as a specific sequence of substanceless bits. In the field of commerce, paper (cheques, exchange, bank notes) took the place of gold at a very early stage. This always begged an answer to the question of the value foundation of money, of the connection between monetary and real value, of the relationship between the monetary and the real economy. This was easy and unambiguous under the gold standard: after all, it was the value of gold metal which formed the basis of the value of money. With the dissolution of the gold standard the value foundation of money is institutionalised everywhere in the central bank, whose responsibility is to maintain institutionally the scarcity of money in order to secure its value internally and externally (in the competition between currencies).[3] That is difficult enough as world exchange and finance markets have become so deregulated after the collapse of the Bretton Woods currency system, which recognised the dollar as the 'gold' anchor of the world currency, that even the power of large and strong central banks to fix the value of national currencies is severely limited.

The foundation of the value of computer money proceeds, as with paper money, by means of the institutionally regulated scarcity of money. But this is not sufficient, as new regulations to ensure technical and economic security must be developed by the central bank so that computer money cannot be privately reproduced – which in principle is technically possible within a split second – infinitely quickly and in infinite amounts. It severs itself from the rules to which money as 'public property' is subject. Money becomes, and this is the arch-liberal utopia of von Hayek, privatised (Hayek 1978). A look at the financial innovations which have taken place in recent decades does in fact show the scale which the privatising bifurcation of money from real economic relations and from ties to political regulation on the globalised markets has attained. However, the privatisation of monetary assets has a flip side, namely a tendency towards the socialisation of debts. We will deal with this below.

So money, in the historical conditions of the late 20th century, emancipates itself from the substance which gives it a material and local character. Money emancipates itself from work; the monetary and the real economy part company. Money becomes the referent of real relations, which, however, functions like a draconian tablet of laws: money requires social actors to observe the rules. It transforms society into a money society, into a divided society, as'owners of monetary assets draw income from their monetary assets and debtors must bear the costs of their debt service through real production. Money and work thus become opposites.

Monetary Society versus Labour Society

The banality of Marx's observation (in a letter to Kugelmann 11th July 1868) '. . . that any nation would perish which stopped work for, I don't want to say a year, but a few weeks . . .' (Marx, MEW 32: 552) is of course valid; without work, no society. However, the question of the *form of socialisation* has not yet been addressed. For it is clear that not every job is important to society or recognised as such, otherwise capitalist societies would not permit the scandal of high mass unemployment: 17 million people without work in the European Union, 35 million in the OECD and world-wide 700 million people are without work or in unstable employment. Work obviously only proves to be 'necessary to society' when its products are 'turned into value', i.e. when they encounter a solvent demand for money. This process presupposes society's form of value and continually regenerates it. Without money in the modern capitalist society there is no social cohesion. The paradox can consequently be observed in the fact that commodity producing societies are *at the same time both monetary societies and labour societies*. The *substance* of value is formed by labour, the *material form* of value unfolds as money, which then intensifies social relations to the level of material constraints. If interest rates are expected to rise because inflationary tendencies are strengthened by an increase in employment, the rates on the stock market fall: this always happens now when positive US job market figures are published (*Financial Times*, 9 March 1996). Good news for the labour of the *labour society* is bad news for the stock market jobbers of the *monetary society*. The norms of the monetary society define the 'system of societal labour'.

The material form of money is more closely determined by the functions befitting of money. In functional analysis Marx and other theorists of money meet – and they must immediately be separated from one another. This separation is necessary not only because Marx explained and reconstructed the material form of money *before* its functional analysis (a monetary theorist from mainstream economics would give as little countenance to such an endeavour as would sociologists who are 'redis-covering' Simmel over Marx), but also because two fundamental functional determinants can be distinguished: money with regard to the world of commodities (the value of which money measures and through which commodities circulate) *on the one hand*, and money with regard to itself, money as money, *on the other*.

Looking at the latter *aspect*, Marx deals *firstly* with money as wealth, which in this form ('the function of storing value') becomes the incarnation of societal wealth, a powerful means of access to resources and at the same time the object of desire of those who amass wealth. Money controls them, not they the wealth. *Secondly*, money functions as a means of payment, as credits. Money is advanced by the creditor in order to receive more money in return after the expiry of a deadline. Money, with interest, values itself only against itself. It establishes new social relations, namely between the creditor and the debtor. The former owns and disposes over monetary assets, the latter disposes only over liabilities: he has monetary obligations to fulfil. Debtors must obey the logic of money imposed on them by the owners of monetary assets as the personification of monetary rationality. Interest is like a tax levied on production. It enforces acquisitive economic behaviour[4] and the corresponding 'acquisitive economic rationality' (Max Weber). This is also responsible for the enormous capitalist dynamic which neither recog-nises nor acknowledges any behavioural maxims other than the logic of money. For instance, one might have thought that at least creditor-debtor relation in the countryside still might be 'embedded' in the community. But as the farmers debt crisis in the United States during the Reagan era clearly showed this kind of 'embeddedness' in times of globalised financial relations is not more than a 'premodern' relic.

Acquisitive economic effort can founder of course due to real material relations. Creditor-debtor relationships which have foundered in real terms can be kept afloat monetarily by money not only being devalued by the direct loss of assets, but also through inflationary processes. In the course of these a real redistribution occurs: *from* those who have limited chances of securing assets or whose income from contracts is not adjusted to the inflation rate *to* those who dispose over real assets and/or are in the position to switch to stable assets. This possibility becomes greater the further the globalisation of finances is advanced and the easier it is to mobilise monetary assets between currencies. To facilitate the exploitation of this possibility is one of the stimuli for financial innovations on the globalised financial markets.[5]

The thrust towards standardisation on the modern world market is established in many theoretical traditions. 'Society today is unequivocally world society', a 'result of evolution' (Luhmann 1987: 585; 557). Of course, these evolutionary processes affect the forms and functions of money in the global context. For the role of money in the creation of the 'world society' must be ascertained if the form of socialisation is indeed determined more by money than by labour. Money reduces different qualities of commodities to the single one of money, which is then distinguishable from itself merely quantitatively. Qualitative standardisation makes a quantitative differentiation possible and thus implies that national societies have differing possibilities to partake in the gratifications of the world society. Inequality is thus produced in the global context, and actually more markedly than in national units as the implementation of corrective redistributive measures is considerably more difficult in the 'world society' than it is nationally.

Yet, without money the functional difference identified by Luhmann or Durkheim as an element of Modernity could not exist. In Luhmann's analysis money makes itself independent by becoming a series of acts of payment which remains uninterrupted only when the ability to pay is maintained (c.f. Luhmann 1990): 'an economic system [consists] of payments. ... For payments have a double purpose: the creation of the ability to pay for the recipient and the creation of the inability to pay for the payer. Such individual events are only possible in a dynamic system – that means with the precondition that the ability to pay and the inability to pay can be passed on or palmed off [elsewhere]. . .' That Luhmann here still regards money as means of circulation is demonstrated by his reference to the circulation metaphor and to the fact that 'the credit mechanism . . . [creates] a degree of leeway with the possibility of creating the ability to pay even where this does not result automatically from the circulation' (Luhmann 1990: 111). As an abstract measurement, money is such an irresistible object of fascination that it allows, indeed inspires, the abstraction from real economic processes. This occurs even when money is functioning as a means of circulation, in which it is unthinkable without the real commodities (goods and services) which it circulates. With regard to the codification of economic communication through monetary payments, Luhmann does not only exclude all metabolic processes from the economy – 'whenever ... money is involved, the economy is involved ..., but not in the case of the pumping process which extracts oil from the ground ...' (Luhmann 1987: 101) – he also writes that 'the private budget [has been] removed from the capitalist sector of the economy [and that it would become] unable to pay if it did not provide income by other means, mainly through labour' (Luhmann 1990: 110).

The economic system of monetary communication is clearly tied to the social organisation of the *metabolism* between nature and society, even if money bifurcates itself from real relations and imposes its behavioural logic onto all other systems of behaviour. (Exchange) value is worth nothing without utility value, thus the relationship between societal value and money requires as its substratum the real objects with which the variety of individual and social needs is satisfied. The use values have a material and energetic aspect and can be described as materials of low entropy. The fetishism of money, so vividly described by Marx, does allow the abstraction of the material and energetic dimensions of social communication in the social subsystems and the systemisation of these in academic semantics. Yet it does turn out that metabolic processes – labour is an engagement with nature and thus a transformation of material and energy – occur to maintain the communication qualified by payment/non-payment within the economic subsystem. Consequently, a monetary society can only be adequately interpreted as a labour society. To have drawn this out in all its detail is Marx's great achievement; later monetary-theoretical discourses come nowhere near this, neither Simmel's, nor those discourses which refer to Keynes, nor the compartmentalised Luhmannian communication formalism. Thus the money of the market does not merely sever itself from the real economic realm; it also severs the theoretical discourse from real ties. In money, the market's tendency of 'disembedding', of which Polanyi (1979) speaks (c.f. also Altvater/Mahnkopf 1996, chapter 4), attains its full force. This turns out to be the case when we deal more closely with money as a means of payment, i.e. with the world-societal relationship between the owners of monetary assets and debtors.

Monetary Assets and Debts

Debtors must pay the price of money – interest – to the owners of monetary assets, and for this reason they must use money in a capitalist manner and produce a sufficient profit (or have it produced). For interest is settled out of profits. Interest is, in so far as it is ascribed a *real* dimension and not just a *monetary* one, a part of (global) added value. This is – under the given social conditions – normal. It is also normal that creditors become debtors and, vice versa, that debtors can transform themselves into creditors. What is not normal is a one-sided social and economic relationship which is reproduced by a constant flow of interest from debtors to owners of monetary assets, without the debtors in their totality being successful capitalists who can extract a profit to cover the interest from their productively invested money and use credits as 'leverage' to make more profit. Interest thus *forces* increases in the productivity of the production process and it limits the possibilities of altering the distribution relationship of the income produced between waged labour and capital. This is very similar in the relationship between the public sector and private owners of monetary assets. When the public sector has become a structural net debtor, debt service becomes its highest priority, to which all other categories of expenditure, particularly those in the social budget, are subordinated: the secondary budget determines the primary budget's room for manoeuvre.[6]

Figure 1: Delinking of monetary and real accumulation

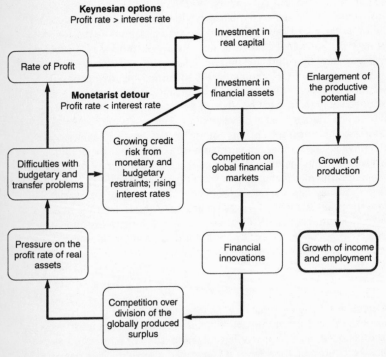

Figure 1 shows, in a highly simplified way, the consequences of the steering of profit use for real and monetary investments. In the national

framework ('Keynesian track') real investments and correspondingly also production, income and employment are stimulated. There are, to be sure, many obstacles to overcome before monetary investments are actually converted into employment. The 'monetarist track' can, however, bring about pathological effects for the economy and for society. When debtors are not in a position to service their debts ordinarily, credit risks increase. As creditors are only moved to lend when the risk can be wiped out, the global interest rate increases by the higher risk component. Thus, financial investments become potentially even more attractive than real investments – until the 'moment of truth' when it becomes clear that in the 'competition for a share of global added value' there is too little 'dough in the tin' for all the claims to be met.

The consequences are not only precarious for debtors, but also for medium and long term economic development which is determined by real investments. This negative effect on growth rates could be counter-acted by redistributing contributions from waged income to real investments. Because of the incentive to invest on financial markets instead of in the real economy, the pressure on mass income increases. The dramatic decline of investment ratios in Latin America since the seventies, which stood at over 22%, to under 17% of GNP in the eighties, the 'lost decade', was accompanied in any case by the transition from high positive growth rates of per capita income to negative growth rates. An important reason for the reduction of the investment ratios was the debt service for external credits.

Derivative capitalism: the 'club society'
The international financial system has developed extremely rapidly over recent decades. Between 1979 and 1984 turnover in world trade increased threefold, and turnover on the currency markets eightfold (Huffschmid 1995). According to the Bank for International Settlements (BIS) the quantities of financial transactions on the international gold, currency and money markets exceed $1200 billion daily (*Die Zeit*, 10.5.96; c.f. also Kulessa 1996: 97), whilst around $10 billion per day would suffice for the circulation of world trade with an annual volume of $3680 billion (based on world exports as of 1993). Financial transactions have thus very little to do with world trade any more: money functions only – if one wishes to express it quantitatively – 1 per cent as a means of circulation and 99 per cent as a means of payment.

The measure of the power of money can be ascertained by a glance at the amounts of derivative financial instruments on the international markets. In 1993 they were estimated to be over $14,000 billion (BIS).[7] That is more than the sum of the social product (1993) of the USA ($6380 billion), Japan ($4190 billion), the Federal Republic of Germany ($1880 billion) and Great Britain ($940 billion). The comparison should not be laboured because flow sizes and stock sizes are being compared. Yet, if one fixes an average interest rate of 6% on derivatives, interest claims of around $840 billion are produced. That is more than the sum of the gross domestic product of Brazil ($409 billion) and Mexico ($334 billion) in 1993, a comparatively good year for both countries. Of course, this relation is an exaggeration because derivatives include reciprocal claims within the global banking system and interest on them is less important than fees on transactions. But when claims or obligations on the derivatives market cannot be settled, for example, because unexpected movements of interest occur, and consequently movements of exchange rates of stocks and shares, the basis of derivatives, contracts can collapse and cause the house of cards of derivatives to tumble. Originally developed as an innovation to secure against risk ('hedge'), derivatives themselves have become increasingly an object for speculation:[8] the 'stock market game of the bankocrats' (Marx, MEW 23: 783).

The financial innovations exist above all in the fact that the elements of financial contracts – the agreed interest, the period of validity, the currency, the modality of repayment, the form of documentation – are combined in a new way ('unbundling' and 'repackaging'). Financial derivatives are 'instruments of the financial market (for instance swaps, financial futures, options) drawn from another financial product (underlying value); they can be utilised for purposes of securing existing positions, arbitrage or speculation. The value or price of the derivative instrument is influenced by the value or price of the financial product which forms its basis' (Deutsche Bundesbank, Monthly Reports, October 1993: 63). Financial futures are fixed-term financial contracts, the basis of which is formed by interest-bearing stocks and shares, that is to say interest rates (interest futures) or foreign currencies (currency futures). Options are the right, but not the obligation, to buy (call option) or sell (put option) at a previously agreed price a certain amount of underlying value either at a specific point in time (European option) or within a certain period of time (American option). Underlying values can be shares (share options), share indices (index options), fixed interest stocks and shares (interest options), foreign currencies (foreign currency options), financial swaps (swaptions) and in turn options (options on options). Options can serve to secure risk-bearing financial operations and also function as an instrument of speculation – as can futures. They are traded either in a form standardised by the stock market, or 'tailor made' outside the stock market, 'over the counter' (OTC) (Deutsche Bundesbank, Monthly Reports, October 1993: 63). According to the BIS, over half of the total sum of derivatives is dealt outside the stock exchange (*The Economist*, 10 February 1996: Survey 9). The amount of interest based futures, options and swaps at the end of 1993, by far the most popular derivative financial instruments, stood at around $14000 billion, having stood at only $1300 billion at the end of 1987.

Table 1: The development of selected derivative financial instruments world wide (nominal amounts in $ billions, final totals)

Position	1987	1993
Forward and futures-type instruments		
Dealt on stock exchange		
Interest futures	4878	4960
Currency futures	14	30
Share index futures	18	119
Dealt over the counter		
Interest swaps	683	6177
Currency swaps	184	900
Options type instruments		
Dealt on stock exchange		
Interest options	122	2632
Currency options	59	81
Options on share indices	26	286
Caps, Collars, Floors, Swaptions	561[a]	635[b]

a) 1990; b) 1992

(Source: Deutsche Bundesbank, Monthly Reports, November 1994: 43.)

In the Federal Republic of Germany alone, the amount of financial instruments not evidenced in the overall trade or financial balance increased almost tenfold from the end of 1986 to September 1994, from DM 875 billion to DM 8267 billion (Deutsche Bundesbank, Monthly reports, April 1995). Since the end of 1990 the trade in financial derivatives (not shown in overall balances) has grown by an average of 53% annually as opposed to an increase of 8% in the total volume of trade. A large part of these investments does not show up in overall balances because the banks no longer act as intermediaries between lender and borrower, saver and investor (financial disintermediation). They still broker the credit relationship, but they are neither the debtor of the savings depositor nor the creditor of the borrower, thus they pay no investment interest nor do they acquire any credit interest, but earn on the brokering fees or, in so far as they do take on a risk (exchange rate or interest risk), on the premiums due. The risks on their side can be secured by options and futures deals. This is the source of the enormous magnitude of the financial derivatives markets; they represent a diversification of the simple credit relationship – between someone who disposes over liquidity and another who requires free liquidity.

The driving wheels of the process of severing of money and market from social and political ties, the bifurcation of the financial from the 'real economic' sphere, are localised in nodal points of the global financial network, where political control is weak and social ties can be neglected offshore: in tranquil Luxembourg, on the Cayman Islands, the Bermudas etc. On the Cayman Islands (20,000 inhabitants) for instance, German banks and companies have applied more direct investment than on the whole of the African continent (660 million inhabitants). A new geography of the world system is emerging in which maps neither of natural features nor of political boundaries can assist orientation, but statistics of global financial transfer can. A '*nodalisation*' of the global economic space is occurring.

The exploitation of higher capital returns abroad, the striving towards risk limitation, towards the avoidance of limitation through regulation or taxes have contributed to the internationalisation and then globalisation of financial markets and – this is the inevitable concomitant – to the fiscal crisis of nation states, although nation states themselves have done everything to support this type of globalisation through deregulation. The actors in this financial network are the personified expression of what Karl Polanyi terms 'disembedding': they have taken their leave from the community of the tax citizens, and as a rule they do not need the solidarity benefits of a welfare state as they can buy these privately. They inhabit shielded ghettos, they have removed themselves from the community and, instead consort in clubs with their own likes. As Edward Luttwak (1994), John Kenneth Galbraith (1992), Robert Reich (1993) establish for the USA, Jens Petersen (1995: 128ff) for Italy, they have as owners of monetary assets a large interest in stable money – for the real value of their assets depends on this – but hardly no interest in state sponsored moves to secure infrastructure and social stability through state expenditure. On the contrary, they oppose this vociferously as (welfare) state activity either endangers the stability of monetary value, when debts are made, or causes the tax burden on the owner of monetary assets to increase. Inflation could not only cause a reduction in the external value of their monetary assets, but could also lead to exchange rate losses if the central bank reacts with an increase in its interest rate. Thus, positive job market figures in the USA are received as negative news on the stock market. Owners of monetary assets can escape devaluation of money and tax burdens by 'fleeing' to tax oases (i.e. by taking advantage of their 'exit option'). Correspondingly, public debts and flight from taxes correlate to a large extent. Jens Petersen describes this tendency for Italy (Petersen 1995: 123ff). With debts of around 120% of GDP the debt service swallows 20% of the state budget and 40% of ordinary tax revenue. Thus, the simultaneity of a growth in private wealth and a corresponding increase in public poverty identified by J. K. Galbraith in the USA of the fifties is repeating itself in a new form. Citizens who hold government bonds (BOT: Buoni ordinari del Tesoro), termed 'BOT-people', have come to form a broad rentier class, which *firstly* is able to mobilise considerable political power in society (no government dares touch income from capital assets), and which *secondly* is a burden to all those who do not own monetary assets. This includes the poorer south of Italy, but it is mainly those who draw income from gainful employment who bear the burden. Here it becomes clear that monetary society[9] weighs heavily upon labour society.

When socialisation is created by money and no longer through labour and communicative dealing, society as a cohesive community tendentially breaks up into '*clubby communities*' and exclusive ghettos. The avoidance of participation in the social costs of the nation is then no longer an asocial or even criminal act, but a normal reaction. Thus, moral scruples or even feelings of guilt are not to be expected with regard to tax avoidance,[10] and even in the public sphere crimes of this kind are viewed only slightly less critically than a small act of shoplifting which involves paltry amounts and not the magnificence of big money. In the 'club society' it is not disreputable to fleece the state budget from those who do not belong to the club.

Yet there does remain a high risk. Derivatives, despite all their detachedness from the real sphere, pose a hardly calculable demand on real flows of income. They are for the large part a matter of zero sum games. They have therefore no (or only a limited) effect on the real world of the economy. But problems arise as soon as open positions cannot be closed on schedule. Then a chain reaction is possible and the sum of interest, fee and premium claims, fictional under 'normal conditions', turns out in 'non-normal' times to be unpleasantly real. It can result in bankruptcy and in losses which can have a detrimental effect on the real world of the economy with production plants and jobs.

Why these risky innovations? Through them the flexibility of the lender and borrower can be increased. Each receives the form of the instrument which corresponds most closely to his or her respective interests. Illiquid capital becomes liquid and flexibly tradable. In this way, permanent production relationships are 'liquidated'. Thus, the 'bifurcation' of monetary and real accumulation expresses itself not only quantitatively as the ascendance of financial contracts over real economic turnover, but also as the qualitative effect of a subordination of real economic and social relations to the financial system. So the global financial system does actually assert itself everywhere as a 'ubiquitous money fetish', exercising its power primarily over those actors (individuals, countries, regions) who are debtors. The financially innovative liquidation of asset holdings facilitates the flexibilisation at the 'locations' which is demanded within the scope of neoliberal deregulation. It is therefore possible to play off production locations against one another on a world-wide scale. The transfer of capital is no longer an empty threat, but a real possibility supported by the new financial instruments.

Financial innovation and the old song of debt

Deregulation and globalisation were the preconditions for the explosive growth of the new financial instruments in recent decades. However, the accumulation of financial assets by the owners of monetary assets on the one hand is of equal importance to the piling up of debts on the other. Through this, social relations in the 'world society' have changed radically in the last two decades. Monetary assets are held mainly in hard currencies (in $, DM, Yen) and it is usual that debt service is settled in these currencies. Similarly, when local investment projects or consumer expenses are financed by external loans the debt service demonstrates relentlessly that local debtors have to follow the rules of the global arena. It makes a difference if people communicate by language or trade on comprehensible commodity markets or if they are linked by monetary claims and monetary obligations on the global market.

The structure of the world society by means of creditor-debtor relations is not particularly spectacular as long as debtors are in the position to service their debts. However, this will only be possible for as long as – other circumstances notwithstanding – the obligations of debt service do not exceed the achievable profitability in the real economy (in the production process). Consequently, debts force a profitability appropriate to interest obligations and thus the corresponding acquisitive economic rational structuring of the production process, i.e. the take-over and completion of 'capital accounting' (Weber 1976: 48ff), the adequate choice of equipment and a distribution between wages and profit which enables the interest to be derived. Debt service in the economy thus forces *economic rationalisation*. Monetary indebtedness forces capitalist economising, and space and time are subordinated to monetary rationality. This was also Keynes's topic, the long history of which is worth repeating with necessary brevity in order to understand better the dynamic of debts.

Aristotle was one of the first to advance a critique of 'acquisitive economics'. Money is the 'element and limit of barter trade. And unlimited, this is thus also wealth ... All profiteers ... wish to increase their money limitlessly ... Because this desire extends into unlimit-lessness, they also desire unlimited possibilities to achieve this' (Aristotle 1989: pp. 95-96). According to Aristotle, the reason for this ethos 'is the industrious endeavouring for life, but not for the good life'. Here, as Max Weber interprets, 'ethical and economic rationalisation' stand opposed to

ELMAR ALTVATER

61

each other (Weber 1976: 352). Interest on lent money which cannot be
used by the debtor as capital for the production of added value is in fact a
foreign body socially and economically, which is subsequently outlawed,
even declared as evil, in all major world religions. Interest functions like a
tax on the production process which for this reason must create a surplus.
This coercion by the economic system, the 'hard budgetary restriction',
causes the subordination of social, political and natural relations to the
economic principle.

This coercion as such is not new. It caused defensive moves in the major
religions and philosophical systems: the Islamic or canonical prohibition of
interest. At the second Lateran Council of 1139 usurers, people who drew
interest, were threatened with severe worldly and divine punishments: they
were to be denied confession and even a Christian burial. Later this
draconian rule was modified; lenders did not go to hell. 'Purgatory' was
invented for them, in which they were to roast for a certain period of time
to cleanse themselves of the sin of drawing interest, in order to gain unconditional entry to heaven afterwards (Le Goff 1988). The pressure to which
debtors are exposed can be so tremendous that their assets are eaten away
and their livelihoods destroyed. The social consequences of such heavy
debts are considerable. In earlier times debtors' bondage and debtors'
prison threatened, today it is other, rationalised forms of dependence and
limitation of one's room to manoeuvre. For this reason, throughout history
there has always been the bankruptcy of debtors or a debts amnesty when
debts got out of hand, such as under Solon in 594 BC.[11] As a rule, a new
cycle of debt could begin after a debts amnesty, until the next regulated –
or critical removal of debts (c.f. Löschner 1983). Bankruptcy or debts
amnesty are so to speak the 'safety valve' when the regulating valve of the
prohibition of interest fails and what is in principle the unlimited augmentation of money begins, be it unregulated or deregulated.

The regulating valve of the prohibition of interest was fixed at a very
low level of the regulating variable, at interest = 0, because the real possibilities for augmentation were very narrow in view of the limited
productivity of societies which operated with biotic energy. Opposed to
this is the experience that interest, when it was charged, was to an extent
exorbitantly high because no market had yet developed which was able to
fix a suitable price for lent money.[12] Both at an interest of zero and at an
extremely high interest rate, capitalist acquisitive effort soon reached the
limits of physical effectiveness and economic profitability. On the other
hand, many cultures viewed the accumulation of wealth without a doubt
positively, but not for turning the wealth into productive capital. Thus,
there are many cultures in which wealth is 'socialised' either through
destruction, collective consumption or redistribution.[13] It was only after
capitalist relations had taken form, and when production could be

increased considerably, above all in the course of the industrial revolution and due to the use of fossil fuels, that it became possible to raise the level of the regulating variable and not only to allow positive interest, but to use it as a positive stimulus to force a surplus of real production. Thus, in principle it must be possible to organise the production process as a process of utilising capital so that interest can be paid by debtors without eating away their capital assets. This possibility became reality with the increases in the forces of production which in the course of industrialisation were no longer linked to limited human resources. The increases in productivity reported annually now enable those interest payments which, in a time when increases in productivity were almost out of the question, had a socially undermining effect.

Money, fossil fuels and capitalist production relations form a triad (c.f. Altvater 1994) which is supposed to have changed the world as radically as never before in human history. It is thus explicable that in the Catholic Church the prohibition of interest has been 'practically annulled despite its eternal validity laid down in the Bible and by papal decrees' (Weber 1976: 340). In Islam too it is valid literally to the present day, only it has been lifted de facto in that, instead of interest, fees and profits are paid on one's participation in a business, and these function economically like interest. Yet the 'regulating valve', has merely been given a higher value and not switched off. If the level of the regulating variable is exceeded, as in capitalist prehistory, the safety valves of bankruptcy and debts amnesty can reduce excessive pressure on the economic system.

Money is always a pecuniary claim which has a corresponding pecuniary obligation. With the growth of financial assets debts also increase and with them the compulsion to produce a surplus in order to be able to service monetary assets. We have seen that derivative financial instruments have increased in the nineties by a yearly average of more than 50%. The underlying values, from which derivatives are drawn, have of course not increased at this rate. A considerable volume of claims has swollen up, the servicing of which could cause problems. Because of money's self-referentiality in the form of the intertemporal interest rate, the Islamic or Christian regulating valve, guided by the debtors' external ability to pay, has in principle been switched off. The increase in the ability to pay is caused by the effect of the hard budgetary restriction of money. The dynamic of money demands a permanent dynamisation of the real economy and society. Admittedly, the possibilities for a growth of the surplus are energetic and material and thus limited by economic (an over-proportional increase in the marginal costs of the progress of productivity) and social (resistance to the 'violence of money' grows) factors; no financial innovation can change them. Then the mounting pressure on the monetary system from bankruptcy, inflation and/or debt amnesty –

expresses itself. The interest claims of the owners of monetary assets must therefore be viewed in relation to increases in productivity and to the profit rate on productive capital.

There are no reliable data on the size of financial assets, disregarding holdings of derivatives, direct and portfolio investments or loans, especially if they are to provide information about global quantities. The sparseness of the data is for its part an expression of the 'disembedding' of global owners of monetary assets (these are above all banks and other financial institutions) from (world) societal bookkeeping. The advantage of free banking zones also lies in the fact that the activities there are not monitored and commonly enough are not even quantified so that our knowledge of them – the basis of rational taxation, political control and social participation – is limited. This is different in the case of public and private debts. These are known to a large extent. In order to gain an overview, let us calculate roughly global debts.

Firstly we will look at the Third World's mountain of debts which towers above everything. Despite a transfer of debt service, the mountain increased constantly from $658 billion in 1980 to around $1770 billion at the end of 1993 (World Debt Tables 1993-94). The group of seven industrialised nations had at the end of 1994 net external debts, i.e. when one totals up credits and liabilities towards other countries, of $278 billion (at the end of 1993 it was $177 billion). The low value is achieved as the net external debts of the USA ($781 billion) or Canada ($214 billion) are balanced by the high net credits of Japan ($688 billion) or the FRG ($213 billion). The USA has therefore the highest external debts of any country on earth.[14] Table 2 summarises the most important data on the external holdings and liabilities[15] of the industrial countries.

The eastern European countries also have serious debts. The external net debts of central and eastern Europe increased from something over $200 billion in 1989 to $290 billion at the end of 1995 (IMF 1996: 173). Thus, the world has without exception net debts. The claims and debts within the global financial system should add up to +/– zero. But the external net debts in the world economy add up to a considerable magnitude even when one can realistically assume that the debts of the Third World and of Eastern Europe are contained in the holdings of the industrial countries. However, a net amount remains which ought not to exist according to the rules of double bookkeeping. An explanation for the mismatch is not easy to find. The most plausible is the assumption that the net debts of the world correspond to private assets which are not measured and thus not contained in the statistics.

Table 2: External credits and external obligations of selected OECD countries (in $ billion, situation at the end of each year)

Country	Status	1981	1986	1989	1992	1993	1994
USA	Assets	899	1308	1752	1913	2268	2378
	Liabilities	630	1391	2145	2525	2926	3159
	Balance	269	−83	−393	−612	−658	−781
Japan	Assets	208	726	1770	2034	2180	2423
	Liabilities	198	547	1478	1522	1570	1735
	Balance	10	179	292	512	610	688
FRG	Assets	244	495	856	1179	1268	1433
	Liabilities	221	405	594	887	1047	1230
	Balance	23	90	62	292	221	203
France	Assets	169	255	472	805	851	979
	Liabilities	141	254	497	885	890	1067
	Balance	28	1	−25	−80	−39	−88
Italy	Assets	96	156	269	371	416	478
	Liabilities	111	192	342	510	525	587
	Balance	−15	−36	−73	−139	−109	−109
GB	Assets	623	1058	1534	1797	2033	2191
	Liabilities	568	916	1446	1761	1998	2168
	Balance	55	142	88	36	35	23
Canada	Assets	69	100	162	181	207	241
	Liabilities	179	234	347	403	444	455
	Balance	−110	−134	−185	−222	−237	−214
G7 total	Assets	2308	4098	6815	8280	9223	10123
	Liabilities	2048	3939	6849	8493	9400	10401
	Balance	260	159	−34	−213	−177	−278
G7 and 8 other OECD countries	Assets	2732	4856	8038	—	—	—
	Liabilities	2563	4836	8324	—	—	—
	Balance	169	20	−286	—	—	—

(Source: OECD 1993b, 1995b (Economic Outlook, December 1993, 1995)).

State debts, or the tradition of public poverty and private wealth

The transition to a capitalism of derivatives and global debts is tantamount to the public sector being taken into the service of the monetary system, which can be seen clearly in the state debts of almost every country. The *private* economic system requires *political* assistance. When financial difficulties become apparent, the political institutions of Bretton Woods, the World Bank and the International Monetary Fund make their presence felt. The political and economic conditionality imposed by them (but also by the EU on its members) in the form of *structural adjustment programmes* is like a world formula which sovereignly disregards distinctions in the various countries and cultures. Globalisation is in fact financial globalisation and it is felt so painfully because the logic of money is asserted without regard for social, political, cultural relations, indeed with a disregard for human dignity itself. Monetary sovereignty lies now with the global institutions. National sovereignty outside the monetary sphere is incomplete as territorial and political borders count for little in the competition between currencies. The *privatisation* of money through deregulation and financial innovations thus corresponds to a *socialisation* of debts. Public institutions therefore do not only lose sovereignty in guiding economic policy, but on top of that they are obliged to act as guarantors for debt service. Public interest payments are becoming more and more the basis of the value of private monetary assets because the public sector is required should private debtors not be capable of coming up with interest and amortisations. Either a 'normal' case of guarantee occurs or the threat of a financial crash requires public intervention in order to avoid negative side effects. It thus occurs that the proportion of public debts in the total external debt in Argentina grew from 60.7% to 96.6% between 1980 and 1989, in Mexico the increase during the same period was from 82.2% to 95.0%, in Chile from 50.3% to 77.5% and in Brazil from 10.6% to 94.4% (Fundap 1993: 25). In the case of public debts it is not a matter of a crowding out bemoaned by neoliberals in the 1970s. On the contrary: from the point of view of bookkeeping, public debts are none other than the flip side of private financial assets. They have taken the place of private debtors, i.e. of companies, who run up too few debts because they invest too little. Debts thus become socialised in order to protect private monetary assets. In other words: because the profit rate on real accumulated capital is too low, private capitalists invest financially in order to secure interest. Finally, in the course of the bifurcation of the financial sector from real accumulation, these are enlarged to a considerable extent from public finances and transferred to the private sector.

Monetary assets are thus secured by transferring liabilities from the regulation of market forces into sovereign domains. Interest, according to Keynes, is like a tax on production. It now becomes apparent that interest does actually become secured and transferred by the removal of taxes if the profitability of the production process is insufficient with regard to interest claims. The state manages this task by means of a kind of socialisation of losses. This is extraordinarily costly both socially and economically because in many state budgets payment of debt service (in the secondary budget) limits enormously room for manoeuvre in policy formation (in the primary budget). As a result of publicly guaranteed liabilities, it is not only the case that social expenditure is under pressure, but – a positive feedback effect – monetary assets increase and along with them interest claims. If monetary assets are not put into productive investments, and if they do not have to expose themselves to the risk of making a loss, the pressure on public budgets in derivative capitalism will not decrease.

Thus, state debts are obviously a functional necessity in deregulated derivative capitalism. Servicing them does certainly cause problems to arise as public debt service cannot be financed by tax on monetary assets, because asset holders under conditions of free convertibility and financial deregulation have the opportunity to transfer their assets to other 'more friendly' places. In other words, they have the power to blackmail democratically elected governments by capital flight. Therefore governments today compete with one another for who will place comparatively low tax burdens on asset holders; for instance, the German Government in late 1996 introduced for this very reason an extreme reduction in taxes on monetary assets and wealth. Consequently, the only remaining strategy is to tap into the income of non-owners of monetary assets, welfare state transfer payments and privatisation of public property. The globalisation of financial markets and the formation of the club society of owners of monetary assets thus leads to the crisis of the welfare state which is erupting in the nineties in all countries, including those with a long welfare state traditions such as Scandinavia and Germany. A dismantling of the welfare state is only possible if a surplus is obtained in the 'primary budget' of state expenditure financed by ordinary (tax) income which can be used to finance the 'secondary budget', i.e. for the debt service. This is of course particularly difficult in times of crisis when growth is slow and as a consequence the relationship between real interest and real growth is particularly unfavourable. Other possibilities of reducing state debts are debt for equity swaps and the privatisation of public property. Both methods are extremely risky and as a rule not very effective as the expected future returns on public institutions are fixed low whilst interest is high, especially in times of crisis. On top of this, it is well known that the 'family silver' can only be flogged once. The last method of debt reduction worth mentioning is the devaluation of monetary assets. If the creditors are foreigners and if the debts the state owes them are in its own currency, then a currency devaluation can provide relief. The USA used this possibility and has halved the external value of the US dollar since the mid-eighties and has thus devalued its external debts (for instance to Japanese investors). Internal debts could be reduced by inflation if both an outflow of capital and interest inflation can be avoided. The *ultima ratio* of a policy which follows this line would be a currency reform. Yet, in normal times, without a change of the political regime, this can only be done if inflation has taken on the scale of hyperinflation as it had in Argentina and Brazil at the end of the eighties and beginning of the nineties.

The competition between currencies: the battle for global added value.
It is precisely the neoliberal deregulation discourse which hides state complicity in this redistribution in favour of the owners of monetary assets. In national societies the regressive effects of 'derivative capitalism' are equally evident as on the global level. The poor have become poorer, the rich richer (cf. statistics on this in UNDP 1994). This mechanism has led to a differentiation within and between countries and regions in countries, also within the so-called Third World in which there have indeed been winners alongside the losers of the 'lost decade' of the eighties.

Keynes' remarks about the 'slips between the cup and the lip' (Keynes 1936: 173) would be supplemented today by the easy evasive possibilities open to liquid monetary capital across borders which reduce the stimulating effect on investment activity, employment and incomes and thus have a negative effect on the ability of public institutions to service their debts 'ordinarily'. It is also precisely globalisation which breaks up the traditional connection between interest rate and profit rate, between the monetary sphere and the real economic sphere. The 'stimulating effect' of money does not lead to more employment and income, if the obstacles cited by Keynes have been removed at all, but to monetary globalisation. This has been indicated schematically in Figure 1. Globalisation is not merely a transnational extension of the nation state's relationship between the monetary and the real sphere, as it was analysed by Keynes. The price of money and the hard budgetary restriction no longer force the *production* of a growing production surplus (and thus of added value); one gains the impression that more real wealth and real income can be 'won' from speculation with financial means. Modern capitalism thus appears to be a kind of perpetual motion.

Interest claims direct themselves on global markets, particularly when official institutions are involved, at the *production surplus which has already been produced*. 'Nation states compete to draw a part of the added value produced world-wide onto their own territory' (Holloway 1993: 23). It is much less nation states which enter into competition with one another, rather the owners of monetary assets (banks, insurance and pension funds, financial service institutions) who take monetary hold of the added value produced in the global (currency) area. However, nation states are imperative for two reasons. To this extent it is justified to talk of states as subjects in this battle of redistribution.

Firstly, private monetary assets must be managed by public institutions because private debtors – companies which produce profits from productive investments and do not themselves belong to the class of owners of monetary assets – do not produce a sufficient production surplus to satisfy interest claims. Thus, public debts are the flip side of insufficient real investment (i.e. investments which do not go into monetary investments), the symptom of a crisis of over-accumulation. Public debts are a response to this. The price is high: it takes the form of the fiscal crisis of states, which has developed into the crisis of social regulatory systems, and this has happened on a world-wide scale. On the other hand, if state expenditure is reduced through cutting interest payment, this will endanger internal and external monetary value. Therefore states must *secondly* ensure that the currency in which monetary assets, and thus the claims on parts of the global added value are denominated, is and remains valuable, its value is increased as much as possible and the owners of monetary assets are presented with an increase, even if they have not produced a real economic profit. Thus, the securing of monetary stability becomes the primary task of the state. *The monetary competition between private owners of monetary assets thus transforms itself into the competition between the currencies of the nation states (or economic blocs).*[16] Because of this, competition on the world market gains a political dimension. At the same time new possibilities of capital investment for the owners of monetary assets open up in the competition between currencies; namely by speculating they can exploit expected changes in exchange rates and once again tap into state budgets, for it is the public sector which bears the losses of devaluation.[17] Globalisation of financial markets also means that the whole world is judged by the sharp gaze of the *rating* of financial markets and those units which are weighed and found to be too light not only arouse interest, but are also plunged into social misfortune, a political crisis and economic difficulties as a consequence of having no alternative other than to be dependent on the goodwill of 'the markets'.

In order to ensure as large a possible portion of added value in the context of global competition, the innovative financial instruments described above were developed. In a national context, money stimulates, as Keynes assumed, real economic activity under certain conditions. In the global context, however, it stimulates first of all financial innovations, and these equally on the side of the creditor (owner of monetary assets) as on the side of the debtor. Financial innovations are the expression of attempts to tap into parts of global added value. They do not necessarily function here as that Keynesian 'drink' which stimulates the system to activity and performance. It is more a matter of levers by which the redistribution process of global added value is influenced. Consequently, the financial innovations are primarily jokers in a global zero sum game. A few become richer and very many poorer.

The Mexican crisis: the first financial crisis of the 21st century
In the competition between 174 currencies on the world market, fewer than five currencies can be evaluated as 'strong'.[18] Other currencies demonstrate either a limited convertibility or they can 'borrow' strength by connecting the exchange rate of the national currency to a strong currency. Of course, this does not only happen when the currency is made attractive by high real interest; in Latin America the interest differential towards treasury bonds from the USA (T-bills) rose from 900 basic points to 1750 from 1994 to 1995 (Banamex-Accival, Monthly Publication, No. 843, February 1996: 50ff.).

The attractiveness of a country or region is reflected in the competition between currencies; it is now hardly a result of the initial allocation of production factors or of the political geographical position unless these are reflected in the strength of the currency. Consequently, a country like Mexico became a popular land for investment in the nineties (rich oil country; NAFTA membership; apparently successful neoliberal stabilisation under President Salinas) until capital returns dropped comparatively and the short term investments of the internationally operating capital were hurriedly withdrawn. Internal and external reasons were decisive in this. The assassination of the presidential candidate Colosio in April 1994, the assassination of Massieu, secretary general of the PRI, in September of the same year and above all the Chiapas revolts destabilised capital, and on top of that the USA increased its interest rate. Thus, the state promissory notes CETES, denominated in pesos, lost attractiveness against the Tesobonos which was an unmistakable sign of an impending peso crisis. This then erupted as a 'Christmas present' in the first two weeks of December 1994. In the course of just four weeks in this 'black' December the peso lost 40% of its value; the official devaluation followed on 20 December 1994 (IMF 1995). Mexico's real values were also worth only 40% in the course of these December weeks, at least when they are measured in world money; and which other binding measure should exist in the international competition between currencies? Money really is the 'true common nature of society' and proves this brutal fact by devaluing the 'real common nature of society'. In 1992, ten years after the outbreak of the debt crisis as a consequence of Mexico's inability to pay, the Third World's successful mastering of its debt crisis was still being celebrated. So for the second time in ten years Mexico once again had to experience an increase in its external debts, now from $128.8 billion to $153.0 billion. The amount remained de facto constant in 1995 but only because a 'stabilisation fund' of almost $18 billion from the IMF had neutralised parts of the external debt. The price for this is a considerable increase in repayments from 1998. Then Mexico must repay $3.1 billion to the IMF and $3.6 billion to the USA (in 1999: $4.3 and $4.4 billion respectively). Whether this will be successful due to the economic crisis is by no means guaranteed (Banamex-Accival, Monthly Publication, No. 842, January 1996).

Conclusion: Tributes to the Ubiquitous Money Fetish

The severing of monetary relations from society is on the one hand the framework within which the transition to neoliberally-inspired political concepts occurs. They give the impression that there are no alternatives to the structural adaptation programmes of the IMF or to 'sequencing' models, to the comprehensive privatisation of public property and to deregulation of prices in the transformation to a market economy in former socialist societies. Neoliberalism is the fitting economic theory at the 'end of history' in the 'new world order', in which alternative visions of the future and cultural plurality are placed under the dictate of competitiveness and culturally neutral acquisitive economic behaviour. However, this kind of liquidation of real relations also results in deindustrialisation, regressive redistribution, destruction of social consensus and the neglect of ecological restrictions. The way financial globalisation functions is an attack on social justice and individual dignity. Even economically strong nations cannot escape this 'material restraint', even if the logic of the material restraint appears to be asymmetrical.

Yet for this extremely high price, one cannot even expect higher economic efficiency from the promises of the neoliberal theorists and politicians. In the seventies they hoped that the lifting of controls would calm down the currency front; but instead the volatility of exchange rates and interest has tended to increase since then. The direction of movements of capital and commodities is influenced by this and the transaction costs of commodity trade and direct investments are growing. Countries compete with regard to the importance of financial transactions by means of interest and of the stability of their currencies in comparison to real economic relations. Through this economic sovereignty is undermined. Under a regime of fixed exchange rates, interest rates in the national context could be fixed to a large extent without regard for world economic conditions in order to influence growth and employment positively. This was the basic idea behind the Keynesian project of expansive employment policy. Whilst in the thirties a *devaluation competition* took place with disastrous consequences for world economic development, political stability and finally world peace, today a *stability competition* for real interest and exchange rates is taking place in the competition between currencies in order to attract capital which is extremely flexible as a result of the financial innovations. The consequences are similarly destructive. The owners of monetary assets can open their club anywhere as society no longer means anything to them. This is also a reason for the fact that they are not prepared to pay for it and enter into tax flight. The rules of monetary globalisation force a 'common nature of society' consisting of payment and non-payment which excludes a sense of community unless it can be instrumentalised and used as a resource in the improvement of international 'competitiveness' to pay tribute to the material restraints of the 'ubiquitous money fetish'. But, because the value foundation of money occurs as a result of the labour of society, limits are laid down for the bifurcation of the monetary from the real sphere. The limits also assert themselves as currency and financial crises in capitalism on the threshold of the 21st century. Thus, representatives of international institutions require structural reforms to be tackled in order to secure the stability of money. These are mostly understood to be reforms with the purpose of redistributing resources in favour of the globalised financial system. Against this background, the remark of the director of the IMF Michel Camdessus that Mexico's financial crisis of 1994/95 is the 'first financial crisis of the 21st century' is not without some irony.

It is not a simple task for political institutions to control financial processes, for the reasons this essay has pointed out. The sovereign power of nation states on financial markets is extremely limited and on an international or even global level there are no mechanisms of control besides the institutions of Bretton Woods - which only act to make assets (monetary wealth) secure, if necessary even by partly socialising the debt and the debt service. A way back to non-convertibility of currencies and control of capital transfers by nation states cannot be found amidst globalisation, so in order to prevent financial crises, the control of financial flows would have to be institutionalized on the international level. One instrument occasionally proposed is a tax on international capital transfers ('Tobin tax') in order to calm down speculative short term capital movements, but it is by no means clear how efficiently such a tax would even work in preventing speculation since there is no guarantee that further financial innovations by markets would not quickly neutralise a Tobin tax. 'Re-embedding' of 'disembedded' financial flows therefore would have to consist, at a minimum, in more transparency in financial relations, minimum standards of reserve requirements for financial business, and the undermining of the resort to tax havens and offshore banking through international requirements on tax payments. But even such a slight reformist programme is very difficult to realise in today's climate, as the European Union shows. So we continue to be led down a path of greater economic and financial integration, on the one side, and on the other financial paradises like Luxemburg, London or Guernsey Island where the regulating power of even powerful central banks ends. The Left in this situation only can make make clear that control of global economic processes at the end of the 20th century is a necessary element of any alternative economic policy project.

NOTES

1. It actually has two prices: the inter-temporal price, interest, by means of which money is comparable over periods of time. It also has an 'inter-spatial' price, the exchange rate, by means of which national moneys (currencies) are comparable.

2. In a Monetary-Keynesian interpretation money is understood as a 'nothing' which is 'enthroned' by the institution of the central bank (since without the availability of this 'nothing' no-one is worth anything). The distinction between this Monetary-Keynesian analysis and Marx's analysis lies principally in the former's misinterpretation of the social genesis of the material form of money which is the centrepiece of Marx's analysis. It is because they have no account of the social roots of money, that the Monetary-Keynesians have to put such emphasis on the institutional genesis of money, i.e. the crucial role of the central bank.

3. For this reason, Monetary-Keynesians ascribe such central importance to the central bank. This goes as far as an idolisation of the central bank as a god-like demiurge of money (c.f. for instance Riese 1995).

4. *Der Spiegel* (7/1996:98) puts it thus: 'Capital scours the surface of the globe for investment possibilities. Whoever wants to be interesting for the investors may, like Schrempp, only follow one goal: 'profit, profit, profit' and the employer who demonstrates too much social commitment is punished with a withdrawal of capital.'

5. However, according to a survey of US firms, only 13% of smaller firms (turnover under $50 million) could use this escape route; amongst larger firms (turnover over $250 million) it was 65% (figures from: *The Economist* 10.2.1996: survey 5).

6. This can also be seen in the convergence criteria of the Maastricht treaty, in which firstly only monetary convergence criteria are contained, and of which secondly two refer explicitly to the debts of the public sector.

7. The data are not precise and in some respects differ from each other considerably. In 1994, according to BIS, they were estimated at around $20 billion (*The Economist*, 10.2.96: Survey 9). In *Die Zeit* the volume at the end of 1995 was quoted at $40.7 billion (*Die Zeit*, 10.5.1996).

8. *The Economist* (10 February 1996) printed a list of losses on the derivatives market which, although incomplete, does give an impression of its volatility. The biggest losses since 1993 have been made by Showa Schell Sekiyu ($1.4 billion), Metallgesellschaft ($1.3 billion), Kashima Oil ($1.5 billion), Orange County ($1.7 billion), and Barings Bank ($1.4 billion). It caused the bankruptcy of Barings Bank. *Der Spiegel* reports of the banking group Trinkaus & Burkhardt that dealers are 'proud whenever their group is described as Germany's biggest betting office' (*Der Spiegel* 7/1996: 94).

9. In Argentina the ironic and fitting term 'patria financeira' has been coined: financial fatherland.

10. Ulrich Beck summarises very nicely: 'Entrepreneurs have discovered the touchstone of riches. The new magic formula is: capitalism without labour plus capitalism without taxes... Many entrepreneurs become virtual taxpayers ('Kapitalismus ohne Arbeit', in *Der Spiegel*, 20/ 1996, 13.5.1996).

11. In his portrayal of the history of the Athenian Constitution, Aristotle summarises Solon's achievements to the effect that the 'abolition of debtors' bondage' ranked in first place

even before the possibility of the court's recognition of interests and the introduction of the right of appeal before a people's court (Finley 1976: 30). It is no coincidence that the Lord's Prayer in German contains the line: '... vergib uns unsere Schuld, wie wir vergeben unseren Schuldigern ...' (forgive us our trespasses as we forgive those who trespass against us), where the German word Schuld means both guilt and debt.

12. In the late Middle Ages in Europe, interest increased, despite the prohibition of interest, to considerable heights which had nothing to do with the debtor's real ability to pay, i.e. to 100% and even more. The church's ban on usurers thus lost its practical relevance and was lifted in the early 15th century. The usurer became an 'assistant to the birth' of the emerging capitalist society (Marx, MEW 23: 782ff).

13. For instance the 'Potlatch' of the Kwakiutl (on the west coast of Canada) was an opportunity 'for passing on inheritance and ceremonial wealth to oncoming generations ... Enormous amounts of gifts were given out ... Even aside from generosity, chiefs had an incentive to give away as much as possible ...' (Kirk 1986: 59f).

14. This is to be judged differently from high external debts of other countries for three reasons: firstly the USA is a large country in every way and thus can cope with high debts more easily than smaller countries. The proportion of debts in GDP of 10.4% in 1993 is considerable, however, especially when its dynamic is observed. In 1985 credits were 1.0% of the national product. Secondly the USA's debts are in their own currency, dollars. Thus, they are not subject to the problem of transfer which all countries must solve who must acquire foreign currency by means of export surpluses or capital imports (new debts) to settle their debt service, and thirdly the conditions of interest service are not identical on credits and liabilities. Interest on credit is higher than interest on deficits so that net debts have led to an external flow of liabilities only above a net value dependent on interest differentials (at the beginning of the nineties this was around $400 billion). Interest on credit is higher than interest on deficit because the USA is regarded as a good debtor and thus gets by without paying extra interest ('spread'), which is sometimes fixed at a very high rate by US banks towards third world debtors.

15. External debts can be defined in three ways: firstly according to the place where the debt titles were issued, secondly according to the place of residence or company headquarters of the creditor, thirdly according to the currency in which the debt is to be repaid and serviced. The first criterion is no longer valid due to the globalisation of financial markets, the second is important but not decisive. Thus, the third criterion is of central importance. Depending on the choice of criterion, a country's external debts can vary. For instance, when the third criterion is employed, the debt titles of a country which are not denominated in its own currency form part of its external debt. This is for instance the case with the Mexican 'Tesobonos', state promissory notes indexed in dollars.

16. In the competition between currencies it is not nation states which count as political units, but currency regions. Nation states are consequently more like a territory which covers the same area as a currency region. Thus the deutschmark was more important in the course of German unification than was the flag.

17. In the pound crisis of 1994 the Bank of England lost several billion pounds sterling to international speculation, particularly to George Soros, the 'man who broke the Bank of England'.

18. From the International Organisation for Standardisation cited in Deutsche Bundesbank: Exchange Rate Statistics, Statistical Supplement to Monthly Report, 5 November 1995.

REFERENCES

Altvater, Elmar (1994): Die Ordnung rationaler Weltbeherrschung oder: Ein Wettbewerb von Zauberlehrlingen, in PROKLA 95 - Zeitschrift für kritische Sozialwissenschaft, Jg. 24, H. 1 (1994): pp. 186-225.

Altvater, Elmar/Mahnkopf, Birgit (1996): Grenzen der Globalisierung. Politik, Ökonomie und

74   THE SOCIALIST REGISTER 1997

Ökologie in der Weltgesellschaft, Münster (Westfälisches Dampfboot).
Aristotle: *Politics.*
Finley, Moses I. (1976*): Die Griechen. Eine Einführung in ihre Geschichte und Zivilisation*, München (Becksche Verlagsbuchhandlung).
Fundap (1993): Fundacao do Desenvolvimento Administrativo de Sao Paulo/Instituto de Economia do Setor Publico: *Processo de Privatizacao no Brasil: A Experience dos Anos 1990-92*, Sao Paulo.
Galbraith, John K. (1992): *Die Herrschaft der Bankrotteure*, Hamburg (Hoffman und Campe).
Hayek, Friedrich August von (1978): *Denationalisation of Money – The Argument Redefined*, (Washington D.C., Institute of Economic Affairs).
Holloway, John (1993): Reform des Staats: Globales Kapital and nationaler Staat, in *PROKLA 90 – Zeitschrift für kritische Sozialwissenschaft*, Jg. 23, H. 1 (1993): pp. 12-33.
Huffschmid, Jörg (1995): Eine Steuer gegen die Währungsspekulation, in: *Blätter fur deutsche und internationale Politik*, 40. Jg., H. 8, (1995): pp. 1003-1007.
IMF (International Monetary Fund) (1995): *International Capital Markets. Developments, Prospects and Policy Issues* (Washington D.C.).
IMF (1996): *World Economic Outlook, May 1996* (Washington D.C.).
Keynes, John M. (1936): *The General Theory of Employment, Interest and Money*, London/Melborne/Toronto (Macmillan, Repr. 1964).
Kirk, Ruth (1986): *Wisdom of the Elders*, Vancouver (Douglas & McIntyre).
Kulessa, Margareta E. (1996): Die Tobinsteuer zwischen Lenkungs- und Finanzierungsfunktion, in: *Wirtschaftdienst*, II (1996): pp. 95-104.
Le Goff, Jaques (1988): *Wucherzins und Höllenqualen. Ökonomie und Religion im Mittelalter*, Stuttgart (Kletta-Cotta).
Löschner, Ernst (1983): *Souveräne Risken und internationale Verschuldung*, Wien (Manzsche Verlags- und Universitätbuchhandlung).
Luhmann, Niklas (1987): *Soziale Systeme. Grundriss einer allgemeinen Theorie*, Frankfurt/M. (Suhrkamp).
Luhmann, Niklas (1990): *Ökologische Kommunikation. Kann die moderne Geseelschaft sich auf ökologische Gefahrdungen einstellen?* Opladen (Westdeuscher Verlag).
Luttwak, Edward (1994*): Weltwirtschaftskrieg. Export als Waffe - aus Partnern werden Gegner*, Reinbek bei Hamburg (Rowohlt).
Marx, Karl, MEW 23: *Das Kapital. Kritik der politischen Ökonomie*, Erster Band Buch I: Der Produktionsprozeß des Kapitals, in K. Marx/F. Engels, *Werke, Band 23*, Berlin 1970.
Marx, Karl, MEW 24: *Das Kapital. Kritik der politischen Ökonomie*, Zweiter Band: Der Zirkulationsprozeß des Kapitals, in K. Marx/F. Engels, *Werke, Band 24*, Berlin 1970.
Marx, Karl, MEW 25: *Das Kapital*, Dritter Band, in K. Marx/F. Engels, *Werke, Band 25*, Berlin 1968.
Marx, Karl, MEW 32: *Letter to Ludwig Kugelmann*, 11 July 1968, in: K. Marx/F. Engels, Werke, Band 32, Berlin: pp. 532-554.
Petersen, Jens (1995): *Quo vadis, Italia? Ein Staat in der Krise*, Munchen (Beck).
Polanyi, Karl (1979): *Ökonomie und Gesellschaft*, Frankfurt/M. (Suhrkamp).
Reich, Robert (1993): *Die neue Weltwirtschaft*, Frankfurt/M./Berlin (Ullstein).
Riese, Hajo (1995): Geld - Das letzte Rätsel der Nationalökonomie, in: H. Schelke, Waltradu/ M. Nitsch (Hg),: *Rätsel Geld. Annäherungen aus ökonomischer, sozialogischer und historischer Sicht*, Marburg (Metropolis): pp. 45-62.
UNDP (United Nations Development Program) (1994): *Human Development Report* (Oxford, New York, Oxford University Press).
Weber, Max (1976): *Wirtschaft und Gesellschaft*. Studienausgabe, Tubingen (J.C.B. Mohr).

GREEN IMPERIALISM:
POLLUTION, PENITENCE, PROFITS

Larry Pratt and Wendy Montgomery

The more pressure that we put on ourselves, on Mexico and on every place else in the world to do something about the environment, the more they're going to reach out for environmental technology. And where are they going to get it? They're going to get it from us!

The late Ron Brown, US Secretary of Commerce. June 1993.

Introduction

That good money and a clear conscience can both be earned cleaning up the detritus, pollution and hazardous wastes generated by the global capitalist economy has never been plainer. If a rivalry over the market for environmental degradation seems a weak substitute for the older inter-capitalist struggles of the Cold War era, the production and marketing of 'green' technologies nevertheless represent major business for capital and state in North America, Western Europe and Japan. Increasingly, the demand for environmental technologies and services is coming from the so-called 'emerging markets' of Asia, Latin America and East Europe.

In the years since the 1972 United Nations Conference on the Environment in Stockholm, the advanced capitalist states have adopted (albeit with far too many steps backwards and with much procrastination) a major part of the agenda of the environmental movement. Concurrently, and virtually unremarked on the Left, a large pollution control and waste treatment and remediation industry has grown up in the Northern states in response to pressure from environmental groups and tough new regulations and enforcement. The clean-up thus far has involved enormous sums of money – $2 trillion, it is estimated, to settle asbestos and hazardous waste claims in the United States alone. Indeed, the increasing awareness by industry of environmental liabilities is driving demand for new green technologies and services. Avoiding litigation through the use of hazardous waste treatment technologies is a good investment of corporate funds.

The environmental technology industry is still very much a dirty or brown 'end-of-pipe' business involved in site clean-up, solid and hazardous waste management, water pollution control and water supply, air pollution control, and consulting and engineering services, but it has been profitable enough to attract some familiar corporate players with dubious environmental reputations. Mitsubishi, scourge of many of the world's greatest forests, has cornered the market on air pollution control equipment in Asia through its subsidiary, Mitsubishi Heavy Industries. In the United States, part of the environmental industry is drawn from the old military-industrial complex: corporations that once designed and manufactured weaponry for the Pentagon now work for contract on Superfund sites. Westinghouse, which once thrived on nuclear weapons contracts, now competes for Department of Energy bids to clean up the radioactive dumps the nuclear industry left behind. Several of General Electric's factories have been cited as dangerous sources of air pollution, but G.E. is now among the top manufacturers of air pollution equipment. Chemical giant DuPont, which produced some 350 million tons of waste in 1989, has developed its own toxic waste management business. The Swedish-Swiss engineering transnational, ABB Asea Brown Boveri Corp., ranked the world's third largest environmental technology company in 1995, sells coal-fired boilers to Indonesia, already coping with serious air pollution, because the US utilities market has dropped due to a shift to low-sulphur coal. In June 1996, over objections of environmental advocacy groups, Malaysia awarded a contract to ABB to build the Bakun Dam deep in the rainforest of the state of Sarawak: the dam will flood 69,000 hectares of forest, dislocate 9,000 tribal people and vastly increase the risk of disease.[1] The situation is much the same in France, Britain, Canada and other developed capitalist states: many of the dominant firms in the environmental technologies industry are involved in the competition to clean up the hazardous wastes, control the pollution, repair the damage which as resource producers, chemical manufacturers and utilities they themselves created – pollution, penitence, profits.

However, this is an industry nearing maturation in the North. The heady days of hazardous waste clean-up are over. The global environmental industry generated more than $400 billion in revenues in 1994, and these are expected to rise to $600 billion by 2010. But our thesis is that the industry, especially in its classic end-of-pipe structures, faces rising costs and problems of overcapacity, and in order to maintain its growth it must export its technologies and services, together with Northern legislation and regulations, to the rapidly-industrializing emerging markets, particularly in Asia and parts of Latin America. Close to 90 percent of the environmental industry's revenues and profits are concentrated in North America, Western Europe and Japan, but recession, government cutbacks and right-wing attacks on major environmental statutes have slowed the industry's expansion. Threatened by stagnation in the developed states and pulled by the competition for market opportunities overseas, the environmental industries entered the era of globalization in the early Nineties, moving to China, India, South Korea, Mexico, Brazil, Poland, the Czech Republic with the strong support of their home governments and multilateral development banks. The North American Free Trade Agreement, the prospect of a European Union incorporation of post-Communist states, such as Poland and the Czech Republic, and the advent of the World Trade Organization have accelerated capital's shift to environmental exports and the transfer of universal norms.

The following pages attempt to analyze the expansion of the Northern environmental industries and the growing technological and financial rivalry among the leading transnational environmental corporations of Japan, the US and Europe for world market share in the major sectors and regions. Our interest is in the political economy of green technology diffusion from the advanced centres of capitalism to East Asia, Southeast Asia, Central and Eastern Europe, and Latin America: what drives the market for these technologies, and what is the nature of this oligopolistic rivalry in which the capitalist state has such an interest? This is a highly *politicised* struggle for global market share in which the governments of advanced capitalism – supported by multilateral banks and, in some cases, prominent environmental groups – try to generate demand for environmental technologies by first exporting their laws and administrative capacity to emerging markets. Having exported models of industrial development via free trade and open markets, Western environmental norms are then offered to clean up the excesses of growth, and finally environmental equipment and services are sold to service the regulations.[2] 'Our ability to export environmental technology depends very much on our ability to export environmental legislation', noted a senior German official in June 1995,[3] while a manager with the US Environmental Protection Agency has remarked that 'EPA can create a market for environmental technologies and services overseas by helping other countries develop their regulatory and enforcement capabilities that drive the demand for environmental technology'.[4] As will be seen, the push to universalize Northern regulatory norms is abetted by some of the large and influential environmental non-governmental organizations. It is a good question whether the practice promotes the cause of transnational ecology or of transnational capital.

The United States and the Global Environmental Industry

The scope of the environmental industry is much less important to the present study than is the understanding of what the industry is – and is not. The industry, which is still primarily an American industry, is concentrated overwhelmingly in the regulated brown end-of-pipe activities of control, clean-up, waste management and remediation rather than in pollution prevention and process innovation, which are riskier, more difficult to finance and have longer-term paybacks. The industry, as it has evolved historically from municipal waste hauling, specializes in solid and hazardous waste management, water quality treatment, the mitigation of air pollution, recycling, and so on. The global leaders of the end-of-pipe environmental industry do not prevent pollution; they collect the wastes of capitalist production and consumption, recycle it, destroy it, or not infrequently dump it in the neighbourhoods of the poor. It is a very profitable business.

The world's largest environmental services corporation, with 1994 revenues of $10 billion and some 74,000 employees, is the US-owned Waste Management Technologies (WMX), which has grown from a collection of trash-hauling companies into North America's biggest solid waste company and a global corporation bigger than Lockheed. Through its subsidiaries, WMX provides high-technology waste treatment systems to countries such as Spain, the Netherlands, Hong Kong and Singapore; it is in engineering and consulting, site remediation, hazardous wastes, and much else. Its international activities account for about one-fifth of WMX's revenues. When in the early Nineties it decided to move to Asia, it took as its partner one of China's large state-owned investment companies and its first project a chemical waste treatment facility for Hong Kong's notoriously polluted harbour. In the United States, WMX has been attacked by Latino and African-American communities for locating hazardous waste sites near their communities, and the corporation's record of fines, penalties and out-of-court settlements was described by a San Diego District Attorney as 'a combination of environmental and anti-trust violations and public corruption cases which must be viewed with considerable concern'. An ecological critic of WMX adds:

> The vast majority of [such] companies are not investing in clean technologies and products such as emissions free, hydrogen-powered cars; non-polluting, closed system industrial factories; or solar and wind energy plants. Instead they create substitutes for CFCs that are not ozone-friendly and that contribute to climate change; they spend billions of dollars on smokestack scrubbers instead of replacing the smokestack with a clean technology; they build toxic waste dumps which are delayed-action time-bombs because they will eventually leak into the groundwater; and they build hazardous waste incinerators that spew millions of pounds of poison into the air and leave behind a toxic by-product of dioxin-laden ash.[4]

The end-of-pipe structure of the US environmental industry is not an accident. It – and most of the legal and regulatory system that underpins it – evolved in the 1970s and 1980s because of concerted pressures from the oil, coal, chemical, auto, steel and utility industries to shape the legislative agenda on environmental reform. In 1974, DuPont and Dow, the two largest producers of toxic waste in America, argued against proposals that legislation should focus on the source of pollution and that industry should be forced into a basic transformation toward clean production; granting Congress the authority 'to control production, composition, and distribution of products' would devastate free enterprise and trade.[6] The corporate position prevailed and Congress proceeded to enact a broad range of statutes and regulations that over the next 20 years brought into being an industry of some 110,000 firms and 1.2 million employees to clean up toxic wastes and mitigate – but not prevent – pollution.

The environmental industry has been defined 'as all revenue generation associated with environmental assessment, compliance with environmental regulations, pollution control, waste management, remediation of contaminated property and the provision and delivery of environmental resources'.[7] It can be divided into three categories: a) *Environmental services* – testing and analysis; water treatment; solid waste management; hazardous waste management; clean-up of contaminated sites; consulting and engineering; b) *Environmental equipment* – water and chemical equipment; instrument manufacturing; air pollution control; waste management technology; process and prevention technology; c) *Environmental resources* – water utilities; resource recovery; and alternative energy resources. The biggest revenue earners, as the following breakdown shows, are solid wastes and water-related activities; the smallest is pollution-prevention technology at half of one percent of industry revenues.

Table 1: US industry revenues by segment (1995)

	Segment	Revenue (%)
1.	Solid waste management	22
2.	Water utilities	16
3.	Water treatment works	15
4.	Resource recovery	9
5.	Water equipment	8
6.	Consulting and engineering	7
7.	Waste management equipment	6
8.	Air pollution control equipment	6
9.	Hazardous waste management	4
10.	Remediation	3.6
11.	Instruments & information	1
12.	Environmental energy sources	1
13.	Analytical services	0.8
14.	Process & prevention technology	0.5

(Source: Environmental Business International.)

The leading 50 environmental corporations in the world are all North American, West European or Japanese. The top 50 firms represent close to $75 billion in revenues or 18% of the market. There are 15 American firms in the list, mostly representing solid waste and engineering (led by WMX, Browning Ferris Industries and Bechtel); 12 German corporations, mostly involved in waste management, air pollution control, and engineering and consulting (RWE Enstorgung, Noell, Phillip Holzman, Alba, etc.); all of the Japanese firms in the leading 50 are high-technology companies (Mitsubishi Heavy Industries, Ebara Corp., Kurita, Hitachi Zozen and Kubota); and there are two French and seven British water companies, all privatized in the late Eighties and now operating internationally. France's leading water companies (Generale des Eaux and Lyonnaise des Eaux) and Britain's (such as Thames Water and Severn Trent) have become the most competitive exporters of the integrated package of designing, building and owning water infrastructure in the developing world, having won major projects in Brazil, Malaysia and Taiwan. There are a few other important transnationals to be noted: Laidlaw, a US-owned Canadian corporation specializing in solid and hazardous wastes; Asea Brown Boveri Corp., the Swedish/Swiss engineering and equipment operator; and the Dutch firm Heidemij, a consulting and engineering company.

Table 2: Revenues & Market Growth: 1993-4 ($ bil)

	1993	Growth (%)	1994
USA	158.5	4.2	165.5
Canada	10.4	3.8	10.8
L. America	6.0	10.4	6.6
W. Europe	124.6	2.2	127.4
E. Eur./Rus	6.0	6.0	6.0
Japan	64.2	1.7	65.3
Rest of Asia	11.9	16.4	14.2
Oceana	5.9	5.6	6.2
M. East	3.6	4.0	3.8
Africa	1.7	8.0	1.8
TOTAL	392.8	3.9	408.0

(Source: Environmental Business International, 1995.)

As Table 2 illustrates, the United States is by far the largest market in the world and generates something like 40% of the industry's total revenues – an estimated $170 billion out of a total $408 billion in 1994, according to a major study of the industry.[8] More interesting is the data on regional market growth: the industry is stagnating in the developed capitalist states, booming in Asia-without-Japan, and growing in Latin America, Eastern Europe and Africa. Within Asia, the fastest-growing environmental markets are China, India, Thailand, Indonesia; in Latin America, Brazil, Mexico, Argentina. Between 1994 and 2000, Asia-without-Japan, it is estimated, will gain $22 billion in environmental revenues, and Latin America markets to grow by $6.5 billion.

Table 3: Hazardous Waste Management Spending ($ mil)

Market Area	1991	%	1995	%
Superfund	2,350	19.0	2,888	17.0
Dept. of Defense	1,176	10.0	2,643	15.5
Dept. of Energy	1,610	13.0	3,567	21.0
State Gov'ts	932	8.0	948	5.5
Industry	3,940	32.0	4,620	27.0
Leaking storage tanks	2,211	18.0	2,352	14.0
TOTAL	12,219		16,998	

(Source: William T. Lorenz & Co., Concord, N.H. (1993))

The main 'market-driver' for this industry in the United States and elsewhere has been government legislation and enforcement. The market for environmental services and technologies is driven by political waves of environmentalism and the introduction of new, stringent regulations. The industry cannot thrive without a strong environmental movement; and the absence of such movements in many developing countries has been a barrier to the export of green technologies. Like the defence sector, the industry also benefits from large government expenditures. In the US, the Clean Water Act, the Clean Air Act, the Superfund legislation of 1980[9], the Resource Conservation and Recovery Act, and subsequent amendments induced thousands of firms to bid for clean-up and other work from municipal, state and federal agencies. The environmental industry has also been targetted for federal monies designed to convert the US defence industry to civilian technology production; and California, the state most negatively affected by military cuts, is also the state with the largest environmental industry and has benefitted from spending by the Departments of Energy (DOE), Defense (DOD), and Superfund. DOE and DOD have emerged as two of the largest benefactors of the US environmental industry, in part because of their sponsorship of technology research but also because they control the funds and lands to contract for the huge environmental clean-up and restoration projects. A federal remediation market, in which public monies are committed to private contractors to restore contaminated sites to something approximating their original state, has helped some military contractors offset losses from reduced defence spending. The Federal Defense Technology Conversion Reinvestment and Transition Act of 1993, which appropriated $471 million to encourage the military and private industry to develop and share technology, led several members of the military-industrial complex, seeking compensation for the end of the Cold War, to go into the environmental clean-up business.[10] Table 3 provides some estimates of the three big federal spenders in one key US environmental market – hazardous wastes.

The US environmental industry experienced its most rapid era of growth, ironically enough, in the late 1980s during the Reagan and Bush administrations. The industry tends to thrive when economic growth is rapid and environmental degradation has been at its worst, and these were the years of Bhopal, Chernobyl and sharp environmental conflicts in the US over issues surrounding hazardous wastes. The insurance industries made multi-billion dollar settlements of hazardous waste cases, and the environmental industry grew in excess of 15% per year. Though it was promoted as recession-proof on Wall Street, no sector of US capitalism was spared when the recession struck in the early Nineties. Many big environmental projects were cancelled as firms world-wide eliminated discretionary spending on clean-up and pollution control, and the Bush administration sought to appease business by gutting such measures as the 1990 Clean Air Act Amendments. Big cuts in appropriations for govern-mental programmes followed as the Right singled out key statutes such as the Clean Water Act, thereby threatening the erosion of environmental regulations as a market-driver for the industry. This was to be the cause of the industry's decision to globalize more of its operations in the early Nineties. More fundamentally, it can be argued that the environmental industries as traditionally organized have matured in the United States and much of the developed capitalist world, and that some of its big revenue-earning segments are unsustainable because capitalism in the developed North is finding it too costly to pay for the end-of-pipe treatment of waste and pollution. Profits in the regulatory-driven segments, such as hazardous waste management and pollution control, are expected to decline. As one study put it, 'these segments face the fundamental long-term challenge that the environmentally negligent and resource-rich environment will no longer exist. We are no longer creating Superfund sites at the rate we once did; we no longer use asbestos, each new manufacturing or industrial facility is now designed with material efficiency and pollution prevention in mind'. Many of the industry's clean-up and control sectors in services and equipment 'face a soberingly finite life cycle':

Faced with the significant costs associated with emissions reduction, resource intensive, waste and pollution producing industries have been seeking ever more efficient means of conducting their operations. Unwanted environmental emissions are increasingly viewed not only as a potential liability but, more importantly, as a sign of economic and production inefficiency ... This transition within industry has, in turn, begun to drive change within the environmental industry itself as traditional 'end-of-pipe' customers begin to demand more comprehensive and simultaneous solutions to both their economic and environmental problems.[11]

The Germans take a very similar view of the industry's future. Spurred by public pressures and the strictest environmental laws in the world, in the 1980s Germany was able to 'decouple' economic growth from increased pollution flows. Chancellor Helmut Kohl has argued that traditional end-of-pipe environmental protection must give way to production-and-process oriented environmentalism, and that government must help lower capital's risk in making this transition. The Japanese, having made major reductions in pollution levels and created new markets for energy and environmental technologies, demonstrated that the states with the most rigorous anti-pollution limits and the most investment in green technology become more efficient and competitive, more likely to dominate the export market. Green technology development and diffusion would strengthen, not weaken, national competitiveness. The Clinton administration set out its Environmental Technology Initiative within weeks of taking office in early 1993; the initiative was designed to accelerate environmental protection while strengthening America's industrial base by increasing the export potential of US environmental technology. 'This investment will aid in the transition away from a defense-oriented economy, by stimulating the increased use of private sector R&D resources for environmental quality-related purposes.'[13]

These ideas might be called the progressive conventional wisdom of the environmental industry since the Rio Earth Summit – the UN Conference of Environment and Development (UNCED) of 1992. The Rio summit, as Pratrap Chatterjee and Matthias Finger argued in *The Earth Brokers*, was about Western science and technology, Western training, Western money and Western institutions – the very forces that have caused the environmental crisis now dominate the process that is expected to resolve it.[14] There was a large turnout of transnationals at Rio, a veritable meeting-ground for penitent polluters, such as DuPont, the world's biggest producer of CFCs and now an environment protection company. They were eager to promote market forces, corporate self-regulation and full-cost pricing of resources, especially as an alternative to more radical solutions. The consensus view of big business at the Earth Summit was set out in Swiss billionaire Stephan Schmidheiny's influential book, *Changing Course*, written as head of a transnational advocacy group, the Business Council for Sustainable Development. A central idea of the study is that capitalism is moving into a stage of sustainable growth and 'eco-efficiency' – a term that applies to a corporate strategy of adding value to the firm while reducing the use of resources and the creation of pollution. Science and technological change can prevent pollution or lower its costs to capital rather than simply clean it up. The other key idea in Schmidheiny's study is that green technologies must be diffused to the South via commercial markets; through the transnational corporation rather than as aid from governments. 'Technology cooperation' replaces technology transfer.[15]

These ideas were particularly addressed, it would seem, to US business. A vulnerability of the American environmental industry is that, unlike its Japanese and German counterparts, it has a weak record in exporting its technologies and services to the rapidly-growing emerging markets. In 1990, US exports of environmental protection equipment were less than one-half of one percent of all merchandise exports. The US environmental industry has made some progress internationally, yet it earns just 6% of its total revenues from offshore markets, whereas the Europeans, Japanese and Canadians earn between 15% and 25% of their revenues from sales and investments abroad. Germany, the leading exporter, has in some years earned 40% of its revenues from environmental technologies from markets abroad: it dominates most of Europe and its largest transnationals are active all over the world. Japan internationalized its pollution-control industry in the late Eighties and now dominates Asian markets. Since those who successfully make the strategic alliances and transfer the technologies are creating value in their companies and also positioning themselves for future opportunities, it would appear that the US industry has been insular in its attitude to trade and overseas investment. The huge size of the mostly-regulated US market made the idea of exports a luxury, and the environmental industries were not included in national export planning until the Clinton/Gore administration took office in 1993. This is an industry that thrives or dies according to the degree of state support it receives, and American free-trade ideology is frequently in conflict with what needs to be done in the real world to match the Germans and Japanese. The US environmental industry frequently complains that American firms, though competitive on price and quality, lose contracts because they cannot compete with the low-interest 'soft loans' offered by, say, the big Japanese trading companies in negotiating with countries such as China. Japan certainly combines green aid and financial incentives with its foreign investment–it is also highly flexible in adapting technologies to local needs – but US firms also have a very wide range of export-promoting and aid-dispensing agencies to draw upon, such as the US Export-Import Bank, US Aid, the Overseas Private Investment Corporation, the Environmental Protection Agency's Technology for International Solutions (US TIES) programme, and a number of multilateral development banks and regional institutions.[16]

Pollution and Inter-Capitalist Rivalry

'The Earth is one but the world is not.'[17] And nor, we might add, is transnational capital. The world of oligopolistic rivalry and international competition is with us still, though it is certainly veiled by the smog of liberal interdependence and co-operation ideology. It is the multinational corporation's drive for technological and capital accumulation, combined with the pressures to globalize in conditions of liberalized trade and financial markets, deregulation and privatization, that is at the core of the inter-capitalist rivalry over environmental markets in East Asia, Southeast Asia, East and Central Europe and parts of Latin America. Maturation of the industry and slower rates of GNP growth in the industrial countries weakened profits; deregulation removed some market-drivers; and privatization brought new corporate players – such as the French and British water companies – into the global industry as competitors. Returns (and risks) would be much higher in the emerging markets of, say, rapidly-growing Asia or Latin America than in Europe. Percy Barnevik, president of Geneva-based ABB, a company with heavy investments in India and other Asian markets, has noted that the emerging markets pose the single greatest challenge to the global environment. 'These people see not only a dream of lifting living standards not 50 or 100 percent, but five or ten times. The question is will they [emerging markets] waste in industry as they build it up – like Eastern Europe?' Funds spent on fine-tuning emissions in developed countries should be diverted to address far worse pollution in developing countries like India:

> What do we talk about in the developed world? We talk about if the ppms [parts per million] of coal-fired power plants in Germany should go down from 25 to 15, while we have 500ppms in India. It costs less to go from 500 to 50 than it does from 25 to 15.

An examination of the rivalry for environmental technology markets must begin with the real-world constraints; then we survey the competition for environmental exports and investments in some of the 'emerging markets' on which data is available. In all of the discussion, we will note the crucial role of the state – developed capitalist as well as developing capitalist – in the environmental industries as they have evolved. The state's role is basic at the international level as well, and this is partly because market forces cannot deliver the environmental goods, but also because national governments perceive that the conflict for market-share in the global environmental industries is part of a wider rivalry over who will shape and benefit from industrial development in the so-called emerging markets.

1) To begin with some of the barriers to green technology diffusion, there is first the question of capital markets and the financing of environmental

technologies. A technology exporter that does not offer a financing package to a developing country has little hope of making a sale. Asia (excepting Japan) needs to invest about $1 trillion in its infrastructure by 2004, with 70% of this in power and transport-related areas. Much of this will have to be raised from financial markets in the North. Most of the electricity to be generated in new power plants will be based on the cheapest energy source – coal with a high sulphur content. Will financial investments in the infrastructure requirements in the fastest growing region of the world be made conditional on better environmental practices? Some pressures might come from agencies such as the World Bank, but for private investors and bankers, who are competing with one another in this rich market, the answer is no: they will not impose such conditionality so long as the loans do not raise serious liability issues for banks or insurers. If anything, financial markets encourage a short-term outlook and the accelerated use of resources for higher growth-rates: they favour even faster growth as opposed to 'eco-efficient' technologies and development. With low resource prices, financial markets encourage the tendency of firms to externalize their polluting activities. Foreign portfolio investment is motivated by the need for short-term results, and this encourages it and the borrowers of the capital to undervalue common property resources, such as water, energy, air, and to use them up in an unsustainable manner: thus the globalization of investment flows has actually speeded up the destruction of the world's forests.[19]

2) Financial markets are not just excessively oriented to the short run, they are highly volatile as well; and this can be ruinous for any developing country planning major environmental investments. The market for environmental infrastructure projects in Mexico is estimated to exceed $30 billion over the next decade, an estimate based on the high rate of discharged pollutants and the lack of adequate treatment infrastructure.[20] There is an enormous need for water, air, hazardous waste and solid waste projects in Mexico, yet many of the projects cannot be financed. In the early Nineties, Mexico's government was eager to obtain financing for environmental technologies, if only to placate the critics of the NAFTA pact and dispel the country's image as a haven for polluters. But US financial markets proved unwilling to accept the foreign-exchange risks after the huge currency devaluation in 1994-5 when portfolio capital fled Mexico in search of more stable currencies. The subsequent very high interest rates meant that no private sector capital became available for environmental projects. With lower government revenues, Mexico has forced local projects to operate on a stand-alone financial basis; but because residential users have low incomes, which places further constraints on financing, many badly-needed environmental projects are

not regarded as viable by investors. Yet, it is notable that while American corporations did not even bid on a 1993 tender to operate part of Mexico City's vast water supply system, a recently-privatized British water company, Severn Trent, formed a joint venture with a Mexican partner, SAMSA, and was a successful bidder, in part because it addressed the state's political interests in Mexican ownership. The Mexican state assumed much of the risk in constructing and financing the IASA system, which was taken in stages, and it was completed despite the peso crisis that struck in late 1994. Strategic alliances with local capital and the state are one way of lowering risks and capital requirements while adding value through technology transfer.

3) Environmentally sustainable growth requires long-term investments in highly-populated poor countries, but there are high-risk premiums on such investments. Foreign direct investment via multinationals moves overwhelmingly toward the areas of higher growth and incomes, which in the case of the developing world means a handful of rapidly-growing countries. Environmental Business International, a leading industry consultant, writes off all of South Asia, with the exception of India, as 'pre-emerging markets' that are 'severely constricted by the lack of financial resources in the public and private sectors and the failure thus far of their governments to promote a larger role for private sector development of environmental infrastructures'.[21] Environmental protection services do not flow toward the areas of worst degradation but to the most promising environmental markets, ie, where there are well-defined regulations, a capacity to enforce them, and the financial ability to pay for anti-pollution measures. There is an observed 'direct correlation between the size and robustness of individual environmental [economies] and their per [capita] income and capital in each country,'[22] and this is a key determinant for investments by the world environmental industry.

4) A further barrier to the diffusion of environmental technology and investments is political and administrative: many Southern governments lack an 'indigenous capacity' to assess their countries' conditions, to create institutions, and to enforce regulations. An important factor in the demand for the environmental industry's technology is tough legislation backed by stringent enforcement, and this entails the development of environmental protection agencies staffed by well-trained officials. The Germans believe that they may have to export their own strict ecology laws before Germany's environmental industry can win new overseas markets. Germany's drive for tighter environmental laws abroad complements its need for export markets for this highly competitive sector. Strict laws fostered a green technology sector in Germany; now the regulations must

be transferred abroad. 'Production,' states Germany's environment minister, 'often began to develop only after state requirements, norms and restrictions gave the orders and guaranteed a certain minimum need.'[23] US Commercial Officers in their reports from prospective markets complain that a market for environmental technology cannot develop in the absence of a framework of laws that are enforced. South Korea has such legislation, 'in many regards similar to US law', but:

> Enforcement of environmental laws in Korea has been inconsistently applied across regions and industries and, in general, not carried out with sufficient rigor to ensure that compliance is achieved. Lack of enforcement is largely a function of insufficient technical and manpower resources (as well as insufficient authority to sanction) for those policing the standards, in addition to lingering national policies that continue to emphasize unhindered economic growth at the cost of the environment.[24]

In 1993 President Clinton established the Environmental Technology Initiative (ETI) to increase the competitiveness of the US environmental technology industries; the international component of the initiative is known as US TIES – Technology for International Environmental Solutions. US TIES is designed to create demand for American technology via a 'market pull' approach by assisting foreign governments in developing environmental standards and norms, training technical staff and regulators in the US with American technology and solutions.

To say the least, the business and political elites of developing states, particularly in Asia, are suspicious of such strategies. Malaysia, Indonesia and China have warned that the Americans and Europeans want to impose costly environmental legislation on the Asian economies in order to slow the region's rapid growth. They are fearful that environmental conditionality agreements will be introduced into trade and financing negotiations,[25] and they resent the efforts of Northern environmental NGOs to use trade restrictions as a lever to force them to accept universal norms and standards. This 'green imperialism' has taken a number of forms, but a good example would be the efforts of one politically-active group, Earth Island Institute of San Francisco, to use American courts to require enforcement of US environmental statutes and to extend the extraterritorial reach of American environmental statutes to all who wish to have access to the US market. In one celebrated case, Earth Island litigated successfully (with domestic fishing interests) to prevent Mexican fishermen from fishing for tuna in Pacific waters because their drift-nets were destroying dolphins; GATT struck down the US ruling. In another case, Earth Island, supported once again by domestic fishing interests, obtained an order from the US Court of International Trade, pursuant to an amendment to the Endangered Species Act 1973, banning imports of all wild shrimp caught by fishing boats not equipped with technology to protect sea turtles (so-called turtle excluder devices): this extension of US conservation law caught more than 50 countries in the legal drift-net, almost all developing nations: Thailand, India, Honduras prominent among them. The embargo protected the US shrimp industry from foreign competition while universalizing US environmental norms.[26] The point is not that sea turtles are undeserving of conservation efforts; rather, it is the combination of brazen protectionism and the unilateral imposition of American standards that belies the claim that Western environmentalism actually represents a form of global civil society.

Asia's Dirty Air

The real heart of the inter-capitalist competition for the global market in environmental services and technologies is in East Asia, and air pollution control (APC) is perhaps the most dynamic aspect of the rivalry. Asia has the world's most polluted air, and it contributes between a fifth and a quarter of the world's emissions of greenhouse gases. China alone does half the damage. Some of its cities are so blackened by air pollution that they cannot be seen by satellite. Among the causes: the massive use of indigenous high-sulphur coal for industrialization, the growth of enormous cities choking with automobile traffic, the high costs of installing efficient environmental technologies, the weakness of the environmental movement in Asia, the ubiquitous illusion of policy elites that rapid growth is a solvent for all problems. China's energy demands are increasing and the country, already the world's leading burner of coal, is expected to double its use in the next two decades in order to meet its ambitious economic growth targets. In its Ninth Five Year Plan (1996-2000), China has identified SO_2 emissions as a major environmental priority, with over 300 projects identified, many of them involving acid rain control ($1.6 billion) and with APC in key cities ($5.7 billion). If the worst of the air pollution is in the largest cities, this is also where the best sales prospects are for transnational green technology manufacturers, provided financing can be secured:

> The sulphur dioxide created by Shanghai's coal burning power plants is now regarded as the most serious pollution problem in the city. The technology for desulphurization is also one of the most needed technologies in China. The central government will be forced to implement harsh controls on sulphur dioxide emissions in the future and plans to levy heavy fines on power plants that fail to meet the tougher standards. For example, under proposed regulations, a typical 300,000 kilowatt power plant operating without any pollution control measures would face an annual RMB 17 million (US$ 2.04 million) in fines, high enough to force it to look for adequate equipment . . . A complete set of desulphurization equipment for a 300,000 kilowatt power plant costs somewhere around US$ 18 million to US$ 20 million, equal to almost half the cost of the total investment in such a power plant. It is impossible at present for local power stations to afford such equipment . . . The Mitsubishi company of Japan is interested in localizing the manufacture of this equipment and is seeking Japanese government funds to support such a project.[28]

Asia is the world's leading regional market for APC equipment, with a 37% share of an estimated $15 billion total and almost 60% of all sales of flue gas desulphurization equipment and electrostatic precipitators for new power plants and heavy industries.[29] Privatization has led to the rapid growth of independent power projects in many Asian countries, and this has pushed the market for APC technologies. Japan itself is by far the largest market in the region and it also has the strictest regulations. Japanese transnationals, such as Mitsubishi Heavy Industries, Hitachi and IHI, having developed their technologies in the domestic market, internationalized to protect their lead and today hold the major shares of the APC equipment market in China, South Korea and a number of other heavily-polluted Asian nations. If the enforcement of regulations improves and the lack of hard financing can be resolved, through a combination of local capital, multilateral bank lending, aid and foreign investment, India and China represent exceptionally large and lucrative markets for the environmental industry, albeit for the medium and longer term. Given the damage that their coal-fired generation of power from hundreds of plants can do to the global atmosphere and to human health well beyond their borders, it seems probable that international financing will be found. The threat posed to Japan by acid rain emanating from southern China in the early 1990s was one of the determinants in the decision of the Japanese state and its environmental technology sector to internationalize the industry: having developed the strictest standards in the region, it would use its technological advantage, supplemented by overseas aid, to become the dominant exporter of anti-pollution equipment and services. This would allow it to promote the continued rapid industrialization of China and the rest of Asia from which it draws such economic benefit, and without suffering from external damage.

Japanese APC companies now not only have a strong lead in China, they dominate the Asian APC market and stand to be beneficiaries of the adoption of anti-global warming plans. They are flexible on financing, willing to adapt costly technologies to local needs, and have long-established trade ties in Asia. Japan's Overseas Development Assistance for environment-related projects began in China in 1991 and has focussed on the transfer and commercialization of cleaner, more efficient technologies. MITI – Japan's Ministry of International Trade and Industry – operates a Green Aid Plan that funds joint research and development in such areas as clean-coal technology and energy efficiency. The projects benefit Japanese manufacturers because they lower the cost and risks of adapting technologies to the Chinese market, and they foster long-term joint ventures and licensing agreements with Chinese business. MITI involves Japan's major industry associations in the Green Aid Plan and in technology transfer arrangements. MITI's strategy (unlike that of the US) emphasizes support for less costly, simplified technologies: for example, developing an affordable flue-gas desulphurization (FGD) technology for use on new coal-fired power plants. FGD technology reduces the incidence of respiratory disease and acid rain, but it can add up to 25% to the cost of a power plant – say an additional $125 million to a $500 million plant – and the Chinese, who plan to build 100 new power plants, have resisted fitting them with this environmental technology. As a way of preventing acid rain that could damage Japan, but also as a response to the obvious business opportunities, MITI and Mitsubishi Heavy Industries have worked with the Chinese to produce a simplified, cheaper desulphurization technology. Long-term, low-interest loans from Japan's Overseas Economic Cooperation Fund (OECF) can be used to finance the installation of such technology on a commercial scale.[30] Fifteen out of 40 of the projects in the first part of Japan's fourth five-year low-interest yen loan were environment-related, though the Chinese reportedly had to be persuaded to request the 15 projects.[31] Japan's environmental ODA expenditures, which have become the dominant segment of its assistance overseas, focus on air pollution control in Asia; and since most of it is untied, it has become a key financing vehicle for Western multinationals financing projects in the region.

In China's largest city, Shanghai, where pollution is an undesirable companion to a 20% annual growth rate and to which much environmental technology is imported, the US lags well behind Japan and Germany. The Japanese have 37% of the import market share for Shanghai's environmental sector, the German's 34%, and the US just 5-7%. US firms, although competitive on quality and price, lose out, the Americans claim, because the governments of Germany and Japan have provided grants and 'soft' low-interest money, amounting to a 30-40% discount, in favour of their exporters. 'Government aid is a principal aspect of several countries' long-term market strategies. Japanese and German companies have become the most successful equipment suppliers to municipal infrastructure projects. They sell their wares at or below cost and train personnel to use their equipment . . . the investment may be viewed as an "entrance fee".'[32]

Japanese transnationals enjoy a similar market strength in all of South Korea's environmental sectors, and Germany is highly competitive there in solid waste management and air pollution control. With a total market of $5 billion and an estimated annual real growth rate of 25%, the import market share in Korea stood in 1995 at: Japan: 42%; US: 20%; Germany: 18%; France: 12%; and others: 8%.[33] In Taiwan, where imports of anti-pollution equipment are expected to reach $1.7 billion by 1997 and total environmental spending is growing at close to 12% per year, foreign suppliers control 80% of the market, but the US, with an import share of 27%, lags behind Japan.[34]

But the Japanese face intense competition in the rest of the Asian market from European and American manufacturers of APC technology, notably from Swiss-based Asea Brown Boveri, Noell of Germany, Babcock and Wilcox of Ohio, and General Electric. These four, together with Mitsubishi Heavy Industries, dominate Asia's growing air pollution control market. And because some countries want to diversify supply sources and reduce their trade deficits with Japan, US and European transnationals are in a position to contest Japan's technological dominance. They are doing so by making strategic alliances with some of Asia's leading businesses and with the governments of the region; when Waste Management International, a subsidiary of WMX Technologies of Illinois, moved to Asia in the early Nineties it settled in Hong Kong, notorious for its polluting industries and chemical wastes; it made a partnership with one of China's state-owned investment agencies, China International Trust and Investment Corp.[35] Ebara Corp., one of Japan's premier environmental corporations, has a partnership with AEA Technology, a huge and remarkable privatized British firm spun off from the Atomic Energy Agency that has 3,500 scientists and engineers and much of Britain's environmental expertise under its roof. Asea Brown Boveri, Bechtel, ERM and Heidemij NV, Western multinationals operating in Taiwan's environmental market, have all formed joint ventures with local firms in the interest of 'localization', while Babcock and Wilcox are partners with Hyundai in South Korea's APC market. India's environmental markets are characterized by collaborations between the country's technical firms and many of the transnationals already mentioned. Flakt India of Calcutta, an iron and steel concern, has a long-standing partnership with the ubiquitous ABB; these two could emerge as dominant in India's environmental technology market. ABB holds a 20% share of the global air pollution control market for power generation, and in the Asia-Pacific region, about 60-70% of its business is tilted towards new coal-fired power plants. Half its annual APC revenues of $1 billion derive from its Asia operations. Another European transnational heavily investing in the Asian air pollution market is Noell of Germany, a subsidiary of the giant Preussag Group, with investments in Taiwan power plants and a hazardous waste facility in Pusan, South Korea.[36] Asia, with its accelerating growth rates and environmental crises, is at the heart of inter-capitalist rivalry near century's end; and environmental technologies are merely one aspect of a struggle among the dominant groups of capital and their respective states for control of the world's fastest-growing markets.

Conclusion: Sustainable Hegemony

Vandana Shiva has noted that our conception of a 'global' environmental crisis, whose resolution can only come from the North's leadership, has transformed the problem of ecology into a problem of technology transfer and finance. 'Since the North has abundant industrial technology and capital, if it has to provide a solution to environmental problems, they must be reduced to a currency that the North dominates.'[37] Thus, the financing that flows from Northern states for the technology for CFC substitutes ends up as subsidies to the same transnational chemical firms that developed and used the CFCs. The transnationals that manufacture Asia's new coal-fired power plants also produce the air pollution control equipment that limit the acid rain and respiratory disease caused by the use of coal as an energy source. In Shiva's framework – and ours – global ecology is about sustainable hegemony: Northern states over Southern; transnational capital over local initiative; green technologies as an alternative to the slowing of capitalist growth and consumption. The environmental technology industries of North America, Europe and Japan basically oil the global development machine by supplying the apolitical technical solutions that allow the huge industrial projects, the nuclear and coal-fuelled power plants, the vast clear-cuts of forests to proceed to the great benefit of transnational capital.

None of this obviates the need to address the environmental crisis of the South through means that do not reinforce the North's hegemony. Few would deny that cleaning up pollution and the toxic disasters created by, say, the *maquiladoras* on the US-Mexican border or by rapid growth in China or Poland is an important contribution to human health and development. Many cities in the South desperately require anti-pollution control and waste-disposal technologies. There is a critical need for potable water supplies and for waste water facilities in much of the developing world. But the South's environmental crisis is also a social crisis rooted in class exploitation, poverty and the unequal control of resources and political power. The growing involvement of the oligopolistic environmental industry in the ecological affairs of developing countries – at least those countries that can attract its investments – offers little more than the greening of global reach, a new colouration of the same old imperialism.

NOTES

1. Joshua Karliner, 'The Environmental Industry: Profiting from Pollution', *The Ecologist*, Vol. 24, No. 2 (March/April 1994); and J. Doyle, *Hold the Applause: A Case Study of Corporate Environmentalism as Practised at DuPont* (Washington DC, Friends of the Earth, 1991). On the ranking of environmental companies, see Environmental Business International.
2. *Ibid.*
3. The speaker was Gerhard Gumbel, President of Germany's Envitec 95 Trade Fair, which is held in Dusseldorf every three years. Reported by Reuters, 19 June 1995.
4. Sarita Hoyt, 'EPA's US Ties Program Diffusing Technologies Overseas', *Business America*, (April 1996), p. 56.
5. Karliner, *op. cit.*

6. A. Szasz, ' In Praise of Policy Luddism: Strategic Lessons from the Hazardous Waste Wars', *Capitalism, Nature and Socialism*, Vol. 2, No. 1.

7. Environmental Business International, Inc. and US Environmental Protection Agency, *The Global Environmental Industry: A Market and Needs Assessment* (San Diego, 1995), p. 3.

8. Environmental Business International, *The Global Environmental Market and United States Environmental Industry Competitiveness* (San Diego, 1995).

9. In 1980, as part of a response to the discovery of the Love Canal hazardous waste site in Niagara Falls and a toxic industrial fire in Elizabethtown, New Jersey, Congress enacted sweeping legislation, the Comprehensive Environmental Response, Compensation, and Liability Act, or the 'Superfund' Act. This legislation and subsequent amendments give federal environment agencies sweeping powers to intervene and impose settlements in hazardous waste sites throughout the USA.

10. See *US Industrial Outlook* January 1994. ch. 19: 'Environmental Technologies and Services.' From Lexis/Nexis database.

11. Environmental Business International, *The Global Environmental Industry: A Market and Needs Assessment*, pp. 7–9.

12. Curtis Moore and Alan Miller, *Green Gold: Japan, Germany, the United States and the Race for Environmental Technology* (Boston, Beacon House, 1994) chaps. 1 and 2.

13. United States, Environmental Protection Agency, *Environmental Technology Initiative FY 1994 Program Plan*.

14. Pratrap Chatterjee and Matthias Finger, *The Earth Brokers: Power, Politics and World Development* (London, Routledge, 1994), p. 60.

15. Stephan Schmidheiny with the Business Council for Sustainable Development, *Changing Course* (Cambridge, Mass., The MIT Press, 1992).

16. The US Department of Commerce reported in late October 1996 that US exports of environmental technology rose 50% between 1993 and 1995 to $14.5 billion, and much of the increase was attributed to the Clinton administration's export-promotion efforts. The Export-Import Bank's support for environmental projects overseas – egs. China, Poland and Venezuela – increased sharply. Exports were responsible for 40% of the industry's 1995 growth. *The Financial Times*, 29 October 1996.

17. From the World Commission on Environment and Development, *Our Common Future* (Oxford, Oxford University Press), p. 27.

18. Remarks made at a conference at Stavanger, Norway, and reported by Reuters, 22 August 1995.

19. Stephan Schmidheiny and Federico Zorraquin with the World Business Council for Sustainable Development, *Financing Change: The Financial Community, Eco-efficiency and Sustainable Development* (Cambridge, Mass., The MIT Press, 1996).

20. US Dept. of Commerce, International Trade Administration, *Financing Environmental Projects in Mexico: Barriers, Resources, & Strategies*, (May 1996).

21. Environmental Business International, *The Global Environmental Industry: A Market and Needs Assessment*, p. 67.

22. *Ibid.*, p. 129.

23. Comments made at an environment trade fair at Dusseldorf in June 1995. Reported by Reuters, 19 June 1995.

24. US Dept. of Commerce, Commercial Officer (Seoul), 'Korea – Pollution Control Equipment', 21 Nov. 1995. National Trade Data Bank. Market Reports.

25. See the discussion in C. Ford Runge, *Freer Trade, Protected Environment* (New York, Council on Foreign Relations, 1994).

26. Cf. the rulings of the United States Court of International Trade in Earth Island Institute, Todd Steiner et. al., plaintiffs against Warren Christopher, Secretary of State, et al defendants, of 5 June, 1995; Jack Rudloe and Anna Rudloe, 'Shrimpers and lawmakers collide over a move to save the sea turtles', *Smithsonian*, (Dec. 1989); *Earth Island Journal*,

(Summer and Fall 1996). The founder of Earth Island Institute, David Brower, also founded Friends of the Earth, and was for many years Executive Director of the Sierra Club. The most potent and uncompromising leader in the American environmental movement, Brower has been called the 'Archdruid' – druids sacrifice people to save trees. See John McPhee, *Encounters with the Archdruid* (Toronto, Macarlane, Walter and Ross, 1971).

27. Among others, see Paul Wapner, *Environmental Activism and World Civic Politics* (Albany, State University Press of New York, 1966).

28. US Dept. of Commerce, Senior Commercial Officer (Shanghai), 'China – Pollution Control Equipment', 16 January 1996. National Trade Data Bank. Market Reports.

29. *Asia Environmental Business Journal*, (May/June 1966), p. 1.

30. Peter Evans, *The China Business Review*, Vol. 21 No. 4 (July 1994); American Embassy Beijing, Commercial Service, 'Hard Currency Financing for Environmental Projects in China', 18 May 1995. National Trade Data Bank. Market Reports.

31. US Dept. of Commerce, NTIS Update, Foreign Technology, 15 July 1995.

32. US Dept. of Commerce, Senior Commercial Officer (Shanghai), 'China –Pollution Control Equipment', 16 January 1996. National Trade Data Bank. Market Reports.

33. US Dept. of Commerce, Commercial Officer, 'Korea – Pollution Control Equipment', Nov. 21 1995. National Trade Data Bank. Market Reports.

34. *Business America*, (April 1996).

35. *Asia Environmental Business Journal*, (July/August 1996), p. 12.

36. *Ibid.*

37. Vandana Shiva, 'The Greening of Global Reach', in Wolfgang Sachs, ed., *Global Ecology: A New Arena of Political Conflict* (Halifax, Fernwood Books, 1993), p. 153.

CHINA'S COMMUNIST CAPITALISM:
THE REAL WORLD OF MARKET SOCIALISM

Gerard Greenfield and Apo Leong

It seems that we have entered an era of silence and forgetting. The silence involves the uncritical acceptance of the logic of capitalism, despite the economic violence and social and cultural destruction wrought by its neoliberal vanguard; while forgetting that 'actually existing socialism' never was socialism. The collapse of authoritarian Communist regimes should have reinvigorated our commitment to revolutionary socialism rather than have served as a justification for compromise and retreat. Rather than 'overcoming subalternity', state socialist societies under Stalinist regimes (re)created new experiences of subordination and alienation, which were intensified and expanded in the capitalist transformations of the 1990s. Instead the Left is not only retreating in the face of the onslaught of neoliberalism, but is transforming itself through a series of long-term compromises which dispel both the project of overcoming subalternity and the very notion that subalternity is a problem in the first place. Overcoming alienation, exploitation, subordination – this is stuff of times past. Under the compulsion of pragmatism, engagement, or plain common sense, we are to believe that there is no alternative to capitalism or that any alternative we dare to imagine should *use* capitalism – not overthrow it.

Market socialism is precisely this alternative. In China, when the Four Modernisations programme was launched in 1978, it was announced that rapid development and growth would be achieved by 'using capitalism to develop socialism', necessitating the development of what would later be called 'market socialism with Chinese characteristics'. The ideological legitimation of 'Deng Xiaoping thought' in the post-Mao era of market reforms relied in part on Lenin's New Economic Policy, which, it was claimed, proved that under certain conditions it was both necessary and desirable to facilitate capitalism in order to further the socialist project.[1] Most important of all, 'Deng Xiaoping thought' declared that exploitation would be tolerated, especially in the Special Economic Zones and 'open cities' which would act as 'windows' on the global economy, by attracting foreign capital to a disciplined and 'competitive' labour force.[2] Indeed, there was a great deal of such tolerance, with over 30 million workers employed in these zones under the systematic repression of labour rights and unrestrained capitalist accumulation.[3] Market socialists in the advanced capitalist countries who glorified the success of China's economic reforms all too often overlooked this even after the massacre of students and workers in Tiananmen Square.[4] This tolerance for exploitation was not shared by the workers whose involvement in the mass protest was driven largely by the sentiment expressed in a worker's letter to the students in Tiananmen Square: that 'the wealth created by the sweat and blood of hundreds of millions of compatriots is squandered by the bureaucrats, China's biggest capitalists.'[5]

Both before and after the 1989 events there were widespread public demonstrations, self-organising among workers leading to the creation of autonomous unions and genuine workers' associations, and riots and protests by hundreds of thousands of peasants across the country against corruption, excessive taxes, and the continued abuse of privilege and power by the Party-state bureaucracy. Violent repression by the Party-state, including mass arrests and the imprisonment of so-called 'subversives' occurred alongside ever-increasing tolerance for the displacement of peasants from their land and the unregulated exploitation of workers in a free labour market. While liberal human rights campaigners in the West have organized public campaigns around a few victims, labour activists and organisers who remain committed to marxism and socialism are not among them. Market socialists and the liberal left, who have praised the reform process in China for its 'gradualism' and the ability of the Communist regime to prevent the economic decline and political chaos witnessed in parts of Eastern Europe and the former Soviet Union, ignore the widespread resistance and protest by China's subordinate classes. They fail to understand that the very same 'gradualism' that the progressive Left has praised as a conscious decision on the part of China's policy-makers to ensure that the transition to a market economy is not a violent and socially destructive process is itself a product of that protest and resistance forcing the political elite and the emerging capitalist class to moderate their strategy. Yet however moderated, the violence of the market cannot be hidden amidst the dismissal of some 50 million workers from their jobs. This is epitomised by the observation that the old three irons – the iron rice bowl, iron armchair and iron wage (representing job and wage security and lifetime employment) – have been replaced by the iron heart, iron face and iron fist.[6] Yet, mass protests, such as the demonstration by 40,000 miners and their families in November 1996[7], as well as strikes and the activities of independent workers' movements continue to challenge both the neoliberal capitalist agenda and the privilege and power of the Party-state bureaucracy – the two elements of what constitutes actually existing market socialism in China.

Constructing Market Socialism: The (Re)Commodification of Labour

High among the promises of wealth and progress in the transition to a socialist market economy, is the claim that workers will be 'liberated' from the bureaucratic allocation and control of employment and excessive egalitarianism in wages perceived to have hindered productivity and undermined the incentive to work. It is taken for granted that this new 'freedom' to work for individual material rewards is guaranteed in a free labour market: '[T]he labour force will enjoy a free-flowing in the market [sic] according to the demands of enterprises and individual preferences. This means that the labour force will also become subjective and objective factors in the market.'[8] According to this neoclassical discourse on the free labour market, the prospects for greater individual material rewards would coincide with greater individual freedom. As Du Haiyan, a leading proponent of the free market in China, has claimed, by 'giving people a completely free hand in choosing their own jobs, an environment of equal opportunity and fair competition will be created, with labourers bearing the economic risks for their own decisions on labour inputs.'[9]

In constructing this new environment, the responsiveness of labour to free market forces can only be ensured if the systems of job security (the iron rice bowl) and egalitarian wages ('eating from one big pot') are dismantled. In the early reform period this impacted on the wages system, with an increasing proportion of wages and bonuses designated as 'floating wages' directly tied to individual performance.[10] While basic wages were combined with 'over-quota' bonuses, this was rapidly overtaken by the reduction of basic wages and the introduction of piece-rate wages. Although bonuses were intended to act as individual incentives, workers continued to demand an equal distribution of bonuses which blunted their effect. Piece-rate wages, on the other hand, would impose a regime of time-work discipline, encourage competition between workers, and undermine workers' sense of security by establishing an uncertain and fluctuating system of remuneration. In 1983, proponents of market reform called for the generalisation of the piece-rate wages system in all sectors and industries to raise productivity and overcome the rigidities of administrative allocation of employment and wages. In fact – as with most official discourse on reform – this shift in policy was an *ex post* recognition of the introduction of piece-rate wages in 1979-80 by state and collective sector managers – a transformation of the relationship between wages and work which economists such as Feng Lanrui and Zhao Lukuan praised for achieving a breakthrough in productivity: 'Each piece of work in the section was contracted to each individual worker and wages are calculated on the basis of actual fulfilment of the work contracted. The result was a 20 per cent increase in efficiency.'[11] Of course this achievement was contingent on the destruction of guaranteed wages as well as job security, with the latter collapsing in the shift from lifetime employment to a system of labour contracts. Under the new system workers must sign and renew their contracts with the management annually on an *individual* basis. There was strong resistance by workers to the labour contract system, though in official discourse the failure to implement the Labour Contract Law of 1986 in state-owned and collective enterprises was attributed to bureaucratism and poor understanding of why or how it was to be done. Although managers acquired even greater powers in 1988 with official recognition of their power of dismissal, they did not overcome resistance to the labour contract system on the shop floor. In 1986 only six percent of state-owned enterprise (SOE) workers were placed under the contract system, increasing to a quarter of all SOE workers in 1994.[12] By 1995 market socialist economists still lamented that among the 'lingering problems' of the reform process was that the 'so-called practice of "eating from the same big pot" still exists for employees in a number of enterprises.'[13] For a decade these changes were resisted, and only in 1996 have the institutionalised rights of workers finally been abolished, with a final shift towards the privatisation or liquidation of state and collective enterprises, the predominance of foreign capital in shaping the labour process, and unemployment reaching tens of millions.

Workers had also strongly resisted the neoliberal privatisation programme, though this resistance too was widely interpreted in terms of institutional constraints and the combined resistance of state sector officials, managers and workers. Many narratives on the impediments to privatisation ignored the profound conflict in interests between managers and workers, instead subsuming workers' interests into that of the 'enterprise' – which is then personified by the manager. For managers the linkage between political power and capital accumulation is such that direct connections to political authority and political modes of coercion in the social relations of production are necessary to retain power over workers and ensure the transfer of wealth and power to the private sphere through the systematic exclusion of workers. Workers, on the other hand, have asserted their desire for greater control of the production process, resistant not to decentralisation and enterprise autonomy as such, but to the particular form that this decentralisation and (managerial) autonomy has taken. Thus workers have struggled to increase the power of the workers' congress within the enterprise, and to acquire autonomy from the Party and trade union bureaucracy. However, while workers in SOEs have continued to resist privatisation, they have been unable to resist *de facto* privatisations which have been carried out through subcontracting, out-sourcing or the formation of partnerships with local and foreign capital. In foreign-invested factories and joint ventures a strict regime of discipline is encoded in workers' contracts and notices are posted in factories listing fines and physical punishments for speaking or drinking water during working hours, being late, wearing name tags incorrectly, sitting or resting, going to the toilet too often, and so on.[14] In a factory where there is a complex system of 46 rules and regulations, 80 per cent of the workers are fined monthly.[15] This system is policed by private security guards and officers of the Public Security Bureau and local militias within a wider system of surveillance that relies on 'bird-cage management systems' (where workers are locked in factories and dormitories) and other forms of physical control and isolation both during and after working hours.[16]

Workers' resistance to these reforms is also undermined by the massive migration of displaced peasants and rural workers to industrial districts and Special Economic Zones in search of work, which has created a floating workforce of 80 to 100 million 'blind' migrant workers without contracts or welfare rights. Undocumented migrant workers are paid less and are under constant threat of being turned over to officials by employers. Even those migrant workers who are working 'legally' are forced to hand over their ID cards, residency documents and entry permits to their employers, which prevents them from being able to leave of their own accord.[17] Strict control over migrant workers was further institutionalised in 1996 when laws were introduced requiring that migrant workers be registered under family planning centres. Proof of sterilisation cards issued by family planning centres must be held by migrant women workers when they apply for jobs in the 'economic miracle' province of Fujian.[18]

In official discourse this migration in search of work is testimony to the effectiveness of labour market reforms. Following massive lay-offs from SOEs in 1993 it was announced that retrenched workers would be 'directed to the market'.[19] In effect this massive increase in unemployment contradicts claims by the ruling political elite that market reforms were intended to reduce unemployment, instead proving unequivocally that the overriding objective was to raise productivity and profit at any cost. As Howard and Howard have noted, in this new neoliberal economic discourse the 'elimination of redundant labour' in itself would raise productivity levels, leading to the immediate retrenchment of over eight million workers from SOEs and the designation of another 20 million workers as 'surplus labour' to be laid off under state enterprise restructuring (now estimated at 50 million workers).[20] The fate of these workers is reflected in the results of a survey in the north-eastern province of Jilin which showed that two thirds of workers retrenched under this programme have not been able to find jobs.[21] The majority of workers who are able to find new jobs, particularly women workers, end up earning less than half the minimum wage. According to a survey of 2,727 women workers laid off from 23 state-owned and collective enterprises, all of them earned less than the minimum wage, with half earning half the minimum wage and a quarter earning nothing at all.[22]

The capitalist dynamic of these changes is based on the reconfiguration of authoritarian factory regimes (for they were never genuinely democratic), consolidating the power of managers and their exclusionary control over production. Direct modes of labour repression and control are underpinned not only by the freedom of managers to hire and fire workers, but also by the enforcement of new systems of discipline and punishment and the close alignment of Party and trade union officials with management. As a worker wrote in a letter to the underground workers' newspaper, *Zhongguo Laogong Tongxun*, recently:

All this concentration of power and responsibility in the hands of party members means that the long arm of party influence stretches even further into the lives of workers at the plant. The 'three visits, one chat' system is a way of ensuring that absolutely nothing interferes with production at the factory. A party representative will visit the home of an employee when: 1. He or she is ill (to check that they are really ill); 2. If they show signs of not being 'satisfied' at work (to make sure that any dissatisfaction doesn't spill over into a collective dispute); and 3. If there are domestic problems at home (thus removing any vestiges of privacy). The 'one chat' is simple and covers all three visits: any problems or contradictions that may affect productivity must be discussed with management.[23]

There are important continuities in this changing regime of production. As Arif Dirlik has argued, the objectives of 'change and progress' as national goals had already led state-socialist regimes from their very beginning 'to mimic the economic achievements of capitalism, goals that not only distorted socialism but, because capitalism is obviously much better equipped than socialism to achieve capitalist goals, undermined the legitimacy of the system as well.'[24] The economic criteria of efficiency and cumulative growth in earlier decades were inspired largely by the centrality of the national economy in the construction of Chinese marxism and the adoption of what Steve Smith labelled in the Soviet case 'technicist Bolshevism' – a version of Taylorism which underpins the regime of labour control in the Stalinist model of industrialisation.[25] Technicist-Bolshevism demanded greater control over the organisation of production and the labour process by a managerial and technical elite presiding over a 'backward' and 'undisciplined' proletariat which had yet to achieve a higher stage of class consciousness. The bargaining process which developed at the point of production involved a mixture of coercion and consent – with a decisive shift to coercion in the pursuit of Taylorist productivity. Combined with the bureaucratic intervention of the Party-state and trade union apparatus to enforce discipline, this regime of production alienated workers and generated quotidian forms of resistance which found expression in laziness, indiscipline, theft, absenteeism - 'irrational' acts interpreted as proof of the need to give managers absolute power to break workers' resistance to the ever-increasing pace and intensity of work. It is precisely the consolidation of this managerial-technicism and the reassertion of control over labour that underlies market reforms. In this sense, as Dirlik is right to conclude, there is an important continuity in the post-Mao era of 'using capitalism to develop socialism'.[26] Moreover, as Pat Devine has argued, insofar as 'market socialism seeks to replace the coercion of administrative command planning by the coercion of market forces', this coercion precludes any possibility of a labour process that is genuinely socialist: 'No less than Soviet-style command planning, the coercion of market forces, whether capitalist or market socialist, reinforces and reproduces alienation. In both cases, workers in enterprises experience powerlessness and non-involvement in relation to crucial decisions that affect them.'[27]

Legitimizing Market Socialism: The Contortion of Marxism

In the post-Mao era of market reform there remained a need for the market socialist project to establish its theoretical and ideological legitimacy. Central to reconciling a market economy with socialism was the question of the commodification of labour and the social antagonisms implicit in it. As market socialist theorists for the Chinese Communist regime have indicated, the commodification of labour power in practice required a rethinking of socialist theory if reforms were to continue: 'The development of China's labour market is faced with an important theoretical obstacle – the theory that under the socialist system labour is not a commodity.'[28] This obstacle was dealt with in a vast literature on market socialism. Lin Zili, one of the leading theorists of Chinese economic reforms, justified the creation of a free labour market and the dismantling of egalitarian wage policies and restrictions on wage differentials (the same 'labour market rigidities' identified in Hu Zu-liu's report for the IMF[29]) by doing away with the very notion of exploitation:

> [T]he exchange of equal amounts of labour is complex. It includes the exchange of unequal amounts of labour, with producers who have relatively advanced material production conditions still able to obtain a certain differential income, and the suppliers of capital able to obtain interest. These things are both unequal exchange of labour, involving the 'possession' of other people's labour, though they generally do not occupy an important position. If at a certain time their role expands, then we can regulate and control them through macro-economic measures, so that polarisation and class antagonism do not result. Therefore, we consider it inappropriate to speak of unequal exchange of labour in the socialist commodity economy as 'class exploitation'. Rather, it is more

appropriately termed 'non-labour income'.[30]

As such the socialist commodity economy has 'broken through the traditional doctrine of only being able to have exchange of equal amounts of labour via the direct exchange of labour' and 'has enabled the abstract principle of exchange of equal amounts of labour to become united with reality.'[31] In Lin's reading of Marx, 'socialism is unity among the workers, and exchange of equal amounts of labour', and for Lenin, 'socialism meant equal pay for equal work, which is also the meaning of exchange of equal amounts of labour.' Having equated socialism with equal exchange, Lin cites the shortcomings of Marx's notion of 'natural labour time' as a means for measuring this equal exchange, arguing that with the complexity of the quality and social division of labour in modern economic systems only through the market can this exchange be carried out. Therefore 'the exchange of equal amounts of labour must be characterized by the exchange of commodities of equal value, becoming a new form of equal exchange of value relationship: this is the socialist commodity economy.'[32] Without any explanation of what compels workers to sell their labour power and the social relations determining this, Lin achieves a link between Marx and Lenin's conceptions of socialism (as constructed in the official narratives of the Chinese Communist Party) and the rational economic necessity of the market. Thus the *inequality* and *polarisation* generated by the divergence between earners of non-labour income and sellers of labour-power reflects the *fairness* and *equality* in exchange envisaged by Marx: 'The principle of exchange of equal amounts of labour involves equality in buying and selling different amounts of labour and in exchanging different average values. This causes people's economic benefits to depend on the amount and efficiency of their labour so that this kind of equality encourages efficiency.'[33]

In this market socialist mode of 'equal exchange' which claims to be different from capitalism, equality is subordinated to the imperatives of efficiency and workers are subordinated to the threat of impoverishment and unemployment. While Marx understood the equal exchange of labour power as being complex, the solution did not lie in fostering existing inequalities, but in recognising its primary determinant – the structures and systems of power which shape the social relations of production and distribution. Furthermore, Marx's conceptualisation of the equal exchange of labour is premised on the social working day, where the social division of labour, the length of the working day and productivity (intensity of labour power) is collectively decided and regulated by workers' councils. The rationale of the Chinese socialist market, on the other hand, is premised on the commodification of labour power and the distribution of power in favour of managers and technicians to increase labour productivity. The social regulation of the working day gives way to the intensification of the pace of work and the extension of the working day, with only the decisions of managers and supervisors and the physical limits of human endurance to bring it to an end.[34]

Implicit in Lin's assertion that the macro-regulation and control of a nascent capitalist class by the state will prevent polarisation and class antagonism is the assumption that the political regime will not become enmeshed in the accumulation of 'non-labour income', and that the state itself is not the source of this emerging class of 'possessors of other people's labour'. Yet the state apparatus which exercises policies of regulation or containment is precisely the same social power base from within which the new capitalist class and partners of global capital are emerging. Mayors of cities, city and provincial officials, military and police officers, are also managers of state-owned and private businesses, as well as being joint venture partners in the foreign-invested factories in the regions or industrial sectors in which they exercise political authority.

The legitimation of the accumulation of non-labour income (which includes interest and 'risk income') is central to Lin's conceptualisation of market socialism. The accumulation of non-labour income (that is, profit) is merely a form of 'complex labour', a fact not understood since '[s]ome comrades do not acknowledge that business is a form of labour.'[35] By treating capital in the neoclassical sense of accumulated material wealth or money rather than a social relation, capital becomes income, then a form of complex labour. Through this device, exploitation and class antagonism is dissolved in theory at the very moment at which it has become more and more a reality in state and collective enterprises. As Apo Leong has observed elsewhere, the theoretical legitimation of exploitation coincides with the reconfiguration of the relationship between labour and capital from antagonism to partnership: 'Class struggle is no longer a byword within the ruling Communist Party and the official trade union. "Stability and harmonious relationship" between the employer and the employee has become the new catch phrase in the country's "historical mission of building a socialist market economy".'[36] Given the monopoly on Marxism-Leninism and the production of official knowledge exercised by the Party elite and their entourage of officially sanctioned intellectuals, the marxist rationale of market socialism formed the basis of a new political economy of truth – the basic principles of which would be beyond debate. This is epitomised by Lui Guoguang's pronouncement that socialism and egalitarianism are incompatible: '[S]ocialism promotes the development of the productive forces, whereas egalitarianism hinders them. Therefore socialism and egalitarianism are not compatible. This is not a new form in theory, but merely a reversal of the reversed Marxist truth.'[37] Whether or not this statement makes sense is less important than the power with which the proposal to abandon all state policies directed at ensuring social equality achieves immunity from criticism by claiming to embody a 'Marxist truth.' As Yan Sun has argued, the rethinking of socialism within official discourse in China 'deliberately makes use of selected parts of Marx's works, in particular Marx's later works that emphasise historical materialism, without considering Engels' mechanistic interpretation of them or early Soviet influences in Chinese absorption of Marxism.'[38]

Wang Ruoshui's famous essay, 'In defense of humanism', written in 1983, had such powerful resonance precisely because of the way in which Marx's later works were used to indirectly challenge the logic of market reforms. Wang indicated that many of the elements of early or young Marx that the Party had rejected could be found in later works, particularly the notion of the alienation of labour. This stood in direct conflict with theorists such as Lin who had appropriated 'late Marx' to justify the commodification of labour. Wang pointed out that 'the mature Marx's *Communist Manifesto* criticises "transforming the dignity of human beings into exchange value" and "leaving no bond between human beings other than naked interest and unfeeling cash transactions"', leading to the conclusion that 'Marx all along connected proletarian revolution and communism with questions of human value, dignity, emancipation, and freedom.'[39] The official response was not a debate of these issues, but Wang's dismissal as deputy editor of the *People's Daily* in a campaign against 'spiritual pollution'.[40] This closure of alternative ways of understanding and resolving the social and economic crisis in China is aptly described by Howard and Howard as the 'epistemological violence of reductionist economics'. They argue: 'Instead of a discussion of options, there is the suggestion that there is one best way to optimize the utilization of labour power. That one best way, it is repeatedly asserted, is the self-regulating market mechanism. Again and again the market's capacity for automatic adjustment is exaggerated and fetishised. This notion of automaticity is reinforced by the constant reference to "mechanisms".'[41] It is the assumed automaticity and neutrality of the market (a concept associated with Deng's theorisation of economic reforms) which does away with any sense that socialism and the market are mutually exclusive. Ultimately market socialist theorists such as Lin see new forms of inequality and the unequal distribution of profit as part of a socialist system where 'these differentials must be arrived at through the market, i.e., through social evaluation an objective, realistic outcome is arrived at.' For labour in particular, the 'market objectively appraises differentials in labour quality, leading to widening differentials in labour income.'[42] Since this process is understood only within the sphere of distribution, it is concluded that the outcome is 'equal'. As with all market socialist perspectives, there is no sense here of the systems of power and social relations of production which determine this 'objective' appraisal by the market. The material interests of nascent capitalists and political power-holders is further euphemised as a type of 'complex labour' and hence differences in the material rewards received by capitalists and workers is understood not as exploitation, but as a manifestation of an objectively determined wage differential.

A similar observation is made by John E. Roemer, one of the leading proponents of market socialism, who asserts that since 'people are differently skilled and educated, wage income will be quite unequal in the population' and so 'labour must be allocated largely by the market'.[43] This reflects the wider convergence of the proponents of market socialism in advanced capitalist societies with the market socialists of the authoritarian Communist regime in China in conceptualising the 'problem' of labour productivity and excessive egalitarianism and advocating the solution of a 'free' labour market. A global discourse on market socialism has both informed and been informed by China's political and economic elites. In these convergent discourses the explanation of how this is *not capitalism* remains unclear. Lin Zili offers the following distinction between China's market socialism and capitalism: 'The essence of the capitalist market economy is the capitalist commodity economy. The form assumed by the socialist commodity economy is the socialist market economy.'[44]

Actually Existing Market Socialism: Township and Village Enterprises

It is significant that in one of the most important works on market socialism in recent years, Roemer's *A Future for Socialism*, China's Township and Village Enterprises (TVEs) are exemplified as 'the first indigenous and competitive form of socialist enterprise' the world has seen, the experience of which provides a model for the future of socialism.[45] Alongside modern corporations in advanced capitalist societies, TVEs in China 'allow us to begin to understand that aspects of economic development which the received theory has attributed to the right to the unfettered accumulation of private property may in fact be due to competition and markets instead.'[46] Using the market-socialist paradigm of Bardhan and Roemer, Paul Bowles and Xiao-yuan Dong have argued that China's 'remarkable economic success' is contingent not on privatisation, but on 'local state activism' and social ownership which has produced 'a decentralized, developmental market-socialist system'.[47] Local state activism is understood as a combination of 'classic entrepreneurial skills' and 'social ownership of the means of production' under which 'these governments have exhibited considerable entrepreneurial skills defined as the ability to seize new opportunities and take advantage of disequilibrium market situations', allowing them to 'enter into previously monopolized markets and capture a share of the monopoly profits.'[48] Like Roemer,

Bowles and Dong have understood this 'classic entrepreneurship' by the local state as a genuine of form of 'socialist entrepreneurship' which 'has led the local state to behave in ways which are different from, and more economically beneficial than, a capitalist alternative.'[49]

Township and Village Enterprises (*xiangzhen qiye*) originated in the commune brigade enterprises (*shedui qiye*) of the 1950s, although they only became known as such when the market reform policies of 1984 recognised their *de facto* profit-making activities and encouraged the pursuit of profit and unrestrained accumulation. This led to a proliferation of these enterprises, increasing from one and a half million in 1978 to 25 million in 1993, employing over 123 million workers.[50] There can be no doubt that the rapid expansion of TVEs has played a critical role in generating new employment and contributing to the growth of national industrial output. However, the extent to which this is based on the proliferation of *socialist* enterprises depends largely on the question of ownership and control. This is partly answered by Bowles and Dong themselves who allude to 'the fact that TVEs are not worker-owned firms operating on democratic principles'.[51] Furthermore there is 'a discernible hierarchy of claims of the profits of enterprises', though no attempt is made to explain the power relations which determine this hierarchy.[52] Even where they explicitly recognise that it is local officials 'who in practice control property rights of TVEs' this is assumed to be a manifestation of local state power and not the power of local political elites.[53] What are referred to euphemistically as 'local connections' are in fact the linkages between the power and authority of the local Party-state and the accumulation of wealth by TVE directors and their agents.[54] Such linkages allow the legal-institutional representation of TVEs as a form of 'collective ownership', which enables TVE managers to avoid taxes and maintain access to state resources, including state loans and contracts, while at the same time exercising effective private control over the accumulation and distribution of profit. But concerned as market socialists are with refuting the neoliberal position on the need for a system of private property rights, Bowles and Dong exercise the same institutional fetishism they are criticising. The possibility of effective private possession and control of production in the absence of declared private ownership or its articulation in legal-institutional arrangements is not considered. Nonetheless they conclude that TVEs 'behave differently from capitalist firms' which is sufficient reason to declare them socialist.

Roemer himself only suggests that there are several possibilities in this new form of social ownership: 'Who owns TVEs? The answer is vague – ownership forms probably cover the gamut of possibilities, from the disguised private firm in the hands of a few partners to ventures that are genuinely owned by local governments.'[55] But it seems that the answer is only vague because the reality – that the vast majority of TVEs are in fact privately owned, with only an estimated seven percent under the collective ownership of townships and villages – cannot be reconciled with socialism of any type.[56] In addition, these local officials who are assumed to exercise the property rights of TVEs are in fact closely aligned to – and sometimes appointed by – local capitalists who have accumulated enough wealth to lend money to the local state to pay the salaries of the staff of the local state and Party bureaucracy.

What also cannot be reconciled with socialism is the 'fusion of local and foreign capital interests' in the relationship between TVEs and foreign capital.[57] Treated unproblematically by market socialists, it is assumed that the interests of foreign capital cannot determine the conditions of production and distribution. Yet even in legal-institutional terms, most joint ventures between TVEs and foreign capital (mostly with Hong Kong-based capital) involve boards of directors in which foreign joint venture partners are dominant, or agreements in which strategic control of the enterprise is held by foreign capital. In addition to this, local political authorities including the local Party secretary often derive a *direct* income from these foreign joint ventures, thereby guaranteeing the partnership of interests between the local state and foreign capital.[58] Ironically having admitted to the 'fusion of local and foreign capital interests', and praising the success of China's integration into the global economy, Roemer, Bowles and Dong fail to situate TVEs within this global context, instead treating them as if their socialist dynamic works in isolation, affected only by the local political economy. Yet the local state itself has been significantly transformed by the drive to attract foreign capital. This involves direct linkages with foreign capital through joint ventures and subcontracting, as well as a restructuring of the state to facilitate the influx and expansion of foreign capital. As Dirlik has suggested, for the Chinese Communist regime 'the recognition of the local in marketing strategy does not mean any serious acknowledgement of the autonomy of the local but is intended only to incorporate localities into the imperatives of the global'.[59] This is exemplified by the local state's 'restructuring' of 13,000 enterprises in the Guangxi Zhuang Autonomous Region over the next three years based on 'entire or part of the assets and workforces of the local enterprises in the form of buying or even holding of the stock by foreign investors or selling of the property rights in part or in whole to foreign investors.'[60]

In Chang Chun and Wang Yijiang's study of TVEs, framed within a liberal view of capitalism, it is concluded that 'the TVE is controlled by the township-village government (TVG), not by its nominal owners, the local citizens.' They point out that while workers 'sometimes do have a nominal right of voting to approve or disapprove' the manager appointed by local authorities, 'this right seems to be largely cosmetic.'[61] In the first instance a vote must be initiated by the local political leadership, which means there will be no vote as long as the township or village leaders support the manager. Therefore, 'the manager can thus remain in office indefinitely.' In practice the authoritarian arrangement of political power ensures that the legal-institutional ownership rights of local citizens can never be translated into effective control over TVEs. In addition, the local state 'controls many other aspects of a local citizen's life ... including who can work in the TVE', and so workers in TVEs 'would rarely want a confrontational relationship with the TVG.'[62] Wages too are beyond the control of workers, 'even collectively.'[63] As such there is even less scope for workers' control over TVEs, particularly since the alignment of the interests of the local Party-state to TVE managers in creating the conditions for the maximisation of profit continues to prevent the emergence of any radical democratic practices necessary to exercise genuine workers' control.

In his contribution to *Market Socialism* published in 1993, Roemer overcomes this problem by redefining socialism altogether: 'Why not define socialism more radically, as a system in which the entire national income, rather than just profits, is divided equally among the population, or is divided according to criteria that society might democratically specify – for example, according to need?'[64] Consequently socialists should support any set of property relations that deliver 'a kind of egalitarianism.'[65] Whereas there is an extensive market-socialist literature on the capitalist practices of 'incentives' and 'competition', the socialist content of this is reduced to a vague egalitarianism. Having sidestepped the issue of ownership, Roemer finds the socialist character of TVEs in the distribution of profit. But even here there is little certainty: '*If it is correct* that the profits of the TVEs go primarily into financing local public goods, such as schools and roads, then a large part of the transformation of the Chinese economy since 1979, only partially indicated by a real GNP growth rate averaging 9 per cent per year since then, will have been due to a new form of property appropriately described as market-socialist.'[66] Roemer also fails to explain how a community or society can 'democratically specify' the division and use of this collective or national income. This is no small matter in a context where, as Bowles and Dong recognise, 'the Chinese township or village is by no means democratic',[67] let alone in the broader context of the authoritarian system of 'democratic centralism' maintained by the Communist regime. While Western market socialists may have different approaches to the question of democracy than the market socialist theorists of the Chinese Communist regime, by leaving the process of democratically specifying collective needs undefined we can see that these differences are clearly tangential to their concerns.

In keeping with Bardhan and Roemer's reduction of socialist aspirations to a system which 'would have a more egalitarian income distribution, and would be more sensitive to social needs, such as education, health care and environmental protection',[68] Bowles and Dong argue that profit maximisation is not the only objective of local governments and that 'local preferences, especially for employment, do seem to play an important role in determining the behaviour of TVEs.' While admitting that bankruptcy and closure leading to the loss of jobs does occur, 'TVEs engage in distinct employment practices and their profits are regarded as a source for funding welfare programmes for the whole community.'[69] Not only does the assumption of the existence of a cohesive, homogenous community exclude 'outside' workers employed in TVEs, but the concern for full employment in official discourse becomes the basis of their socialist vision. While full employment is an important goal – and a particularly critical issue given the massive unemployment crisis in China – it is not necessarily motivated by a socialist agenda. Rather than being consciously chosen by local leaders in response to a socialist process of articulating workers' needs and interests, policies aimed at full employment are an element of the hegemonic strategy of the local ruling elite to maintain its hold on power in a period of economic crisis.

It can also be argued that the threat of social instability and perceived political crisis caused by massive migration to coastal and urban-industrial areas has led the central state to encourage the development of TVEs as a means of stemming the tide of migration and re-establishing control by generating new forms of employment. The fact is, most of this employment is temporary. In a case study of a garment TVE which formed a joint venture with a Hong Kong-based company in 1988, the neoconservative economist Liu Xiao Meng indicates that nearly 40 per cent of the workers are temporary and that despite the need for approval by the Township Industrial Office before firing permanent workers, their contracts allow them to be easily terminated for 'incompetence'.[70] In other cases the director is free to hire and fire workers and the only employee who cannot be dismissed by the director without the approval of the Township Industrial Office is the chief accountant.[71] At the same time workers must pay security deposits when they begin work at TVEs, sometimes paying the equivalent of two months' wages which is only refundable after a couple of years or, more commonly, only if the director permits them to resign. In a similar study of a TVE paint factory, only eight of the 78 workers have permanent employment, and the rest are contract and temporary workers who are 'available on the labour market'.[72]

As a study of actually existing socialism, and a proposal for a working alternative to capitalism, there is a remarkable omission: the labour process. Whether or not TVEs 'behave differently from capitalist firms'[73] can only be determined by the nature of the labour process, the extent to which workers exercise control over the conditions under which they labour, and the structure of power and authority at the point of production. Part of the problem stems from a tendency in the literature on the political economy of 'transition' to treat the 'enterprise' as the basic unit of analysis; a social actor in its own right. This collapses the material interests and the distinct social identity of workers with that of managers into a single, homogenous entity of 'the enterprise', implying the absence of social conflict and relations of domination and subordination within the enterprise. Consequently, for market socialists it is the behaviour of the homogenous enterprise which determines whether it is a manifestation of capitalism or socialism, and not the social relations of production within it. In fact the only insight into the experience of workers in Bowles and Dong's study (gleaned from an article in *Business Week*) is negative. In coastal areas: '... TVEs have hired both local and non-local labour with the latter often being hired as wage labourers on terms less advantageous than the local "insiders". These developments may rob the TVEs of any progressive and meaningful role as agents of socially-desirable development.'[74] Having alluded to the subordinate position of 'non-local labour' and their apparent exclusion from certain benefits, Bowles and Dong fail to examine the implications of this for their thesis that TVEs are fundamentally socialist in character. The extent to which migrant workers are in fact excluded from the social welfare functions of the state and from participation in the operation and redistribution of profit of TVEs is revealed by Han Dongfang's explanation that the experience of exclusion and marginalisation is inherent in the identity of migrant workers: 'Migrant workers from the poor rural areas have become known as *mingong* (literally peasant worker) which is an abbreviation of the category 'worker with peasant status' i.e. an employee without an urban residence permit. Although these workers are often employed in big cities, they are there solely on the understanding that they sell their labour power and otherwise count for nothing.'[75] In the conclusion to their study on TVEs, Chang and Wang mention *mingong* in passing, observing that, 'wages paid to a worker who is a local citizen will have a higher value than the wages paid to a worker who is an outsider', while assuming that they are employed because local full employment has been achieved.[76] Yet in recent protests over unemployment and low living standards, local peasants have complained that *mingong* are brought in to work in TVEs, even though unemployment in the townships and villages is already high.[77] The use of *mingong* is so extensive that many of the TVEs praised as 'small economic miracles' have built dormitories to house migrant workers. While this falls within the category of expenditure on social welfare, there is a contradiction here between 'satisfying local needs' and bringing in migrant workers to replace local workers, which directly challenges the logic of 'community' and localism in market socialist perspectives.

In their criticism of Richard Smith's claim that TVEs are capitalist enterprises, Bowles and Dong argue that bonuses and wages were higher for workers in TVEs in the late 1980s, (based on knowledge constructed by the World Bank).[78] However, case studies of TVEs and reports in local newspapers show that on average TVE workers earn basic wages which are lower than the minimum wage and must earn the rest through overtime and piece-rate quota bonuses. Even the basic wage is not guaranteed since the minimum wage is set by local township authorities whose material interests – both institutionally and privately – are tied up in the maximisation of profit. It is also common practice for TVE management to keep separate records for 'book profits' (*zhangmian*) and 'accounting profits' (*jiesuan lirun*) to lower the taxes they pay to the local state. The power of the director and chief accountant to decide this, and the exclusion of workers from having access to this information, is another example of the 'lack of democratic principles' which Bowles and Dong recognise, but fail to see as significantly affecting the socialist nature of TVEs.

According to Bowles and Dong 'the wage-productivity link is stronger in TVEs', having 'successfully addressed the monitoring problem (i.e. how workers and managers have been induced to work efficiently)'.[79] In identifying the relationship between workers and efficiency as a 'monitoring problem' (and as 'labour monitoring'), Bowles and Dong fail to break from the productivist goals of capitalism. The implications of this are epitomised by a case reported in *Hunan Workers' News* in which the manager of a TVE in Hunan carried handcuffs and an electric truncheon in the factory to deal with 'dissenting workers'. Since 1993 the manager has kept a guard dog which is used to threaten and attack workers. While the workers' monthly wages were reduced to 50 rmb (less than half the legal minimum wage of 125 rmb), the factory pays 120 rmb in monthly expenses for the dog. One of the workers lamented that: 'Our lives cannot compare to that of a dog!'[80] While this is an extreme case of the managerial despotism in TVEs, it illustrates the fundamental character of these market-socialist sites of production: the excessive power of managers, the centrality of discipline and punishment in controlling workers, and the physical and social violence embodied in the inducements and incentives (threats and coercion) praised by market socialists as the engine of productivity. It is precisely this unconditional drive for maximising labour productivity that has created hazardous working conditions and a high rate of industrial accidents and occupational diseases in TVEs.[81] According to *China Women's Daily* over a third of all TVEs violate official standards on health and safety.[82] When a TVE lighter factory in Guangdong province burned down in September 1995, 23 workers were killed and over 60 were injured. All of them were women workers with the youngest only 15 years old.[83]

In addition to their omission of any discussion of the labour process, Roemer, Bowles and Dong neglect issues of gender and power in the social relations of production in TVEs and in the wider political economy. As Elisabeth Croll has noted: 'One of most striking impressions of any official visitor to China continues in the 1980s and 1990s to be the predominance of men in the leadership committees at all administrative levels of the government and the Party.'[84] These patriarchal power structures have been consolidated by the feminisation of factory labour throughout China, driven by a low-wage strategy of national accumulation and both new and old gender ideologies which undervalue the labour-power of women. Many TVEs in fact only hire unmarried women under 20 years of age, who are dismissed when they reach 25 or marry.[85] The experience of women workers in TVEs is described by Croll in the following way: 'Where the labour process is fast, fragmented and repetitive, the payment calculated according to piece-work, there is evidence to suggest that women work longer lower-paid hours, conditions of work are cramped and there are few provisions for the implementation of new and improved labour-protection regulations.' She cites a survey of TVEs in 1989 which revealed that half had not implemented laws protecting women workers and 44 per cent 'did not reduce the heavy work of pregnant women or take them off night-shift.' Though the majority of women on maternity leave were being paid their wages in full, 'their bonuses and other benefits were not guaranteed, leading to a decrease in income by one third.'[86] More recent studies show that the average wage of women workers is only three quarters that of men, and, more significantly, the percentage of women earning less than 100 rmb per month is three times higher.[87] So for women workers the future of socialism envisaged by market socialists such as Roemer promises to be bleak. Along with other capitalist practices market socialists have appropriated for this socialist project, it seems they will also retain the patriarchal systems of power and domination that have become integral to the capitalist system.

In Roemer's glorification of TVEs in China, he cites an article in *The Economist* to elucidate the success of competition and hard budget constraints in facilitating liquidations and mass closures. The 'amazing growth' so important to this capitalist productivism is coupled with the collapse of three million TVEs in 1989 under the government's austerity programme – a natural outcome of market competition. In fact, despite the supposed local-communal benefits generated by these TVEs and the promise of full employment, Roemer welcomes the demise of these uncompetitive TVEs as good for actually existing socialist enterprises.[88] The fate of workers in these three million liquidated TVEs is not mentioned in Roemer's account, nor is the process by which they were disbanded explained. Did workers collectively decide that liquidation was necessary? Were alternatives discussed? Were productive materials and equipment divided among the workers? Were outstanding debts inherited by the local state? Were the factories and workshops purchased by private interests, and if so was payment distributed among workers? Did workers have the option of staying on? Consideration of such questions requires reflection on the extent to which workers and the local community actually made decisions about the operation of these TVEs. Finally, we must ask whether the promise of social welfare for the local community is a sufficient reason for supporting the new political economy of the local state and TVEs, particularly if the prioritisation of efficiency over all else leads to a destructive process of liquidation and mass dismissals. Bardhan and Roemer reassure us that: 'Most small firms, as under capitalism, either die after some time or are bought by large firms, and the same trajectory could be expected under market socialism, where large corporations would purchase successful private firms.'[89] Having already subsumed workers into the homogenous entity of the enterprise, they neglect to tell us whether, with the death of enterprises, workers are expected to follow suit. In fact workers only figure in this scenario as a potential problem since 'the major constituency opposed to liquidation or scaling down of unprofitable enterprises is the workforce.' To overcome workers' resistance to being laid off they propose that profit sharing arrangements outweigh the 'attraction of clinging to the job'.[90] There is no understanding here of working class identity and resistance, or the social and cultural construction of job security, work and wages in the lives of working people. This reinforces Ernest Mandel's criticism of the market-socialist alternative:

> The fact that no market economy has been able to avoid the ills of periodic economic catastrophes like mass bankruptcies (mass destruction/devalorization of capital/productive equipment), mass unemployment, periodically declining living standards and periodically increasing moral misery for millions, is of course not accidental. It is related to the very nature of that economic system.[91]

Now let us think this through. Here we have TVEs which, we are told, are socialist. At the same time we are told that workers exercise only nominal ownership over the means of production and even then only as local citizens. In effect they exercise no control over the conditions under which they are exploited. In addition, there is hyper-exploitation of women workers and displaced migrant workers, as well as closures and mass lay-offs in response to the vagaries of the market. Thrown in with this there is corruption and bare self-interest among those who do exercise ownership and control, and there is no democracy on the shopfloor, in the local political setting or in the national context. There is even evidence of protest and resistance by workers and peasants. We are then expected to believe that this is socialism, this is the alternative to capitalism! The distinction between this vision of socialism and the 'faint hoofbeats of barbarism' is difficult to discern.[92] In defending this paradigm, Roemer claims that 'the theory of capitalism has made concessions to socialist critiques in the realm of economic theory', leaving one to wonder how much the theory of socialism has conceded to the logic of capitalism in the realm of practice.[93]

Workers under China's Market Socialism: Another Road to Barbarism

Although depicted as a gradual process of reform and readjustment, the market socialist system has met with considerable resistance from below. Throughout the state and collective sectors, in TVEs, private enterprises and foreign joint ventures, growing resistance to new modes of coercion and exploitation has emerged to challenge the very logic of the capitalist regime of production. In 1994 there were 135,000 reported labour disputes, and another 150,000 in the first six months of 1995. In addition to this the All China Federation of Trade Unions (ACFTU) admitted that there were 25,000 strikes involving 450,000 workers in 1995. Although presented in the dominant development discourse as a manifestation of demands for higher wages under conditions of rapid economic growth, the vast majority of strikes in foreign-invested factories, private enterprises and TVEs are due to serious violations of workers' rights, including forced overtime, beatings, and physical and sexual harassment.[94]

The predominance of the issue of workers' rights in these collective actions is exemplified by the strike by workers in the Japanese-invested Panasonic Corporation factory in Zuhai in 1995, where they demanded that copies of the new national labour law (introduced a year earlier) be made available to them – a demand which led the official trade union to attack the striking workers. In SOEs strikes have been undertaken in protest against unpaid or late payment of wages, and not higher wages.[95] The response of the new capitalists and state sector managers has been based on attempts to fragment the workforce and break down the collective social and cultural identity of workers. In the Special Economic Zones and open cities migrant workers were initially hired from the same provinces, which enabled them to (re)establish a collective identity within factories based on their common dialect and notional kinship ties. This formed the basis of a powerful sense of common interests and a tendency toward collective action which often challenged the power of managers and supervisors. In response, managers have implemented policies of segregation, ensuring that workers from the same province are broken up into different sections in the factory.

While the strikes reflect a resurgence in workers' collective resistance to domination and exploitation by the Party-state and capital, the possibility that these sporadic collective actions will form the basis of an organised working class movement is severely limited by counter-mobilisational strategies aimed at displacing any forms of self-organisation. State power continues to be exercised through the centralised trade union apparatus, with violent repression of labour movements organised outside of these structures. Official trade unions have continued to carry out many of their functions of the pre-reform era: mobilising workers to raise productivity and output, enforcing labour discipline and consolidating managerial control over labour, in accordance with the productivist goals of Stalinist industrialisation. In the transition to capitalism these functions have been redeployed to enforce capitalist discipline, and consolidate the power of the capitalist entrepreneurs aligned with or emerging from within the Party-state. Hence the demand by the Secretary General of the ACFTU, Xiao Zhen-bang, in 1994 that 'unions must try all means to eliminate instability' and ensure that 'unexpected incidents' be prevented by working with the Party and state to consolidate control from above.[96] These incidents and moments of instability refer to the strikes and other self-organising activities of workers. While the role of the trade union in defending workers' rights and interests was reiterated at the Twelfth National Congress of the ACFTU, it was also stated that trade union activities should not conflict with the 'legitimate rights of investors'.[97] Thus official trade unions seek to manage workers' responses to the capitalist labour process, claiming to be protecting workers' rights and interests on the one hand, while having indirect linkages to capital (maintaining labour discipline and industrial peace for the sake of national economic growth) and direct linkages (involvement in profit-making business activities with domestic and foreign capital). Although there are isolated cases of local trade union officials actively supporting workers' demands once they have gone on strike, trade union officials have generally sought to bring an end to spontaneous strikes as quickly as possible. In fact state enterprise managers continue to be members of trade union committees and are seen by the ACFTU as a legitimate segment of its constituency. The ridiculousness of this situation is reflected in a labour dispute in late 1995 in which: '[A] young worker at the Hao Wang Dajiu restaurant in Shanghai decided to take her case to the local Labour Disputes and Arbitration Committee (LDAC), only to find that the chairman of her local ACFTU branch was representing *the employer* at the hearing!'[98] The implications of this for workers' self-organising activities should not be underestimated. As we write, two independent labour organisers are standing trial for 'subversion', and if convicted will be sentenced to 10 years in prison. Li Wenming's crime was to have organised (along with Kuang Lezhuang and Liao Hetang) a workers' night school to teach literacy and to raise workers' awareness of labour laws and their rights. Though legal, the school was closed by the Public Security Bureau. Later they founded the Workers' Federation and Workers' Friendship Association and published a journal called *Workers' Forum*. It was in this journal that the poem of one of the workers who survived the Zhili toy factory fire in 1993 (in which 87 workers were killed) was published. Finally all three were arrested in May 1994 along with another activist, Guo Baosheng. Li and Guo are now standing trial, while Kuang and Liao have been sentenced to 're-education through labour'.

This system of state authoritarian trade unionism is reinforced by a global discourse on the political economy of development which sees the experience of the East Asian Newly-Industrialising Countries (NICs) as a model for economic growth and development. That is, rapid industrialisation overseen by authoritarian political regimes, and the exercise of state power to repress and displace working class struggle, creating conditions for the expansion of state capital and large agglomerations of domestic and foreign capital in partnership with the state. In their praise of 'socialist state-led development' in China, Bowles and Dong assert that the same kind of 'national development ideology' which underpinned state-interventionist strategies in the East Asian NICs is evident in China where 'the provinces and lower-level governments are similarly endowed with a developmentalist ideology which has led them to intervene in the development process by actively sponsoring growth in their regions.'[99] Within China neoliberal and market socialist economists alike are attracted to the East Asian NIC model because it legitimates the systematic state repression and coercion required to impose their agenda. Even dissident Chinese intellectuals in exile have begun to speak of the need for a 'new authoritarianism' to maintain stability during the period of 'shock therapy' and to break down the entrenched power of workers and overcome their indiscipline. Giving tacit support for the 'neo-authoritarian solution', market socialists such as Paul Thompson have argued that in the current stage of 'disorganised socialism', China requires '[d]ecisive political leadership.'[100] Roemer is more explicit in his support for the authoritarian political regimes of the East Asian NICs, arguing that not only have these regimes exercised the sort of state management of the market economy proposed in the market socialist paradigm, but have successfully achieved the conditions for a transition to bourgeois democracy: 'Authoritarian developing capitalist countries with high rates of growth (such as South Korea and Taiwan) are more likely to become democratic capitalist countries in the near future, for those economies have succeeded in dramatically raising the standard of living for almost everyone during the last generation.'[101] In effect this argument converges with the demands of China's political and economic elite for even greater collective social and economic sacrifice by the mass of the working people in this period of market socialist 'transition'. For the subordinate classes this promises to be a permanent transition, and the market socialist vision of Western marxists differs little from Deng's promise of wealth for all – eventually. Western market socialists may still claim that unlike the incumbent Chinese Communist regime they promise an end to authoritarianism, since the wealth generated by market socialism will give rise to democratic processes. But the notion of democratic processes – like the labour process – is borrowed from capitalist experience. As with 'liberal marxist' opponents of the Chinese Communist regime such as Su Shaozhi, the forms of democratic participation envisaged by market socialists are derived from the institutional forms which exist in capitalist societies, and presumes a separation of the political and the economic that mimics the ideologies of capitalism.[102]

By invoking the liberal teleology which charts an inevitable trajectory from economic development to political pluralism (which then justifies political authoritarianism in the interim period of rapid industrialisation), Roemer obscures the remaking of authoritarian political elites as hegemonic ruling classes exercising new strategies of domination and control in the transition to bourgeois democracy. What is also obscured is the history of violent repression of the labour movements and other social movements in these countries in the period of rapid growth, and the current crisis of wage cuts and job losses which have followed the relocation of industrial production to countries such as China and Vietnam, and the casualisation of work in the service industries. Regardless of this, Roemer sees the experience of the East Asian NICs as sufficient justification for the authoritarian political regimes within which TVEs operate in China since – as microcosms of the East Asian NICs – democratic transition will be an inevitable outcome of economic growth generated by the local state. Again, their vision threatens more than it promises.

The proponents of 'actually existing market socialism' in China offer us less a coherent conception of a feasible socialism, than they do a political strategy and intellectual paradigm that obscures the social violence and exploitation inherent in capitalism, and gives it another name. For a socialist alternative to be imagined and realised a ruthless, sustained critique of capitalism in all its variants is as important now as it has always been.

NOTES

1. Yang Zhuhua (ed.), *Liening: Lun Jicheng, Jiejian Liyong Ziban Zhuyi* (Lenin: On Inheriting, Adapting and Using Capitalism) (Zhengzhou, Henan People's Publishing House, 1994).
2. See Wu Jie, *On Deng Xiaoping Thought* (Beijing, Foreign Language Press, 1996).
3. 'Zone workers', *Asian Labour Update*, 18 (May-July 1995), pp. 5-7.

4. It is important to distinguish this market socialist perspective, which sees a democratic process emerging in the political economy of towns and villages at a local level, and continued support for the centralised Chinese Party-state from those elements of the left more closely aligned to Stalinist forms of Marxism-Leninism. While the violent repression of the student and workers' movements in Tiananmen Square in 1989 confirmed the belief held by most socialists that the Chinese Communist regime was not socialist at all, it was this latter element of the left which continued to support the Chinese Communist Party. An example of this is the support for the Chinese state's actions in Tiananmen Square by the Communist-aligned trade union, Kilusang Mayo Uno (KMU) in the Philippines. Although their statement of support was claimed to have been an error, it was quite clear that KMU was entrenched in its support for the Chinese Communist regime, regardless of its actions. For a discussion see Kim Scipes, *KMU: Building Genuine Trade Unionism in the Philippines, 1980-1994* (Quezon, New Day Publishers, 1996), pp. 68, 186, 190.

5. 'A worker's letter to the students', Gregor Benton and Alan Hunter (eds.), *Wild Lily, Prairie Fire: China's Road to Democracy, Yan'an to Tian'anmen, 1942-1989* (Princeton, Princeton University Press, 1995), p. 270.

6. Changkai (ed.), *Laodong Guanxi, Laodongzhe, Laoquan: Dangdai Zhongguo de Laodong Wenti* (Labour Relations, Labourers and Labour Rights: Contemporary Chinese Labour Issues) (Beijing, Chinese Labour Publishing House, 1996), p. 111.

7. Jasper Becker, 'Layoffs trigger rise in protests', *South China Morning Post*, 28 November 1996.

8. Sun Xiuping, Zhu Huayou and Yao Tiejun, *Theory and Reality of Transition to a Market Economy* (Beijing, Foreign Language Press, 1995), p. 161.

9. Du Haiyan, 'Interim Report on Research Project Entitled "The Question of Staff and Workers in Reforming State-Owned Enterprises"', *Jingji Yanjiu*, 1, 20 January 1983 pp. 58-65; cited in Pat and Roger Howard, 'The campaign to eliminate job security in China', *Journal of Contemporary Asia*, 25, 3 (1995), p. 348.

10. Feng Lanrui and Zhao Lukuan, 'Urban unemployment and wages', in Yu Guangyuan (ed.) *China's Socialist Modernization* (Beijing, Foreign Language Press, 1984), pp. 569-618.

11. *Ibid.*, pp. 616-17.

12. Shek Ping Kwan, 'The new poor in Chinese cities', *Change* (August 1996). Translated by Chan Ka Wai.

13. Sun Xiuping *et al.*, *The Theory and Reality of Transition to a Market Economy*, p. 164.

14. 'Notice to all workers of the Enterprise Company Limited', *Asian Labour Update*, 21 (April-July 1996), p. 24; *The Flip-side of Success: The Situation of Workers and Organising in Foreign-invested Electronics Enterprises in Guangdong* (Hong Kong, China Labour Education and Information Centre, 1996), p. 7.

15. Asia Monitor Resource Center, *Labour Rights in the Pearl River Delta* (Hong Kong, Asia Monitor Resource Center, 1996).

16. *The Flip-side of Success*, p. 11.

17. Apo Leong, 'Beasts of burden', *Asian Labour Update*, 16 (July-September 1994), pp. 5-8.

18. *South China Morning Post*, 4 July 1996.

19. *China Daily*, 22 March 1993 p. 2. Cited in Howard and Howard, 'The campaign to eliminate job security in China', p. 342.

20. *Ibid.*, p. 343.

21. *China Women's Daily*, 13 March 1996. Translated in *China Labour Bulletin*, 28 (July 1996), p. 9.

22. *Hunan Workers' News*, 8 March 1996. Translated in *China Labour Bulletin*, 28 (July 1996), p. 9.

23. Translated in *China Labour Bulletin* (October 1996), p. 4.

24. Arif Dirlik, *After the Revolution: Waking to Global Capitalism* (Hanover, Wesleyan University Press, 1994), p. 44.
25. Steve Smith, 'Taylorism rules OK? Bolshevism, Taylorism and the technical intelligentsia in the Soviet Union, 1917-41', *Radical Science Journal*, 13 (1983), pp. 3-27.
26. Dirlik, *op. cit.*, p. 34.
27. Pat Devine, 'Beyond market socialism', *New Politics*, 2, 4 (Winter 1990), p. 112.
28. Sun Xiuping *et al. op. cit.*, p. 178.
29. Zu-liu Hu, *Social Protection, Labour Market Rigidity, and Enterprise Restructuring in China* (Chicago, International Monetary Fund, 1994).
30. Lin Zili, 'Privatization, marketization and polarization', in Peter Nolan and Dong Fureng (eds.) *Market Forces in China: Competition and Small Business – The Wenzhou Debate* (London, Zed Books, 1990), p. 167.
31. *Ibid.*, p. 166.
32. *Ibid.*, p. 166.
33. *Ibid.*, p. 170.
34. Our discussion of Marx's own writings is limited to the argument presented by Lin Zili. For a critical discussion of the contradictions between market socialism and Marx's work, see David McNally, *Against the Market: Political Economy, Market Socialism and the Marxist Critique* (London, Verso, 1993).
35. Lin, *op. cit.*, p. 168.
36. Apo Leong, 'Masters no more', *Asian Labour Update*, 14 (January-March 1994), p. 1.
37. Lui Guoguang, 'Socialism is not egalitarianism', *Beijing Review*, 28 September-4 October 1987).
38. Yan Sun, *The Chinese Reassessment of Socialism, 1976-1992* (Princeton, Princeton University Press, 1995), p. 267.
39. Wang Ruoshui, 'In defense of humanism', in Benton and Hunter (eds.), *Wild Lily, Prairie Fire*, pp. 515-16.
40. Benton and Hunter, *op. cit.*, p. 312.
41. Howard and Howard, *op. cit.*, pp. 338-55.
42. Lin, *op. cit.*, p. 168.
43. John E. Roemer, 'Can there be socialism after communism?', in Pranab K. Bardhan and John E. Roemer (eds.), *Market Socialism: The Current Debate* (Oxford, Oxford University Press, 1993), p. 90.
44. Lin, *op. cit.*, p. 174.
45. John E. Roemer, *A Future for Socialism* (London, Verso, 1994), p. 127.
46. *Ibid.*, p. 126.
47. Paul Bowles and Xiao-yuan Dong, 'Current successes and future challenges in China's economic reforms', *New Left Review*, 208 (November-December 1994), p. 62.
48. *Ibid*, p. 55.
49. *Ibid.*, pp. 51, 60.
50. *China Statistical Yearbook 1995* (Beijing, China Statistical Publishing House, 1995), pp. 363-64.
51. Bowles and Dong, *op. cit.*, p. 58.
52. Bowles and Dong, *op. cit.*, p. 57.
53. Bowles and Dong, *op. cit.*, p. 74.
54. Bowles and Dong, *op. cit.*, p. 58. They also conflate the local state and local government, reducing the systems of power and institutions embodied in the state to one particular set of institutional arrangements, that of government. As a result they are exclusively concerned with one dimension of state power – authority – and fail to recognise the constellation of interests and social forces acting upon the state. Only through this conceptual framework can the role and power of the local Party apparatus be ignored so completely.
55. Roemer, *A Future for Socialism*, p. 128.

56. John Wong and Yang Mu, 'The making of the TVE miracle: An overview of case studies', in *China's Rural Entrepreneurs* (Singapore, Times Academic Press, 1996), pp. 16-17.
57. Bowles and Dong, *op. cit.*, p. 75.
58. The content of joint venture agreements is discussed in Liu Xiao Meng, 'Zhen dier nilong fuzhuang chang diaocha (Survey of a garment factory)', and Shi Xiu Yin, 'Zhen yulong zhong chang diaocha (Survey of an eiderdown factory)', in Marong and Wuqing Duan (eds) *Zhongguo Xiangzhen Qiye Diaocha* (Survey on Township and Village Enterprises) (Oxford, Oxford University Press, 1994), pp. 165-195; pp. 343-395.
59. Dirlik, *op. cit.*, p. 72.
60. *China Economic News*, 15 July 1996.
61. Chun Chang and Yijiang Wang, 'The nature of the Township-Village Enterprise', *Journal of Comparative Economics*, 19 (1994), p. 435.
62. *Ibid.*, p. 438.
63. Martin L. Weitzman and Chenggang Xu, 'Chinese Township-Village Enterprises as vaguely defined cooperatives', *Journal of Comparative Economics*, 18 (1994), p. 133.
64. Roemer, 'Can there be socialism after communism?', p. 90.
65. Roemer, *A Future for Socialism*, p. 125.
66. Emphasis added. Roemer, *A Future for Socialism*, p. 128.
67. Bowles and Dong, *op. cit.*, p. 59.
68. Pranab Bardhan and John E. Roemer, 'Market socialism: A case for rejuvenation', *Journal of Economic Perspectives*, 6, 3 (1992), p. 103.
69. Bowles and Dong, *op. cit.*, pp. 59-61.
70. Liu Xiao Meng, 'Zhen dier nilong fuzhuang chang diaocha (Survey of a garment factory)', in Marong and Wuqing Duan (eds.), *Zongguo Xiangzhen Qiye Diaocha* (Survey on Township and Village Enterprises) (Oxford, Oxford University Press, 1994), pp. 183-85.
71. Liu Xiao Meng, 'Zhen neiranji peijianchang diaocha (Survey of an engine components factory)', in Marong and Wuqing Duan *op. cit.*, pp. 100-104.
72. Liu Shi Ding, Liu Ke Bai, Shi Xiu Yin and Wang Han Sheng, 'Zhen tuliaochang diaocha (Survey of a paint factory)', in Marong and Wuqing Duan *op. cit.*, p. 413.
73. Bowles and Dong, *op. cit.*, p. 58
74. Bowles and Dong, *op. cit.*, p. 75.
75. Han Dongfang, *Workers: The Great Losers in China's Reform Process* (Hong Kong, unpublished mimeo, November 1996), p. 5.
76. Chang and Wang, *op. cit.*, p. 450.
77. Shek, 'The new poor in Chinese cities'.
78. Bowles and Dong, *op. cit.*, p. 61; Richard Smith, 'The Chinese road to capitalism', *New Left Review*, 199 (May-June 1993), pp. 87-90.
79. Bowles and Dong, *op. cit.*, pp. 58; 61-3.
80. *Hunan Workers' News* (August 2, 1996).
81. *China Labour Bulletin* (April 1996), p. 12.
82. *China Women's Daily* (January 3, 1996). Translated in *China Labour Bulletin* (July 1996), p. 7.
83. *China Labour Bulletin* (April 1996), p. 4.
84. Elisabeth Croll, *Changing Identities of Chinese Women: Rhetoric, Experience and Self-Perception in Twentieth Century China* (Hong Kong, Hong Kong University Press, 1995), p. 131.
85. Liu Shi Ding, Liu Ke Bai, Shi Xiu Yin and Wang Han Sheng, 'Zhen tuliaochang diaocha (Survey of a cable factory)', in Marong and Wuqing Duan *op. cit.*, pp. p. 368.
86. Croll, *Changing Identities of Chinese Women*, pp. 122-23.
87. *China Labour Bulletin* (June 1996), p. 13.
88. Roemer, *A Future for Socialism*, p. 128.

89. Bardhan and Roemer, 'Market socialism', p. 108.
90. *Ibid.*, p. 113.
91. Ernest Mandel, 'The myth of market socialism', *New Left Review*, 169 (May-June 1988), p. 110.
92. This phrase is borrowed from Manfred Bienefeld, 'Capitalism and the nation state in the dog days of the Twentieth Century', in Ralph Miliband and Leo Panitch (eds.), *Between Globalism and Nationalism. Socialist Register 1994* (London, Merlin Press, 1994), p. 94.
93. Roemer, *A Future for Socialism*, p. 36.
94. *Guangdong Labour News* (December 3, 1995); *Workers' Daily* (July 29, 1995).
95. Shek Ping Kwan, 'Labour disputes in China', *Change* (October 1996). Translated by Chan Ka Wai.
96. 'Repression of independent unions by the ACFTU', *China Labour Bulletin* (November 1995), p. 10.
97. Apo Leong, 'Masters no more', p. 1.
98. Original emphasis. Han Dongfang, 'Workers'.
99. Bowles and Dong, *op. cit.*, p. 61.
100. Paul Thompson, 'Disorganised socialism: State and enterprise in modern China', in Chris Smith and Paul Thompson (eds), *Labour in Transition: The Labour Process in Eastern Europe and China* (London, Routledge, 1992), p. 254.
101. Roemer, *A Future for Socialism*, p. 129.
102. Su Shaozhi, *Democratisation and Reform* (Nottingham, Spokesman, 1988). See also Su Shaozhi, *Shinian Fengyu* (Ten Years of Wind and Rain) (Taipei, Times Cultural Publishing House, 1995).

TAKING STOCK OF A CENTURY OF SOCIALISM

George Ross

Donald Sassoon's *One Hundred Years of Socialism*[1] reads like a classic in the sense of Tolstoy's *Anna Karenina*. Sassoon does not dispose of his central character in front of a train, but what happens to European socialism is something rather similar, he thinks. European socialism tragically miscalculated and misunderstood until its enemies did it in. On Sassoon's evidence the socialist movement is today moribund. There is still a body left – contemporary social democracy – and it still breathes. But this is a case of mistaken identity: the body is an imposter.

Sassoon's book is weighty in all ways, with 780 pages of text, 1000 with supporting materials. Its size is commensurate with the tasks it sets. Indeed it could have been even longer. Sassoon wants to review 100 years of socialist movements in fourteen different European settings – Northern European and Scandinavian social democrats (including Austria, but not Ireland) plus Latin movements, both socialist and communist. If this breadth does not give plenty for experts to critique, his relative disinterest in organizations and political institutions probably will. His signal virtue, however, is starting where a first class socialist scholar would start, with the political economy of socialism.

As far as this reviewer is aware, this is the first such interpretative effort since the end of the 'Golden Age' of European capitalism and the arrival of the new ice-age of neo-liberalism in our time. It is certainly the most thorough, up-to-date and by far the best comparative history of European socialism that we have. Beyond Sassoon's multiple and fascinating comparisons, he tells a single story. If he is correct, and his evidence indicates that he is, he is saying something very strong about the present situation of the Left. The best way for a reviewer to do justice to these accomplishments is by recounting this story, therefore. Underneath the story is a 'Leninist-Gramscist' perspective on socialist history which also deserves reflection.

Expansion

The first fifty years of Sassoon's century is covered in only a little over 100 pages, one seventh of the entire book. What really matters about this first period of 'expansion' is how it prepares us to understand more recent events. The late 19th century Marxist conceptual 'vulgate' which shaped most socialist reflection is Sassoon's point of departure. He simplifies it to three points – the capitalist state is unfair; history occurs in comprehensible stages; and the working class is a homogeneous group. The power of these three propositions was huge, he thinks: it shaped anti-capitalist Left radicalism into socialism. But each of these grand propositions was problematic. The capitalist state was certainly unfair, but too much emphasis on the state was likely to be a liability. That history occurred in clear stages led to the beliefs that history's movement could be understood in a positivistic way, that outcomes could be projected and that history was on socialism's side. This credo may have been psychically comforting, but could mislead socialists about who and where they were. Finally, the notion of the homogeneous working class was 'heuristically' useful in bringing together disparate groups, but it masked differences along skill, sectoral and gender lines, and that some 'workers' were better than others at institutionalizing a definition of 'worker' biased towards their own interests.

Sassoon does a solid job portraying the socialist movement's inability to move from this holy trinity to practical ideas and strategies. The insurrectionary dream, in particular as defined and codified by the Bolsheviks, was no way out. Indeed Sassoon asserts strongly that the Bolshevik-inspired Communist movement had little or no strategy about confronting and transforming capitalism at all.[2] On the social democrat side Eduard Bernstein's 'revisionist' insight that capitalism was capable of self-regulation was partially correct, yet the insight made the movement's problems worse because it minimized the fact that capitalist self-regulation often happened in harsh crises, immense misery, illiberal politics and brutal war. Quite as significant, the insight pointed revisionists towards a bland parliamentarism in which socialists did politics exactly as done by non-socialists. Others tried to fill in the gaps in the inter-war period, but with little success. 'Planists' advocated using the state and neo-corporatist managerialism in workers' interests. Gramsci contributed an important theory of the socialist movement's decline in the face of fascism – upon which Sassoon draws heavily – but provided few positive lessons to move in the opposite direction. Perhaps the most important new sources of reformist ideas came from outside the socialist movement altogether, from Keynes, for example.

Sassoon provides readers with both facts and analytical distance. The original vulgate lacked, but had promised, effective linkages between theory and practice. As flaws in the original trinity became clearer many flowers, and a number of weeds, grew, but adequate new answers were hard to find to link everyday struggle and movement towards socialism. This did not prevent the socialist movement from growing very large, however. Socialists thus 'practised' – with some erroneously confident of the theoretical correctness of their actions and others simply improvising. In general movements were involved in daily struggle for what their supporters seemed to want and this began to cumulate into vaguer large programmes. Thus the SPD clearly wanted a welfare state and a managed economy, for example, before being swamped by Hitler. Nordic social democrats moved more successfully in similar directions, laying the foundations for their post-war 'models' in the 1930s. Almost everyone knew that legal protection for trade unionism was essential.

Sassoon's central thesis might thus be qualified as 'Leninist-Gramscist.' What has been determining in the history of the socialist movement is an inability to establish linkages between theory and practice which would lead every day resistance beyond short-term demands towards socialism. As Lenin, among many others, understood, these linkages did not spontaneously emerge. It was up to socialists to perceive them theoretically and then forge them into practices which made sense to workers. By the Second World War there was a substantial socialist movement in existence across Europe with high aspirations but insufficiently clear ideas about how to turn them into reality. History refused to wait for the movement to articulate its thoughts, however. The War, along with the Great Depression and Fascism which preceded it, shattered the credibility of capitalism and created new openings for the mass Left. In many places the Left was in an even stronger position to promote its solutions because of its admirable role in national struggles against Nazism and Fascism. For the first time it would be called upon to respond to the demands of power.

Constructing Social Capitalism

Rather than moving to socialism, Socialists surged towards what Sassoon calls 'social capitalism.' To Sassoon the immediate post-war reformist period was a moment of policy improvisation by labour and socialist movements. For the first time presented with real power, socialists had to find things to accomplish. For the most part they pursued programmes that had no clear linkage with any socialist future, the tragic flaw of the movement, according to Sassoon. Instead, they found their policies either in the spontaneous desires of their bases or borrowed them from bourgeois reformists.

The expanded welfare state was perhaps the most noble of all Left accomplishments. Workers needed protection against the predictable accidents of their own lives – healthcare, disability insurance, old age pensions – plus shelter from the harshness of the capitalist market – correctives for inequalities in cultural capital through education, poverty and unemployment. 'Social citizenship' was the answer. But the specific forms of these programmes were often borrowed from non-socialist sources. The British took over the proposals of Beveridge, the Swedes those of the Myrdals. On the continent there was an expansion of existing Bismarckian or Jacobin-Republican programmes. The results, although progressive, were often contradictory. Where universality and promoting equality were goals, programmes were often paternalistic in 'social engineering' ways, bureaucratic and vulnerable to underfunding and budget squeezing. Where the social insurance principle prevailed, the programmes were corporatistic and discriminatory in different ways. In almost all cases welfare states were gendered in favour of males. More generally, the relationships of such programmes with the class structure and the market were ill-conceived.[3]

Increased state intervention in the coordination of national economic life and regulation of the market, often through public ownership, was another Left answer. What the Left insisted upon, for obvious reasons, was full employment. The theories of state intervention for full employment and other purposes were, however, once again either provided by reformist intellectuals like Keynes and Woytinsky or came from long-standing statist traditions (as in Jacobin France, where statism was rejuvenated by a new generation of technocrats). As with the welfare state, the articulation of different forms of state intervention with existing economies was more or less creative. In the UK 'planning' was invoked but never seriously implemented except as wartime controls. 'Public ownership' was a mantra without strategic content, a magical hope that change in legal ownership would shift economic logics. The nationalizations which occurred mainly responded to worker grievances against certain employers and tended to fall in exhausted rustbelt sectors. Elsewhere things were different, but hardly more promising for socialist transition. In France, for example, nationalizations were used for indicative planning which was both successful and acceptable to a weak capitalist class used to statist leadership. In Sweden, with a small, open economy dominated by a few large corporations which demanded flexibility on the international market, there was little public ownership at all. In Austria, public ownership was a legacy of Nazism rather than a product of the Left. In general, where there was public ownership, there were few socialist ideas about its connection to transcending capitalism.

The only exceptions to this absence of linkage between socialist theory and reforms were found, on occasion, in Communist parties, but they were hardly comforting. Communist parties, particularly in France and Italy, saw reforms in terms of consolidating political alliances that would be useful in advancing Soviet interests. When they thought about the domestic political directions of these 'united fronts,' it was in terms of 'national roads' to socialism or, in the parlance of the immediate post-war period, to 'popular democracy.' The theory connecting to practice here was, alas, crude. Reforms would be manipulated to place Communists in beachheads in the state. When these beachheads were strong enough, the Communists would assert hegemony, then control, over the state. From there movement to emulate the Soviet model would be the objective. The 'national road' idea was not implausible for a brief post-war moment, but it was profoundly undemocratic. In any event, Western communists were never able to implement the idea, and not only because of the Cold War. In fact, it contradicted their higher priority: promoting Soviet diplomatic goals.

Welfare states, public sectors and state economic management were all profoundly national. The Left, where it had influence, used it to construct reformulated national 'mixed' political economies. The limits of the Left's profound 'nationalization' were nowhere more evident than in the realm of foreign affairs. As Sassoon points out, socialist ministers 'realistically' followed 'national interests' in their diplomatic pursuits as if they had read Henry Kissinger from cover to cover. There was no such thing as a 'socialist foreign policy,' in other words. The Labour Party provided the classic illustration of this with its pursuit of an Empire-based strategy at the very great costs of British absence from the processes of European integration, but other socialist administrations did analogous things. There was, however, one enormous constraint. The coming of the Cold War meant that social democrats could express their national interests only under an umbrella of anti-Sovietism and pro-Nato Americanism. This caused considerable neutralist anguish among the social democratic rank and file, but there was little choice. The Americans were playing a very skilful game. Post-war reforms could not be consolidated on the basis of available national resources in Europe, since everyone was flat broke. With the Marshall Plan and other incentives, the US granted social democrats the cash to do the job of consolidating, but at the price of Cold War pro-Americanism.

Revelling in an Age of Gold

Sassoon's central historical claim is that the cobbled-together nature of post-war reformism, its improvisation, borrowing and catering to populism, set the socialist movement up to be outmanoeuvered by capitalism in the Golden Age. The quarter century beginning in 1950 was the most extraordinary period of growth in capitalism's history. One dimension of this was the 'catch up' replication in Europe of the American

Fordist-Consumerist model within the reformed frameworks that the Left had helped build in the immediate post-war years. The Left's inability to link theory and practice after the War left it vulnerable to the recovery and renewal of capitalism itself. The Left's reforms could be reconciled with the booming market of the Golden Age, together becoming the 'Keynesian welfare state.' Extraordinary growth allowed redistribution of part of profit and taxes to support an expanding welfare state and created space for the higher wages that unions were in a position to demand. Many workers could thus become 'affluent' and fuel the consumption boom which, in turn, pumped up profits. State intervention allowed demand management to promote fuller employment which also fuelled growth.

Socialist movements were also coopted theoretically by the Golden Age through an exquisitely simple logic. Because post-war reforms flourished, capitalism was growing rapidly and it now seemed eminently steerable by the state, social democrats concluded that capitalism and the needs of ordinary people were compatible – capitalism and full democracy were compatible. Basic social transformation was therefore no longer needed and the search for connections between theory and practice to lead toward the transcendance of capitalism could be abandoned.

'Revisionism' in its first post-1945 variant thus triumphed. One favourite revisionist was Anthony Crosland who, Sassoon notes, at least had the good grace to insist that further reform towards greater equality was desirable. Others settled for managing the system as it was. Amidst Bad Godesberg and Gaitskell there was thus considerable variation in revisionism. There was also a lot of conflict inside the Left about it. But the revisionists spoke an important language to social democratic politicians and leaders who could henceforth proceed by promising slightly more than the Right to get elected – and in the 1950s socialist parties were doing much less well at the ballot box than they had after 1945. The opponents of revisionism were vociferous and numerous. Alas, they rarely defined clearly enough what it meant politically to have socialist commitment in the 1950s. Sometimes, they still even based their positions on traditions, scriptures and the imagery of satanic mills.[4] Revisionists could retort that their opponents were hopelessly 'old-fashioned.'

The moment was tragic. The revisionists were fundamentally wrong in their analyses of capitalism and its futures. Quite as significant, however, both sides of the debate, in different ways, were oblivious to the basic social changes brought by the Golden Age. Socialist democrats had long since given up efforts to develop counter-hegemony among wage-earners, leaving culture open to profiteers. Multiple battlefields were thus surrendered with little struggle to consumerism, the onslaught of media, and commercialized youth culture. Few socialists noticed the changes in the position of women and the rapid rise of female labour force participation.

No one of importance foresaw the coming of a threatening autonomous intellectual and new middle strata radicalism, even when they were de facto part of it. Revisionists and their opponents both overlooked the environmental costs of the new capitalism. Most had but limited clues about the deeper meanings of decolonization and non-Western development. Sassoon claims, a bit hyperbolically, '. . . not one novelty worth writing or thinking about had been envisioned or predicted by the European socialist movement.' (p. 197). Taken in by the Golden Age, socialist leaders committed to a new consensus politics around a transient stage of capitalism in the belief that it was permanent.

Navigating with Bad Maps – The 1960s

The 1960s displayed the destructive contradictions of capitalist paradise. There were numerous short circuits built into the 'virtuous circles' of Golden Age political economies. The most important was the system's vulnerability to wage drift and inflation. Relatively full employment and high levels of unionization gave workers unusual market power. If they did not use it 'well' (by accepting that the health of capitalism was more important than their own interests) wages would rise faster than productivity, and resulting inflation would produce currency and trade imbalances. Different countries developed different ways of handling this problem. The most successful were 'neo-corporatist,' where large, powerful union movements, employers' associations and governments (or equivalent institutions) agreed on non-inflationary wage levels and tradeoffs to persuade workers to accept them. Neo-corporatism was most likely to be found in small, internationally open economies like Sweden and Austria, where excess inflation meant immediate and serious international trade problems. But they also existed, in different forms, in certain larger societies like Germany.

Problems thus emerged first in other settings like France, Italy and the UK. In such places militant labour movements existed which were either unwilling or organizationally unable to play the neo-corporatist game fully. Rising labour market tensions, usually fuelled by employer refusals to bargain seriously, led to very large strike movements in the 1960s and 1970s – concentrated in intense periods in France and Italy, spread out in the UK. But even where neo- and other-corporatisms were effective there were rising tensions. Workers demanded more money, but also new reforms like industrial democracy and investment control which, implemented, might have unbalanced their systems. So much, then, for the full institutionalization and decline of class conflict which leaders of the socialist movement had pronounced to be at hand. Workers were pushing strongly against the edge of the 'neo-capitalist' envelope. Quite as important, capitalists understood this and began to recalculate benefits against the costs of the Golden Age order.

Simultaneously, and more mysteriously for both revisionists and their socialist opponents, there were major new middle class rebellions, the student movements of the 1960s and their issue-oriented sequels. Here, despite declaratory Marxism from young activists, the motivations and underlying themes were very different from anything the socialist movement had known in the past. Individual liberation, rather than collective representation, was an essential theme. This new libertarianism connected with strong anti-bureaucratic and anti-statist outlooks, coupled with an anarchist insistence upon direct participation. The fact that these new social movements had to coexist in Europe with labour movements, themselves rebellious, confused the picture but, more important, sometimes led to gigantic social explosions, as in France and Italy. But the new movements occurred everywhere, bringing their new modes and themes to 'Left' politics.

The final ingredient in the crisis of the 1960s was an international situation strained to the limit by the very same factors that had earlier held 'neo-capitalism' together. The American war in Vietnam was a major event. It caused and fed the largest student rebellion of all in the US, which spread quickly to Europe where it was essential in stimulating Europe's own youth movements. The war, the political difficulties of the American government, and the profligate economic policy which followed from them, contributed massive new inflationary tensions to an increasingly global economy and further fed European problems. On top of this the Americans were no longer able, and willing, to administer an international capitalist monetary system without narrowly pursuing their own interests, another disaster in the making.

None of what occurred in the 1960s fit the various models of revisionism. The revisionist-led movement had assumed that all conceivable problems could be handled by clever management within the parameters of Golden Age capitalism. Most socialist leaders, and many communists as well, believed that working class conflictuality could be 'contained' (the operative word) by fine-tuning macroeconomic management and coaxing unions into deals to moderate wages in exchange for incremental labour market reforms. New middle strata and new social movements were also understood in managerial ways. Everything could go on as before if the movement could adjust its electoral appeals to buy support from these new libertarians. Finally, disruptions in the international system were seen as but temporary, manageable by conciliating the Americans, adjusting currency values and negotiating new trade agreements. There was an important additional dimension. The revised socialist movement, which had lived so long within specific national cocoons, blindly believed that nothing could possibly occur to attenuate the integrity of national political economies. All in all, as Sassoon shows, the official Left, socialist and communist (witness the Italian Communists' disastrous pursuit of 'historic compromise' in the 1970s), was wrong about the situation every step of the way.

Done in by the Stages of Capitalism?

Far from being able to connect theory and practice most of the socialist movement was eager, by the end of the 1970s, to manage capitalism, just at that point where Golden Age capitalism was about to rejoin other golden ages as fond memory and fantasy. What resulted was genuine 'crisis.' And, to cite Sassoon, '. . . when this model of capitalism entered into crisis, so did the concomitant model of social-democratic politics . . .' around which the official left had convened. The result was that '. . . by the early 1990s, the Left had been comprehensively defeated in the West, while in the East the smouldering ruins of the communist experiment marked the apparent global triumph of the system of private capitalist accumulation.' (p. 446) The socialist movement, out of practical ideas, let alone socialist ideas, was approaching the end of its century.

Why did the Golden Age end? Growth levels and productivity levels dropped steeply and unemployment rose. Experts conflict in explaining this, however. One group cites new market internationalization. Even if disagreements remain hot and heavy about how much, and what, 'globalization' has occurred, there has been financial transnationalization, a shift of semi-skilled Fordist employment away from Europe, an accentuation of the importance of transnational corporations, increased foreign direct investment throughout the advanced capitalist areas and, finally, increasing international trade. Another group asserts that the new wave of technological change destroys jobs more than it creates them. A third group points to political decisions by elites to move away from a full-employment macroeconomic policy towards price stability. Similarly, the renewal of European integration in the '1992' programme – involving fundamental political decisions in the making of which 'socialists' were central – was constructed around the premise of market deregulation. The decision for Economic and Monetary Union (EMU) has made monetarist price stabilization and market liberalization practically inevitable into the third millennium.

Capitalist elites had decided that the era of regulated capitalism was over. The time had come to 'return to the market.' They also decided that the capitalist system could live quite well without strong unions, social protection programmes and efforts to limit inequality. The consequences for socialists were catastophic. Unemployment weakened unions and made it easy for governments and employers to dispense with trade union help in controlling wage drift and inflation. 'Trends towards corporatist interme- diation' became 'trends towards market intermediation.' Everywhere deregulation and privatization came onto the table. Rolling back the welfare state was difficult because of its popular support, but the costs of rising unemployment, constraints on budgetary deficits and longer-term debt plus elite hopes placed it under strong indirect pressure. Above all, the seductive dream which brought socialists into the Golden Age consensus, that the national state could manage the flows of national economies to promote mild redistribution and social protection, completely foundered. The 'nationalization' of socialists, perhaps the most important 'heavy tendency' in their history, now played strongly against them. Even the 'third way' models like Sweden and 'Modell Deutschland' faltered under these pressures.

This provides the setting for the end of Sassoon's *One Hundred Years* when the body impersonating socialism enters. Different socialist movements confront this crisis in particular ways, and Sassoon is exhaustive in providing the details, but most have a standard package of ideas with no pretence of promoting socialism. In our times, theory consists of watching opinion polls while practice is to follow these polls wherever they lead. Social democrats – for now everyone who counts polit- ically is a social democrat – thus present themselves slightly to the left of centre in political spectra which have shifted dramatically to the Right. But they promise little but austerity and sacrifice in the short run, allegedly in the service of 'enhanced national competitiveness in the global market- place' that will later allow modest reforms, slight reflation, slightly less pressure on the welfare state, slightly less contemptuous practices towards the less fortunate and so on. 'Positioning,' rather than principle, is the new name of the game. Class discourses and workerist vocabulary have all but disappeared and as workers and workerism decline in salience, fighting over the new middle class (even, indeed, over the old middle classes) has become the road to salvation, which now means only victory in elections.

None of this has occurred without quite dramatic conflicts *inside* socialist parties. Here the British Labour Party, or perhaps the Italian Communists, are models. By and large, however, opponents of the new course have been marginalized, leaving the Blairs, Jospins, d'Alemas and others in charge. 'New Labour,' the 'rally of the middle classes,' is also typical in seeking its inspirations in President Bill Clinton. American Democrats, once regarded as exceptions because the US had no socialist tradition, are now regarded as the model to be emulated. In the meantime, workers, whose emancipation in socialism was the express goal of the socialist movement, desperately try to protect their threatened positions, sometimes voting for the conservative Right, sometimes for a new populist right which could well become a grave danger for democracy itself.

Century's End?

The century of socialism is over, Sassoon concludes. What is Left is no longer socialist. The body remaining is an imposter for which most of us vote when the time comes since there exists no viable alternative to limit the damage of neo-liberalism. Yet few of us are naive about what our votes will produce. They may, or may not, stave off the worst. Sassoon's conclusion is gloomy in the extreme, therefore. The story is worse than the old 'social democrats were never any good' line that most of us have used, usually in the belief that there were other, more promising ways of proceeding. What has happened, Sassoon claims, is that socialism's inability to link transformative theory to daily practice with a transformative logic has, over time, been fatal.

To recapitulate, the story begins with an expanding, although nationally and doctrinally divided, European socialist movement that was successful at imposing its presence. Sassoon's thesis contends that this movement's failure was at translating these abstractions into actions to link peoples' everyday struggles to the coming of a socialist future. Despite this failure socialism became the reigning opponent of capitalism after its first half century. Thus when Fascism, Depression and war discredited capitalist elites, if not capitalism itself, and post-World War II Western European societies adopted democratic institutional forms, socialists came to power. Without socialist policy answers they improvised reforms. These post-war reforms were then consolidated as part of the most successful period of capitalist expansion in history. Consolidation led socialist leaders, and many socialists themselves, to accept the capitalist self image of the period and believe that prosperity had become permanent. This, to Sassoon, was not a simple 'betrayal' but a tragic turn into an historic cul de sac. From being the confused reigning opponent of capitalism socialism thus became the loyal opposition within capitalism. For a very brief time this allowed some redistribution, enhanced social protection for many workers, rising living standards, not to speak of credibility for socialist politicians and considerable power for trade unions and socialist parties. Socialism installed itself *within* capitalism, trading away its self-ascribed vocation for transforming it, at huge costs.

The Golden Age was not the end of capitalist history. Instead it was an exceptional moment whose own internal contradictions foreshadowed its end. When it did end abruptly it gave way to a new period defined by, among other things, governmental elites and capitalists dismantling the processes, structures and reforms which socialists had believed to be permanent. Socialist movements, chasing Europe's political shift to the

Right, then abandoned everything except opportunism. If workers were no longer likely to be a 'universal class,' and if their desires for protection from market cruelties seemed to stand in the way of global competitiveness – whatever this meant – then so be it, these kind of workers were no longer needed. Indeed, the concept of class should be dropped altogether because vote hunting involved turning to middle classes who, as Marx shrewdly noted, refused to see themselves as parts of any class, even if their interests conflicted with those of workers and almost always with those of the poor. This meant abandoning all but marginal prospects for providing the kinds of policies that workers and the poor needed. In response workers began to instrumentalize Socialists in their votes and attitudes, just as Socialists had come to instrumentalize them. A 'crisis of politics' thus opened in which ordinary people lost hope and either became targets for nationalist and populist mobilizations or hunkered down in cynicism.

Has Sassoon therefore cast socialism, as Tolstoy cast *Anna Karenina*, in front of a moving train? His message is bleak. Things have gone well beyond ousting misleaders and correcting their mistakes. The post-war choices made by different movements have led to the liquidation of movement credibility and resources. Hope for socialist transformation and belief in the dimensions of what Sassoon labelled the 19th century 'vulgate' have become marginal phenomena. The decline of 'class' has already been mentioned. The belief that history can be understood rationally is in full retreat before the twin epistemological terrors of our time, neo-Smithian or neo-Benthamite methodological individualism and post-structuralism, with the latter having wrought particular havoc on the Left. That the capitalist state is unjust is widely recognized, but misunderstood now to mean 'captured by special interests' (which it is, but there is a deeper logic at work). Recognition of the state as a systematic source of injustice is a mixed blessing, however, since it has nourished ferocious anti-statism on both Left and Right. We perceive it most easily on the Right where it manifests itself in the credo that markets are the only way to decide and distribute. On the Left, in anarchist and communitarian forms, it is more subtle and perhaps more congenial, but still not very useful for working change.

This destruction of long-standing socialist beliefs has been accompanied by the decomposition of socialist organizations. Mass parties, originally meant as microcosms of new democracy and centres for a more humane counter-culture, have given way to elitist organizations for electoral engineering. After elections, political managers take over to pursue their trade statistics, input-output matrices and deal-making with big interest groups. Leaders are manufactured to be 'stars' in their own firmament. Trade unions still exist and are still held to their traditional mission of producing real returns for their supporters, but they, too, have

lost much strength since the Golden Age and often they represent memberships of older males, with women, young people and 'a-typical' workers
left more or less to their own resorts.

Sassoon's exhaustive and detailed discussion obliges us to recognize the
magnitude of the problems that the next 100 years of socialism face,
beginning now. Can a plausible socialist movement be rebuilt? At least in
European societies the relative decline and fragmentation of workers, the
rise of alternative progressive vocabularies from new middle strata
movements constructed around 'oppressed category' themes, the
deepening of self-affirming individualism and the anti-statism that accom-
panies it, are all realities that must be confronted. And whatever the extent
of globalization, decline in the economic and social policy capacities of
most nation states is real.

The decomposition of large collective identities since the 1970s has
been extraordinary, and certainly no accident. Capital and elites have
discovered a mine of new ways to divide populations into conflicting and
isolated groups. Can a new coalition of different salaried groups be put
together over time that will have the cultural and political salience of the
old 'working class?' This is vital, not only to socialism but to the future of
democracy. The present dismantling of social and political citizenship
promoted under the guise of marketization is premised on exploiting
divisions between less and more secure groups and it is menacing indeed.
Next, is there a socialist method to transcend the 'oppressed category'
debate? However much this has been important to the Left in underlining
the complexity of social life and the ways that traditional socialist
discourse simplified it, it is now clear that this debate leads to a reformulated interest group politics that technocratic and capitalist elites can
master through divide and rule tactics. Then how can rampant individualism be confronted? Socialists should not deny the positive side of large
numbers of people recognizing that there can be a vast range of creative
human biographies. Capitalists and their media prey on this, however, to
provide contrived, controlling, profitable and very often demeaning
contents for these noble aspirations. Finally, 'national' questions are fundamental. The nationalization of socialism in its first century was profound
and its costs have been huge. How can socialism reconstitute its national
capacities – something which implies a desperately serious effort to find
the precise margins of manoeuvre for reform and change which remain –
without creating new nationalist divisions? Underlying all of these matters
are the eternal basic questions. What should equality and democracy be in
our time?

It is to the credit of Donald Sassoon that we cannot avoid such
questions. His work poses even deeper theoretical issues, however. Recall
his organizing thesis. The socialist movement has been defeated by its own

inability to conceptualize its settings in an intelligent strategic way. The first century of socialism demonstrates consistent, and devastating, failures to construct linkages between theory and practice which would lead every day struggle towards socialism. The perspective posits that such linkages did not spontaneously emerge from ordinary working class life but had to be perceived and forged into struggle by Socialists. Historically, however, socialists were largely unable to counteract the material and cultural powers of capitalism over ordinary peoples' lives. Ultimately, most gave in to these powers.

This is a classic thesis, but Sassoon, like many socialists before him, presents it in a fundamentally ambiguous way, leaving it open to two different interpretations. The first is that there actually *were* such linkages between theory and practice waiting to be found. It would follow from this that the failure of the socialist movement occurred because it was unable to find them. The second is that there were no such linkages. This would mean that a socialist movement constructed in terms of searching for the linkage between theory and practice was bound to fail in any event. This basic ambiguity leads to further questions. If the first interpretation is correct, then we are entitled to ask what socialists should have done differently, in quite specific terms, and why they did not do so. Sassoon very carefully does not do either. If the second interpretation is more accurate, then Sassoon is really telling us that socialism was a collective dream rather than a realistically constructed transcendance of capitalism. If this is the case, why was the dream so widely believed and what have been its true historical functions? He does not answer these questions either. Herein lie the most important criticisms to be made of the book.

The first version of the 'Leninist-Gramscist' thesis has been central to serious socialist thought in one way or another throughout the past century. Positing that different realities can follow from different conceptual and strategic choices, and that humans are not simply constrained by what exists, helps us remove ourselves from the worst kind of positivism (which, moreover, has always been a fundamental servant of the capitalist status quo) and also gives us hope and some optimism, both qualities that progressives cannot live without. The problems with it are quite as obvious. While it is sound epistemologically to argue that the future is not entirely constrained by the logics of the present and that conceptual and strategic choices do make a great difference, there do not seem to be solid reasons to believe that any particular 'socialist' choices flow from this observation. In other words, individuals and collectivities have choices, but the logic of these choices cannot be connected to a state of affairs in the future, however desirable. This is a different question, of course, from whether it is or is not possible for a complex social movement to accumulate hegemonic momentum. But whether this momentum is targeted to achieve

1

'socialism,' or something else that its proponents want to label socialism, cannot be known.

The first version of Sassoon's thesis is unverifiable, therefore. The second version of it is more satisfactory philosophically, but much less uplifting politically, since it gives us no guarantees. Capitalism as a social order is oppressive and generates its own opposition, which it then has to channel and control. Sometimes it is very successful at this, sometimes less so. Sometimes it can co-opt and neutralize a large movement of opposition. This is Sassoon's argument about socialism in its first century. Sometimes it is effective at fragmenting opposition so that no large movement emerges at all. This seems to be what has been happening since the end of the Golden Age. Above all, Sassoon's story shows that the impatience of socialists about the rapid movement of history has been problematic. The first century of socialism might correctly be labelled 'One Hundred Years of Socialism in a World of Capitalist Nations.' The relative collapse of this particular world has opened a long, complex moment during which the socialist movement will be on the defensive. Socialists would do well to act accordingly. If they do so, and resolve some of the basic issues raised in Sassoon's deep, rich reflections, then their second century will be devoted to the construction of a genuinely international movement.

NOTES

1. Donald Sassoon *One Hundred Years of Socialism* (Hbk: London, I.B.Tauris, 1996; Pbk: Fontana, 1996), (New York, New Press, 1997).
2. At first the Bolsheviks were confident that capitalism was about to collapse into universal revolution around them. When this did not happen Bolshevism became 'socialism in one country', such that the strategy of Western Communism came to be built around the use of European communist movements to protect the Soviet Union. This degenerated quickly into the instrumentalization of European workers for Stalinist great power politics at huge costs in terms of dividing the socialist movement in Europe.
3. This is historically true despite much subsequent Left 'functionalist' reflection which insists upon seeing welfare states as neatly designed social safety valves for capitalism. One of Sassoon's many virtues is to reject these visions.
4. Some, like the French communists, even argued that workers were facing worsening impoverishment, just as the changes of consumerism and boom appeared.

THE MARGINALITY OF THE AMERICAN LEFT: THE LEGACY OF THE 1960s

Barbara Epstein

By virtually any definition of the term, the US left is not doing well. In the sixties the left was intertwined with a series of progressive social movements; these movements and the left within them attracted enormous numbers of young people, many of whom changed not only their ideas but the way they led their lives through this experience. A vibrant left politics and culture flourished in every major city in the North and in many in the South; few college or university campuses were untouched by it. The left was a major presence in national politics and in intellectual life, outside as well as within academia. The left brought a freshness, honesty and moral integrity to national discussion that compelled attention and respect. Today this is virtually all gone. Though there are many organizing projects concerned with specific social problems, there are only the remnants of a left able to link these issues and call for systematic social change. In national politics the left has little if any influence. There is a subculture that identifies itself as left, but it is insular and dispirited, and too often preoccupied with policing the attitudes and language of those in or close to the left. The staleness of the left's perspective and its political marginality in the nineties stand in sharp contrast to its attractiveness and influence in the sixties.

The mistakes of the left are only one reason for its decline: the left has also been undermined by the rising power of global corporate capital and discouraged by the collapse of the Soviet Union and the apparent victory of capitalism over socialism. But this article will focus on what the American left has contributed to its own marginalization because while the left cannot reverse these trends, it can rethink its own perspective. In the sixties, the left was intertwined with a set of social movements. In the nineties, the left has come to be an intellectual milieu, a climate of opinion, with no coherent, collective relationship to movements for social change. What holds this milieu together is a common memory of or identification with the radicalism of the sixties. Many of the ideas that the left has drawn

138

from the sixties do not fit the conditions of the nineties very well. Gradual dissociation from social movements and increasing immersion in academia over the last thirty years has also led large sections of the left to revise the legacy of the sixties in ways that isolate the left and divert it from issues of social change.

In the realm of electoral politics, where 'the left' designates an arena that includes programmes with even faintly social democratic overtones, left perspectives have almost disappeared from sight. In the 1996 elections the left was barely visible. In 1984 and 1988 the Rainbow Coalition was strong enough to have some impact on the party's programme, and in 1992, even without the Rainbow Coalition, Clinton still felt enough pressure to present a health care programme that was partly addressed to the left. In 1996 there was no visible left within the Democratic Party, and Clinton's welfare reform programme reflected pressure from the right but not from the left. Meanwhile Pat Buchanan and the extreme right more generally were a major presence within the Republican Party. Ralph Nader and the Green Party ran a minimal campaign. Though many people on the left voted for Nader out of a sense of utter disillusionment with Clinton, the Nader campaign had no significant impact on national politics.

At the other end of the spectrum, the explicitly socialist left (representing the most restrictive definition of the term) is also in serious decline. The major organizations of the socialist left are at best stagnant. Since the late seventies the most prominent socialist organization in the US has been the Democratic Socialists of America. Formed out of a merger of two previous organizations (one, the New American Movement, consisting largely of people with histories in the New Left, the other, the Democratic Socialist Organizing Committee, made up of social democrats oriented toward the left wing of the Democratic Party), through the late seventies and early eighties DSA had many members who were engaged in community organizing as well as a group of Democratic Party and trade union luminaries who were willing to lend their prestige to the organization.

DSA has ceased to be an organization of activists. It still has a large paper membership, and it has a staff which conducts various campaigns; in the recent national elections DSA helped mobilize progressives in Congress around a programme for a living wage, and held a series of hearings on the economy. When John Sweeney was elected head of the AF of L he publically joined DSA as a statement of his break with the right wing Democrats who had been Meany's associates. But despite the fact that DSA still speaks for the left in some Democratic Party and trade union circles, it is a shadow of its former self. In the recent past, one of the things that distinguished left organizations from liberal or mainstream organizations was the role played by the membership. The direction of left organizations was determined by their memberships; that of liberal and mainstream organizations, by a staff, which sent out mailings to, and collected dues from, a paper membership. DSA now fits the latter model.

DSA is probably the most widely known explicitly socialist or left organization in the US. Other than DSA, there are various small sectarian groups which have little if any influence. There are the Committees of Correspondence (CoC), formed in 1992 by dissidents leaving the Communist Party along with leftists from other backgrounds, in the hope that the left could be revitalized by creating a common ground and transcending sectarian divisions. Over four years the CoC has dwindled from roughly two thousand at its founding convention to a few hundred at its last convention. There are a number of left projects oriented toward combining electoral politics with community organizing: the New Party, the Labor Party, the Green Party, the Alliance. It is possible that a movement could emerge out of one or more of these. But at the moment they are small and struggling.

Left journals in the US are in only slightly better shape than organizations of the left. A few left journals have collapsed, a few have either been forced to cut back or have shifted toward academic issues and audiences, a few are holding their own. In 1992 the *National Guardian*, an independent left weekly newspaper with a large audience, including people in many left and progressive organizations, folded. Nothing has emerged to take its place. Soon after *In These Times*, another independent left paper but with an audience weighted more towards academics and professionals, was forced to cut back from weekly to biweekly publication and from newspaper to magazine format. *Socialist Review*, which at one time was a leading theoretical journal of the independent socialist left in the US, has located itself in the academic field of Cultural Studies and employs a jargon so obscure that only those steeped in this literature can hope to understand it. The leading journals of the left, *The Nation, The Progressive, Z, Monthly Review, Dissent, New Politics*, are stable but stagnant.[1]

The relationship between left journals and their readers has been transformed in more or less the same way as the relationship between left organizations and their members. In the sixties and seventies, and still to some extent in the early eighties, readers of the left press cared a great deal about what appeared in its pages, because what was said in the left press affected what positions organizations took, what people on the left did. In the nineties the left press is read with considerably less passion. What appears in its pages may affect what people think, but it has little impact on what anyone does.

It would be too narrow to restrict one's definition of the left, in the US, to the electoral left and/or organizations, publications, projects that are explicitly socialist. In the late sixties and early seventies there was a large ideologically and politically diverse arena of organizations, groups, individuals, who called themselves radical or left, who were opposed to a society based on inequalities of wealth and power, and believed that a better society could be attained through collective action. Among people who regarded themselves as left or radical there were differences over which structures of inequality were fundamental, which issues needed to be attacked first, and also over how a better society would be organized. Though probably most people in this arena regarded class as one dimension of inequality, there were many who were more concerned with gender or race. Some people in this arena would have called themselves socialists. Many others would not have, often because they associated socialism with a highly centralized, state-controlled society, which clashed with their vision of decentralized, small-scale communities. Though there were sharp disagreements among the radicals of the late sixties and early seventies, nevertheless anarchists and socialists, radical feminists, anti-imperialists and radical anti-racists were all in some loose way part of a broader movement that was opposed to all of these dimensions of inequality.

The diverse radical movement that was so strong in the late sixties and early seventies now barely exists. At that time there was a cohort of radical or left activists, stretching across the civil rights/Black Power movement, the women's movement, the anti-war movement; despite their differences these people talked to each other, influenced each other's thinking, and in some very broad way regarded each other as part of a common struggle. In each of these movements it was radicals who led, who set the agenda. Participants in these movements were by no means predominantly leftists – but through their involvement they were likely to develop more radical views.

In the nineties nothing comparable to this exists. In one movement after another the liberal sector has become dominant, the radical sector, barely visible. In the late sixties and through at least the first half of the seventies the radical wing of feminism,[2] based largely among students and other young women close to the anti-war movement, was equally or more visible than liberal feminism, whose constituency was older, more cautious, more removed from radicalism. Members of liberal feminist organizations such as the National Organization for Women were more likely to be drawn toward radical feminism than were radical feminists to be drawn to liberal feminism. Today the large bureaucratic liberal feminist organizations, such as NOW, are at the centre of the women's movement. These organizations tend to consist of paid staff and large paper memberships. What was once the radical sector of the movement has evolved into, on the one hand, an arena of alternative social and cultural organizations for women, and, on the other, women's studies programmes and a diffuse feminist presence in the universities.

In one arena of progressive politics after the next, a once-vibrant radical wing has faded. In the late sixties and early seventies black radicalism, taking up the slogan of Black Power, challenged the cautious integrationism of the established black organizations. By the early eighties the movement for Black Power had subsided into valuable, but often not especially radical, electoral efforts. In the nineties the African-American movement is divided between the socially and politically conservative nationalism of the Nation of Islam and the beleagured integrationism of the NAACP. Many black intellectuals speak and write eloquently for a radical perspective, but this does not constitute a movement. In the gay and lesbian movement, the radicalism represented in the eighties by organizations such as Act Up and Queer Nation has subsided. Since the war in Vietnam solidarity movements, through their opposition to US interventionism, have been a major focus of radical activism in the US. In the late seventies and early eighties, leftists played a major role in mobilizing against US intervention in Central America. Since the end of the Cold War this sector of the US left has disappeared.

This does not mean that progressive efforts no longer exist. Community organizing remains strong. There is a widespread environmental justice movement, made up of local groups concerned with environmental hazards, often along with other community social justice issues. There are networks of activists concerned with housing and tenants' rights, with immigrants' rights, with capital flight and workers' rights. There are groups concerned with violence against women, defending the right to abortion, opposing racism and the right. There are many people of the left scattered through these movements, and many of those involved in these movements for any substantial length of time move toward the left by coming to see connections between various issues and forms of injustice, and coming to believe that these problems call for a fundamental transformation of society.

These tend to remain, however, private beliefs rather than the public positions of organizations. In the case of the environmental justice movement, for instance, it is clear to many in the movement that doing away with environmental toxics would require drastic government control over the process of production; it would mean putting public welfare ahead of the right of corporations to make a profit. This would mean a dramatic turn away from market values; it would mean moving toward at least a radical form of social democracy. This view is at most hinted at in public statements. Leftists as well as others point out that taking such a position would undermine the movement's effect in the public arena and also narrow its base: local groups rely on drawing people with a range of political views. All of this makes perfect sense. Community organizing efforts can mobilize constituencies that the left sees as important (poor and working class people, people of colour, women), and many leftists are involved in these efforts. But community organizing in relation to specific issues, for particular, limited reforms, is not the same thing as a left, which implies a broader social analysis, an agenda for system-wide social change.

In the nineties the term 'the left' has come to describe people who read more or less the same journals, hold opinions that fall within an identifiable range, people who are part of more or less the same subculture. The left is more visible in academia than anywhere else in society, and the arena of Cultural Studies, where a left or radical perspective is more or less part of professional identity, is the most visible part of the broader academic left. What makes the left visible is not social action but access to publishing. In the sixties the left was bound together by common involvement in a broadly defined common project. In the nineties it is held together mostly by a common relationship to the past, by having participated in, supported, or having subsequently come to identify with, the movements of the sixties.

The left's mistakes are only one source of its problems. The left has declined around the world: clearly there are forces at work that go beyond anything that the US left could have brought upon itself. It is difficult to think of any nation, in the mid-nineties, where the left has a strong base, exercises real influence, and has a clear sense of direction. When the Soviet Union collapsed, some on the left hoped that the end of a Stalinist form of socialism would create an opening for democratic socialism, in the former Soviet Union and Eastern Europe, and possibly in the West as well. So far these hopes have not been borne out. Though capitalism has failed to bring the prosperity that its advocates predicted (and in fact in many places has made the economic conditions of the majority worse), challenges to the market system have not succeeded, and do not seem to be gathering momentum. In the seventies and eighties left movements emerged in Western Europe that inspired the left in the US and elsewhere. In the seventies Eurocommunism seemed to be combining Marxism with a commitment to democracy; in the late seventies and eighties the Greens held out the hope of a politics that addressed social and environmental issues. Both for a time combined local activism with electoral politics. But both failed. Eurocommunism was unable to break out of the bureaucratic mould of the Communist parties that it tried to reform, and the Greens were swept aside by the unification of Germany. Nothing has emerged to take the place of these efforts. In Central America, the revolutionary movements that flourished in the seventies and early eighties have faded. The PRD, in recent years central to the Mexican left as a whole, is in decline. Even in South Africa, where the Communist Party and non-Communist leftists played a major role in the movement against apartheid, and continue to exert influence in the governing ANC, the left is on the defensive.

Movements of the left everywhere have been weakened by events and forces beyond their control. The collapse of the Soviet Union demoralized the left around the world, including the US left, despite the fact that the Soviet Union had long since ceased to be regarded as any kind of model by the vast majority of leftists. Nevertheless, the Soviet Union did hold capitalism at bay, and provided a counterweight to the international power of the US. With the Soviet Union gone it became difficult to argue convincingly that socialism was possible or that capitalism could be replaced by any more humane system. The view that capitalism is natural and inevitable has been reinforced by corporate capital's success in spreading its tentacles around the globe. By weakening states' control over their national economies, globalization weakens social welfare systems. Heightened international economic competition makes it difficult to defend spending on existing programmes, let alone propose new ones. In this environment movements of the left easily come to look like relics of the past.

Despite the real difficulties that it causes for progressive politics, globalization does not eliminate the possibility of a left. The late twentieth century is, after all, not the first instance of the globalization of capital. Through its history capitalism as a world system has alternated between periods in which national economic development took precedence and periods of intense international competition for world markets. The most recent instance of heightened international competition took place during the last decades of the nineteenth, and the first decades of the twentieth, centuries. As is now the case, corporate capital crossed national boundaries, disrupted existing social and economic systems, and let loose waves of international migration. In that instance social and economic disruption strengthened the left rather than weakening it, leading to heightened conflict between capital and labour and the emergence of revolutionary movements.[3]

In the decades surrounding the turn of the twentieth century the contest between capital and labour seemed to many people to be more or less equal. Many people hoped (or feared) that a radicalized working class would win this battle, that capitalism would not survive its surge of international development. The extravagant hopes that the Bolshevik Revolution inspired in leftists in Europe and North America (and the equally extravagant fears that it inspired in advocates of the status quo) reflected the widespread assumption that socialist revolution could spread through the capitalist world. By the early twenties it had become clear that this was not going to happen, and it is possible that capitalism had been stronger than either the left or the right thought throughout the preceding decades. But the rapid growth of the left during this period of expansion of international capital shows that there is no automatic equation between globalization and a decline of the left. The industrial system that was taking shape around the turn of the century created the basis for working class solidarity by sharpening divisions between capital and labour, bringing large numbers of workers together and pitting them against a common capitalist enemy. In the late twentieth century capitalism is being transformed in ways that so far at least seem to mostly undermine working class unity, by heightening divisions among working people, by dispersing workers into smaller workplaces and replacing many stable full-time jobs with temporary or part-time employment. The way work is being reorganized poses real problems for the left. But globalization is not in itself the problem.

Though the current transformation of capital discourages working class consciousness and collective action by fragmenting the work force, it might be creating the basis for a different sense of solidarity by widening the gap between rich and poor, by worsening the living standards of the majority and fostering social and environmental crises that are likely to impinge on virtually everyone. In the US, the standard of living of the majority has gradually declined over recent decades: most people work harder for less real pay, at less secure jobs. Meanwhile the social welfare net that was created by popular struggles during the thirties is being pulled out from under the feet of those who need it, excluding those on the bottom rungs from participation in the economy, and undermining whatever loyalty they may have to society. The social consequences of these policies and of decades of environmental degradation will undoubtedly escalate. A left is likely to re-emerge in the US because the US needs a left. The existing left does not have the power to stop the process of globalization. But it can make the re-emergence of a large left easier by rethinking mistaken approaches.

For the left of the nineties, the movements of the sixties remain the point of reference, the basis for conceptions of what constitutes radical politics. The radical politics of the sixties included a critique of liberalism that was very appropriate for the sixties, but left radicals utterly unprepared for the subsequent revival of conservatism; a rejection of electoral politics which made sense in the context of the sixties but is no longer a viable left position. It also included a cultural radicalism which in the sixties meant extending protest against injustice to the realm of personal relations, and expressed a utopian vision of a better society. In the nineties cultural radicalism has been recast, particularly by the academic left, as a deconstructionist stance that pursues criticism for its own sake, regards truth as an illusion and values as matters of preference. This cultural radicalism has little connection to movements for or visions of social change, and is mostly driven by the internal pressures of academia.

The conception of radicalism that was developed by the movements of the sixties also contained elements that by the end of the decade were causing problems for those movements themselves. In the more politically oriented wing of the movement it was widely assumed that there could be a revolution, when in fact interest in revolution was almost entirely limited to young people, and only a sector of youth at that. In the counter-cultural wing of the movement cultural or personal change tended to be equated with social change. Throughout the movement it was assumed that it was always better to be more radical than less, and radicalism was often taken to mean challenging limits because they were there and/or escalating standards of militancy. Radicalism also came to be equated with a politics of separatism that did not merely call for organizing particular groups separately, but included a tone of hostility toward outsiders, especially former friends and allies. Unfortunately some of the aspects of sixties radicalism that were most destructive to the movements of that period continue to be part of what is understood as radicalism or left politics. This article is intended as a plea for rethinking the legacy of the sixties in the light of the nineties, distinguishing between those aspects that remain valuable in the nineties and those that do not (and which may not have been such good ideas even at the time), building on the former and discarding the latter.

The movements of the sixties began as expressions of liberalism, as protests against violations of liberal values, but over the course of the sixties came to regard liberalism as the enemy, and developed a critique of liberalism that was accurate, insightful, and constituted a major contribution to left social and political analysis. The conception of radicalism which by the late sixties constituted a loose intellectual framework for movement culture as a whole evolved out of a passionate, enraged rejection of liberalism that took place in one movement after the next. The passion and rage expressed a widespread sense of betrayal, based on a growing perception of liberalism as an ideology of social control. Student and youth-based movements for social change found themselves in conflict with a liberal establishment that defended the status quo, saw themselves as betrayed by liberal allies unwilling to cut their ties to liberals in power, and came into conflict with liberal organizations, mostly made up of older people, that resisted the movement's confrontational approach to the authorities and egalitarian internal culture and organizing style.

Both the civil rights movement and the Northern student movement revolved around liberal perspectives and demands: the civil rights movement demanded equal rights for blacks, especially the right to vote, and SDS (Students for a Democratic Society) pointed to the hypocrisy of official claims that the US was a model of democracy given the realities of racism, poverty, and a foreign policy that promoted the Cold War. There were individual leftists in both movements, but in their early years both were dominated by young people who believed in liberal values, were outraged that they were being violated, and wanted them put into practice. Both movements found themselves pitted against Democratic administrations that called themselves liberal and defended their policies on this basis.

For the civil rights movement, the critical moment in the shift from liberalism to radicalism was the Democratic Party convention of 1964, in Atlantic City, where the Mississippi Freedom Democratic Party (MFDP), whose delegation, representing black voters registered by civil rights workers, demanded that it be seated. In the ensuing negotiations liberal allies of the civil rights movement within the Democratic Party swung their votes to a proposal that the MFDP be given two token seats, a 'compromise' that the MFDP rejected. Many civil rights workers concluded that anyone within the system was inevitably beholden to it, that in order to bring about change it was necessary to oppose the system from the outside. This rejection of liberalism was underscored by the realization, on the part of many civil rights workers, that liberal administrations might well give blacks the vote, but that that would not be enough, that real equality for blacks required questioning racism more broadly, and also challenging the class divisions that made achieving the right to vote a somewhat hollow victory.[4]

For the anti-war movement, the critical moment of disillusionment with liberalism came at the 1968 Democratic Party convention in Chicago. Anti-war Democrats were silenced on the floor of the convention by being shouted down or finding, when they rose to speak, that microphones had been disconnected. Meanwhile anti-war demonstrators on the streets outside the convention were being beaten by police. The convention nominated a liberal candidate, Hubert Humphrey, who maintained the party's support for the war. Many in the anti-war movement came to the same conclusion that civil rights workers had arrived at four years earlier: one could not bring about change from within the system, one had to work outside the system for its overthrow.[5]

In fact the view that liberalism was the problem had been developing within SDS, the main organization of the New Left, for several years. Early New Leftists had resisted calling the system that they opposed capitalism, partly out of uneasiness about adopting a Marxist vocabulary, and partly because the term 'capitalism' did not convey the problems of faceless bureaucracy and meaningless lives that they were concerned with (and to which socialism was not in itself a solution). They tended to prefer vague terms like 'the establishment' or just 'the system.' But by the mid-sixties many New Leftists were coming to the conclusion that doing away with racism, poverty, and war required structural changes in society, that students alone could not accomplish these changes, and that they needed an analysis of society in order to identify potential allies and construct strategies for change. In 1964 Paul Potter, then president of SDS, gave a speech at the first March on Washington against the war in Vietnam in which he said that it was necessary to name the system in order to change it, but stopped short of saying what that name might be. A year later, at the next March on Washington, Carl Oglesby, the next president of SDS, recalled Potter's speech and proposed a name for the system: corporate liberalism. He pointed out that the war in Vietnam was being run and defended by liberals, and argued that liberalism served to justify the actions of the corporate state, protect it from criticism, and prevent change.[6] This made sense to young people in whose experience liberalism had mostly served to defend the status quo. The radicalism that the movements of the sixties moved toward in the latter half of the decade was shaped by the widespread view that liberalism was the ideology that needed to be discredited, corporate liberalism (or liberal capitalism) the social system that needed to be dismantled.

The movement's critique of liberalism made sense in the sixties. It was true that conservatism was no longer the problem. The depression had destroyed the confidence of those in power that capitalism could run itself. Through a combination of fears of revolution from above and demands from below for government action, laissez-faire economics had been replaced by a consensus in favour of a liberal welfare state. In foreign policy conservative isolationism had been replaced by what was called liberal internationalism, meaning a policy of extensive economic and/or military intervention to extend US influence and protect the interests of US corporations. The critique of liberalism was important not only because it described the exercise of power in the postwar era more accurately than older conceptions of a ruling class wedded to conservatism, but also because it emphasized the importance of ideology: liberalism protected the status quo by giving it moral justification.

There were, however, problems with the critique of liberalism. First, it was easy to gloss over the difference between liberalism as a strategy for social control or as a justification for the status quo, and liberalism as a commitment to democracy, as the basis for popular demands for reform. The people who developed the theory of corporate liberalism noted these distinctions. When Carl Oglesby called the system 'corporate liberalism' he pointed out that it rested on values that were opposed to those of authentic humanist liberalism, which he said were more genuinely repre-sented by the movement. The two histories that traced the development of liberal reform as a strategy on the part of large corporations and the state (James Kolko, *The Triumph of Conservatism*,[7] and James Weinstein, *The*

Corporate Ideal in the Liberal State[8]) both distinguished between demands for reform by popular movements and the appropriation of reform by those in power. But when the theory of corporate liberalism was adopted by movements that were more interested in distinguishing themselves from liberals than in making alliances with them, these distinctions were easily forgotten. In many parts of the movement the word 'liberal' became an insult.

The second problem was that it was easy to infer, from the theory of corporate liberalism, that conservatism had been permanently discredited, that people in ruling circles had become convinced that an extensive welfare state was crucial to the functioning of the system and would never allow it to be dismantled. Many people on the left also thought that widespread prosperity was a permanent feature of advanced capitalism, that the main problem for the left was and would continue to be persuading people to rebel against a system that showered them with material rewards. Herbert Marcuse, in his book, *One-Dimensional Man*, which was widely read throughout the movement, argued that advanced industrial society rested on technical advances that had solved earlier problems of scarcity. Such societies, he argued, produced repressive or false needs, especially desires for unnecessary consumption, and that the endless cycle of the production and satisfaction of false needs squelched independence of thought, dissent, true democracy. Marcuse saw the welfare state as prototypical in a society that produced total administration and fostered total dependence.[9] There was a large grain of truth in this argument, and good reasons for the widespread appeal of anarchist visions of a stateless society and an economy in which production and need would be brought back into balance. But the critique of liberalism and the confidence in continued prosperity that accompanied it created a left unprepared for the political and economic shifts that have followed the sixties, the decline in standards of living, the appeal of conservatism and its gains in political power, the dismantling of welfare systems.

In the sixties the intransigence of the Democratic Party and the stability of the two-party system prompted the movements largely to abandon the arena of electoral politics and focus instead on direct action, protest in the streets, and cultural radicalism. The fact that the renunciation of electoral politics came to be regarded by many people as a measure of radicalism was not a major problem at the time. The problem is that continued lack of interest in the electoral arena on the part of the left has meant abandoning that arena to the right. Since the late seventies the right has put a great deal of effort into electoral campaigns ranging from the local to the national level, and has become a major force in politics. Though the left has participated in local elections in many places, it has not been a significant factor in national politics, and it has not accomplished anything remotely comparable to the achievements of the right in any arena of politics.

In the late seventies and eighties, while the right was reappearing as a political force in the US, postmodernism was becoming a major influence in the academic left and Michel Foucault in particular was being widely read. Through the eighties and into the nineties 'Foucaultian theory,' a distillation of sometimes contradictory assertions drawn from his (actually much more complex) writings, was widely coming to be regarded as the intellectual framework for radicalism. One tenet of Foucaultian theory, summed up in Foucault's image of the panopticon from which a guard surveys the surrounding prison yard, and from which he is able to observe virtually every motion of every prisoner, is that the state is nothing but an instrument of surveillance and discipline. This implies that resistance consists of avoiding the gaze of the state and fleeing to the margins of society. Another tenet of Foucaultian theory is that power is diffused everywhere in society, infusing everyday life, the family, sexual relations.[10] In the late seventies and eighties many feminists, gays and lesbians were drawn to this perspective because it provided a theoretical basis for a radical critique of personal relations and culture, a justification for the path already being pursued by radical feminist and gay and lesbian organizations.

Foucaultian theory, however, did not merely extend politics to the local and the personal, it substituted these arenas for the state as the arena of radical politics. The Foucaultian equation of the state with disciplinary surveillance left no room for struggle in that arena and no possibility that people might need state services. This view of the state had something in common with the view held within the radical anti-nuclear movement of the late seventies and early eighties, that radicalism meant changing people's ideas, not seeking political power through the state. People who held this view rejected the conception of revolution as a seizure of state power, which had taken hold within the anti-war movement of the late sixties. But the conception of radicalism as operating mostly or entirely outside the arena of the state was linked to the cultural radicalism of the sixties.

In the nineties, the absence of a left presence in national electoral politics in the US has more to do with the left's habit of focussing elsewhere than with explicit arguments against entering the electoral arena. It is still possible to find arguments from the cultural left against electoral politics. Amarpal Dhaliwal, for instances, in an article in a collection of essays on *Radical Democracy*, condemns democracy as a 'modernist project,' liberalism as a strategy of inclusion aimed at silencing critics of racism, and the vote and other democratic rights as means of cementing state power.[11] But most people on the left understand that liberal democracy is no longer the main problem, that the rightward tilt of mainstream politics has to be taken seriously. The problem is that the left has little in the way of a vocabulary or set of concepts for addressing this. The full title of the collection in which Dhaliwal's article appears is *Radical Democracy: Identity, Citizenship, and the State*. Despite the title, there is little discussion of the state; most of the articles focus on issues of identity, the construction of subjectivity, and cultural conflict.

The cultural radicalism of the movements of the sixties, which consisted of a range of critiques of prevailing culture and also of the radical culture (or more accurately, cultures) that were constructed within the movements, was a great strength of those movements. Much of the movements' moral authority came from their commitment to egalitarian values, and much of their appeal to young people had to do with the degree to which the movements themselves became alternative communities in which these values were put into practice. The cultural critique developed by the movements was at least as important and lasting an achievement as their more practical contributions to achieving voting rights for blacks in the South and ending the war. Liberal aims were so thoroughly intertwined with radical ideas, especially by the late sixties, that distinguishing between the two is a little artificial, but on the whole one can say that what was radical about these movements was their ideas: their social analysis, their vision, their attempts to realize that vision themselves. The movements of the sixties that lasted past the end of the war and went on to flourish were feminism, gay liberation, environmentalism – each of which, at least during the sixties, was primarily oriented toward cultural critique. The cultural radicalism of the sixties also had its problems. By the late sixties in large parts of the movement radicalism had become an end in itself. In the anti-war movement this led to an upward spiral of militancy and the adoption of revolutionary theories that were doomed to failure in the US, giving rise to sectarian battles and authoritarian behaviour. Through the movement as a whole it prompted tendencies to reject limits of all kinds because they were there, and an equation between radicalism and a separatism infused with hostility toward former and potential allies. Unfortunately the cultural radicalism of the nineties often has more in common with the weaknesses than the strengths of the cultural radicalism of the sixties.

Movement culture, both in the civil rights and the Northern student and anti-war movements, included an emphasis on authenticity, which meant putting aside dogmas and thinking for oneself, speaking honestly, relating to others with openness and trust. The equivocations of government officials and anti-Communist liberals unwilling to admit that there were social problems in US society or government policy contrasted sharply with the movements' eloquent protests against racism in the South and a senseless war in Vietnam. The movements' emphasis on creating what in the civil rights movement was called 'beloved community,' a band of brothers and sisters committed to struggle for a better society and to each other, contrasted sharply with postwar middle class culture, with its materialism and its emphasis on social convention, its elevation of family life and the privacy of the home. These conceptions of authenticity and community had a good deal in common with some versions of anarchist thought. In early SDS, at least, Paul Goodman's *Communitas* was read widely, and anarchist conceptions of a society made up of small, self-governing communities were taken seriously. In the early sixties especially a large part of the appeal of the movements (or of 'the movement,' as it was gradually coming to be called) was that many people found it a better place to live than mainstream society. Movement people who had previously been isolated dissidents were glad to have found each other. On the whole people listened to each other with respect, and treated each other with more care than they were likely to find outside the movement.

Over the course of the sixties frustration and anger grew and began to erode or at least transform the idealism of the early period. In the South this partly had to do with the difficulty of maintaining non-violence, or passive resistance, in the face of continued violent assaults and the failure of the federal authorities to provide much help. In the second half of the sixties the tone of the movement in both the North and the South was changed by the war, which enraged movement activists as well as increasing numbers of young people generally. For many in the movement the context of war undermined the appeal of non-violence, replacing it with a pursuit of militance. The rapid influx of angry opponents of the war into SDS and the movement generally changed the tone of movement culture, giving it a harsher quality, a rebelliousness that involved rejecting conventional limits, loosening sexual constraints and taking the lid off anger.

By the late sixties a logic had taken hold within the anti-war movement that measured commitment to ending the war in terms of an escalating standard of militancy. Demonstrations became occasions for skirmishes with police and there was increasing talk of violence. To the extent that this was guided by strategy rather than emotions, the idea was to force the repressive apparatus of the state to show its true character (as in provocations designed to force 'pigs' to act like pigs), and also to create enough disruption to force the government to end the war. The disadvantage of this approach was that it tended to isolate the radical anti-war youth movement from other sectors of the population, and it also drove away some young people. But by the late sixties there were enough students and young people angry enough about the war to give escalating militance a mass base.

The escalation of tactics that took place in the late sixties rested on the widespread but largely unexamined assumption that revolution was possible and could be brought about by finding the right revolutionary theory and applying it vigorously enough. There was little discussion of how this revolution would actually take place, what the post-revolutionary society would look like, or why anyone should expect that the majority of the US population would support a revolution. Rigid and dogmatic versions of Marxism circulated; vanguard parties were formed; many people looked to revolutions in the Third World as models to be imposed on the US, overlooking the authoritarian elements of those models, and ignoring the fact that the same approaches might not work in an industrialized liberal democracy. SDS, the centre of the anti-war movement, was taken over and destroyed by debates between factions, in effect sects, putting forward equally implausible revolutionary scenarios.

There were many people in the anti-war movement who had no interest in the fantasies of armed struggle and seizure of state power that had swept so much of the movement's leadership. This conception of revolution had little appeal in the emerging women's movement or in the counter-cultural left. But the idea that some kind of revolution was possible was part of a broader belief, or at least hope, that the movement could accomplish whatever it wanted, that external constraints did not really matter, a fantasy summed up in the slogan of May '68, 'all power to the imagination.' Throughout the movement, if one doubted that a radical transformation of society was likely any time soon one was likely to keep quiet about it, because saying such a thing was tantamount to distancing oneself from radical politics.

The rapid decline of the left after the war came as a shock to many people who had expected that it would remain strong and would turn its attention to issues of domestic social justice. The movement declined quickly when there was no longer a war to hold it together partly because of the recession of 1973, which undermined the youth culture that had sustained the movement. The youth culture and the movement had been sustained by low rents, low prices, the ease of obtaining and supporting oneself on part-time work, and confidence that one could go back to school or resume a career. The movement had also been weakened from within in its last years, partly by the sectarianism and fantasies of violence that had taken hold in the anti-war movement and partly by the growing equation of radicalism with a separatism that was laced with hostility to outsiders.

The turn toward separatism began in the civil rights movement. In 1966 the Student Nonviolent Co-ordinating Committee (SNCC) expelled whites, urging them to return to their own communities and organize there. SNCC also renounced non-violence and soon after adopted the slogan of Black Power. There were reasons for blacks to exclude whites. Whites who joined the movement were mostly from the North, middle class, and college educated, and they could easily dominate discussions in the movement and intimidate the poor blacks whom the movement wanted most to reach. The fact that most whites could return to lives distant from the conditions that faced Southern blacks at times affected the roles they played in the movement. There were good arguments for an exclusively black organization. But while it would have been one thing to have created such an organization from the outset, expelling whites already there, and urging them to leave the movement and return to their own communities, had quite different implications. The effect of this decision, along with the renunciation of non-violence and the shift to Black Power was to weaken or destroy ties with white organizations that supported civil rights and with black organizations that wanted to maintain those alliances. These changes isolated SNCC and led to its destruction: in the rural South a black movement could not survive without support from the black church and the black community generally. But many young black radicals in the North adopted the slogan of Black Power and, to one degree or another, the separatist stance associated with it.[12]

Radical feminism also took a separatist stance. As in the civil rights movement there were good reasons for women to organize separately from men. Life in the anti-war movement had become very difficult for women, and for some men; in the movement climate of the late sixties men with streaks of authoritarianism tended to rise to leadership. When women began to raise the issue of women's rights, most men in both the civil rights and the anti-war movement were quite resistant. It did not seem likely that a feminist politics could be developed in these arenas. But as in the civil rights movement, feminist separatism meant not just organizational autonomy but suspicion and hostility, not just the formation of organizations for women only but a conception of radicalism that involved attenuating or breaking ties with men. A rhetoric took hold that described men as the enemy. Women who openly disagreed were likely to be seen as supporters of the patriarchy; women who were in relationships with men often found it easiest to belittle their importance.[13] For heterosexual women, at least, a separatism laced with hostility to men was at best a half-truth, a partial or temporary stance.

The equation of radicalism with separatism first by blacks and then by women more or less sealed the link between the two. In the seventies and eighties identity politics largely took over the realm of progressive politics, meaning a politics organized around claims based on identity by race, gender, sexual orientation, and a tendency to reinforce such identities by emphasizing differences with other groups. In this sense identity politics is something new. The civil rights movement was not an example of identity politics; its goal was racial equality, not the assertion of black identity or the redefinition of black culture, though both took place as side effects of

the struggle for equality. The women's movement can be seen as transitional, between an older politics in which identity itself tended not to be in
question and movements based on particular groups would be likely to
seek alliances, and a newer politics in which the need to assert identity, and
defend its boundaries, is more salient, and often discourages alliances.

The cultural politics of the left in the nineties echoes aspects of the
cultural radicalism of the sixties that least deserve to be emulated, and
which, in the context of the nineties, tend to isolate the left. In the academic
left, particularly in Cultural Studies and elsewhere in the humanities,
radical politics is mostly understood in terms of a cultural radicalism, for
which postmodernism, or more specifically the poststructuralist theory by
which it is informed, is the intellectual basis. In the early eighties the term
'postmodernism' was widely used to refer to what was at that time a
relatively new literature that pointed to widespread changes in culture and
at times tried to connect these to changes in society. But the term came to
be seen as not very useful because it covered too much: trends in popular
culture, avant-garde art and architecture, literature that criticized,
commented on, celebrated, or showed the influence of these trends. The
term poststructuralism refers more specifically to a set of theories that
originated in France in the sixties which address issues of language, culture
and society.

The association of poststructuralism with political radicalism is based
on the poststructuralist emphasis on flux, instability, fragmentation, and its
critical stance toward everything it addresses: the social order, prevailing
culture, existing theory. Poststructuralism's association with political
radicalism also has to do with its origins with a group of French intellectuals who were associated with the radical student movement of the '60s
and tended to see May '68 as a formative moment in their intellectual and
political development. Poststructuralism does express many aspects of the
ethos of May '68: its anti-authoritarianism, its rejection of Marxism, its
celebration of the imagination, its resistance to all constraints or denial of
their existence. As the influence of poststructuralism has faded in France,
it has been taken up by intellectuals in the US who are attracted to this
stance and also to the fact that it places language, discourse, culture at the
centre of social analysis.

The problem with equating poststructuralism with political radicalism is
that poststructuralism's stance of across-the-board criticism of all claims
and all values leaves it without any set of values against which existing
society might be measured or which might provide the basis for a vision of
a better society. Poststructuralism puts forward an extreme epistemological
scepticism according to which, because our perceptions of reality are
filtered through our categories of understanding, we cannot attain any
accurate, reliable knowledge of any reality, and we have no basis for

judging alternative accounts. If one takes this seriously one cannot claim that the left's view of society has any greater validity than that of the right. The poststructuralist campaign against 'essentialism,' meaning the belief that things, beings, social or natural processes or relations, contain any inherent qualities which might resist being recast by human discourse, pushes poststructuralism and the academic world guided by it toward a fascination with language and interpretation and a disinterest in reality, natural or social. Poststructuralism's stance of suspicion toward all values discourages efforts to define a progressive set of values and remove any basis for questioning or attempting to check the marketplace values that are invading academia generally. In the sixties cultural radicalism was tied to movements engaged in social struggles and also had its feet solidly planted in a set of social values. In the nineties radicalism might have a wider appeal if it included an essentialist component of this sort.

When movements are too weak to bring about the social changes that they want, or find themselves too isolated to even try, they are often tempted to retreat to the arena where they do have some power, and conduct campaigns for correct attitudes among their own memberships or constituencies. In the late sixties, when the unrealistic goal of revolution took hold within the anti-war movement, sects proliferated and discussion within the movement as a whole took on a strongly sectarian flavour. Over the last decade or so a different kind of sectarianism has become widespread in left and progressive circles. In the absence of a movement that is capable of effectively challenging racism, sexism, and other forms of injustice opposed by the left, it is easy to turn to a symbolic or vicarious politics that consists of hunting for bad attitudes and rooting them out in an arena where one has some influence, which means among others who are also on the left. Campaigns to police language stand in for more substantial efforts throughout the left; this accords with views of language and discourse as the central concerns of radical politics. Such campaigns impede free discussion, promote intellectual conformity, and drive people away from the left. Authoritarianism is always a danger in social movements, and the record of twentieth century revolutions shows that left authoritarianism can become a very serious problem when movements of the left gain power. The best antidote is combatting authoritarianism on the basis of democratic values, including freedom of speech. This again requires a radical culture with a streak of essentialism, a left willing to assert and insist upon a set of values.

The left does best when it is connected to a popular movement, or a set of popular movements, with clear agendas. In this context the left can provide a social analysis and articulate the social vision and set of values that make it possible to formulate strategy and to develop a progressive culture. The left is also much more likely to revise outdated views when it is connected to popular movements than when it is not. The social analysis and cultural views of the left were developed in important ways in the thirties and transformed in the sixties. In periods in which the left is disconnected from popular movements there is the danger that left analysis will remain static while society changes.

There is no mass movement with a clear agenda today, and the left cannot wish one into existence. There are some hopeful efforts, projects which deserve attention from the left, such as efforts to form a progressive third party by groups such as the New Party, and the signs of a possible revival of labour, where there are the beginnings of a campaign to organize the unorganized, and overtures to left organizations and left intellectuals to contribute their skills. But these are still no more than signs of hope. Fundamentally the left in the US is in the anomalous position of having become mostly an intellectual arena with stronger ties to movements of the past than to any in the present. Under these circumstances it seems like a good idea to take a careful look at how that legacy is being cast, what aspects of it might be most helpful to left politics in the present.

NOTES

1. This is not intended to be an exhaustive list of publications that are important within the left. I have left out journals with particular foci (such as those concerned with political economy, in particular *URPE Review* and *Dollars and Sense*), despite their contributions to left analysis, because of their specialization. However my point holds here too: interest in left political economy is not growing.
2. In relation to the women's movement of the sixties terminology poses some problems. What I am calling the radical wing of the women's movement contained two tendencies, one socialist feminist, the other calling itself radical feminist. Radical feminists put gender first, and either did not accept the class analysis of the socialist feminists or saw class as less important than gender. Socialist feminists and radical feminists often had links to or at least histories of involvement in the civil rights and/or anti-war movements. Both were quite distant from the liberal feminist National Organization for Women, which had been organized by somewhat older, professional women associated with the Democratic Party. Women in what I am calling the radical wing of the women's movement generally referred to this wing of feminism as 'the women's movement.' Elsewhere in this piece I use this term myself. The same problem exists in describing the movements of the sixties, which by the end of the decade had become sufficiently intertwined that many people spoke of 'the movement.' Though there were liberal organizations that addressed the same issues that young radicals were concerned with, these were not usually part of what people meant by 'the movement.'
3. Giovanni Arrighi describes the history of capitalism in terms of successive waves of globalization in *The Long Twentieth Century: Money, Power and the Origins of Our Times* (London, Verso, 1994).
4. Clayborne Carson describes this conflict and its consequences for the civil rights movement in *In Struggle: SNCC and the Black Awakening of the 1960s* (Cambridge, Harvard University Press, 1981).
5. Todd Gitlin, *The Sixties: Years of Hope, Days of Rage* (New York, Bantam, 1987), ch. 14, 'The Crunch.'

6. Carl Oglesby 'Trapped in a System,' *The New Left: A Documentary History*, ed. Massimo Teodori (New York, Bobbs-Merrill, 1969), pp. 183-188.
7. James Kolko, *The Triumph of Conservatism: A Re-interpretation of American History, 1900-1916* (New York, Free Press of Glencoe, 1963).
8. James Weinstein, *The Corporate Ideal in the Liberal State, 1900-1918* (Boston, Beacon Press, 1968).
9. Herbert Marcuse, *One-Dimensional Man: Studies in the Ideology of Advanced Industrial Society* (Boston, Beacon Press, 1964).
10. The identification of the state with of surveillance, discipline, and repression, and the image of the panopticon, can be found in Michel Foucault, *Discipline and Punish: The Birth of the Prison* (New York, Vintage, 1979), and the conception of power as diffused through society and resistance as necessarily local, especially from Foucault's *The History of Sexuality, Volume 1: An Introduction* (New York, Random House, 1978), though this idea can be found elsewhere in Foucault's work as well.
11. Amarpal K. Dhaliwal, 'Can the Subaltern Vote? Radical Democracy, Discourses of Representation and Rights, and Questions of Race,' in *Radical Democracy: Identity, Citizenship, and the State*, ed. David Trend (New York, Routledge, 1996), pp. 44, 52.
12. For an account of the decision to expel whites from SNCC, the political shift associated with it, and the impact of this on SNCC, see Clayborne Carson, *In Struggle: SNCC and the Black Awakening of the 60s* (Cambridge, Harvard University Press, 1981). For the subsequent history of Black Power, see Manning Marable, *Race, Reform and Rebellion: The Second Reconstruction in Black America, 1945-1990* (Jackson, University Press of Mississippi), pp. 84-119.
13. For an account of the internal culture of radical feminism, see Alice Echols, *Daring to be Bad: Radical Feminism in America 1967-1975* (Minneapolis, University of Minnesota Press, 1989).

CLINTON'S LIBERALISM:
NO MODEL FOR THE LEFT

Doug Henwood

Leftists, me included, have often gotten a perverse kick out of pointing out that what Henry Luce in the 1940s famously christened as 'The American Century' died in the mid-70s at an age well short of a hundred, a victim of the Vietcong and stagflation. But maybe the beast didn't really die. After all, despite the U.S. loss in Vietnam, that war marked pretty much the end of the post-World War II cycle of anticolonial conflicts. The U.S. foreign policy establishment learned a lot of lessons from that disaster, among them never to fight another war with an army of draftees. It destroyed the revolutions in Central America, most importantly that in Nicaragua, during the 1980s, using death squads and proxy armies.

More broadly, the economic rebellions in the Third World – calls for a new world economic order and a global redistribution of resources – have been utterly crushed. In fact, Washington-friendly policies prevail now in virtually every country in the world. State enterprises have been massively privatized, and goods and capital traverse borders with a freedom unknown since 1914. The mildest social democracy seems impossible, and socialism is the weakest it's been as an intellectual and political force in 150 years. U.S. planners who've been designing the world since 1945 have gotten pretty much everything they ever wanted.

Even the global business cycle is kind to America at the beginning of 1997. Fears that the country was being overtaken by the more organized capitalisms of Japan and Western Europe now look quaint, with Japan still suffering from its bubble-bursting and the Old World up to its neck in slack. Sure, U.S. household incomes have been flat-to-down for 20 years, its manufacturing wages exceeded by ten European countries and Japan,[1] employment security is notably minimal, its poverty rate is the highest in the First World, and its income distribution most unequal[2] – but in some circles, these are reckoned as precisely the cause of U.S. economic strength. In the new world ruled by tight money and free trade, 'flexibility' is the prime virtue, and there's no room for sentimental moaning about living standards and polarization.

In other words, the U.S. economy has become a model for the world, with the most minimal of welfare states, the weakest of regulations, and the maximum of freedom for private capital to do as it pleases. The IMF and World Bank have brought the model to the South, and the architects of European economic union are bringing it – slowly, and not without popular resistance – to the cosseted welfare states of the EU. Maybe Henry Luce was right about the American Century after all.

Not only has the U.S. economy become a model for the world, at least among elite academics and policymakers, the U.S. political system is even gaining admirers. And Bill Clinton and his Democratic Party have become objects of study, and even admiration, for left-of-centre parties. What exactly does this mean?[3]

Democrats Move Right

If there's one historical figure most closely associated with capital's recent triumph, it's Ronald Reagan. Obviously the phenomenon is far more complicated than a single celebrity, but Reagan's political genius was to disguise a cruel and backward-looking agenda as the very stuff of optimism, appropriating a lot of classically leftist language about revolution and possibility for a very right-wing programme. In the 1960s and 1970s, capitalism had lost a good bit of the revolutionary aura that Marx and Engels celebrated in their contradictory way in the *Manifesto*. The Reagan years changed all that – not only in the United States, but around the world – and the left is still reeling from this historical reversal.

But Reagan left office eight years ago. He's disappeared from public view, and for all his world-transforming achievements, scores remarkably low in retrospective polls. For example, his overall presidential approval ratings are only a bit higher than Jimmy Carter's, who was widely thought of as a disaster, and are below George Bush's, who suffered the worst defeat of any incumbent president since Herbert Hoover. On so-called 'feelings thermometers,' in which pollsters ask people to rate figures on a scale of 0 (very cold) to 100 (very warm), Reagan (57) barely outscored Bill Clinton (56) and, surprisingly, had only a few degrees on Hillary Clinton (52) and the TV character Murphy Brown (52). Again, he was bested by George Bush (59). While his economic policies were rated as mostly good by 48% of the public in an NBC News/*Wall Street Journal* poll, they were rated as mostly bad by 35% – hardly a landslide of approval.[4]

But maybe that's the wrong place to look for the Reagan legacy. When I interviewed Sir Alan Walters, Margaret Thatcher's former economic advisor, he (somewhat surprisingly) said that the Iron Lady's most lasting achievement was the transformation of the Labour Party. One can say pretty much the same thing about Reagan and the transformation of the Democratic Party (allowing for the fact that the Dems could never even qualify as a mildly social democratic party, compared to Labour). Again, this probably personalizes too much; Thatcher, as much as Reagan, was the highly effective agent of a broad rightward shift in elite opinion. Still, it's impossible to imagine carrying out a comprehensive, sustained attack on popular living standards without such political figures able to sell the task – and not merely to sell it, but to drum up some genuine enthusiasm for it.

But Walters' political insight is quite illuminating, even if he does spout lots of nonsense on economic policy. Clinton is not only the leader of a party that has almost completely repudiated its better history, the heritage of the New Deal and civil rights revolution – he was one of the architects of its rightward move. He was one of the founders, and spent a year as the leader, of the Democratic Leadership Council (DLC), a corporate-funded organization of conservative Democrats, almost invariably described in the mainstream press as 'moderate,' whose ideological and electoral aim has been to distance itself from the poor and the black in order to woo the rich and white.

I have to emphasize that in reviewing this history, I don't want to idealize the Democrats' pre-DLC record. The major achievements of the New Deal are tarred by the party's appeasement of Southern racists; for example, FDR's social legislation excluded domestic and agricultural workers because they were overwhelmingly black, and any extension of federal benefits to them would undermine the Dixie social order. The World Bank and IMF were founded by Democrats, as was the CIA. Kennedy was a rabid anti-Communist, and Johnson's administration, despite passing important civil rights laws, prosecuted a murderous war on Vietnam. The precedents for Reagan's domestic austerity programmes and military buildup were well-established during the Carter years. At the sub-federal level, state and city Democratic machines have been the corrupt pawns of real estate developers and other local potentates. Still, despite these qualifications, Social Security, minimum wage laws, Medicare, and the civil rights laws of the 1960s were all established under Democratic regimes (though food stamps and the Environmental Protection Agency were Nixon initiatives, a measure of just how far right things have moved since the mid-1970s).

The DLC was founded in 1985, the year after Reagan's landslide re-election. Its cause was quickly endorsed by pundits, who universally held that the Democrats lost because their candidate, Walter Mondale, had been too 'liberal.' In fact, Mondale was a tediously moderate figure who had nothing on offer but a hair shirt. This habit of blaming Democratic losses on excessive liberalism began in 1972, with Nixon's trouncing of George McGovern. McGovern is the only Democratic presidential candidate of the last 24 years who could accurately be labelled 'liberal,' but that hasn't stopped professional opinion managers from applying the label to his successors.

Jimmy Carter won in 1976 largely because the memory of Watergate was still fresh in the popular mind, and his opponent, Gerald Ford, was an embarrassment, painfully inarticulate and dim. Carter, despite his Southern conservatism and born-again Christianity, did show a bit of populism that gained him votes: he denounced the corruption of politics by money and even spoke on occasion about busting up Big Oil. But his early populism waned, and he matured into a president of military expansion, balanced budgets, and lowered expectations – something of a proto-DLC figure. Faced with an inflationary crisis and a run on the dollar, he appointed Paul Volcker as chair of the Federal Reserve. Volcker promptly drove up interest rates into the high teens, causing the worst recession since the 1930s, and assuring Carter's retirement in 1980. Given the centrality of that experience to the neocapitalist ascendancy, it's yet another reason to count Carter in the conservative camp, even if he was an early personal casualty of the right's ascendancy. Chalk him up as a self-sacrificial lamb.

After Reagan took office and instituted his famous adventure in deficit spending, the Democrats became the party of fiscal orthodoxy. Their candidates in 1984, Mondale, and 1988, Michael Dukakis, were full of rhetoric about a country living beyond its means, and held out the promise of little more than tighter belts. A bizarre kind of political cross-dressing was in full swing. The Republicans had become the party of optimism, growth, and exuberance, and the Democrats had become the party of gloom and restraint – a near-reversal of their clichéd images of earlier decades. During the 1988 Democratic convention, the film biography of Dukakis showed the candidate mowing his own lawn with a manual mower – an image that, whatever its cardiovascular or ecological virtues, exuded an anal-retentive austerity. Late in the campaign he did flirt with some class war rhetoric, and picked up a bit in the polls, but it was too late, and too half-hearted (so half-hearted in fact that Dukakis actually rebuked a speechwriter who submitted a draft characterizing Bush as a 'country-club' candidate). Still, pundits dutifully circulated the DLC line that the party was losing because of its excessive liberalism.

In 1992, the pundits celebrated the DLC's own Bill Clinton as the party's best hope, the very embodiment of the 'New Democrat,' freed of all that embarrassingly antique welfare state/civil rights baggage. Though Bush had seemed invincible in 1990 and 1991, thanks to his bold leadership in the destruction of Iraq, the grim economy, burdened by the debt hangover from the 1980s, made a Democratic victory seem more possible than at any time since Reagan's election in 1980. Bush's approval rating, as measured by Gallup, which was 89% in February 1991, sank to a low of 29% by July

1992 – the greatest collapse in the history of regular polling, which began in the late 1940s.[5]

While Clinton did campaign as a 'New Democrat,' he did so coyly. Yes, he promised to 'end welfare as we know it,' a promise that came to cruel fruition in 1996; yes, he made a point of signing the execution warrant of a brain-damaged prisoner in Arkansas, to show just how tough on crime he was; and yes, he visibly distanced himself from the party's leftmost and blackest celebrity, Jesse Jackson. But, unlike his predecessors, he did not run as the candidate of austerity. Quite the contrary – his economic message was expansive. He would raise the levels of public physical and social investment, rebuilding a tattered national infrastructure, jack up spending on education and health care, and propose policies (details largely unspecified) to boost employment and wages. The numbers were tiny, but at least greater than zero. Politically, he had in large part appropriated the optimistic mood, if not the substance, of Reagan's economic message, leaving Bush looking doddering and obsolete, and Perot, cranky and weird. Once elected, however, all this went out the window.

Clinton, Arkansan

Before dissecting the achievements of Clinton's first term, a little detour into his performance as governor of Arkansas would be highly instructive. In a phrase, it was a disgrace, but a good foretaste of what kind of president he would turn out to be. Governor Clinton's record was nicely summarized by Ramesh Ponnuru, writing in the conservative magazine *National Review:*

> As governor, he soaked the poor and scattered tax exemptions on business interests; increased the government's use of what is charitably called 'creative finance'; created public-private partnerships with little public accountability; weakened conflict-of-interest and sunshine laws; and strengthened his own control of law enforcement. He was thus able to construct a political coalition including not only labor and the welfare establishment but also bankers, bond counsels, developers, and owners of heavy-construction companies. Every interest group was invited to the table, except for taxpayers and consumers.[6]

The right-wing bias of the author is visible in the uncritical inclusion of 'labor' and the 'welfare establishment' among the interest groups, since Clinton has a history of indifference or hostility towards organized labour, and he's importantly responsible for the grotesque welfare 'reform' of 1996. In 1986, Bill Becker, head of the Arkansas AFL-CIO, told the *Wall Street Journal* that Clinton's treatment of workers in his state was 'reminiscent of what Reagan is doing to us.' Most notoriously, Clinton's state Industrial Development Commission – which eagerly advertised the state's right-to-work law in the business press in an attempt to lure investment, a law that Clinton defended as the state's attorney general in 1976 – made a $300,000 loan to a company to build inventory so that it could survive a likely strike. As a result of that, Becker uttered his famous description of Clinton: 'This guy will pat you on the back and piss down your leg.'[7]

But all the rest of it is true – and we haven't even mentioned yet the Arkansas scandals. For the benefit of non-American readers who are unfamiliar with the more famous scandals, they include Whitewater, a complicated, smelly land deal, in which Bill and Hillary got favourable financing from a banker whose failing savings and loan was regulated by Clinton's government, the intent of which was to make the family rich; and Hillary's fixed commodity trading, in which a broker cooked her account to allow her to turn $1,000 into $100,000 – a very unusual sequence, since novices who trade commodities are more likely to turn $100,000 into $1,000.[8]

Let's forget the personal stuff, though, and look high-mindedly at Clinton's policies in Arkansas. Under his reign, the state was a paradise for despoilers of nature and exploiters of labour. To take a notorious example, one of Clinton's favourite targets for tax and regulatory indulgence was the chicken industry, a major player in Arkansas. So indulged was the industry that corn intended for chickens was exempted from sales tax, but not that for human consumption. The industry relies for raw material – i.e., living birds – on networks of 'independent contractors' who raise chickens under conditions of virtual indentured servitude, who buy or rent specialized equipment from corporate chicken processors and marketers like the one eponymously run by Clinton intimate Don Tyson. The processing plants are staffed by grossly underpaid workers who suffer a 20% chance of injury every year. And the chickens' wastes are dumped into the state's rivers, making the state's waters among the worst in the country. In fact, an environmental scorecard of the 50 states compiled by the Institute for Southern Studies had Arkansas 48th in its composite 'green index' and 50th in government environmental policies – not surprising, considering that the state usually comes in near the bottom on most social indicators, like income, poverty, literacy, and education spending.[9] The real surprise is Clinton's unearned national reputation as a friend of nature.

Arkansas has a long history of impoverishment, so Clinton isn't the only guilty party (though coming in dead last in environmental policy is no mean achievement). But how did he handle the matter of economic development while governor? In a way that gave a foretaste not only of his presidency, but of the scandals that have since come to plague him. Take, for example, the Arkansas Development Finance Authority. Clinton established it in 1985 to stimulate the state's economy and to create jobs. It did create jobs – 2,700, by its own count, or about one a day between its founding and the time of Clinton's election as president. It did so by floating tax-free bonds and lending the proceeds to businesses investing in

Arkansas. To float those bonds, it needed the services of lawyers, investment bankers, and commercial bankers – each of whom got generous fees. Clinton appointed all the Authority's board members – that is, those with the authority to choose which bankers and lawyers got the state's business, though always subject to being overruled by the governor. This way, noted executives of the Little Rock-based investment bank Stephens Inc., Clinton could have 'total control,' thereby 'politiciz[ing] the bond selling process.' And why would Clinton want to do that? To maximize his fund-raising powers. Some 1,300 grateful members of the circle favoured by the Authority contributed $2.7 million to various Clinton campaigns.[10]

First-term Betrayals

As President, Clinton has continued this strategy – running a business-friendly economic policy, assuring that the contribution checks keep rolling in. Of course, all U.S. politicians do this, but Clinton has done it with an unprecedented personal enthusiasm and involvement.[11] His late Commerce Secretary, the former corporate lawyer-lobbyist Ron Brown, famously shepherded U.S. CEOs around the world, cruising for lucrative contracts. The public justification was always job creation, but such gains are minimal, and with far less social payoff than building high-speed railroads or offering college tuition subsidies would offer.

For all the talk about Clinton representing a turn away from Reaganomics, the old trickle-down logic persists. One of his most cherished domestic programmes, the Earned Income Tax Credit, which offers a tax refund to low-income workers, is actually a public subsidy to low-wage employers (even though it does put a few dollars into the pockets of people who desperately need it). One of Clinton's proposals for 'fixing' the welfare reform bill he signed in 1996 is to offer direct subsidies to employers for hiring former welfare recipients – a quite-literal form of corporate welfare. Instead of a public jobs programme, with decent pay and benefits, and with public-spirited aims like offering child care or building parks, Clinton would subsidize the important work of flipping burgers and parking cars.

His budget-making has been a direct betrayal of his campaign promises.[12] Instead of a modest investment and stimulus programme, he's become the president of deficit reduction.[13] I don't mean to argue that running big deficits year in, year out is a good thing – far from it. Borrowing money from rich people and paying them interest for the privilege is a cowardly substitute for taxing them. And, over time, building up big debts only increases the political power of the creditor class; it's unlikely that the bond market would have become the arbiter of almost all state policy in the U.S. had outstanding debt not tripled during the Reagan-Bush years.

But 'deficit reduction' is rarely the neutral accounting exercise it sounds like on the surface: it's almost always an excuse to cut back on the decent things that government does while leaving the punitive things untouched. The only exception to this rule in Clinton's case was the tax increase on the richest 1% of taxpayers – not enough, for sure, but the best way to cut back on red ink. Typically, though, Clinton subsequently apologized for this move to an audience of rich Texans.

Otherwise, the budgets he's proposed have been achingly austere – even before the Republican takeover of Congress in the 1994 elections. In a budget sent to Congress in early 1993, only months after his inauguration, Clinton proposed a deficit reduction totalling 2.5% of GDP – with a revenue increase of 1%, and spending cuts of 1.5%. The budget proposed in early 1994 was even more austere. Federal investment, the centrepiece of his 1992 economic platform, would have fallen to the lowest level, measured as a share of GDP (the measure in all subsequent references), since 1950. Spending on conservation, pollution control, agricultural research, energy research, public housing, food stamps, income security, and community and regional development, would all fall relative to GDP. And what would rise? Subsidies to business, known in budget lingo as 'advancement of commerce.'[14]

After the 1994 elections, Clinton's budgeting got even more austere. The document he submitted in early 1996 was full of high-flown rhetoric in its prose introduction, but the actual numbers on offer were stringent. Despite saying that 'we' need to 'invest in education and training, the environment, science and technology, [and] law enforcement,' spending on all categories but the last was projected to fall as a percent of GDP. (Clinton, or whatever copywriter was speaking in his name, did brag about helping states 'build more prisons.') Had his budget been adopted as proposed, spending on education in 2002 would decline to half what it was when Reagan took office, to the lowest level since 1966. Spending on 'pollution control and abatement,' in budget-speak, would sink to the lowest level since 1972; on federally sponsored R&D, to the lowest level in history. Overall spending would decline to the lowest level since 1966. Of course, there's no virtue to higher spending in itself, but public services in America are already threadbare enough.

Liberal Clinton apologists respond by saying that he has no choice, given the country's allegedly conservative mood and Republican Congressional dominance. We'll look at the allegedly conservative mood in a moment, but it's a strange view of politics that urges pre-emptive compromise, before the struggle with the opposition even begins. But of course Clinton doesn't view the Republicans as the opposition – a contrast with most Republicans, who view him with inexplicably bitter contempt – but simply as friends he hasn't quite made yet.[15]

Let's move from these macro budgetary abstractions to several specific pieces of policy. In budget and other administration documents, Clinton and his surrogates have bragged that their major economic achievements were cutting the deficit in half and the passage of NAFTA and GATT. This makes him indisputably the president of the bond market and free trade – classically 'liberal' positions in the European sense.

True believer free marketeers reject this categorization of Clinton as one of their own. One reason they do is the failed health care proposal of his early months in office. This incomprehensibly complex piece of legislation would have created some sort of privatized national health scheme, with giant insurance companies and medical conglomerates at its centre. There would have been a role for government in regulating the beast, and insuring the poor, but the vastly inefficient private sector would have been given the lead role. The scheme was so complex and contradictory it alienated virtually everyone. Liberals and leftists who would have supported a single-payer, Canadian-style scheme could offer little more than a weak endorsement at best. Small insurance companies correctly perceived they would be frozen out, and mounted an intense campaign against the plan. The right objected to the very notion of a universal health insurance scheme. It was the worst of all possible worlds, and discredited the whole notion of radical health care reform.

And, as the physician and writer David Himmelstein has argued, it was a sign to the health care industry that the threat of 'socialized' medicine, on the national agenda at least in potential since the Truman years, had finally been lifted. With that all-clear sounded, the industry embarked on the most rapid and extensive merger and acquisition binge in economic history. Within the space of a couple of years, the old fee-for-service model of U.S. medicine has largely been replaced by 'managed care' – a system run by large insurance companies and health maintenance organizations (HMOs) with an interest in minimizing treatment and maximizing profit. While pressures had been building for such a transformation, Clinton's repudiation of national health insurance, part of Democratic Party platforms for 40 years, was directly responsible for this stunning corporate takeover. The restriction of access and choice that had been spuriously cited as the drawback of public health insurance schemes by the propagandists of private health care had become reality under a system of pure profit maximization, thanks importantly to Bill Clinton.

The other appalling achievement of Clinton's first term was the passage of welfare 'reform.' The federal government's principal income support programme, Aid to Families with Dependent Children (AFDC), established as part of the Social Security Act of 1935, was abolished. AFDC was stingy, but it did offer cash income to the very poorest single mothers and their children, and did so as a matter of right ('entitlement') for all those who qualified.[16] That system was abolished in 1996, and replaced with time limits and harsh work requirements. Recipients are limited to no more than five years on welfare – not consecutively, but in a lifetime – though states are free to impose shorter limits if they like. States and localities are increasingly using welfare recipients in place of public sector workers – cleaning parks, clearing snow, picking up trash. Additionally, cutbacks in the previously sacrosanct food stamp programme will reduce benefits from 80 cents per meal to 66 cents over the next several years.

According to (conservative) estimates by the Urban Institute, 11 million families will lose income under this grotesque reform, fewer than half of them the widely detested single-mother kind. Over half will be the working poor. In all, the Institute estimates, some 2.6 million people will be rendered newly poor (by official poverty measures), and the already poor will be rendered 10% poorer. Aside from this direct effect, the indirect effects of throwing millions of desperate people onto the labour market will be to depress wages for the worst-paid third of workers.

Clinton bears great moral responsibility for this 'reform,' perhaps the cruellest bill to become federal law in this century. During the 1992 campaign, he famously promised to 'end welfare as we know it.' Though he and his advisors spoke of job training and assistance as part of any reform package, no one with any sense of political reality could imagine that these half-decent intentions would survive in the prevailing environment of fiscal sadism – not to mention the racism and sexism that power the hatred of welfare recipients – assuming they were even seriously meant at all. All that the pundit class and the moneyed elite heard was the 'ending' part, and the political momentum became irresistible. And, Clinton signed the legislation. If his conscience was the least bit troubled by impoverishing millions, he has given no public sign of it.

And I haven't even mentioned other highlights of the first Clinton term – like an environmental record far more damaging than Reagan's and Bush's (this on the word of no less than the environmental icon David Brower), and a policy of blowing up 100,000 units of public housing. The destruction of public housing is based on the theory that poverty is caused by the concentration of poor people in poor neighbourhoods; dispersing them will reduce their exposure to social toxins, namely, each other. Where they are to go when their housing is destroyed is anyone's guess. But real estate developers are hungrily eyeing the soon-to-be-vacated sites for gentrified re-development.

It's tempting to say that Clinton is empty and unprincipled, a creature of pure political opportunism, but that lets him off too lightly. In fact, he's probably quite serious about his historical mission of purging the Democratic Party of its last humane traces. It's questionable whether a Republican president could have accomplished what he's accomplished for the corporate class: NAFTA, GATT, welfare 'reform,' fiscal stringency, and the rest. Had a Republican proposed any of this, there would have been a firestorm of outrage. But because Clinton did, advocacy groups for the poor, unions, environmental organizations, and the liberal weeklies were all silenced. It looks like the major economic goals of his second administration will be admitting Chile to NAFTA and privatizing, partly or fully, the Social Security system. Again, Bush or Dole probably would have had a difficult, maybe even impossible, time with such an agenda.

Electoral Models

With such an awful record, why was Clinton re-elected? There are several reasons for this. First of all, only 49% of the voting age population actually cast a ballot in November 1996, the lowest share since 1924 (which was only the second election women were allowed to participate in, and when restrictions on black voters still prevailed).[17] Behind that low turnout is a sharp class skew: nonvoters are disproportionately poor, and voters, disproportionately affluent. Though there are three times as many households with incomes under $15,000 as there are with incomes over $100,000 (21% vs. 7%, respectively), both extremes of the income spectrum are about equally represented in the electorate (11% vs. 9%). This class skew was more apparent in 1996 than 1992: the share of the over-$50,000 households in the electorate rose, and that of the under-$50,000s fell.[18] So, elections in the U.S. are competitive sports played out before a fairly well-heeled audience; those harmed by Clinton policies simply stayed home.

Second, an incumbent president running with a reasonably healthy economy has a very hard time losing. A simple electoral model I devised correctly predicted the outcome of 11 of the last 13 presidential elections using just two inputs – real disposable personal income, and the president's Gallup approval rating, both taken in the second quarter of the election year (six months before the election).[19] With the economy in decent, if not boomy, shape, the election was Clinton's to lose.

The table shows how Clinton's economic record stacks up against his predecessors. In sum, labour has done OK, but capital has done swimmingly. Employment growth is respectable, but less impressive than the Kennedy, Johnson, and even the Carter years. Unemployment is lower, on average, than the 1970s and 1980s, but still well above Golden Age levels. Real hourly earnings are about flat, a triumph by recent historical standards, but again, nothing sterling in a longer view. But the Clinton years have been very good ones for creditors and stockholders, and the 'fiscal shift' – the change in the deficit, expressed as a percentage of GDP – is the most dramatic in modern history.

Table 1: Presidential Economics

	employ-ment	unem-ployment	real hourly earnings	stock market	real inter-est rate	CPI	GDP	fiscal shift
Roosevelt III	5.0%	4.4%	3.4%	0.3%	–3.5%	6.0%	7.2%	+0.1%
Roosevelt-Truman	1.7	3.4	0.6	–4.1	–6.0	7.8	5.1	–2.8
Truman	2.9	4.4	2.7	11.4	–0.1	2.6	6.6	–1.2
Eisenhower I	1.4	4.3	3.2	13.6	2.3	1.0	2.1	+2.0
Eisenhower II	0.3	5.5	1.3	5.1	1.6	1.8	1.9	–0.6
Kennedy-Johnson	2.6	5.8	1.8	8.2	2.8	1.2	4.9	+0.6
Johnson	3.9	3.9	1.5	1.0	1.9	3.3	4.4	+0.3
Nixon I	2.2	5.0	1.7	–0.8	1.3	4.6	3.2	–2.4
Nixon-Ford	1.6	6.7	0.0	–10.6	–1.3	8.3	1.8	–1.2
Carter	3.1	6.5	–1.4	–3.6	–1.1	10.4	2.6	+0.8
Reagan I	1.4	8.6	0.2	1.6	6.0	4.9	2.3	–1.8
Reagan II	2.7	6.5	–1.0	9.7	5.8	3.5	3.2	+1.5
Bush	0.6	6.2	–1.3	6.7	3.9	4.2	1.2	–2.7
Clinton I	2.5	6.0	0.1	11.6	4.1	2.8	2.6	+2.7
averages								
Democrats	3.1	4.9	1.2	3.5	–0.3	4.9	4.8	+0.1
ex-Roosevelt III	3.0	5.3	0.9	5.7	1.5	4.1	4.3	+0.6
Republicans	1.5	6.1	0.6	3.6	2.8	4.0	2.3	–0.7

Major economic indicators by presidential term. Averages are arithmetic averages; average growth rates are compound annual growth rates. Beginning and end of term are January, for monthly figures, and first quarter for quarterly GDP figures. *Employment* is the average annual growth rate in civilian employment measured by the Bureau of Labor Statistics (BLS) establishment survey. *Unemployment* is the average civilian unemployment rate, also from the BLS. *Real hourly earnings* is the average hourly pay for nonsupervisory workers in manufacturing from the BLS's establishment survey, deflated by the CPI. (Manufacturing is used because the series for all private workers is available only from 1964 onwards.) *Stock market* is the real average annual growth rate in the Standard & Poor's 500 index, deflated by the consumer price index (CPI). *Real interest rate* is long-term rate on U.S. Treasury bonds, reported by the Federal Reserve, deflated by the CPI. *CPI* is the compound annual growth in the consumer price index. *GDP* is the compound annual growth rate in real gross domestic product; annual figures for Roosevelt's third term, and quarterly figures thereafter. (Quarterly real GDP figures are available only from 1947 onwards.) *Fiscal shift* is the change in the federal surplus/deficit as reported in the national income and product accounts; a positive number is a move towards lower deficits or higher surpluses. Roosevelt's third term began in 1941 and ended in 1945. Figures for Clinton are the latest available as of December 1996, and are subject to minor revision over time.

Source: author's database.

But these half-decent economic numbers have not translated into electoral success for Clinton's party. The DLC's move to the 'centre' – which really means to the right – is often justified as a vote-getting move, but there's little evidence to support this claim. Clinton's re-election masks a truly dismal performance by the Democrats. According to the pundit Michael Barone, starting from the day Clinton was elected in 1992, the Democrats have lost 12 Senate seats, 60 seats in the House of Representatives, 11 governorships, and 500 legislative seats. Noted Barone, 'No Democratic president has seen such harm come to his party since Grover Cleveland in his second term 100 years ago – and that was followed by 34 years of Republican dominance.'[20] Tellingly, Clinton is often described as the most conservative Democratic president since Cleveland.

Of course, it may be that the country has moved so far to the right that there's nothing the Democrats could do to stem these losses, or that they'd be even worse had Clinton not moved to the right. But it's hard to read that analysis out of the public opinion data.

A poll taken just after the election by Clinton's former pollster, Stanley Greenberg, showed that Clinton won because he was perceived as more likely to protect domestic programmes, particularly Medicare, Social Security, education, and those relating to the environment. His margin of victory was provided not by the upscale voters the DLC has been targetting, but by non-college-educated lower- and middle-class voters. Voters were relatively positive about the overall state of the economy, but were nervous about the future, and very friendly towards an agenda including comprehensive health care, significantly higher spending on education, and a programme of regulation of corporate behaviour.[21] But no national political figure is articulating anything like these goals.

Ironically, Clinton is best positioned to cut those very programmes that people elected him to protect – and his whole political philosophy has essentially rejected the idea of government programmes altogether. The great guru of the second half of his first term, Dick Morris, was famous for this advice. In the words of a *New York Times Magazine* profile of Clinton: 'Morris contends that the most enduring problems facing the nation, from the collapse of the family to the decline in civility, are behavioral ones against which Government programmes can make little headway, but Government persuasion can lead the way. "The problems we face, not the symptoms, but the causes, are fundamental causes best dealt with by altering the way people think and act and do." '[22] In other words, the president should be a preacher and storyteller, but not a political leader in the conventional sense. Ironically, the married Morris himself was forced to resign from serving his president when it was revealed that he'd been carrying on with a prostitute, showing a particular fondness for sucking her toes. Values are for the masses, not their rulers.

A rich insight into the cynicism behind the 'values' strategy was offered by Greenberg himself, in an article in the liberal magazine, *The American Prospect*[23]. According to Greenberg, 'progressives' harp too much on their (accurate) diagnosis of the ills experienced by working and poor Americans. Yes, people suffer from stagnant, even declining, incomes, stress, and profound insecurity. But what 'progressives' need to acknowledge in their rhetoric is the day-to-day heroism demonstrated by ordinary people in simply making ends meet. People have little faith in institutions like government, unions, or parties; only one in ten people in Greenberg's polls even have any faith in their friends. All they have to rely on are their own resources and the support of their families.

Successful politicians, then, need to craft 'narratives' that appeal to people with such constricted expectations. Thus, Clinton talks about tax credits for education and training – an extremely minor programme in every sense, but one cynically designed to appeal to this exhausted, despairing self-reliance. Clinton and Greenberg have embraced Margaret Thatcher's famous declaration that 'There is no such thing as society. There are individual men and women, and there are families.' And so has Clinton, the first president from the party of the New Deal and Great Society to achieve re-election since Roosevelt, embraced the liberalism of the Manchester school.[24]

The Clinton–Morris–Greenberg strategy is an obvious descendant of the Reagan-Bush appeal to 'values.' In their version, the Republicans embodied the good middle American way of life – monogamous, family-centred, religious, and patriotic – and the Democrats the opposite of all this – polyamorous, polymorphous, godless, and in secret league with America's enemies. It was a very effective technique for gathering the votes of folks who would be harmed by their actual policies.

Clinton has had to change the content of the values pitch, obviously; he's an admitted adulterer, but the public doesn't seem to care. There's a bit less emphasis on religion, though Clinton himself claims to be deeply religious, as does his wife, whose earnest social-workerish Methodism gets under the skin of libertarians, and not all of them on the right. Alexander Cockburn, for example, has quite properly denounced Hillary Rodham Clinton for her passion to intervene in people's private lives in the interests of 'therapeutic policing' – to guarantee their physical and mental health when they're not managing the task in a manner pleasing to the First Lady and her beloved 'social workers, shrinks, guidance counselors, the whole vast army of the helping professions.' As Cockburn points out, Hillary and her husband frequently refer to children as an 'investment,' a turn of phrase that reveals their coldly monetized view of the world.[25] All in all, a nicely Victorian combination of Manchester economics and hypocritical moral uplift.

What might we expect of the second Clinton term? I've already suggested some of it, particularly the partial privatization of Social Security. For more hints, we can turn to a speech he gave to the DLC on December 11. In it, Clinton promised to govern from 'the vital center,' which in America always means the centre-right. He listed his priorities as 'finishing welfare reform,' whatever that means; putting more people in jail; 'keeping America strong,' which presumably means buying more weapons; promoting free trade; and, of course, 'balancing the budget.' Balancing the budget is a code-phrase for deep cuts in civilian services, but coming out and saying that would ruin Clinton's image as the friend of the quotidian heroes. To offer narrative support to the lonely masses, Clinton actually suggested the following: 'I think we should expand Family Leave in a very limited way so that parents can take some time off to go to regular parent-teacher conferences at school and to take their children to regular doctor's appointments, not just when they're desperately ill.'[26] This stirring vision came from the president who claimed repeatedly during the 1996 campaign that his administration was building a bridge to the 21st century.

If this is a model for left-of-centre governments around the world, then the left is in even deeper trouble than we ever imagined.

NOTES

1. In 1995, U.S. manufacturing wages were exceeded by those of Japan, Austria, Belgium, Denmark, Finland, France, Germany, the Netherlands, Norway, Sweden, and Switzerland, and were 15% below the OECD-less-Mexico average. U.S. Bureau of Labor Statistics, 'International Comparisons of Hourly Compensation Costs for Production Workers in Manufacturing, 1995,' Report No. 909, September 1996.
2. Based on Luxembourg Income Study (LIS) data computed for *Left Business Observer* by LIS research director John Coder, and reported in LBO #61, 13 December 1993.
3. I've been following Bill Clinton obsessively since 1992 for *Left Business Observer.* In cases where sources are not formally cited in this essay, they can be assumed to be based on reporting for that newsletter.
4. Polls are from 1995 and 1996, except the Murphy Brown number, which was from 1992. They come from the Roper Center's computerized poll anthology, Public Opinion On-Line (POLL), available on Knowledge Index, through Compuserve.
5. Approval ratings are from my own historical database of Gallup polls, assembled from raw material on the Roper Public Opinion On-Line (POLL) database.
6. Ramesh Ponnuru, 'Running in Place: How Bill Clinton Disappointed America, *National Review,* July 29, 1996.
7. Alexander Cockburn and Ken Silverstein, *Washington Babylon* (London and New York, Verso, 1996), p. 258. 'Right-to-work' laws are laws common in many U.S. states that prohibit closed union shops.
8. The land deal is reminiscent of the one that Ronald Reagan's Hollywood cronies concocted to make him rich – except that that one worked, and was on a much larger scale. Clinton's cronies, unfortunately, were incompetent provincials whose schemes came to naught.
9. Doug Henwood, 'The Change Agents,' *Left Business Observer* #54, 4 August 1992; Bob Hall and Marry Lee Kerr, *1991–1992 Green Index: A State-by-State Guide to the Nation's Environmental Health* (Washington, Island Press, 1991). The composite index was based

on 256 indicators, covering air and water quality, energy use, toxic waste risks, environmental infrastructure, noxious emissions, environmentally related health indicators, protected areas, and state spending and regulatory policies.

10. Michael J. Goodman and John M. Broder, 'Clinton's Rein on Bonds Linked to Contributions,' *Los Angeles Times,* 29 June 1992.

11. In the cautious words of Stephen Hess, a very mainstream scholar of the presidency, 'You can't say that [Clinton] is the only one who was ever interested in raising money. [But] most of them have an awful lot of insulation between them and big money. [With Clinton,] there was a lot less insulation than we expected.' Quoted in Glenn R. Simpson, Leslie Chang, and Marcus W. Brauchli, 'Clinton Dinner Illustrates Fund- Raising Perils,' *Wall Street Journal,* 6 January 1997.

12. The analysis of Clinton's budgets that follow is based on official budget documents published by the Office of Management and Budget, and computer spreadsheets distributed by the administration from the White House web site (http://www.whitehouse.gov).

13. The stimulus program he proposed in early 1993 was extremely tiny, and almost half of it consisted of an expansion in tax breaks for corporate investments.

14. Non-U.S. readers, and even a few U.S. ones, may not be aware of how budgets are made in the U.S. Unlike Britain, where the Chancellor's word usually becomes law, the budget submitted by the president to Congress every February is only a starting point at best. The real budget-making work is done by a gaggle of committees in both houses of Congress, in an orgy of dealmaking and high-stakes lobbying. In recent years, it's been common for Congress not to finish its budgetary work by the beginning of the fiscal year, October 1, so the government runs for a time on what are called 'continuing resolutions' – extensions of the previous year's budget into the new fiscal year. The process is extremely messy. Deals are cut, often secretly, and strange pet projects get funded when Congresspeople slip phrases into legislation without their colleagues being fully aware of it. Budgets are often approved late at night in a rush to adjourn without any legislator having read the final document that's being voted on.

15. One of the mysteries of contemporary American politics is just why the right hates Clinton so much, given his conservative record and his evisceration of the liberal wing of his party. Explanations generally turn on culture more than policy – Clinton and his wife represent some unpurged heritage of the 1960s, that of sex, drugs, and rock and roll. Rumours abound about Hillary's alleged lesbianism – supported by no evidence of course. That she was a very establishment corporate lawyer in Little Rock earns her no credit on the right. Clinton's own (hetero)sexual appetites are well-known, and the rumours there are on firmer evidentiary ground. But both are drug-free, and Clinton's taste in rock and roll is extremely tame, even banal. He listens to Fleetwood Mac, Elvis, and Kenny G., not the Sex Pistols, Bongwater, and Bikini Kill.

16. In practice, state welfare authorities often did all they could to deny assistance, but legally the presumption was that if you qualified you were eligible. As is often the case, welfare in the U.S. is largely a state responsibility, though the federal government did provide funding for AFDC, and will provide funding for its successor programme, Temporary Assistance for Needy Families (TANF). Details and administration of TANF will be left to the states. Funding for AFDC was elastic – it would expand and contract with demand, which was usually a function of the business cycle. TANF funding is capped, and will not expand with a recessionary increase in demand. For more, see Doug Henwood, 'Demote the General Welfare,' *Left Business Observer* #74, 7 October 1996, and briefing papers prepared by the Urban Institute (various documents) and Center on Budget and Policy Priorities ('The New Welfare Law'), available from their web sites (http://www.urban.org and http://epn.org/cbpp/, respectively) or from their offices in Washington.

17. The turnout numbers are based on press reports. My own computations, using reported vote totals and Census Bureau population estimates, are even lower. But I'll go with the

higher number out of caution.
18. Income figures from U.S. Bureau of the Census, *Money Income in the United States: 1995* (Current Population Reports, P-60–193, September 1996). Turnout figures from exit poll data gathered by Voter News Service, reported in the *New York Times*, 4 November 1992, and 6 November 1996.
19. The exceptions were 1960, when it's quite likely that vote fraud gave Kennedy the election, and 1976, when Ford lost for reasons cited earlier. I made the first 12 'predictions' retrospectively; the 13th, a prediction of Clinton's victory by a 6 percentage point margin, appeared in both *Left Business Observer* and *Barron's* in August 1996, three months before the election. The actual margin of his victory was 8 points. As pleasant as it is to take credit for such prescience, the real news is the predictability of presidential elections despite the apparent volatility of the campaigns.
20. Quoted in Alan McConagha, 'Inside Politics,' *Washington Times*, 10 December 1996, p. A8.
21. Robert L. Borosage, 'Statement' accompanying release of a poll by Greenberg Research, Inc. (Washington: Campaign for America's Future), 12 November 1996, and background documentation provided by Greenberg Research, Inc. Despite the rather healthy-looking macro numbers, just 2% of the respondents to Greenberg's poll – limited to professed voters, a disproportionately upscale group – rated the economy as excellent, and 56% as good, with 31% calling it not so good, and 8% poor. And this, remember, is about as good as it gets, in business cycle terms.
22. Todd Purdum, 'Facets of Clinton,' *New York Times Magazine*, 19 May 1996, p. 40.
23. Stanley B. Greenberg, 'Private Heroism and Public Purpose,' *The American Prospect*, No. 28 (September-October 1996), pp. 34-40.
24. Johnson and Truman were elected to second terms, but both entered office on the death of their predecessors. Clinton is the first since Roosevelt to have been elected twice.
25. Alexander Cockburn, 'Beat the Devil,' *The Nation,* 12 February 1996. See also Cockburn's response to a letter criticizing that column in the 11th March issue of the magazine.
26. 'Remarks by the President to the Democratic Leadership Council,' Sheraton Washington Hotel, Washington, D.C., 11 December 1996, White House transcript. Family Leave was one of the great legislative achievements of the first Clinton term; it allowed people to take time off without pay to tend to newborns and family medical emergencies.

THE IDEOLOGY OF 'FAMILY AND COMMUNITY': NEW LABOUR ABANDONS THE WELFARE STATE

Joan Smith

The past seventeen years of New Right hegemony in the USA and the UK have led to a systematic undermining of the 'old settlements' of the Keynesian Welfare States. These settlements, accepted by both Conservatives and Labour politicians in the UK and federally imposed on recalcitrant States in the US, have been destabilised by twenty years of tax cuts and welfare restructuring in both countries. In the US the reduction and reconstruction of public assistance welfare, already exceptionally parsimonious for an OECD country, has created a model for other Western societies, including the UK. The welfare and labour law systems of both countries now carry global capitalist seals of approval for fiscal propriety, low wages and employer-friendly labour laws. In the United States income inequality is at its highest since the 1920s, and in the United Kingdom all the redistributive gains of the Second World War and after have now been reversed.

Unfortunately both the US Democratic Party and the UK Labour Party, re-marketed as New Democrats and New Labour, have accepted the 'reality' of an increasingly minimal welfare system and labour protection and argued that there is a need for a 'New Settlement' to replace the old Keynesian Welfare States. In the United States welfare 'reform' has particularly targeted the cheap social assistance programmes for single mothers and the unemployed (Aid to Families with Dependent Children – AFDC – and other anti-poverty programmes), rather than social security programmes (pensions, Medicaid) with widespread support. In August 1996 Clinton finally signed the Republican-drafted *Personal Responsibility Act* which dismantled federal regulation of AFDC and other poverty programmes, allowing States to set their own conditions and level of benefits. Under the new Act social assistance is limited to five years' support in a lifetime, with a maximum of two years' support at any one time. Clinton also set the federal block grant for these programmes at lower levels than the inflation rate over the next five years. As one Italian -

newspaper headline put it 'Clinton Abolishes Roosevelt'.

In the United Kingdom there has been very little check to New Right policies which have cut both social insurance and social assistance welfare programmes. National Insurance cover for periods of unemployment, maternity leave and sickness all lost their earnings-related element as early as 1980; these payments were uncoupled from rising earnings and tied instead to the retail price index as was the basic old age pension. In 1986-1988 a further programme of welfare 'reform' led to the abolition of grants for necessities (cooking, bedding, clothing) for the poorest, turning them into loans, and to the abolition of the right to income support for young people aged 16-18 years. Further welfare 'reform' in 1996 has led to the rolling together of both social assistance (funded through general taxation) and social insurance for the unemployed (for which workers have paid through their National Insurance stamp) into a new Job Seeker's Allowance (JSA). Under the JSA claimants have to prove they have been looking for work – a re-enactment of the 1930s 'genuinely seeking work' clause – and have to take any job no matter how unsuitable.

It seems unlikely that an incoming Labour Government in the UK would reverse any of these reductions in the welfare safety net. From the 1980 Social Security Act through to the new Job Seeker's Allowance, the Labour Party has accepted welfare 'reform' with barely a fight. Labour's one positive promise, to restore the Old Age Pension to the level it would have been if it had continued to be linked to average earnings, has been dropped in favour of a Labour version of 'no new taxes'. The 'windfall' tax they hope to raise from a one-off tax on the privatised utilities will only cover some additional spending in the health and education sectors, and the training of a quarter of a million young people.

The argument for a 'New Settlement' for welfare in both the UK and the US derives from the acceptance of three economic 'facts' by centre-left politicians. The first 'fact' is that budget deficits are caused by spiralling welfare payments rather than by lowered tax receipts. The second is that the provision of health and welfare services is being jeopardised by an ageing population in both societies.[1] The third is that welfare payments are being swelled by scroungers and an 'underclass' of welfare dependants. It has been one of the notable success stories of the UK New Right that budget deficits created through unemployment, the under-taxation of companies and the redistribution of the tax burden away from the rich, have been successfully presented as a crisis of welfare rather than of capitalism, and that the Centre-Left have accepted this view of the economy.[2] At the heart of the argument for a 'New Settlement' in Britain is the promise by Blair, Brown and others to accept this new tax and welfare regime as largely irreversible. Their aim is to deliver, as Clinton has done, a decrease in the budget deficit and a growth in employment and, as Clinton once wished, a more equitable society through economic growth, rather than redistribution.

But in both countries the decay of the social fabric (apparent in unrepaired and over-crowded state schools and hospitals and breakdowns in social order) has reached a crisis point in the poorest areas and presents increasing problems for the rest of society who are not part of the 'overclass'. The 'new theory' that the centre-left has been searching for in order to combat the ideological hegemony of the New Right, turns out to be a theory that locates the responsibility for the fracturing of society not in the privatisation and inequitable programmes of the past twenty years, nor in government policies and deregulated free markets, but in the families and communities that suffered most from those policies. In the US and the UK 'New Democrats' and 'New Labour' have found communitarian theory useful in constructing a political discourse that it is in the community and in the family, not in the 'commonwealth' (civil society as government), that responsibility lies for social disorder and disintegration. The communitarian position appears to expect that poor, and growing poorer, parents will be able to impose order on their children, and rebuild their own communities. It is therefore important to consider the assumptions underlying the communitarian theory which now provides the theoretical justification for the new consensus between the 'left of centre' (as Blair once described himself), centre *and* right.

From the New Right to Communitarianism

From the mid-1970s when Conservative think tanks in both the United Kingdom and the United States began writing their dreams of a free market future of private wealth and public poverty, the exchange of theory on free market economics was accompanied by an exchange of theories exploring problems of poverty and social order. In the early 1970s the then leading UK free market politician, Keith Joseph, put forward a version of Oscar Lewis' 'culture of poverty' thesis to explain the existence of impoverished claimants in a welfare democracy. This attempt to counter Peter Townsend's rediscovery of poverty was easily discredited. But by the late 1980s it was possible for UK Conservative politicians to successfully adopt the language of the 'underclass' from US writers such as Auletta and Murray.[3] Whereas the terms of the poverty debate in the 1960s and 1970s were set by the poverty lobby in both the US (Michael Harrington) and the UK (Peter Townsend and Brian Abel-Smith), by the 1990s the poverty debate had been captured by the 'underclass' lobby seeking the abolition of welfare 'dependency' through the abolition of welfare. The central feature of New Right social thought has been the successful presentation of welfare recipients as the creators of the problem of social order rather than its casualties, as dependants on society rather than claimants from society.

In the United States the term 'underclass' became synonymous with black Americans living in ghettoised neighbourhoods. The most liberal version of the increasingly popular theory of the underclass was that of William Julius Wilson, who argued that the underclass was caused by an absence of a 'marriageable pool' of traditional bread-winning males (because of rising unemployment and rising crime) which left women to raise children as single mothers. Although liberal in its attempt to shift the argument from behaviour to social conditions, Wilson's thesis allowed for a redefinition of poverty as a problem particularly affecting ghetto dwellers rather than rural and urban workers and suburban Americans without work, and those Americans in jobs where the pay was too low to raise them over the poverty level.[4] In all versions of underclass theory, poverty became associated with crime and disorder rather than need and was no longer obviously connected to the welfare and unemployment crises of deregulated free markets.

In first the US and then the UK Charles Murray presented the extreme right-wing version of the 'underclass' thesis. His argument was that welfare payments *created* an underclass of dependants with welfare dependent expectations and attitudes. As well as being enormously influential in the US, these ideas were taken up in the UK in 1990 and particularly after the election of 1992.[5] Just as in the US, where two conservative US think-tanks were important in pushing the underclass argument and targeting welfare payments (the American Enterprise Institute[6] and the Heritage Foundation), the UK's Institute of Economic Affairs aided by the *Sunday Times* created a platform for Murray. In 1994, in a series of articles for the Murdoch-owned London *Sunday Times*, Murray described the unemployed and single parents of the UK as a 'new rabble' unlike the 'New Victorians' of self-help savers. Just as the existence of Aid to Dependent Families was the '*cause*' of a black underclass in the United States, so in the UK the existence of the right to permanent social housing for homeless parents of dependent children, and to housing benefit and income support, was the 'cause' of a white British underclass, living on local authority housing estates and subsisting on income support.

On both sides of the Atlantic 1996 saw the first, but not the last, legislative culmination of the scape-goating of single parent mothers, and other welfare recipients. As Clinton finally signed the Republican *Personal Responsibility Act*[7] despite the previously successful veto campaign, the Job Seeker's Allowance was introduced in Britain with new powers to take people off benefit. Peter Lilley, UK Minister for Social Security, also unveiled a new 'cheats hotline' for members of the public to phone in and inform on 'scroungers', and paid for it by closing the Benefits Agency telephone advice service for welfare claimants. The repeal of the Homeless Persons' Legislation under the new Housing Act 1996 took away the right to permanent social housing for homeless applicants, including parents with dependent children who may now be assessed for two-year temporary accommodation only; if a local authority wishes to offer further support it can, but it is only allowed to house the homeless in local-authority owned or controlled property for a maximum of two years out of three.

Rather than confronting these New Right policies both New Democrats and New Labour have sought to construct a 'New Settlement', one which is acceptable to Conservatives, industrialists and bankers. Unable to answer the question of how they would regenerate the economy and mend the social fabric without reinflating, spending more on welfare and raising taxes, the New Democrats have mined certain aspects of communitarian writings to provide a distinctive theory of social crisis, which would leave lowered tax rates and cuts in welfare unchanged, while offering proposals for the restoration of the 'good society'. The role played by Charles Murray in promoting the underclass thesis in both the US and the UK has now been taken over by Amitai Etzioni on behalf of the communitiarian position. Following well-received works by Robert Bellah (*The Habits of the Heart* and *The Good Society*), Etzioni undertook the task of producing a general statement of communitarian philosophy and sociology. He produced first *The Moral Dimensions: Towards a New Economics, 1988,* and then *The Spirit of Community*.[8] *The Spirit of Community* in particular provided a popularised account of communitarianism in which the origins of the present-day social crisis could be found in a parenting deficit, inadequate education systems, the weakening of community ties and rampant individualism.

The appeal of communitarian theory to the 'centre-left' has been that it appears to offer an alternative to both destructive free market individualism (allied with social authoritarianism), and 'expensive' social democratic welfarism and liberal civil rights programmes. In his 1988 text Etzioni claimed communitarian thought as a middle way[9], seeking to wrest the high ground from both individualism (a term used to slide together both libertarian neo-economic theory and liberal 'rights' theory) and social-conservatism:

> We are now in the middle of a paradigmatic struggle. Challenged is the entrenched utilitarian, rationalistic-individualistic, neo-classical paradigm which is applied not merely to the economy but also, increasingly, to the full array of social relations, from crime to family. One main challenge is a social-conservative paradigm that sees individuals as morally deficient and often irrational, hence requiring a strong authority to control their impulses, direct their endeavours, and maintain order. Out of the dialogue between these two paradigms, a third position arises, which is advanced in this volume. It sees individuals as able to act rationally and on their own, advancing their self or 'I', but their ability to do so is deeply affected by how well they are anchored within a sound community and sustained by a firm moral and emotive personal underpinning – a community they perceive as theirs, as a 'we', rather than as an imposed, restraining, 'they'.[10]

Indeed, the general argument in *The Moral Dimension* seemed to offer a happy alternative for centre politicians: a critique of the social results of free market economics which nevertheless accepted the central premise of the free market; an argument against the individualist fallacy at the core, it is claimed, of both free market economics and liberal 'rights' traditions; a plea for community without social authoritarianism, and for the moral regeneration of society without financial costs to the state. In *The Moral Dimension* Etzioni offered a basis for a standstill 'new settlement' which attempted, with goodwill and moral persuasion, to rebuild crumbling communities.

By 1993 however, Etzioni's argument had changed in significant ways from his 1988 position and a 'standstill' interpretation was no longer possible. In *The Spirit of Community* (1993) Etzioni displayed an almost complete acceptance of the New Right agenda on social order and of the critique of 'rights talk' that had come to be so fashionable in the United States, whilst arguing that the worst of New Right policies could be avoided. *The Spirit of Community* begins with a series of claims that the New Right agenda of restoring law and order, saving the family, restoring schools as moral educators, and rebuilding communities could take place without an authoritarian state, Puritanism, educational indoctrination, women's inequality and the growth of vigilante/separatist communities. However there must be a moratorium on the growth of individual rights and of government responsibilities. Although Etzioni initially states in *The Spirit of Community* that 'strong rights presume strong responsibilities' his real message, published at the time when a national American healthcare system was being debated, was that there should be 'no new rights':

> When asked whether certain things are a 'a privilege that a person should have to earn, or a right to which he is entitled as a citizen' most Americans (81 per cent) considered health care a right (versus 16% who said it was a privilege). Two-thirds (66 percent) considered adequate housing a right (as opposed to 31 percent who called it a privilege). Indeed, why not? Until one asks, as there are no free lunches, who will pay for unlimited health care and adequate housing for all? The champions of rights are often quite mum on this question, which if left unanswered makes the claim for a right a rather empty gesture.[11]

Etzioni goes on to the litany that rights presume responsibilities, that there are some responsibilities without rights, and that there needs to be careful adjustments between rights and responsibilities. He then presents his central purpose in writing *The Spirit of Community*, which is to argue for the moral reconstruction of America through the re-generation of shared values in family and community life. For Etzioni, the degeneration of family life is at the heart of the moral malaise of society. Whilst paying lip-service to the argument that one good single parent can be better than two inadequate ones (a lip-service recently repeated by Tony Blair), Etzioni goes on to argue that the two parent family is a 'two-piston engine of effective education' for the child.[12] Having a child is a moral commitment yet he argues, parents have steadily reduced the number of hours they spend with their children in a week (from 30 hours a week in the 1960s to 17 in the 1980s) and have increasingly used substitute child-care to enable them to work. Etzioni states clearly that child care provision, staffed by temporary under-paid workers, is no substitute for parents who should be prepared to work less, to spend less money, to stop moving and to settle in a community. Both flexitime and home working are positive developments for parenting, according to Etzioni.

His two 'radical' proposals for state support for parenting are for paid maternity leave in the United States (a welfare benefit that Western Europe has had for decades) and child allowances. There are no proposals to reduce the hours of the working week or to create a network of subsidised high quality child care facilities. Instead there are proposals for a waiting time before marriage (ignoring the decline of marriage as an institution even within the much married United States), a waiting time before divorce, that families should eat meals together, that both parents should contribute to child support, and that welfare laws should be reformed so that they do not discriminate against the married.[13] A further proposal for the remoralising of the young and development of self-discipline is for the return of the form teacher. Thus, the violence and drug-dependent cultures that have swept through schools in poor areas in both countries during the past decade are to be dealt with by parents and by teachers, the very people who have been trying to deal with them all along.[14]

Etzioni's most controversial proposal is for a year of national service for all young people in order to overcome the demoralising experience of unemployment.[15] This year of national service would provide an experience of living in a unified community, reinforcing American values among all cultural groups.[16] Despite this proposal for a re-construction of a national community Americans, in a world designed by Etzioni, would still not be able to turn to that national community for social justice. They would have to rely on themselves and their families:

> A communitarian position on social justice (for all groups) includes the following elements: First, people have a moral responsibility to help themselves as best they can ... There is, as conservatives keep reminding us, something deeply degrading about being dependent on others.
>   ... The second line of responsibility lies with those closest to the person, including kin, friends, neighbours and other community members. They are next in line because they know best what the genuine needs are (they are much less likely to be cheated than are welfare bureaucrats) and are able to tailor the help to what is required.
>   ... as a rule every community ought to be expected to do the best it can to take care of its own ... Charity – and, more broadly, social responsibility – ought to begin, but not end, at home ...
>   ... Last but not least, societies (which are nothing but communities of communities) must help those communities whose ability to help their members is severely limited ...

Providing federal unemployment insurance, which is partially funded by taxes that are paid by all Americans is here fully justified.[17]

Among measures that Etzioni finds acceptable for the development and protection of communities are the introduction of curfews and of national identity cards.

In Etzioni's *The Moral Dimension* the critique of excessive individualism was aimed both at the libertarian theorist Nozick, who would seek to end welfare in the name of liberty, and at the radical liberal John Rawls, who sought a liberal theory of justice in order to promote redistributive justice and civil rights.[18] The arguments for 'no new rights', 'no rights without responsibilities', are arguments that have been deployed successfully against the left's previous commitment to redistributive justice and to civil rights. These arguments have been used to reconstruct centre-left policies in the US and UK. Exhortations to return to family values and to rebuild communities have played an increasingly important role in the speeches of the Labour leadership in Britain because they address two obvious realities – increasing poverty among young families and increasing social disintegration among poor communities – without requiring the restoration of social justice through redistributive policies, or the restoration of a justice system in which prison is a last resort rather than a first.

Seventy American academics signed the 'Responsive Communitarian Platform' drafted by Etzioni, Mary Ann Glendon[19] and William Galston in 1991. This programme for moral regeneration with families as the first line of defence, followed by schools and communities, demonstrated that communitarianism had not only taken heed of New Right critiques of 'welfare dependency', 'welfare scroungers', and 'disintegrating communities' but had accepted them all. It is this perspective that has been taken as a radical re-statement of centre and centre-left values in both Clinton's camp and in some Labour Party circles. In Clinton's 1992 election campaign workfare proposals were placed alongside commitments to good child care, jobs for those who needed them, and to healthcare reform, but in 1996 it was only the commitment to workfare that survived. Similarly, policies put forward by the Social Justice Commission, set up by the late labour leader John Smith, have been diverted away from proposals for the reversal of increasing inequality, to discussions of community, family and crime. There is now growing pressure within the British Labour Party to accept the 'necessity' to means-test the remaining universal elements of the British welfare state in order to provide adequately for the poorest, and to accept the increasing privatisation of future welfare provision and job training. The dualism of the 1992 Clinton position is now being reproduced in the 1997 British Labour Party in the run-up to the General Election of 1997.

The British Labour Party, the New Settlement and the Stakeholder Vision

Many of the original Institute for Public Policy Research (IPPR) pamphlets were written in language that wavered between the New Right map of contemporary society and 'Old Labour' commitments to equality and social fairness.[20] The concept of welfare 'dependency' appeared in several pamphlets alongside tables depicting the growth in poverty. In two of them, the 'problem' family reappears. The idea that people on benefit were 'claimants' from society had largely been replaced by a mixture of ideas from both right and left. It was in this context that communitarian arguments became important inside the Labour Party, offering a theoretical legitimation for the New Right perspectives on social welfare but dressing them in the language of family and community responsibility, and increasingly of 'law and order'.

In his 1993 IPPR essay 'Sharing Responsibility for Crime', Blair argued for a perspective that was neither conservative, blaming individuals for crime, nor 'left', blaming society, but one in which 'rights and responsibilities go together'. Blair described this as a 'left of centre' position and in it perspectives of family responsibility and society responsibility jostled one another:

> . . . a child brought up in a stable, well-balanced family is more likely to develop well than one who is not, and that it is likely to be harder, financially and emotionally, to bring up children alone . . . raising a child well is made easier if a family has a decent income, lives in pleasant surroundings, is well housed, and has access to high quality education.[21]

Blair ended by arguing that the country was now prepared for a 'sensible, balanced and modern view of individuals, family and community, of the right balance between individual responsibility and social action'.

Blair was still careful not to commit himself totally to the idea of an underclass. In *New Britain*, his recent major collection of political essays, he consistently used the phrase 'what some call an underclass'.[22] But increasingly the themes he addresses are ones of family and community values. In October 1996 a speech delivered in South Africa (much to the audience's surprise) was almost entirely devoted to his view of the 'decent society':

> At the heart of everything New Labour stands for is the theme of rights and responsibilities. For every right we enjoy we owe responsibilities. That is the most basic family value of all. You can take, but you give too.[23]

His tough stance on crime, he said, derived from his concern for the suffering of people on council estates:

> . . . whose lives are made hell by teenage tearaways, vandals, drug-dealers, muggers, graffiti artists and the culture of despair that has been spawned by the break-down in the decent values on which Britain was built.

This was why he supported Jack Straw's curfew on children in these estates at night.

> Families have the right to live in secure communities that are orderly and safe for their children to live, learn and play in. But parents have a responsibility to know where their children are and what they are doing.
> ... Some call it curfew. I call it child protection.
> A visit to a juvenile court would prove to anyone the direct link between the break-up of family and community bonds and the breakdown of law and order.

Despite Blair's emphasis on the need for family values, he also tried to distance himself from the 'back to basics' position of the Conservatives. He was adamant that a return to family values did not mean a return to women in the kitchen or to homophobia or to Victorian society. In his very next statement, however, that position was qualified:

> But the absence of prejudice should not mean the absence of rules, or order, or stability ... Let our social morality be based on reason – not bigotry. But let us not delude ourselves that we can build a society fit for our children to grow up in without making a moral judgement about the nature of that society...
> Any decent society is founded on duty, responsibility. A philosophy of enlightened self interest in which opportunity is extended ... greater security, safer streets, motivated young people.[24]

Linking law and order and family values together Blair is pulled closer and closer to the Right.

With respect to some other polices, Blair's speeches and writing differ considerably from the more right-wing communitarian statements of Etzioni.[25] Blair's original arguments on the stakeholder economy, society and politics began from the global challenge to British capitalism rather than the destruction of the inner cities and family life. Many of his speeches refer to a quite different ideological tradition in British politics, that of 'one nation'.[26]

> Social justice, the extension to all of a stake in a fair society, is the partner of economic efficiency and not its enemy ... We live in a world of dramatic change and the old ideologies that have dominated the last century do not provide the answers. They just do not connect with a new world of global competition, abrupt technological advance, a revolution in the world of women, new environmental danger, and widespread demands for a new more empowering and open form of politics.
> But there is a big ideal left in politics. It goes under a variety of different names – stake-holding, one nation, inclusion, community – but it is quite simple. It is that no society can every prosper economically or socially unless all its people prosper, unless we use the talent and energies of all the people rather just the few, unless we live up to the ambition to create a society where the community works for the good of every individual, and every individual works for the good of the community.[27]

For Blair the nation is the ultimate community and communitarianism is presented both as a new version of much older British traditions that were the foundation of the 'old' settlement (one nation and social citizenship theories), and as a version of the social inclusion perspective of

European, particularly French, socialism. In his writings, communitarianism, social inclusion, social citizenship and a 'one nation' perspective are all compatible with the British ethical socialist tradition:

> Since the collapse of communism the ethical basis of socialism is the only one that has stood the test of time. This socialism is based on a moral assertion that individuals are inter-dependent, that they owe duties to one another as well as to themselves, that the good society backs up the efforts of the individuals within it, and that humanity demands that everyone be given a platform ... the good of each does depend on the good of all. This concept of socialism requires a form of politics in which we share responsibility both to fight poverty, prejudice and unemployment, and to create the conditions which we can truly build one nation – tolerant, fair, enterprising, inclusive. That, fundamentally was Attlee's kind of socialism and it is mine.[28]

Just as with Clinton in 1992, Blair has appeared to be facing in two directions at once since his election to the leadership of the Labour Party. To his left there are several radical statements on the stakeholder perspective, including Will Hutton's book *The State We're In* and the Trades Union Congress 1996 statement *Your Stake at Work. Proposals for a Stakeholding Economy*. To his right are Labour Members of Parliament such as Jack Straw, Shadow Home Secretary, and Frank Field, Chairman of the Social Security Select Committee and highly influential across all parties in the formation of policy on welfare and social security.

The essence of the more radical stakeholder vision is to ally a modernised 'social citizenship' theory with European perspectives on social inclusion:

> The right to be a member of a functioning economic community is among the most important of individual rights. The key stakeholder value is inclusion, rather than the equality sought by the Old Left or the individual autonomy of the New Right.[29]

In this view, put forward by Hutton and Kay, businesses are social institutions, not creatures of the stock market, and ownership confers obligations, including that of paying tax.[30] A business discharges its franchise through a network of co-operative working relationships, and wealth creation depends on building institutions that allow co-operative relationships and embody trust and commitment. Moreover, successful market economies rely on a host of intermediate organisations in order to function, such as voluntary organisations and quangos, hospitals and firms; it is this institutional infrastructure that generates, nurtures and sustains social capital.

Arguments derived from Hutton and Kay on the short-term nature of British capitalism, seeking higher dividends rather than long-term investment, are repeated in the first chapters of the TUC's pamphlet *Your Stake at Work*.[31] The thrust of this pamphlet is to summarise the lack of investment in Britain industry and to compare the governance of British companies unfavourably with that of other European countries, particularly

Germany and France. The TUC pamphlet outlines a range of policies designed to create a new deal for workers within British companies (who now have the weakest legal protection in Western Europe), and for a reversal of the rising tide of inequality, redundancies and low-paid part-time working prevalent in the UK since 1979. Their proposals include schemes for workers to own shares in the companies they work for (the Employee Share Ownership Plans of the US are one potential model), greater investment in workforce skills, implementation of changes in Company Law already proposed by official inquiries, and greater control over institutional funds by investors. These proposals, and those of Hutton and Kay, are ones which seek a more efficient capitalism that can provide work and welfare to its citizens, and also seek to democratise capitalism in the name of 'stakeholding'.[32]

In Frank Field's version of stakeholding, as expressed in *Stakeholder Welfare*, there is little that any Conservative could take exception to.[33] This right-wing version of stakeholder theory draws heavily on both new right and communitarian arguments about family and community values. Field begins by outlining the seven principles which underpin his perspective:

* Welfare influences behaviour by the simple device of bestowing rewards (benefits) and allotting punishments (loss of benefits) . . . The nature of our character depends in part on the values which welfare fosters.
* Welfare should aim to maximise self-improvement without which all is lost. Work, effort, savings and honesty must all be rewarded rather than, as so often at present, being penalised by welfare's provisions.
* Welfare has to reflect the pivotal role which self-interest plays within our motivations. . .
* Welfare has to work with the changing labour market, giving people incentives and support to maximise their opportunities and thereby their rewards from work.
* Welfare should openly reward good behaviour and it should be used to enhance those roles which the country values. Those individuals who wish to buck the system and oppose the verities of civilised life should not be encouraged.
* Welfare should be given a central role in guaranteeing citizenship in an age of stake-holder democracy.
* The aim of welfare's reconstruction therefore is to hold fast to inclusiveness which was the central objective of post-war reforms, offering new institutions popularly owned and controlled by the membership, which will win the enthusiasm of the majority.'[34]

The first five statements demonstrate Field's complete acceptance of the underlying premise of the underclass/welfare dependency thesis that welfare undermines the character and morals of its recipients. Field is clearly in no doubt that there is an 'underclass' in Britain and that 'welfare continues to play a part in recruiting to and solidifying the underclass'[35], particularly through the provision of means-tested benefits. His alternative to the current welfare system is one which is based on a mixture of private and public funding. Households would 'own' a portfolio of private benefits through the ownership of individual pension funds and individually allocated insurance contributions and benefits; income support would

become work to welfare programmes (aimed particularly at the reintroduction of single parent mothers to the labour market as well as at the
unemployed). Underlying his argument is a central belief, peculiar for a
self-proclaimed Christian, that individuals are not motivated by altruistic
sentiments but by self-interest[36]. His argument that each household in
British society would ultimately own its own assets is coupled with an
explicit acceptance that in the short term there will not be significant
increases in help going to the poorest in our society.

Field also accepts the return of a division between the deserving and the
undeserving poor[37] and, as in the United States, single mothers on welfare
are the group of claimants he is most prepared to target. How a single
mother will actually draw up the life-time work plan that Field envisages,
and work her way off welfare when three-quarters of current employment
is part-time and UK wage rates for new low-paid jobs have fallen to the
level of the early 1980s, it is hard to imagine. Field does offer the proposal
that any person who can not fund their own pension or insurance at any
time should have their entitlement paid for by the State. What he does not
propose is the one important reform that some other European welfare
states use to deal with the 'poverty trap', an income disregard which allows
claimants to stay on benefits and supplement their benefits through work
up to a set level.[38]

Field's influence inside the Labour Party, as one of their most well-
known experts on welfare provision,[39] is to create disarray within the
Labour Party as to what their actual welfare policies should be. The
speeches of Tony Blair and other Labour front-benchers are now littered
with references to welfare 'reform', the word used by the Conservatives as
code for the dismantling of universal protection and earnings-related
benefits. At the 1996 Labour Party Conference, references to the stakeholder economy and society were absent from Blair's speech, and the 'old
left' lost the fight for the restoration of the state pension to 1979 levels,[40]
let alone other benefits. Increasingly Blair's speeches emphasise family
values and our duties and responsibilities to British society, rather than our
stake in the economy and political life. The shift to responsibilities, rather
than rights and responsibilities, is a very short step, one which was always
embedded in the communitarian perspective. At the beginning of the
election year Tony Blair has finally announced his policy, adopted directly
from the US, of 'zero tolerance' of crime, including zero tolerance of
homeless beggars on the street.[41]

Conclusion

In the short period of ten years ideas originally put forward in *The New
Consensus on Family and Welfare* (1987), by Michael Novaks among

others, have become accepted as given fact among politicians of the centre-left on both sides of the Atlantic. In the 1980s these ideas were carried by New Right ideologues and promoted by the American Enterprise Institute and the UK Institute of Economic Affairs. However, by the early 1990s, as the social consequences of economic deregulation, unemployment and rising inequality became obvious, these ideas had became tainted by their source in the think-tanks of the New Right. In the mid-1990s many of the earlier New Right thinkers and fellow-travellers in the UK have jumped ship into 'civic conservatism' (David Willetts), and the search for 'virtue' (David Green) and the 'moral community' (John Gray). Communitarian ideas on 'virtue' and on family and community values have become the common currency of political discourse and of newly formed think-tanks such as the Institute for Civic Society.[42] It is through communitarian writings and arguments that New Right perspectives on the family and community have conquered the US Democrats and the UK Labour Party.

The influence of American politics on the British Labour Party is particularly pernicious given the current debate on the future of the welfare state in the UK. The total expenditure of the United States on social welfare was extraordinarily low throughout the 1980s (1.5% of Gross Domestic Product in the first half of the 1980s), and the US tax and transfer system provided almost no redistributive element, according to the only major authoritative comparison of welfare systems in the OECD countries.[43] Of all welfare systems the United States tolerated the greatest level of child poverty in the mid-1980s. It is this system of employment and welfare that has been taken as a model for Britain by the UK Government and it is therefore no surprise that the level of child poverty in the UK rose from one in ten in 1979 to one in three in 1992.[44]

Although the right of both Conservative and Labour Parties are now locating the rise of poverty in the rise of single parenthood, the rise in poverty has as much to do with the economic conditions young parents face as with changes in family structure. All young adult households in the West, whether single parents or not, faced an increased threat of poverty during the boom years of the 1980s: German Dutch and British poverty rates among household heads aged 20-29 rose by 13.4% and 15.3% from the end of the 1970s to the middle of the 1980s (compare these rates with those of the 30-55 year old heads of households for whom poverty rates rose between 5.1% and 11.8 %).[45] In these years single parent poverty was particularly high in both the United States and Canada. In the UK, however, single parents and others on benefits were protected from the worst excesses of cost-cutting New Right governments through the extensive availability of the non-means tested benefits of free healthcare and social housing. Although UK cash benefits were low by Northern

European standards, the UK was the only country in which poverty rates were significantly lowered once non-cash benefits were taken into account.[46] It is, of course, precisely these non-cash benefits that have been targeted by the Conservatives in their last years of office, in the almost certain hope that the Labour Party will not reverse their cuts in social housing provision or make full restitution to the under-funded National Health Service.

Cutting benefits to mothers and children in the name of 'family values' is only possible if public support for mothers struggling to bring up children on very little money (either from benefits or wages) is undermined through a constant barrage of argument that it is these mothers who are actually promoting the disintegration of the family and community. In the West we are all living through an accelerated decomposition of the 'modern family'. Scandinavian countries now have nearly a majority of children born outside of formal marriage, the UK and France have 30%, Germany, Ireland and Portugal all have 16%. Everywhere across the European Union marriage rates have fallen since 1960. Although the UK still has a relatively higher marriage rate, it also has the highest divorce rate.[47] The United Kingdom's pattern is therefore similar to that of the US. Indeed in the US in 1993 over half of all women aged between 15 and 44 were not married. As the number of married couple with children households has declined, the proportion of single parent household families has risen to nearly a quarter of all households with dependent children in both the US and UK.[48]

Almost certainly the fall in marriage rates and rise of single parenthood is not just associated with changes in young peoples' adopted lifestyles. Much of the change has also been thrust upon them by the fall in real wages in the US for those who did not complete high school and for those who only completed high school,[49] and a rise in unemployment and in the numbers on low part-time wage rates in the UK. This has not just changed the options for marriage but also for successfully leaving home. In the United States the percentage of young people living at home at age 24 has steadily increased to 54%, and to 30% at age 29, which are similar levels to the 1950s. In the UK the government Housing Survey discovered a 6% similar rise in the proportion of young men aged up to 24 years living at home between the years 1990-3/4, the first rise for generations.[50] Those young people who cannot continue to live 'at home' (i.e. in their parent's home) swell the increasing numbers of homeless young people in cities in both the UK and the US. These young men and young women also join the list of those to blame for disintegrating communities.

The centre-left in the UK, like the Right, have sought their solution to problems of welfare need and crises of social order in the politics of the United States of America rather than in Europe, and this has led to a politics of 'blame', particularly of blaming single parent mothers on welfare for crises of both family and community.[51] Etzioni's argument that the responsibility to help those in need lies first with themselves and then with their family and their community is a dangerous one. The fairest element of the 'social assistance' welfare state of the UK is the general principle of individual or couple claiming. Young people living in a household in the UK do have rights to income support once they are 18, albeit at a lower level than adult claimants over the age of 25 years; a lone mother can have a man staying overnight without Social Security officials seeking to prove that he is keeping her and her children and so removing benefit. Only in the case of families is the right to assistance assessed across adults, and many feminists have pointed out how detrimental to the economic welfare of women and young children this can be. Etzioni's vision of welfare could ultimately lead to the implementation of a welfare regime like the UK 1930s Household Means Test, a family means test.

The Responsive Communitarian Platform has had more impact on both Democrat and Labour policies than the many radical community initiatives in the United States and the United Kingdom led by local activists seeking to counter the devastating effects of the social policies of the past two decades.[52] Accounts of the rise of poverty and inequality in the United States during the past 20 years, of the rotting social infrastructure as state citizens vote to withdraw taxation support from higher education and welfare, of the rise of middle class ghettos defended by private security, have never been central to Etzioni's version of communitarianism. Instead, the core of the Responsive Communitarian Platform appeal was to an anti-rights front. It sought to justify the 'new settlement' in welfare through the principle of 'no new rights' and stands back from engagement when the rights of illegal immigrants and programmes of affirmative action are being cut down. Proposition 209, which repealed the civil rights legislation of California, including its affirmative action programmes, was not instituted by Communitarians but their argument of 'no rights without responsibilities' certainly has helped to create disarray among Democratic opposition to the repeal.[53]

In the run-up to the 1997 General Election in the UK Blair's speeches increasingly shift to the moral high ground rather than the welfare low ground. Recent proposals by Gordon Brown, Shadow Labour Chancellor of the Exchequer, have included the proposal to means-test universal child benefit for young people aged 16-18 in order to target the less well-off. Noises about the means-testing of the inadequate old age pension are no longer accompanied by promises to divert that money towards poor pensioners. Beyond the US and UK the influence of 'underclass' and 'welfare cheats' arguments have been more muted, but debates on the problem of dependency and the 'unaffordability' of real welfare states have spread with the transmission of these ideas through organisations like the OECD and the World Bank.[54] As the British Labour Party is now the largest social democrat party sitting in the European Parliament, it is in a position to introduce this new perspective, to the right of the European social exclusion perspectives on welfare, into the European debate. There is thus a danger that Britain's low standards of welfare provision could become a standard for other European countries, just as the US minimalist provision has become a standard for the UK. For European social democracy this would be a tragedy.

NOTES

1. The ageing population argument is actually less true of the US and the UK than of most other Western European economies.
2. A consequence of this success has been that cuts in welfare assistance for the unemployed and single mothers have been passed on to the elderly and those with disabilities. In the UK it has been possible to reduce entitlements to old age pensions and to disability pensions because the distinction between social assistance and social welfare is much weaker in the UK welfare system than in the US.
3. K. Auletta, *The Underclass* (Random House, 1982); Charles Murray, *Losing Ground. American Social Policy 1950–1980* (Basic Books, 1984).
4. W. J. Wilson, *The Truly Disadvantaged: The Inner City, the Underclass and Public Policy* (University of Chicago Press, 1987).
5. By the Institute of Economic Affairs in London and *The Sunday Times*, leading to seminars and discussion across a wide range of academic institutes. See Charles Murray, *The Emerging British Underclass*, Choice in Welfare Series No. 2 (London, IEA, 1990) and Murray, *Underclass: The Crisis Deepens*, Choice in Welfare Series No. 20 (London, IEA, 1994). Both have commentaries by other social policy thinkers.
6. Michael Novaks co-ordinated the academic group who wrote *The New Consensus on Family and Welfare: A Community of Self-Reliance*, 1987, published by the American Enterprise Institute for Public Policy Research, Washington D.C. This pamphlet largely consolidated the particular targets for the right's assault on welfare in the name of 'a community of self-reliance'.
7. Mimi Abramovitz., *Under Attack, Fighting Back. Women and Welfare in the United States* (New York, Cornerstone Books/Monthly Review Press, 1996) provides the best introduction to the assault on welfare for women and children in the US.
8. Robert Bellah et al, *The Habits of the Heart* (Berkeley, University of California Press, 1985) and *The Good Society*, 1988; Amitai Etzioni, *The Moral Dimension: Towards a New Economics*, 1988 published by Free Press, NY and *The Spirit of Community, 1993*, published by Free Press, New York and in the UK part published in Britain as the pamphlet *The Parenting Deficit*, through the centre-left think tank DEMOS.
9. Both Keynes and Harold Macmillan also claimed the old welfare settlement as a 'middle way' between Communism and Capitalism in the 1930s. Macmillan's 1938 book was called *The Middle Way* whilst Keynes put forward the argument in the final chapter of his *General Theory*. Since the fall of Communism in the USSR the 'middle way' has taken a giant step to the right on ground already prepared by the New Right.
10. Etzioni, *The Moral Community* pp. 8-9.
11. Etzioni, *The Spirit of Community: The Reinvention of American Society* (New York, Touchstone, 1993), p. 5. This book is still considered a basic text of political communitarianism although since then Etzioni has followed it with two edited texts, Etzioni (ed.), *New Communitarian Thinking: Persons, Virtues, Institutions and Communities*

(Charlottesville, University of Virginia Press, 1995), and Etzioni (ed.), *Rights and the Common Good* (New York, St. Martin's Press, 1995).

12. *The Spirit of Community*, p. 61.

13. *Ibid.*, pp. 83-5.

14. Amongst the earliest and most pertinent critiques of Communitarianism were some women philosophers who thought it wise to be cautious when male politicians, sociologists and economists were making claims about family, community, self and virtue. Besides Amy Guttman, Marilyn Friedmann was among one of the first to point out that theories of a gendered self, such as those developed in the work of Chodorow and Gilligan, do not appear in Communitarian writings, which nowhere acknowledges that the narrative self can be constructed differently for women and for men. See M. Friedmann, 'Feminism and Modern Friendship: Dislocating the Community', in S. Avinieri and A. de Shalit, *Communitarianism and Individualism* (Oxford, 1992), pp.121-136. Friedmann also pointed out that communitarian emphasis on the moral claims of community over its members ignores the question of how legitimate those claims are. Quoting MacIntyre's argument that we all inherit 'debts, inheritances, rightful expectations and obligations' from our family, community and nation, Friedmann argues that many communities exclude and oppress outsiders while also oppressing the women within. Communitarian emphasis on family, neighbourhood and nation raises the issue of how far these structures have been oppressive of women in the past and in the present. As Friedmann argues, any mature person can chose to shape their community and join new communities rather than accept the ones they were born to. Both modern friendship and the possibility of adopting many roles in the urban environment are liberating for men and women fostering 'not the constitution of subjects but their reconstitution'. See also A. Guttman in the same collection, p. 121 *ff.*

15. 'A year of national service would remove many unemployed youths from the streets; it would provide them, often for the first time, with legitimate and meaningful work; and it would help protect them from being enticed into crime.' *The Spirit of Community*, p. 113

16. *Ibid.*, p. 114.

17. *Ibid.*, pp. 144-147.

18. It is important not to underestimate the intent of Communitarian philosophy to undermine radical liberalism. Rawls's argument in *The Theory of Justice*, 1971, was a radical restatement of liberalism designed to promote welfareism and the extension of civil rights *within* the United States. Rawls presented a theory in which society is created through a contract establishing the 'principles of justice for the basic structure of society'. Rawls's assumption of an 'original position of equality' is purely hypothetical (corresponding to the state of nature of Hobbes' contract theory) but allows him to consider what type of society would be constructed if the members of that society were all equal and also if they all did not know their own place in society when they made the construction ('the veil of ignorance'). Blair finds it necessary, as someone whose socialism was initially inspired by Kant's philosophy among other influences, to distance himself from John Rawls Kantian conception of social justice. 'The Left was captivated by the elegance and power of Professor John Rawls's *Theory of Justice* . . . His manifesto for an egalitarian society is a brilliant exposition of the argument that an equal society is in the interests of anyone who does not know which position in that society they would occupy. But it is derived from a highly individualistic view of the world'. Tony Blair, *New Britain, My Vision for a Young Country* (London, Fourth Estate Limited, 1996), p. 299.

19. Mary Ann Glendon is the author of *Rights Talk: The Impoverishment of Political Discourse* (New York, Free Press, 1991).

20. The output of Institute for Public Policy Research (IPPR) had been intended to rival the work of the right-wing think tank IEA and to produce an alternative perspective on welfare. In the years immediately after 1992 IPPR published a series of papers covering taxes and benefits, social insurance, racial equality, work benefits in a flexible labour

market, disabled people and social justice, housing, pensions, and work and welfare. Some of these pamphlets looked across to Europe rather than to the United States and references to welfare systems of the United States did not seek to emulate their features, and yet other pamphlets published by the IPPR included a restatement of the commitment to family and community by Michael Young, not dissimilar to the pamphlet produced by Norman Dennis and George Erdos for the Institute of Economic Affairs.

21. Blair , 1993, in A. Coote (ed.), *Families, Children and Crime*, p. 89, IPPR.
22. Blair, *New Britain*, pp. 114, 142.
23. *The Guardian*, October 15 1996, p. 2.
24. *Ibid.*, p. 2, Jack Straw has picked up every American idea on the social control of poor communities in a bid to outflank the law and order policies of the Conservative's reactionary Home Secretary, Michael Howard. Whilst the Audit Commission has suggested a radical overhaul of juvenile justice, through the introduction of the type of Children's Hearings introduced in Scotland thirty years ago, Jack Straw has been campaigning for curfews on housing estates. It is bizarre that the major opposition to Government policies on juvenile justice should be launched by its own civil service rather than by the Labour Party.
25. Etzioni accepted this in an article called 'New Values' in the *New Statesman and Society*, 12 May 1995 (London), when he admitted that there was no communitarian economic agenda. 'The drive was, and is, to provide a democratic inclusive alternative to the Christian right that provides authoritarian answers to issues raised by the decay of the moral infrastructure and the decline of shared values ... Our agenda so far has been cultural so it may be that the British will add a socio-economic agenda to ours'.
26. In the US more radical communitarian visions are available in the community activists movement and among some philosophical writings such as Walzer's, but there is a lack of any Conservative one-nation tradition as in the UK.
27. Blair, *New Britain*. Preface.
28. Speech to the Fabian Society, July 1995, republished in *New Britain*. The above quotation demonstrates why communitarian ideas been so acceptable to the Centre and to the Left. One of the central ideas, that of the 'narrative self' is derived from, and close to, all Marxist and social democratic theories of the development of self and the 'inter-dependent self'. There is a world of difference, however, between a Marxist theory of personality which presents an understanding of the way we are all formed through class, race and gender placement, within a particular household form in a particular historical conjuncture and the communitarian argument that the community or 'tribe' one lives in is the source of tradition, belief and morality.
29. *The Observer*,13 October 1996. Will Hutton is the editor of *The Observer* and wrote this article jointly with John Kay. John Kay is an economist who has written extensively on corporate governance both for the IPPR and elsewhere. See John Kay and Aubrey Silberston, 'Corporate Governance', *National Institute Economic Review*, August 1995.
30. Hutton and Kay's argument is very similar to Ralph Nader's argument in the US, that Business Corporations are the real recipients of tax breaks and welfare handouts.
31. See W. Hutton, *The State We're In* (London, 1995) and TUC, *Your Stake at Work, TUC Proposals for a Stakeholding Economy* (TUC Congress, 1996).
32. TUC, *Your Stake at Work*. Many of the proposals derive from previous work by Will Hutton and John Kay, and also John Hill's work for the Joseph Rowntree Foundation on wealth and income inequality in *Inquiry into Income and Wealth*, Vols. 1 and 2 (York, Joseph Rowntree Foundation, 1995).
33. The pamphlet is a short restatement of Field's perspective on the future of welfare presented in *Making Welfare Work* and *How to Pay for the Future* available from the Institute of Economic Affairs (2, Lord North Street, London, SW1P 3LB). The fact that Field has chosen to publish through a Conservative think-tank is notable. *Stakeholder Welfare*, Choices in Welfare Series No. 32. (London, IEA, 1996). Field's text is accom-

panied by commentaries by Alan Deacon, Peter Alcock, David Green and Melanie Phillips. Deacon's commentary focuses on the importance that character and morality play in Field's theory of welfare, whilst Alcock seeks to shift the discussion back to the purpose of welfare in relation to social solidarity.

34. F. Field, *Stakeholder Welfare*, Choices in Welfare Series No. 32.

35. 'The underclass is as difficult to define as it is easy to recognise when confronted with it. The major cause is the collapse of full employment and particularly the radically transformed employment position of those with brawn and little developed intelligence. F. Field, *Ibid.*, p. 17.

36. *Ibid.*, p. 19. 'No welfare system can function effectively if it is not based on a realistic view of human nature. Self-interest, not altruism, is mankind's main driving force ... Labour's failure to hold a balanced view of human nature presented a picture to the electorate of a party completely out of touch with reality'. See also the essay 'Welfare and Character' by Alan Deacon in the same pamphlet, pp. 61-70.

37. As Labour M.P.s move to the right in their discussions of welfare so the entire debate has jumped to the right. In the most recent radio discussion in the UK on welfare 'Liberal Britain' Radio 4, 10 January 1997, Digby Anderson openly argued that it was necessary to reduce all benefits and to make distinctions between the 'deserving and undeserving'. On the same programme David Marsland and others discussed the requirement of the family to look after their kin and Frank Field's views on Stakeholder Welfare, which he also presented, were much closer to Anderson and Marsland than to the local welfare activists and to Bea Campbell.

38. This is one of the proposals put forward by Michael Young and A. H. Halsey in their IPPR monograph, *Family and Community Socialism*, 1995, which argues for a re-distribution of social resources towards children, as a real expression of family values, while at the same time regretting the decline of the family.

39. This is a role he has played before. In 1976 he was the first Labour welfare expert to speak up for the sale of council houses, the Conservatives' first and most successful privatisation of public assets.

40. They also lost the argument that the State Earnings Related Pension (SERPS) should remain the cornerstone of an additional second pension. This leaves the way clear for Field's argument that everyone should be personally responsible for their own additional pension (the basic pension is only £61 a week) through private personal pension schemes. *Which*, the UK Consumer Magazine, has discovered that most pension providers charge as much, or more, than the actual tax relief on pension contributions to run these pensions and that the majority of people would have been better off saving in other ways. With high charges and falling annuity rates, private pensions have become one of the worst buys, except for those tax-payers who receive higher rate tax relief.

41. *The Guardian*, 7 January 1997.

42. 'New Money, Old Values', *The Guardian*, 8 January 1997. One $35 million donation founded this institute in Boston in 1996.

43. T. Smeeding and L. Rainwater, 'Cross-National Trends in Income Poverty and Dependency: The evidence for young adults in the eighties'. Working Paper 67, (Luxembourg Income Study, Luxembourg).

44. V. Kumar in *Poverty and Inequality in the UK. The effects on Children 1993*, (London, National Children's Bureau), produced the first evidence of the trebling of levels of poverty among children. Three years later Department of Social Security officials have also produced an estimate that 30% of children born in the UK are born into poverty. The latest study of child poverty in the UK has now revealed that 2 million children are undernourished or malnourished; this is a direct consequence of the low levels of benefits and of the abolition of nutrition standards for school-meals in 1980. *The Observer*, 12 January 1997.

45. V. Kumar, *ibid*.

46. The Luxembourg Income Study has found that the only significant change in the ranking of national poverty rates occurs in the United Kingdom, where non-cash income has the largest (absolute and proportional) impact on poverty. The ranking of all other countries stays much the same whether non-cash income is included or not.

47. V. George and P. Taylor-Gooby (eds.), *European Welfare Policy* (London, Macmillan, 1996), see Table 9.3 Family Trends in Europe, quoting Hantrais.

48. National Research Council, *Losing Generations. Adolescents in High-Risk Settings, 1990* (Washington D.C., National Academy Press), p. 44.

49. National Research Council, *Losing Generations. Adolescents in High-Risk Settings, 1990* (Washington D.C. , National Academy Press), p. 27.

50. H. Green et al, *Housing in England 1994/5*, (HMSO, London, 1996), p. 107.

51. T. Eardley, J. Bradshaw, J. Ditch, I. Gough and Peter Whiteford. *Social Assistance in OECD Countries: Synthesis Report.* August 1996 (London, Department of Social Security, HMSO). The authors report that 'The English-speaking world with extensive social assistance do report a range of issues in common. These include the costs of assistance, work disincentives, fraud and the issue of targetting ... These patterns are to be expected given the high cost of programmes and the large welfare clienteles in this group of countries. However, the question of behavioural incentives in welfare – to discourage marriage or remarriage and to encourage teenage pregnancy and welfare dependency more generally – appears to be a defining feature mainly of the stigmatising and divided public assistance system of the USA. The concept of assistance as creating a new 'underclass' is relatively absent in Australia and New Zealand, and while present in debates in Britain and Canada it has not achieved ideological dominance.' p. 171.

52. There has, however, been a range of Comprehensive Community Initiatives, led by local activists outside of organised party politics in the United States. Local activism has also been important in the UK for the establishment of credit facilities and bartered-work schemes in local areas abandoned by the private institutions Field believes in.

53. *The Guardian*, 6 November 1996, for a description of the passing of this amendment, whose very title confused voters, as an addendum to the voting schedule for President. Dole came out in its support whilst Clinton did not.

54. T. Eardley, J.Bradshaw et al, *Social Assistance in OECD Countries , op. cit.*, p. 103.

THE DECLINE OF SPANISH SOCIAL DEMOCRACY 1982-1996

Vicente Navarro

At the beginning of the 1980s when social-democratic parties in northern and central Europe were considered to be in decline, the southern European Socialist parties flourished politically. One of them, the Spanish Socialist Party (Partido Socialisto Obrero Español, or PSOE), was re-elected four times (three of them by majorities), a record for political longevity among European Socialist parties. Only the Swedish social-democratic party had lasted more than 14 years in government. As a result of its electoral success, the influence of the PSOE among the parties belonging to the Socialist International grew substantially. The centre of gravity of social-democracy in Europe shifted, then, from the north to the south during the 1980s, with the electoral victories of social-democratic parties in Spain, France, Greece, Italy (in coalition with Christian-Democratic and other parties), and Portugal. Among these parties, the one with the largest electoral support was the PSOE, whose average electoral support during the 1980s was an impressive 44%.[1]

The PSOE's electoral success was attributed to its breaking with traditional social-democratic policies such as state intervention in economic development and a preferential relationship with the trade unions. This became a new strategic point of reference for other social-democratic parties in Europe. Felipe Gonzalez was asked to preside over a committee of the Socialist International to revise the principles of socialism for the 21st century. The PSOE deliberately and explicitly de-emphasized state intervention to resolve some of the serious economic problems inherited from the Franco regime, and its relationship with the trade unions became extremely adversarial with four major general strikes, an unprecedented number for a Socialist government. According to Carlos Solchaga, Minister of Economy in the second Socialist government, 'the trade unions should not have any privileged relationship with the Socialist government. They should be treated like any other interest group, such as the College of Physicians, for example.'[2] And Ludolfo Paramio, director of the PSOE's foremost intellectual institution, the Pablo Iglesias Institute, and member of the party's Executive Committee, wrote that 'a socialist party should downgrade the trade unions to the same level as any other interest group, such as professional colleges or philatelical societies.'[3] The Deputy Prime Minister in the Socialist government, Narcis Serra, declared that the social constituency of the government and of the PSOE was the middle class, that the working class was a disappearing class, and that the U.S. Democratic Party was a middle-class party worth emulating.[4] While these views were resented by the grassroots of the PSOE, they were widely accepted among large sectors of the leadership.

The Spanish Socialist government also became a major point of reference in another debate, the political transition from dictatorship to democracy that was occurring in eastern and southern Europe and in many countries of Latin America. According to Bresser, Maravall and Przeworski, the most successful transitions have occurred in those countries, like Spain, where the government has liberalized the economy, diminished the role of a strong and too embracing state, and facilitated the full growth of constrained market forces while developing a safety net to take care of those social groups most affected by these economic changes.[5] According to Jose Maria Maravall (a leading theorist of the PSOE), the Socialist government in Spain inherited an excessively interventionist state that was constraining the economic growth and competitiveness of the Spanish economy. The government therefore had to modernize the Spanish economy by diminishing the role of the state, allowing market forces to develop more fully. This modernization (and the human costs of its accompanying unemployment and dislocation) was tolerated by the Spanish electorate because of the growth in the social network that took care of marginalized sectors.[6] Thus, a foremost characteristic of the Spanish Socialist government, until recently quite atypical for social-democratic practices, has been its reduction of the economic role of the state. Although many social-democratic governments have incorporated into their policies a whole array of monetarist and liberal policies, none has done so to the same degree as the PSOE administration. As Wolfgang Merkel concludes in his detailed survey of social-democratic governments, state intervention in the economy fell under the PSOE government to a level unknown in other European social democracies.[7]

The purpose of this essay is to explain the continuities and changes that occurred during the 1982-1996 period when the PSOE was in government, and to analyze why the successive Socialist governments chose certain public policies over others. The article also analyzes the reasons for the subsequent electoral decline of the PSOE that culminated in their defeat in 1996. Against what prominent interpretations of social democracy like that of Przeworski and Sprague[8] would lead us to expect, we show that the primary reason for the decline of the PSOE government in particular and of Spanish social-democracy's fortunes in general was the adoption of public policies that conflicted with the interests of large constituencies of their electorate, including both the working and middle classes.

The Historical and Political Context

One of the most unexpected developments in recent Spanish history was the fast electoral growth of the PSOE after the establishment of democracy. The PSOE had played only a minor role during the anti-fascist struggle led primarily by the Communist Party (PCE). Mistakes made by leaders of the PCE during the democratic transition (in which the PCE had a moderating effect, lowering the level of popular expectations), together with the historical memory of the Spanish population (the PSOE had traditionally been the party of the working class) explains this sudden upsurge in the PSOE's popularity. By 1977, in the first election following Franco's death, the PSOE already received 29.3% of the electoral vote while the PCE received only 9.4%.[9] In 1979 the PSOE obtained 30.5% of the electoral vote, the PCE 10.8%.

The overwhelming victory of the PSOE in 1982, when it received the support of 48.4% of the electorate, had several causes. One was the collapse of the Right due to the enormous tensions among the various factions of reformists known in Spain as the 'post-Francoist' forces. They had coalesced around Adolfo Suarez, the founder of the right-wing UCD, wherein Christian Democrats, liberals, and fascist sympathizers established an alliance with the primary purpose of stopping the Left, in particular the PCE. It was principally the disagreements within the UCD around the divorce law, together with the delegation of authority to the Catalan and Basque regions, which led to the coalition's collapse. It obtained less than 3% of the overall vote. In addition to receiving the votes of the disenchanted supporters of the UCD, the PSOE benefited from the participation in 1982 of first-time, young voters (overall participation jumped from 67% in 1979 to 80% in 1982) who voted massively for change, which they identified with the PSOE.[10]

The most important reason for the PSOE's success, however, lay in its having become the electoral beneficiary of working-class resentment against attempts to clamp down on labour militancy that had been so important to effecting the transition to democracy in the first place. Spanish labour in the mid-1970s was the most militant in Europe, with the largest number of strikes and mobilizations on the continent, forcing the transition from dictatorship to democracy. From 1975 to 1977, 7,514,000 workers, representing 88% of all salaried workers, participated in the strikes.[11] The employers were clearly on the defensive, fearful of the underlying challenge to the social order. Wages increased at a much higher rate than productivity during the 1975-1977 period, with declines in the rate of profit, in investments, and in the rate of job production.[12] Labour militancy also resulted in a series of legislative interventions granting the right to strike in 1975, the prohibition of dismissals without cause and indemnization (granting 60 days pay for every year of service) in 1976, and the right to establish unions and political parties, including the Communist Party (PCE), in 1977.

After the transition to democracy, increasing labour costs combined with a reduction in productivity and investments, a high inflation rate, and the beginning of job destruction pushed the new political establishment in search of a new social accord which could respond to these deteriorating conditions. Accordingly, the *Moncloa Pacts* (1977) were aimed at lowering labour costs while increasing job-creation in the private and public sectors. Although labour stood by its commitments to wage restraint, the employers and the right-wing government did not. In addition, a whole series of laws were passed to permit new types of contracts (for new entries into the labour market). These laws allowed short-term contracts – referred to by the unions as 'contratos basura' ('shit contracts') – which offered very little social protection and a salary level that was on average 40% that of permanent jobs. They also made the process of dismissal rather easier by reducing compensation from 60 to 45 days of pay per year of service for employees at enterprises of 25 or more workers and half that compensation for employees at enterprises of less than 25 workers (83% of all workplaces in the private sector). Also, workers' dismissals could be resolved on a case-by-case basis by new government appointed agencies rather than through the court system, the former being far more amenable to grant cause for dismissal than the courts. Despite workers' rebellions and mobilizations against these laws (according to official figures, 2.5 million workers participated in these strikes), they were finally codified in the *Estatuto del Trabajador* and affirmed by the Spanish Parliament in 1980.[13] As a consequence, unemployment tripled from 5.32% in 1977 to 16.45% in 1982, while wages and salaries declined. It is this labour situation that especially explains the enormous support among the working class for the PSOE, whose programme called for a massive job creation with expansionist policies that included increases in public and social expenditure to expand the welfare state: 85% of the working-class vote went to the PSOE in 1982. The PSOE discourse – a discourse of class struggle – was more radical than that of the PCE which, besides being involved in a fratricidal struggle among its various factions, was the strongest voice in support of the *Moncloa Pacts*, while the PSOE kept a certain distance.[14] The radical discourse of the PSOE and very much in particular of the Secretary General of the PSOE, Felipe Gonzalez, contrasted with the moderate tone adopted by Santiago Carrillo, the Secretary General of the Communist Party. As a consequence of these factors, the Communist Party received only 4.1% of the overall vote, and only 12% of the working-class vote.

At the time the PSOE won the 1982 elections, the Spanish situation was characterized by the following features:

1) An economy in great disarray, with a negative rate of growth (-1.2% per year), a high unemployment rate (16.2%, more than double the OECD-Europe average[15]), and a high rate of inflation (14% per annum, above the OECD-Europe average).

2) An underdeveloped state with a public employment rate (4% of total employment) much lower than the OECD-Europe average (9%), and a public expenditure rate much lower than the OECD-Europe average, with only half of the employed population paying taxes. The state, besides being underdeveloped, was highly centralized due to its Jacobin inheritance from the Bonapartist state (when Napoleon ruled Spain) strengthened by 40 years of fascism that borrowed heavily from the Italian fascist state. For example, the Instituto Nacional de Industria (the National Institute of Industry, or INI), established in 1945, was modelled after its Italian equivalent whose role was to direct the industrial development of the country.[16]

3) A state that was not only underdeveloped and centralized but highly unpopular because of its repressive nature and its limited social sensibility. In 1975, social public expenditures represented only 9.9% of the GDP, much lower than the European Community's average of 24%. Another element (left unchanged by all democratic governments, including the social-democratic ones) was the composition of the civil service. All civil servants – from judges to university professors – had to sign an oath of loyalty to the fascist regime during the 1950s, 1960s, and 1970s, representing a core of resistance to change in the public administration.

4) An underdeveloped economic infrastructure that was ill-prepared to integrate into the developing European economy, given the state's heavy subsidization of unprofitable sectors. These subsidies were justified in the name of avoiding unemployment but were not used to promote restructuring within economic sectors.

5) The most regressive taxation system, with the largest amount of fiscal fraud, in Western Europe.

When the Socialists won the elections in 1982, it was widely expected that they would make the state a key element in economic transformation, following a radical expansionist programme similar to that of the Mitterrand government in France elected in 1981. The Spanish Socialist government, however, chose not to follow this strategy, quickly adopting the conventional wisdom that Mitterrand's U-turn was inevitable.[17] The PSOE government also embraced the conventional view that the defeat of the British Labour Party in 1979 and 1983 was due to its dependency on the trade unions. These interpretations reflected the thinking of the economic team within the Socialist government. Most of these professionals were functionaries of the Ministries of Economy and Public Finance who have traditionally been very closely connected with the Bank of Spain.[18] They had been chosen on the basis of their proximity to the financial sector in order to reassure that sector and promote its further development. Accordingly, most members of the first Socialist government in Spain (and in particular the Cabinet members responsible for economic policy making) did not have a close relationship with the trade unions. The distancing from the unions and the working class – a distance that bordered on contempt in many cases[19] – may in part be explained by the petit bourgeois origins of much of the leadership of the Spanish Socialist government, educated for the most part in some of Spain's most exclusive private schools within a very class-conscious society. Sixty-eight percent of the members of the Socialist government went to private schools and the majority of them send their children to private schools. These percentages are even higher among the members of the economic teams of the successive Socialist governments.[20]

But beyond these kind of factors, it must be said that an additional determinant of the PSOE's trajectory was the unpopularity of the state, for the reasons mentioned above. Making the state sector the motor of the economic modernization would have required a significant transformation of most of the central administration. This would have resulted in major confrontation with the corporatist interests embedded in the bureaucracy – a group that the Socialist government had no intention of antagonizing despite their well-deserved reputation as rigid, user un-friendly, and inefficient. No major reforms were introduced to the central public administration, a contributing factor to this having been the large percentage (38%) of members of the Spanish Parliament who were functionaries themselves. The major changes in the apparatuses of the state took place in the autonomous regions and in the municipalities.[21]

These factors help to explain why the PSOE government did not entertain the possibility of an alternative strategy in which the state would play a key role in the nation's modernization by means of a public industrial sector which could stimulate overall industrial development and generate employment. Instead, the government forced the state into a subsidiary and minimal role.

The Policies of the PSOE Governments, 1982-1996

Privatization
The Socialist governments considered the country's experience with public

enterprise to be particularly negative. Most public enterprises were part of the INI, which had accumulated an enormous deficit during the fascist period and until the transition to democracy. Its primary function was to absorb the sectors in crisis, such as steel and shipbuilding, in order to avoid further unemployment. Its production structures were obsolete, unproductive, and over-staffed. It was not entirely surprising, therefore, that the Socialist governments did not favour any further nationalizations or an expansion of the public sector. But their success in reducing the size of the public sector by privatizing large public industries even extended to profitable public enterprises such as SKF Española, Enturba and others. The only exception was the nationalization of the financial group Rumasa whose imminent collapse would have had a disastrous impact on the Spanish economy. Once made profitable, however, Rumasa was privatized again. Otherwise, the number of employees in public enterprises declined, from 4.9% of all employment in 1981 to 4.6% in 1985, due to the reduction of the number of public enterprises and of employees per enterprise.

Complementing these privatizations, the Spanish Socialist governments considerably reduced subsidies to the public enterprises, from 3.7% of GNP in 1984 to a low of 0.7% in 1987, with the explicit objective of introducing entrepreneurship and systems of evaluation associated with the private sector to public enterprises, thereby reducing the role of the state to a bare minimum. The primary concern of these economic policies was to increase the competitiveness of the public sector, not to create jobs. This explains why several authors have defined these policies as Thatcherite.[22] This characterization, however, is inaccurate. The PSOE government, while carrying out policies that increased unemployment, expanded public funds for unemployment insurance from 2.59% of GNP in 1982 to 2.85% in 1985, whereas the Thatcher government reduced such payments from 1.7% of GNP in 1980 to 1.0% in 1990 (almost halving them in ten years). Also, the privatization of public enterprises in Spain was accompanied by provisions for gradual dismissal and generous compensation, and with credit and fiscal policies aimed at stimulating private investments in affected areas to create employment.[23]

These policies, however, were insufficient to reverse the growing unemployment. A major contributor to job destruction was the Reconversion and Reindustrialization Act of 1983, which besides reducing public employment stimulated the competitiveness of the private sector by reducing private employment as well. Spanish enterprises became more lean and mean; consequently, 70,500 jobs were eliminated in steel, coal, shipbuilding, and textiles (the sectors experiencing the greatest crisis) during the 1982-1985 period. These government policies were complemented by others which facilitated early retirement (both in the public and in the private sectors) and increased unemployment compensation funds.

Such policies, as indicated above, were aimed at softening the harshness of reforms while stimulating private industry, via fiscal policies and subsidies, to invest and create jobs in the zones considered particularly affected by these measures (zonas de urgente industrializacion, or ZUR), such as Galicia, Asturias, and Basque Country. Yet these measures did not prove particularly successful, as employment in these areas continued to decline through the mid-1980s.

The privatization policies, carried out with a considerable harshness, contrasted with the Socialist government's softness towards powerful groups entrenched in the public administration and in the private sector. For example, the Socialist governments never confronted the financial and energy monopolies responsible for some of the highest prices for energy and communications and the highest returns on capital in Europe.[24] The emphasis put on adding flexibility to the labour market, which continued during the whole period until 1996 (to a point where Spain has reached the highest rates of temporary employment and unemployment in the European Union), has not been accompanied by the curtailment of the privileges of well-entrenched economic groups.[25] During the UCD government a close relationship could be seen between contributions by energy companies to the UCD and the increases in electricity bills, regulated by the government.[26] One factor contributing to the Socialist government's unwillingness to confront banking and energy monopolies was the handsome financial support these groups also provided for PSOE electoral campaigns. Banking and the electrical companies were among the major funders of all the political parties, including the Socialist party (but excluding the Communist Party), during the democratic transition and after. They provided 20,000 million pesetas to these political parties from 1977 to 1986, with most assistance provided to the governing party. Jose Sevilla Segura, a top official in the Ministry of Public Finances during the first Socialist government, admitted that the focus of the government's economic policies had become very similar to the policies of the previous right-wing government. The main emphasis was on forcing flexibility in the labour market and confronting the trade unions, while leaving untouched the rigidities of the large employers, which continued their oligopolistic behaviour, responsible for the high costs of energy, communications, and money.[27] This differential treatment eventually generated considerable resentment from PSOE members and supporters.

Public expenditures policies

While public employment diminished during the first Socialist government, public expenditures grew considerably, from 38.1% of GNP in 1982 to 42.30% in 1985. Of these expenditures, the most rapidly increasing were social transfers, in particular the pensions public funds, which increased from 9.10% of GNP in 1982 to 9.93% in 1985. Health expenditures, however, declined from 4.70% of GNP in 1982 to 4.60% in 1985 (see Table 1). With this exception, the Socialist government followed expansionist public expenditure policies in social transfers and in services.

Table 1: Public Expenditures (% GNP) in Spain (constant currency)

	1980	1982	1985	1986	1988	1990	1992
Public Goods							
Defence	1.99	2.25	1.99	2.28	2.00	1.71	1.56
General Services	3.29	3.58	4.06	3.97	4.10	4.50	4.70
Goods and Services							
Education	3.29	3.01	3.56	3.55	3.80	4.14	4.30
Health Services	4.55	4.70	4.60	4.54	4.50	4.99	5.42
Housing and other	1.16	1.40	1.83	1.81	1.79	1.50	1.60
Social Transfers							
Pensions	8.62	9.10	9.93	9.80	10.0	10.6	10.9
Unemployment Insurance	2.24	2.74	2.85	2.68	2.49	2.65	3.13
Economic Expenses	5.5	8.26	8.28	7.64	7.78	8.30	8.95
Interest on the Debt	0.73	0.97	3.20	4.08	3.70	3.82	4.50
Total Public Exp	33.32	38.10	42.30	42.17	41.93	43.69	46.77
Total Social Exp	21.76	23.04	24.77	24.20	24.36	25.37	27.06

(*Source:* Tabla 9.39 'Clasificacion Funcional del Gasto de Administraciones Publicas. Participacion sobre el P.I.B. (%)' in G. Rodrigo Cabrero, 'Politicas de Rentas' *Capitulo 9 del Informe Sociologico sobre la Situacion Social en Espana,* Fundacion FoESSA, Vol. 2, 1995, p. 1458.)

These expansionist policies, however, were reversed during the second Socialist government, with a reduction of public expenditures including social expenditures. From 1985 to 1988, public expenditures were reduced from 42.30% of GNP to 41.93% and social expenditures from 24.77% of GNP to 24.36%. Decreased social spending meant stagnant expenditures on pensions (with a significant decline in pensions per capita due to the growth of the elderly population, a decline facilitated by the Pensions Reform Act of 1985); a decline in unemployment expenditures; and a continuation of the reduction in health-care public expenditures that had occurred during the previous period (1982-1985). This reduced spending coincided with the expansion of the National Health Service to cover almost the entire population (expanding from 88% to 98% of the population), an outcome of the *Ley General de Sanidad,* approved by the Spanish Parliament in 1986. This expanded coverage with reduced expenditures meant a dramatic lowering of per capita health-care public expenditures, with a deterioration in the quality of services (particularly acute in primary care, the Cinderella of the health services) and in the working conditions of health-care personnel, which generated widely supported strikes among health-care workers in 1988.[28]

The government justified these austerity measures as necessary for the reduction of the public deficit and inflation and to better prepare the country for its entry into the EC in 1986. The decline in public and social expenditures, along with the decline in the disposable income of workers and the continuous growth of unemployment, generated large protests, culminating in the general strike of 1988 organized by the Communist-led Workers Commissions (CCOO) and Socialist-led Union General de Trabajadores (UGT). For one day the whole country came to a halt. It was the first general strike against a Socialist government in Spain, and signalled a definitive break between the union movement and the PSOE. As a result of the enormous popular support for the general strike, Alfonso Guerra, Deputy Prime Minister in the PSOE government, called for a major readjustment in the government's economic and social policies. From 1989 to 1992 (the period of the third Socialist government), public expenditures expanded from 42.77% to 46.77% (of GNP) and social expenditures rose from 24.78% to 27.06%, reaching levels of expenditures comparable with those in most countries of the EC. These increases in expenditures were facilitated by the economic boom that occurred with Spain's integration into the EC in 1986, fuelled by a large increase of foreign investment.

The growth of social expenditures continued into the 1992-1996 period. This was a response to continuous pressure – expressed through mobilizations and strikes – from a population still frustrated with the underdevelopment of the Spanish welfare state. According to a recent poll, 69% of the Spanish population believes that pension payments are far too low, 69% believes that unemployment compensation is insufficient, and 72% believes that the National Health Service is underfunded.[29] The statistics provided by government and voluntary agencies substantiate this popular opinion. Fifty-two percent of widow pensioners and 71% of non-contributing unemployment insurance recipients received pensions below the minimum wage, and the health-care expenditures per capita are among the lowest in the EU.[30]

Tax policies
One indicator of the class nature of fascism was the fiscal policies of the Franco regime, characterized by the most regressive system of taxation in Europe, worse than in Greece and Portugal, and the low level of public revenues. In 1975, the revenues to the state (including Social Security) represented 21% of GNP, much lower than the average (34%) for the countries of OECD-Europe.[31] Most of these revenues were generated by indirect and regressive taxation: sales taxes represented 31% and payroll

taxes 47% of all tax revenues; income tax, of very limited progressivity, represented only 14% of all tax revenues. Fiscal fraud was the highest in Europe. The two main fiscal reforms after 1975, the first carried out by the Suares UCD government and the second by the 1982 PSOE government, changed this picture somewhat. By 1986, tax revenues represented 32.1% of GNP, with income taxes representing 19% of all taxes. Sales and payroll taxes continued to represent the larger proportion of state revenues (73% of all state revenues: 33% sales taxes and 40% payroll taxes). By 1990, tax revenues represented 35% of GNP, with income taxation representing 33% of all tax revenues, a considerable increase in revenues derived from this source (the average for the OECD countries was 45%).[32] The tax system remained highly regressive; Spain still had one of the lowest levels of state revenues in the EC. And tax fraud continued to be the highest in Europe. According to the Internal Revenue Agency of the Ministry of Finances, the average employer declares less income than the average labourer, while the average professional declares the same income as the latter. During the period of austerity under the second Socialist government when significant cuts were made in social expenditures in order to reduce the deficit, the respected Foessa foundation estimated that the revenues lost due to tax fraud amounted to more than half (68%) the public deficit in that period.[33] This situation was recognized by the then Vice-Minister of Finances (Secretario de Estado), J. Borrell.[34] The preparation of the Spanish state for entry into the EC meant sacrifices primarily for the salaried and wage-earning sectors of the population, while for the liberal professions, rentiers, and employers incomes grew considerably, although such growth did not appear in their income tax returns. All this reflected the limited nature of the transformation of the Spanish state: despite improvements such as the considerable growth in the percentage of state revenues derived from income taxes, the patterns of power relations within the state changed little.

Employment policies
In 1982 the PSOE government inherited a very high unemployment rate of 18%, but this further increased during the 1982-1985 period, reaching an impressive 21.1% by the end of the first Socialist government. This increase was the result of a continued destruction of private and public employment, an outcome of the privatization of public enterprises analyzed earlier. The economy was stagnant during this period. It was not until the entry of Spain into the EC that there was any reversal of this job destruction. The subsequent economic boom, facilitated by the economic expansion of the capitalist world at that time, increased job creation at an average rate of 2% per year, one of the highest rates of growth in the OECD. This high rate of job creation, however, did not match the even higher growth in demand for work due to the massive entry of the young

and of women into the labour market in this period. During the second half of the 1980s, women's employment increased by 5% while men's employment declined by 1.1%. Most of the growth in women's jobs occurred in the private sector, in contrast to the experience in most OECD-Europe countries where women's job creation has mainly taken place in the public sector and particularly in the social services, a situation that continues today.[35] In Spain, however, the government did not have a policy of public employment through expansion of the social services sectors, an omission that was particularly surprising given the highest unemployment rate in OECD-Europe and the underdevelopment of the welfare state. Many tasks carried out through the welfare state in other EU countries are, in Spain, still the responsibility of families – that is, women. Community and home social services for the elderly and handicapped are virtually non-existent in Spain, leaving the burden of these functions to wives, daughters, and mothers. As a consequence, stress-related morbidity among women 35-55 years of age is higher than in any other group, male or female.[36]

In the majority of OECD-Europe countries, however, the growth of employment in the social sectors has been and continues to be the main source of job growth in the last 15 years. Rather than expand this type of employment (public employment growth in 1982-1992 was only 1.2% per year), the Spanish Socialist government based all its employment policies on the neoliberal assumption that the high costs of labour and labour rigidities were the primary causes of slow job production. The theory sustained by the Ministers of Economy and Labour was that the price of labour was too high, and that the increase in salaries should be lower than the increase in productivity. This position was a constant in the economic policies of the Spanish Socialist governments, despite the fact that declining real wages and increasing productivity (both higher than in other EU countries) were accompanied by a greater rate of job destruction over the last 20 years than elsewhere in Europe.[37] The other objective of the employment policies of the Socialist governments was an increased flexibility of the labour market, which had been extremely rigid during the fascist regime's paternalistic and corporatist type of labour relations. The *Moncloa Pacts* and subsequent government interventions changed the pattern of labour relations, producing a highly flexible labour market with one of the highest levels of precarious jobs in the EU. At the end of the 1980s, the percentage of precarious jobs (contracts without job security) was at an all time high: 38%, the highest in Europe. In particular, the majority of new positions during this period were precarious, a situation that continued into the 1990s. It is important to note that in spite of the labour flexibility laws passed at the beginning of the 1980s, the job destruction rate has remained the same, reversing itself only in the second half of the 1980s when the rate of economic growth increased significantly. Still, during the 1991-1993 recession the level of unemployment increased considerably, reaching an all-time high of 23%.[38] Exacerbating the situation, the Socialist governments carried out very restrictive monetarist policies aimed at reducing the rate of inflation, one of the most important objectives of the Ministry of Finances, whose policies in this respect mirrored those of the Bank of Spain. Despite the rhetorical flourishes by the government, job creation never became a primary objective of government policies except (in an indirect and not very successful way) by stimulating the job creation potential of the private sector. The pattern of job creation and destruction followed the economic cycles, without government intervention to reduce unemployment. It was this passivity of the public sector *per se* in the face of the serious social problem of unemployment that characterized the employment policies of all four Spanish Socialist governments.

The PSOE and the Unions

The victory of the PSOE led to the establishment of a social pact between the two major employer associations – large (CEOE) and small (CEPYME) employers – and the UGT and the CCOO, starting with the *First Interconfederal Agreement* (AI) of 1983. This was followed by a tripartite agreement in 1984 with the inclusion of the government: the *Acuerdo Economico y Social* (the Social and Economic Agreement, or AES). This three year arrangement involved acceptance of both the salary guidelines dictated by the Socialist government and further measures of labour flexibility, with the establishment of a job creation programme paid for by the salaried and wage-earning sectors of the population. Employers agreed to reduce the extra hours of work required from employees and to increase employment-producing investments, while the government committed itself to expand unemployment coverage and increase employment-producing public investments. Of the three parties to the AES, the trade unions were the only party that continuously and consistently honoured its side of the agreement, keeping a lid on salaries and collaborating in the labour flexibility measures. They did so at their cost: the rate of unionization declined substantially during those three years. Both the government and the employers, on the other hand, failed to deliver on most of their promises. On the contrary, and as shown above, public and social expenditures declined during 1984-1986, while job destruction continued in both the public and private sectors. This failure to deliver and the continuing deterioration of labour (in spite of some improvements after 1986) led to a growing frustration which exploded in the 1988 general strike. The tensions between the unions and the government never diminished and the trade unions' profound distrust of the Socialist government is rooted in this history.

In these agreements, the trade unions agreed to accept salaries increasing at a lower rate than the rate of inflation, the employers agreed to increase job-producing investments, and the government agreed to increase the minimum pension to the minimum wage level and increase the level of coverage of the unemployed (only 38% of the unemployed were covered at that time). The employers, however, did not increase their investments. The substantial improvement in their rate of profit and overall profit levels did not translate into new jobs but rather into speculative activities. Furthermore, the government eased legal steps that employers had to take before dismissing workers and permitted a very broad interpretation of the laws allowing for the 'shit contracts.' Unemployment reached a high of 22.2% in 1985. To further aggravate the situation, the government introduced legislation in Parliament (where it had a majority) revising the pension law, increasing the number of years of worker contributions required before the enjoyment of pensions. This was read by the CCOO as the starting point for the government's reduction of the welfare state, which led in 1985 to a call for a general strike – one that had varied success in different regions of Spain.

The focus on lowering the price of labour and increasing labour flexibility as the twin pillars of employment policy has lost substantial credibility among the PSOE electorate and among the trade unions. In this regard it is remarkable that Maravall and other Socialist leaders continue to accuse the trade unions of non-solidarity and corporatist behaviour, putting their interests above the interests of the nation. As a matter of fact, both the UGT and the CCOO accepted wage controls and labour flexibility for the entire duration of the first Socialist government. Their labour discipline, accepting that wages were to increase at a slower rate than productivity, was part of their contribution to the democratic transition and to the success of the first left-wing government elected after that transition.

The UGT did not join in the strike, but the relationship between the UGT and the Socialist government also began to deteriorate. Nicolas Redondo, Secretary General of the UGT, resigned from his position as a Socialist Member of Parliament. Shortly before his departure, the UGT lost the trade union elections to the CCOO, which in 1987 became the largest trade union. In 1986 major changes followed the entry of Spain into the Common Market. Attracted by low salaries and high labour flexibility, an enormous flow of foreign investment stimulated (through increased competition) Spanish employers to invest. Starting in 1986, there was for the first time since 1977 a real increase in Spanish salaries and wages, increasing workers' disposable income; salaries increased at a higher rate than inflation. Unemployment was also reduced with the creation of one and a half million jobs during the 1985-1989 period, but that was due primarily to the increase in temporary jobs. The temporary economic boom strengthened labour, which was further consolidated with the virtual union of the major trade unions, CCOO and UGT. Together they were better able to stand up to the government and employers, particularly in protest against the significant cuts in public and social expenditures that led to the December 14th, 1988 general strike which forced the major social turn in the policies of the Socialist government.

But it was not enough to undo the damage that had been wrought by the overall strategic orientation of the PSOE since its election in 1982. According to the Institute for Labour Statistics of the Spanish Ministry of Labour, the disposable income of the wage sector of the labour force has declined 1.5% during the last 15 years.[39] Unemployment has increased by 58% and poverty – although it has declined due to the universalization of pensions and health services – still affects 20.7% of the population.[40]

The Electoral Decline of the PSOE

As we have seen, despite the programme on which it was elected, the first PSOE government gave priority not to the creation of employment but to the control of inflation and the capitalist modernization of industry in preparation for the entry of Spain into the EC. This resulted in a continuation of job destruction, with clear reluctance on the part of the Spanish capitalists to invest. Not until 1986 and 1987 was there any considerable increase in job-creating investments, and even then most was stimulated by foreign investments. Public expenditures, however, continued to expand in the two areas that mattered most for electoral purposes: pensions and unemployment insurance – although the percentage of unemployed covered declined due to the large increase in unemployment.

The 1986 election witnessed another majority sweep for the PSOE, although its share of the vote declined to 44.4% from 48.4% in 1982. Though it still received the majority of the working-class vote, two important warning signs of workers' discontent with Socialist government policies had already appeared: a significant increase in working-class abstention from voting and a major decline in the working-class vote for the PSOE. The PCE benefited surprisingly little from this working-class disillusionment. The other major change in the 1986 election was the middle class's reluctant vote for the PSOE, out of fear of a right-wing victory under Manuel Fraga, the presidential candidate of the Conservative Party who had been a minister in the fascist regime. Old memories kept alive during the PSOE's electoral campaign did the trick. The discrediting of the Right, still perceived as a forceful political successor to the fascist regime, was the best card played by the PSOE in the 1986 elections; and it was the weakness of the Right together with that of the Communists that provided the space for the rightward shift of the PSOE government.

The PSOE was once again victorious in the 1989 election, but with a significantly lower vote of 38.7%. It might seem paradoxical that just one year after a most successful general strike the electorate returned the PSOE to power. The victory was in part the result of the social turn that the strike had forced on the government, creating the impression of a new sensitivity to working-class demands. Also, disposable income was increasing after a long period of decline, with the unemployment rate now falling. Still, working-class support for the PSOE continued to decline. Moreover, two new and notable developments occurred. The middle-class sectors became more reassured by changes in the right-wing party, the Popular Party (PP), when Fraga was replaced by Jose Maria Aznar. Aznar, although a tax collector lacking in charisma, was nevertheless a new face with no connections to the former fascist regime.[41] The PP received a considerable increase in the vote in 1989, up to 32%, and the PCE (now regrouped within an alliance of leftist forces and disaffected groups in the Izquierda Unida, or IU – the United Left) finally started benefiting from the working class's discontent with the Socialist government, gaining 9% of the electoral vote. But as working-class frustrations continued, there was a general pre-election perception in 1993 that the PSOE would lose. That perception was strengthened by the very poor performance of Gonzalez in a debate with Aznar. For the first time since 1982 it seemed that the post-Francoist Right – represented by the PP – was going to win. A panic spread among the Left, with the battle cry 'no pasaran' ('they will not pass!'), the resistance call of the Republican forces in Madrid under siege during the Civil War. On election day, however, to everyone's surprise, the PSOE won again, primarily because – as exit polls showed – many left-wing people who intended not to vote, or to vote for the IU, changed their minds at the last minute and voted for the PSOE. It won 38.7% of the vote, while the PP received 35%. The IU was the loser in that last-minute transfer of votes: it received practically the same proportion (9.6%) as in 1989. The message, however, was clear: the left-wing voter did not want the PP in government while preferring a shift to the left by the Socialist government. According to the polls, this was also the desire of the majority of the electorate, including those who abstained.

Rather than ally itself with the IU, however, the PSOE government allied with the centre-right Catalan nationalist party, pressing for a new labour reform that would further increase the flexibility of the labour market. This proposal was opposed by the unions, which called for another general strike that had a considerable following among industrial and construction workers. In the 1994 European elections, the PSOE lost three and a half million votes, reaching the lowest level since democracy was established. The working class abstained *en masse*, although the IU vote increased to 13% and for the first time a significant number of workers (over 14%) voted for the PP, particularly in the red suburbs of the big cities. The only sectors that remained loyal to the PSOE were the pensioners (25% of whom voted PSOE) and small farmers and farm workers (more than half), the chief beneficiaries of the expansion of the pension system and of the National Health Service.

Table 2: Electoral Behaviour by Occupation and by Size of Town in the 1996 Election

Electoral Behaviour by Occupation in 1996 Election

OCCUPATION	PARTY		
	PSOE	IU	PP
Employers	20%	6%	63%
Farmers	32%	2%	52%
Liberal Professions	30%	7%	51%
Industrial Workers	40%	15%	26%
Administrative Personnel	38%	14%	32%
Civil Servants	26%	12%	51%
Unskilled Labour	48%	12%	32%
Unemployed	38%	18%	32%
Pensioners	48%	4%	38%
Housewives	49%	6%	39%
Students	32%	20%	34%

Electoral Behaviour by Size of Town in 1996 Election

POPULATION	PSOE	IU	PP
Less than 10,000	42%	8%	35%
50,000–100,000	38%	12%	38%
More than 500,000	32%	13%	45%

(*Source: El Pais*, 6 April 1996, p. 14.)

In the March 3rd, 1996 national election, the PP finally won with 38.78% of the vote while the PSOE received 37.62%. The PP received 9,700,863 votes versus 9,419,530 votes for the PSOE, a difference of only 281,333; the total left-wing electorate however numbered one million more than the right-wing as the majority of the electorate (51.2%), taking into account the votes of the left-wing regionalist parties, voted left. The PSOE and the IU received a total of 48.1% of the vote, almost identical to their aggregate vote in 1993 (48.4%). A transfer of votes from the PSOE to the IU had occurred, and since the electoral system favours large parties over small,[42] the number of left-wing elected representatives was much smaller in 1996 than in 1993, declining from 177 parliamentary seats to 162. This explains why the PP favoured the IU over the PSOE during the electoral campaign. The enormous sectarianism within the Left had led to its defeat. Had the IU voters supported the PSOE candidates in those districts where the IU candidates had no chance of being elected, and had the PSOE voters voted IU in those districts where the PSOE had no chance of being elected, the PSOE would easily have won.[43] Still, for Julio Anguita, President of the IU and Secretary General of the PCE, the largest political force in the IU, the main 'enemy' (a term he used frequently) was the PSOE rather than the PP. Table 2 shows the occupational and regional support for the IU, PSOE, and PP. The strongest PSOE supporters continued to be the pensioners, unskilled labourers, industrial workers, and rural dwellers. The PSOE lost in most of the autonomous regions except for Andalusia and Catalonia.

The PP had run a campaign presenting itself as a 'centre' party, renouncing some of the most extreme 1993 positions such as the privatization of Social Security and the National Health Service, even though the latter had already been initiated in some of the regional autonomies controlled by the PP. The PP appeared as the party of Jacobin Spain with anti-Catalan and anti-Basque positions, calling on the support of the immigrant Spanish-speaking working class in Catalonia and in the Basque country. Still, the major advantage of the PP was the unpopularity of the PSOE government. On election day, 35% of PP supporters declared they voted for the PP as a way of getting rid of the PSOE government. An important group that deserted the PSOE in droves was the young. In the 1982 election the young (18-27) represented 25% of the PSOE vote; in 1996 they represented only 16%. For the first time since democracy was established in Spain, more young people voted for the PP than for the PSOE.[44]

The IU did not benefit much from the unpopularity of the PSOE. Its share of the vote rose only slightly, from 9% to 11%. This outcome was primarily a result of the position taken by the leadership of the PCE, the major force in the IU whose anti-PSOE strategy (accusing the PSOE leadership of being the major enemy of progress in Spain) indirectly favoured the PP. This alienated considerable sectors of the PSOE grass-roots who, while in disagreement with the economic policies of the PSOE government, did not accept Anguita's position that the social-democratic government was worse than a PP government would be. The systematic anti-PSOE policies of the IU had been responsible for an ultra-right-wing member of the PP (a member of the fascist group Guerrilleros de Cristo) becoming governor of Asturias, the coalmining region of Spain and the main left-wing region of the country. Both the anti-communism of Felipe

Gonzalez and the anti-socialism of Anguita caused disgust among large sectors of voters of both parties. On election day the number of protest votes (ballots left blank) against the sectarianism of both parties of the Left was larger (367,198 votes) than the PP's margin of victory over the PSOE (281,333 votes). During the 1996 election, Anguita had declared that the primary objective of the PCE was to defeat the PSOE government, making it indistinguishable from the PP.[45]

The election of the PP government with the support of the right-of-centre Catalan and Basque nationalist parties has further accentuated the neoliberal economic policies initiated by the previous Socialist government, adding new public policies aimed at reducing and even dismantling the rather undeveloped Spanish welfare state. The Bank of Santander, the second largest bank in Spain and a major funder of the PP, has been calling for the full privatization of the Spanish social security system, as happened in Chile during the Pinochet dictatorship.[46]

Moreover, the victory of the PP has empowered the Right, including the fascists, quite considerably. Open expressions of fascist fervour and support are tolerated by the PP. Shortly before the March 3rd, 1996 elections, for example, a municipal counsellor from Albacete (Andalusia) protested the 60th anniversary of the arrival of the International Brigades by calling them criminals, killers, butchers, and the scum of the earth, without being censored by the PP leadership.[47] The PP-governed municipality of Malaga opposed a popular proposal to name a street after one of its best known sons, Pablo Picasso, because he was a 'red.' And the President of the University of Sevilla, Mr. Medina, awarded the National Prize in Literature in 1975, recently spoke very highly of Franco, Hitler, Mussolini, and Pinochet, referring to fascism as the highest level of development of a society.[48] In all these cases, the national leadership of the PP has remained silent. While the PP wanted to appear as a moderate party of the centre, the far Right and the Francoist forces campaigned actively for the party, and Aznar, its presidential candidate, welcomed their support. He avoided distancing himself from the Franco era and denounced the Socialist party's anti-Francoist pronouncements as exaggerated and unfounded. When asked in an interview during the 1996 campaign whether in 1936 he would have supported Azaña (the head of the democratically elected Republican government) or Jose Antonio Primo de Rivera (founder of the fascist party), Aznar replied that fortunately he did not live during those years and did not need to make a choice. When the interviewer persisted and asked whether Franco had been a positive or negative force in Spanish history, Aznar replied that it was not up to him to judge Franco's tenure, that was history's role. His own strongly conservative pro-Catholic view had been a trademark of his campaign, calling for 'men who know what responsibility is and for women who know their place as women in society.'[49] At the economic level, major financial centres, which are very influential in the leadership of the PP, have called for what amounts to a dismantling of the Spanish welfare state.[50] And the economic team of the government reads like a Who's Who in the world of large Spanish employers.[51] The PP named Margarita Mariscal as Minister of the Interior, an ultra-right-wing lawyer and daughter of a well-known rightist judge who defended the fascist branches of the Spanish civil guard that planned the (failed) military coup of 23 February 1982. Three other members of the Cabinet belong to the ultra-right-wing religious order Opus Dei, including a newly established Undersecretary for Religious Affairs.[52]

The fact that the PP has attracted the support of the fascist movement of Spain, thought to represent approximately one-third of the PP vote, explains why Spain is the only country in southern Europe that does not have an explicitly fascist party as such. It also explains why the PP government has not distanced itself from the fascist regime of General Franco. The PP's economic team, however, belongs to the liberal branch of the party and is committed to further increasing labour flexibility and reducing the social protection of the working class – but without reaching the extremes put forward by large sectors of the employers' association who called for the dismantling of the welfare state. Supporting this restraint is the Catalan Christian Democratic Party, or CIU, which fears that such measures would threaten the social peace of Spain.

So far, the PP has reduced taxes on dividends and the taxes of the wealthiest 20% of the Spanish population; privatized the still existing major public enterprises; deregulated urban zoning (a central government responsibility in Spain), greatly favouring real estate interests; reduced social expenditures (except pensions); and further liberalized capital and labour markets. For this last measure the PP government has the support of all the previous Ministers of Economy of the successive Socialist governments.[53] There is, therefore, a clear continuity in the economic policies of the PP and PSOE governments, although they will likely be taken to more unrestrained levels by the PP. The seeds of those policies, however, were planted during the PSOE governments.

Interpreting the Decline of Spanish Social Democracy

The experience with the Spanish Socialist government enables us to test one of the main interpretations of the decline of social democracy in Europe. Przeworski and Sprague[54] attribute the fall of social democracy to the decline of its basic constituency, the working class and the trade unions, and its subsequent attempt to reach out to the middle class in order to maintain its electoral base. This reaching out to the middle class, however, alienates the shrinking but still essential working-class base, which puts these Socialist parties in an impossible situation. According to this position, then, the decline of the Socialist government in Spain would be the result of the decline of the Spanish working class and the alliance of the party with the middle-class electorate.

Table 3: Evolution of the Intention to Vote Among Various Classes in Spain, 1986 and 1993

		YEAR	
CLASSES	PARTY	1986	1992
Old Middle Class*	PP	20.8	17.5
	PSOE	20.2	19.9
	IU	1.7	3.6
New Middle Class†	PP	14.4	16.0
	PSOE	42.1	26.3
	IU	3.3	7.8
Working Class	PP	5.1	11.5
	PSOE	45.1	36.1
	IU	2.9	5.8
Small Farmers and	PP	16.0	12.0
Farm Workers	PSOE	33.0	56.0
	IU	–	–
Inactive in the	PP	13.1	16.0
Workforce (primarily	PSOE	25.0	25.2
pensioners)	IU	0.8	1.9

(*Source:* J.F. Tezanos, Tabla 9, 'Socialismo y Clases Medias,' *Sistema*, Nov. 1994, p. 29.)

---

*Owners of small industrial, agricultural, and service businesses, liberal professionals and self-employed.
†Administrative employees, commerce employees, and salaried professionals.

Przeworski and Sprague's explanation is wrong on many different counts. First of all, their definition of the working class as 'the wage earners and salaried who realize manual labour in mining, industry, construction, transport and agriculture, and their inactive family members'[55] is extremely narrow. It excludes service workers in both the private and public sectors, a key segment of the working class. Yet even within their narrow definition of working class, the very slow decline of those sectors in Spain has been less than the decline in workers' support for the PSOE. Actually, the working class in Spain, according to both structural and subjective definitions, has been expanding rather than declining. Between 1975 and 1992, the percentage of the working population declaring themselves to be members of the working class increased from 39.8% to 50%, while the percentage declaring themselves to be middle class declined from 60% to 45%.[56] Moreover, while the percentage of the working population that is unionized was falling during the first half of the 1980s (coinciding with the trade unions' agreement with the Socialist government), that percentage later increased when the unions took a more militant stand. The most militant among them, the CCOO, gained many new members and became the leading union in Spain. It was precisely at this time of trade union growth that working-class support for the PSOE declined.

Moreover, the period of maximum working-class support for the PSOE coincided with the period of maximum support among the middle class (Table 3). In the majority of the middle class (administrative personnel, salaried professionals, and commerce employees), the decline of support for the PSOE paralleled the decline among the working class, although the middle-class decline was somewhat slower. There was no trade-off, therefore, between middle-class voters and working-class voters.

None of Przeworski and Sprague's theses are proven correct in the case of Spain. As shown in this article, the decline of the Spanish social-democratic government is primarily a political, not a structural, problem. It is due to the implementation of public policies, documented above, that have antagonized a large segment of both the working class and the middle class. The welfare state and its parallel policies of full employment, for example, can benefit both classes when the welfare state is based on universal policies in which social transfers and services are provided as citizens' rights, and when the funding of these interventions is progressive rather than regressive, with the level of benefits satisfying the standards of the middle class.[57] The policies of the PSOE government, however, antagonized both the working and the middle classes. While that government did not deserve the sobriquet of 'Thatcherite socialism,' it did follow policies that were too close to the interests of capital rather than to the interests of the working and middle classes. It got away with this for a long time, given the revulsion these classes felt for the right-wing alternative. But it could not avoid the political and electoral decline that must eventually attend a social-democratic party that accepts the main economic tenets of neoliberalism.

NOTES

1. It is important to clarify that while southern European social-democratic parties (in Spain, Italy, France, Greece, and Portugal) were winning government elections, the overall level of electoral support (32.9%) received was, on average, lower than the electoral support (39.7%) obtained by northern European social-democratic parties (in Sweden, Norway, Denmark, and Austria), and only slightly higher than support (28.6%) for central European social-democratic parties (in Western Germany, Belgium, Holland, and Switzerland) – see W. Merkel, 'Evolución Electoral de los Partidos Social Demócratas', *Final de la Social Democracía?* (Edicions Alfons el Magnanim, 1995), Tabla 3, p. 62.
2. 'Declaraciones de Solchaga', *El Pais*, 15 January 1989.

VICENTE NAVARRO 219

3. L. Paramio, 'El Socialism y los Sindicatos Hacia el Divorcio?', *Sistema*, No. 82, 1988.
4. 'Declaraciones del Vicepresidente Serra', *El Pais*, 28 October 1988, p. 12.
5. See L.C. Bresser, J.M. Maravall and A. Przeworski, *Economic Reforms in New Democracies: A Social Democratic Approach* (Cambridge University Press, 1993).
6. J. M. Maravall, 'Politics and Policy: Economic Reforms in Southern Europe' in L.C. Bresser, *et al.*, *op. cit.* See also J.M. Maravall, *Los Resultados de la Democracía: Un Estudio del Sur y del Este de Europa* (Alianza Editorial, 1995).
7. W. Merkel, *op. cit.*, p. 227.
8. A. Przeworski and J. Sprague, *Paper Stones: A History of Electoral Socialism* (University of Chicago Press, 1986).
9. There is an extensive bibliography on the Spanish transition. The best known accounts are P. Preston, *The Triumph of Democracy in Spain* (Methuen, 1987), and J. M. Maravall, *The Transition to Democracy in Spain* (Croom Helm, 1982). See also chapter 21, 'The End of Authoritarian Regimes in Western Europe' in D. Sassoon, *One Hundred Years of Socialism* (I.B. Taurus, 1996). Sassoon's explanation, however, relies too much on the interactions among the personalities involved in the transition, without analyzing the key role played by popular mobilizations.
10. The PSOE had received substantial financial aid from the Socialist International and from the German S.P.D. which enabled it to establish an impressive network of local offices throughout the country. See the chapter on Spain in P. Anderson and P. Camiller, *Mapping the West European Left* (Verso, 1994).
11. J. Albarracin, 'La Politica de los Sindicatos y la Dinamica del Movimiento Obrero' in M. Etxezarreta, *La Restructuración del Capitalismo en España 1970-1990* (Icaria, 1991), p. 467.
12. Due to the difficulties in firing workers during these years, the considerable growth in unemployment in this period was primarily a result of new entries into the labour market (300,000 new job seekers): women, in particular, whose rate of labour force participation had been historically very low; youth whose numbers had increased substantially due to the 1960s baby boom; and Spanish immigrants returning to Spain as Europe experienced its first major post-war recession after 1973.
13. F. Miguelez and C. Prieto (eds.), *Las Relaciones Laborales en España Siglo XXI*, 1991, p. 82.
14. The radical discourse of the PSOE and its subsequent overwhelming electoral victory at first frightened the monarchy and the Spanish establishment. The King had already expressed his concern about the PSOE's growing popularity during the UCD government, writing a letter on 22 June 1977 to the Shah of Iran requesting a gift of 10 million dollars for the UCD in order to strengthen Suarez's party, 'the guarantor of the monarchy and of Spanish stability and the only force to stop socialism.' See A. Missé, 'La financiacion de los partidos', *Memorias de la Transicion*, No. 23, *El Pais*, 1996, p. 413. The Shah of Iran replied that he preferred to answer the King of Spain orally rather than in writing.
15. In 1982, the active population included 13,237,000 adults of which 2,120,000 were unemployed.
16. It is important to stress that the Franco state was indeed a fascist state, despite the formal political discourse of Spain (accepted by the major political parties) which refers to that fascist state as a Francoist state and the fascist regime as a Francoist regime. This is a political project to reinterpret that regime as a personal dictatorship of General Franco, denying or at least downplaying its class nature. In reality, the Spanish state during that period was a dictatorship that sustained an extremely repressive class dominance with the collaboration of allied social strata that shared in the control of the state. The post-Franco transition resulting from a pact between left and right political and social forces left the state apparatus practically unchanged, including its public administration. The democratic institutions were appendages to a public administration that went unchanged. The maintenance of the monarchy was a symbol of that continuity. This point merits emphasis

because of recent attempts to deny the class character of fascism and the fascist character of the Spanish regime. (For a discussion of this topic see V. Navarro, 'Fascism and Antifascism: Yesterday and Today', *Monthly Review*, Vol. 47, No. 8, 1996, pp. 14-27). The major supporters of the fascist coup and the fascist movement were the capitalist class, both the modernizing sector of that class (in banking and industry) and the oligarchic sector based on land ownership (plus the Church, and the middle classes). The key funder of the fascist coup was the financier Joan March who had been a leading member of the Liberal Party and founder of the liberal paper *Libertad* (*Liberty*), and was presented during the second republic as the model of a modernizing entrepreneur. When March felt threatened by the expansion of working-class power, he funded the fascist military coup with the assistance of his collaborator, John Olrich, a top executive of the Exxon Oil Company, and with the approval of the U.S. State Department. Joan March was the main supporter and defender of the Franco regime. Today his family continues to be prominent in the finance sector in Spain and they fund the liberal Foundation March, which counts among its leadership (as co-director of the Foundation's Research Center on Social Sciences) Jose Maria Maravall, one of the most influential theoreticians of the PSOE, and a Minister of Education during the first Socialist government.

17. French events have always had an enormous impact in Spain, partly the result of common traditions, partly because most of the political establishment traditionally spoke French rather than English as a second language. (This situation began to change during the 1980s when English became the primary foreign language, with *The Economist* and the *International Herald Tribune* quickly replacing *Le Monde* as the most influential foreign newspapers within the political establishment.) Mitterrand's early policies were, in fact, responsible for France having an unemployment rate of only 2% of the total labour force, compared with 4% for the EC (and 5% for West Germany). Also, the public deficit in France was the lowest among the G-7 countries and the balance of payments was 2% of GNP, similar to the average for the OECD countries. Although inflation increased, alternatives to the austerity policies imposed were available to counter this trend, including more progressive fiscal policies and measures to reduce high rates of consumption by the wealthy. Instead, the Mitterrand government followed austerity policies that affected most negatively the working class and popular masses, increasing unemployment and social inequalities. As Rocard, who along with Jacques Delors was an early advocate of these reforms, was later to recognize, 'an income redistribution took place with a considerable decline in the disposable income of the popular classes, mass unemployment and labour insecurity ... all to the benefit of financial capital who won completely!' See M. Rocard, 'L'heure de verité', *France*, 25 April 1993, p. 2.

18. Even under the Socialists the Bank saw its sole function as controlling the rate of inflation; it has never considered the reduction of unemployment to be one of its primary objectives.

19. This attitude towards the unions by influential figures within the PSOE has been noted by several observers as a rather peculiar and atypical position for socialist leaders to take. See, for example, the comments made by Margaret Hodge to the leading PSOE members, in M. Escudero's contribution to the collection edited by D. Miliband, *Reinventing the Left* (Polity Press, 1994), p. 245.

20. See 'Quienes son muestros gobernantes?', *El Pais Semanal*, 22 August 1994, p. 12.

21. Employment in the former increased from 3.85% of the total public employment in 1982 to 34.97% in 1996, and in the latter – the municipal government – increased from 14.47% in 1982 to 23.96% in 1996. Central government employment actually declined from 77.59% of total public employment in 1982 to 34.25% in 1996. 'El Estado de Bienestar Exige Más Funcionarios,' *La Vanguardia*, 4 February1996, p. 18.

22. See especially J. Petras, 'The rise and decline of southern European socialism', *New Left Review*, 146, 1984, pp. 37-52.

23. C.A. Zaldibar and M. Castells, *España Fin de Siglo* (Alianza Editorial, 1992), p. 79.

24. World Competitiveness Institute, 1994.
25. M. Etxezarreta, *op. cit.*, p. 45.
26. A. Missé, 'La financiacion de los partidos', *Memorias de la Transicion, El Pais*, Vol. 23, March 1996, p. 416.
27. J.V. Sevilla Segura, *Economía Política de la Crisis Española Critica*, Capitulo 5, 1985, p. 123.
28. V. Navarro and J. Elola, 'Las Politicas Sanitarias en España 1970-1995', *Sistema*, Vol. 102, 1995.
29. See G. Rodrigo Cabrero, *Informe Sociologico sobre la Situacion Social en España*, Capitulo 5, 1995, p. 1450. The main complaints have to do with poor quality of the hotel side of hospital services, bureaucratic administration and NHS insensitivity to users, and minimal time that primary-care doctors spend with patients (3 minutes on average).
30. S. Sarasa and L. Moreno (eds.), *El Estado de Bienestar en la Europa del Sur* (Consejo Superior de Investigaciones Cientificas, 1995), p. 70.
31. *Revenue Statistics of OECD Member Countries 1965-1985* (OECD, Paris, 1986), p. 83; and *OECD España 1988-89*, M.66.
32. Presión Fiscal y Componentes en % del PIB: Comparación Internacional, in M. Etxezarreta, *op. cit.*, p. 194.
33. G. Rodriguez Cabrero, 'La distribucion de la Renta en España en la Decada de los Años Ochenta. Las Politicas de Redistribucion Fiscal desde la Fiscalidad' en *Informe Sociologico Sobre la Situacion Social en España* (Fundacion Foessa, 1994), p. 1433.
34. J. Borrell, 'De la Constitución a Europa: Una Decada de Politica Fiscal', *Información Commercial Española*, Vol. 680, 1990, pp. 9-37.
35. Employment Survey, OECD, 1995.
36. *Encuesta Nacional de Salud*, Ministerio de Sanidad y Consumo de España, Tabla 5.
37. C.A. Zaldibar and M. Castells, *op. cit.*, pp. 320, 99.
38. R. Marimon, ed., *La Economía Española* (Antoni Bosch Editions, 1996), p. 23.
39. 'El poder adquisitivo de los salarios cedio un 1.5% durante los últimos quince años', *Cinco Dias*, 12 January 1996, p. 14.
40. Informe FOESA, 1993.
41. Even though in an unguarded declaration to the press in 1980 Aznar had criticized Guernica, the Basque city destroyed by Nazi bombers and immortalized by the Picasso painting that bears its name, for removing the names of General Franco and Jose Antonio Primo de Rivera, founder of the fascist party, from the city's streets.
42. C. A. Zaldibar and M. Castells. op. cit.
43. 'Votos de IU en favour del PP', *El Pais*, 10 March 1996, p. 19.
44. J. Montero, L. Nuño and S. Paloma, 'El comportamiento electoral de los jovenes: Reflexiones sobre las elecciones legislativas de 1996', *Temas*, No. 19, 1996, p. 24.
45. 'Anguita situa a Gonzalez como el autentico enemigo de la izquierda', *El Pais*, 27 February 1996.
46. 'Botin colseja les pensions', *Els Temps*, 4 March 1996, p. 28.
47. 'Un concejal del PP tacha de 'asesinas' a las Brigadas Internacionales', *El Pais*, 26 February 1996.
48. 'Elogio del fascismo', *El Pais*, 10 May 1996, p. 30.
49. Entrevista con Jose Maria Aznar, *El Tiempo*, 24 February 1996, p. 1. In the March 3, 1996 election, young women (25-44 years) favoured the PSOE over the PP by a higher margin (3 to 2).
50. 'Un libro contra un estado', *El Pais*, 16 June 1996, p. 49.
51. 'Nombramientos made in PP', *El Pais*, 17 June 1996, p. 62.
52. 'Los nuevos ministros', *El Pais*, 5 May 1996, p. 19.
53. 'Cuatro ex-ministros de economia debaten las perspectivas de la union monetaria', *El Pais*, 12 July 1996, p. 62.
54. A. Przeworski and J. Sprague, *op. cit.*

55. *Ibid.*, pp. 34-35. For a similar criticism of the very restrictive definition of working class used by Przeworski and Sprague, see L. Panitch, 'Capitalism, Socialism and Revolution', *Socialist Register 1989*, (Merlin Press, 1989), p. 20.
56. F. Tezanos, 'Socialismo y Clases Medias', *Sistema*, Vol. 123, Nov 1994, p. 24.
57. For an elaboration of this point see V. Navarro, 'La Economia y el Estado de Bienestar', *El Futuro del Socialismo*, (Fundacion Sistema, 1995).

CARDOSO'S POLITICAL PROJECT IN BRAZIL: THE LIMITS OF SOCIAL DEMOCRACY

Paul Cammack

It seems to me that this is a crucial question for the 1970s: how to link the economic objectives of development to political practices which are neither authoritarian nor totalitarian.

An identical form of state – capitalist and dependent, in the case of Latin America – can coexist with a variety of political regimes: authoritarian, fascist, corporatist, and even democratic... It is simplistic to imagine that a dependent capitalist process of industrialization can take place only through authoritarianism.

It is difficult – if not wrong – to imagine that without substantive or social democratization, political democratization is a deception. Sometimes 'pure' liberal democracy (or, better, the actual practice of democratic liberties) constitutes a favourable condition for the advance of social democratization.

But I was never a neo-liberal.

If these statements, made at various times between 1971 and 1996, make an appropriate starting point for a consideration of political alternatives in Brazil, it is because they were all made by Fernando Henrique Cardoso, the sociologist turned politician who is now its President.[1]

Cardoso's work as a sociologist and political scientist from the early 1970s reflects a coherent political project with which his political practice over the last two decades has been consistent. It centres upon the democratization of the state and society in Brazil, and has consistently been social democratic rather than socialist in character. My argument is that thinking about an alternative socialist political project in Brazil entails understanding and engaging critically with this project. In doing so, we should avoid the easy but false impression that it represents a capitulation from a former radical to neo-liberalism. But at the same time we should consider its limitations, and explore the possibility that its role and significance today, in a very different conjuncture from that in which it was first proposed, are necessarily no longer what they were at the outset.

Cardoso's social democratic project was articulated at the height of

Brazil's military dictatorship, when the fortunes of representative institutions (although these were never entirely discarded by the military) were at their lowest ebb. In the context of the general mood of disenchantment with democratic values, and the endorsement of authoritarianism by the United States as a sound basis for accelerated development and a defence against subversion, the social-democratic project was radical, oppositional and counter-hegemonic in character. It was realistic in its assessment of the deficiencies of the liberal democratic tradition in Brazil and Latin America, and the limited potential of the 'privileged agent' of democratic revolution – the industrial bourgeoisie. Above all, it was clear on the need for a long and patient effort of independent self-organization by social democratic forces outside the ambit of either traditional political elites or the state. If we are to judge by the frequent pronouncements Cardoso has made on the subject since he became president, it remains progressive in intent. However, time has moved on. The international and domestic forces against which Cardoso's initial project was aimed have themselves become fervent advocates of the adoption of liberal democratic political institutions, which now seem an appropriate vehicle for furthering their own interests. Significant sectors of the Brazilian bourgeoisie have opted to support Cardoso, but neither they nor their allies abroad attach great priority either to the democratization of state and society, or to the pursuit of social reform. At the same time, the logic of Cardoso's own position has led him to adopt a range of neoliberal economic policies – to become, in fact, the most successful Brazilian architect by far of the 'normalization' of the economy which O'Donnell once saw as the privileged task of the bureaucratic-authoritarian state. This is not surprising, as his project aims to democratize what he himself has termed 'associated-dependent development', not to go beyond it.

Although the rhetorical commitment to the democratization of Brazil's state, political regime and society remains, the narrow neo-liberal agenda has contained it, and converted it into a more limited project for bourgeois hegemony. At the same time, Cardoso's growing conviction that the continuity of his economic policies can only be guaranteed by his own re-election to the presidency (which in turn requires a major constitutional reform) has persuaded him to look to support from the politicians of the right and centre-right whose backing brought him to the presidency. The politics of official clientelism to which this has given rise run directly counter to his previous insistence that democratic reform could be a prelude to social reform. In these circumstances, the part played by the social-democratic project over the last two decades can be played today only by an explicitly socialist project. In the context of the global ascendancy of neo-liberalism and the limits it places on social democracy, only an uncompromising socialist project can provide the basis for the radical, oppositional and counter-hegemonic alternative which the social democratic project represented during the dictatorship.

At the same time, socialists can draw valuable lessons from the trajectory of Cardoso's social democratic project. Today, in the context of internal debate and pervasive loss of faith in socialist ideals, socialists can learn from the commitment demonstrated by Cardoso and others in equally unpromising circumstances to the ideals of social and democratic reform. We can also be guided by two central principles of Cardoso's own analysis – commitment to the democratization of the state and society, and recognition of the need to assign priority to a long and patient effort of self-organization. On the present evidence Cardoso's insistence on placing neo-liberal economic reform before political democratization has led him to abandon these two principles. There is all the more reason, therefore, for the left to take them up.

Finally, the conjunctural circumstances in Brazil are such that substantial tactical space exists within which a socialist project can be advanced. As noted above, Cardoso's distinctive social democratic project is currently threatened with assimilation to a narrower neo-liberal project. The obliteration of the distance between the social democratic project and the alternative project of the bourgeoisie and its international allies can be avoided only through a tactical alliance with the left to advance the project of democratization of the state and the regime. Indeed, should Cardoso secure the change needed in the constitution which will allow his re-election, there may be no other basis on which such a project might proceed. And to the extent that the process of democratization of the state and the political regime does go forward, the conditions for the left to advance an alternative socialist project will improve.

It follows that socialists should unreservedly support the democratization of the state and the political regime. At the same time, we should argue uncompromisingly that a project that began with the assertion (itself virtually a heresy at the time) that dependent capitalist development could proceed under a political regime of representative democracy is always likely to find that its limits are reached at a point when 'political democracy' is achieved, while dependent capitalism still remains intact. In these circumstances, the task of the alternative socialist project is not only to identify these limits, but also to insist that it is essential to go beyond them. In other words, where Cardoso has proved willing to compromise on political democratization in order to safeguard neo-liberal reform, and hence blocked a possible passage from neo-liberal reform to social democratic reform, the left should insist upon political democratization, thus re-opening the possibility that democratic pressure may bring about pressure not only for much-needed social democratic reform, but also for more radical departures which do not respect the limits imposed by capitalism. With these thoughts in mind, I first analyse the origins and development of Cardoso's social democratic project, then examine its fortune during his presidential period.

Cardoso's Social Democratic Political Project

The presentation from which the first quotation at the head of this article is taken was made in New York in the spring of 1971.[2] It was delivered at the height of the military dictatorship in Brazil, with Médici in power, when the economic boom which had begun in 1967 was in full swing, Congress purged and sidelined, and the prospects for the restoration of democracy as remote as they would ever be. It was a public statement which articulated a political position and made a political intervention, as the reference in the titles to 'political alternatives' makes clear. It therefore offers an appropriate point of departure for an account of Cardoso's academic and theoretical work as a political intervention.

Speaking, then, at the height of the dictatorship, Cardoso chose to address the issue of representative democracy in Latin America, noting first the virtual absence in the region of the political conditions associated with it (representative parties, institutional mechanisms to allow the interplay of interests and the resolution of conflict, the separation and harmony of powers, basic individual guarantees, and legitimacy arising from the legal and rational basis of power); and second the absence of appropriate social conditions (given massive urban and rural poverty, small middle classes, and a small dominant sector remote from the rest of society). In these circumstances, he argued,

the novelty of the present situation is not in the 'end of liberal democracy' (or, as some would have it, of the regime of bourgeois liberalism) as an effective form of political organization, as this has only ever had a brief existence in virtually the whole of the region; it is rather in the fact – and this is new – that the ideology of democracy is losing force.[3]

What was more, he argued, in official circles in the United States the rejection of liberal democracy as a guiding ideology was cynically welcomed as evidence of pluralism, and the legitimacy of alternative paths to development. The critique of liberal democracy slid over, therefore, into a justification of authoritarian and even totalitarian ideologies of development.

In the 'autocratic-bureaucratic' states committed to associated development, and generally among elites around the region, Cardoso noted the generalization of the belief that 'it is not possible to have accelerated economic growth with popular participation in the political process and with liberty.'[4] Against this, he argued that under capitalism and socialism alike the protection of individual liberties was essential:

Recent historical experience reveals two processes which are only apparently contradictory: that substantive democracy does not depend upon the formal organization of a
liberal-bourgeois regime but that, on the other hand, neither the capitalist nor the socialist
pattern of development, or their intermediate formulations, are sufficient by themselves to
guarantee that same substantive democracy.[5]

This commitment to individual rights and civil liberties prompted a
critique of the 'autocratic-bureaucratic' model of development – not only
on moral grounds but also on the grounds that it would lead to the isolation
of the political elite, the replacement of debate by manipulation, and the
collapse of any capacity to govern effectively. It also prompted a call for
political organization: the prospects for democracy depended upon the
capacity of political leaders to defend basic ideas of liberty with intransigence, but also upon the capacity of social groups to define their own
interests and to organize themselves:

The elitist vision linked to the state, among Latin American intellectuals and politicians
alike, has made it difficult to strike the right balance with regard to the political problems
of society. We think more easily of solutions at the top than of the arduous, patient and
lengthy tasks of organizing and preparing the popular sectors, the professional groups, the
masses, for the construction of freer and more equal societies.[6]

At the same time, Cardoso recognized that liberal democracy was
simultaneously a regime of representation founded upon the idea of civil
liberties and individual guarantees, and a means through which the
interests of the bourgeoisie were imposed upon other classes:

The great political issues in Latin America are not exhausted with the problem of liberty
and individual guarantees. The problem remains of viable models of organization of the
state and its relationship with society and with economic life. It is in this more concrete
context that the previous issue of fundamental liberties should be placed, because we fall
otherwise into the error which the critique of liberal democracy correctly identifies: that
of supposing an abstract and absolute political order which does not take into consideration the real conditions of the relation of forces prevailing in society and their
contradictions.[7]

A month earlier, participating in a workshop at the University of Yale,
Cardoso had offered an analysis of the theoretical and *practical* implications of associated-dependent development in Brazil which complemented
the general analysis reviewed above.[8] This important text identified the
specific features of Brazilian society and politics which would dictate the
nature of the political project with which the military regime was to be
opposed. Here too the presentation was a political intervention, intended
'to suggest the range of possible futures for the Brazilian development
model, and to offer some useful insights both for people actively involved
in politics and for analysts'.[9]

According to Cardoso, the populist developmental model rested upon
an alliance in the first place between the Brazilian state and domestic

capital, and assigned a secondary role to foreign capital. But the pursuit of industrialization and the concentration of policy on expanding the market for manufactured goods among the middle classes meant that the social bases of the regime (largely 'popular' in character) had begun 'to correspond less and less to the class sectors controlling the productive forces'.[10] At the same time, changes in the international capitalist economy meant that international corporations were seeking to base manufacturing production in the periphery. This had the double consequence that the limits of 'dependent development' were extended, and power shifted towards 'groups expressing the interests and modes of organization of international capitalism.' As a result, the 'antipopulist sectors of the military and technocracy... gained in influence,' while 'the older ruling sectors. . . lost their relative power position in the total structure.' The most decisive change, however, was the direct repression of the popular sectors, which was a response to the fact that 'the accumulation process required that the instruments of pressure and defense available to the popular classes be dismantled.'[11]

We should remind ourselves just how categorical Cardoso was, in the context of analysis firmly grounded in principles of political economy, that in this new phase of international capitalism the limits of 'dependent development' were extended:

> Assuming as it does the immersion of industrial capital into peripheral economies, the new international division of labor puts a dynamic element into operation in the internal market. Thus, to some extent, the interests of the foreign corporations become compatible with the internal prosperity of the dependent countries. In this sense, they help promote development. Because of this factor, the growth of multinational corporations necessitates a reformulation of the traditional view of economic imperialism which holds that the basic relationship between a developed capitalist country and an underdeveloped country is one of extractive exploitation that perpetuates stagnation. Today, the massive investment of foreign capital aimed at manufacturing and selling consumer goods to the growing urban middle and upper classes is consistent with, and indeed dependent upon, fairly rapid economic growth in at least some crucial sectors of the dependent country'.[12]

One of the implications of this situation was that 'as long as the economy maintains its present growth rate, it is even possible that some sectors of the lower strata (workers in the more modern sectors, and so on) will share in the prosperity.' But at the same time, and in direct contrast to other analyses at the time which stressed the economic limitations and the political efficacy of the regime, Cardoso questioned the *political* efficacy of the 'bureaucratic-authoritarian' state, arguing that 'it is true that the regime has been able to generate effective policies and to keep order. It has not, however, solved its fundamental problems, particularly those of a distinctly political nature. It has not devised means to broaden and firmly establish its legitimacy in the society at large'.[13] In casting doubt upon the political solidity of the regime, however, he simultaneously denied that 'the outside opposition, armed or verbal, ha[d] any ability to cause the regime's breakdown,' and argued that the 'reconstitution of popular representative organizations' seemed only 'a remote possibility in the present horizon of political choices'.[14]

At the same time, this analysis developed further a line of argument familiar in Cardoso's previous work, concerning the nature of Brazilian society and politics prior to the implantation of the bureaucratic-authoritarian regime after 1964. The central theme of this analysis was the relative backwardness of social classes and political institutions, reflected in the lack of autonomy of both the bourgeoisie and the working class, and the general reliance upon the state and upon anachronistic institutional arrangements in political organization on all sides and at all levels. Cardoso had argued earlier that in the populist period 'in not assuming the political responsibilities of an economically dominant class, the [Brazilian] industrial bourgeoisie [became] in part an instrument of the political domination of traditional groups'.[15] On this basis he had concluded, on the eve of the 1964 coup, that faith in a developmentalist alliance which would unite a progressive bourgeoisie with the working class was illusory. He now repeated his previously expressed view that 'the bourgeoisie never had effective political organization and pressure instruments,' and added that with the support it had given to the coup, it had 'lost all leverage to shape its more immediate political interests'.[16] However, this was only one aspect of a broader analysis of the political system before 1964, in which the potential of the working class for independent political activity was equally problematic:

> The populist alliance through which some sort of attempt was made to bring together the masses, middle-class groups, and the national entrepreneurs was itself dependent on the state. It was caught up in a web of interests and relationships ultimately based upon an economic foundation that was not only intrinsically nonrevolutionary, but also backward. Furthermore, one of the structural anchorages of that alliance was the nonincorporation of the rural population, leaving it politically unorganized and economically overexploited. This made it possible to count on the support of the conservative clientelistic parties, particularly the Social Democratic Party (PSD).[17]

It followed that the masses, selectively organized from above by the state and tied into various clientelistic political systems orchestrated either by the state itself or by the rural elites, were as little prepared for autonomous political activity as the bourgeoisie:

> Economic and urban development has mobilized the 'masses,' but it has not filled the historical vacuum of a society and culture in which they have never been organized, never politically educated, never enabled to claim their fundamental rights on an equal footing: bread as well as freedom.[18]

Some further considerations pertinent to the social democratic project are found in a discussion of the new authoritarianism in Latin America in which Cardoso condemned the tendency to generalize the model of 'bureaucratic authoritarianism' to include such cases as Mexico, and to abstract away from the institutional form of a *militarized* political regime.[19] At the same time, he insisted upon the need to distinguish between the *state* and the *political regime*. The state was defined as 'the basic alliance, the basic "pact of domination," that exists among social classes or fractions of dominant classes and the norms which guarantee their dominance over the subordinate strata.' It included state institutions as the organizational reflection of the political practice of the dominant classes as they sought continually 'to articulate their diverse and occasionally contradictory objectives through state agencies and bureaucracies.' In contrast, the political regime was defined as 'the formal rules that link the main political institutions (legislature to the executive, executive to the judiciary, and party system to them all), as well as the issue of the political nature of the ties between citizens and rulers (democratic, oligarchic, totalitarian, or whatever).' All Latin American states were capitalist; it made no sense to speak of a bureaucratic-authoritarian *state*; and only a few Latin American capitalist states had bureaucratic-authoritarian *regimes*.[20] On the basis of this distinction Cardoso argued – strikingly in retrospect – that the principal characteristic of the bureaucratic-authoritarian *political regime* was not that it represented a particular "pact of domination," as this was not a characteristic exclusive to it, but that it was 'politically profitable for the civilian and military bureaucrats that hold state office'.[21] It was in this context that Cardoso made the argument highlighted at the head of this paper that 'an identical form of state – capitalist and dependent, in the case of Latin America – can coexist with a variety of political regimes: authoritarian, fascist, corporatist, and even democratic'.[22] We should pause again here, remembering the conjunctural context in which these remarks were made, and note the significance of the conjunction in Cardoso's position of the two ideas that dependent development could produce both prosperity (albeit of a limited kind) and political democracy.

The possibility and the conjunctural significance of democracy varied from case to case, in accordance with local historical and institutional circumstances. In Brazil, there were few available resources in the historical legacy of a tradition of 'a strong state plus elitist political control'.[23] Despite this, the goals of the military had not been achieved. Tensions existed between the military as an institution and the executive, and the state apparatus was heavily factionalized, and penetrated by private interests whose access nevertheless remained precarious. In these circumstances, there was in civil society 'an awareness of the illegitimacy of the regime and a conviction that sooner or later the political organization of society [would] have to be reconstituted.'[24] Even in the unpropitious circumstance in which politics was 'the exclusive preserve of an elitist bureaucracy,' a party created by the military regime to fill a purely formal role of opposition – the MDB – had ironically become an effective opposition party. In sum, Cardoso continued to argue that the Brazilian regime was not solidly established, and that a social democratic alternative remained viable, reasserting arguments he had advanced at the beginning of the decade. 'It is simplistic,' he asserted, 'to imagine that a dependent capitalist process of industrialization can take place only through authoritarianism.' The functioning of authoritarian regimes and the achievement of proposed economic goals created new challenges and new forms of opposition which they could not overcome. The likelihood of change might depend, therefore, on 'the political capacity of opposition groups to propose creative alternatives of power that address these same challenges by offering different, and better solutions'.[25]

It seems clear, in the light of the evidence provided by these related presentations, that the political project advocated by Cardoso for Brazil called from the early 1970s for an explicit commitment to liberal democratic values and a democratic ideology, and argued that even within the prevailing economic model of associated-dependent development the potential existed for such a democratic political regime. It also recognized that a liberal democratic political system was at the same time a system of class domination, and called for a sustained effort to organize a cross-class coalition under democratic leadership to pursue the democratization of state and society. The project rested upon the following seven propositions: that *political democracy and civil rights had always been lacking in Brazil;* that *they were worth having for themselves and for what they made possible in social terms;* that *they were in principle compatible with "associated-dependent development;"* that *the Brazilian bourgeoisie was neither willing nor able to launch its own democratic project*; that *the low level of organization of the masses precluded a popular or socialist alternative*; that *armed opposition did not offer a credible option*; and that *the only realistic alternative which progressive intellectuals could espouse was independent activity within the institutions of the existing system to promote, through slow and patient organization, the democratization of the state, the political regime, and society.*

This was, then, essentially a project aimed at producing substantial *organizational* and *institutional* change as a necessary precondition for future social reform within the limits (assumed to be somewhat flexible) of associated-dependent development. In other words, it was a project for the *social, institutional and political democratization of the associated-dependent model of capitalist development,* inspired, as noted at the head of this paper, by the view that priority should be attached to finding ways of pursuing the existing pattern of economic development within a democratic framework. As such, it can be distinguished from four alternative projects. The first, the *consolidation of military authoritarianism* through the achievement of durable political legitimacy, was not only unwelcome but was ruled out by the failure of the military to develop effective political institutions. The second, the *return to national developmentalism* through a regime based on 'the assumption of an active, entrepreneurial sector bound up with a state structure that serves as a bridge to the popular masses', was ruled out by the contradictions which had bedevilled it in its first incarnation, and by subsequent changes in the domestic and international political economy. The third, the *installation of a popular regime based directly on the masses*, was ruled out by the economic potential of associated-dependent development and the strength of the social forces behind it, the failure of armed revolution, and the lack of preparation of the masses themselves. The fourth, whose identification is crucial if the progressive character as well as the limits of Cardoso's project are to be correctly assessed, was the *introduction of a narrowly defined liberal democratic regime* which excluded the prospect of social and economic reform. This alternative was rejected.

Cardoso and O'Donnell

One mistake we should not make, therefore, is to identify Cardoso's social democratic project with the more conservative model of 'political democracy' espoused by Guillermo O'Donnell and others since the mid-1980s. The essential difference between them was apparent as early as 1979, in O'Donnell's contribution to the collection on the new authoritarianism in Latin America already cited above. In direct contrast to Cardoso, O'Donnell denied that any social democratic project could emerge within the political economy of dependent development. Maintaining this perspective, he later endorsed precisely the narrowly defined liberal democratic regime without social mobilization or reform which Cardoso rejected, and which he himself had condemned in 1979.

O'Donnell's discussion of the new authoritarianism addressed the political process in the capitalist state, which 'maintains and structures class domination, in the sense that this domination is rooted principally in a class structure that in turn has its foundation in the operation and reproduction of capitalist relations of production'. Here the state is 'first and foremost, a relation of domination that articulates in unequal fashion the components of civil society, supporting and organizing the existing system of social domination.' At the same time, in order to secure this purpose, the institutions of the state are required to pose as 'the agents of a general interest of a community – the nation – that transcends the reproduction of daily life in civil society'.[26] Within this framework O'Donnell identified two other fundamental political mediations, these being citizenship (in the double sense of the abstract equality implied by universal suffrage and the right to recourse to the law), and *lo popular* (which involves concrete rights which apply equally to all those who belong to the nation without respect to their position in society, and is hence 'a carrier of demands for substantive justice which form the basis for the obligations of the state toward the less favored segments of the population'.[27] The partial recognition of these substantive rights in 'normal times' was an important source of consensus in capitalist society.

In this context the implantation of the bureaucratic-authoritarian state was described as 'an attempt to salvage a society whose continuity as a capitalist system was perceived as threatened'.[28] O'Donnell argued that the 'BA state' was unable to legitimize itself as it was narrowly based and founded upon coercion. It suppressed both citizenship and *lo popular*, and because of these exclusions it could only appeal to the 'nation' as a project to be created, rather than an existing reality. The alliance of the forces of repression and the technocrats who ran the economy made the connection between coercion and economic domination transparent. As a result it could not achieve hegemony, and was bound to depend upon instilling fear in the great majority of the population. O'Donnell clearly saw no prospect at this time, then, that the economic model pursued by the BA state could prove compatible with a social democratic political regime. It is equally significant that he ruled out at the same time the possibility that a purely capitalist state – in other words one which rejected the call for substantive social justice embodied in the concept of *lo popular* – could ever achieve sufficient legitimacy to restore the rights embodied in the concept of citizenship. Seemingly, it never occurred to him that the project of a truly internationalized capitalism could actually succeed sufficiently on its own terms to introduce and maintain a narrowly liberal democratic political regime. He appeared to believe that orthodox (anti-statist) economic policies were only required and could only be sustained in the short term, and that a return to statist national development at some point was both desirable and inevitable. And he seemed to reject the possibility that liberal capitalist development open to the international economy could redefine the nation, achieve hegemony, and win the consensual support of citizens through liberal democratic institutions. Concluding the essay, O'Donnell ruled out both a PRI-style dominant party and an inclusive corporatist solution, and proclaimed democracy as the only option. With the restoration of political democracy 'at the very least the mediation of citizenship would reappear,' the problem of executive succession would be resolved, and the upper bourgeoisie would be freed from direct reliance upon the armed forces. However, one insoluble problem remained:

> But what kind of democracy? It would have to be one that achieves the miracle of being all this and that at the same time maintains the exclusion of the popular sector. In particular, it would have to be one that sustains the suppression of invocations in terms of

pueblo and class. Such suppression presupposes that strict controls of the organizations and political movements of the popular sector are maintained, as well as controls over the forms of permissible discourse and rhetoric on the part of those who occupy the institutional positions which democracy would reopen. The search for this philosopher's stone is expressed in the various qualifying adjectives that customarily accompany the term 'democracy.' ... The philosopher's stone would be a form of democracy which is carefully limited, in the sense that invocations in terms of *pueblo* or class are prohibited, but which at the same time is not such a farce that it cannot provide the mediations and, ultimately, a legitimacy that could transform itself into hegemony. The question of how this form of democracy will be achieved poses an enigma that severely tests the ingenuity of the 'social engineers' who offer their expertise to accomplish a task which amounts to squaring the circle. Yet the goal which the most enlightened actors in this system of domination seek to achieve is clearly this kind of democracy.[29]

Reality, one might say, is compelling. The O'Donnell of 1978 saw this option as a 'distorted and limited democracy,'[30] but he has since become one of the 'social engineers' who propose political democracy with no promise of social justice.[31] The exceptional and transitional phase of economic 'normalization' has become the norm, and the thrust of the ideological effort behind attempts to reformulate Latin American democracy these days is precisely to impose this limit, promoting citizenship and excluding *lo popular*.

There is a vital and fundamental contrast between the approaches of O'Donnell and Cardoso. O'Donnell failed to distinguish between state and political regime, and as a result came to a mechanistic and over-deterministic understanding of the available political alternatives. From this point of departure he at first identified a narrowly liberal democratic political regime as the only solution compatible with the interests of the dominant elites, but declared it unwelcome and scarcely realizable in practice. In short order, however, he endorsed it himself. In contrast, Cardoso identified himself with a distinctively social democratic political project from the start, declared it to be realizable in practice, and set about contributing to its realization. It remains now to be seen what has become of the project in the 1990s.

The Social Democratic Project in the 1990s

More recently Cardoso has defended the social democratic project in the context of the ascendancy of neo-liberalism and the transformation of the Soviet Union and Eastern Europe. Social democracy, he argues, should follow the Austrian social democrats of the beginning of this century, criticizing both liberalism and Bolshevik socialism. He certainly cannot be accused of underestimating the extent of this challenge as it presents itself in contemporary Latin America:

Apart from the challenges of that ideological battle, social democracy struggles in Latin America with a political tradition that is unfavorable to it, and it confronts the emergence of a new democratic practice that is frequently confused with the success of liberalism. This all happens in a context of economic stagnation (the decade of the 1980s is considered, from this point of view, a lost decade) and increasing social inequality.[32]

The unfavourable political tradition to which Cardoso refers is once again populism, or national developmentalism. 'In Latin America,' he argues, 'the demand for social rights – through populism – and the search for greater opportunities for economic development – through anti-imperialism – emerged before serious democratization and, up to a certain point, with disdain for it'.[33] On the left, the formal aspects of democracy were given little importance in comparison to hostility to poverty and imperialist exploitation, while across the political spectrum developmentalists gave less attention to the rule of law than to the need for industrialization and economic development:

> The so-called progressive bourgeoisie was more statist and nationalist than liberal-democratic. Therefore, the forces that could have been expected to criticize clientelism and patrimonialism in the name of democracy and the extension of human and political rights, until the mid-1970s, emphasized the 'efficiency of the state.' A strong state, in their view, would serve the accumulation process and eventually, better the living conditions of the masses. Direct social action by the state, even for more critical progressives, had precedence over questions of democracy, autonomy of class movements and direct political representation. In this way, the idea of social well-being was intimately tied to the defense of state action.[34]

In sum, Latin American progressivism practised selective redistribution to favoured groups (often through the perverse method of inflation) rather than the reorientation of state policies and public expenditures through fiscal and income policies, and neglected the question of the democratic control of the state. The according of privileges to select corporate groups, a minority of wage earners among them, constituted an impediment to the univeralisation of social conquests, and therefore a direct contrast with the European welfare state. The original sin of Latin American progressivism was that it was 'more statist than democratic.'

The subsequent installation of repressive bureaucratic-authoritarian regimes, the emphasis on accumulation and investment over redistribution, and the debt crisis, led to an anti-statist reaction which was reinforced by the resurgence of liberalism on a global scale. As Cardoso argues it, this had the problematic effect that 'the criticism of statism got mixed up with the criticism of populism,' threatening to sweep away the argument that structural reform carried out by and through the state is a necessary precondition for development along with the necessary critique of the deficiencies of populist national-developmentalism. In these circumstances, social democracy in Latin America today must offer a critique both of neo-liberalism and of the distorted progressivism of the past. In addition Cardoso remains explicit, as argued above, in recognizing the limits imposed by acceptance of a capitalist model of development: *'while defending the workers' and salaried employees' points of view, one needs to recognize the necessity to restrict corporatism and respect the requirements of production in terms of efficiency, productivity and necessary link between distribution and production'.*[35] Hence social democracy 'needs to oppose, in the name of economic growth and medium-term rationality, demands that, as just as they may be, will interrupt the continuity in the provision of desired benefits in the future.' Nevertheless, it will have failed unless it can combine prosperity with income redistribution. In sum

It is a critical posture toward the present type of development – combined with responsible positions concerning the necessity of accumulation and economic growth, added to its qualities as a moral and concrete political force in favor of income redistribution and social welfare policies – that will distinguish Latin American social democracy from populism, national-statism and renovated liberalism.[36]

Thus

the real question for contemporary social democracy concerns knowing how to increase economic competitiveness – leading to increases in productivity and the rationalization of the economy – and how to make the vital decisions concerning investment and consumption increasingly public ones, that is, how to make them transparent and controllable in society by consumers, producers, managers, workers and public opinion in general, not only by impersonal bureaucracies of the state or the private sector.[37]

In sum, therefore, social democracy in Latin America

should insist on democracy as an objective in itself (in the past, something done only by liberals) and, at the same time, dedicate itself to the institutionalization of practices of liberty, creating the arenas where reforms can be decided and implemented.[38]

On the eve of Cardoso's accession to the presidency, then, the project which he sought to carry forward was clear. It recognized and accepted the limits imposed by the need to accept the imperatives of global capitalism, but it argued that within those broad limits a process of political democratization would allow a degree of redistribution and social reform. The 'national project' advocated by Cardoso as president of Brazil has been largely consistent with the project outlined above. At the same time, engagement with concrete issues in national and international politics has led to a closer definition of the implications of the project at the close of the twentieth century. In particular, Cardoso has taken every opportunity to spell out the character and potential of social democracy in the context of 'globalization' – the increasingly compelling character of capitalist competition throughout the global economy. Extended statements made by Cardoso as president during 1996 confirm that the project remains the same, and identify both the progressive intent behind it, and the limits placed upon it by its acceptance of the current character and dynamics of global capitalism.[39] So much is this so, in fact, that Cardoso may be seen, and seems increasingly keen to project himself at an international level, as the architect of a modernized social democratic project which has come to terms with 'globalization.' Four main elements dominate his current discourse: a 'porous' state which is accountable and democratic, and which cooperates with civil society and non-governmental or 'neo-governmental' organizations to create an enlarged public space; an economic policy which accepts the context and discipline of globalization but gives the state an active role in regulating the market; a social commitment reflected in a domestic priority accorded to spending on education and health, and an international commitment to socially progressive global regimes; and an insistence that any project developed by the left must be universal rather than sectional, and therefore cannot focus on a single class or a privileged minority. Each point can be briefly illustrated from recent public statements.

The Porous State
Cardoso accepts that the state operates on behalf of the most advanced capitalist interests, but argues at the same time that it will only serve the interests of the bourgeoisie if it succeeds in integrating excluded sectors into society. He argues the need to replace the old clientelistic state created to serve the interests of the elites and the political class with a 'porous' state, a state in partnership with civil society, by-passing regional and local politicians to deal directly with voluntary bodies and independent citizens:

> The state has to be open. A porous state, so that the organizations of civil society have a presence – the so-called non-governmental organizations, which were looked on with great suspicion by the bureaucracy[40]

The national project which this proposal represents, and which Cardoso seeks to crystallize,

> is a democratic project, participatory, distributive, in which you have a growing public space. To reduce the size of the state means to increase the public space, it's not a question of reducing the size of the state in order to enlarge the market. It's reducing the size of the state to increase the public space[41]

An Active Economic Policy
At the same time, Cardoso argues that the hallmark of globalization is that capital is much more profitable in the periphery than at the centre. Not all areas of the periphery will benefit, but Brazil has a chance of doing so, and if it succeeds the consequence will be an increase in the forces of production, leading to development. In these circumstances, the Brazilian regime is not at the service of monopoly capital or state capital, but necessarily of 'that capital which is competitive in the new conditions of production.'[42] Within this broad context, however, it seeks to regulate the market, and to channel resources to small and medium enterprises, as we;; as to underdeveloped regions of the country. It does not simply accept the

discipline of the market, as a neo-liberal strategy would, but seeks to regulate it in order to overcome its deficiencies, and to create the social harmony without which the system would be threatened.

Social Commitment

In essence, then, Cardoso's project is aimed at achieving reform within a given system of production:

> Today, without changing the mode of production, we are trying to increase welfare. We have not found another mode of production capable of offering greater welfare. The failure of socialism led to the conclusion that changing the mode of production does not resolve the problem. The option is to try to increase welfare without altering the mode of production. To increase welfare it is necessary to make programmes universal. It is necessary to be willing to put order at risk in order to promote universalization.[43]

This is not simply a moral or normative commitment, but a real need which is as pressing for the bourgeoisie as it is for the excluded sectors themselves. In other words, the integration of the excluded is in the interests of all. In the long run, exclusion will be reduced by investment in education, and secondarily in health. It will also be mitigated by such projects as land reform, which are to be carried out specifically because they redress exclusion, despite the fact that the productivity they allow cannot hope to match that of the most advanced capitalist sectors in agriculture.

At an international level, this perspective leads Cardoso to call for new 'rules of governance' of the global order, characterized by greater democracy, the participation of a larger number of countries, and the development of new (and as yet unspecified) instruments to control the process of globalization. This is accompanied by a specific commitment to the inclusion of 'social clauses' in international agreements and regimes, from which Brazil will benefit because it will promote the development of a better-protected, better-educated and more productive workforce.[44]

A Universal Project for the Left

On this logic, the only feasible project for the left today is precisely a social democratic project which accepts the broad contours of capitalist production and competition on a global scale, but seeks to advance within it universal access to the advances in welfare which growing development and prosperity can bring. Hence Cardoso claims that 'I am against inequality and against injustice, so I consider myself of the left',[45] and argues that with the abandonment of faith in the alternative proposed by revolutionary socialism, 'The left today is the trend towards growing equality, which makes programmes universal'.[46]

Cardoso as President

On any assessment, the progress made by Cardoso as president towards the realization of his social democratic project by the end of 1996 was disappointing. This is so, I would argue, not only because priority has been given to economic stabilization and broadly neo-liberal readjustment (it is after all the stated logic of Cardoso's position that these changes have to be given priority in order to make subsequent social reform possible), but also because Cardoso has gone backwards on the parallel reforms that might have made social reform a reality. At the same time, the prospects for political reform have been dealt a mortal blow by Cardoso's reliance on the right and centre-right PFL and PMDB in preference to his own Social Democratic Party, the PSDB.

At the end of 1996 the Plano Real, the stabilization programme in place since mid-1994, which had secured the lowest inflation Brazil had known for four decades and proved the bedrock of Cardoso's continuing popularity, remained firmly in place, with inflation looking set to drop to single figures in 1997. At the same time, the privatization programme which had been pursued with stops and starts from the Collor presidency onwards was nearing completion, with Cardoso insisting that the sale of the giant mining complex Companhia do Vale do Rio Doce (CVRD) remained a top priority for the coming year. In addition, the opening up of Brazil's economy to foreign competition continued, notably with legislation in July to open up the market for cellular telephones, initially with a three-year period in which foreign companies would be limited to 49 per cent holdings. Even so, this last measure represented only a small step to the opening up of the telecommunications industry, and the petroleum sector remained off limits. On the whole, these major economic reforms could be said to be on course, albeit progress against the background of apparently lasting stabilization was slow. In themselves, however, they simply made up the neo-liberal package deemed essential to success in the global capitalist economy. Self-evidently, they did not in themselves either promise or advance a social democratic agenda.

Three further reforms, themselves the centre of Cardoso's frequently proclaimed package of administrative reform, remained stalled or subject to slow and piecemeal progress. These were the reforms of the tax system, the social security system, and the civil service. The first of these, fundamental to any redistribution of wealth and income in notoriously inegalitarian Brazil, was virtually abandoned despite the high priority it had initially been given at the start of Cardoso's term of office. Failure to secure progress on a fundamental overhaul of the tax system allowed the public deficit to swell, and prompted hand-to-mouth measures such as the tax on financial transactions, with the proceeds earmarked for spending on the health service. In the meantime, little progress was made on social security reform, a measure that in any case was largely an attack on rights acquired by workers in the 1988 constitution. Plans introduced early in 1996 were eventually severely scaled down after unsuccessful negotiations with workers' leaders, with key proposals held over for 1997. Legislation to remove the employment rights of civil servants, many of them employed through the wide-ranging patronage powers of state and local governments, fared no better, and towards the end of the year, Cardoso's government brought in stop-gap measures by provisional decree which again failed to address the bulk of public employees with lifetime tenure and generous pension rights.

None of these three reforms, it should be noted, were straightforwardly social democratic in character. A fundamental tax reform had the most obvious claim to be central to a social democratic project, depending on the extent to which it might be progressive, and the use to which increased revenue might be put. But the social security and civil service reforms were at best indirect steps towards universal provision, on the logic of Cardoso's analysis, as they would remove islands of privilege which created obstacles to universal provision aimed at the most needy. Only the introduction of a somewhat strengthened land tax towards the end of the year, following upon successive peasant massacres, increasingly widespread land invasions, and heightened tension throughout the countryside, suggested limited and belated progress on the long-delayed commitment to land reform.

Not only was progress slow on these measures, but such limited advances as were achieved were purchased at substantial cost, with Cardoso's government, despite his long history of opposition to the abuse of state resources to purchase support, resorting to trading financial favours for votes on the floor of Congress as very limited social security reforms were voted through in March. This characteristic of Cardoso's government, stemming from his initial election with right and centre-right support and his subsequent reliance on the PFL and the PMDB, has been significantly reinforced as the project of constitutional amendment to allow for Cardoso's re-election to the presidency has taken shape. It runs quite contrary to the logic of the social democratic project sustained from the 1970s onwards, and therefore demands particular attention. To the extent that the project espoused by Cardoso has been progressive, after all, it has been because it links a 'realistic' assessment of the imperatives of capitalism in an age of global competition to genuine democratic political reform which offers the hope of empowerment and limited redistribution to the majority. This was to be achieved, according to the formulation in Cardoso's original project, by the democratic reform of the unaccountable clientelistic state, and the self-organization of the majority. Cardoso's past political trajectory faithfully reflected this project. He attached himself to the opposition MDB, then chose to stay with its initially social democratic successor, the PMDB, at the time of party reform in 1979, rather than enter the newly-formed working class-based socialist PT (the Workers' Party).[47] At the same time, though, he left the PMDB to found his present party, the PSDB, when the PMDB was invaded by successive waves of former supporters of the pro-military PSD in 1982 and 1986, and the ability of the party to follow a principled line was destroyed by the systematic use of patronage by Sarney after his accession to the presidency. One of the most significant consequences of Sarney's lavish use of patronage in order to pursue his own aggrandizement, it will be recalled, was the hijacking of constitutional debate as Sarney sacrificed all other objectives in pursuit of a vote in favour of a five-year presidential term.

Cardoso has shown himself to be well enough aware of the contradiction involved in his own resort to the traditional practices of pork-barrel politics in order to achieve his ends. 'We have to create the new on the basis of the old,' he remarked in an interview given at mid-year, adding that 'of the allies that we have, some don't accept the market, while others accept it but continue to take a clientelistic attitude towards the state.' In sum, he concluded, 'There are few who accept the market but don't want anything to do with clientelism.'[48] The change of position with regard to the original reformist project is striking. In the original project, the democratization of the unaccountable authoritarian state was to be the mechanism by which the modernization of the capitalist class would be achieved, along with such redistribution as was possible within the confines of respect for the principles of capitalist accumulation. On that basis it was legitimate to argue, as Cardoso did, that 'sometimes "pure" liberal democracy (or, better, the actual practice of democratic liberties) constitutes a favourable condition for the advance of social democratization.' Cardoso's revised position, reflecting as it does the embrace of clientelistic politics in order to achieve even the very limited progress in promoting reform during his presidency, rests upon the opposite logic. As the surreptitious campaign to promote a constitutional reform to allow his re-election has proceeded, it has further strengthened the reliance of the government on the utterly clientelistic PFL and PMDB, divided, weakened and demoralised the PSDB, and recreated precisely the situation which prompted Cardoso's departure from the PMDB to found the PSDB.

Conclusion

Cardoso's social democratic project, as developed from the early 1970s onwards, deserves to be taken seriously. It is a fundamental mistake to assume that Cardoso came to power as a convinced neo-liberal.

Nevertheless, on the evidence assembled here, Cardoso the sociologist remains the most acute critic of Cardoso the president. Cardoso came to power with the popular legitimacy derived from the success of the Plano Real, and the ascendancy it gave him over elites and the capitalist class in Brazil. In power, he has accommodated himself to the archaic state which his earlier analysis had consistently condemned, and it is that capitulation, more than anything else, which has stripped the social democratic promise from his project, and reduced it to a recipe for the consolidation of neo-liberalism in practice. What is more, the resort to personalism and the repeated spectacle of the destruction of a new party which briefly represented a vehicle for social democratic reform has set back the prospects of long overdue institutional reform. In these circumstances, Cardoso's repeated and pained insistence that he is not a neo-liberal are bound to ring increasingly hollow. Quite possibly he gambled on his ability to escape once in office the implications of the initial alliance with the retrograde forces on the Brazilian right which brought him to power. Perhaps he still believes that once re-election is secured it will be possible to re-launch a social democratic project on a new basis. The danger, however, is that he will replicate the past he has condemned. Just as the populist state extended limited social rights and a modest degree of economic redistribution without achieving significant political democratization, Cardoso seems set on course, at best, to achieve a neo-liberal reform of the populist state without achieving significant political democratization.

NOTES

1. The quotations come from 'Alternativas Políticas na América Latina', in *O Modelo Político Brasileiro e Outros Ensaios* (Sao Paulo, DIFEL, 1973), p. 20; 'On the Characterization of Authoritarian Regimes in Latin America', in D. Collier, (ed.), *The New Authoritarianism in Latin America* (Princeton, Princeton University Press, 1979), pp. 39, 55; 'Régimen Político y Cambio Social', in N. Lechner, (ed.), *Estado y Política en América Latina* (Mexico City, Siglo XXI, 1981), p. 290; and 'Entrevista: Presidente Fernando Henrique Cardoso', *Esquerda 21*, January-February 1996, p. 42.
2. 'Alternativas Políticas na América Latina' was the opening presentation at a seminar held at the Centre for Inter-American Affairs in New York in May 1971.
3. 'Alternativas Políticas', *op. cit.*, p. 6.
4. *Ibid.*, p. 28
5. *Ibid*, p. 20.
6. *Ibid.*, p. 28.
7. *Ibid.*, p. 9.
8. 'Associated-Dependent Development: Theoretical and Practical Implications' , published in A. Stepan, (ed.), *Authoritarian Brazil: Origins, Policies, Future* (New Haven and London: Yale University Press, 1973), first presented at the Yale workshop organised by Stepan in April 1971.
9. *Ibid.*, p. 143.
10. *Ibid.*, p. 144.
11. *Ibid.*, pp. 146-7.
12. *Ibid.*, p. 149.

13. *Ibid.*, p. 171.
14. *Ibid.*, p. 175.
15. *Empresario Industrial e Desenvolvimento Economico no Brasil* (Sao Paulo, DIFEL, 1964), p. 180.
16. 'Associated-Dependent Development,' *op. cit.*, p. 148.
17. *Ibid.*, pp. 160-161.
18. *Ibid.*, p. 175.
19. 'On the Characterization of Authoritarian Regimes in Latin America', in D. Collier, (ed.), *The New Authoritarianism in Latin America, op. cit.*, pp.33–57.
20. *Ibid.*, pp. 38-9.
21. *Ibid.*, p. 51.
22. *Ibid.*, p. 39.
23. *Ibid.*, p. 46.
24. *Ibid.*, pp. 46-7.
25. *Ibid.* pp. 55, 57.
26. 'Tensions in the Bureaucratic-Authoritarian State and the Question of Democracy', in D. Collier (ed.), *The New Authoritarianism in Latin America* (Princeton, Princeton University Press, 1979), pp. 287–8.
27. *Ibid.*, p. 289.
28. *Ibid.*, pp. 299–300.
29. *Ibid.*, pp. 314–5.
30. *Ibid.*, p. 317.
31. See in particular G. O'Donnell and P. Schmitter, *Tentative Conclusions About Uncertain Democracies* (Vol. 4 of G. O'Donnell, P. Schmitter and L. Whitehead, (eds), *Transitions from Authoritarian Rule, op. cit*), especially pp. 11-14.
32. 'The Challenges of Social Democracy in Latin America', in M. Vellinga (ed.), *Social Democracy in Latin America: Prospects for Change* (Boulder, Westview Press, 1993), p. 275.
33. *Ibid.*, p. 278.
34. *Ibid.*, pp. 278-9.
35. *Ibid.*, p. 284, emphasis mine.
36. *Ibid.*, p. 286.
37. *Ibid.*, p. 287.
38. *Ibid.*, p. 293.
39. 'Entrevista: Presidente Fernando Henrique Cardoso', *Esquerda 21*, January-February 1996, and 'Para lembrar o que ele escreveu', Interview, *Folha de Sao Paulo*, 13 October 1996.
40. 'Entrevista', *op. cit.*, p. 42.
41. *Ibid.*, p. 52.
42. 'Para lembrar o que ele escreveu', *op. cit.*, p. 6.
43. *Ibid.*, p. 6.
44. 'Entrevista', *op. cit.*, p. 39.
45. *Ibid.*, p. 36.
46. 'Para lembrar o que ele escreveu', *op. cit.*, p. 5.
47. M. Keck, *The Workers' Party and Democratization in Brazil* (New Haven and London: Yale University Press, 1992), pp. 54, 57–8.
48. *Exame*, 3 July 1996, p. 23.

THE STATE AS CHARADE: POLITICAL MOBILISATION IN TODAY'S INDIA

Ananya Mukherjee-Reed

Introduction

Several rather distressing characteristics seem to define India as she enters the fiftieth year of her Independence. Of these the most apparent is the triumph of capital; having maximised the advantages of the Nehruvian 'mixed economy', it has now entered into a new phase characterised by an increased leverage over both state and labour. No less apparent at the end of these fifty years is the demise of the idea of the state itself, absolutely central to which is the rise of right-wing religious fundamentalism. Even though the fundamentalists articulate their critique of the state in terms of religious oppression, as I will show below, that critique is actually wedded to a particular version of the neo-liberal project that meets the interests of Indian capital.

The event which most clearly marks the emergence of fundamentalism as a significant political force in India is the series of violent communal riots that occurred in the north Indian city of Ayodhya on December 6, 1992.[1] Between the riots in 1992 and the national elections in May 1996, the Bharatiya Janata Party (BJP), the main political vehicle of the Hindu Right and the primary force behind the events at Ayodhya, continued its attempts to consolidate political power. Their efforts resulted in victories in a number of provincial elections, most notably in the country's two richest and most industrialised states, Maharashtra and Gujarat, and not surprisingly, these victories generated a sense of euphoria among the party faithful heading into the 1996 national election campaign. The anticipation of success was not entirely without foundation: the BJP (and its allies) received the largest percentage of the popular vote and won the largest number of seats in parliament, which put them ahead of both the Left Alliance and the Congress Party. However, the BJP failed to win an absolute majority. While it was invited to form the government, it was unable to bring together a viable coalition and was voted out of office within two weeks. The United Front government which was subsequently formed consisted of a coalition of the Congress and the Left Alliance, where the members (often called the 'Third Force') share the common goal of resisting the rise of Hindu fundamentalism.

Despite its failure to form the government, the BJP continues to be an important force in India's political-ideological terrain, and whether it can eventually establish itself as the ruling party at the centre remains the most important question for Indian politics today. Indeed, in many circles there is a belief that the Hindu Right has appealed to an 'authentic' and long-suppressed Hindu religiosity that characterises the Indian masses, and for that reason, it will from now on claim its permanent – and indeed, legitimate – space in Indian politics. Marxists and liberals, on the other hand, disagree with the view that there exists such a repressed Hindu psyche; instead, they see the BJP's success as arising out of the same fascist tactics that characterise the rise of fundamentalisms elsewhere in the world today, namely, the portrayal of a common enemy – in this case, the Muslims. Despite the quite substantial differences between them, both these arguments see the element of religiosity as being central to the strategy of the Hindu Right, and in that sense, perceive it as constituting a sharp break with India's 'secular' political tradition.

I wish to argue instead that an analysis of the strategy of the Hindu Right must go beneath its apparent appeal to religiosity to uncover a tried and tested mobilisation strategy that has a long tradition in India. This strategy consists of two equally important components: (a) an appeal to the experience of social, political and economic oppression of the Indian people, and (b) a proposal for redressing that oppression that pre-empts any serious change in the existing relations of property. In other words, the success of the religious Right – or any political strategy for that matter – derives as much out of its appeal to the masses as its appeal to the elites, and more precisely, out of its ability to develop a narrative that precludes the necessity for a conflict between the two.

Let me clarify one point at the outset. In emphasising the processes through which support is mobilised by political elites, we must see these processes as dialectical: elites respond to dominant currents in the popular psyche as much as they seek to mobilise popular opinion along desired lines. As such, these efforts at mobilisation necessarily involve processes of co-optation, re-channelisation and even demobilisation of genuine and organic social movements that arise out India's deeply inequitable structure. Since I focus on these processes of manipulation, it might appear that I am depriving the 'subaltern' of its subjectivity and denying to it the ability to participate in the creation of their own objective situation. In my view, whatever epistemological position one adopts, it is impossible to sustain the empirical argument that the Indian subaltern classes are bereft of subjectivity and have been the passive victims of the elites. There are too many instances in which the political consciousness of the 'unfed, illiterate Indian' has asserted itself against structures of power. That said, however, I must immediately insist that the subaltern's consciousness has been conditioned and manipulated by all types of elites and hence has to a large extent been denied the opportunity to create (or even objectively interpret) its own circumstance. Despite the potential allegation that such an assertion 'desubjectivises' the subaltern, I believe this to be a valid epistemological position. For, to impose subjectivity (or agency) on those who are confronted by fairly immutable structures of domination can easily lead us to an individualistic, anti-modernist, inegalitarian, neo-liberal position which requires the victim to accept unqualified responsibility for her misery. Such an unrelenting preoccupation with subjectivity, I will argue below, is untenable.

The BJP: History, Truth and Political Power

There are various explanations for the rise of religious fundamentalism in contemporary India. Let us begin with the most polemical of these, the one that is used by the political party of the Hindu Right, the BJP itself.[2] Basically, the BJP contends that its popularity derives out of the deep frustration that the Hindu majority feels with respect to the pro-minority policies of the Indian state. According to this explanation, the allegedly 'secular' ethic that forms the basis of the Indian constitution has been used primarily as a tool to get the minority vote. In practice, Indian secularism has thus meant much more than simple formal equality and non-discrimination on the basis of religion (or caste), but has endorsed a form of distributive justice for the minorities. Yet, the argument goes, since it was the Muslims who had ruled India until the onset of colonisation, injustice could only have been inflicted by the Muslims on the Hindus. At the very least, Muslims have jeopardised all efforts by Hindus towards Hindu-Muslim unity and have retained the same separatist vision that led to the creation of a separate Islamic Republic of Pakistan. The conclusion the BJP draws is that it is necessary to end the 'charade' of the secular state.

It is not only Muslims who have benefitted by this charade, according to the BJP. The state has also 'pampered' the lower castes and other ethnic minorities in the name of formal equality and universal rights. Such pampering of the lower castes was particularly favoured by Mrs Indira Gandhi, when she sought to 'include' members of the lower castes (and classes) into the units of local self-government. The momentum generated by this process was picked up by Mrs Gandhi's successor V. P. Singh, who tried to implement very aggressive affirmative action policies. In accordance with a rather controversial Report by the Backward Classes Commission submitted to the Singh government, 50 per cent of public sector jobs were to be reserved for members of lower castes and other backward classes. These reservations led to the much-discussed urban upper-class 'backlash' in Northern India during which two college students coming from upper class families in Gujarat set themselves on fire. This incident, along with the generally tactless manner in which the problem of affirmative action was approached by the Singh government, secured a permanent place for BJP-led rightist, reactionary fundamentalist politics in contemporary India.

In addition to such 'wrongs' in the realm of political-economy, a second (and, within the Hindu worldview, even more offensive) use of the secular ethic against Hindus has occurred in the realm of culture and identity. In effect, it is argued, the Hindu worldview has been eliminated from the public realm by 'pseudo-secular' nationalists like Nehru. From the perspective of the 'classificatory and divisive' Western modes of thought upon which Nehru and others relied, India appeared as a patchwork of irreconcilable worldviews. The only way in which this complexity could be 'rationalised' according to the requirements of the 'modern state' was to banish these diversities from the public realm.[3] This, the BJP alleges, resulted in the creation of a state based upon a fundamental denial of the one homogenous culture which 'truly' represents India , viz. *Hindutva*, i.e. the essence of Hinduism.

Now, how is one to assess the BJP's claim that its political support is rooted in the political, economic and cultural oppression of the Hindu majority by the 'pseudo-secular' state constructed by a Westernized elite? This argument has certainly resonated well among many sections of the Hindu upper and upper-middle classes who perceive themselves to the victims of government policy. Perhaps the most powerful class that felt victimised by the oppressive hand of the state is the landed elite. The grounds for their disaffection can be traced back to Indira Gandhi's encouraging of lower castes and classes to enter local government (a strategic move designed to establish a permanent Congress stronghold in rural constituencies). This shrewd politics of empowerment (unmatched by any material change), unleashed a demand for democratisation of feudal structures by lower castes (and classes). Throughout the seventies and eighties, the resistance from below became increasingly well organized. Initially led by and composed of low-caste Hindus who identified themselves as the proletariat, it attracted oppressed peoples from all religions and established links with various labour and peasant insurrectionary groups in different parts of the country. Known commonly as the *Dalit* Movement (*Dalit* literally means the 'downtrodden'), this upsurge was influenced by a combination of different strains of Marxism (especially Maoism) and an unusual variety of radical revivalism which structurally linked cultural, economic and gender oppression. Although the Dalit movement must be credited with questioning the very basis of caste and class rule, it was not able to bring about any significant shift of power away from the landed elite. It did, however, provoke a backlash from the agrarian upper and middle classes.[4]

Like the agrarian classes, yet another key section that has felt 'oppressed' by the 'pseudo-secular' state was the upper echelons of the state bureaucracy who strongly resent the infiltration of the bureaucracy by 'semi-literate low class officials'. Their opposition has been especially manifest in the debate that has been sparked by the recent election of Phoolan Devi, the former 'bandit queen,' to India's parliament. Feelings of oppression may also correlate with age: young men between ages 16-40 from Hindu upper-and middle class homes have been most strongly attracted by the BJP's agenda. The reason behind this relate to the recent resurgence of an aggressive achievement orientation, which feels itself stumbling against affirmative action policies for lower classes. While the onset of economic liberalisation has stimulated the material ambitions of the middle-classes, opportunities for realising these ambitions have not progressed in any significant way. In this situation, the (lower caste and minority) beneficiaries of affirmative action provisions inevitably become the targets of wrath of the middle classes who feel themselves to be the victims of such policies.[5]

Yet, while it is true that the BJP has garnered support among some Hindus who feel wronged by the secular state, three facts undermine their claim that their support is spontaneous and widespread. First, there is the fact that the base of their support tends to be limited to upper class and middle class Hindus. It is hard to sustain the claim that these groups have been oppressed by the state. Nor have the lower classes substantially benefitted by state policy. Any political 'empowerment' that has occurred among these lower classes has not been accompanied by any significant betterment of their living standards, and there is absolutely no evidence whatsoever that any economic gains that have been won, have come about at the cost of the upper classes. Second, support for the BJP shows great geographical variance. In the rural areas, in the states of the south (especially in Kerala, where a majority of the populace is Christian), or in the eastern state of West Bengal (where a significant part of the urban populace is left-leaning), the BJP's exclusivist Hindu agenda has been received with little or no enthusiasm. This is even more true of the responses to the issue surrounding the Ayodhya riots of 1992. Third, and perhaps most interestingly, the various political strategies employed by the BJP indicate its own awareness of the limitations of the class-biased nature of its religious platform. This is indicated most clearly by the fact that most of the BJP's political victories have come out of consciously forged alliances with local political parties which were led by and represented oppressed lower castes.[6]

Exploring the BJP's elitist and regional biases leads us to the puzzling problem of explaining the BJP's electoral success. Here, let me suggest first a somewhat obvious but critical point: casting the ballot does not necessarily reflect an acceptance of the party's political agenda. In this case, many of the electoral gains made by the BJP reflect losses suffered by the Congress, and in that sense, constitute a vote for the BJP only by default. Second, in the two Indian states with the largest Muslim population, namely West Bengal and Kerala, the BJP or its allies have made no dent in the voting behaviour of the general Hindu populace; it has, however, considerably influenced the Hindu upper and upper-middle classes, especially young males in urban areas. Third, since the BJP government fell at the centre, the party has suffered further losses in the provincial elections of October 1996, indicating a serious lack of ability of the party to sustain its electoral success. In Uttar Pradesh (UP), one of its strongest constituencies, the BJP has failed to win an absolute majority and lost 91 of the 177 seats it had won in the 1993 provincial elections. In Gujarat, the BJP government, which has been in power since 1993, had to be suspended and President's Rule imposed as violence marred parliamentary proceedings.[7] Fourth, several important variables that may explain its electoral success are only now beginning to be researched. These include, but surely are not limited to: (a) an extensive cadre-based organisational machinery; (b) a series of pre-electoral populist measures (like soup kitchens and shelters for the poor); (c) the use of terror;[8] and, (d) the resort to widespread conversion to Hinduism in the states of Gujarat and Rajasthan, in two of the five states where the BJP has made its electoral conquest. Even in their efforts to convert, it seems that the missionaries of the Hindu Right 'have shown an inordinate interest in converting the socially dominant and powerful Muslims, and not the 'lower' Muslim castes who form the majority of the Indian Muslim population.'[9]

All this leads us to question the claim that the BJP's electoral success reflects an 'authentic' resistance to a synthetic, Western secularism imposed illegitimately on Indian society by the post-Colonial state. The formula for its success should not, therefore, be sought in ability to articulate a general interest, but in its ability to articulate particular interests within a broader rhetoric of resistance with which it seeks to make the masses identify. In this respect, it tries to draw into its fold as many diverse groups as it can, viz., women, workers, caste minorities, Non-Resident Indians (NRIs), upper class Hindus, young men belonging to urban elite groups etc., but it is especially its link with the nationalistic bourgeoisie opposed to foreign capital that provides the key to understanding its strategy. This is what I will analyse in detail later in the essay, but first I want to examine another explanation of the rise of the Hindu Right.

The 'Subalternists'

Writing from a distinctly postmodernist perspective, members of the editorial collective known as the 'Subaltern School' in India have raised the issue of Hindu fundamentalism in the larger context of a critique of the Western ideal of the secular nation-state.[10] The basic premise of this subalternist explanation of the success of the BJP is that the modernist-universalist ethos inscribed in the secular nation-state is inappropriate for India.[11] The source of this inappropriateness lies in an incorrect understanding of religiosity and the importance it has in the consciousness of the subaltern. The failure of Marxists (and secular liberals) to understand the significance of religiosity reflects not only an unquestioned adoption of the premises of the European Enlightenment, but an uncritical acceptance of the primacy of economic and political equity over all other kinds of equality. This refusal to problematise the notion of modernity is what is said to characterise the *hyperliberal colonial modern*.[12] Given his inability to problematise modernity, the 'hyperliberal colonial modern' is unable to understand how the secular state is experienced by the masses as a violation of the right to religious freedom. It is this experience of an oppressive secular state, these postmodernists argue, that has led to a spontaneous eruption of popular support for the BJP.

In sum, the supposedly universal forms of the modern state do not meet the demands of cultural diversity and/or religious freedom in the Indian context (or that of other post-colonial states). Partha Chatterjee, for example, claims that the modern secular state is riddled by a series of anomalies due to the fact that its basic principles (viz., liberty, equality and neutrality) cannot be implemented without serious contradiction (and impingement on the rights of minorities). Instead of striving after an unattainable neutrality, the state should instead advocate tolerance.[13] Thus, in place of the secular state and its uniform civil code, Chatterjee suggests that religious communities need to be given the political space to regulate their own practices. This would guarantee minorities the 'right against governability, i.e., a right not to offer reasons for being different,' and to expect tolerance of its 'unreasonable' ways. The major constraint which Chatterjee would impose on this right is that 'each religious group will publicly seek and obtain from its members consent for its practices insofar as those practices have regulative power over members.' What this means at the institutional level for religious communities, is that its 'institutions must have the same degree of publicity and representativeness that is demanded of all public institutions having regulatory functions.'[14]

There are several rather serious problems with the general position advanced by postmodernists as well as with Chatterjee's specific proposals for an alternative to the liberal-democratic secular state in India. We can begin with some of the institutional implications of this position and the likely effects which they would have. First, if one accepts the existence of incommensurate discourses and the corresponding 'right against govern- ability,' as Chatterjee advocates, then what we are left with is a minimal state. The basic concern here is that, if the decision as to what constitutes valid religious praxis is to be decided strictly within a religious forum, then this minimal state cannot legitimately protect its citizens from any 'abuse' done in the name of religion, since the state cannot legitimately *define* abuse. What this means is that such questions as whether a Muslim woman is entitled to alimony on desertion by her husband will be decided within a patriarchal religious forum dominated by conservative male theologians. While Chatterjee and others will argue that the oppression of Muslim women in India at the hands of chauvinist male theologians occurs only because of the lack of democracy and representativeness in the religious forums, this is not a solution to the problem. Rather it is to ignore the reality. Is one to expect democratic procedure in a religious forum which is governed by religious laws, where the power to interpret these laws is restricted? As the Indian experience has already shown, it is all too conve- nient for the state not to address such abuses even when it has the constitutional power to oppose them. Ceding the right to religious bodies to define such questions will only give the state further excuses for not intervening.

A second important institutional implication of the postmodern position is that by favouring religious communities, it inhibits and delegitimises attempts by other non-religious collectives (e.g., trade unions) to claim their democratic space. Thus, for example, if a Hindu 'religious forum' like the World Council of Hindus decides, on an 'authentic reading' of the *Vedas*, that lower caste Hindus are inherently more suited to manual rather than intellectual labour, then trade unions cannot intervene on the part of its lower-caste Hindu members – since the postmodern state will be unable to challenge such a ruling.

Underlying the unsavoury institutional implications of the postmodern position are some fundamental problems. The first of these is the general postmodern presupposition of the incommensurability of discourses across cultures. A second problem among subalternists like Chatterjee is a basic tendency to 'essentialise' the colonised consciousness as immutably and uncritically religious. These two factors account for the privileging of equal liberty for religions over equal political, social and economic rights for individuals and all social groups. In effect what is being argued is that while other countries might engage in 'democratic revolutions' which demand the same standards of equality for the coloniser and the colonised (e.g., a liberal democratic state with a uniform civil code for all citizens), India must continue to derive its politics of equality from an essentialised politics of religious difference.[15] In other words, the subaltern is incapable of learning from her experience as a political being: she is incapable of detecting manipulation by self-interested elites who act as often in the name of religion as in the name of secularism; in particular, the subaltern is incapable of deciphering how both these types of politics are inherently opposed to any serious change in the material conditions of her existence. The denial of this fundamental aspect of the subalterns' experience, and how that experience might enable a different, *a-religious* politics of equality, is what gives post-modernist politics its reactionary content.[16] In this it bears an uncanny resemblance to the revisionist phase in the development of psychoanalytic theory in Europe: as Marcuse has so eloquently summarised in his epilogue to *Eros and Civilisation*, this revisionism helped in many ways to justify and diffuse the true colours of fascism in Europe.

Moreover, and here we return to our original question, ignoring key aspects of the subalterns' experience leads to an inadequate account of the rise of the BJP. By essentialising subaltern consciousness, postmoderns are not able to appreciate the fact that subalterns may support Hindu fundamentalism (to the degree they do at all) with a great deal of ambiguity and for much more complex reasons than a desire for greater religious freedom from the state. [17]

Toward an Alternative Explanation: Gandhi and the Hindu Right

Marxists and other radicals have also sought to offer explanations of the upsurge of Hindu fundamentalism in India. These accounts have taken either of two forms. One strand, explicitly Marxist in its orientation, develops a political-economy analysis that indicates how mixed Hindu-Muslim communities that historically existed in more or less harmonious relations, have been made to compete with each other for increasingly scarce resources in order to stave off poverty. Thus, historical processes of pauperisation, destruction of village communities and the subsequent ghettoisation of the urban communities produced by 'predatory commercialisation' are held responsible for communal conflict.[18] The other strand focuses on ideological critique. Within this strand, one explicitly Marxist theorisation has sought to explain the rise of the Hindu Right as the culmination of a long process of ideology formation which was consciously designed and executed by three related organisations (viz., the RSS, the VHP and the BJP).[19] Another radical analysis, this one by critical feminists, has argued that the Hindutva doctrine's ability to abort the modernist-feminist project before its fulfillment lies at the root of its popularity. [20] A third approach to ideological critique comprises an analysis of the 'myths' and 'histories' on which the Hindu Right bases its claims. This analysis, especially the version outlined by the eminent historian Romila Thapar reveals how, in keeping with its inherently fascist character, the ideologues of the Hindu Right have attempted to homogenise the essentially divergent character of Hindu myths and histories. As Thapar illustrates, the Hindu myths have traditionally taken on substantially different contents according to the different social contexts in which they are rendered, very often reflecting radical critiques of structures of oppression; central to these diverse renditions is a refusal to treat epics, myths or histories as immutable, given, or sacred 'texts'. Thapar argues that this is precisely what *Hindutva* attempts to emasculate, and purging it of its radical content – seeks to replace it with a single homogenous, conservative text that suits particular interests. Even though it is backed in this endeavour by the very latest developments in the media, its very efforts at homegenisation have restricted its political appeal.

In what follows, I will draw on some of these approaches to offer an integrated account of the recent rise of the Hindu Right in India. While agreeing with the view that its appeal has been restricted, I believe that the Hindu Right *has* appeared as a powerful ideological contestant in India. Central to the ideological appeal of the Hindu Right is its critique of the Indian state which in essence, is a critique of the failure of the state to respond to the particular needs of domestic capital as well as the needs of the new propertied classes that have been unleashed by the coming of neo-liberalism. In other words, I would contend that too much emphasis has been placed on religiosity as the distinguishing characteristic of the Hindu Right, and on the break it constitutes with India's secular past. I wish to argue that it is not so: the strategy of the Hindu Right, as unprecedented as it might seem, is characterised by a basic commonality that all mobilisation strategies hitherto have shared. In particular, the thrust of the strategies used by the Hindu Right derive out of similar ideological constructs developed by Mahatma Gandhi, who, as is well-known, is associated with a set of ideals quite substantially opposed to that of the Hindu Right. While Gandhi idealised non-violence, communal harmony and a secular state based on religious toleration, the BJP, using some of the very same strategies as the Mahatma, strive towards a theocratic state based on religious exclusion. How is this possible? These apparently opposed goals are actually united by their essentially anti-egalitarian ontology, central to which is a strategic measure to accommodate the needs of the propertied. The commonality between Gandhi and the Hindu Right stems from their mutual profound antipathy towards all modernist and especially Marxist principles of equity.

One fundamental parallel between Mahatma Gandhi and the Hindu

Right constitutes the fact that both see religion as the major instrument with which to de-radicalise popular consciousness.[21] In Gandhi, the essentially conservative nature of his religious ideology is most evident in his conception of the 'ideal state' which he denotes as *Ramrajya* (literally, Rama's kingdom): a state based on religious-moral authority of the virtuous ruler.[22] The *Ramrajya* is characterised by harmony – a harmony between religions, sexes, and castes, between capital and labour and between the landed and the landless. The model is one of an extended family: a 'naturally' constructed organic unit where each member is 'naturally' assigned a certain role in the unit. Moreover, exactly as in a family, society (or the state) is characterised by a certain hierarchy, a hierarchy to which every member of the family submits voluntarily. This emphasis on harmony and hierarchy feed, in turn, directly into Gandhi's model of 'trusteeship', which Gandhi proposed as an alternative to the socialist state. In this model, the rich would consider themselves as trustees of society, and offer their wealth for the use of those less fortunate. With such a moral regeneration of the propertied classes, Gandhi argued, there would be no need for the propertyless to demand justice through violent political means (e.g. confiscation, nationalisation or land reform as in Soviet Russia), except in the special circumstance where the trustees failed in their role.

In addition to this general framework within which property was to be legitimated, Gandhi went even further to accommodate the ambitions of capital. On the one hand, the domestic bourgeoisie of his time sought freedom from the reigns of imperial capital. On the other hand, they actively searched for ways in which to suppress any radical structural change that could frustrate their ambitions of capitalist growth. Trusteeship, non-violence and insistence on familial relations between opposing classes (especially capital and labour) provided the ideological tools through which Gandhi sought to pre-empt thoroughgoing structural change, the demand for which had gained considerable momentum at that time. The indigenous elites, both the industrialists and the landed classes, were beginning to feel pressure and needed a strategy that would be able to legitimate a capitalist state. In the industrial sector, the Indian labour movement, which was fostered initially by colonial capitalism and grew steadily during the 1920s, gained a new momentum in the 1930s. The number of strikes increased, the number of unions and union membership rose steadily, while the two largest federations of trade unions initiated a process of gradual rapprochement from a previous position of antagonism. Growing labour unrest caused the Congress to lose seats in the provincial legislatures and eventually forced them to pass a series of labour welfare measures in 1937 at the meeting of the Congress Labour Committee. However, Congress was very careful 'not to hit the capitalist interests too hard', while taking care of some of the immediate legitimation needs. Inquiry committees were set up to look into the question of wages, wage indexation, legislation on the settlement of disputes, and most importantly the question of representation of labour in management.

A similar situation prevailed in the farm sector. Demographic pressures on the fixed landed base greatly increased the number of the landless and the virtually landless, many of whom had been pushed out of subsistence farming. In the 1920s and the 1930s their situation was becoming impossible, being subject to the vagaries of an incomplete market system for securing a minimum supply of their basic needs. The situation came to a climax during the Great Depression, which, while temporarily providing them with wage bonuses, initiated a structural shift from permanent and patronage-based employment patterns to short-term, more casual, and insecure employment patterns. This growing misery of the rural poor resulted in a series of agrarian riots and violent confrontations with landlords. There was a 'perceived danger that not only would the agrarian elite not be able to hold down the countryside but that some of its members might even join and sponsor an attack on the extant state institutions.'[23]

It was under the stress of these developments that industrialists like Birla generously agreed to finance Gandhi's nationalist movement, while Muslim landlords, who might have otherwise been troubled by the rising Hindu militancy within the Congress Party, renewed their ties with the Congress. In one of his letters to a friend, G. D. Birla wrote 'I need hardly say I am a great admirer of Gandhiji. In fact I am one of his pet children. I have liberally financed his khadi (cottage industry) movement and untouchability activities . . . I wish I could convert the authorities to see that he is greatest force in the side of peace and order . . . He alone is responsible for keeping the left wing in check.'[24] Industrialists also began to indulge increasingly in charitable activities, as trusts for the advancement of education, healthcare, women, Harijans and the poor became the order of the day. Such activities, in addition to fulfilling the ethical obligations of noblesse oblige, helped to meet the most immediate needs of the lower classes and, thereby acted as an antidote to radicalisation amidst the poor.

On the question of freeing domestic capital from the reins of imperial capital, Gandhi's ideology was used in support of the Indian industrialists demand for an end to discrimination in favour of British capital. At one level, Gandhi's *Swadeshi* (Nationalist) movement encouraged the patronising of domestic firms and purchase of domestically produced goods, supplemented by a large-scale boycott of foreign goods.[25] Here Gandhi invoked a full-fledged critique of imperialism, quite distinct from his other theses in its radical tone.[26] At a deeper level, Gandhi invoked *Swadeshi* to symbolise the suppression of the indigenous by the invasion of the 'foreign'. '... But for me', Gandhi wrote, 'real freedom will come only when we free ourselves from the domination of Western culture... because this culture has made our living artificial ... Emancipation from this culture would mean real freedom for us'.[27]

We are now in a position to see more clearly the similarities between the Gandhian doctrine with that of the contemporary Hindu Right. Of obvious significance here is their invocation of the contradiction between the 'indigenous' and the 'foreign': Gandhi invokes this contradiction as a rhetoric with which to resist British capital, whereas the Hindu Right, as we shall see, uses it for a more complex task of legitimating a somewhat 'bastard' form of neo-liberal capitalism demanded by the contemporary bourgeoisie. Gandhi was faced with a relatively straightforward task of protecting national capital from colonial capital; for the Hindu Right, it is a more complex task of finding a rhetoric within which domestic capital can choose and dictate the conditions under which it interacts with global capital. In other words, the BJP wants to protect the interests of a domestic capitalist class that favours neo-liberalism to the extent that it reduces state control, but feels seriously threatened by those elements of neo-liberalism that open it up to foreign competition. The question that first needs to be answered, however, before going into this in more detail, is why after fifty years of secularism in an independent India religious ideology revives as a means of dealing with this problem for capital.

Indianising Neo-liberalism: From Secularism to The Hindu Right

In direct opposition to Gandhi's ideal of *Ramrajya*, Nehru and Mrs Gandhi established and consolidated 'a secular socialist Indian republic', where the role of the state was to integrate across all 'primordial' cleavages, projecting poverty as the factor that unified these 'different' groups. The primary political strategy was the promise of alleviating poverty, and it was in order to fulfill this strategy that the state undertook its developmental role. As is well-known, the developmental role comprised a politics of accommodation, played out through an elaborate mechanism of public economics. First, there were massive doses of public investment and soft financing to aid the development of capitalism. Second, there were huge subsidies to the farm sector necessitated by its rising militancy and political power that came in the wake of the Green Revolution. Even though an increasing amount of subsidies went to the farm sector (and continue to go even after liberalisation), agricultural incomes stubbornly remained outside the purview of taxation. Finally, there were subsidies, grants and transfers, public works programmes, and relatively high levels of social sector expenditures incurred in order to satisfy the political needs of 'legitimation'.

By the end of the 1960s, severe contradictions emerged in this secular and state-led developmental strategy. The scale and content of the above programmes lent credence to the state's political promise – but it came with the growth of monopoly houses, gross inequalities in land reform, rising public sector losses, and ever-increasing poverty. This provoked, on the one hand, a resurgence of left forces and radical ideologies in different parts of India. On the other hand, it added new layers to the social stratification that already existed. Developmental planning directly increased the size of the urban upper middle classes (through the development of both public and private sectors), the petty bourgeoisie, and a nouveau riche agrarian class which was born directly out of the Green Revolution. While these new classes provided Mrs Gandhi with a new base of legitimation, at the same time their support discredited her claim to be a populist leader.

It was the deepening of these contradictions for which Mrs Gandhi returned to 'primordial' politics and again sought mobilisation along ethnic/religious/ communal/caste lines. It was not surprising, then, that for a substantial period between this point in the late seventies and 1984 when she was assassinated, the 'Punjab' problem (which eventually emerged as the Hindu-Sikh religious conflict) became her (and the nation's) major preoccupation. In addition, Mrs Gandhi attempted to shift focus away from the economic failures by focusing once again on a rhetoric of political empowerment of the lower castes and classes, especially in the rural areas. Thus, in order to maintain Congress strongholds in rural constituencies, she took up a policy of allowing increased access of these classes into units of local self-government. This provided the much-needed political vent for growing economic demands of the increasingly marginalised rural populace, and was quite successfully chanelled into an aggressive 'lower caste politics.'[28]

Indira Gandhi's successor, her son Rajiv Gandhi (1984-89) continued with this style of particularistic politics, entering into special accords with each particular religious/ethnic/regional group that approached him with their demands. Symbolic of his preference for the decentralisation of excessive federal power, this particularistic approach helped Rajiv appeal to a common experience of oppression exactly as his predecessors had done: this time, the oppression of the Nehruvian state.[29] Rajiv sought to address two aspects of this oppression (a) its restriction on private enterprise; and (b) its restriction on consumption, especially 'luxury' consumption, which was a direct outcome of its emphasis on the capital goods sector as the primary agent of development. Invoking the exact same rhetoric of *Ramrajya* as Gandhi, Rajiv now defined this ideal state as one characterised by free enterprise, high technology, and a consumerist middle-class. In order to encourage free enterprise, Rajiv embarked on a programme of liberalisation that not only removed the Nehruvian controls on capital, but also sought profitable linkages with global capital. In order to promote the middle-classes, Rajiv's government negotiated one of the highest pay increases for the uppermost echeleons of public sector workers (who provided the effective demand for the consumer goods 'revolution' that subsequently swept the country). However, the essential elitism of this approach needed somehow to be countered, especially because of the way in which the ideologues of Hindutva were already garnering support for a more 'indigenous', mass-based politics.

Again, in the exact same manner as his predecessors, Rajiv resorted to an appeal to communal sentiments in order to offset the inherently class-biased nature of his agenda. On the one hand, Rajiv overrode decisions of the Supreme Court (with respect to the rights of Muslim women) and passed a law that accommodated the conservative demands of Islamic fundamentalists. On the other hand, he wholly adopted the rhetoric of Ramrajya which was being used by the Hindu Right and participated actively in the ceremony for laying the foundation stone for the proposed temple at Ayodhya.[30] With these twin acts, he opened up space for the kind of anti-modernist religious politics sought by the Hindu Right, at the same time that he catered to the needs of the bourgeoisie with the policies of liberalisation. Rajiv's successor V. P. Singh (1989-90) continued to add momentum to the aggressive politics of the Hindu Right by putting into place a policy to reserve almost fifty percent of public sector jobs for lower castes and other minorities. This provoked an anti-secular backlash amongst the Hindu upper castes which not only helped justify the claims of the Hindu Right, but also deeply divided the populace along 'primordial' lines. [31]

It was precisely through the backdoors of this amorphous and fragmented polity that both Hindutva and neo-liberalism entered the political space in India. Rajiv Gandhi's governments proved crucial in bringing about the marriage between the Hindu Right and neo-liberal economics, predicated as they were on the common rejection of the state intervention. In particular, neo-liberalism matched perfectly the Hindu Right's insistence that the Nehruvian model was 'too interventionist', obstructing not only free enterprise but also Hindu religion and culture. How did this apparently strange marriage actually come about?

For this we need to understand the shifting political preferences of Indian capital. While it lent strong support to the post-V. P. Singh Congress government headed by Narsimha Rao and his finance minister Dr Manmohan Singh for going even further than Rajiv in dismantling controls on capital, Indian capital quickly came to the opinion that they were proceeding 'too fast' with respect to inviting foreign capital in. At issue was the Congress government's policy to allow foreign companies to increase their stakes in their Indian subsidiaries by up to 100 per cent. As a result of this policy, most MNCs have managed to increase their stakes in their Indian subsidiaries with minimal capital outlay. (Colgate-Palmolive, for example, has increased its stake from 40 to 51 per cent by purchasing shares at one-twelfth of the ruling market price.) Further, most of these 'restructured' subsidiaries have plans to enter the lines of business that are the most profitable and are growing at the highest rates: i.e. the consumer non-durables like beverages, cosmetics, fast food etc. Finally, instead of bringing fresh capital into the country, these MNCs plan to raise capital in the Indian stock markets, thereby threatening to reduce the availability of funds for Indian businesses.

It was no surprise, therefore, that the resistance by Indian capital to this 'foreign invasion' culminated in a 'revolt' by the Bombay Club, an informal association of the top industrialists in the country. The basic thrust of the Club's demand was that the Rao government should provide domestic capital with a 'level-playing field' vis-à-vis foreign capital. The Bombay Club's resistance to global competition has since reflected itself in the numerous proposals put forward by various chambers of commerce.[32] For example, the Federation of the Indian Chambers of Commerce and Industry (FICCI), which is one of the two major chambers in the country, has proposed that MNCs which enter with a majority holding in Indian companies be mandatorily made to disinvest after a predetermined time-frame.[33] Similarly, the President of the other leading chamber of commerce, the Confederation of Indian Industries (CII), has suggested the need for invoking Swadeshi in order to resist the onslaught of transnational capital.[34] Most importantly, despite the government's effort to woo foreign capital, several highly acrimonious battles have occurred in the recent past between Indian business houses and MNCs looking to increase their stakes in those houses. As a result, the Indian corporate sector has come to resist rather strongly any universal policy change which make for an unfettered entry of foreign capital. Instead, it has articulated a preference for particular deals, joint ventures and financial partnerships the merits of which are to be decided on a case-by-case basis.

And this is precisely what the BJP represents in the party political arena. Interestingly enough, this particularistic approach to foreign firms is especially favoured by one faction of foreign capital looking to invest in India, viz., the non-resident Indians (NRIs). They see a rather unique possibility for gaining special treatment by the Indian state and Indian capital and have preferential access to the Indian market and the cheap, yet relatively skilled labour force. From the point of view of Indian businesses, the NRIs provide a way to establish linkages with global capital without having to succumb totally to uncertainties of unfettered foreign competition. This fortuitous coincidence of interests was probably first noted by Rajiv Gandhi, the official author of post-Nehruvian political-economy in India; however it is the BJP, along with its cultural outfit, the World

Council of Hindus, which have been actively trying to build bridges between the NRIs and their motherland. In fact, a new organisation called the *Overseas Friends of the BJP* was formed to launch the Saffron Vision 2000 in the US. The aim of this project is to educate NRIs in the US about the economic policies of the BJP.[35]

Two main elements of the BJP's economic policy are particularly appealing to capital: privatisation and protectionism. The philosophical roots of this protectionism are derived from a synthesis of Gandhian socialism and the thoughts of a lesser known nationalist ideologue, Deendayal Upadhyaya, both of whom emphasise *Swadeshi* and self-reliance.[36] In line with the idea of self-reliance, the BJP's economic policy recommends restrictions on the entry of foreign capital into consumer goods sectors and only qualified entry into other sectors of production. This is where the BJP most sharply distinguishes itself from the Congress, and thereby draws support from the largest faction of Indian domestic capital. Further, the BJP also endorses a policy of preferring investment by NRIs over other types of foreign capital. In the states governed by the BJP and its alliances, explicit policies have been pursued to attract NRI investment. Between 1991 and 1995 about Rs.4 billion (approximately $119 million) of NRI investment have flowed into Gujarat, which is one of the richest and most industrialised states in India ruled by the BJP.[37] This impressive inflow of capital is a result of the Gujarat government's special incentive package for the NRIs, which a special branch of the Ministry of Industries of the Gujarat state has been set up to administer. The incentives include priority in allotment of cash subsidies and loans from financial institutions, as well as special allotment of resources like electric power and land. At the national level, NRI investment constitutes 44 per cent of the total foreign direct investment in 1995-96.[38]

Apart from this preferential policy with respect to NRI capital, the rest of BJP's economic policy is unqualifiedly neo-liberal. It favours, for example, a total deregulation of all kinds of control on Indian industry and recommends drastic cuts in deficit spending. It also suggests steady privati-sation in all areas, including sale of state-owned land in rural areas, the proceeds from which are to be used to retire national debt. In terms of its trade policy, the BJP's primary aim was to limit imports of consumer goods. In 1993 for example, some BJP stalwarts planned a 'boycott' of goods manufactured by MNCs, which was to be initiated with a public burning of foreign goods that would replicate the occurrences during the nationalist struggle. The BJP had also planned a negative list of sectors where foreign investment would not be allowed and imports were to be restricted.[39] This mix of protectionism and privatisation in favour of domestic capital amidst globalisation is something that has in general been far too much ignored, by no means only in India.

Conclusion

This essay has contended that there is a certain continuity between past strategies of political mobilisation in India and those of the Hindu Right, however disparate they may seem at the first instance. This continuity lies in the way in which the Hindu Right embodies the class politics of its time, and attempts to protect the interests of property from whatever immediate forces may seem to come in conflict with it. To stress the discontinuities between the Hindu Right and the past trajectory of Indian politics is to ignore the increasing triumph of property that comprises the very essence of this trajectory. It is in this specific sense that I see distinct similarities between the Gandhian model of communal harmony and the exclusivist theocracy of Hindutva, and between the developmentalism of Nehru and Mrs Gandhi and the neo-liberalism of Rajiv Gandhi. Essential to all of them is not only the desire to capitalise on the democratic consciousness of the Indian people but also the perverse ability to co-mingle apparently contradictory forces and structures, and thus in the end, to stall any serious crisis of legitimation that might unleash a serious demand for structural change. Placed within this 'meta-narrative', it is not clear that the Hindu Right's ideological onslaught can be fought only at the realm of ideology, i.e. by either invoking the secular values of Gandhi and Nehru or by advocating toleration that pre-empts non-religious communities. This is precisely why one needs to celebrate the whole array of creative and genuine resistance, that oppose, in whatever meagre way possible, the oppression of capital as well as that of manipulative politics.

NOTES

1. Ayodhya is the supposed birthplace of Ram, a popular and much revered Hindu God. According to the BJP's representation of history, the Mogul ruler, Babur, had constructed a mosque on Lord Ram's birthplace. The BJP wanted the mosque destroyed and replaced by a Hindu temple dedicated to Lord Ram.

   In its efforts to mobilise public opinion, especially in Northern India, the BJP organized a huge procession through the heart of New Delhi in which party stalwarts, dressed up as warrior-gods set out towards Ayodhya in order to 'set history right'. Organised brilliantly with the help of their dedicated cadres, the BJP was highly successful in increasing its visibility throughout India through such theatrics.

2. For the purposes of this paper I will be referring to the Hindu Right as the main analytical category. The Hindu Right in India comprises the RSS (The Rashtriya Swayamsevak Sangha, i.e. the National Organisation of Volunteers), the VHP (The Vishwa Hindu Parishad, i.e. the World Council of Hindus) and the BJP (the Bharatiya Janata Party). The RSS claims to be a cultural, and not a political organisation. It is the principal ideological apparatus of the Hindu Right. The BJP (and some of its allies like the Siv Sena which currently rules the state of Maharashtra) are political parties of the Hindu Right. The VHP is an international organisation that provides a common forum for Hindus all over the world.

3. T. Basu et al., *Khaki Shorts and Saffron Flags: A Critique of the Hindu Right* (New Delhi, Orient Longman, 1993), p. 37.

4. See Gail Omvedt, *Dalit Visions: The anti-caste movement and the construction of an Indian identity* (New Delhi, Orient Longman, 1995).

5. While both upper and middle classes disapprove of affirmative action for minorities, the resentment of the middle classes is much stronger, since middle-class youths compete more directly for government jobs and seats in educational institutions and are more dependent on these for the fulfillment of their material ambitions than upper-class youths.

6. This was necessary because the very nature of the BJP's agenda restricted its appeal to the Hindu elites in the Hindi-speaking areas of the country where the Hindu myths (especially that of Ram) were the most popular. Paradoxically, this is also the region where the Muslim minority is concentrated and where caste and class oppression by the Hindu landed elites is the starkest. Logically, therefore, these were also the areas where Indira Gandhi's empowerment politics was most actively received and seized upon by the victims of oppression. As such, the BJP had no other option but to forge alliances with parties that represented lower-caste interest. In these cases the BJP legitimised itself through its anti-Muslim agenda. One must note, however, that most of these 'alliances' were simply deals struck between opportunists seeking to consolidate their political-ideological territory.

7. 'Amidst total chaos and unruly conditions leading to physical removal of all Opposition members from the Gujarat Assembly, a few of them beaten up mercilessly, the Suresh Mehta Ministry claimed to have won the vote of confidence today, after the sudden hospitalisation of the Deputy Speaker, Mr Chandubhai Dabhi. Journalists boycotted the proceedings after a press-police confrontation. While nothing was audible in the din, an official spokesman of the Government claimed that 93 members, including the Acting Speaker, Mr Dolatbhai Desai, and two independents, voted in favour of the confidence motion with none against, clearly establishing the Ministry's majority support in the House of 179 members.' *The Hindu*, 11 October 1996.

8. See Sumit Sarkar, 'The Fascism of the Sangha Parivar,' *Economic and Political Weekly*, vol. 27, no. 5, 1993 for a comparison between the the the BJP and its alliances like the Siv Sena and the fascist regimes in Italy and Germany, especially, in terms of their resort to open terror. Particularly important in the Indian case are the seemingly unconnected incidents like the murder of Shankar Guha Neogy, leading labour leader of unusual zeal, the beating up of journalists, the bombing of the Bombay Stock Exchange, each of which have occurred within the BJP's territory. The use of terror in order to whip up communal conflict amongst Hindu-Muslim communities which have co-existed perfectly harmoniously over long periods of time have been eloquently portrayed in a number of documentaries.

9. 'Muslims in many parts of India live in constant fear of attacks by Hindu mobs in which, especially in recent years, the police is known to have played an extremely partisan role, often actively assisting the Hindu rioters'. In 1994, the VHP, the ideological outfit of the Hindu Right that actually performs the conversions, claimed to have converted 20,000 Muslims in Gujarat and were eyeing the 500,000 strong population of Muslims in central Gujarat. Most of these Muslim groups that the Hindu Right seeks to convert are actually low-caste Hindus who had converted to Islam to escape the tyranny of the caste system. See Y. Sikand and M.Katju, 'Mass Conversions to Hinduism among Indian Muslims', in Economic and Political Weekly, 20 August 1994, pp. 2214-2219.

10. Dipesh Chakraborty, 'Radical Histories and Questions of Enlightenment Rationalism: Some Recent Critiques of Subaltern Studies,' *Economic and Political Weekly*, 8 April 1995.

11. Partha Chatterjee, 'Secularism and Toleration,' *Economic and Political Weekly*, 9 July 1994, p. 1768.

12. Chakraborty, *op. cit.*

13. Chatterjee, *op cit.*, p. 1772.

14. *Ibid.*, p. 1775.

15. These democratic revolutions include not only the bourgeois revolutions of the west, but more importantly, the socialist revolutions in various parts of the world which contested 'Western' liberal-democratic principles of equality. In most of the Third World, it is precisely these revolutions that have challenged colonial and neo-colonial relationships, and more generally all forms of oppression that arise out of structures riven with inequity. Ironically, some of the earlier works by these same subalternists had demonstrated this 'radicalised' consciousness, especially peasant consciousness, which had developed as a response to feudal-colonial oppression and had been in existence in India prior to intervention by the nationalist leaders like Gandhi. Some subalternist studies had also demonstrated the co-existence of this radical-revolutionary element with the religious element, and how each had served a function in resisting oppression.

16. This proposition, that the subaltern is essentially resistant to modernist principles of equality, one may argue, is simply empirically unsustainable in the Indian context. Several movements that have been more representative of the subaltern's view than the Hindutva movement have clearly demanded equity in the modernist and, indeed, Marxist sense. The Dalit movement, the Naxalite upsurge, the current movement against the American MNC Enron, are all clearly demonstrative of a demand for actual structural change. The denial of these realities as constituting the subaltern's psyche reflects, I believe, not only the essential anti-modernism of this particular brand of subaltern studies, but also its ontological opposition to Marxism.

17. While it is beyond the scope of this paper to go into a full-fledged critique of the notion of coloniality, I am tempted to make one observation. It seems that contemporary subalternists' anti-enlightenment position is based, paradoxically, on the very same 'colonial' assumptions that it critiques. For, the subalternist seems to accept the colonisers' belief that religiosity and communalism are so deep-rooted in the mind of the colonised that its needs for equality cannot be served by the 'modern' state. Thus it is not the modernist postion but the anti-modernist position that actually concurs with the colonisers' perception of the colonised. The concurrence is with respect to the following proposition: the 'culture' of colonised is essentially different from the colonisers'; so different that it negatively affects the former's ability to grasp (and much less institutionalise) the notions of political and economic equality that inform the colonisers' world; it follows therefore that the colonised must continue to be ruled by institutions that are premised on 'different' principles of equality.

18. A. K. Bagchi, 'Predatory Commercialization and Communalism is India,' in S. Gopal (ed.) *The Anatomy of Confrontations* (New Dehli, Oxford University Press, 1995), pp. 193-218.

19. Basu et al., *op. cit.*

20. Sangari, *op. cit.*; R. Kapur and B. Cossman, 'Communalising Gender/Engendering Community: Women, Legal Discourse and Saffron Agenda,' *Economic and Political Weekly*, 24 April 1993, pp. 35-43.

21. The empirical examples of this are many. Gandhi's intervention in the Ahmedabad mill-workers' strike, in the proposed rent-strike in Awadh, are all examples of his anti-radical stance.

22. 'By political independence', wrote Gandhi, 'I do not mean an imitation of the British House of Commons.... We must have ours suited to ours.. I have described it as Ramrajya, i.e., sovereignty of the people based on pure moral authority. It means the rule of dharma.' M. Gandhi, *The Moral and Political Writings of Mahatma Gandhi* (vol. 3), Raghavan Iyer, ed. (Oxford, Clarendon Press, 1987).

23. See Washbrook, D.A, 1981. 'Law, State and Agrarian Society in Colonial India' in *Power, Profit and Politics: Essays on Imperialism, Nationalism and Change in Twentieth Century India*, pp. 649-721.

24. *In the Shadow of the Mahatma* (New Delhi), p. 46.

25. Gandhi, *op. cit.*, p. 326-342.

26. *Ibid.*, p 287-289. See especially the piece entitled Imperialism, Exploitation & Freedom.
    At the same time, however, he constantly reassured the British that there was no possi-
    bility of an armed revolt, and that it was his belief that imperialist exploitation could be
    righted through moral considerations.
27. *Ibid.*, p. 234
28. Brass, P. *The Politics of India since Independence* (Cambridge, Cambridge University
    Press, 1990).
29. *Ibid.*, chapter 6.
30. Banerjee, S. 'Sangh Parivar and Democratic Rights', *Economic and Political Weekly*, 21
    August 1993.
31. *Ibid.*, ch. 7.
32. Chandrashekhar, C.P., 'Invited Invasion: Levelling the Playing Field', in *Frontline*, 8
    November 1993.
33. 'FICCI Moots Mandatory Disinvestment by MNCs', Press Trust of India, New Delhi,
    October 6.
34. 'The Return of Xenophobia', in *Business Today*, 22 June-6 July 1992; 'The CII's MNC-
    Bashing,' Business Today, 7-21 April 1996.
35. 'Building Bridges', in *Business Today*, 22 July-6 August 1993.
36. Basu et al.
37. *The Economic Times*, 3 August 1996.
38. *Business Line*, 3 December 1996.
37. 'Building Bridges', in *Business Today*, 22 July-6 August 1993.

MARXISM, FILM AND THEORY: FROM THE BARRICADES TO POSTMODERNISM

Scott Forsyth

Introduction

From the sixties onwards, the study of media and culture has increasingly moved from the pages of journalism and fan mags into the expanding 'mass' universities of advanced capitalist countries. The new or para-disciplines of film, communications and cultural studies, related but usually institutionally distinct, emerged from English and Sociology departments to occupy considerable space in the academic landscape. The revitalised Marxism of the sixties and seventies was important across the humanities and social sciences; but in these new fields, Marxism – married to related radicalisms like Third World anti-imperialism and socialist feminism – was virtually hegemonic. The most influential critical work in film and cultural studies was specifically understood as Marxist (of varying strains and combinations) and located in the politics of socialist transformation. Thus an enriched Marxism helped to understand how this century's massive growth and consolidation of media and cultural industries not only transformed the face of world capitalism and the everyday lives of its peoples, but how they altered the way capitalism rules politically and reproduces itself culturally.

Little more than twenty years later, the 'retreat of the intellectuals' from this apparent position of strength seems a rout. Amidst the dominance of poststructuralism, postmodernism, aesthetic formalism and genre populism, academic radicals, if cultural theorists, now textually rebel with their favourite rock videos or thrillers. Vulgar anti-Marxism is common currency. And connections to social movements, let alone anything so materially crass as class, are little mentioned. What happened?

As a tale of the travails of Marxist intellectual fortunes, this has been told across various academic disciplines. Many commentators have emphasised the limited nature of the New Left built in the sixties and seventies, the passage of some of its cohorts into expanding universities and the relationship of intellectuals to the upturns and downturns of social

movements. Clearly, there have been disappointments as the movements of
the sixties and seventies waned, revolutionary hopes faded and the right,
with aggressive neo-liberal strategies, took government power. The
collapse of the Soviet Union has doubtless reinforced any rightward and
anti-Marxist trajectory among intellectuals. However, the politics of the
intelligentsia cannot be simply read off the swings in direction of working
class and other social movements. Ellen Wood directs attention to, among
other factors, the 'sociology of the academy' which becomes the institutional context of these theoretical developments.[1] Additionally, the waning
of cultural radicalism must be related to the limitations and flaws of the
particular Marxist theory which seemed so powerful. More generally, all
leftist intellectuals have been challenged by the complex transformations
of global capitalism, codified as 'restructuring' and 'globalizing', but in
film and cultural studies, theorists have seen their object of study radically
transformed in the dramatic globalizing of cultural industries; aesthetic and
cultural specificity seem obliterated by new media technologies of
production, distribution and consumption. To many academic theorists, the
nature of this changing cultural politics superseded the axis of class
struggle which motivates Marxism.

Marxism in Film History

But there are distinct features germane to the case of film studies and
theory. For in this arena of modern culture, Marxism and socialist struggle
are not newcomers; they are central to film history. The theory and practice
of socialism have always catalysed important cultural production and
Marxism has a rich and variegated aesthetic tradition, but film is unique,
among all arts and mass media, in the defining role those traditions have
played. Any intellectual comprehension of film required confrontation
with a powerful Marxist and socialist legacy.

The Soviet cinema of the '20s has inspired artists and audiences for
decades and still is the foundation for many theoretical and aesthetic
debates. Those films remain crucial not because of their role as revolutionary propaganda – that was largely recuperable by Stalinism – but
because they embodied the ambitions of a thriving cultural avant-garde to
ally with a revolution and its vanguard. The enduring social realism of Jean
Renoir in the thirties was specifically created within the cultural politics of
the Popular Front and the French Communist Party. In the thirties and
forties, an international documentary movement was built with ties to
movements of international solidarity, the mass organisation of trade
unions, various Communist Parties and Popular Front organisations. The
traditions of the committed documentary still define contemporary work.
The intense interchange between leftist workers' theatre and popular film

in many countries in the '30s and '40s is important in historical comprehension of popular cultural radicalism. Surrealism, that archetypal avant-garde, was shaped by bohemian anti-capitalism struggles within organised Communism and Trotskyism and by Breton's highly original cultural Marxism. At the same time, particularly in cinema, Surrealism was appropriated and popularised in commercial industries and this continues even in the present. Any historical account of the most powerful national and international industry, Hollywood, must analyse the integration of a generation of European exiles, particularly from Weimar Germany (strongly influenced by the ideals of Marxism and the various artistic avant-gardes of the '20s and '30s), as well as the successful intervention of the CPUSA in Hollywood and the profound and devastating impact of the purge and blacklist against a generation of radical film artists.

Contemporary analysis has begun to go beyond that brutal political eviction and see leftist politics shaping the transformation of genres in the '40s and their prevalent, if shaded, critique of the social order. The great filmmakers of Italian neo-realism made their finest films within the field of influence of the Italian Communist Party and the contradictory terrain of the post-war Historic Compromise. The vast and diverse movement of filmmakers and activists labelled the Third Cinema was built in the violent waves of anti-colonialist liberation struggle from the fifties onwards, shaped by Marxism and third world nationalism and most inspired by the Cuban revolution and its famed cineastes. In a more subterranean fashion, from the fifties to the early seventies, the Lettrist and Situationist Internationals attempted to fuse Dadaism and anarcho-Trotskyism in manifestos, scandalous events, sloganeering graffiti and a few rarely-seen films. In '68, Jean-Luc Godard formed the Dziga Vertov Group, nominally gesturing to the Soviet twenties but inspired by the events of May and specifically grounded in the Marxist film theory being developed by the famed journal *Cahiers du Cinema*.[2]

This listing travels through the heart of filmmaking this century, encompassing a huge array of the most celebrated artists – from Brecht and Piscator to Bunuel and Visconti to Chaplin and Welles – and the most successful and coherent movements and national industries. Mainstream film criticism has partially rewritten the story in humanist, aesthetic and romantic terms, but can't ignore the Marxist and socialist tradition. However, it is important to see that this 'tradition' is not linear, not a glorious red thread. Stalinism crushed the innovations of the great Soviet filmmakers. Much of the vitality of the documentary movement was absorbed and tamed in the bureaucracies of state propaganda of Canada, the United States and Britain. The Popular Front's collapse, caught between liberalism and Stalinism by the turns of Party strategy, and the subsequent Hollywood blacklist and purge, did much to destroy an

American cultural left and to make even the idea of a popular radical cinema impossible for a generation. The Situationist International dissolved in '72 (but its champions still celebrate its sparking role in May '68; and Debord's analysis of mass media's authoritarian spectacle remains challenging and relevant). Godard's collective collapsed in '72 in Maoist groupuscule squabbles and a disavowal of Marxism and, eventually, politics of any kind. Nonetheless, this has been a powerful tradition, not a fortunate string of geniuses or great films. The contribution of Marxism to film has been emblematic of a cultural politics defined and revitalised by activist political practice, by the interplay among intellectuals making films, both for instrumental local and internationalist use and for successful popular commercial industries, by active debate in party and related cultural journals, by experiment and ferment in acting and film workshops and schools, in cine-clubs and film societies. Generalising, we can see cultural work which traversed and negotiated – or tried to – boundaries between realist and modernist aesthetic practices, between so-called high and low culture, between cultural and political avant-gardes. Moreover, it needs to be underlined that this tradition of cinematic cultural politics developed and flourished, for the most part, outside the universities.

The Revolution in Theory? From May 68 to the Academy

This impressive history allowed historians, sociologists and critics influenced by Marxism to play central roles in writing about film through these decades and doubtless prepared the way for what seemed to be the intellectual hegemony of the Left in the early seventies. This was signalled by the manifestos for a new Marxist film theory and criticism announced by *Cahiers du Cinema*, the most important film journal in the world, in the late '60s and early seventies. In the fifties, that journal had influentially redefined film criticism around *la politique des auteurs*, the discovery and celebration of great authors within the Hollywood studio system, hitherto scorned by most cultural critics. It was largely conservative criticism which defined itself against the cinema of the Popular Front and sociological and political themes, while romanticising and promoting favoured directors and the stylistic signatures of their *mise en scene*. The journal's fame was secured when its key critics – Truffault, Godard, Chabrol, Rohmer, Rivette – burst into international success with the films of the New Wave at the end of the '50s. It was thus all the more sensational when young Marxists took over the journal and when Godard, newly radicalised, subsumed his celebrated auteur status into the collective of the Dziga Vertov Group. These filmmakers and intellectuals played an important role in '68, filming key demonstrations, establishing the militant Estates Generaux de Cinema, campaigning to save the Paris Cinémathèque and closing down the Cannes

Film Festival. Intense debates with militant Maoist groups were held, even in some of the films of the Group. However, the relationship of this new film theory to activism and film practice proved conjunctural and its elaboration and later development occurred within the institutionalising of film studies as an academic discipline in the seventies.

Cahiers' project was strongly defined by Althusser's structuralist Marxism. While a vast historical rewriting was proposed, the project was more defined by structuralism's infamous 'exorbitation of language' (to deploy Perry Anderson's phrase), and the complex techniques of semiotics and Lacanian psychoanalysis were enlisted to 'scientifically' dissect film as a language. The complexities of film's narrative traditions, even its technologies of production and perceptions were reduced to a common 'realism' which repetitively fixed subjected spectators in their ideological positions. Unconscious deployments of style and form, revealed by textual analysis, allowed some films to express and expose contradictions in ideology and within this realism. In film theory, as in other fields, Althusserianism bore the faults of an emphasis on intellectualised ideological struggle, a distance from the subjects dominated by ideology and an elevation and aggrandisement of the role of intellectuals.[3] Only an interpretative cadre could unpack the ways ideology dominates, expose the gaps and 'structuring absences' and resist the 'interpellation' of the subject. However, *Cahiers'* grand synthesis proved unmanageable; while Marxism was gradually eclipsed, its theoretical ambitions and, perhaps failures, pepared the way for the endless construction of Theory itself as a hermetically obscure specialisation. An amalgam of structuralism, semiotics, psychoanalysis and deracinated extracts of Marxism – usually labelled poststructuralism – dominates film theory today. The last Situationist film, made in 1973 by René Viénet, was acerbically prescient on the political trajectory of these intellectual developments. *Can dialectics break bricks*? is a Japanese samurai epic, hilariously re-dubbed into a battle between revolutionary workers and state capitalist bureaucrats. The Situationists called this rearrangement of popular culture for political purposes *detournement*. (Readers may recall the Woody Allen film *What's Up, Tiger Lily*? which used the same formal joke several years earlier.) In the Situationist epic, the rebellious workers are warned by the most evil of the bureaucrats:

> I don't want to hear any more about class struggle. If necessary I'll send in my sociologists. And if that's not enough, my psychiatrists ... my Foucaults! My Lacans! And if that's not enough I'll even send in my structuralists!

Institutionalising Formalism

This theoretical project was translated, popularised and dramatically developed for the English-speaking academy in a number of influential books, particularly by Peter Wollen and Noel Burch, by the journal *Screen* in Great Britain and then by journals like *CineTracts* in Canada and the more politically militant *JumpCut* in the United States. *Screen* undertook a missionary role in relationship to the advanced theories of Continental Marxism, structuralism and post-structuralism in much the same way as *New Left Review* in the same period.[4] While most of these new intellectuals identified with the movements and cultural politics of the '60s and '70s, particularly in the women's movement, gay liberation, anti-racist and third world solidarity struggles, the central debates rapidly became highly specialised methodological controversies, not specifically or topically political, and were largely directed into the institutionalisation of film studies in the universities of Britain, France and North America. Key articles were collected into a small number of highly influential textbooks which gave pedagogical coherence to the rapidly developing field. In the USA alone, several hundred film departments were established in the sixties and seventies; the number of film dissertations rose from several hundred to more than two thousand in less than 15 years. (Despite this growth film studies remains a comparatively small, even fragile discipline – perhaps a few thousand faculty in the relevant American associations, little more than one hundred in Canada.) A dizzying melange of poststructuralist and psychoanalytic orthodoxies hurtle through the academic mills in the form of papers, journals, conferences, graduate courses. Barthes, Kristeva, Deleuze and Guattari, Metz, Lyotard, Irigay, Derrida, Baudrillard, Baktin and lesser lights enjoy celebrity and inspire acolytes. An uncharitable observer at a film studies conference these years might find panels of *idiot savants*, masters of techno-linguistic jargon, exchanging truncated snippets of much grander theoretical systems, battling over dissected husks of Hitchcock or television. This was, and is, criticism whose audience necessarily becomes other like minded academics, little interested in material social processes. What is argued over is an impoverished prototype of cinema and an almost parodic reduction of the political to the textual, the radical to metatextual rhetoric. One of the key editors in the North American process, Bill Nichols, writing in the mid-eighties, decried the apolitical and obscurantist direction of much of this dominant poststructuralist theory, its lack of effect and reach outside the academy. He sees this as a regrettable, but probably necessary, part of the bureaucratisation of scientific knowledge in institutions where 'difficult' language is utilised to distinguish territory and enforce hierarchy. Debates over methodologies have supplanted any politically substantive issues, virtually as a sign of institutional status. The novelty and uncertainty of film as a distinct field of study perhaps intensified this specialisation as an institutional and professional strategy; the process involves the social positioning and commodification of both ideas and intellectuals themselves superseding any relationship to active social movements and struggles.[5]

It is the fate of this self-described advanced theory to co-exist, more or less happily, with older, humbler kinds of academic practices, as in other disciplines: authorial and generic criticism, localised historical research, phenomenological approaches, or even with schools of filmmaking and screenwriting. Despite considerable differences – between humanist and anti-humanist rhetoric or empirical against metatextual methodologies – film studies connects them all through shared formalism, a text-centred interpretative focus that downplays social context and social transformation. A fierce critic of the discipline, Ma'sud Zavarzadeh, comments 'The dominant (poststructuralist) film theory ... has institutionalized a mode of textualism that has effectively suppressed all but formalist readings of film ... this new orthodoxy has allowed contemporary film theory to focus exclusively on the immanent negotiations of the sign in the film and to bracket the political economy of signification and subjectivity that relate the local immanent politics to global social struggles.'[6] Demarcations between approaches take on the competitive territorial divisions typical of any departments in the institution. Judiciously, a prodigious amount of interesting and challenging work has been produced but the socialist necessity of connecting the explanatory and the transformative no longer defines this disciplinary project. Rather, the field is characterised by Byzantine interpretative competition. The pretensions and cant of much of this theory have been attacked by both cautious and conservative approaches and by several strong voices who re-assert and insist on the politics of opposition, against the academic grain.[7]

Zavarzadeh's important denunciation needs to be qualified in a number of ways. It was the critical work, in the early '70s, of those on the Left, even though, as we shall see below, not entirely eclipsed, which prepared the ground for the formalism and obscurantism of this institutionalisation, even when the critics purported to be ultra-radical. For example, Colin McCabe's analysis of 'classic realism' as authoritarian narratives, irredeemably bourgeois, repetitively fixing spectators passively within dominant ideology, became an axiom of a theoretical dismissal of Hollywood and narrative itself, forestalling crucial investigations into the importance of narrative in relationship to politics. Peter Wollen argued that the film text makes authorship simply an effect of the text; intention and commitment are dismissed as romantic humanism. It seems that both the author and the spectator are dead. The necessity of agency for an effective politics is marginal to this cultural critique and it is obviously only steps from this towards the dominance of discursivity wholesale. In a powerful feminist extension, Laura Mulvey analysed the pleasures of Hollywood as entirely organised upon the masculine gaze and male pleasure, subsuming aesthetics to ideology and film criticism to Lacanian psychoanalysis. While this challenge to necessarily include gender and sexuality in any paradigm of analysis was positive, psychoanalytic critiques of this kind were bereft of any historical context other than thousands of years of patriarchy and also foreclosed attention to the priority of social context. Noel Burch constructed a similarly reductive and hostile analysis of Hollywood's so-called realism and developed a set of formal counters to this bourgeois form, modelled on Brecht, but with a specific critique of Brecht's insistence on content and context. Wollen echoed this with a prescriptive manifesto for a counter-cinema inspired by Godard's Dziga Vertov Group. Burch and Wollen called for a radical modernist inversion of the reviled realism, particularly through the tropes of intertextuality and self-referentiality and their deconstruction of narrative and imagistic pleasures, their 'disruption of the dominant signifying practices'. A courageous spectator would be exposed to the workings of ideology – on other passive spectators; the model of this spectator is the intellectual critic himself.

When Godard's project collapsed, a few Theory films were made, notably by Mulvey and Wollen in England in the '70s. But these were films suitable only for film theorists and a viable tradition did not develop. It is worth noting that these calls for practice ascetically dismissed much of the socialist tradition in film as hopelessly bound up with bourgeois narrative and realism. Important contemporaneous work in committed documentary was similarly marginalized as naively realist by the chimera of a radical modernist counter-cinema inspired more by theory than by activism and political urgency. Even the historic avant-gardes of the '20s and '30s were seen as inspirational for their daring form not their command of narrative, commitment and political analysis. The avant-garde theories of juxtaposition and confrontation of form and content, or collage and montage, within an acute sense of the audiences' place in a dialectic of changing popular culture, were reduced to stylistic markers. All of this critical work in the early '70s proved challenging and provocative – indeed in a small discipline remained enormously influential – but its impact was entirely within the increasingly academic debates of the field, not outwards to activists, filmmakers and radicalising audiences in the traditions that Marxism and socialism had formerly brought to film. Within academic debate, its intellectual direction was to reduce the complexity of film narrative and its relationship to ideology to issues of form and textuality. Politics took place within the text itself. The institutional ground was readied for poststructuralism's more politically acceptable formalism.[8]

Populism and the Postmodernist 'Thing'

Of course, there is also a seemingly radical politics in much of the dominant academic work as well; it is, in fact, a strangely elitist brand of populism. In an anti-dialectical swing from absolutist condemnation of

Hollywood and its audiences, film studies, particularly from the mid-eighties on, is more likely to celebrate Hollywood now with taxonomic devotion. The once-passive spectator now likely negotiates a resistant reading or subcultural rebellion. Subversion is everywhere in academic comprehension of popular culture in the '80s and '90s. Most genres, and even whole decades, of mainstream cinema have been 'discovered' as belatedly transgressive, subversive, progressive – textually. The positive impulse to investigate how popular culture relates to political ideology and everyday life is diffused, with the particular influence of Foucault, into an omnipresent dance with Power. A recent authoritative textbook collection defines this populism within the rule and triumph of the market, categorising and belittling Marxist contributions as tied to an outdated ideology of the State.[9] Much of this work has shifted attention from film to television and video and found optimistic textual politics in the constantly new choices and identifications of consumer liberties in music videos, soap operas, pornography, situation comedies. Entertainment is therefore suddenly championed, as if 'active' consumption has not always been located within capitalist social relations. The title of another collection catches the swing from elitism to populism – *High Theory/Low Culture*.[10] The authoritarian narratives of derided realism somehow transform, as if in compensation for the earlier reductionism, through what Zavarzadeh calls 'ludic postmodernism'.

Many of the now familiar themes of postmodernism – the fragmentation of subjectivity, the antagonism towards 'grand narratives' (and narrative altogether), the discursive evacuation of material social processes, the resistance to Power, all framed by the 'epochal novelty' of the postmodern and the ways of thinking which comprehend it – reverberate, perhaps incubate, through the poststructuralist theorising in film studies. From the mid-eighties, it is postmodernism that gives a relative coherence to much of this theory, providing a narrative of change and an infinitely replenished subject matter in the endlessly novel products of expanding cultural conglomerates. The postmodernist discourse – or 'thing' as a cinematic champion inelegantly put it – has moved beyond debate.[11] Its tropes are presented without argument or demonstration, in an arrogant idealist barrage, simply ruling out potential critics not at this cutting edge. As academic commodity, it has prolonged the sway of Theory fashion trends, providing exchangeable intellectual currency transnationally in an increasingly globally connected academic community. In film studies, the particular dominance of poststructuralism presaged the later importance of postmodernism.

Most Marxists have understood this postmodernist discourse broadly, as part of the rightward drift of intellectuals in the Second Cold War through the collapse of the Soviet Union. But the discourse has its own logic and momentum within the 'sociology of the academy'. Indeed, it must be understood as the language and ideology of a fraction of the intelligentsia, sharing markers of specialisation and prestige. The rhetoric defines a stratum with little sense or hope of social influence but universalising its perceptions of meaninglessness and futility. When capitalist culture presents itself as more triumphant and unassailable than ever, postmodernism offers an exegesis of that culture; what began as scathing denunciation with Jameson or with the earlier work by Debord has become delirious celebration in Baudrillard.[12]

The most substantive issues originally raised by Jameson concerned the relationship of style and form to epoch in the Marxist lineage pioneered by Lukacs and developed by Goldmann. Drawing on a vast array of examples from architecture to films to novels, he attempted to periodize culture homologously with Mandel's famed analysis of 'Late Capitalism', that is, of the postwar boom and its extension of automation into all sectors of production, marked by technological innovation in computers, nuclear energy, electronics, chemicals and genetics. This was a serious effort to think culture historically, albeit with a sophisticated reductionism of culture to economy. Jameson insisted on the centrality of narrative to social and cultural life and to Marxism's defining comprehension of history. But the trajectory of postmodernism is now towards fashion and journalism and a rhetoric of newness, a simpler replication of the culture of consumption. Diversity and difference are now commonplace marketing strategies, in the promotional world of Bennetton and Calvin Klein. As periodization, postmodernism now increasingly appears to be in the line of bland techno-utopian designations of a contemporary moment in Progress, akin to the Information Society or Post-Industrialism. Within that limitation, the postmodern is offered as stylistic shorthand for the kinds of narratives, experiences of spectatorship, complication and multiplication of modes of distribution and exhibition and diversification of products and technologies offered by the vast media/cultural conglomerates that have been such a central part of postwar capitalism. Postmodernism gives us, in Francis Mulhern's clever phrase, 'the theoretical self-consciousness of satellite television and the shopping mall.'[13]

The left's predominant political stand today, a merely defensive opposition to capitalist restructuring, obviously lacks the overarching and transformative vision socialism (and even social democracy) once claimed to offer. This logically fuels the inverse faith in micro-politics or individualistic rebellion that runs through so much of the postmodernist literature. It is capitalism's triumphal globalization that subordinates such residual radicalism, not its evident and ongoing crisis, or even decline, that more careful analysis reveals. Postmodernism's political posture within this rightward drift has two characteristic moves. In one, it repeatedly directs its fire at Marxism, caricatured as necessarily totalitarian and bound to epistemological and aesthetic realisms outdated by the advance of Theory. This now resembles nothing so much as the bargain of Cold War liberalism, purchasing space for a species of radicalism by joining in the chorus of red-baiting. This is most telling in the ridiculous attack on 'grand narratives', a code for Marxist historicism, while the capitalism of the Triumph of Globalization, There Is No Alternative, and the Death of Socialism shows no signs of any faltering of its faith in Big Stories; it is of course the intellectuals themselves who have lost faith in socially significant and effective narratives, individually and historically.

In a second, more 'progressive' move, postmodernism identifies the new social movements as hope for social change – this has been especially important in film studies which concentrated so strongly on issues of sexual and racial identity and was inspired by those very movements of gender, sexuality and race. However, rather than directly connecting to those continuing movements, postmodernism's micro-politics has increasingly focused on the identity politics of race and gender, refracted through the competitive professionalism and bureaucracy of the universities themselves. It is hard to imagine a more suitable home for theories of discursivity, fragmented subjectivity and refusal of ambitious narratives of social change. The Foucauldian analysis of power and institutions discovers countless opportunities for limited activism and the promotion of a regulatory regime of radical liberalism. We know this phenomenon partly through the media campaign against so-called 'political correctness' – a particularly authoritarian continuation of red-baiting the minimal gains of the movements of the sixties and seventies and the modest emplacement of the Left in the academy. But the Left also knows this as damaging internecine struggle, where the sectoral perspectives of race, gender and sexuality battle each other, refusing traditions of solidarity and socialism. Not surprisingly, the direction of much of the academic left is to disappointment and cynicism.

Marxism – Why it Failed and Why it is Still Needed

It is useful to underline how the 'radical' turn in much cultural theory and practice is distanced from most of the Marxist cultural – and cinematic – tradition's vital, if uneven, exploration of the power of the aesthetic, the social knowledge of narrative, the dialectic between producer and audience, the relationship of art and class struggle, even the concern with the audience's pleasure and involvement (even in Brecht's much referenced alienation effect). But Marxists should not smugly judge the fault lines of this increasingly faux-radicalism. Perhaps, most importantly, Marxists have not developed a convincing anti-Stalinist politics that has been able to comprehend the Soviet Union, and its collapse, in a persuasive and radical-ising fashion for new generations. The roadblock of Stalinism, and its cultural reductionism, certainly marks the stops and starts in the socialist cinematic tradition, as strong as that tradition is. Similarly, the Marxist cultural politics associated with Trotsky and the revolutionary modernism of, for example, Breton and Rivera, doesn't survive the '40s and the brutal twists and turns of the Left. Important work by Alan Wald and Serge Guilbault has historically analysed the disappointing retreat of anti-Stalinist cultural politics to formalism and conservatism in the United States. That thread is picked up again, by the Lettrists and Situationists of France, especially Debord, in the '50s and '60s, in brilliant and inspiring ways, but collapses again with an incoherent relationship to political practice and parodic comprehension of both class relations and the role of the revolutionary party in contemporary capitalism.[15] These failures find their way into the narrative of theory and the academy I have been recounting; in fact, many of the deficiencies and dead ends of the higher theory and lower postmodernism replicate or descend from the blockages and failures of Marxist cultural theory itself. The entire Western Marxist tradition can be seen to have over-estimated the power of ideology and the centrality of cultural struggle, perhaps correcting classical Marxism's neglect, but also de-emphasising the theoretical attention to organisation, movements and political economy so vital for the socialism we need.[16] A number of commentators note that the Frankfurt School's themes of cultural pessimism (denunciation of cultural industries and their production of benumbed authoritarian personalities, despair over collective agency and pallid call for the negations of theory or an idealised aesthetic) are echoed in much of the structuralist and poststructuralist cultural theory of more recent years. The critique of the commodification of culture has obviously been crucial to Marxism – in the Frankfurt School, in Lukács, in Benjamin – but we can see its increasing abstraction from a wider analysis of social totality and class relations in its extension to sign, image, spectacle and simulacrum in Debord and Baudrillard. Indeed, much of this cultural critique circles the dilemmas of consumption and hyper-consumption which characterised the postwar boom years but has failed to adapt to the capitalism of *crisis, alongside consumerism* we have faced for several decades.

Change in these decades in the media and cultural industries have been crucial to the process and mythologizing of globalization and this devel-opment is the material frame for film studies' short intellectual and institutional history. Behind the smug determinism of its ideologues, capitalism has responded to its long wave of crisis with the relentless neo-liberal offensive in politics, but also with immense changes in its global organisation and power: strengthened transnational corporate structures, incorporation of new technologies into production, enhanced flexibility and mobility of capital and shifting international divisions of labour – both for national proletariats and the beginnings of transnationally connected bourgeois and petty-bourgeois. These are certainly familiar to Marxists, both as the culmination of the post-war epoch and in continuity with the global logic of capitalism for a very long time. They are capitalism's relentless and destructive revolutionising of the world.

All the media industries are enormously successful examples of these dramatic changes. But they are also crucial to the cultural realisation of this revolution in massive changes to consumption world-wide. That is a revolution carried by the intensified commodification of information and entertainment. Obviously, these have been pivotal to the trade negotiations of NAFTA and GATT and will continue to be at the very forefront of restructuring. These industries have introduced a dizzying range of techno-logical innovations and new media over the last decades, intensifiying, albeit in brutally class-riven and globally unequal fashion, all aspects of cultural consumption. All the media are increasingly interpenetrated and converging in corporate structure, production, distribution and consumption. We are witnessing the automation of culture. Much of cultural theory tracks these developments, from phone sex to the Internet and, shaped by postmodernism, celebrates the exhilarating and perpetual novelty of each commodity innovation's momentary incorporation of the techno-utopianism of capitalist progress. Ignoring the continuity of capitalist logic and the striking similarities across the history of modern mass media from the nineteenth century onwards, theory trails the creativity of capital; its enervation mimics the passivity long associated with both postwar consumerism and structural enhancement of corporate power.[17]

Film, in particular Hollywood, is in the vanguard of an increasing globalization of cultural revolution. The entertainment industry, led by Hollywood's dominance in film, video and TV programming, is among the leading export industries of the United States, second only to aerospace.[18] Throughout the eighties, Hollywood dramatically widened its international dominance and increased its revenues and profits. Film studios are central in the small number of concentrated communications mega-conglomerates that increasingly dominate global culture through the '80s and '90s. Film studies' historic irony is that it attempts institutional and intellectual consolidation as its object of study and aesthetic desire seems to dissolve into this mixed and multi-media convergence of toys, videos, CDs, CD-ROMs, advertising, cable TV, books and comics, home computers and VCRs and on and on. The self-referentiality and intertextuality which the theorists of *Cahiers du Cinema* and *Screen* politically valorised is neces-sarily embodied in any cultural commodity as it travels across media and industries in these widening fields of consumerism. Film aesthetics takes on the character of nostalgic lament and the categories of formalism are even further de-politicised.

However, films have not disappeared into the 'mediascape', they remain exceptional commodities which lead and organise converging, multiplied and multilayered distribution and consumption. Within the giant conglomerates, Hollywood films are central to corporate strategies which are transindustrial, synergistic and global.[19] But, for all the important changes and hype of the last decades, the cultural industries still rest on the same social relations and the same century long process of intensifying consumption that Hollywood emblematized. This continuity in capitalist logic is as remarkable as any claims to postmodern novelty. Similarly, Hollywood remains ideologically and aesthetically important to American capitalism and imperialism. and how it understands its place in the world. In fact, Hollywood films provide us with some of the most coherent constructions of the continuity of capitalism through its restructuring reinventions of itself and utopian announcement of new benevolent world orders and irresistible globalization.

For illustration, we can look briefly at a selection of action thrillers, all ready to hand at your local video store, soon to be downloaded on your home computer: *True Lies, Speed, In the Line of Fire, Hard Target, Crimson Tide, Broken Arrow, Clear and Present Danger, Fair Game, The Rock, Mission: Impossible, GoldenEye*, the *Under Siege, Die Hard, Lethal Weapon* series. The list could be multiplied. As corporate productions they are typical: lavish budgets, massive promotion and distribution, investment right on screen in famous stars, spectacular special effects, aestheticised violence, stunts and explosions. Their theatrical success initiates likely sequels and imitations and cross media circulation as home videos, comic books, video games, TV shows, toys and countless inventive marketing campaigns and tie-ins from fast food to fashion. Historically, they are in a tradition of spectacular Hollywood filmmaking and marketing that is almost a century old; generically they reproduce propulsively simple variations on masculine adventures, hybridizing conventions historically developed in Westerns, gangster, spy and horror films, science fiction and, even, screwball comedy – consistently demanding audiences have a playful sense of the intertextual and self-referential nature of the product they are consuming. The narratives are organised to sequentially highlight the machinery of filmmaking itself, emphasising dazzling artifice, the willing immersion in believing, the expensively produced nature of the experience purchased. Most contemporary film studies dismiss these films as commodities beneath consideration or dissect them as paragons of postmodern style, but they are exemplary products of the cultural revolution of late twentieth century capital.

At the same time, as ideological narratives, these films are in striking continuity with the films of the seventies and eighties labelled as 'Reaganite entertainment'.[20] Those films mobilised super-masculine American heroes, most famously Rambo, in the service of the American Right's programme all over the world; invading Grenada, bombing Libya, re-fighting the Vietnam war repeatedly, fighting Communists, Arab fundamentalists and Latino drug dealers all over the world. The same, or similar heroes continue to battle a wave of threats to America in the nineties, often with similar plots or threats – to hostages, of nuclear blackmail, with several interesting changes.

Intriguingly, Hollywood has avoided dramatising the crucial events in the supposed success of globalization and the New World Order – the collapse of the Soviet Union and the destruction of Iraq in the Gulf War. Rather, these films reprise an America vulnerable and beleaguered in the world, still as insecure and threatened, beset right in its home territory with a succession of terrifying villains; they show up right in the airports and streets of America, a paranoid inversion of first world triumphalism. It has become axiomatic that America looked for new enemies as the real world threat of the Soviets gave way to detente and collapse. These films present the menace of ubiquitous terrorism. Crazed Arab fundamentalists and Latino drug dealers draw on racism historically constitutive of Western and American imperial conquest and provide satisfyingly tamed variation of the coloured hordes who have peopled imperial adventures and nightmares for generations. But America is also still fighting Russians. Post-communist social and economic disaster has produced the newest ethnic stereotype in many years, the Russian Mafia – literal characterisation of 'bandit capitalism'. In other films, plot contrivance allows a restaging of the terms of the Cold War conflict as America battles recidivist Russians; the nostalgia for the moral politics of the Cold War is palpable. Even more innovatively, many of these villains are Americans themselves. In numerous thrillers, a rogue CIA agent goes mad or mercenary and threatens the most heinous crimes against America. While the implicitly useless or unemployed institutions and bureaucracy of the Cold War produced this monstrous treason, the films uniformly exonerate and recuperate the institutions themselves in the vanquishing of these rogues.

Perpetual war against perpetual insecurity is America's post-Cold War fate in these representative films. They tell us that the Cold War's state and culture continue fundamentally unchanged, putting us in the perspective of the armed men of that state. Danger to America is everywhere but depoliticised, resistance mutated into criminality and madness with violence its primary motive. While the military readiness of America is dramatised as viscerally necessary to peaceful everyday life, that necessity is only circuitously connected to the instability of international relations, the gross inequalities of wealth and power that globalization intensifies. Succinctly condensing the brutality and hubris of imperialism, the spunky heroine of *Speed* jokes about a demented villain, 'What did we do, bomb his country?'

Most powerful visually, these films represent the military technology of imperialism – its weapons, computers, surveillance trickery, satellites and especially nuclear power – as the most alluring and frightening feature of Cold War continuity. The war economy and capital investment of corporate filmmaking fuse in the ostentatious special effects, the eroticised weaponry and the amusing fright of nuclear weapons temporarily in the wrong hands. Military, corporate and Hollywood imagery, technique and ideology converge and reinforce each other. The imagery advertises the most advanced technology in filmmaking and war, overwhelming their audiences with the wealth and power of first world capitalism, even while their narratives offer an America threatened by the world it is dominating. The films neatly show what is novel, unchanging and powerful in the culture and economy of imperialism in its contemporary conjuncture. They also display some of its continuing weakness and anxiety about the resistance it inevitably produces. Perhaps *Independence Day* is the most complete and extreme culmination of these ideological and aesthetic trajectories. The most authoritarian American nationalism and egregious xenophobia – directed to the universe at large – is lionised in a pastiche of Reaganite films and themes and with the most elaborate screen pyrotechnics possible. Its cultural globalization is specifically defined as American – the whole world will celebrate July 4th – but it is still an America vulnerable to near-total defeat, whose audiences cheer when aliens obliterate the White House.[21]

Popular culture is tremendously complex and Hollywood, of course, offers countervailing and parallel cycles and genres as well. Any analysis must also consider what kinds of contradiction or even resistance are emerging. Changing conditions of production or evolution of genres and conventions do not allow the reading of culture to be any less confusing or ambiguous than when Marx celebrated the social realism of the novels of the royalist Balzac. Hollywood, even within the giant conglomerates of today, can still subtly market and integrate liberal feminism in women's melodramas, such as *Steel Magnolias* and *Fried Green Tomatoes* or further market 'difference' to black women with *Waiting to Exhale*. The conventions of hyper-masculine action thrillers can adapt to proto-feminist super-women, as in *Terminator 2* or *Aliens*. Or those conventions can accommodate an interesting critique of the barbarism of contemporary capitalism, as Van Damme battles heroically for the homeless in *Hard Target*. The neo-noir thrillers of Quentin Tarantino and his many imitators can be seen as white trash/underclass critiques of a media-drenched and degenerating America heading for disaster. The aesthetics of grisly violence – Tarantino's particular talent in the special effects of exploding blood bags and mutilated prostheses – perhaps reflects the increasing social decay and brutality of class-riven America. Film studies more typically celebrates Tarantino as stylistic postmodern auteur, pastiching the surface of Hollywood history and the detritus of pop culture, 'ironic' champion of fragmented, if not entirely vacuous, masculine subjectivity. The cycle of near-future science fiction films – from *Blade Runner* to *Robocop* to *Demolition Man* to *Strange Days* to *Escape from LA* continues to dramatise a contradictory 'New Bad Future', obliquely attacking the neo-conservative devastation of the '80s and '90s while savouring the collapse of the social order with cheerful and inventive hopelessness. The radical black nationalism of Spike Lee and John Singleton has proven popular and entertaining to young radicalising audiences, but readily amenable to neo-conservative incorporation, while the politics of the Civil Rights movement remains moribund and coded racism vitalises, and vitiates, the political discourse of the American mainstream.

Back to the Barricades?

The face of imperial culture – even in its powerful globalizing dominance, in its efforts to show us, to paraphrase Marx, 'a world in capital's own image' – is powerful, but also contradictory, belligerent but fearful, homogenising but unable to silence emerging and opposing voices, images and stories. It is within and out of such complexities and contradictions of bourgeois culture that oppositional and socialist culture has developed in the past; the struggle remains as difficult and as possible as ever. The politics of dominant film remains important to understanding class rule and to the building of cultural and political opposition. Perhaps the failures of academic 'radicalism' seem worst in this realm of collective pleasure and imagination – the failure to imagine any order other than capital's dazzling domination. Beyond movies, beyond criticism, the development of a more vitally socialist cultural politics will require an articulation of intellectual work, cultural practice and the revitalisation of mass movements which can challenge imperialism, even in its apparent globalized triumph.

We can see this process maturing in the concerted opposition to the ruling class's crisis and restructuring solutions increasingly taking shape in the general strikes in France, in Spain, in Italy, in Greece, in Ontario, in many countries of the third world, in the peasant insurrection in Mexico. It is also apparent in the best activist legacies of the so-called new social movements – in, for example, the Canadian and American women's movements struggles around abortion rights or the gay and lesbian movements battle for equal rights and against state bigotry and indifference to AIDS. Wider resistance is proving to be class-based and union-led, but with coalitions drawing in wide layers of the oppressed and marginalized, re-articulating the relationship between class organisation and social movements. It is possible to see the often-claimed opposition – a favourite postmodernist shibboleth – between class struggle and resistance based on social relations of gender, sexuality and race being overcome in struggle. Clearly, there are dramatic differences and deficiencies in the strategies and programmes of these emerging movements and in the cohesion and radicalism of these mobilisations, but they are rising; this is where the dialectic between defensive resistance and transformative confrontation can develop.

The challenge in filmmaking and in the intellectual study of film will be to relate to and contribute to these growing movements of resistance. Despite the might of Hollywood and the dominance of poststructuralism and postmodernism, there are grounds for confidence in the continuity of radical traditions in film. The persistence of political critics in the field, from the '70s to the '90s, as a significant 'counter-current' to poststructuralism, as Nichols puts it, will be of particular importance. Journals like *Cineaste, CineAction* and *JumpCut* defined themselves, with some success, against the orthodoxies of the academy. Important and withering Marxist attacks on the Lacanian and poststructuralist hegemony were made in the late '70s, particularly by Andrew Britton and Terry Lovell.[22] Fredric Jameson's highly original analysis of class allegories in film narratives opened up interpretative terrain neglected by the field's narrower concentrations.[23] Feminist work remains central in film studies, widening and challenging all methods of film interpretation and popularising the possibilities of alternative women's cinema. Mulvey's Lacanian feminism is debated and challenged from diverse perspectives.[24] Important gay critics, like Andrew Britton, Richard Dyer and Robin Wood broaden film analysis on issues of sexuality in important and innovative ways.[25] Similarly, the focus on representation extended logically to identities of race and ethnicity in film, taking up and refining cultural critiques associated with anti-racist movements of the '60s and '70s. While some of this cultural identity politics has severe limitations, its continuity with the roots of the sixties radicalisation remains a crucial achievement for the cultural Left.

Considerable new work has begun to analyse the intricacies of popular genres, styles and conventions, to confront the historic and social contexts of films, their makers and viewers. Some of this work is directly inspired by its relationship to social movements, particularly anti-racism, feminism and gay liberation. A few historians address the historical changes in popular culture across the neo-conservative years in detailed political analysis and political economy of various national cinemas.[26] The many books, articles and lectures of Noam Chomsky, Michael Parenti and bell hooks have made sharp political analysis of the media popular and accessible to wide audiences, appealing to the simmering resistance to the neo-conservative years, fostering media activism all over North America. Little remarked in the academy (with the partial exception of hooks), these public left intellectuals have helped keep the field of a leftist critique of media vital and relevant. In the 'left wing' of film and media studies, Marxism remains influential if no longer dominant and while this work may often slide into the theoretical swamps of poststructuralism or the political vagaries of liberalism, its enduring terrain is an important gain for the intellectual Left.

Much of this critical work relates to and is inspired by continuing radical film practice from the '60s to the '90s. Most important, perhaps, activists are consistently making committed documentaries intimately tied to the labour, women's, gay and lesbian, anti-racist, anti-war and solidarity movements, to liberation struggles, to celebrating and excavating the history of the Old Left. Alternative networks of production, distribution and exhibition are built and sustained. This oppositional practice continued in countries all over the world, consistent with the Left's partisan traditions in film history. Poststructuralist theory largely ignored this work or gave it marginalizing condescension. But political critics, notably Bill Nichols and Thomas Waugh, and some journals, take up the history and critical analysis of this crucial part of the Left's tradition. In more recent years, documentaries have even forged a small presence as theatrical features widening audiences even more; the successes of *Roger and Me, Hoop Dreams* and *Manufacturing Consent* in North America are especially notable. Perhaps no body of work stands out so strongly as the remarkable career of Ken Loach; from the '50s to the '90s, his searing film and television dramas speak to the strongest traditions of working class and socialist culture, searingly confronting the most difficult social despair, political defeats and enduring hopes. A few independent and Hollywood fiction films are inspired by and related to these radical roots, most consciously in the work of John Sayles, but also notably by women and filmmakers of colour. The new black American cinema, ranging from independents like Julie Dash and Charles Burnett to the commercial success of Spike Lee, is particularly prominent. The work of Sankofa and Black Audio Collective in Great Britain stands even more clearly in the traditions of leftist film culture. It arose in response to struggles by black communities and with a specific political analysis of culture and media, particularly indebted to the intellectuals of Third Cinema, to the traditions of Black Marxism and to the Marxist roots of cultural studies. Their films ranged formally from documentary to experimental to fiction and thematically across racial, sexual, imperial and class conflict. From these co-ops, the work of Isaac Julien (*Looking for Langston, Young Soul Rebels*) has been especially inspirational to young radical filmmakers in Britain and North America. *Looking for Langston* evokes the historic avant-gardes to inspire contemporary resistance, reverently and beautifully commemorating Langston Hughes, the gay black poet of the Harlem renaissance. (The difficulties and blockages in the socialist tradition are perhaps inadvertently signalled in the film's complete silence on Hughes' intimate relationship with the CPUSA.) In the '90s, the dramatic explosion in queer – gay and lesbian – cinema and video continues this burgeoning radical sub- if not counter-culture; along with Julien, the militant and provocative films of Derek Jarman in Britain, Greg Araki in California and John Greyson and Bruce LaBruce in Canada have probably received the most acclaim. A few important critics and journals continue to promote and cheer the important developments in Third World cinema, even while brutal economics and increased Western cultural globalisation threaten the gains of earlier years. The survival and achievements of the Cuban revolution and its cinema, in the face of the post-Cold War onslaught of American imperialism, was emblematized by the international acclaim for the last films of the great Tomas Gutiérrez Alea – *Strawberry and Chocolate* and *Guantanamara*.[27]

In creative and intellectual work, we can see the contours of oppositional culture and the continuation of the radical and socialist traditions – sometimes in crude emergent forms, sometimes with eloquent sophistication – and some of the ways they can relate to and be inspired by active social and political struggle. This is not a simple or automatic process but this is the terrain of engaged debate and creative differences where Marxism can continue, and reinvigorate, its own intellectual and political contributions and where a cultural politics of solidarity and resistance can challenge the pictures and reality of capitalism's hollow triumph.

NOTES

1. See Ellen Wood, 'A Chronology of the New Left and Its Successors, Or: Who's Old-Fashioned Now?', *The Socialist Register* (London, Merlin Press, 1995).
2. See, among a large number of historical accounts: Jay Leyda, *KINO: A History of the Russian and Soviet Film* (New York, Collier, 1960); Chris Faulkner, *The Social Cinema of Jean Renoir* (Princeton, Princeton University Press, 1986); Thomas Waugh (ed.), *'Show Us Life': Toward a History and Aesthetics of Committed Documentary* (New Jersey, Scarecrow Press, 1984); Larry Ceplair and Stephen Englund, *The Inquisition in Hollywood: Politics in the Film Community 1930–1960* (New York, Anchor, 1980); Thom Anderson, 'Red Hollywood' in Suzanne Ferguson and Barbara Groseclose (eds.), *Literature and the Visual Arts in Contemporary Society* (Columbia, Ohio University Press, 1985); John Downing, ed., *Film and Politics in the Third World* (New York, Autonomedia, 1987); Julianne Burton, *The New Latin American Cinema* (New York, Smyrna, 1983); Michael Chanan, *The Cuban Image* (London, BFI, 1986); Charles Musser and Robert Sklar, (eds.), *Resisting Images: Essays on Cinema and History* (Philadelphia, Temple University Press, 1990).
3. Among many works on Althusser, see Simon Clarke (ed.), *One Dimensional Marxism*, (London, Allison and Busby, 1980).

4. See Nick Brown (ed.), *Cahiers du Cinema: 1969–72 The Politics of Representation* (London, Routledge, 1990); Peter Steven (ed.), *JumpCut: Hollywood, Politics, Countercinema* (Toronto, Between the Lines, 1985); *The Sexual Subject: The Screen Reader on Sexuality* (London, Routledge, 1992); Noel Burch, *Theory of Film Practice* (New York, Praeger, 1973); Peter Wollen, *Signs and Meaning in the Cinema* (Bloomington, Indiana University Press, 1972). Sylvia Harvey, *May 68 and Film Culture*, (London, BFI, 1980) is an excellent account of the period in Paris. James Roy MacBean, *Film and Revolution* (Bloomington and London, Indiana University Press, 1975), conveys the revolutionary excitement of Godard's, and others, work in that period.

5. Bill Nichols (ed.), *Movies and Methods, Volume 1*, (Berkeley, University of California Press, 1978) and *Volume 2*, 1985, contain most of the key works in this theoretical institutionalisation. He comments on the process critically in the Introduction to *Vol. 2*.

6. Mas'ud Zavarzadeh, *Seeing Films Politically* (Albany, State University of New York Press, 1991), pp. 2–6.

7. David Bordwell, *Making Meaning: Inference and Rhetoric in the Interpretation of Film* (Cambridge and London, Harvard University Press, 1989), is an entertaining tour of the interpretative maze in film studies, albeit in service to his own 'neo-formalism'; Noel Carroll, *Mystifiying Movies: fads and fallacies in contemporary film theory* (New York, Columbia University Press, 1988) is a thorough attack on Theory, though he mistakes Althusser for Marxism *tout court* and offers a literal refutation of psychoanalysis that misses its strength as textual hermeneutic; Zavarzadeh, Faulkner, Sklar, *op. cit.*, and Michael Ryan and Douglas Kellner, *Camera Politica: Politics and Ideology of Contemporary Hollywood* (Bloomington, Indiana University Press, 1988) hold up the lineage of political criticism from various perspectives. Zavarzadeh, Faulkner and Sklar argue strongly for the continuing importance of Althusser's redefinition of ideology and social totality.

8. See Colin McCabe, 'Realism and the Cinema: Notes on Some Brechtian Theses', *Screen* 15, 2 (1974); Noel Burch, *op. cit.*; Peter Wollen, 'Godard and Counter-*Cinema: Vent d'est*, *Afterimage*, no.4, (Fall 1972); Laura Mulvey, 'Visual Pleasure and Narrative Cinema', *Screen*, 16, no.3 (Autumn 1975). On the failures of counter-cinema, see D. N. Rodowick, *The Crisis of Political Modernism: Criticism and Ideology in Contemporary Film Theory* (Urbana and Chicago, University of Illinois Press, 1988).

9. See Introduction, Manuel Alvarado and John Thompson, (eds.), *The Media Reader* (London, BFI, 1990).

10. Colin McCabe (ed.) *High Theory/Low Culture* (New York, St.Martin's Press, 1986); the work of John Fiske, Dick Hebdidge and E. Ann Kaplan on television, sub-cultures and music videos have been particularly influential in this populist turn.

11. In the introduction to Christopher Sharrett (ed.) *Crisis Cinema: The Apocalyptic Idea in Postmodern Narrative Film* (Washington, D.C., Maisonneuve Press, 1993).

12. See particularly, Fredric Jameson, *Postmodernism, or, The Cultural Logic of Capitalism* (Durham, Duke University Press, 1991); Jean Baudrillard, *In the Shadow of the Silent Majorities* (New York, Semiotexte, 1983); Andrew Britton, 'The Myth of Postmodernism: The Bourgeois Intelligentsia in The Age of Reagan', *CineAction* 13/14 (Summer 1988), is a particularly powerful critique; also, see In Defence of History: Marxism and The Postmodern Agenda, special issue of *Monthly Review* (July/August 1995).

13. Francis Mulhern, 'The Politics of Cultural Studies', *Monthly Review* (July/August 1995).

14. See Serge Guilbault, *How New York Stole the Idea of Modern Art: Abstract Expressionism, Freedom and the Cold War* (Chicago and London, University of Chicago Press, 1983); Allan Wald, *The New York Intellectuals: The Rise and Decline of the Anti-Stalinist Left from the 1930s to the 1980s* (Chapel Hill, University of North Carolina Press, 1987); Mexican director Paul Leduc's brilliant *Frida* recreates this moment of revolutionary modernism in its dramatization of the relationship of Rivera and Kahlo with Trotsky and with Stalinism; an important cinematic version of this passage was Maya

Deren's migration from revolutionary activism in the '30s – secretary to Max Eastman, correspondent with Trotsky – to key founder of the American experimental, and deeply formalist, cinema in the '40s; her work has since been retrieved for the politics of women's cinema by contemporary feminists; see Lauren Rabinovitz, *Points of Resistance: Women, Power and Politics in the New York Avant-garde Cinema, 1943–71*, (Urbana and Chicago, University of Illinois Press, 1991).

15. On the Situationists and Lettrists, see Greil Marcus' famed tour de force from dadaism to punks and back, *Lipstick Traces: A Secret History of the Twentieth Century* (London, Secker and Warburg, 1989).

16. See Perry Anderson, *Considerations on Western Marxism* (London, New Left Books, 1976).

17. Jonathan Crary, 'Capital Effects', *October*, 56 (Spring 1991), offers a lucid historical perspective on the whirl of technology and commodities characterizing this latest re-articulation of mass media and their relationship to one another. Ellen Wood, *op. cit.*, comments astutely on the importance of the consumerism of the ascendant capitalism of the '50s and '60s to the politics of the New Left in the academy.

18. Janet Wasko, *Hollywood in the Age of Information* (Austin, University of Texas Press, 1994), p. 222.

19. *Ibid.*, pp. 241–254.

20. Andrew Britton, 'Blissing Out: The Politics of Reaganite Entertainment,' *Movie*, No.31-32 (1986); Scott Forsyth, 'Evil Empire: Spectacle and Imperialism in Hollywood,' *The Socialist Register* (London, Merlin Press, 1987).

21. These comments are an abbreviation of 'The Cold War Forever? Hollywood Thrillers and Imperial Ideologies', presented to the Conference of North American and Cuban Philosophers and Social Scientists, Havana, Cuba, June, 1996. It is also useful to recall Mandel in discussing the arms race economy regarded it as a product of the decline and crisis ridden nature of American capitalism.

22. Andrew Britton, 'The Ideology of *Screen*', *Movie*, No. 26; 1978–79, Terry Lovell, *Pictures of Reality: aesthetics, politics, pleasure* (London, BFI, 1980).

23. Fredric Jameson, *Signatures of the Visible* (New York and London, Routledge, 1992).

24. See, for example, Patricia Erens (ed.), *Issues in Feminist Film Criticism* (Bloomington, Indiana University Press, 1990); Rabinovitz, *op. cit.*

25. See Robin Wood, 'The Responsibilities of a Gay Film Critic,' in Nichols, *Volume 2, op. cit.*

26. To cite a small sample, Greg Waller, (ed.), *American Horrors: Essays on the Modern American Horror Film* (Urbana and Chicago, University of Chicago Press, 1987); Richard Dyer (ed.), *Heavenly Bodies: Stars and Society* (London, BFI, 1982); Ryan and Kellner, on Hollywood in the Reagan years, *op. cit.*; Ted Magder, *Canada's Hollywood: The Canadian State and Feature Films* (Toronto, University of Toronto Press, 1993); Peter Stead, *Film and the Working Class: The Feature Film in British and American Society* (London and New York, Routledge, 1989); on black film, among many key books, see Mark Reid, *Redefining Black Film* (Berkeley, University of California Press, 1993); Vivian Sobchak, *Screening Space: The American Science Fiction Film* (New York, Ungar Press, 1988); Carol J. Clover, *Men, Women and Chainsaws: Gender in the Modern Horror Film* (Princeton, Princeton University Press, 1992).

27. See Thomas Waugh, *op cit.*; Bill Nichols, *Newsreel: Documentary Film on the American Left (1970–75)* (New York, Arno Press, 1980); Bill Nichols, 'Voice in Documentary' in *Movies and Methods, Vol. 2*, is one of the initiating theoretical discussions focused on documentary. For more recent discussion of committed documentary, see Peter Steven, *Brink of Reality: New Canadian Documentary Film and Video* (Toronto, Between the Lines, 1993) and Richard Fung, 'Colouring the Screen: Four Strategies in Anti-Racist Film and Video', *Parallelagramme* Vol.18, No. 3, 1992, pp. 38-53; on gay and lesbian work, see Martha Gever, Patribha Parmar and John Greyson (eds.), *Queer Looks:*

perspectives on gay and lesbian film and video (Toronto, Between Lines, 1993); on black and third world cinema, see Chanan, Downing, Burton, *op cit.*, also Teshome Gabriel, *Third Cinema in the Third World: The Aesthetics of Liberation*, (Ann Arbour, UMI Research Press, 1982) and Michael Martin (ed.), *Cinema of the Black Diaspora: Diversity, Dependence and Oppositionality* (Detroit, Wayne State University Press, 1995), an exceptional collection of critical articles, interviews with filmmakers and manifestoes. Journals like *JumpCut, CineAction* and *Cineaste* in North America consistently address committed documentary and 'Third Cinema'. On the current crisis in Cuban cinema, see Scott Forsyth, 'Cuban Films and the Crisis of Socialism' *CineAction*, 39, (Winter 1995).

CYBORG FICTIONS:
THE CULTURAL LOGIC OF POSTHUMANISM

Scott McCracken

The *fin-de-siècle* crisis in socialism has coincided with the reappearance of
the cyborg. Cyborgs are everywhere, in films, fiction, politics and theory.
Three strands of cyborg discourse can be identified. First, there is the use
of the cyborg to represent the increasingly complex relationship between
humanity and technology. Implants, transplants, prostheses, hormonal
treatment, cosmetic surgery and genetic engineering all blur the boundary
between body and machine. Second, there are cyborg fictions: the narratives that explore the imaginative possibilities inspired by new technology.
These include the cyberpunk fiction of William Gibson and films like
Terminator and *Terminator II*. Thirdly, there are the theoretical extrapola-
tions of these fictions which map the relationship between the inhuman,
global systems of the new world (dis)order and the kinds of hybrid
identities that are one of its characteristics. Here the most influential writer
is Donna Haraway, who sparked many of the critical debates with her
article, 'A Manifesto for Cyborgs: Science, Technology and Socialist
Feminism in the 80s', first published in *Socialist Review*.[1]

Haraway is a historian of science who has devoted most of her work to
interrogating that concept of the human which acts as an unquestioned
assumption in most scientific research. Her cyborg project contains three
central elements. Firstly, she wants to problematise identities rather than
reinforcing them. In her 'Cyborg Manifesto', she describes herself as
'Once upon a time, in the 1970s . . . a proper, US socialist-feminist, white,
female, hominid biologist, who became a historian of science to write
about modern Western accounts of monkeys, apes, and women'. Now she
'has turned into a multiply marked cyborg feminist, who tried to keep her
politics, as well as her other critical functions, alive in the unpromising
times of the last quarter of the twentieth century'[1]. In this role she wishes
to replace traditional science history with narratives that are also 'multiply
marked'. That is, they mark difference rather than masking it, highlighting
the identities that constitute and are constituted by science. The second

element is an attempt to relate those scientific narratives to the larger contexts of scientific research, contexts which include neglected questions like gender and race. Thirdly, she wants to interrogate the central role of the liberal individual as the assumption around which most science works. Significantly, she writes that her transition to cyborg status occurred in response to the challenge of anti-racist and postcolonial critiques of 'Euro-American feminist humanism'. It was, in other words, part of the same suspicion of 'grand narrative' that has upset many of the carefully constructed projects of emancipation of the twentieth century.

In what follows, my two main examples of cyborg manifestations will be Haraway's collection of essays, *Simians, Cyborgs, and Women: the reinvention of nature*, and 'The Winter Market', a short story by William Gibson. If I am more concerned with cyborg fictions than cyborg realities, then this is not to deny the actuality of the new relationship between humanity and technology. One of Haraway's claims is that the cyborg is 'a creature of social reality as well as a creature of fiction'.[2] I will argue that, at a time when the limits of existing socialist narratives are clear, cyborg fictions perform an important and 'real' cultural function. They operate as what Fredric Jameson has called, 'narrative as socially symbolic act'.[2] That is, they provide the kinds of transformative metaphors through which the cultural conflicts of the late twentieth century are mediated. In Jameson's words, 'history is not a text, not a narrative, master or otherwise, but . . . as an absent cause, it is inaccessible to us except in textual form, and . . . our approach to it and the Real itself necessarily passes through it prior textualization, its narrativization in the political unconscious'.[3] The proliferation of cyborg metaphors means that we ignore them at our peril, because it is through such forms that new kinds of consciousness (both empowering and disempowering) arise.

Unfortunately, suspicion of 'cyberhype' has led some marxist commentators to categorise all cyborgs as reactionary. Julian Stallabrass sees the paradigm as the opening shot in *Terminator*: a robot crushing human skulls.[4] However, to accept this Orwellian vision at face value is to throw away a long tradition of anti-capitalist criticism. Despite the fact that cyborgs are frequently cited as a postmodern phenomenon, cyborg metaphors have appeared regularly in one form or another at moments of social crisis from the industrial revolution to the present day. From Mary Shelley's monster to Carlyle's image of the shuttle that 'drops from fingers of the weaver, and falls into iron fingers that ply it faster' to Marx's description of the proletariat as 'an appendage of the machine', cyborg fictions have mediated the evolving relationship between humanity and technology. Rita Felski points to examples of male cyborgs during the last *fin de siècle* in the work of Rathchilde. Andreas Huyssen writes of the robot's use as a figure for feminised mass culture in Fritz Lang's

Metropolis; and cyborgs have appeared again at the end of the twentieth century.[6]

There is, however, little doubt that, in the 1990s, most cyborgs are working for the enemy. The absence of socialist alternatives has seen a conservative version of the technological fix run rampant. The unseen hand of the of the free market is advocated as the inhuman machinery that will resolve all economic problems. A catalogue of cyberconcepts, the information superhighway, the internet, artificial intelligence, virtual reality, interactive programs, cyberspace, cybersex, all function as happy endings to the problems that an untrammelled capitalism is building up for the twenty-first century. They are the cheerful recourse of films like *Mission: Impossible* or thrillers like Tom Clancy's *Debt of Honour*, where the search always provides an instant answer, the technology always works and the smart weapon always hits its target. In politics the story is Newt Gringich's idea of universal access to the internet, Bill Clinton's slogan 'a computer in every classroom', or Al Gore's global network of fibre-optic cables as the solution to economic development.[7]

In an increasingly uncertain world, these conservative visions offer the hope that, after all, progress and human happiness are not mutually exclusive. They function because they have a powerful utopian impetus and, despite their limitations, even the most facile provide an imaginative space in which new forms of consciousness can be explored. But, like all popular fictions, they would not work if they did not first arouse the anxieties they are designed to quell. To be successful each must provide the means through which a workable, coherent identity can be put together in the context of social and economic forces which fragment the rational self.[7]

By contrast, progressive cyborg fictions problematise the question of identity. They give precedence neither to inhuman machinery, nor to a conservative version of human nature. Instead, they explore the transformations of what it means to be human. The impact of globalisation is an important factor here. While some socialist commentators have been sceptical about the actual degree of change,[9] it is undeniable that in the latter half of the twentieth century the speed of global interactions, both human and economic, has been unprecedented. This has had real cultural effects. Global population movements and information networks have created a new environment in which the sense of self is radically different to earlier phases of capitalism. From an older Left perspective, a phenomenon like identity politics seemed like a regression, or the special interests of small privileged sectors in the United States and Western Europe. Eric Hobsbawm, for one, has been quick to condemn what he sees as sectional interests over the Left's need for a universalist project.[10] But, from a contemporary perspective, the levels of dislocation and alienation currently experienced by large numbers of people mean that identity must be understood as a vital focus for political activism.[11] Cyborg fictions explore the kinds of identities needed to live in the new world; and interest in them is not confined to elites. New and old concepts, for example, the mestiza, hybridity, double consciousness and queer politics[12] might all be described as radical cyborg fictions. Each attempts to think through the problem of the self in the context of a world where cultural boundaries are constantly shifting.

The most influential body of work, and the most obviously indebted to popular (science) fiction, has been that of Donna Haraway. Haraway's 'Cyborg Manifesto' deliberately courts the extreme. Haraway argues for a revolution in our understanding of the human.

> Cyborgs are post-Second World War hybrid entities made of, first, ourselves and other organic creatures in our unchosen 'high-technological' guise as information systems, texts, and ergonomically controlled labouring, desiring and reproducing systems. (1)

The thrust of Haraway's argument (and of much of the work that has followed the Manifesto) has been avant-garde in the modernist sense of working at the boundaries of the culturally accepted. Partly, one suspects, this is because the context of many of the debates has been Northern California, a region of the United States strongly influenced by Silicon Valley and the lesbian and gay culture of San Francisco. In the Bay Area changing the sexed body through piercing, tattoos, scarification, hormonal treatment, cosmetic surgery and implants is a practical form of posthumanism that exists alongside the technological advances of Apple-Macintosh and Hewlett Packard.

> Bodies have become cyborgs – cybernetic organisms – compounds of hybrid techno-organic embodiment and texuality. (212)[13]

In her collection, *Simians, Cyborgs and Women: The Reinvention of Nature*, the reader traces Haraway's development from socialist-feminist to cyborg-feminist through her accounts of how primatologists have studied apes. Science, in her account, becomes a story told to regulate and legitimate certain forms of social organisation. The funding and institutionalisation of research produces certain results. Most telling is her account of how a focus on male dominance amongst apes was changed by feminist primatologists who pointed to the importance of the mother-child relationship. She marks the shift from the dominance theory of the 1930s to a theory of stress-management in the postwar period so that, 'Primate studies are motivated by, and in turn legitimate, the management needs of a stressed society' (33). In the same way, she notes a change in the biological model from one characterised by metaphors from engineering before 1945, to sociobiology's postwar 'theorizing of nature as a communications or control machine' (61). The communications revolution opened the way to 'a logic of control appropriate to the historical conditions of post-Second World War capitalism' (58).

The cyborg illustrates this situation, one where the organism is no longer the unit of analysis. Instead the concept of the individual organism is abolished in favour of biology as communications system: 'The cyborg is text, machine, body, and metaphor – all theorized and engaged in practice in terms of communications' (212). In the absence of the comforting and familiar units of liberal individualism, critical analysis becomes a question of boundaries.

> . . . bodies as objects of knowledge are material-semiotic generative modes. Their boundaries materialize in social interaction. Boundaries are drawn by mapping practices; 'objects' do not pre-exist as such. Objects are boundary projects. But boundaries shift from within; boundaries are very tricky. What boundaries provisionally contain remains generative, productive of meanings and bodies. Siting (sighting) boundaries is a risky practice. (200-201)

Haraway writes of the relationship between bodies and machines as a 'border war' (150). Science fiction, speculative fiction and fantasy are useful modes in this context because their subject is the point at which the boundaries between what is 'real' and what is possible are drawn (201). Cyborg fictions are ways of theorizing and narrating these boundaries. The consequence is monster stories: 'Monsters have always defined the limits of community in Western imaginations' (180). Cyborgs are the monsters which populate the margins of discourse: 'These boundary creatures are, literally, monsters, a word that shares more than its root with the word to *demonstrate*. Monsters signify' (2). At this point, analysis of the narrative, of the fiction, becomes as important as the discovery of the facts, which have themselves been constituted as a story. Science, as the 'most respectable legitimator of new realities' (78) can provide the narratives society needs to resolve 'the contradiction between, or the gap between, human reality and human possibility in history' (42). But Haraway is not content to let those narratives be authoritative. They are always fictions, mediating social reality.

The key element here for future socialist narratives is the challenge these monsters present to the liberal individualist self. In an essay on theories of the immune system ('The Biopolitics of Postmodern Bodies: Constitution of the Self in Immune System Discourse'), prompted by social and scientific discourses around AIDS, Haraway shows how the body's boundaries cannot be clearly defined as an organic whole against an exterior not-self: 'In a sense, there could be no *exterior* antigenic structure, no "invader" that the immune system had not already "seen" and mirrored internally. Self and "other" lose their rationalistic oppositional quality and become subtle plays of partially mirrored readings and responses' (218). This has consequences for conceptions of identity in the late twentieth century, when the 'constructions of an organism's boundaries, the job of the discourses of immunology, are particularly potent mediators of the experiences of sickness and death' (208).

These are challenging enough ideas in themselves, but it is Haraway's persistent correlation of the problem of the self in medico-scientific theory with the inadequacy of the concept of the individual that presents the greatest challenge of all. To follow the Cyborg Manifesto's call to arms would be to concede that we do, after all, live in a posthuman world, where the old straitjacket identities no longer have force. However, the grandeur of Haraway's claims need to be examined more closely before they can be accepted. Two critical points need to be made. Firstly, the mediation between scientific paradigm and 'postmodern world' is highly complex and, at times, Haraway's essays seem to posit an unmediated base-super-structure model.[14] Secondly, there are the avant-garde qualities of Haraway's writing already mentioned, qualities that are developed further by some of her followers who argue for a posthuman, postgender, post-identity politics of monstrosity.[15] These concerns might be cited as the preoccupations of a small privileged minority, whose organic intellectuals have the advantage of tenured jobs in California's still generously funded academic institutions.

Both these objections are serious ones, but both can be countered. The first is probably flattened by the weight of Haraway's extensive study, *Primate Visions: Gender Race and Nature in the World of Modern Science*, which has won widespread praise. The book examines the social and cultural forces that shape one particular discipline, primatology, in the United States, Japan and India. In the context of *Primate Visions*, the extravagant claims of the Cyborg Manifesto appear as a working through of the implications of the bigger study. The second is more complex, because it raises the vast debate about the relationship between cultural elites and mass culture, a debate that extends back to the earlier moment of modernist aesthetics.[16] In the case of Haraway (who currently holds the post of Professor at the History of Consciousness Board, University of California, Santa Cruz), the validity of her claims must depend on how successful they are in providing a language that can relate changes in cultural identity to the context of globalisation.

Significantly, one of her key cultural reference points is the work of chicana women writers like Gloria Anzaldúa and Cherríe Moraga. They write of the permeable and shifting identities that come into being in the human and cultural border traffic between the United States (particularly the state of California) and Mexico. These are the kinds of hybrid identities that are developing as a consequence of globalisation. Of Moraga, Haraway says, her 'language is not "whole"; it is self-consciously spliced, a chimera of English and Spanish, both conqueror's languages. But it is this chimeric monster, without claim to an original language before violation that crafts the erotic, competent, potent identities of women of colour' (175-6). Her other example, Anzaldúa, writes, in her collection, *Borderlands/La Frontera*, of 'the new mestiza' as on the border between two cultures:

> Because I, a *mestiza*,
> continually walk out of one culture
> and into another,
> because I am in all cultures at the same time,
> *alma entre dos mundos, tres, cuatro,*
> *me zumba la cabeza con lo contradictorio.*
> *Estoy norteada por todas las voces que me hablan*
> *simultáneamente*
> (soul between two worlds, three, four,
> my head buzzes with the contradictory
> I am Northernised by all the voices that speak to me
> simultaneously)[17]

The new mestiza is not defined by an essentialist identity, but by '*una lucha de fronteras*/a struggle of borders'. This mapping of boundaries has much in common with comparable 'postcolonial' projects, fictional and theoretical, which have attempted to engage with the intensifying pace of global interaction. Salman Rushdie's *The Satanic Verses*, for example, charts the metamorphoses that occur in the process of migration from the Indian subcontinent to the former imperial centre, a process that creates, in the words of the postcolonial critic, Homi Bhabha, a kind of third space of cultural hybridity:

> for me the importance of hybridity is not to be able to trace two original moments from which the third emerges, rather hybridity to me is the 'third space' which enables other positions to emerge. This third space displaces the histories that constitute it, and sets up new structures of authority, new political initiatives, which are inadequately understood through received wisdom.[18]

Paul Gilroy's concept of the Black Atlantic constitutes a similar attempt to think outside the fixed and misleading boundary lines of nation states and to create a space in which a double consciousness that is both inside and outside modernity can be thought. The point here is not, of course, to say that the new mestiza, Bhabha's hybridity, or Gilroy's development of Du Bois's double consciousness delineate the same space. It is rather to suggest that current conditions create the same kinds of problems for meaningful narratives in different parts of the globe. Gloria Anzaldúa, between Mexico and California, tackles similar kinds of dislocation as (albeit in a very different way) Salman Rushdie between Bombay and London. Chicana poetry and magical realism are both, in a sense, cyborg fictions because they foreground the imperfect stitching that reveals them as monstrous.

Haraway's use of the cyborg as transformative metaphor is productive because it embraces, rather than runs away from, these new realities. Her concept of the cyborg engages with the kinds of hybrid identities that are being produced by the new global economy. Experience is now both local and global, regional and transcultural, biological and technological. The cyborg, as transformative metaphor, provides the figure through which the possibilities, as well as the limitations, of the new can be thought.

In fact, the problem for the Left is not the difficulty of finding cyborg fictions. As I claimed in my opening paragraph, cyborgs are everywhere and, at the same time, evidence of the inapplicability of the liberal individualist ideal is abundant. The problem lies in trying to read the embarrassment of riches that is postmodernist culture for evidence of a new emancipatory project. William Gibson's work, which forms part of the original 'cyberpunk' movement, is a good place to start. Cyberpunk has been described by Fredric Jameson as, 'a new type of science fiction . . . which is fully as much an expression of transnational corporate realities as it is of global paranoia itself'.[19] The movement is true to its name in its skilful self-promotion. It extrapolates from the cut-throat consumer society of the 1980s and that decade's increasing divide between rich and poor. Gibson's fictional world describes a recognizable geo-political system, characterised by weak nation states and dominant transnationals. Its inequalities reflect the long term outcome of the present crisis predicted by David Harvey: 'heightened international and inter-regional competition, with the least advantaged countries and regions suffering the severest consequences'.[20] But, while inspired by the development of new technologies like virtual reality, personal computers and the internet, Gibson's narratives focus as much on the social contradictions thrown up by technology as the machinery itself. On the one hand, cyberpunk is resolutely posthumanist. It delights in the transformation of what is meant by being human: Gibson's characters employ genetic engineering, drugs and advanced forms of surgery to transform themselves. On the other hand, the cyberworld is peopled with the descendants of postwar countercultures who represent a persistent romanticism.

Gibson bolts this romanticism onto a Chandleresque sense of style. A consequence is that the most marked aspect of his world is a sense of lack, or unfulfilled potential. His novels and short stories explore the forms of hybrid, 'cyber' consciousness that arise from the employment of new technologies as a means of domination. His most famous contribution to the science fiction genre is the idea of 'jacking in'. Using a jack into their central nervous system, his characters are able to plug themselves directly into the 'matrix' (an enhanced form of the internet) and explore a virtual world of information, described as:

A graphic representation of data abstracted from the banks of every computer in the human system. Unthinkable complexity. Lines of light ranged in the nonspace of the mind, clusters and constellations of data. Like city lights, receding . . .'[21]

We are meant to take this no more or less seriously than Mary Shelley's readers might have taken the possibility of animating the reassembled parts of dead bodies by electricity. Rather, the matrix acts as a metaphor for the kinds of cultural collisions and re-inventions of the self that might now be possible. Thus, it is quite wrong to argue, as has Julian Stallabrass, that cyberspace is 'merely the literal expression of the situation of the individual in contemporary society, and more specifically of business people and their camp followers (engineers and intellectuals) spinning universalizing fantasies out of their desire to ride the next commercial wave'. On the contrary, its deployment by all sides in the battle over future meanings has been anything but literal and its politics are in still in dispute.

Some of Gibson's best writing is in his shorter fiction. In his short story 'The Winter Market' the main character, Lise, is akin to the old-fashioned robot, a descendant perhaps of the female robot in Lang's *Metropolis*. She is the victim of a wasting disease and can only move with the aid of a polycarbon exoskeleton. She is, thus, already a hybrid being: part-human and part-machine; and, as in *Metropolis*, she embodies both a fear of the feminine and a technophobia.[23] She first appears to the narrator, Casey[24], as a sexual threat when she approaches him at a party:

> But she found me again. Came after me two hours later, weaving through the bodies and junk with that terrible grace programmed into the exoskeleton.[25]

As a robot, Lise belongs to an earlier era. Her other more up-to-date talents are not revealed until Casey takes her home. Lise's unconscious creates the kind of raw material which, through 'jacking in', can be recorded and used as mass-market entertainment. Casey is a skilled editor of the kind of dreams she can produce. He fashions the raw material into a saleable commodity. Lise's dreams turn out to be the most powerful he has ever encountered:

> You never felt that hunger she had, which was pared down to a dry need, hideous in its singleness of purpose. People who know *exactly* what they want have always frightened me, and Lise had known what she wanted for a long time, and wanted nothing else at all. (147)

The narrative works over some of the now canonical aesthetic binaries that characterise discussions of modernism and postmodernism: for example, the modernist divide between high and low culture. Lise's mass-market talents are compared to the modernist artist, Rubin. His raw material is *gomi*, the Japanese word for rubbish: we are told that islands have been built out of gomi in Tokyo bay. In Rubin's studio, 'One box is filled with the severed heads of hundreds of Barbie dolls, another with armored industrial safety gauntlets that look like space suit gloves' (150). Rubin makes his art from physical detritus, while Casey makes his with the waste products of people's minds. For Rubin, 'everything he drags home must have been new and shiny once, must have meant something, however briefly, to someone' (161). The suggestion is that Lise's mind contains similar waste, she and it are cast-offs of a society that is extraordinarily wasteful, both of goods and people. But, where Rubin's art-works are displayed in galleries, Casey's editions of Lise's dreams become mass-produced commodities. Modernism's elitism is transformed into a direct relationship with the desires of mass society. Her hunger becomes not just her own, it now belongs to all the dispossessed: 'Those kids back down the Market, warming their butts around the fires and wondering if they'll find someplace to sleep tonight, they believe it' (158). Lise's unconscious is in tune with the collective desires of her audience.

Whether we treat this relationship as productive or oppressive hinges on whether mass culture is seen as a total system or as a contested terrain. In the first case, the 'consumer' of popular culture is understood to be a passive recipient of whatever the culture industry churns out. In the second, she or he is understood to be critically engaged in an imaginative relationship with the popular text, one where that relationship is productive of a workable, coherent identity which allows him or her to live in a (perhaps otherwise intolerable) world. One strand of mass culture theory, developed from Adorno in his most negative and least utopian dialectical mode, might see Lise's abilities as no more than a metaphor for the way in which the culture industry absorbs and defuses popular dissatisfaction in capitalist society. For example, Julian Stallabrass sees the video game (the form which comes closest to Gibson's vision of Lise's products) as overwhelming the agency of the player: it is a 'phantasmagoric experience of total immersion'.[26] Stallabrass's image of 'immersion' is symptomatic of the tendency in mass culture theory to conceive of the subject as powerless in the face of a great wave of pap. It denies the crucial role of fantasy in the formation of a critical subjectivity, where the active 'reader's' needs and desires are projected onto the setting provided by the popular text. Thus, the term 'consumption' is itself problematic because, in Paul Gilroy's words, it 'accentuates the passivity of its agents and plays down the value of their creativity as well as the micro-political significance of their actions in understanding the forms of anti-discipline and resistance conducted in everyday life'.[27]

The persistent strain of mass culture theory in left-wing thought reproduces a static model of culture. It obscures dominance as the product of a continuing social process and it effectively denies the importance of culture in political struggle. However, if power relations are not permanently fixed, but are part of an ongoing (albeit unequal) conflict, then the struggle over meaning is an integral part of any form of politics. Moreover, mass culture theory's model of culture denies the utopian potential of popular texts. The importance of consent as well as coercion means that some kind of compensation is necessary for those whom power excludes. Popular texts must contain a surplus of meaning over and above their instrumental function, which satisfies our needs and desires and provides an element of hope for a different world.

The transformative metaphor of the cyborg permits a different, more complex understanding of the relationship between reader and text than that provided by mass culture theory. In 'The Winter Market' the narrative unsettles a traditional understanding of the opposition between human agency and the dehumanising effects of the culture industry. Lise's fate provokes a reflection on the reader's imaginative relationship with the popular text. On the verge of death, as a consequence of the disease and her addiction to amphetamines, she arranges to have her personality downloaded into a computer. In this Faustian bargain, she will escape the physical limitations of her life, but is beholden to the company, which will not pay for the amount of memory needed to store her unless she continues to produce the hits that make her so valuable. The ambivalent effect on the reader is produced by a semi-comic account of Lise's status as undead.

> Because she was dead, and I'd let her go. Because, now, she was immortal, and I'd helped her get that way. And because I knew she'd phone me, in the morning. (140)

Casey is left, like the reader, waiting for a voice of uncertain status, but, as Rubin points out, engagement with the machine is inevitable: '. . . you have to edit her next release. Which will almost certainly be soon, because she needs money bad. She's taking up a lot of ROM on some corporate mainframe' (166). For both Lise and Casey, artist and editor, the future holds no clear borderline between creativity and the machine. Their future selves will both be, to different degrees, posthuman cyberselves. Thus, Gibson's short story maintains the element of ambivalence that is essential to a creative encounter with the future, exploring the new boundary positions that are emerging.

The downloaded Lise even disrupts mass culture theory's persistent gendering of mass culture as feminine, where the fear of the masses is 'always also a fear of woman, a fear of nature out of control, a fear of the unconscious, of sexuality, of the loss of identity and stable ego boundaries in the mass'.[28] Her position as artist in the machine suggests a new hybrid that does not fit well with any form of gendered identity. The possibilities this creates have meant that, despite accusation that cyberpunk is fiction for boys, the movement includes women writers like Pat Cadigan and the feminist writer, Marge Piercy. Piercy has returned to the genre in *Body of Glass* (1992, published as *He, She and It*, 1991, in North America) after being credited with creating the first cyberworld in *Woman on the Edge of Time* (1976).

Not all cyborgs are as challenging as Gibson's or Piercy's, but they are now ubiquitous in popular fiction. Tom Clancy's recent thriller, *Debt of Honour* (1995), is a paranoid fantasy that sees a weakened United States overcome a military threat from an aggressive Japan using a variety of smart weapons co-ordinated through the use of satellites and computer technology. Satellites that are able to track fugitives and carry laser weapons turn up in a contemporary horror novel, Dean Koontz's *Dark Rivers of the Heart* (1994). In Clive Barker's fantastical tale of parallel universes, *Everville* (1994), the forces of evil are tracked with a computer database that receives information from every possible source. Even Michael Crichton's bestseller about sexual harassment, *Disclosure* (1994), involves a scene where the protagonist enters a virtual world to retrieve the information he needs to prove his 'innocence'.

This constitutes a quantifiable shift, comparable with earlier moments in the postwar period that demonstrate that popular culture is not about standardised products but is subject to process. John Sutherland has noted the increase in international themes in the bestsellers of the 1960s and 70s.[29] Andrew Billon has observed the rise and fall of the 'sex and shopping' or 'bonkbuster' novel with the consumer boom of the late 1980s.[30] Feminist critics have charted the changes in the romance novel that accompanied second-wave feminism in the 1970s, when heroines became less passive and began to challenge some of the earlier assumptions about a woman's role.[31] We now see a proliferation of popular narratives where the protagonists come to an understanding of their position in the world through new technology. In this popular texts are not just reflecting techno-logical change. In order to be successful, popular fiction must do more than perpetuate the powerful ideologies that govern our lives. It must also relate the generalised and impersonal semantic horizons of the new global order to the personal life and self-identity of the reader. Thus, the popular text must perform the difficult and impressive job of relating the personal to the political. Although the popular text is a commodity it is not just a commodity. It must also answer some of the needs of its readers.

Thus, popular fictions, whether in paperbacks, films or political rhetoric need to be recognised as an important terrain of struggle. Simplistic accounts of their function under capitalism fail to explain their range and scope. Narratives are now emerging that do, however inadequately, give a structure to the new relationship between identity and globalisation. Rather than ignoring them, we need a socialist politics that is able to popularise the radical insights of cyborg fictions and to challenge and subvert the reactionary popular narratives that already exist. It is no accident that the two most successful left-of-centre politicians of the moment, Bill Clinton and his shadow Tony Blair, both tell 'stories' about the relationship between national and global economies; but they are not the ones we need.

If the reality is closer to Gibson's vision of the dispossessed than Al Gore's vision of development, to Anzaldúa than to the rhetoric of NAFTA, and to Rushdie's schizophrenic London than to the blandishments of EMU, then the Left needs a narrative that is both innovatory and popular, its own cyborg fiction that doesn't hide the joins, to challenge the ones that do.

NOTES

1. *Socialist Review*, vol. 15, 80 (1985), pp. 65-107, later published as 'A Cyborg Manifesto: Science, Technology and Socialist-Feminism in the Late Twentieth Century' in Donna J. Haraway, *Simians, Cyborgs, and Women: the reinvention of nature* (London, Routledge, 1991). From here on page references from the latter are included in the text.
2. Fredric Jameson, *The Political Unconscious: narrative as socially symbolic act* (London, Methuen, 1981).
3. *Ibid.*, p. 35.
4. Julian Stallabrass, 'Just Gaming: Allegory and Economy in Computer Games', *New Left Review*, 198 (March/April 1993), p. 82.
5. Thomas Carlyle, 'Signs of the Times' in *Selected Writings* (London, Penguin, 1971), p. 64; Karl Marx, 'The Communist Manifesto' in Eugene Kamenka (ed.), *The Portable Karl Marx* (Harmondsworth, Penguin, 1983), p. 211.
6. Rita Felski, 'The Art of Perversion: Female Sadists and Male Cyborgs' in *The Gender of Modernity* (Cambridge, Mass, Harvard UP, 1995); Andreas Huyssen, 'The Vamp and the Machine: Fritz Lang's *Metropolis*' in *After the Great Divide: Modernism, Mass Culture, Postmodernism* (Bloomington and Indianapolis, Indiana UP, 1986).
7. On Al Gore's vision of the future see Herbert I. Schiller, 'The Global Information Highway: Project for an Ungovernable World' in James Brook and Iain A. Boal (eds.), *Resisting the Virtual Life: the culture and politics of information* (San Francisco, City Light Books, 1995). The collection as a whole provides an excellent survey of the political uses of cyberculture.
8. For more on the nature of contemporary popular fictions see Scott McCracken, *Pulp: an introduction to popular fiction* (forthcoming, Manchester University Press, 1997).
9. Andrew Glyn and Bob Sutcliffe, argue that the 'the world economy is considerably more globalized than 50 years ago; but much less than is theoretically possible. In many ways it is less globalized than 100 years ago.': Andrew Glyn and Bob Sutcliffe, 'Global But Leaderless? The New Capitalist Order', *Socialist Register 1992*, p. 91. For example, they point out that 'Even within Europe, where the thrust towards trade liberalization was strongest, export shares by the end of the 1980s were only a little above those of 1913' (p. 79).
10. Eric Hobsbawm, 'Identity Politics and the Left', *New Left Review*, 217 (May/June 1996) pp. 38-47.
11. Jürgen Habermas identifies this moment as a gap between 'the systems world' and 'the life world' and looks to a time when 'social movements [are] no longer orientated to the system's steering needs, but to the *processes at the boundaries* between system and lifeworld': *The Philosophical Discourse of Modernity* (Cambridge, Mass., MIT Press, 1987), p. 357. It is at these boundaries, at the intersection between the machinery of modern institutions and the uncertainty of everyday life that cyborg fictions emerge. In the very last pages of *The Philosophical Discourse of Modernity* Habermas writes that the 'changes with the language of general systems theory that has developed from cybernetics . . . come a lot closer to the sociocultural form of life than classical mechanics' (pp. 384–5). Interestingly, this is not far from the line taken in Haraway's 'Cyborg Manifesto'.
12. Gloria Anzaldúa, *Borderlands/La Frontera: the new mestiza* (San Francisco, Ann Lute,

1987); Homi Bhabha, *The Location of Culture* (London, Routledge, 1994); Paul Gilroy, *The Black Atlantic: Modernity and Double Consciousness* (London, Verso, 1993); Eve Kosofsky Sedgewick, *The Epistemology of the Closet* (Hemel Hempstead, Harvester, 1991); Judith Butler, *Bodies that Matter: on the discursive limits of sex* (New York and London, Routledge, 1993).

13. When Haraway concludes the Manifesto with the statement that she 'would rather be a cyborg than a goddess', she is opting for engagement with the cutting edge of new technologies rather than evasion through that other Californian alternative, New Age philosophy.

14. See, for example, the correlation between the communication revolution and the logic of postwar capitalism cited earlier (*Simian, Cyborgs, and Women*, p. 58).

15. See for example Judith Halberstam (ed.), *Posthuman Bodies*, (Bloomington, Indiana UP, 1995).

16. See Fredric Jameson, *Postmodernism, or, the cultural logic of late capitalism*, (London, Verso, 1991), pp. 2-3.

17. Anzaldúa, *Borderlands/La Frontera*, p. 76. I am grateful to Nuria Triana Toribio for help with the translation of this passage.

18. Homi Bhabha, 'The Third Space' interview with Jonathan Rutherford in Jonathan Rutherford ed. *Identity: Community, Culture, Difference* (London, Lawrence and Wishart, 1990), p. 211.

19. Jameson, *Postmodernism*, p. 38.

20. David Harvey, *The Condition of Postmodernity* (Oxford, Blackwell, 1989), p. 183.

21. William Gibson, *Neuromancer* (London, HarperCollins, 1986), p. 67.

22. Julian Stallabrass, 'Empowering Technology: The Exploration of Cyberspace' in *New Left Review*, 211 (May/June 1995), p. 32.

23. See Huyssen, 'The Vamp and the Machine' *op. cit.*

24. The great-great-grandson, perhaps, of Casey Jones whose relationship with a machine was legendary.

25. William Gibson, 'The Winter Market' in *Burning Chrome* (London, Harper Collins, 1993), p. 144 (from here on page numbers in text).

26. Julian Stallabrass 'Just Gaming: Allegory and Economy in Computer Games', p. 84. For a longer discussion of mass culture theory and bestselling fictions see Scott McCracken, *Pulp: an introduction to popular fiction.*

27. Paul Gilroy, *The Black Atlantic*, p. 103.

28. Andreas Huyssen, 'Mass Culture as Woman: Modernism's Other' in *After the Great Divide: Modernism, Mass Culture, Postmodernism*, p. 53.

29. John Sutherland, *Fiction and the Fiction Industry* (London, Athlone Press, 1978), p. 56.

30. Andrew Billon, 'Getting Up on the Wrong Side of Bed', *The Observer Review*, (3 Jan 1993), pp. 3-4.

31. See Ann Rosalind Jones, 'Mills and Boon meet Feminism' in Jean Radford (ed.), *The Progress of Romance: the politics of popular fiction* (London, Routledge Kegan Paul, 1986).

RESTORING THE REAL: RETHINKING SOCIAL CONSTRUCTIVIST THEORIES OF SCIENCE

Meera Nanda

As we come to recognize the conventional and artifactual status of our forms of knowing, [we realize] that it is ourselves and not reality that is responsible for what we know.
(Stevan Shapin and Simon Schaffer, 1985)

It always seems to me extreme rashness on the part of some when they want to make human abilities the measure of what nature can do.
(Galileo Galilei, *Dialogues Concerning the Two Chief World Systems*, 1632)

Introduction

One of the oldest urges in Western intellectual tradition is to think that reality and truth should coincide, that our knowledge be certified in the end by the structure of reality itself. Modern science, which best embodies this urge, aims at justified knowledge which can faithfully track the contours of the natural world. The logic of science, however, has been severely challenged by a set of doctrines which deny that what we take as scientific facts bear any necessary relation to the causal processes and theoretical entities they claim to describe. Often referred to as 'social construction of science' or 'sociology of scientific knowledge,' these doctrines claim that because science's methods, like any other way of knowing, are wholly relative to a theoretical framework and a world-view, science amounts to a construction, and not a discovery, of reality: we know what we ourselves construct and there can be no warrant that our constructs can progressively come to map the world as it really is. Understood sociologically, the practice of science becomes a matter of conventions, and truth a matter of how we 'garland consensus with authority.'[1] If meaning-conferring power can be imagined as distributed along a triangle whose three sides are the natural world, the individual knower and cultural practices, social constructivism tends to collapse the first two into the third: facts once seen as due to the world's own determination are instead seen as projections upon a much thinner world by the cultural practices of communities of inquirers. While constructivist approaches to science have revealed how deeply our perceptions, conceptual categories and modes of reasoning are embedded in our social life, they have exacted a heavy price: they have inflated the role of cultural practices in fixing our beliefs to such an extent that the world and the self have virtually disappeared as constraints on the content and logic of our beliefs and cultural practices.[2]

This essay offers a critical exposition of some of the most influential sociological and feminist theories that purport to see the natural world, experimental evidence, scientific facts and objectivity as social constructs.[3] I will call constructivist any theory of science that includes in its purview 'the very content and nature of scientific knowledge... [and] not just the circumstances surrounding its production.' While the earlier structural-functional tradition of Karl Mannheim and Robert Merton only studied the social conditioning of the agenda of science (the foci of interest and the rate of advance), the newer socio-cultural theories aim to explain the technical *content* of science in terms of social variables (class, gender and/or professional interests, among other things). Although they differ in emphasis, the various schools within the constructivist stream adhere to three tenets. First, what makes a belief true is not correspondence with an element of reality, but its adoption and authentication by the relevant community of inquirers.[5] Thus, there is no hard and fast philosophical difference between a society's fund of knowledge and the beliefs currently held and disseminated by certified authorities. Second, science is a socially located praxis that creates the reality it describes, rather than a detached description of a pre-existing reality external to its own practice. Science not just describes 'facts', but actually constructs them through the active, culturally and socially situated choices scientists make in the laboratory.[6] Third, the constructivist theories examined here admit of no analytical distinctions between knowledge and society, the cognitive dimension and the socio-cultural dimension: people's *knowledge of the world* and their *organization of life in the world* constitute each other, the two are 'co-produced.'[7] From the obviously true and undeniable premise that science is done in definite socially located institutions by socialized individuals, constructivist theorists tend to deny any meaningful distinction between what is inside and outside of science and between things natural and social.

We will encounter these assumptions in their strong, moderate and weak versions as we cast a critical look at the major schools of SSK. All through the exercise, I will argue for a recovery of the real through a dialectical, mutually self-correcting relationship between the real world, the knower and her/his cultural assumptions, each helping to determine the content and meaning of the other two. Even though I don't present a comprehensive realist theory of science in this essay, I do try to show the desirability and the possibility of a robust (though fallible and non-foundational) contextual realism which admits the role of culture and social interests in our perceptions, but never loses sight of the discipline the real world imposes on our cultural conventions and interests. Recognizing the social nature of scientific practice does not have to lead us to give up the commonsense idea that a belief is true because the state of affairs to which it refers is in fact the case, and not because it is believed by a community of certified inquirers, as the constructivists would have it.

Political and Philosophical Arguments Against Deconstruction of Science

I decided to undertake this critique *not* because I doubt that sometimes what we accept as an immutable truth about nature is actually socially constructed. There is no question in my mind that scientists can be, and often have been, led by their unconscious biases and conscious material interests to project the existing social order onto the order of nature. Such science-certified 'findings' can, in turn, give socially created differences a gloss of unalterable destiny, sanctioned by the very structure of nature itself. It is a singular achievement of feminist and radical science critics to have drawn attention to the fact that science at times has been used to naturalize unequal and hierarchical social relations of gender, caste/race. I share the impulse behind these critiques of science insofar as they seek to turn the self-critical rationality of science on science itself. Such an exercise, if combined with a realist epistemology, can identify the blinders of conventions, interests and ideologies so that we can know the truth about the world and our place in it.[8]

It is precisely because I *value* the impulse of emancipatory self-critique that the constructivist science-critics start out with, that I *reject* the position they arrive at, namely, a complete merging and mutual constitution of the social order and the order of knowledge. Once we come to see the very content of natural sciences as not merely conditioned, but constituted by the culturally sanctioned social practices, scientific knowledge becomes a matter of prevailing and ever-changing conventions, with no necessary relation with the natural order and no *critical* relation with the social order. This conflation between the real and our accounts of it jeopardizes the entire project of a progressive critique of ideology, for as Frank Farrell puts it:

> When reality itself has become a manufactured image…it can no longer make sense to measure our beliefs against how matters really stand. When selves are understood to be cultural artifacts, then the notion of self discovery or self emancipation is a delusion. If rational practices must occur within a nexus of power and taken-for-granted biases, then the goal of coming to have a more objective account of reality and of ethical relations is a foolish one.[9]

Social constructivist doctrines have moved from the critical function of truth, to a critique of the very possibility of true knowledge, or as Michele

Barrett puts it, following Foucault, from an analysis of 'the economics of untruth [ideology] to a politics of truth' itself.[10] Starting with a suspicion that social interests can sometimes occlude truth, they have concluded that social interests always-already *constitute* it, and that knowledge whose validity can transcend our local context and interests is *in principle* impossible. Starting from the materialist insight that science is a socially mediated practice, constructivist theories have come to see logic, evidence, truth and even external reality itself as social, having no content independent of their sociality.

I am especially concerned with the exhaustion of ideology-critique in contemporary feminist and postcolonial writings on science and society. These critics have turned their backs on the earlier science-for-the-people initiatives that used the findings of modern science to critique the false and inadequate knowledge that legitimizes the existing social hierarchies. They have instead turned their critical tools on modern science itself in an attempt to expose science's own unacknowledged social values and ideologies. Having found Western, patriarchal and capitalist assumptions going 'all the way down' into the very logic of modern science, the only alternative these critics can consistently support is that of a multicultural collage of 'ethnosciences' or 'situated knowledges' justified by the world-views and interests of women (for feminists), the non-West (for post-colonials) or non-Western women (for post-colonial and multicultural feminists). But given that neither 'women,' the 'non-West' nor 'non-Western women' make up uniform categories, situated knowledges end up privileging the most hackneyed stereotypes of feminine ways of knowing and the 'wisdom' of non-Western traditions over scientific methods of inquiry. What gets lost in this discursive affirmative action is a critical appraisal of these parochial, localized perspectives, many of which are deeply implicated in legitimizing age-old oppressions.[11]

As a one-time biologist and a feminist from a non-Western country, I find the neo-traditionalism condoned, tolerated and, indeed, often celebrated by feminist and postcolonial science critics extremely troubling. It may be appropriate at this point to disclose my personal investment in a defence of scientific rationality. I learned to do science as a young woman in India, received a doctorate in molecular biology and later worked as a science writer in close collaboration with science for people movements in India. I found in science the intellectual resources for rationally questioning – and rejecting – many of the Hindu assumptions regarding caste and gender hierarchies. Indeed, it would be no exaggeration to say that training in modern science marked the beginning of humanism and feminism for me. I cannot consent to the radical deconstructionist theories of science for the simple reason that they *completely misdescribe* the science I did in the lab, and the science I did on the streets as an activist and a writer in New Delhi, circa mid '70s to the mid '80s. Most progressive intellectuals in the West at the close of the twentieth century have come to see scientific rationality as the 'mantle of those in power, those with authority.'[12] But coming from where I come from, I can see the missing half of the dialectic: scientific rationality *also* contains the resources to challenge those in power, those with authority.

The sociological theories of science which see natural science as purely local and context-specific practice contradict the very rationale that made it possible for me to learn modern science while growing up in a small and rather provincial city in Punjab. The entire idea of adopting modern scientific education in non-Western countries is premised on a belief in the universality or trans-contextuality of scientific knowledge.[13] Social constructivist theories embrace a deep and radical relativism which undercuts all epistemological grounds for transcultural appropriation of the methods, theories and worldview of modern science. These theories reduce the obvious spread of modern science beyond the Western world to an epiphenomenon of the West's imperialism – a sign of the West's cultural hegemony which must be *resisted* in the name of national liberation, cultural survival and the recovery of the civilizational projects interrupted by colonialism. Framing science as Western cultural imposition on non-Western others undercuts the very rationale of progressive people's science movements in Third World whose primary commitments are not to the nation, but to universal human values of justice and equity; not to cultural survival, but to cultural change that promotes these values; not to a resumption of inherited civilizational projects, but to new futures. These movements are committed, in other words, to an internal critique of local knowledges in the light of the best available and the most humanly accountable values, regardless of the place of origin.[14] By treating the best confirmed scientific theories simply as local constructs of the West, *no different in their basic logic* than the local cultural constructs of the rest (i.e., pre-scientific folk knowledges), constructivists undercut epistemological grounds for the critique of the latter from the vantage point of the former.

Let me hasten to clarify that by wishing to defend the universality of scientific rationality, I am by no means suggesting that science is insulated from its social context. While science has specialized, knowledge-seeking aims which *differentiate* it from the rest of the society, these goals are met through institutions and practices that are not *separate* from the apparatus of social power, material production and cultural belief. I am not denying that as a hegemonic, state- and corporate-sponsored activity, science is shaped by a society's dominant interests: wrenching scientific knowledge away from hegemonic institutions and making it available to those standing outside the gates was my reason for preferring journalism and activism over doing science. Not for a moment am I denying that scientists carry their gender, race/caste and class biases with them into the lab – as one among a handful of women in a biotechnology lab in an elite technology institute, I am only too painfully aware of the cultural conti-nuity between the lab and the world outside.

But – and this is crucial – I am equally strongly aware of how *funda-mentally contra-conventional the content of science can be.* Scientific *practice* is culture- and context-bound, but the content of science is not always so. The prevailing paradigm leads a scientific community to selec-tively pick out a certain (and not any other) natural object/phenomenon from the entirety of the natural order. It is also true that scientists approach this object/phenomenon with time- and context-dependent questions, theory-laden methods and rules of evidence. *But the results of scientific inquiry quite often confound the conventions from which we begin.* As any self-reflective working scientist can attest, often the methodological conventions, the theoretical postulates and the larger goals of the inquiry are re-evaluated in the light of what we learn about nature starting from our local conventions, goals, and values. Science is simply not so circular and question-begging an affair as social constructivist theories make it out to be, where social conventions determine what we can see and accept as true. Scientific knowledge depends upon social institutions and cultural conven-tions for its *existence* but not for its *truth*. The truth of a belief, as we shall see, is not a matter of internal relations or coherence within a framework of beliefs, but a matter of the relationship of the belief to something else prior to and independent of the framework. And we can arrive at succes-sively approximate descriptions of this relationship through a constant revision and modification of our conceptual categories and theories in the light of newly discovered features of the world.

Indeed, it is precisely because the findings of science are a constant threat to the spontaneous consciousness of everyday life sanctified by the authority of culture, that doing and teaching science had a subversive quality in my social milieu. It is the contra-conventional character of science that made it an ally of those of us engaged in an internal critique of some of the inegalitarian elements of our culture. The findings of modern 'Western' science enabled us to show – with empirical evidence that was publicly testable – that *no matter what the consensus of the local community is, no matter what the powers-that-be claim, some social values and some facts of nature that these values are informed by, are wrong and must be rejected as false.*[15] Our project of denaturalizing socially-created, religiously-sanctified inequities (especially of gender and caste) was not different in spirit than that of feminist and other progressive critics of science in the West. But where they see science as an agent of natural-ization of social differences, we sought in modern science evidence that the facts of nature were not what they were assumed to be by our community, and that a different social order, in tune with a different understanding of the natural order, was possible.[16]

Some would – as indeed, many postmodern/postcolonial critics of modern science, both in India and the West already do – doubtless think of our attempt to challenge the traditional order from the vantage point of 'Western' science as an act of treason against our natal civilization, and consider us 'internal colonizers' bringing the diverse local narratives under the sway of a eurocentric metanarrative. But as long as we could argue that the *content* of modern science was not 'Western' or Eurocentric in any substantive way, and that it gave us a picture of the natural world that was as true for us in India as it was for the bearer of any culture anywhere on the planet earth, we could defend ourselves against the charges of imperialism. But now, the social constructivist theories that claim that the particular content of scientific knowledge cannot transcend the context of its production have pulled the rug from under our feet. Those of us who believed in science for social revolution are left with no principled defence against the shrill accusations of our cultural nationalists and our fundamentalists, the sophisticated among whom silence us by citing the authority of (the much misunderstood) Kuhn and (only too well understood) Foucault, Rorty and Latour.

So much for the political grounds of my dissatisfaction with social constructivism. My *philosophical* disagreements with it centre on the fact that it denies a *rational self-correction either of scientific knowledge in the laboratory or in the values of the larger culture in the light of evidence from the natural order*. Social constructivism holds that the evidence from nature is never free from contextual values and thus cannot override or contradict the scientists' enculturation. What gets demarcated as 'science' from the other everyday cultural meanings and practices has no necessary or essential features (falsifiability and/or institutional norms that allow for replicability and critique of others' findings) that increase its probability of being a true(er) explanation of a phenomenon. The ever-changing ('contingent') boundary between science and non-science, sociologists tell us, is a consequence of rhetorical games through which socially powerful groups draw cultural maps for the rest of us to live by, charting some knowledge that serves their interests in the cultural space marked as 'science.' Because science's claims of approximation to the actual causes and underlying mechanisms of manifest phenomena through an open and dispassionate attempt to falsify all evidence take place through culturally embedded practices, there can not be a progressive march toward truth. Science, like any other cultural practice, is a struggle over institutional accreditation of what is meaningful and true, a struggle that simultaneously stabilizes knowledge and social power.

In this essay I will be concerned with two consequences – namely, anti-realism and relativism – of the constructivists' attempt to explain scientific rationality *ultimately* in terms of cultural meanings and social power. Anti-realism in constructivist theories does not deny the existence of the real world, but only denies that what we accept as scientific facts necessarily correspond to it. Epistemological relativism claims that, as Martin Hollis and Steven Lukes put it, that 'what counts as good reasons for holding a belief depends upon the context,' or as Karl Popper put it, 'truth is relative to our intellectual background or framework and it may change from one framework to another.'[17] Relativism and anti-realism are intimately related. Larry Laudan, one of the staunchest opponents of relativism, indeed defines relativism as the flip side of the constructivist creed that 'the natural world and such evidence that we have about the world do little or nothing to constrain our beliefs.'[18] When our beliefs are 'liberated' from the constraints of reality, or when the external reality is seen as malleable enough to be moulded into any shape dictated by our conceptual schemes, what is real and true for one social group ceases to be so for another.

When reality is 'thinned out' and not allowed to constrain our beliefs, social relations end up carrying the entire weight of justification of our beliefs. Obviously, no ensemble of social relations can be deemed irrational – for the very fact that they allow societies to sustain themselves confers upon them a 'natural rationality.'[19] It follows that all beliefs are as rational and true as the social relations that undergird them. The problem of rationality for sociologists and anthropologists of science is not sorting out mere beliefs from beliefs that are justified to hold by virtue of the traditional epistemic virtues of truth, rationality, success or progressiveness.[20] Sociologists of science believe that all these virtues are honorifics that a community confers on some beliefs *after* they have been accepted by a community of scientists and the rest of the society through a process that can be fully explained in terms of sociological and cultural variables (e.g. class and gender interests). *Constructivist theories of science, in other words, prohibit us from using correspondence truth as a regulative ideal of our inquiries into the nature of knowledge in different societies and different historical contexts.* All one can justifiably do is to study the empirical conditions under which different communities of inquirers accredit (or de-accredit) their respective beliefs. Without any evaluation of beliefs' correspondence with any given object/phenomenon, we are forced into a relativist position.

I will contend that anti-realism and relativism are two sides of one basic philosophical fallacy which, following Roy Bhaskar, I call the 'epistemic fallacy.'[21] or, following Philip Kitcher, IRA or 'Inaccessibility of Reality Argument.'[22] The epistemic fallacy consists of assuming that our socially derived conventions have ontological consequences, or that *how we know determines (or at least, crucially shapes, or delimits) what exists.* The widespread tendency to derive conclusions about reality from our representations of it follows from the basic philosophical assumption that underlies all social constructivist and postmodern thought, namely, that all the reality we can ever really get at is the reality that is internal to our system of representation. Our representations thus constitute reality for us and what falls outside of our representations is relegated to the Kantian noumena, things-in-themselves, which cannot be known.

Moreover, because IRA is supposed to apply equally to social reality as well as natural reality, constructivists believe that there is no philosophical difference between natural and social sciences, and that both are equally interpretive.[23] One logical conclusion of this equivalence is that, as John Searle correctly surmises, for constructivists, natural reality (for example, a mountain) is socially constructed in a way that, say, money is socially constructed.[24] In both cases, it is our representations that confer the particular status to a physical entity: our representations make the object real for us.

There are various versions of the epistemic fallacy and IRA, but all lead to the same result: thinning out and disempowering reality in relation to socially-situated knowers. Very many features of the world once seen as a result of the world's own determination are seen as projections upon a much thinner world by the powers of the subject. This thinning out and contraction of the world is recommended by constructivists as liberatory, for they seem to believe that it gives human subjects more power to change what they take to be reality, by changing their conceptual schemes and discursive practices. The political dead-ends that such prioritization of discourse has led the academic left into are by now well understood.[25]

As a scientist, I am also concerned with how the thinning and disempowering of reality urged by social constructionists completely belies the basic assumptions of natural scientists. A realist ontology, as Roy Bhaskar argues, is presupposed by the social activity of science.[26] A belief in the existence of a law-abiding and comprehensible world, made up of material things and structures forms a kind of background which gives meaning to science. Any activity properly deemed science seeks to get nearer to the truth of the underlying causes and structures of the manifest phenomena and thus provide an account of what's going on behind the phenomena that we experience.

Most working scientists would agree with Gross and Levitt, a biologist-mathematician duo who have recently taken issues with constructivism, that 'science is, above all, a reality driven enterprise.'[27] As the outpouring of working scientists' critique of constructivism that followed the recent hoax by the physicist Alan Sokal indicates, most agree with Sokal's statement that ' there is a real world; its properties are not merely social constructions; facts and evidence do matter.'[28] Indeed, to tell a physicist that laws of nature are not explanations of natural phenomena but projections on nature of our social concepts is like 'telling a tiger stalking prey that all flesh is grass,' as Steven Weinberg put it.[29] It is scandalous how feminist and sociological critics of science have never paused to wonder why most working scientists fail to recognize the science they do in the picture of science that emerges in constructivist accounts. I am not suggesting that all science critique *must* obtain a seal of approval from working scientists – there may well be aspects of their work (especially science's social history) that scientists may not be aware of, or may not immediately recognize. But at the same time, surely something is amiss in a critique that assumes the actors to be so deluded as to consistently confuse their own constructions for facts of nature.[30]

The realism that I'll defend aspires to capture the robust realism of most natural scientists. I will argue that scientists find out things about the world which are independent of human cognition; they advance true statements, use concepts that conform to natural divisions and develop schemata that capture objective dependencies. One of the most rigorously argued defences of such a realism has been recently provided by Philip Kitcher whose definition of science I will follow: science aims to 'produce structured accounts of causal structures of the world, by delineating the pre-existing natural kinds and uncovering the mechanisms that underlie causal dependencies.'[31] Such realism rejects 'deflationary realism,' a recent favourite in science studies circles, which grants the existence of entities described by science, but does not accept that successful scientific theories are progressively truer accounts of these entities.[32] The great virtue of the realist philosophers whose work I will use is that their account of realism does not require an appeal to some ideal, a priori notion of rationality involving either a semantic relationship between our words and the world, or a god-like transcendence of the social context. The realization that we can only access the world through our cultural and social categories by no means vitiates knowing the world in a manner that can transcend our cultural and social categories.

The Uncritical Naturalism of Social Constructivism: The Trap of Epistemic Fallacy

Paradoxically, the seeds of social constructivism were contained in the demise of logical positivism. Once the distinctions between pure observation and theory, and between the context of discovery and the context of justification became impossible to maintain – as it was after the critiques of positivism by realists like Karl Popper and historicists like Thomas Kuhn – it became impossible to maintain that we can know the world as it is and mirror it in our theories. Conventionalism can be understood as one answer to the scepticism that resulted: we know, constructionists say, what we ourselves construct. We make 'facts' and project them onto nature, for nature itself is too generous and can live with any number of contradictory explanations. It cannot be any other way, for there is no pristine, theory-free data to judge our theories against. Knowledge is inescapably a construction and constructivist science scholars claimed to be 'only' working out the consequences of this human condition. It is for this reason constructivists take great umbrage at their critics who read them as attacking science by reducing its rationality to social relations. In this section, I will argue that while constructivist theories have forced scientists and philosophers of science to rethink their mirror-of-nature descriptions of science and experimental evidence, they have exacted an unacceptable price by denying any normative distinction between knowledge and belief.

There were undoubtedly good historical reason – the Nazis' denouncement of 'Jewish science' for one – that led the logical positivists to try to keep the social-psychological genesis of ideas separate from questions of their validity.[33] But for the next generation of science scholars, whose formative experience was the Vietnam War and the civil rights struggles, the separation between context and content of science lost emotional and intellectual appeal. They came to see science as deeply implicated in inegalitarian social theories that legitimated the exclusion of women and racial minorities and supported an imperialistic military indus-trial complex. This generation experienced the separation of social context from the logic of science as an ideological justification of what Jeffrey Alexander calls 'absent reason'[34] – that is, reason located outside the concrete, everyday life of embodied human beings as they go about making sense of their lives. Because human motives, aspirations and biases were not admitted into the logic and methods of science, the objective knowledge that positivists celebrated was experienced by their heirs as alienating.

Alexander suggests that post-positivist social theory can be understood as a search for 'positive reason' which views reason from *within* the totality of lived life with all its sensuality, its conflicts and its here-and-now goals. In philosophy of science, this search for positive reason started with Thomas Kuhn's *The Structure of Scientific Revolutions*. The individualistic perspective of a knower dramatized by Descartes as a solitary being contemplating the indubitability of his consciousness could not be sustained in view of Kuhn's historical analysis of how scientists absorb ideas from their predecessors and are epistemically dependent on them. After Kuhn, scholars of science became more concerned with the actual processes of science, and it came to be widely accepted that, as Hilary Kornblith put it, 'questions about how we *actually* arrive at our beliefs are relevant to how we ought to arrive at our beliefs.'[35] By offering to study the everyday work of scientists, sociologists and anthropologists of science claim to hold the key to questions about rationality which were earlier considered a matter of philosophical speculation alone.

Post-Kuhnian science studies, in other words, naturalize reason: scientific reason is seen not as some special and privileged style of thought that must be protected from all other aspects of life in society, but as inseparable from the general spirit of the times that informs the ensemble of social institutions and interests. Naturalists treat science as a part of our interactions with nature and with our peers – a process which can be understood without any *a priori* assumptions regarding the certainty of our consciousness or our sense.[36] While the naturalistic turn has had a salutary effect of emphasizing the materiality and historicity of scientific rationality, it has opened the door to radical historicism as well. As Thomas Nagel suggests, there have been two responses to the historicization of scientific rationality, 'to recognize the limitations that inevitably come from occupying a particular position in the history of a culture.. or to convert these into non-limitations by embracing a historicism which says there is no truth except what is internal to a particular historical standpoint.'[37]

The realist naturalism of Roy Bhaskar, Philip Kitcher, Ronald Giere, Dudley Shapere and Richard Boyd that will be defended in this essay represents the first response, which admits the contextuality of knowledge but tries to show that is not an insurmountable problem in getting to the truth about a context-independent reality. The second alternative is followed by the social constructivist critics who play the sceptic. The crucial difference between the two approaches consists in this. A realist can accept the social nature of science without, at the same time, denying that science is a special kind of an institution with a special function: namely, to discover truth about the natural world.[38] A realist sociologist then goes on to appraise the social relations and norms that operate in the institutions of learning in terms of whether or not they generate reliable knowledge most of the time. Constructivists, on the other hand, are anti-essentialist about truth, reality and aims of science. They believe that different groups of people at different times and places will light up the world differently, see different aspects of the mind-independent world as real, and come to define what is true about their particular view of reality differently. On this view, there is no one a priori criterion of truth that serves as the goal of all inquiry, but rather knowledge is simply whatever emerges when 'men operate in the interest of prediction and control, shaped and particularized by their situation.'[39]

So far, a realist sociologist may agree and demarcate science in terms of the norms that regulate scientific institutions instead of universal and unchanging philosophical first principles. That, indeed, was the approach of Robert Merton who demarcated science from non-science in terms of institutionalized norms of *communism, universalism, disinterestedness* and *organized scepticism* that help to detect and correct the errors introduced by ideologies, interests and political interest.[40] But the post-Mertonian constructivists are anti-essentialist about these (or any other) norms, and hold that institutional practices and norms of science are themselves open to varying interpretations contingent on the distribution of power (e.g., gender, class and nationality) that prevails in the rest of the society. Thus, they see the social activity of science as no different from the play of power in other institutions of society. For the constructivists, the social can provide no more of a ground for truth than the philosophical, for the social itself is always in the process of being produced simultaneously with knowledge; or, as Shapin and Schaffer put it, 'the solution to the problem of knowledge is embedded within practical solutions to the problem of social order.'[41] The entire project of demarcating science from non-science is superseded in favour of showing continuities between the two. The boundary is not between truth and falsehood but between what socially powerful groups provisionally (depending on the historical context) decide to label as truth, or as Foucault put it, 'the problem is not in drawing the line between that in a discourse which falls under the category of scientificity or truth and that which comes under some other category... but in seeing historically how effects of truth are produced within discourses that are themselves neither true nor false.'[42]

The 'Strong Programme' (SP) of the new sociology of scientific knowledge (SSK) inaugurated by David Bloor at the University of Edinburgh in 1976 aspired to extend the scope of sociology to the very 'content and nature of scientific knowledge,' as the opening sentence of his influential *Knowledge and Social Imagery* declared. Bloor accused his predecessors of a 'lack of nerve and will' for treating 'science as a special case' and assuming scientific rationality, validity and objectivity to be 'absolute and transcendent.' Instead, Bloor called for treating *all* knowledge, regardless of its validity or objectivity, 'purely as a natural phenomenon,' *amenable to the same type of explanation*. In other words, if sociological factors were evoked to explain those beliefs which were not rational, then the SP required that social factors be used to explain rational beliefs as well. Any prior distinction between rational and non-rational was declared to be an unscientific value judgment on the part of the sociologist. The strong programme's hyper-rationalist emphasis on value neutrality and even-handedness was not unlike, in Roy Bhaskar's words, 'an undercover agent who works on both sides of the fence... playing the game of reason to undermine the authority of reason.'[43]

The SP set the ground for all other social and cultural critiques of science. Even as they try to distance themselves from the relativism of the

SP, all important feminist critiques of science, including the works of Evelyn Fox-Keller, Sandra Harding and Helen Longino, accept the basic idea behind the SP that the very content of science requires a social explanation. The so-called postcolonial critics make the same move and, often without directly citing the constructivist works, simply assume that science is a Western and imperialist way of knowing the world and for that reason, lacks any universal purchase. Indeed, it is only after they accepted the assumption that the identity of the knower makes a difference not just to the questions asked but to the answers given as well, that the radical science critics could justify the demand for 'different sciences for different people,' which has gradually replaced the earlier radical agenda of 'science for all the people.'

It is only their prior commitment to the defence of 'difference,' that can explain how self-identified radicals can continue to overlook the normative anemia of constructivist views of knowledge. Theories inspired by the SP refuse to distinguish between justified beliefs (*episteme*) and mere beliefs (*doxa*) and treat all knowledge simply as 'what people take to be knowledge... without regard to whether the beliefs are true or false.'[44] The reasons that, say, a tribe believes in a shaman to cure a certain illness are equally rational for the tribe, as the reasons why someone in a different society may believe in, say, a neurosurgeon. It isn't as if better or worse correspondence with nature makes one belief more rational than the other: believers in both cases actually see correspondence with *what they take to be* nature. There is simply no tribunal higher than the culture and custom of the members of a particular group in deciding what is rational to believe in, or as Barry Barnes describes his 'tolerant' theory of rationality:

> Different bodies of natural knowledge carry conviction in much the same way... All of them alike are made credible to reasonable human beings by contingent aspects of their context. It is not that some are sustained by reasons and other by causes, or that some are accepted because they correspond to reality and others despite their lack of such correspondence. Rather it is that *every body of accepted belief carries conviction as the established account of reality employed by a culture or community . . . Those beliefs that count as knowledge are those sustained by custom.* (emphasis added)

This seemingly egalitarian and tolerant view of knowledge is, however, hopelessly inadequate for critique of inherited knowledge 'sustained by custom,' for it is incapable of drawing a distinction between what is current in the society and what is genuine knowledge. It leaves no room for the possibility that a community may find some beliefs credible even though there is not sufficient warrant for them, or in other words, some beliefs of a community could be false and irrationally held. It is this inability to demarcate warranted beliefs from accepted beliefs that makes constructivist theories normatively anemic.

The normative anemia of social constructivist theories is not unrelated to their anti-realism: the two spring together from the epistemic fallacy that afflicts all varieties of constructivism to various degrees. Epistemic fallacy, recall, is the chief mechanism through which meaning-conferring powers move from the world to our discourses: the properties of the world are supposedly delimited from an unstructured substrate by the knowers' culturally given categories. The real difference between constructivists and realists is not that the former affirm and the latter deny the presence of these culturally sanctioned conventions in the practice of science. The difference is that the constructivists affirm, while the realists deny, that 'in a relevant sense, social conventions in science determine the causal structures of the phenomena scientists study.'[46] In other words, while the realists admit the conventional nature of scientific knowledge, they hold these conventions to be 'ontologically innocent,' while the constructivists see them as 'world constituting.' Thus, for the constructivists, there is no contradiction between saying that the real world constrains our knowledge and still holding that the knowledge is constitutively social, for the socially constructed reality is as real as any real thing can ever be. We cannot ever know the world as it is, and the only world we can ever know is the world we grasp through our conventions. The tolerant views of rationality espoused by constructivists crucially depend upon giving our discourses the meaning conferring power, for otherwise one would have to admit that the structure of reality itself decides which account is more rational to hold and that some beliefs are false and irrational. Thus the collapse of what it is into how we know it is of fundamental importance to all varieties of constructivism.

Such a collapse has disastrous consequences for the concept of truth. All varieties of constructivism urge science to divorce truth from the world as it exists, and marry it to what we may believe about the world.[47] Such a scenario where truth and reality are made internal to the social context will leave both science and society impoverished, and the worst victims will be precisely those who the constructivists want to stand up for: the dominated groups, people on the margins, especially those in the Third World, who need the findings of modern science to question some of the inegalitarian ideas of their own cultures. Truth, understood more traditionally as a degree of fit between *what is said* and *what is* requires the most strenuous defence by all those interested in justice.

The Increasingly Radical 'Symmetry': From the Strong Programme to Actor Networks

'Since the mid-1970s, each new variant of SSK has tended to be a little more radical than the one before. Each new variant has stood longer on the relativist road,' according to Collins and Yearley.[48] What has made the successive variants of SSK ever more 'radical' is their growing degree of 'symmetry.'

Symmetry is a key tenet of David Bloor's 'strong programme' (SP) for sociology of scientific knowledge. It requires sociologists to treat correct and false beliefs symmetrically as caused by sociological factors. While the original idea behind symmetry (as espoused by the Edinburgh school scholars including Bloor, Barnes, Collins and Shapin) made truth and falsity equally amenable to social explanation, the more recent idea of symmetry (the Paris School, associated mainly with Bruno Latour and Michel Callon) makes nature and society symmetrical, that is, if one wants to explain beliefs about nature in terms of social conventions, they also have to explain social conventions in terms of beliefs about nature. Neither the social nor the natural can be taken to be given a priori.

The work of the Edinburgh School is premised on a basic anti-essentialist assumption that nothing necessary or essential distinguishes science from any other social activity – 'science *is* social relations,' as a well-known slogan in SSK goes.[49] Thus the beliefs scientists come to hold must be explained in the same terms as are used to explain the consensus between social actors in any other social institution. The first, the *causality* tenet of the strong programme demands that sociologists treat knowledge 'purely as a natural phenomenon' and 'study the conditions which bring it about' with the methods of natural sciences, which are held up as an exemplar of value-neutral inquiry.[50] One consequence of mimicking a scientific value-neutrality is that the SP admonishes sociologists to remain *impartial* (the second tenet) between true or false, rational or irrational, successful or unsuccessful knowledge, and to seek *symmetrical* (third tenet) explanations for true and false beliefs: for to seek a different explanation for true belief would amount to allowing one's value judgment to affect one's analysis.[51] The sociologists' task is to dispassionately examine how different social interests and cultural conventions determine where the boundary between true and false knowledge gets drawn in different societies and in different historical periods. Finally, because the SP seeks to scientize the sociological study of science, sociologists are obliged to *reflexively* (the fourth tenet) apply the tenets of the SP to their own activities as well.

The symmetry tenet of the SP is the most controversial. It states that sociology of scientific knowledge 'would be symmetrical in its style of explanation. The same type of cause would explain, say, true and false beliefs.' That is: whatever causal mechanism we find useful for explaining in naturalist terms how someone came to have a belief, we should invoke it regardless of whether we think the belief in question is true, false, rational or irrational. The idea that the truth, rationality or pragmatic success of an idea is irrelevant to why one should hold a belief is expressed more succinctly by Barry Barnes:

> What matters is that we recognize the sociological equivalence of different knowledge claims. We will doubtless continue to evaluate beliefs differentially ourselves, but such evaluations must be recognized as having no relevance to the task of sociological explanation; as a methodological principle, we must not allow our evaluation of beliefs to determine what form of sociological accounts we put forward to explain them.[52]

The symmetry principle is meant to challenge the immunity the traditional philosophers of science (the 'teleologists,' as Bloor calls them) and pioneers of sociology of knowledge (Marx to some extent, but especially Mannheim and Merton) had granted to natural sciences. According to these theorists, the findings of natural science were to be explained by rationality – that is, reasons based on evidence and logic which 'glowed by their own light,' and needed no further explanation. Bloor castigates this asymmetry in favour of science as akin to treating science as sacred, and the rest of the social life of politics and power as profane. By demanding that truth or rationality be irrelevant to how we explain belief, Bloor is denying the legitimacy of this distinction and claiming that science be dragged down into the dirt, so to speak, with all the rest of social life. And since it is patently the case that not all aspects of social life and beliefs (myth for instance) can be explained in terms of reasons, but require social-cultural causes, the symmetry principle requires that scientific beliefs be explained in terms of social-cultural causes as well – to do otherwise will amount to violating the scientific neutrality that the symmetry principle wishes to bring to SSK. The corollary is that *reasons* that a scientist might cite for arriving at a belief are not to be accepted as the final explanation, but a sociologist must provide a *social-cultural cause* for a scientist accepting any given evidence as reasons for his or her theories. Reasons are mental states and not material causes, and sociologists like all good scientists, must strive to reduce the former to the latter without regard to the truth or falsity of a belief. This, in short, is the mandate of the SP.

Apart from initiating a flurry of historical studies trying to show causal connections (or at least congruence) between scientific theories and social interests,[53] the symmetry tenet has been embraced by feminist and other radical epistemologists who champion science from the standpoint of women, racial minorities and non-western cultures. There are two reasons for the attraction the symmetry thesis holds for all 'liberatory epistemologists.'[54] First, the demand that all beliefs – good or bad, true or false – be explained sociologically gives these critics an opening to argue that social biases are not eliminable by following the norms of good science, but instead structure all knowledge including, in Sandra Harding's words, 'the very best beliefs any culture has arrived at or could in principle discover.'[55] Thus, Harding argues that if class, race and gender are called upon to explain the social beliefs of 'health profiteers, the Ku Klux Klan or rapists' then it is safe to assume that race, class and gender have 'probably shaped the 'empirically supported,' 'confirmed by evidence' results of our fine research projects as well.'[56] Secondly, it is only when social values are seen not as just conditioning the context of discovery, but structuring the cognitive norms for deciding what constitutes appropriate experiment, data and evidence etc., can it be claimed that science done by different social groups (women, working classes, non-western people) will 'look different' (Sandra Harding's phrase) in its very content.[57]

It is only on accepting these assumptions which were first formalized by the SP that the feminist and postcolonial science critics could justify their call for jettisoning the traditional view of objectivity as value-neutrality in favour of doing science explicitly and self-consciously as feminists and/or non-Western scientists: because our social context causes our all beliefs, including our best validated scientific beliefs, we should choose the 'correct' social arrangements in order to maximize the truth of our beliefs. Once knowledge is seen as an effect of social causes, social location ceases to be an unwanted source of bias but becomes a 'resource' for more (or 'stronger') objective knowledge. The problem with these radical episte-mologies is not their feminism and/or anti-imperialism. The problem instead lies in the assumption that science will 'look different' and possess a 'stronger objectivity' when done from these political perspectives. I will examine the calls for socialization of objectivity in a later section; at this point, I am more interested in showing that disclaimers notwithstanding,[58] science critics who accept the symmetrical explanation of truth and false claims alike, cannot escape the rather strong epistemological relativism that follows from it.

It is true that unlike the classic relativism of truth, the relativistic programme of the SP does not assume that all knowledge claims are equally true or equally false against their particular contextual web of beliefs and standards. Instead, the SP posits an equivalence or symmetry not between the *veracity* of all beliefs, but 'only' with respect to the '*causes of their credibility*.'[59] Yet in the end, the SP supports a judgmental relativism no less earnest – a relativism that claims that there is no way to distinguish between beliefs held for good reasons of evidence and logic and any other beliefs held, say, for reasons of custom and habit.

In their attempt to naturalize knowledge and to study it with the methodology of science, the proponents of the SP eschew all ready-made, philosophical criteria of truth. In the interest of scientific (i.e., value-free) study of science, they even claim to set aside their own evaluation of truth or falsity of the belief in question. Thus, Bloor treats the symmetry tenet more like a methodological injunction: 'all beliefs are to be explained in the same general way regardless of how they are evaluated.'[60] The next step toward epistemological relativism is taken when the strong programmers deflate the conception of truth by redefining it *instrumentally* as a 'conventional instrument for coping with and adapting to our environment'[61]; and *epistemologically* as depending not upon a statement's 'correspondence with reality but the correspondence of the theory with itself ... that is, for interpreting experience for internal consistency with the theory.'[62] A very similar idea was expressed by Barry Barnes' defence of natural rationality which is to be evaluated not in terms of how it relates to reality but to the 'objectives and interests a society possesses by the virtue of its historical development.'[63] And again:

> Knowledge cannot be understood as more than the product of men operating in terms of an interest in prediction and control shaped by the particularities of their situation ... Wherever men deploy their cultural resources to authentic tasks of explanation and investigation indicated by their interest, what they produce deserves the name of knowledge.[64]

All beliefs produced in the course of 'men' operating on the world to ensure survival and sustenance are supposed to stand at par with each other. It is not, as Barnes affirms more recently, that some carry more conviction because of greater correspondence with nature but all of them 'alike are made credible to reasonable human beings by contingent aspects of their context.'[65] This is the 'liberal sensibility'[66] toward knowledge that is affirmed by other scholars associated with the Edinburgh school.

So far, the SP has only disabled correspondence truth, but not relativized it: one could argue that different groups find different beliefs more or less credible in their own cultural frameworks, but still hold that only one of them is supported by better evidence and is more rational to hold – that is, given more empirical investigation and arguments derived from already established science, one will emerge as warranted knowledge. In an influential paper, Barnes and Bloor embrace an earnest relativism of truth by making *evidence and reasoning themselves internal to the social context*. Recall that the symmetry thesis had enjoined the sociologist to disregard truth or falsity but only search for causes of a belief's *credibility*. But then, Barnes and Bloor take a further step and announce that there is no sharp distinction *between credibility and validity*. They declare that for the relativist, 'there is no sense attached to the idea that some standards of beliefs are really rational as distinct from merely locally accepted as such.'[67] The 'real rationality' they wish to deny is what is traditionally understood by validity based upon evidence and reason. Barnes and Bloor's claim is that 'evidencing reasons themselves are contingent and socially variable, and what counts as evidencing reason in one context will be seen as evidence for quite a different conclusion in another context [because] something is only evidence for something else when set in context of assumptions which give it meaning.'[68] If this is so – that is, if some data and some other is taken as evidence for some hypothesis on the basis of social convention – then it follows that what is considered valid may turn out to be invalid in other historical or transcultural circumstances where other contextual assumptions prevail.

By internalizing the very criteria of demarcating the true and the false, science and myth, fact and superstition to the social context of inquiry, the SP goes beyond historicism – and Marxism – and joins the postmodern agenda.[69] Marx's historicism, for instance, recognized the situatedness of all human practice, including science, but also held that historically located practice revealed scientific laws that could be discovered once and for all. The warrant for these laws did not change through history. Postmodernism understood most broadly, and the strong sociologists of science, see the standards of justification of beliefs themselves as co-produced with the specific regimes of power. Because both postmodernism and the SP allow no super-cultural norms of rationality, no special tribunals set apart from the sites where inquiry is practised or no perspective-independent rules of evidence, they leave no grounds for preferring one form of rationality to another. Thus we end up with a monism that berates the rationalist dualism between truth and falsity, and fits in very snugly with the postmodernist move away from the economy of untruth to the politics of truth, that is, form a critique of ideology to a critique of truth itself.

Moving from symmetry to 'radical' symmetry are the Paris School followers of Bruno Latour. Latour finds Bloor's tenet of symmetry rather asymmetric for it uses society to explain nature, but takes society as given prior to nature. Latour wants to correct this asymmetry through his 'radical symmetry' and proposes to explain 'nature and society in the same terms.'[70] He announces his opposition to all dualisms, including those that juxtapose the rational and the irrational, belief and knowledge *and* the social and the natural. To that end, he proposes a 'counter-Copernican revolution that forces the two poles, Nature and Society to shift to the centre and fuse together [because] we do not make Society, any more than we make Nature, and their opposition is no longer necessary.'[71]

But what co-produces both nature and society? The short answer is power. Social actors do not confront Nature and Society separately but in a seamless web. This web is made up not of discrete entities called humans, non-humans, machines, facts, science and society impacting on each other but of 'heterogeneous associations' or networks of all of these. And given Latour's counter-Copernican revolution, *any* element of the network – from the Anthrax bacteria that Pasteur isolated to the instruments in the lab – can be seen as an actor with its own interests. Reality and truth get defined in a war of strength between actor networks.[72] Scientists simply have more rhetorical and material resources, and consequently get to create alliances large enough that nobody can question their power within their domain.[73]

This is a decidedly surrealistic picture of science and society and it faces considerable resistance from those committed to the SP.[74] Contrary to some who find signs of realism in Latour's inclusion of actants from nature in his networks, I believe that Latour's conflation of nature and society represents one of the purest expressions of 'superidealism' (Bhaskar's term) which denies the intransitivity of nature, i.e., that external reality is prior to and independent of all intentionality and human activity in the sense that the world would remain unaffected even if there were no one to represent it. Marx, whose name constructionists (although not Latour, who is more given to discourse theories and semiotics) often invoke to support their claim for radical construction of the 'sensuous world' through labour, allowed the primacy of nature before human practice.[75] Latour's counter-Copernican revolution, in contrast, denies all distinctions between the ontology of the world and our social relations by a fiat.

Social Construction of Nature

> Reality itself does not constrain rule use, even when the rules are those for the proper application of empirical concepts or natural kind terms. *Reality will tolerate alternative descriptions without protest. We may say what we will of it, and it will not disagree.* Sociologists of knowledge rightly reject realist epistemology that empowers reality.[76]

Barry Barnes' words capture the kind of anti-realism – or what Barnes himself prefers to call 'single-barrel realism' – that has become the dominant view of constructivist studies of science. So taken-for-granted is the idea of silent compliance of nature with our descriptions of it that in most science studies scholarship it serves as a background assumption requiring no further justification. Nature is disposed off rather easily with a set of scare quotes like in 'the world out there' as if it was somehow naive, or worse, to believe that our theories tell us about the theory-independent world. In this section I will discuss and critique two sets of argument most commonly used to bracket reality, or at least to put it within scare quotes, signifying irony and unreality. The first set leads to nominalism that claims that the way we categorize the entities of the natural world are human and cultural creations with no necessary relation to any essential features of the material entities. The second set includes arguments adapted from Gaston Bachelard, a French philosopher who asked how experiments which crucially depend on human labour can lead to knowledge about a human-independent reality.

Nominalism first. While Barnes and his fellow strong programmers pride themselves in being 'realists' and chastise the adherents of radical symmetry for their idealism, they are more accurately described as 'fig leaf realists'[77]: that is, while they are willing to admit the world exists independently of our concepts and conventions, they give it a diminishingly small role in the way we categorize it and what we believe about it. They instead adhere to a doctrine they call 'finitism,' supposedly the 'most important single idea in the sociological vision of knowledge.'[78] Finitism holds that the relation between the finite number of our existing examples of things and the indefinite number of things that we shall encounter in the future is indeterminate and underdetermined by nature, but depends upon how *we* decide to develop it. Communities of knowers in different cultures, or in the same culture at different times, do indeed group, order and pattern objects of nature according to perceived similarities and differences, but the sensory input from nature can be classified in any number of possible ways which parallel a community's social relations: as Bloor puts it following Durkheim and Mauss, 'classification of things reproduces the classification of men.' Moreover, the theory of finitism holds that every occasion on which a concept is applied to an object in the world, it must be accounted for by reference to specific, local contingencies, which are none other than utility for the purposes of 'justification, legitimation and social persuasion.' In all of this, we are told again and again, nature does not mind what conceptual frame we put on it: it remains 'silent,' 'indifferent' and 'tolerant' in the face of alternative accounts of it. In other words, our accounts do refer to the reality, but the strength of that reference and its future extension is determined by habit and custom.[79]

If one pauses to think about it, finitism is a startlingly radical idea. It claims that our social conventions (which ultimately serve the function of control and dominance) reach all the way down to the very names we give to things. The furniture of the world comes without labels and in an infinite profusion of variety. It is we who determine what belongs with what other objects. The labels we decide to put on things, furthermore, can be explained 'entirely from the collective decisions of [their] creators and users.'[80] The order of the world is not given but made by us for the sake of, among other things, controlling our fellow beings.

An even more radical nominalism follows from the work of another group of scholars who take the metaphor of social construction of reality to apply equally to social objects (like our classification schemes, above) and to *material objects themselves*. Most of these scholars are associated with the participant-observer or 'lab-study' tradition and include well-known works by Knorr-Cetina, Latour and Woolgar. This brand of neo-Kantian nominalism, represented here by the work of Knorr Cetina, goes on these lines: nature is undifferentiated, featureless and 'malleable,' and one cannot assume the existence of natural kinds in this infinite, malleable, constantly changing complexity. Scientists bring bits and pieces of nature into the laboratory to 'delimit' the specific entities (including the unobservables like electrons, genes, etc.) that they claim exist in it. The process of delimiting the actual objects of nature is cultural and social because 'what pre-exists before scientifically delimited objects are culturally delimited objects, those humans pick out and encounter and deal with in everyday life,'[81] or as she puts it elsewhere, in the laboratory, scientists 'align' the natural order with the social order by selectively noticing and 'reconfiguring' aspects of the world depending upon their own location in time and place. Thus, Knorr-Cetina insists that we take the metaphor of 'manufacture of knowledge seriously,' and see science as a 'way of world-making... [science] secretes an unending stream of entities and relations that make up the 'world.'... this known world is a cultural object, a world identified and embodied in our language and our practices.'[82] In other words, our conceptual schemes and conventions are not ontologically innocent, but have world-constituting powers.

Knorr Cetina's basic idea that 'this known world is a cultural object' is quite widespread among radical critics of science, even though it may not always be couched in the same theoretical terms. Various standpoint epistemologies that seek to empower specific groups of knowers begin with an attempt to loosen the grip of the given over our conceptual schemes, in order that knowers can freely exercise the totality of cultural and other subjective/interpretive resources that they may have.[83] That the contents of the real world are cultural creations appears in many guises in feminist writings on science. Harding, echoing Donna Haraway, ascribes intentionality to nature because 'nature-as-object-of-human knowledge never comes to us naked, but only as *already constituted in thought*... and simulates an intentional being.'[84] Likewise, Fox-Keller sees good science as 'the science that brings the material world in closer conformity with the stories and expectations that a particular 'we' bring with us as scientists embedded in particular cultural, economic and political frames.'[85] The growing postcolonial literature on science is defining new groups of 'particular we' who should define nature according to our own metaphysical categories. This route leads to 'ethnosciences' which end up affirming cultural essences of civilizations, often in ways that benefit the local elite more than the people.

Notice, in all these theories there is a deep-seated anthropocentrism at work. The direction of determination is from human subjectivity to the world: the limits of our culturally embedded beliefs are taken as the limits of the knowable world. For something to exist, we have to be able to *say* that it exists and as a result there is a tendency to think of nature itself as 'already constituted in thought.' It is true that as language using animals, we grasp the world only through language, but what we say is often *about* a language-independent state of affairs. Not recognizing the distinction between our concepts and the objects that exist independent of these concepts is far from empowering, for the simple reason that the aspects of reality that have not been realized yet in our discourses continue to impact on our lives.

Nominalist theories in both their Humean (Barnes and Bloor's 'finitism') and Kantian (Knorr-Cetina's 'delimiting') guises claim that there are no natural kinds: nature is mute and does not dictate our categories. The natural reaction of the scientist in me is: nature is far from mute. It tells us when we get it wrong. A child dying of a misdiagnosed disease, a bridge not holding up, rains not following prayers – all of these are nature's ways of talking to us, telling us to revise our classification and to check our rules. And in natural science, the scientist in me wants to affirm, we have figured out a way to learn more systematically and efficiently from experience so that we constantly correct the conceptual framework we started out with, and learn to distinguish natural kinds from social kinds. It is precisely this article of faith of working scientists – that science *improves* our abilities to listen to nature's messages – that is denied by the fore-mentioned scholars and constructivists in general. The most advanced laboratory science is no different from, say extra sensory perception, for *in principle*, we can only know the world by imposing our prior beliefs which are enmeshed in our 'form of life.'

But the obvious progress in scientific knowledge over the last three centuries shows that it is simply not the case that modern science is trapped by the existing web of beliefs, continuous with our everyday common sense or cultural habits. As Ernest Gellner suggests, the success of modern science in 'insisting upon treating like cases in a like manner ... in bringing about a marked 'rationalization' in our attitude to nature' shows that there may have been a *'diminution of that conceptual opportunism* which allows the classification of things to be at the service of too many and too varied a set of social ends.'[86] What is even more remarkable is that not only have we learned to perceive and classify the regularities in the world but we have also begun to understand the processes and entities responsible for these regularities. As many philosophers, notably Wesley Salmon and Ernan McMullin have argued, science has moved beyond description to explanation: it can not only tell us *what* but also *why*. Science has moved to an 'ontic conception' of explanation in which it is increasingly able to open the black boxes of nature to reveal the underlying causal mechanisms at work. To take a couple of trivial examples, we understand very well the atomic structure on the basis of which we classify the elements in the periodic table; we know what makes for a perception of a colour. Our classification schemes are not only able to group objects into the natural kinds but can explain why they constitute a natural kind.[87]

Furthermore, the idea that we have as great a measure of freedom in applying our rules as social constructivists would have it, is blind to all the accumulated knowledge of evolutionary biology. As Giere argues, the constructivists assume 'a Humean view that there is no natural connection between two impressions. The only connections are those we impose.' But such a view, he argues is 'rooted in pre-Darwinian empiricism.'[88] Humans, being intelligent, talking primates, can at least be assumed to be capable of the kind of 'fine discriminations in among objects in our environment without the benefit of social conventions' that other animals can accomplish. Thus Giere points out well-known facts about some universal categories (colours, e.g.) that all human beings, regardless of culture are capable of distinguishing. It appears that at least for some perceptual judgments, the fact of widespread agreement does not require a social explanation and the explanation of evolutionary biology is sufficient.

To turn now very briefly to arguments from the artificiality of the phenomena produced in the laboratory, Gaston Bachelard insisted on the crucial significance of the human labour that goes into conducting experiments and asked: how can experiments tell us anything about a human-independent reality, when they are not a part of nature but produced in the laboratory by very specific and intricate work? This question forms the basis of many ethnographic studies of laboratory work. Using participant-observation techniques Knorr Cetina tries to deconstruct the artificiality and the constructedness of the entire laboratory and claims that a laboratory is a site of action from which 'nature' is as much as possible excluded rather than included.' This, she explains, is a sign of the power of the lab to 'enculture natural objects. The laboratory subjects natural conditions to a social overhaul.'[89]

A very similar logic is evident in the story that Latour and Woolgar (L&W) tell of the Nobel Prize winning discovery of Thyrotropin Release Factor (TRF), a peptide hormone which regulates the production of thyrotropin by the thyroid gland. From their participant-observer study of how Roger Guillemin (the co-discoverer of TRF) and his colleagues went about standardizing a test for the putative TRF, L&W conclude a. that the bioassay was chosen as a result of social negotiations; and b. 'without the bioassay, TRF could not be said to exist.'[90]

In a trivial sense, it is true that without the bioassay scientists would not be able to assert that the test chemical is actually TRF. But if the claim is the stronger one that 'none of the phenomenon 'about which' participants talk could exist without' the material arrangements in the lab (including the bioassay) and that 'the phenomenon are thoroughly constituted by the material setting of the lab,'[91] then they are obviously equating the very existence of a phenomenon (TRF) with the scientists' ability to isolate and identify it in the lab. Moreover, their second premise that the bioassay is adopted as a result of social negotiation and is a matter of 'interpretive flexibility' simply shows a lack of appreciation of how there are auxiliary theories for checking the suitability of a given bioassay.

There is in fact a parsimonious explanation that can reconcile local human labor that goes into an experiment with an experiment's ability to tell us something about the entities in the world outside the lab. First, the very fact that an experimental result is *reproducible* shows that it is not produced by the work done in any particular local setting.[92] *The human labour that goes into an experiment only actualizes the potential and structures already existing in nature.* As Bhaskar elaborates, the very significance of experiments lies in the fact that they tell us about mechanisms, structures and systems of relations that persist in the object of study even outside the lab when it is not being experimented upon. A strict localism on the lines of Bachelard assumes that our transitive knowledge /practice is the same as the intransitive dimension and exhausts it. Bhaskar correctly points out, experiments 'do not produce its intransitive objects of investigation but only the conditions for their identification.'[93]

Social Construction of Experiments

How much 'interpretive flexibility' scientists enjoy in accepting or rejecting experimental evidence is one of the most hotly debated aspects of sociological theories of science.[94] In this section I'll examine the sociological study of experiments inspired by Harry Collins' Empirical Program of Relativism (EPOR).[95] I will concentrate on Collins' analysis of gravity waves in order to explicate the kind of reasoning sociologists employ to argue that the criteria for distinguishing confirming evidence of a theory depend, in the final instance, not on what the evidence tells us about the phenomenon in question, but on sociologically maintained consensus. Collins' *Changing Order* and other classics in the EPOR tradition have been subjected to severe critiques, leading to newer works in the study of experiments which admit more constraints by nature.[96] Yet, these classics are important, for they are frequently cited as having 'shown' that interpretation of experiments is driven by social interests.

Harry Collins took the radical core of the SP, namely, the tenets of impartiality and symmetry, to a logical conclusion and declared that 'we must treat the natural world as though it in no way constrains what is believed to be.'[97] Starting from this 'methodological relativism,' Collins goes on to study the debate over the existence of gravity waves and concludes that experimental evidence is not sufficient to decide theory choice. Scientific controversies and disputes cannot be resolved by experiments, because the outcome of experiments is itself decided by tacit knowledge and conventions shared by the community of scientists led by a core group of elite scientists. Collins raises the problem of the 'experimenter's regress,' which goes as follows: Suppose evidence determined theory choice. But evidence consists of replicated experimental results. How do we know that the experiment is successfully replicated? When we can be sure of the competence of the experimenter. But the only way experimenters can demonstrate their competence is by replicating experiments.

Thus, in Collins' study of gravity waves (g-waves), how do we know we have a good g-wave detector? By successful detection of g-waves. But how do we know that these are g-waves that we have detected? Because they have been detected by an instrument which a community of scientists thinks detects g-waves.

But controversies do get settled. What breaks the regress? Scientists' prior beliefs that are entrenched in their 'form of life', answers Collins. If a community of scientists already believes in the phenomenon, they will regard confirming experiments as competent, and if they don't, they will regard *dis*confirming experiments as competent. And how does the community come to a consensus about their belief in the phenomenon and the competence of the experiment? Collins believes that a 'core set' of scientists 'funnels all of their competing ambitions and alliances' and certifies whether or not the crucial experiment is competently performed. The involvement of elite scientists in settling a controversy is not a sign of 'bad science,' Collins argues, but is a necessary feature of experimental work: because experiments cannot be evaluated on a criterion independent of the outcome, scientists have no option but to employ social negotiations to resolve the controversy.

Collins' work adds grist to the constructivist mill that science is not a reality-driven enterprise but, in the final instance, a convention-driven one: we choose theories based upon the 'multiple entrenchment' of concepts and rules in our social conventions. If experiments themselves are resolved ultimately by conventions underlying the tacit knowledge of scientists, it is these conventions that make scientists see correlation and causation in nature. Appropriately, Collins offers sociological solution to Hume's problem of induction:

> we perceive regularity and order because any perception of irregularity in an institution-alized rule is translated by ourselves and others as a fault in the perceiver ... it is not the regularity of the world that imposes itself on the world but the regularity of our institu-tionalized beliefs that imposes itself on the world. We adjust our minds until we perceive no fault in normality. It is why our perceptual ships stay in their bottles.

There is a high degree of consensus between Collins and others on this view of experiments in science as an extension of our web of our institu-tionalized beliefs. Shapin and Schaffer's celebrated defence of Hobbes, for instance, is premised upon their assumption that the debate between Boyle and Hobbes was not only about alternate conceptions of knowledge and appropriate knowledge-seeking practices, but ultimately involved different ideas of the entire social order, including the relation between laity, the intellectuals and the authorities. Likewise, Andrew Pickering's study of quarks is meant to show that high-energy physicists accepted the theory of weak neutral current because 'they could see how to ply their trade more profitably in a world in which neutral current was real.'[99] This so-called 'opportunism in context' is a rather cynical and economistic interpretation of scientists' behaviour which has them investing their expertise in areas promising highest returns.

One fallout of this convention-driven view of science is that practicing scientists end up looking like 'reality dupes' who naively believe that their theories are picking out aspects of the real world. But, as Roth and Barrett point out, the anti-realism of the EPOR scholars is not a *conclusion* they reach from their case studies, but rather a *precondition* for their 'phenomenological epoche' (i.e., suspension of natural attitude) regarding scientists' own accounts of doing science. That is the whole point of Collins' famous injunction to constructivists to proceed as if reality does not matter (even though scientists think it does). By bracketing reality, the sociological method is supposed to give factors *other* than the alleged nature of the physical world a chance to be seen at work. It may be the case that the best explanation of why scientists chose one theory over another is to be obtained by omitting references to reality but, as Roth and Barrett correctly point out, it may be that explanation might, at least in some cases, also require reference to reality. The point is that *EPOR sets up rules of the game such that the reality is ruled out by a methodological fiat.* The signature conclusion of EPOR scholars on realism runs as follows:

> SSK offers strong empirical evidence that if our beliefs about controversial features of the world are a consequence of the way the world is, this is not evident during passages of discovery and proof. An account which rests on orderly interaction with the world can be provided only after retrospective reconstruction.[100]

So here we have Collins offering us evidence to the effect that evidence doesn't matter!

All irony aside, I find both of the above cited 'conclusions' (assumptions?) of EPOR – that science is, in the final instance, convention driven, and that the reality is a retrospective 'upshot' of scientific practices – extremely troubling. The views of these sociologists go completely against all that made laboratory work exciting and worth the effort. But there are good reasons to refuse Collins' conclusions. For one, because Collins completely ignores the perfectly rational reasons (wrong calculations, computer errors) why the experiment in question had to be rejected.[101] Furthermore, Collins' premise for experimenter's regress is plain wrong. Experimenters' regress does not exist. It does not exist for this reason: *the reliability of an instrument (or a technique) can be established by connecting its performance to procedures that can be validated by a set of background assumptions and laws that are independent of the claim under test.* Thus it is simply not the case that the test of the g-wave detector depends upon the existence of g-waves, or the existence of g-waves is 'coextensive with' the availability of a g-wave detector. We have a large number of independently justified beliefs – indeed, Einstein's theory of general relativity itself – that predict the presence of g-waves and allow us to hypothesize their nature, and how, in principle they can be detected. Likewise, there are other networks of physical theories that justify the design, functioning, sensitivity etc. of the detector. It is encouraging that the more recent work recognizes the independence of experiments from the theory under test.[102]

Social Construction of Facts

My Lord, facts are like cows. If you look at them in the face long enough, they generally run away.[103]

In the studies reviewed above, constructivists try to stare away the materiality and independence of nature, and experimental evidence thereof, into the interests, ideologies and the prevailing commonsense of scientists and the societies they belong to. The social and the real become inseparable and our knowledge of the real – what we takes as facts – becomes a projection of the social on the real. In this section, I will describe and critique the near total permeability constructivists allow between the social and the real at all times in the evolution of scientific facts. I will argue instead that science is not a seamless web between the outside and the inside, the social context of inquiry is *not* inseparable from the logic of inquiry. Rather, *science separates itself from conventional wisdom by repeatedly testing and revising the wisdom of the conventions in the light of what it learns about the world*. It is this dialectic between the background assumptions and the real world that is independent of these assumptions that makes science a distinctive way of knowing the world. It is this dialectic that allows nature to have a say in our construction of facts.

The point of departure is again the 'strong programme' of SSK. Recall that the SP had argued that evidence cannot be used to determine whether any particular knowledge of any social group is better grounded in reality than the other because what counts as evidence is itself a matter of cultural convention. The claim that 'something is only evidence for something else when set in context of assumptions which give it meaning'[104] plays a prominent role in sociological case studies. These case studies set out to show that scientific theories are accepted because of the congruence between the background assumptions (which serve as reasons for treating an observation as evidence) and the social interests and cultural meanings of the dominant groups at any given time. The SSK literature is replete with case studies 'demonstrating' that the web of background beliefs relevant to science is coterminous with the entire society and includes its religious myths, cultural assumptions and social interests.[105] Or as the recent work on 'technototemism' suggests, science can be seen as the 'highest form of totemism' through which the totemic relations between social groups and natural world get mapped on to, or inscribed into, scientific facts.[106] But this role of culturally embedded background assumptions in construction of scientific facts has been developed most consistently by the feminist critics of science.

Evelyn Fox-Keller, for instance, argues that what counts as knowledge – specifically, 'the kinds of questions one asks and the explanations one finds satisfactory' – depends upon one's prior relationship (more controlling vs. interactionist) with the object of study, which in turn is shaped by the relationship of the knower with other members of the society (especially the mother-child relationship which leads to a more 'dynamic objectivity' among women and a 'static objectivity' among men). Given the metaphoric genderization of science since its beginning in the 17th century and the static objectivity encouraged among men by exclusive parenting by mothers, modern science is permeated with the language of control and domination. Keller ascribes the attraction of metaphors of 'master molecule' that have guided research in molecular biology to a prior commitment to ideas of hierarchy and control that underlie and support patriarchal relations.[107]

Helen Longino provides a more analytical argument on very similar lines and tries to show *how* our prior commitments to certain desirable social relations and political ideals ('contextual values') become a part of the rules scientific reasoning ('constitutional values'). Almost echoing Barnes and Bloor, Longino argues that 'how one determines evidential relevance, why one takes one state of affairs as evidence for one hypothesis rather than for another, depends upon one's beliefs, which we can call background assumptions ... a state of affairs will only be taken to be evidence that something else is the case in light of some background belief asserting a connection between the two.'[108] Thus if our background assumption is that human behaviour is the result of neonatal exposure to sex-hormones which determines the relevant brain structures (the 'linear model' in Longino's terms), then the data on correlation between sex hormone levels and variability of physiology and sexual behaviour becomes evidence for differential exposure to prenatal hormones. But if our background assumption is that human behaviour is a result of inter-action between biology and social factors, (the 'selectionist model' derived from Gerald Edelman's work on neural Darwinism), then the variability of behaviour will be evidence for both biological differences *and* differences in social conditioning. According to Longino, both models can explain the data correlating hormones and behaviour equally well. Thus it is not reality per se that determines which model is better. Rather, 'in the final analysis commitment to one or another model is strongly influenced by values or other contextual features,'[109] with those interested in human autonomy and expansion of human potentiality (as feminists are) favouring the selectionist model over the linear.

As a result, Longino argues that search for a feminist epistemology should be replaced by 'doing research as a feminist' which would require that scientists consciously choose those background assumptions/ explanatory models that are congruent with their political values, or as Longino puts it, 'scientific practice admits political considerations as relevant constraint on reasoning, which through their influence on reasoning and interpretation shape content.'[110] The 'bottom line' requirement of doing science as a feminist, according to Longino, will be to choose background assumptions which 'reveal or prevent the disap- pearance of the experiences of women and/or reveal or prevent the disappearing of gender ... [that is] prevent the erasure from inquiry of a gradient of power that keeps women in a position of subordination.'[111] Feminists, because of their interest in revealing the gender/power gradient in knowledge, will prefer explanatory models which privilege hetero- geneity, complexity of interaction and decentralization of power over ontological homogeneity (i.e. treating difference as aberration), linear cause-and-effect and unidirectional control. These values are equally and simultaneously cognitive and social because they determine what data count as evidence. And if we have to have contextual values to make sense of data, we should choose the 'right' ones and create knowledge that empowers, rather than dominates, human beings. Longino, unlike other less careful critics, does insist that for feminist values to replace the tradi- tional values that guide scientific work, they have to withstand an open and critical scrutiny by the scientific community, that includes feminists *and* non-feminists. But the basic thrust of Longino's contextual empiricism – that standards or values that guide evidential reasoning are inseparable from the social context *and* that these standards ought to serve politically progressive ends – resonates well in science studies where the answer to the question 'whose side are you on?' has become the test of the validity of knowledge.

Is it true that political considerations – or more generally contextual values – decide the choice of background assumptions (or models) in the light of which some observation becomes evidence for a hypothesis? Is it true that cognition can never be free of contextual values and political beliefs? Is it true that cognition is not only socially organized and mediated but is actually driven by social logic?

That an observation by itself proves nothing is not a novel insight. The *condition of relevance*, i.e., the requirement that to count as a reason, a claim must be relevant to the idea to be tested, was among one of the earliest critiques of logical empiricism, most well known among them being Karl Popper. It was recognized by the early critics of empiricism that such relevance is determined by background information and assumptions.

If critical realists like Karl Popper and Dudley Shapere, as well as relativists like Kuhn and constructivists like Bloor and Barnes and the feminist scholars of science can agree on the role of background assumptions in establishing the condition of relevance, and yet come to different pictures of science, the difference obviously must lie in *how they define the domain of the background assumptions.*

For the science studies scholars and most feminist science critics, the domain of the background assumptions is a network of all social and cultural forces that shape the common sense of an era: there is no line between what is internal to science and what is an external influence. These scholars work with what Ernan McMullin has dubbed 'presumption of unrestricted sociality (PUS).'[112] By and large, those who operate with PUS tend to treat background assumptions themselves as givens which don't change in the light of the new knowledge. Reading social values as constraints on scientific reasoning fails to see the other half of the dialectic: the initial common sense and cultural assumptions that lead scientists to seek some kind of evidence themselves get revised in the light of the evidence. Those theorists who collapse the social context of discovery into all the later stages of research tend to see science as a seamless fabric which is stamped forever by the conditions of its origin. They fail to see that all aspects of scientific inquiry are potentially capable of redesign in the light of knowledge derived from the earlier phase.[113]

Recent developments in many disciplines of science-as-we-know-it (that is, without any radical make-over of either the institutions of science or the larger society) provide ample evidence of a constant revision of background conventions, metaphors and philosophical assumptions about our world and life in it. As new empirical findings have revealed new phenomena and structures at successive levels in matter, living organisms and mind-brain relationships, there are signs of a new synthesis between what has been conventionally called reductionism and holism. Understanding of details of mechanisms at one level have led to theories that seek to understand relations between different levels and see how qualitatively new properties emerge through these interactions. Take the case most often cited as the exemplar of reductionist, controlling and patriarchal thinking – the idea of DNA as the 'master molecule,' or the 'central dogma' of transfer of information from DNA to proteins. Almost from the time that DNA structure was discovered, the attempt to understand how it was replicated and translated into proteins involved an understanding of a concert of enzymes and structures involving the entire cell – a far cry from the image of central control and dominance read into the metaphor of 'master molecule' by the critics. Likewise, there was nothing dogmatic about the central dogma of molecular biology: each step of it was subjected to rigorous empirical tests.[114] This is not to say that science-as-we-know-it is free from social interests and influences: the rush to commercialize processes and products of molecular biology has encouraged a race to decode, manipulate and sell genetic information, often at the cost of a deeper understanding of the physiology of the whole organism. But these interests hardly warrant giving the internal logic of molecular biology a gendered gloss.

Or, take the selectionist model of consciousness developed by Gerald Edelman that Longino holds up as a model that feminists should adopt to understand the relative role of hormones and the environment in shaping human behaviour. Edelman's model of neural Darwinism (or the theory of Neuronal Groups Selection) developed as a result of cross fertilization of ideas from immunology, where Edelman had already done Nobel Prize-winning work on how antigens select out the 'right' kind of antibody. Edelman saw an analogy between the immune system and the nervous system, for both of them have to distinguish between self and non-self. His selectionist model, moreover, does not exactly displace the linear model of hormone action. Its appeal for scientists lies in its ability to make sense of diverse observations of a dozen of different fields from artificial intelligence to memory research.[115] To be sure, Gerald Edelman holds strong philosophical views which favour free will and human agency and opposes any attempt to reduce consciousness to molecular or physiological terms alone (although he seeks a purely biological explanation of consciousness).[116] But these philosophical assumptions don't map on to any particular political position, and as far as one can tell from published sources, there is no evidence that Edelman's work was a result of any explicit political allegiances, or that its appeal is limited to a section of the scientific community with any given set of beliefs on gender, race or class. Indeed, there are strong suggestions in Edelman's explication of his philosophical views that he could well have arrived at his strong aversion to reductionism and biological determinism as a result of evidence from modern biology and physics.[117]

What I want to suggest is that a congruence between facts and values may not *always* be evidence of values constructing facts, but can *also* be read as facts leading to values: the two generally grow and change together, and I see no reason to see contextual values as given and prior to the actual work of science. Moreover, I would argue that the very fact that the selectionist model has had the kind of appeal among biologists interested in the development of brain and consciousness shows that the existing scientific institutions are capable of correcting their course and heading out in directions which hold promise for expansion of human abilities – a promise that feminists and other progressives can welcome, as Longino indicates.

One aspect of the give-and-take between our assumptions and the real world in the process of scientific inquiry is that *the domain of background assumptions changes and becomes less social as science matures, and correspondingly, scientists have less choice to pick background assumptions and models that are consonant with their politics.* As Dudley Shapere has argued, for a *mature* science, background assumptions are mostly made up of a set of background *scientific* theories, or 'a body of successful and doubt-free beliefs which have been found relevant to the domain':[118] science becomes more *internalized* in its reasoning process as it grows, and once past its infancy, the external milieu is no longer internal to it. As Kuhn put it, 'compared with other professional and creative pursuits, the practitioners of mature science are effectively insulated from the cultural milieu in which they live their extra-professional lives.'[119] Science aims at becoming more self-sufficient in the sense that 'the more science learns, the more it becomes able to learn' on the basis of its already existing stock of the best, most confirmed, least doubted beliefs. Therefore, *what decides evidential relevance in mature science is not raw social values but scientifically tested reasons*, and the two gradually get demarcated from each other through a process of 'conceptual bootstrapping,' which involves a constant revision of culturally derived assumptions in the light of empirical evidence generated by the hypotheses which are initially based on the cultural assumptions. The increasing demarcation between the scientifically relevant background assumptions and contextual factors need not be based on any a priori and universal criterion but is itself a product of historical development of a science. The relevance of this dynamic to the question of doing science as a feminist (or as a socialist, as a Third World scientist, or as a Hindu or Islamic scientist) is that as any science matures, background assumptions are *not* up for grabs. After a certain point, the question of the political valence of background assumptions becomes rather meaningless.

Another way to visualize how background assumptions become a part of science – not as raw social conventions which can be changed voluntarily depending upon ones politics, but as a part of the corpus of tested and confirmed results – is to see the growth of science in any domain as a progressive filling out of a crossword puzzle. In this crossword puzzle, as Susan Haack argues, experimental evidence serves as the analogue of the clues, while background information serves as already completed entries.[120] How reasonable a new entry in the puzzle is depends on how well it is supported by the clue and any other already-completed intersecting entries. Once a new entry is accepted, it becomes a part of the background against which other clues are read and new entries made.

Now, it is entirely possible that some particular entry might be put in place without sufficient support from the rest of the solved and unsolved clues for reasons of ideology, political interests, aesthetics or the pressure to complete the puzzle as soon as possible: that is, a scientific claim might be accepted without sufficient warrant. And it is a legitimate role of the social and humanist critics to investigate and show, *on a case by case basis*, when claims get accepted not because they are warranted by evidence, but because of social interests. But in order to show that, it is necessary to believe that *in principle* how good a piece of evidence is (i.e. warrant) does *not* depend on whether or not it gains acceptance: a statement may be true even if no one believes it at any given time. But if one follows Haack's analogy, it becomes clear that the constructivist critics that we have been examining in this essay collapse warrant of a claim into its acceptability: they argue that it is *because some privileged members of a community of inquirers find a claim acceptable to their prior beliefs that the claim becomes warranted*.

According to Haack, it is due to the strength and distinctiveness of the social and communal nature of science that warrant does *not* get determined by acceptance. Because science is the work of many persons, spanning different generations and different cultures (increasingly so in today's globalized science), scientific knowledge gets accepted through a process of checking and criticism. Here, one would happily agree with the constructivist critics that the more open and inclusive the social institutions of science, the better it would be for science, since inclusion of diverse view points will improve the quality and degree of mutual criticism. Thus the argument for equal opportunity for women and minorities with adequate interest and training, makes not just social but epistemic sense. The more open and inclusive communities of knowers are, the more likely they will be to pass on true(r) beliefs rather than falsehoods.

What does *not* make sense is the claim that the gender, race or ideology of the knowers will (or should) make any difference to the assessment of the evidence and the conclusions derived therefrom. The idea that the social location of the knower makes a difference to scientific reasoning does not make sense because, just as someone solving a crossword puzzle is limited by the grid of already-completed entries and the clues, the *scientific community is not at liberty to change any entry at will without destroying the integrity of the puzzle*. In the final instance, this integrity is crucially dependent on the structures and mechanism of the world itself. Only those who would simultaneously deny the integrity and independence of reality would have no qualms in treating the social character of science as necessary *and sufficient* to explain the entire logic of science.

Before I move on to my next – and final – task, namely, a critique of the radical call for socializing objectivity, I will very briefly examine how the adherents of the Paris School explain the social construction of facts. To recapitulate, the Paris School theoreticians, notably Bruno Latour and Michel Callon, assume a more radical symmetry that sees both nature and society as being produced together as a consequence of the network of human and non-human actors.

In this actor network model, a statement becomes a fact if it is inserted in network of other sentences that 'black box' it, or remove it from any further inquiry: or as one face of Latour's Janus announces in his famous *Science in Action*, 'when things hold, they start becoming true.'[121] A fact is a consequence, and not a cause of our coming to believe in it; treating a statement as a fact, causes it to be a fact.

But what makes statements 'hold'? The strength of the alliances of a sentence with other actants in the network which as we have seen before includes, without any ontological distinctions, bits and pieces from nature, culture and society: bacteria, X-rays, hormones and machines (inscription devices), scientists, other scientists, their sponsors and the rest of us. To the extent a scientist succeeds in establishing a strong enough network to the point that no further questions are asked regarding the actants, he/she succeeds in defining reality and the truth about them. And since the resources required for this network building are so many and so expensive, only elite scientists in elite labs located in elite countries get to define the truth for the rest of us.[122]

At one level, this model of making of facts can be read as a Machiavellian description (Latour's own label) of what scientists do. It can't be denied that a good part of scientists' time, effort and resources are taken up by mundane, everyday concerns of the kind that occupy all of us: who to collaborate with? who to trust? whose work to cite? The difference is that for Latour, Woolgar and other lab studies scholars, scientific reasoning *is* this mundane reasoning and that nothing 'scientific' happens inside the laboratory. Any talk of reasoning that links the inscriptions to something independent of the inscriptions (TRF, Pasteur's anthrax bacilli) are treated as so many post-facto rationalizations.

That power legitimizes ideas is hardly a novel insight. Marx famously argued that the ruling ideas of a society are the ideas of the ruling classes. But Marx left open the possibility that those without power can come to a scientific understanding of the true state of affairs, and armed with it, expose and dethrone the ruling ideas. But if truth *by definition* is an effect of power, what hope is left for those without power? If there is no truth but that defined by those with better lawyers, as follows from the actant-network,[123] can the poor ever get justice? Latour is well aware of these concerns but treats them as one more example of the traditional sociologists' lack of symmetry between 'might' and 'right': in his radically even-handed world, 'it is necessary *not* to make any a priori distinction between might and right'[124] (in order to show the might that is implicit in what is accepted as right and reasonable). I fail to see what useful purpose can be served by treating as symmetrical values that *should* be ethically and politically asymmetric.

Socializing Objectivity

Most radical critiques of science tend to display a set of interesting contradictions. While the critics reject the idea of objectivity as authoritarian or worse, they simultaneously want to claim that doing science as a feminist/third world woman/working class will make science *more* objective (or less biased). Moreover, while they have no hesitation in internalizing the very criteria of validity to the social context of any group of knowers, most constructivists simultaneously don't wish to be called relativists. This linking of radical change in social relations with a promise of greater objectivity in knowledge serves to legitimize the critique of science-as-we-know-it, for it casts the critics not as rash rebels against science, but as visionary leaders of a new science and a new society. In this final section, I will examine how the constructivist critics square their radical contextualization of all aspects of science discussed in previous sections with their idea of objective knowledge. I will argue that the resolution they offer ends up distorting those aspects of science which may be most important for a critical self reflexivity of background assumptions that the critics claim to value.

Typically, constructivists argue that while they are epistemic relativists, they are not judgmental relativists: that is, even though they hold that the truth of a belief depends upon the social context of its production, they are not suggesting that all beliefs are equally true or false[125]: some social relations and cultural contexts, they claim, lead to better accounts of the world. Given their antipathy to the realist notion of truth as correspondence of our statements with an independently existing world, constructivists operate with a deflated notion of objectivity which, in the final instance, rests on the social arrangements under which scientific inquiry takes place. They typically offer two sociological criteria for objectivity. First, a statement is objective if the social conditions of its production can screen out purely subjective, arbitrary and idiosyncratic beliefs in assessing the relevance of the evidence to the hypothesis.[126] This sociological criterion of demarcation between science and non-science is perfectly valid and was the cornerstone of Robert Merton's sociology of science. But the raison d'être of the post-Mertonian sociology of science is to 'show' that scientific institutions and social norms cannot screen out biases and social values that are a part of a culture's world-view, or to put it another way, the very reasoning of science (the constitutive values) cannot function without social values (contextual values). Constructivists cannot define objectivity as a total screening of all bias, for then they have no choice but to say that objectivity is a chimera. The only choice that appears to be available to them is to equate objectivity with elimination of 'bad biases': a statement is deemed objective if it serves desirable social ends. Because value freedom is impossible, the constructionist argument goes, we can improve the quality of science by improving the social values that science serves. As Evelyn Keller puts it quite succinctly:

> scientific knowledge is value-laden (and inescapably so) just because it is shaped by our choices ... [thus] why should we even think of equating 'good' science with the notion of 'value-free'? Far from being 'value-free,' *good science* is science that effectively facilitates the material realization of particular goals, that does in fact enable us to change the world in particular ways ... In this sense, *good science* typically works to bring the material world in close conformity with the stories and expectations that a particular 'we' bring with us as scientists embedded in particular cultural, economic and political frames.[127]

It is this logic that leads most constructivist critics to call for *more ideology* as a cure for purported ideology in science, with a difference that the 'particular we' whose stories and expectations that science is supposed to justify are on the 'right' side, whatever that means. My discomfort with making political use-value as the criteria of goodness of knowledge stems from this question: what happens when the 'particular we' turn out to be from the 'other side' who can just as easily use the logic of construction to justify reactionary ideas, as is happening today with religious and cultural nationalists in Third World?[128]

Yet, an explicit call to admit political ideals into the logic and reasoning of science is one of the most important conclusion and recommendation to emerge from constructivist science studies. This recommendation obviously turns the traditional ideal of value-neutrality on its head. Conventionally, objectivity is understood as a 'stepping back' from one's initial view in order to form a new conception which has the earlier view as an object amenable to a scientific analysis. In other words, as Thomas Nagel explains in his classic *The View From Nowhere*, we continually raise our understanding to a new level by forming a new conception that includes a more detached understanding of ourselves, of the world and of the interaction between them. Thus objective understanding is aimed at 'transcending our particular viewpoint and developing an expanded consciousness that takes in the world more fully.'[129] As we detach our understanding of the world from the contingencies of the here and now, the traditional view of objectivity holds, we simultaneously succeed in revealing successive layers of reality. Objective truths are therefore seen as more faithful representations of reality.

The constructivist reformulation of objectivity in terms of use value of knowledge leads them to this practical recommendation: when faced with a choice of 'evidencing reasons,' (i.e., background assumptions) pick the ones which allow the inquirers to criticize increasingly deeper layers of the assumptions of their worldviews. As Sal Restivo puts it, those knowledge systems are to be preferred that have a higher 'capacity for criticism, reflexivity and meta-inquiry.'[130] Here Restivo makes common cause with Sandra Harding's 'strong objectivity' and Helen Longino's 'transformative criticism,' which are aimed at revealing the hidden biases against women and other oppressed people that become constitutive of 'good' (i.e., empirically adequate) science. All three assume one, that science-as-it-is is incapable of spotting those biases which the members of the group share, and secondly, there are certain social arrangements which enhance the scientific community's capacity for self critique of their assumptions and biases. Thus the agenda for a deeper and stronger objectivity becomes 'detection of limiting interpretive frameworks and construction of more appropriate frameworks ... which are consistent with the values and commitments we express in the rest of our lives.'[131]

This project of active 'detection' of the social and political valence of interpretive frameworks and construction of 'more appropriate frameworks' takes different routes for different sociologists of objectivity. For Restivo and his 'weak programme' associates, the most objectivity-enhancing political position is anarchism, while for Harding and Longino, it is feminism. In other words, explicit embrace of these political positions – 'doing science as a feminist,' as Longino exhorts – is justified because these positions offer scientists a better opportunity to question and critique their own taken-for-granted background assumptions. In practice, these proposals translate into striving for a society where individuals can become 'open-ended and self-actualizing epistemic agents' (Restivo), or starting inquiry from the standpoint of marginalized social groups, who presumably can see farther, deeper and clearer than those in the dominant groups (Harding), and organizing scientific institutions such that subjective opinions of no one group dominate and the assumptions of all groups are equally subjected to a 'transformative criticism' (Longino). It is safe to say that all three would agree that as a minimal requirement, scientific community must be maximally inclusive of diverse and conflicting viewpoints and interest, a sentiment expressed well by Longino:

> That theory which is the product of the most inclusive scientific community is better, other things being equal, than that which is the product of the most exclusive. It is better not as measured against some independently accessible reality but better as measured against the cognitive needs of a genuinely democratic community.[132]

There is a weak interpretation of these assorted arguments for a democratized and inclusive science which is totally incontrovertible, and perfectly compatible with a realist epistemology. This weak interpretation would limit the appeals for democratization to the process of discovery – that is the choice of problems, setting the agenda etc. Opening the institutions of scientific and technological learning and research to all those interested in science, regardless of social location is undoubtedly good for science and good for the society. The larger the stock of ideas, view points and experiences, the larger the diversity of questions asked and approaches followed. Such a diversity is needed for compensating for individual biases and idiosyncrasies. Equal access to scientific knowledge is both a political *and* an epistemic good.[133] Undoubtedly, scientific institutions should be open and capable of rigorous critique of ideas without regard to position of the scientists in the pecking order, and ideally, institutions of learning should not be at the service of dictators, generals, and profiteers. And undoubtedly, modern scientific institutions need a substantial course correction in this regard.

But science for all the people is hardly the agenda of the kind of science critique that we are examining here. Indeed, for those who see science as inherently ideological, it makes more sense to *insulate* people from modern science rather than ask for equal access to it for all: that is indeed the demand of the so-called 'post-colonial' critics of science who see modern science as a threat to other cultural meanings. Furthermore, as we have already seen, the partisans of stronger objectivity believe that the context of discovery extends seamlessly into all aspects of science, including the processes of justification. Given this assumption, the constructivist argument for greater democracy and pluralism in science has a much stronger interpretation which extends beyond the institutional arrangements of scientific institutions to the very reasoning of science.

Deeper democracy and pluralism in more and more aspects of society is an ideal I share. But I believe that the demand to democratize science, when carried into the realm of justification itself, may end up making science *less* objective, rather than more. However flawed our contemporary scientific institutions are, they nevertheless allow room for scientists to come together (or at least aspire toward coming together) as a community not based on their sex, race or class, but united in a broadly defined goal – finding truths about the natural world. These institutions are based upon an ethic (however imperfectly adhered to) that demands submission of all claims, regardless of the source, to the toughest empirical tests and critique. Constructivists by and large are suspicious of any such profession of unity of ideas and goals and tend to see them as ideological justification of scientists' bid for power. They would like scientists to be explicit about their 'true' interests (determined by personal identities, interests and histories) and give up 'pretensions' of universalism. This lies at the heart of the demand for discursive democracy, wherein scientists should be free to explicitly invoke their identity-based ideologies and assumptions at all steps of scientific reasoning. Such a demand, I am convinced, will destroy the community of knowers united in an ideal of search for truth and replace it with a Hobbesian war of all ideologies against all others.

I believe that the deeper democracy of society that the radical critics of science seek may require that the process of evidential justification in science *not* be seen as inherently political, and *not* be democratized if democratization means rooting out 'bad' bias (by whose standards?) and inculcating 'good' bias (by whose standards?). If democratization of science requires 'admitting political considerations as relevant constraints on reasoning ... and content' as Longino recommends,[134] or that science be seen as 'politics by other means,' as Sandra Harding advises[135] or that science incorporates anarchist values of 'individual liberty, community life and healthy environments' as Sal Restivo urges,[136] then I am afraid such 'democratization' will end up undercutting the grounds for genuine and deeper democracy in our social relations, because the latter requires reliable knowledge of the structures of the world that exist independently of all partial perspectives.

To insist upon restructuring the social relationships of science – as Restivo, Harding and Longino do – without allowing that science as a social institution may have a social dynamic that is well adapted to its function of generating knowledge of the world, can make science *less* self-reflexive rather than more. The dilemma that these critics face is this: the values they want to promote in scientific practice – deeper critique and reflexivity – may causally depend on social relations based upon an ethos of co-operation tinged with competition. As David Hull's well-known study demonstrates, the apparently self-serving behaviour of scientists in terms of competition for credit and career advancement helps to ensure a higher degree of self-reflexivity and critique in modern scientific institutions as they have developed in the West.[137] The question then is, can we afford to radically alter the social relations of science, and yet continue to desire the advantages the peculiar logic of the existing scientific institutions make possible? There is no doubt that inclusion of women, and all other historically excluded social groups will improve the critical reflexivity of science by increasing the variety of viewpoints. But beyond that, making science more consensual may end up closing off venues for critique and growth of knowledge.

Another major problem with letting go of the ideal of objectivity as neutrality is the sheer unpredictability of how knowledge affects politics. Ideas, as postmodern theorists have been at pains to show, don't have essences. Given the extreme variation in social contexts in which scientific knowledge is received, it is hard to tell in advance which ideas are 'progressive.' To take a few examples, the recent findings that homosexuality may have biological basis was received with much consternation in Germany where the gay community remembered the Nazi solution to unwanted genetic characters, while in the US, many gay activists welcomed the findings, feeling that they may alleviate discrimination. Likewise, the ideological correctness of studying racial and gender differences changes with time and place. After years of agitating against raging hormone theories about women, feminists are now calling for research on how the effect of medication varies with hormones.[138] What political values should the researchers have given consent to at any given time?

Thirdly and finally, despite their valiant efforts to avoid judgmental relativism, I don't think that social theorists of objectivity have given us good reasons why they should not be considered as embracing a variety of village relativism. In the case of Sandra Harding, the superior epistemic standpoint of the oppressed was to protect feminist knowledge from becoming one more kind of knowledge, no better and no worse than any other way of knowing. But Harding has given no convincing evidence to show that marginalized persons possess superior epistemic qualities. It is not clear how her account of knowledge can remain non-relativist in the absence of the epistemic privilege of marginality. Likewise, it is not clear if Longino's view of transformative criticism can avoid relativism for the simple reason that what counts as public scrutiny varies from culture to culture, from one community of experts in one field to another and from one historical period to another.[139]

In view of these problems with the various calls for science produced from the perspective of the oppressed, I prefer C.S. Pierce's frank confession of belonging to 'that class of scalawags who propose to look the truth in the face, whether doing so be conducive to the interests of the society or not. Moreover, if I ever tackle that excessively difficult question, 'what is for the true interest of society?' I should feel I stood in need of a great deal of help from the science of legitimate inference.'[140]

Conclusion

In this essay I have tried to show that while science is a socially *manifested* process, it is nevertheless not a socially *grounded* activity: only a dialectical and progressive interaction between the socially situated inquirers with each other *and* with the mind-independent world can explain the content of scientific ideas.

Unlike the constructionist theorists, I believe that social relations do not play a *constitutive* role, although they do play a crucial *facilitating* role in the practice of science. I have argued that social relations of science have to be studied with an eye toward the overall goal of science, that is the production of structured accounts of the world that actually tell us something true about the world. The validity of these accounts, I have further argued, cannot be completely subsumed into the existing social and cultural context, for that would be reductionist and anthropocentric to boot, as it will make 'human abilities the measure of what nature can do,' something the wise Galileo cautioned against nearly four centuries ago. Scientific knowledge as a purely and ultimately social knowledge, furthermore, cannot avoid a non-trivial epistemological relativism, which is antithetical to the cause of justice: for 'without truth, there is no injustice,' only so many different stories.[141]

In sum, this one-time scientist believes that science is simply too important to be left to those who would only deconstruct it.

NOTES

1. David Bloor, *Knowledge and Social Imagery*, (Chicago, 1991, 2nd Edition), p. 42.
2. The three-sided relationship between the world, the self and culture is from Frank Farrell's *Subjectivity, Realism and Postmodernism: The Recovery of the World in Recent Philosophy*, (Cambridge, 1994).
3. Sociological theories critiqued in this essay include the Edinburgh School's 'Strong Programme' put forth by David Bloor and supported by Barry Barnes and Steve Shapin among others; Harry Collins' 'Empirical Program of Relativism' and the associated work by Andrew Pickering; the lab studies tradition of Knorr Cetina, Steve Woolgar and Bruno Latour and the actor-network theories of the 'Paris School' led by Bruno Latour and Michel Callon. Feminist critics of science examined in this paper include Evelyn Fox Keller, Sandra Harding and Helen Longino. Attention will be drawn to selected postcolonial science critiques as derivative discourses of sociological and feminist theories of science.
4. See the opening lines of David Bloor's programmatic text, *Knowledge and Social Imagery*. For a clearly laid out distinction between the *structuralist* (associated with Robert Merton) and *constructivist* (post-Mertonian and post-Kuhnian) streams, see Harriet Zuckerman, 'The Sociology of Science,' in Neil Smelser (ed.) *Handbook of Sociology* (California, 1988).
5. Arthur Fine labels this as the 'central doctrine' of constructivism. See his ' Science Made Up: Constructivist Sociology of Science,' in Peter Galison and David Stump (eds.) *The Disunity of Science: Boundaries, Contexts and Power* (Stanford, 1996).
6. See Karin Knorr Cetina's writings for programmatic statements regarding the constructive v. descriptive nature of science, especially her paper in Knorr Cetina and Michael Mulkay (eds) *Science Observed* (California, 1983).
7. Bruno Latour is the best known representative of co-production thesis; see his *Science in Action: How to Follow Scientists and Engineers Through Society* (Cambridge, Mass.: Harvard University Press, 1987). For an extended theorization of coproduction of science and social order as 'techno-totemism' see Devid Hess, *Science and Technology in a Multicultural World: The Cultural Politic of Facts and Artificats* (New York: Columbia University Press, 1994).
8. Anthony Giddens interprets postmodern critiques of scientific rationality not as super-seding modernity, but as a deepening of modernity which turns the self-critical rationality of science on scientific rationality itself. See Giddens, *Consequences of Modernity* (Stanford, 1990), p. 50. See also, John Searle, 'Rationality and Realism, What is at Stake?' *Daedalus*, Vol. 122, 1993.
9. Frank Farrell, *Subjectivity, Realism and Postmodernism*, p. 245. I am not suggesting, however, either that truth will always shine through all socially motivated narratives, or that truth is to be valued only insofar as it promises to dispel particular ideologies. I agree with Andrew Collier that 'as far as the politics of liberation is concerned, the cognitive virtues of objectivity, clarity, logical rigor are also political virtues – even though they may conflict with some short-term political advantage. Good politics itself requires that cognitive practices be conducted according to cognitive criteria...' see Andrew Collier, *Socialist Reasoning: An Inquiry Into the Political Philosophy of Scientific Socialism* (London, 1990), p. 148.

10. Michele Barrett, *The Politics of Truth: From Marx to Foucault* (Stanford, 1991).
11. For a selected sample of the vast and fast-growing literature in support of 'ethnosciences,' see Sandra Harding, 'Is Science Multi-cultural? Challenges, Resources, Opportunities, Uncertainties.' *Configurations*, Vol. 2, 1994, Ashis Nandy (ed.), *Science, Hegemony and Violence* (Oxford, 1988); Vandana Shiva, *Staying Alive: Women, Ecology and Development* (London, 1989); Stephen Marglin and Frederique Marglin (eds.) *Dominating Knowledge: Development, Culture and Resistance* (Oxford, 1990); Ziauddin Sardar (ed.), *The Revenge of Athena: Science, Exploitation and the Third World* (London, 1988).

For a critique, see Meera Nanda, 'History is What Hurts: Materialist Feminist Perspectives on Green Revolution and its Ecofeminist Critics,' in Rosemary Hennessy and Chrys Inghram (eds.) *Materialist Feminism: A Reader* (forthcoming). For a defence of science for postcolonial feminism, Meera Nanda, 'The Science Question in Postcolonial Feminism,' *Annals of The New York Academy of Sciences*, vol. 775, 1996. For a defence of popular science movements, Meera Nanda, 'Against Social De(con)struction of Science: Cautionary Tales from The Third World,' in Ellen M. Wood and John B. Foster (eds.) *In Defense of History*, Monthly Review Press, 1997.
12. Sal Restivo *Science, Society and Values: Toward a Sociology of Objectivity* (New Jersey, 1993), p. 55.
13. 'Science, surely, is not limited to national or racial boundaries,' Hans Reichenbach wrote while in exile from Nazi Germany.
14. Science for people movements in Third World countries which look to modern science not just as a means for economic development but also cultural change, operate on a Kantian sense of universal rationality well described by Christopher Norris, 'such is the *sensus communis* as Kant conceived it: the jointly epistemological and evaluative quest for principles of reason that would point beyond the limiting horizon of present, de facto communal belief.' See Norris, 'Truth, Ideology and Local Knowledge: Some Contexts of Postmodern Skepticism,' *Southern Humanities Review*, Vol. 28, No. 2: 109-166, p. 134. For a rigorously argued defence of the project of internal critique of traditions, see Martha Nussbaum and Amartya Sen, 'Internal Criticism and Indian Rationalist Traditions,' in Michael Krausz (ed.), *Relativism: Interpretation and Confrontation* (Notre Dame, Indiana, 1989).
15. Such an objective basis for critique has fallen out of favour with the constructionist and pragmatist critics of science who suggest that we reject a practice not because of its falsity with respect to some actually existing state of affairs, but because of its 'meaning in use' i.e., social effects. The problem is that enculturation habituates people to many injustices, and as a result, often the most odious social practices appear benign in their 'meaning in use.' Besides, the meaning in use differs for different groups of people: the network of cultural ideals, myths and images can make practices that are degrading and harmful to particular groups of individuals appear benign and even necessary for the good of the larger society: clitoridectomy is one example, the practice of untouchability is another.
16. A primary commitment to human values can keep scientism at bay as well: just because we have discovered some facts of nature, it does not follow that we *must* remake society to correspond with them. While we *can* derive our values from facts, that does not *oblige* us to choose only those values that are consonant with facts about the natural world.
17. Martin Hollis and Steve Lukes (eds.) *Rationality and Relativism* (Cambridge, Mass., 1982). Karl Popper's definition of relativism appears in his *The Myth of the Framework: In Defense of Science and Rationality* (New York, 1994). For a review of the variety of anti-realisms and relativisms that appear in the constructionist literature, see Robert Nola, 'Introduction: Some Issues Concerning Relativism and Realism in Science,' in Robert Nola (ed.) *Relativism and Realism in Science* (Dordrecht, 1989).
18. Larry Laudan, *Science and Relativism: Some Key Controversies in the Philosophy of*

Science (Chicago, 1990), p. viii. Despite his uncompromising opposition to epistemological relativism, Laudan is not a realist.

19. Barry Barnes, 'Natural Rationality: A Neglected Concept in the Social Sciences,' *Philosophy of Social Sciences*, Vol. 6, 1976.

20. In his interpretation of the central dogma of constructivism, H.M. Collins explicitly forbids invoking TRASP – that is, truth, rationality, success and progress – for explaining why anyone should hold a belief. Collins, 'What is TRASP?: The Radical Programme as a Methodological Imperative.' *Phil. Soc. Sci.*, 11, 1981.

21. Roy Bhaskar, *A Realist Theory of Science* (Leeds 1975), p. 36.

22. Philip Kitcher, 'Knowledge, Society and History,' *Canadian Journal of Philosophy*, Vol. 23 (1993).

23. For a well-stated case for treating natural science as equally interpretive as human sciences, see Joseph Rouse, 'Interpretation in Natural and Human Science,' in David Hiley, James Bohman and Richard Shusterman (eds.) *The Interpretive Turn: Philosophy, Science, Culture* (Ithaca, 1991).

24. Searle, *Construction of Social Reality* (New York, 1995), p. 190. Searle of course opposes this interpretation and argues that mountains differ from money in the sense that the former 'do not require the existence of representations as part of the conditions of their normal intelligibility', p. 193.

25. For a recent work, see Teresa Ebert, *Ludic Feminism and After: Postmodernism, Desire and Labor in Late Capitalism* (Michigan, 1996).

26. Roy Bhaskar, *Realist Theory of Science*, p. 9.

27. Paul Gross and Norman Levitt, *Higher Superstition: The Academic Left and Its Quarrels with Science* (Baltimore, 1994), p. 234.

28. With an aim of exposing science critics' rather weak grasp of science and even weaker standards for peer review, Alan Sokal, a theoretical physicist as New York University intentionally strung together the most outrageous statements by well-known postmodern theorists and cultural critics, from Derrida, Lacan and Latour to Aronowitz and Haraway to pay exaggerated tribute to how postmodern social theory has shown that the reality physicists study is a social and linguistic construct. *Social Text*, an avant garde journal of cultural critique published the paper (No. 46-47, 1996). Sokal's later explanation for why he perpetrated this hoax makes interesting reading on the gap between scientists and their constructionist critics. See *Lingua Franca*, May/June and July/Aug. 1996. See also Steven Weinberg, 'Sokal's Hoax,' *New York Review of Books*, August 8, 1996.

29. Steven Weinberg, *Dreams of a Final Theory* (New York, 1992), p. 29.

30. For a rare critique of constructionists for ignoring the view point of natural scientists, see Warren Schmaus et al, 'The Hard Program in the Sociology of Scientific Knowledge: A Manifesto,' *Social Epistemology*, Vol. 6, 1992. These critics believe that 'if a scientist does not accept or even recognize our [sociologists'] explanation of his or her actions, this is prima facie evidence of the inadequacy of the explanation.'

31. Philip Kitcher, *The Advancement of Science: Science without Legend, Objectivity without Illusions* (Oxford University Press, 1993), p. 104. For another work by a kindred spirit, see Peter Kosso, *Reading the Book of Nature: An Introduction to the Philosophy of Science* (Cambridge, UK, 1992). A strong realism that retains the notion of truth as constrained and validated by reality also appears in the writings of Ronald Giere, Ernan McMullin, Dudley Shapere and Richard Boyd.

32. For recent works advocating a deflationary realism see, Sergio Sismondo, *Science Without Myth: On Construction, Reality and Social Knowledge* (Albany, 1996); Joseph Rouse, *Engaging Science: How to Understand its Practices Philosophically* (Ithaca, 1996).

33. Insisting as Hans Reichenbach did that 'relation of a theory to facts [is] independent of the man who found the theory.' Quoted from Ronald Giere, 'Viewing Science,' *PSA* 1994, Vol. 2. Giere offers a brief but insightful social history of the rise of social

constructivism.

34. Jeffery Alexander, *Fin de Siecle Social Theory: Relativism, Reduction and the Problem of Reason* (London, 1995).

35. Hilary Kornblith, 'Introduction: What is Naturalistic Epistemology?' In Hilary Kornblith (ed.) *Naturalizing Epistemology* (Cambridge, Mass, 1985).

36. The logical positivism of the Vienna circle was the leading trend among the *first generation* of philosophers of science and reined supreme until around 1960. The historicists, including Thomas Kuhn, Paul Feyerabend and Stephen Toulmin constituted the zeitgeist of the *second generation*. The *third generation* of science scholars are reacting both to positivism and historicism and 'seeking a dialectical synthesis' of the two. See Werner Callebaut, *Taking the Naturalistic Turn: or How Real Philosophy of Science is Done* (Chicago, 1993). For a contrast between traditional and radical sociological naturalism, see Philip Kitcher,' The Naturalists Return,' *The Philosophical Review*, Vol. 10, 1992.

37. Thomas Nagel, *The View From Nowhere* (Oxford, 1986), p. 11

38. As Susan Haack puts it, 'science is not *simply* a social institution like banking or fashion industry, but a social institution *engaged in inquiry*, attempting to discover how the world is, to devise explanatory theories that stand up in the face of evidence.' see Haack, 'Toward a Sober Sociology of Science,' *Annals of the New York Academy of Science*, Vol. 775, June 1996. (emphasis in the original) See also, Hilary Kornblith, 'A Conservative Approach to Social Epistemology,' in Frederick Schmitt (ed.) *Socializing Epistemology*, 1994.

39. Barry Barnes, *Interests and the Growth of Knowledge* (London, 1977), p. 24.

40. Robert Merton, *The Sociology of Science* (Chicago, 1973).

41. Steve Shapin and Simon Schaffer, *Leviathan and the Air Pump* (New Jersey, 1985), p. 15.

42. Michel Foucault, 'Truth and Power,' (ed.) *Power/knowledge* (Brighton, 1980), p. 118. For constructivist literature on boundary-work, see Rouse, *Engaging Science* and Gieryn, 'Boundaries of Science,' in *Handbook of STS*.

43. Roy Bhaskar, 'Feyerabend and Bachelard: Two Philosophies of Science.' *New Left Review*, 94, 1975.

44. Barry Barnes and David Bloor, 'Relativism, Rationalism and the Sociology of Knowledge,' in Hollis and Lukes (eds.). *Rationality and Relativism* (Cambridge, Mass. 1982). The phrase 'normative anemia' is borrowed from Joseph Rouse, *Engaging Science*.

45. Barry Barnes, 'Realism, Relativism and Finitism,' in D. Raven et al, *Cognitive Relativism and Social Sciences* (New Brunswick, 1992), p, 133–134.

46. Richard Boyd, 'Constructivism, Realism and Philosophical Method,' In John Earman (ed.) *Inference, Explanation and Other Philosophical Frustrations: Essays in the Philosophy of Science* (Berkeley, 1992).

47. The new union has many names: pragmatic theory of truth, the coherence theory of truth, the deflationary theory of truth. None of them, as the recent survey by Frederick Schmitt shows, escapes the problem of relativizing truth to a system of belief. See his *Truth: A Primer* (Boulder, CO, 1995).

48. H.M. Collins and Steven Yearley, 'Epistemological Chicken,'in Andrew Pickering (ed.), *Science as Practice and Culture* (Chicago, 1992), p. 303.

49. Attributed to Robert Young. Quoted here from Sal Restivo, 'The Theory Landscape in Science Studies,' *Handbook of STS*.

50. Bloor urges sociologists of science to 'only . . . proceed as the other sciences proceed, and all will be well.' See his *Knowledge and Social Imagery*, p. 157.

51. But as Larry Laudan argues, the SP's reading of value neutrality of scientific methodology clearly runs against the best established precedents in natural science because natural scientists routinely use different models and causal mechanisms to explain related but different phenomena. Larry Laudan, 'The Pseudo Science of Science?' *Phil. Soc. Sci.*

Vol. 11 (1981).

52. Barry Barnes, *Interests and The Growth of Knowledge* (London, 1977), p. 25.

53. For a bibliography, see Steve Shapin, 'History of Science and its Sociological Reconstruction,' *History of Science*, 1982, Vol. xx: 157–211.

54. I do not mean to suggest that feminist critiques of science are derived from sociology of science in general, or the SP in particular. The two have independent, although mutually supportive, trajectories, which have only now begun to explicitly come together at some points. Feminist and social-cultural critics of science increasingly use and cite each other's work to support their distinctive agendas. Feminist scholars of science have tried to distance themselves from the relativist implications of the SP and don't seem to have made much use of the Paris School (at least so far.)

55. Sandra Harding, *Whose Science? Whose Knowledge?* (Ithaca, 1991), p. 138.

56. *Ibid.*, p. 12.

57. Helen Longino provides the most rigorously argued case for the necessity of the social for understanding the cognitive processes of science. See her *Science as Social Knowledge* (Princeton, 1990). Longino uses the SSK literature to bolster her case that observation and justificationary reasoning are social; see her 'The Fate of Knowledge in Social Theories of Science,' in Frederick Schmitt (ed.) *Socializing Epistemology*. Likewise, Evelyn Fox-Keller cites the findings of the SP to argue that 'on every level, choices are social even as they are cognitive and technical.' See her *Secrets of Life, Secrets of Death: Essays on Language, Gender and Science* (New York, 1992), p.26.

58. See Knorr-Cetina and Michael Mulkay, 'Introduction,' *Science Observed* (California, 1983). Prominent feminist science critics, especially Sandra Harding, Evelyn Keller and Vandana Shiva simultaneously treat the content of science as constituted by social location (as sanctioned by the SP) and yet deny that they are arguing for just another story from women's lives: rather, they present feminist knowledge to be superior – i.e., more objective – as compared to 'malestream' science.

59. Barnes and Bloor, 'Relativism, Rationalism and the Sociology of Knowledge,' in Hollis and Luke (eds.) 1982, p. 23.

60. David Bloor, *Knowledge and Social Imagery*, p. 158.

61. *Ibid.*, p. 40.

62. *Ibid.*, pp. 38–39.

63. Barry Barnes, *Interests and the Growth of Knowledge*, p. 2.

64. Barry Barnes, 'Natural Rationality: A Neglected Concept in the Social Sciences,' *Phil. Soc. Sci.* Vol. 6, 1976: 115–126., p. 124

65. Barry Barnes, 'Realism, Relativism and Finitism,' in Raven et al, *Cognitive Relativism.*

66. Steve Shapin, *The Social History of Truth: Civility and Science in the Seventeenth Century* (Chicago, 1995), p. 5

67. Barnes and Bloor, in Hollis and Lukes, p. 27.

68. *Ibid.*, p. 29.

69. For a clear statement regarding difference between historicism and postmodernism, see Linda Nicholson's introduction to her anthology, *Feminism/Postmodernism* (New York, 1990), p. 4.

70. Bruno Latour, 'One More Turn After the Social Turn...' in Ernan McMullin (ed.) *The Social Dimension of Science* (Notre Dame, Indiana, 1992). Latour first described his 'actor-network model' in his *Science in Action: How to follow scientists and Engineers through society* (Cambridge, Mass, 1987).

71. *Ibid.*, 'One More Turn . . .' , p. 280.

72. Military metaphors abound in Latour's writings. One wonders why those who have seen metaphors as vehicles of masculine values in science have accepted Latour's metaphors so uncritically.

73. Latour's favourite example of this Machiavellian process is Louis Pasteur's work on anthrax: because he had the laboratory, Pasteur could win the anthrax bacillus to his side

MEERA NANDA 349

and was able to translate the interest of the farmers in terms that coincided with his own interest in establishing his authority and the interest of the bacillus. In this process, Latour argues, both nature and society were changed simultaneously: the society had to accept a new reality of the microbe and had to go through Pasteur's lab to find a solution.

74. See Harry Collins and Steve Yearley, 'Epistemological Chicken,' in Andrew Pickering (ed.) *Science as Practice and Culture*. Chicago, 1990. See also, Barry Barnes, 'How Not To Do Sociology of Science,' *Annals of Scholarship*, Vol. 8, 1991.
75. See especially, *German Ideology* (New York, 1991), p. 62-63.
76. Barry Barnes, 'How Not to..' p. 331, emphasis added.
77. The term 'fig leaf realism' was coined by Michael Devitt to describe 'an idle addition to idealism.' Quoted from Robert Nola, 'Introduction,' to his *Relativism and Realism in Science*, 1989.
78. Bloor's 'Afterword' to the second edition of *Knowledge and Social Imagery*. See also, Barry Barnes, David Bloor and John Henry, *Scientific Knowledge: A Sociological Analysis* (Chicago, 1996).
79. This summary of finitism is from Barnes, 'Realism, Relativism and Finitism,' in Raven et al, 1992, Barnes, ' On the Conventional Character of knowledge and Cognition,' in Knorr Cetina and Michael Mulkay (eds.) *Science Observed* (California, 1983), and David Bloor, 'Durkheim and Mauss Revisited: Classification and the Sociology of Knowledge,' *Stud. Hist. Phil. Sci.* Vol. 13 (4), 1982.
80. Bloor, *ibid.*, p. 280.
81. Karin Knorr Cetina, 'Strong Constructivism – from a Sociologist's Point of View: A Personal Addendum to Sismondo's Paper.' *Social Studies of Science*, vol. 23, 1993: 555-63. p. 558.
82. K. Knorr Cetina, 'The Ethnographic Study of Scientific Work: Towards a Constructivist Interpretation of Science,' in Knorr Cetina and Michael Mulkay (eds.) *Science Observed* (California, 1983).
83. As Frank Farrell argues, the contemporary social constructionist nominalism is not very different in its motivation from the medieval nominalism. For medieval theologians, 'a world where things have their proper natures and proper modes of actualization seemed to place undesirable limits on God.' With modernity, human subjectivity took the place of God but retained the anti-realist orientation toward the world. With postmodernism, subjectivity itself has become nominal, further diminishing the role of the real in fixing our beliefs. See, Farrell, *Subjectivity, Realism and Postmodernism*.
84. Harding, *Whose Science*? p. 147 (emphasis added.)
85. Evelyn Fox-Keller, *Secrets of Life*, p. 5. For a recent critical review of Keller, see Alan Soble, 'Gender, Objectivity and Realism,' *Monist*, Vol. 77, 1994.
86. Ernest Gellner, 'The Paradox in Paradigms,' *Times Literary Supplement*, April 23, 1982.
87. See Wesley Salmon, *Four Decades of Scientific Explanation*. Minneapolis, 1989, Ernan McMullin, 'Enlarging the Known World,' in Jan Hilgevoord (ed.), *Physics and Our View of the World*, (Cambridge, 1994). Strong arguments for existence of natural kinds based upon 'cluster of properties determined by causal structures of the world' have been provided by Richard Boyd, 'What Realism Implies and What it Does Not,' *Dialectica*, 43 (1989).
88. Ronald Giere,' Toward A Unified Theory of Science,' in James Cushing, C.F. Delaney and G. Gutting (eds.) *Science and Reality: Recent Work in Philosophy of Science* (Notre Dame. 1984), p. 15.
89. Knorr Cetina, 'Laboratory Studies' in Handbook of STS, p. 146. Knorr Cetina justifies lab studies thus: 'detailed description deconstructs – not out of an interest in critique but because it cannot but observe the intricate labor that goes into the creation of a solid entity, the countless nonsolid ingredients from which it derives, the confusion and negotiations that lie at its origin . . .' p. 146.
90. Bruno Latour and Steve Woolgar, *Laboratory Life: The Construction of Scientific Facts*,

Princeton, 1986 (first edition 1979), p. 64. For an excellent description and critique of L&W's project, see Ian Hacking, 'The Participant Irrealist at Large in the Laboratory,' *Brit. Jour. of Phil. Sci.* 39: 277-294.

91. Latour and Woolgar, *ibid.*, p. 64.

92. Hans Radder, 'Science, Realization and Reality: The Fundamental Issues,' *Stud. Hist. Phil. Sci.* Vol. 24(3), 1993.

93. See Roy Bhaskar,' Feyerabend and Bachelard,' p. 53.

94. For a not so recent but illuminating review, see Ian Hacking, 'Philosophers of Experiment,' *PSA*, 1988.

95. Harry Collins's EPOR is also sometimes referred to as the Bath school, after the University of Bath, where Collins teaches. EPOR serves as the hub of a network of well-known sociologists in constant traffic with each other and with the strong programme. Included in this tradition are the sociological history of quarks by Andrew Pickering, study of solar neutrinos by Trevor Pinch and the most well-known of all, Steve Shapin and Simon Schaffer's sociological history of the development of experimental method by Robert Boyle.

96. Roth and Barrett, *ibid.*, James R. Brown, *The Rational and the Social* (New York, 1989); Alan Chalmers, *The Fabrication of Science* (Minneapolis, 1990). For more recent works that admit more constraints by nature see Peter Galison, *How Experiments End* (Chicago, 1987), Allan Franklin, *Experiment, Right or Wrong* (Cambridge, 1990). Later works by Pickering also move toward recognizing 'resistance' from the world. See Andrew Pickering,' Objectivity and the Mangle of Practice,' *Annals of Scholarship*, Vol. 8, 1991

97. Harry Collins, 'What is TRASP? The Radical Programme as a Methodological Imperative.' *Phil. Soc. Sci.* Vol. 11, 1981.

98. *Ibid.*, p. 148.

99. Pickering, quoted from Roth and Barrett, 'Deconstructing Quarks,' p. 594.

100. Collins, *Changing Order*, p. 185.

101. For details, see Gerard Darmon, 'The Asymmetry of Symmetry,' *Social Science Information*, 25(3): 743-755.

102. Notably, David Stump, 'From Epistemology and Metaphysics to Concrete Connection,' in Peter Galison and David Stump (eds.) *The Disunity of Science: Boundaries, Contexts and Power* (Stanford, 1996) and Peter Kosso, *Reading the Book of Nature*.

103. Epigraph from Knorr Cetina, *The Manufacture of Knowledge: An Essay on the Constructivist and Contextual Nature of Science* (Oxford, 1981).

104. Barnes and Bloor, 'Relativism, Rationalism and Sociology of Knowledge,' in Hollis and Lukes (eds.), p. 29

105. See David Bloor, 'Durkheim and Mauss Revisited,' for his interpretation of Boyle's laws as congruent with his conservative political ideas; Barry Barnes and Steve Shapin, *Natural Order*, Beverly Hills, 1979, Steve Shapin, 'History of Science and its Sociological Reconstruction,' *History of Science*, Vol. xx, 1982 for a review.

106. David Hess, *Science and Technology in a Multicultural World: The Cultural Politics of Facts and Artifacts* (Columbia University Press, 1994).

107. Evelyn Fox-Keller, *Reflections on Gender and Science* (New Haven, 1985); especially part III. Keller's book has the status of a classic among feminist science critics. For a more recent defence of constructionist ideas, see Keller, 'Science and Its Critics,' *Academe*, Sept./Oct. 1995.

108. Longino, *Science as Social Knowledge*, p. 43. Longino distinguishes her approach from SSK by distancing her 'contextual empiricism' from SSK's wholist assumptions which tend to explain theory change in terms of gestalt switches and incommensurability. But see her 'Fate of Knowledge in Social Theories of Science' in Schmitt (ed.), *Socializing Epistemology*, 1994, where she describes her affinities with science studies literature in insisting that cognitive is social.

109. Longino, *Science as Social Knowledge*, p. 189.

110. *Ibid.*, p. 193.
111. Longino enumerates six epistemic and political virtues of 'doing epistemology as a feminist' in her 'In Search of Feminist Epistemology,' *The Monist*, Oct. 1994, Vol. 77. See also her recent 'Gender, Politics and Theoretical Virtues,' *Synthese*, 104: 383–397, 1995, for elaboration of feminist values for accepting theories and models.
112. McMullin, Ernan, 'The Rational and the Social in the History of Science,' in J.R. Brown (ed.) *Scientific Rationality: The Sociological Turn* (Dordrecht, 1984). PUS can also stand for the 'presumption of ultimate sociality,' for SSK not only insists that social explanation be sought for all aspects of science but also that ultimately, in the final instance, it is the social that explains the cognitive.
113. See Thomas Nickles, 'Good Science as Bad History: From Order of Knowing to Order of Being,' in Ernan McMullin (ed.) *Social Dimension of Science* (Notre Dame, 1992).
114. See Francis Crick, *What Mad Pursuit* (New York, 1988). See also Paul Gross and Norman Levitt, *Higher Superstition*, p. 141.
115. See Oliver Sacks, 'A New Vision of the Mind,' in John Cornwell (ed.) *Nature's Imagination* (Oxford, 1995). See also Gross and Levitt, *Higher Superstition*, for the compatibility between Edelman's model and the linear cascades of hormone action, p. 147.
116. Gerald Edelman, 'Memory and the Individual Soul: Against Silly Reductionism,' in Cornwell (ed.) *Nature's Imagination*.
117. *Ibid.*, p. 201.
118. Dudley Shapere. *Reason and the Search for Knowledge* (Dordrecht, 1984), p. xxii.
119. Those among constructionists who find Kuhn's ideas congenial to theirs tend to read his work rather selectively, for Kuhn offers one of the sharpest arguments against the presumption of unrestricted sociality. While Kuhn admits that 'early in the development of a new field, social needs and values are a major determinant of the problems on which its practitioners concentrate,' he insists that as the field of inquiry matures, 'the problems on which specialists work are no longer presented by the external society but by an internal challenge . . . and the concepts used to resolve these problems are normally close relatives or those supplied by prior training . . . In short, compared with other professional and creative pursuits, the practitioners of mature science are effectively insulated from the cultural milieu in which they live their extra-professional lives.' *The Essential Tension* (Chicago, 1977), p. 119.
120. Susan Haack, 'Science as Social? – Yes and No,' in Jack Nelson and Lynn Hankinson Nelson (eds.) *A Dialogue on Feminism, Science and Philosophy of Science* (The Netherlands, forthcoming).
121. Latour, *Science in Action*, p. 12.
122. *Ibid.*; and Michel Callon, 'Four Models for the Dynamic of Science,' in Jasonoff et. al (eds.) *Handbook of STS*.
123. Stephen Fuchs and Steven Ward, 'What is Deconstruction, and Where and When does it take place? Making Facts in Science, Building Cases in Law,' *American Sociological Review* Vol. 59, 1994.
124. Bruno Latour, 'Clothing the Naked Truth,' in Hilary Lawson and Lisa Appignanesi (eds.) *Dismantling Truth: Reality in the Postmodern World* (NY, 1989).
125. For a classic statement of the distinction between epistemic and judgmental relativism, see Karin Knorr Cetina and Michael Mulkay's 'Introduction,' *Science Observed*, 1983.
126. See Longino, *Science as Social Knowledge*, p. 62 for a description of this distinction.
127. Keller, *Secrets*, p. 5. (emphasis in the original).
128. Meera Nanda, 'Science Wars in India,' *Dissent*, Winter 1997.
129. Thomas Nagel, *The View from Nowhere*, p. 5.
130. Restivo, *Science, Society and Values*, p. 61.
131. Longino, *Science as Social Knowledge*, p. 191.
132. *Ibid.*, p. 214.

133. For a thoughtful discussion of why an objectivist should welcome pluralism, See Noretta Kortege, 'Ideology, Heuristics and Rationality in the Context of Discovery,' in S. French and H. Kamminga (eds.) *Correspondence, Invariance and Heuristics* (The Netherlands, 1993).
134. Longino, *Science as Social Knowledge*, p. 193.
135. Harding, *Whose Science?* p. 10. The complete quote reads: 'Science is politics by other means, and it also generated reliable information about the empirical world. Science is more than politics of course, but it is that.'
136. See Sal Restivo, *Science, Society and Social Values*. Restivo argues for what he calls the 'weak program' in SSK which would aim at not just explaining science but critiquing science and the social arrangements it is constituted with.
137. David Hull, *Science as Process* (Chicago, 1988).
138. Both examples are from Noretta Koertge, *op. cit.*
139. Critiques of standpoint are legion. For a critique from a Marxist perspective, see Bat-Ami Bar On, 'Marginality and Epistemic Privilege' in Linda Alcoff and Elizabeth Potter (eds.), *Feminist Epistemologies* (New York, 1993); Rosemary Hennessy, *Materialist Feminism and the Politics of Discourse* (New York, 1993). For an incisive philosophical critique see Cassandra Pinnick, 'Feminist Epistemology: Implications for Philosophy of Science,' *Philosophy of Science*, Vol. 61, 1994.
   For a critique of Longino's transformative criticism, see Sharon Crasnow, 'Can Science be Objective? Longino's Science as Social Knowledge', *Hypatia*, Vol. 8, 1993 and Philip Kitcher, 'Socializing Knowledge.'
140. Quoted from C.F. Delaney, *Science, Knowledge and Mind: A Study in the Philosophy of C.S. Pierce* (Notre Dame, 1993).
141. Norman Geras, *Solidarity in the Conversation of Humankind*, p. 107.

POSTCOLONIAL THEORY AND THE 'POST-' CONDITION

Aijaz Ahmad

The End of History is the *death* of Man as such.

Alexandre Kojève

The issue of 'postcolonial theory' shall detain us at some length presently.[1] So, let me start by reflecting on the other term in the title of the discussion at hand: the Post Condition. The phrase itself is taken from Niethammer whose book on the past careers of the concept of 'posthistory'[2] was published in Hamburg barely a few months after Francis Fukuyama, the philosopher from Rand Corporation, published his famous essay which he then went on to revise and expand into the even more famous book that outlines his own tamer version of Kojève's philosophically magisterial statement on *fin de l'histoire*.[3] In political persuasion, philosophical stance and structure of argument, the two authors could hardly be more dissimilar. It is uncanny, therefore, that both should have been concerned – Fukuyama as advocate, Niethammer from a position at once antagonistic and nuanced – with those strands in European intellectual history which have been fond of announcing that History has already ended. Since we hear so much these days about the End of History and its 'metanarratives of emancipation' – from Fukuyama in one register, but in many more registers from postmodernist, deconstructivist and postcolonialist positions – it might be useful to begin by reflecting briefly on some of the political origins of this postist philosophical reflex.

The origins of the idea are obviously traceable to Hegel but then enunciations of this kind, often in versions very different from anything Hegel might have said or thought, became particularly loud and bewilderingly various at two distinct historical junctures: during the 1930s – in the midst of revolution, depression, fascism and world war – and then in the present period of capitalist triumphalism. Meanwhile, the repertoire of posthistorical imaginings has been refracted through complex and competing traditions of thought, and it would be a mistake to identify it all with a singular political stance. In Hegel's reflections on the French Revolution,

353

of course, this idea of the 'End' had the predominant meaning of 'Purpose' or 'Vocation': the proposition, in other words, that History had finally found its vocation in the Idea of Liberty which had become the irreversible ground on which collective human struggles were henceforth to be fought. By the 1930s, however, in the times of National Socialism, three competing versions were to emerge in definitions of *posthistoire*. In Nazi apologetics, the Third Reich itself was portrayed as the EndState, still in the process of its universalisation, towards which history was said to have been tending. Secondly, those who were later disillusioned with the Reich, either with the manner of its progression or with its demise, were then to cultivate a posthistorical melancholy, becoming deeply sceptical not only about the feasibility of collective social projects of any kind but also about what Spengler had already called 'rose-coloured progress,' so that modes of withdrawal ranged from stoical a-sociality, to (to use a Foucauldian phrase for our own purposes) Care of the Self, to quasi-aristocratic clericism of Being.[4]

But, then, in a completely different kind of variant, some of the most powerful thought that arose among the German intelligentsia in opposition to the Nazis, notably the writings of Horkheimer and Adorno, identified a little too easily a critique of the technologically efficient barbarism of the Nazis with a global Eclipse of Reason and Art – identified that particular barbarism, indeed, with a cage-like entrapment in the technological reason of the Modern as such. Adorno's remorseless avant-gardism in matters of Art and Literature, as the reliable refuge from technological Reason and popular culture alike, is of a piece with the stringent pessimism of *Minima Moralia* and a pervasive sense that collective politics of a revolutionary kind is really impossible in the face of the 'massification' of modern culture; 'mass' and 'popular' are, in the writings of Horkheimer and Adorno, words of punctual and irredeemable degradation. What Bourdieu calls Heidegger's 'ultra-revolutionary conservatism' and 'aristocratic populism' meet their contrary and complement, in Adorno's writings, in the form of an avant-gardist aristocratism, in which Art seems often to serve the same function as that of Being in Heidegger's 'effects of priestly prophecy'.[5] In *this* version, the Third Reich, and the pervading techno-logical Reason of which the Reich is seen to be the chief embodiment, spells out the end of History, then, not as its realization, as Nazi apologists would have it, but as its final negation, spelling out the impossibility of either the thinking or the making of History as an emancipatory project in any foreseeable future.

Let us be more precise, though. For much of the leftwing philosophy that came of age in Western Europe between Petrograd and Munich, especially around the years that brought the Depression and the Hitlerite triumph, political reality was grim three times over: Nazi barbarism, surely, but also the dashing of Bolshevik possibilities and revolutionary hopes in Stalin's USSR, *and* the descent of what one knew as 'liberal capitalism' into the Depression on the one hand, great intensification of consumerist fetishism on the other. Faced with such a history, and even though he probably did not quite comprehend the extent of Stalinist revision of Bolshevism, Gramsci, in the loneliness of a fascist prison, did remain attached to the formula he had made his own, 'optimism of the will, pessimism of the intellect'. In contrast, Adorno, who himself seems never to have been intrinsically part of a mass movement, even a defeated one, could identify 'optimism' only with the aesthetic intensities and narrow plenitudes of avant-garde Art; History, in the older philosophical sense of a project in which the emancipation of some was inextricably linked with the emancipation of all, seemed now to have virtually no prospects.

This avant-gardist and academic elitism as a reaction to political disillusion was of course to return on a much wider scale, this time among the Parisian intellectuals who became dominant in the aftermath of May 1968, especially as many of them moved from the Far Left to make their peace with a new and neo-liberal conservatism. The striking feature of this return of cultural elitism, however, was that all those themes of the Frankfurt School – antinomies of the Enlightenment, Eclipse of Reason, the ambiguities of Progress, the massification of culture, the decline of revolutionary possibility – which had produced such disturbance and even moral pessimism for Adorno and Benjamin, were now re-staged as sources of pleasure and signs of a new freedom, as if this new sense of living in the aftermath of the end of meaning, the death of the social, etc., produced an unprecedented range of possibilities for *play* – as if Adorno was being re-read through Daniel Bell, Marshall McLuhan, and Donald Duck. In one major aspect, the hallmark of the postmodern aesthetic is that what was experienced as a source of anguish in the Modernist aesthetic is now staged in the register of infinite gratification. Furthermore, the postmodern is posthistorical in the precise sense of being a discourse of the end of meaning, in the Derridean sense of infinite deferral of all meaning in language and philosophical labour alike, as well as in the Lyotardian sense both of what he calls 'incredulity toward the metanarratives of emancipation' as well as the assertion that there can be no criteria for choosing between different 'language games' that are external to the respective 'games' as such. Characteristically, this postmodern philosophical consciousness distinguishes itself from an earlier, largely existentialist sense of meaninglessness and the Absurd by positing its own discourse of the end of meaning as a happy liberation from the Logos as such.

We thus have not one but two claims regarding the End of History. There is the quasi-Hegelian claim put forth by Fukuyama which itself makes a strong gesture of reconciliation with Nietzsche, as we shall see.

But there is also the deconstructivist, postmodernist claim which has a much more complex lineage: connected not with Hegel but with Heidegger – and through Heidegger, with the philosophical atmosphere of post-Weimar Germany – and descended more or less directly from Nietzsche, but from a Nietzschean strand rather different than the one that Fukuyama invokes. These are philosophically different claims, with distinct modes of argumentation. Yet there are resemblances as well, the most striking of which is that neither is able or willing to think of a possible future for humanity that would be basically different than today's neo-liberalist triumph and consequent universalisation of commodity fetishism. But, then, how is it that philosophers as different as Fukuyama and the postmoderns reach more or less the same conclusion? A common commitment to the existing modalities of capitalist democracy is obviously the more substantial link, but there are also commanding influences, notably that of Kojève, that remind us of some shared philosophical origins for the two strands in posthistorical thinking today, however divergent they may be in other respects.

Now, Fukuyama himself foregrounds his debt to Kojève, and the fact that this influence has been filtered through Leo Strauss and Allan Bloom is also well known. That Kojève should exercise his influence on a section of the U.S. intelligentsia through such solidly reactionary interlocutors is itself significant, and goes some way in explaining how Fukuyama's argument which purports to take seriously Hegel's Master-Slave Dialectic does nevertheless move effortlessly to the jubilant conviction that capitalist democracy, headed by the United States, had not only triumphed over its chief adversaries, principally communism, but had also proved itself to be something of a terminating point in the political evolution of humankind.[6] What is less widely appreciated is the extent and contradictory nature of Kojève's influence in Paris, from the early 1930s onward. His Seminar on Hegel, mainly on the *Phenomenology*, which lasted from 1933 to 1939, was one of the defining events that made Hegel so central a figure in French philosophical debates for the next two decades or so. But it was a very special reading of Hegel, filtered equally through Marx and Heidegger; Kojève may well be credited with introducing Heidegger to the French intelligentsia. Indeed, the pairing of Marx and Heidegger, which became such a convention in Derridean deconstruction, is traceable directly to Kojève, with the key difference that the deconstructivists tend to drop Hegel altogether and claim to 'radicalize' Marx through the superior authority of Heidegger.[7] This 'radicalization' of both Hegel and Marx through the application of Heidegger – whose thought Karl Jaspers, Kojève's teacher and Heidegger's own one-time friend, was to find 'in its essence unfree, dictatorial, uncommunicative'[8] – was one side of the story. During that same phase, Kojève had been, along with Baudrillard, a

Communist.[9] Meanwhile he was also in sympathetic touch with the well-known far-left group, Socialisme ou Barbarie, which included both Lyotard and Castoriadis, and which Walter Benjamin was also to contact through Georges Bataille, a key member of Kojève's seminar. Indeed, Kojève was to have a decisive influence on both Bataille and Lacan, who were among his favourite students and were to emerge much later as seminal figures in poststructuralist thought.[10]

What we are tracing here is not something as direct as a uniform intellectual or political lineage but a certain milieu, a complex ideological matrix, almost an atmosphere, and certain modes of thought that coalesced and collided with each other in complex ways. Heidegger seems to have been a central figure (Kojève conducted his seminar on Hegel in one auditorium while Henri Cobin expounded on Heidegger's *Being and Time* in an adjoining one). Even though Fukuyama's book has merely one index entry for Heidegger it is safe to say that he too is connected, through the influences of Bloom and Strauss, with precisely that intellectual milieu of radical conservatism during the interwar years in Germany whose ideological moorings Niethammer illuminates and which included Heidegger and Schmitt as quite central figures. Kojève himself was greatly influenced by Heidegger's philosophy but there is no indication that he ever drew close to National Socialism, even though his intellectual relations with Carl Schmitt, his close partnership with Leo Strauss, and his philosophical fascination with violence[11] would seem to indicate that the matter of Kojevian formation is not easy to disentangle from that whole intellectual climate that smacks of a widespread authoritarian temper. The matter is rendered even more complex by the fact that if Lyotard and Derrida, whom no one can conceivably accuse of Nazi sympathies, have led the campaign in France to protect Heidegger against any discussion of his work for the Nazis and his subsequent refusal to publicly account for that association, in Germany that same role has been played, among others, by Ernst Nolte. Nolte also takes up specific themes from Heidegger's pro-Nazi political declarations in the course of his revisionist effort to 'normalize' the Nazi experience as an 'understandable' response to the rise of Stalin in the Soviet Union and as one element among others in what Nolte, echoing many Nazi apologists in the past, calls 'an international civil war'.

Finally, there is the matter of the fundamental shifts in Kojève's own career and outlook, which reminds one of so many others. The Kojève that we first encounter as the teacher of the legendary seminar fancied himself a communist, interpreted Hegel's treatment of the twin histories of religion and philosophy through Marxist categories of alienation, false consciousness and, above all, labour. As Roth puts it about that period in his thought, 'For Kojève the dynamic of mastery and slavery is the motor of History: domination sets history in motion and equality will end it.'[12] In that reading, we actually get two versions of what Kojève calls *fin de l'histoire*. In one version, we are said to be living in a posthistorical period in the sense that a *project* of Equality has been set in motion historically by the French Revolution and philosophically by Hegel, and all that remains is the practical completion of that project – to which in any case there are no alternatives. In a stronger version, the End of History could only come with the end of class struggle and the triumph of 'slave ideologies', i.e. the triumph of equality over hierarchy, which is then identified squarely with the EndState of 'classless society'.

By the 1950s, as Kojève recreated himself in the guise of an illustrious civil servant, three major shifts took place. One, class struggle and with that the struggle for 'recognition' was now said to be essentially over in countries of advanced capitalism where most of the surplus value, he said, was returned to the worker: '. . . the United States has already reached the final stage of Marxist 'communism', since, in effect, all the members of a 'classless society' can appropriate whatever appeals to them, without working more than they feel like doing,' and 'the American way of life was the one fitted for the posthistorical period.'[13] Second, however, this End of History was identified with a Weberian sense of complete rationalization of society and a sense of nausea, emptiness and boredom of the kind that was made fashionable in France at that time through disparate fictions of Sartre, Camus, Françoise Sagan *et al*. Third, Kojève's interests shifted increasingly from the philosophy of History to the making of Discourses, and the tonality of his prose also shifted, accordingly, to a register distinctly non-Hegelian and surprisingly similar to that of the poststructuralists: '*"The definitive annihilation of Man properly so-called"* also means the definitive disappearance of Discourse (*Logos*) in the strict sense,' he was to write in a note to the 1969 edition of his book on Hegel.[14]

Two features of this career are worth reiterating. On the one hand, the vertigo of these shifts reminds one, inevitably, of the careers of those luminaries of French postmodernity whom Daniel Singer once bluntly called 'bastards of May' and 'Maoist turncoats.'[15] But, then, it also clarifies for us that Fukuyama, who picks up one strand of Nietzsche while the postmoderns pick up several others, is loyal to Kojève twice over: he picks up Kojève's treatment of the Master-Slave Dialectic from the 1930s but then severs that account from Kojève's Heideggerian Marxism of that period, recombining it with the two-faced quality of Kojève's thought of the 1950s: the celebration of the United States as the EndState which terminates History, but also a lament for the End of History as a Weberian rationalization and the reign of mediocrity. It is on this ground of Kojevian doubleness (duplicity?) that Lyotard's End of all Metanarratives meets

Fukuyama's End of History, and that postmodernity itself becomes yet another version of *fin de l'histoire*, not in Hegel's sense of History discovering its Vocation as Pursuit of Equality and Freedom but in the much more recent and tawdry sense of living, jubilantly, in the aftermath of the end of meaning itself.[16] This complexity in the philosophical lineages of 'The Post Condition' suggests to us that Fukuyama's thought is by no means *sui generis* and that much of his intellectual formation, political conviction and worldview he in fact shares with some of the dominant strands in postmodernity, whether or not he is in any obvious sense sympathetic to those modes of Parisian brashness. It is not only that Lyotard repackages in French philosophical language what we once used to hear from Daniel Bell and others; it is also the case that Kojève's influence in Paris and beyond has included a lot more than Fukuyama, so that if one of the main registers of Fukuyama's declaration of the End of History sounds somewhat like Lyotard's declaration of 'the end of all metanarratives' or Baudrillard's announcement of 'the death of the social', the resemblance is not merely incidental.

This is of course not to deny that Fukuyama's discourse is very peculiarly knotted, with an unbridgeable inner contradiction; for, he attempted to reconcile two contrasting tendencies within the larger philosophical tradition, as they are indicated even by the two terms that he took into the title of his book, 'The End of History', and 'The Last Man'. It might appear, at first sight, that the figure of 'the Last Man' seamlessly represents the moment at which History itself comes to an End. In the actual structure of Fukuyama's argument, however, there is a considerable slippage. The rhetoric of the 'End of History' he takes from Hegel, to assert that what we are witnessing in our own time, in the 1990s, is that much-awaited outbreak of liberty which Hegel had first glimpsed in the figure of the Man on Horseback at Jena and which has now taken, on Fukuyama's account, its final form in the global triumph of neo-liberal capitalism, and in the terminal defeat of its adversaries. The rhetoric of 'the Last Man', by contrast, is descended from the Nietzschean rejection of the intellectual lineages of Humanism and the Enlightenment, as well as his elitist rejection not only of what later came to be known as 'consumer society' but also popular power of any kind. In this way, the narrative of Modernity itself becomes a secular, enraged, agnostic narrative of the Fall of Man, and a narrative, therefore, of the coming of universal mediocrity, the bleakness of it all hardly relieved by the persistence of a spiritual aristocracy comprised of a few such as Nietzsche himself, not to speak of latter-day Nietzscheans.

That Hegelian starting-points in Fukuyama's thought should eventually lead to Nietzschean conclusions is a paradox almost too delicious. Upon reflection, though, this upshot seems less surprising since Hegel and even

Kojève are filtered, in Fukuyama's thought, through an intellectual tradition whose own structure was inseparable from that ideological crucible of the 1930s when not only a hatred of communism but deep distrust of liberal democracy itself became quite compelling in sections of the European intelligentsia under pressure from National Socialism. The figure of 'The Last Man', in Fukuyama's configuration, is thus somewhat Janus-faced. Thanks to the coming of liberal democracy, this Last Man, in his Occidental location, has known true liberty, in the form of a universal recognition granted by the liberal state, and, supplementing the satisfactions of socio-political recognition, he has known also the satisfactions that come with consumerist plenitude. He now seeks emancipation not *through* Reason but *from* Reason, not *through* History but *from* History, in the shape of that Dionysian and privatized Freedom which Foucault has more recently called 'regimes of pleasures.' These satisfactions of universal recognition and consumerist plenitude have, however, even within the ultimate self-realization of the Occident, a catch built into them. The dilemma of liberal democracy, the secret even of its eventual self-destruction, is, according to Fukuyama, that any practice of universal equality can only produce a state of universal mediocrity, because mutual 'recognition' of each by all can be universalized only by accepting the lowest possible denominator for what merits equal recognition. The triumph of liberal democracy is thus for Fukuyama an end of history in two quite different senses.

One very strong sense, of course, is that the Occidental states and societies of advanced capitalism are said to be entirely comfortable in their affluence and the liberal order; that they are relieved by the defeat of their adversaries and no longer imagine any other future for themselves; that the triumph of liberal capitalism is, so far as one can see, definitive. But the second sense then immediately follows: this very End of History seems to produce nothing but an infinity of futurelessness, mediocrity, consumerism, a levelling of all distinctions, equalizing of all political wills in the form of universal franchise, a desert-like future of full homogeneity. He cites Leo Strauss's telling interrogation of Kojève: is it really possible to dissolve Hegel's Master-Slave opposition without producing sheer equality and homogeneity? Fukuyama indicates his support of Strauss's position through three key assertions. One, that since equality can only be based on universal mediocrity, what the human will truly wants is a belonging not to universal equality but to a special community of its own, within a complex system of numerous such communities; not the liberal democracy of universal citizenship, but a heterogeneous system of mutually exclusive communities wherein one takes the satisfaction of recognition only by those whom one recognizes as one's peers. Second, quoting Nietzsche's description of the state as 'the coldest of all cold monsters', Fukuyama asserts that there is far greater human satisfaction in membership in an immediate, directly experienced community than in the equal citizenship within a state; 'politics' is thus dissolved into 'society' and 'society' itself into its constituent units, in an infinite play of heterogeneities. So far does Fukuyama go in this direction as to suggest that the authoritarian regimes which have supervised such stupendous capitalist growth in East Asia may well be humanly more satisfying in so far as they rest not on universal equality in the political domain but on integral and mutually discrete communities within the larger capitalist society.

Far from being a purely triumphalist account, thus, Fukuyama's discourse is in fact self-divided between profound allegiance to liberal capitalism and equally strong temptation to reject it in favour of dictatorial regimes; and the discourse is self-divided also between the polarities of a certain Hegelian optimism about the March of History as an unfolding of the Idea of Liberty on the one hand, and, on the other, the overwhelming Nietzschean scepticism about the very conceptions of History and Liberty as possible or even desirable emancipatory collective projects. These contradictory *philosophical* positions he tries to uphold, simultaneously, in view of his own central propositions, which, as it happens, tend to mutually cancel out each other. Ideologically, he is fully committed, in the first instance, to an unrestrained celebration of the free market and its global triumph; in *this* rhetoric, 'free market' is the essence of Liberty as such. At the same time, however, he also declares that the emergence of *consumption* as the primary ground for the exercise of freedom in today's mass capitalist society, whether in the Occident or in East Asia, degrades the Idea of Freedom as such. The Last Man that has been produced at the End of History, thanks to the global triumph of neo-liberal capitalism, is then, by Fukuyama's own account, a mass of humanity beset by mediocrity, authoritarian rule, and voracious appetite for sheer consumption. Thus it is that even the textures and tonalities of his prose oscillate between a neo-liberalist triumphalism and a posthistorical melancholy. This too is logical, since this bureaucrat-philosopher of the American Empire thinks of himself, formally, as a Hegelian, but encounters at the End of History the figure not of Hegel but of Nietzsche.

Now, Fukuyama takes himself to be neither postmodern nor postcolonial. Unlike so many postmoderns and postcolonials, from Derrida to Spivak, he claims for himself no radical, leftwing credentials in the politics of today. Unlike Lyotard, Kristeva, Glucksman and many other 'New Conservatives' of French postmodernity, Fukuyama has no past as a Trotskyist, Maoist or whatever. He has no qualms about the fact that he is, and has always been, a man of the Right and an advocate of neo-liberalist capitalism; much of his life has been spent, after all, between the U.S. State Department and the Rand Corporation. I begin with Fukuyama in this context for somewhat different reasons.

The first of these reasons is, in today's intellectual climate, the hardest to state, namely that I find Fukuyama as a thinker comparatively more substantial and engaging than those, such as Lyotard and Baudrillard, who have provided so much of the jargon of postcolonial theory. This I say despite the fact that Fukuyama strikes me as being, in the final analysis, wrong on virtually every major count. He is right, for instance, though hardly original, in asserting that capitalism is more universally dominant and more securely entrenched today than at any other point in this century; but he is wrong to equate this capitalist triumph with the outbreak of Equality and Universal Recognition. What has been universalized is neither a universal state of the common good, nor an equalized access to goods and services, but integrated markets for the circulation of capital and the expropriation of labour, and, in the cultural domain, universalisation of the ideology of commodity fetishism.

Indeed, if you subtract commodity fetishism, hardly anything remains in the culture of actually existing capitalism that is fundamentally universalistic. Indeed, the history of this capitalism shows that the dissolution of traditional communities and the mobility of populations under capitalist pressures produce not a universal culture of broadly shared human values and radical equalities, but highly malleable processes of decomposition that constantly recompose identities of nation, race, ethnicity, and religious group, not to speak of freshly fashioned claims of tradition and primordiality. One might even speculate that the great intensification of identity politics and of multi-culturalist ideology and policy demonstrates, in some crucial respects, the living reality of how much contemporary capitalism is in the process of giving up on the idea of Universal Equality even in its advanced zones. The modern state even in these zones may well get reorganized as so many islands of ethnic identity supervised by the benign but ever vigilant gaze of the one ethnicity that is so dominant that it need not define itself as ethnicity. Thus, Fukuyama is wrong even on this count: communitarian ideology as a complement of industrial capitalism is by no means an attribute of East Asia alone; it is ascendant within North America itself; meanwhile, the more strident versions of communitarianism are blowing apart legacies of secular civil government in countries as diverse as Algeria, Egypt and India; and yet, the idea of self-governing religious communities as an alternative to secular citizenship in the modern nation-state is gaining ground in that branch of postcolonial theory which calls itself Subaltern Studies, as is clear from the recent writings of its principal figures.[17]

This is a reversal, in fact, of historic proportions. The idea of universal equality was until quite recently the most potent ideological force in the struggles against European imperialism and against the Eurocentric racisms which have been the necessary supplements of that imperialism. Now, Fukuyama of course advises us that it is precisely the aspiration for universal equality that is producing a culture of universal mediocrity, while Lyotard and his postcolonialist followers such as Gyan Prakash, a late entrant in the Subalternist paradigm, have taken to assuring us that the idea of universality is itself Eurocentric and simply one of those metanarratives of Emancipation that have been rendered obsolete by the entry of the world into postmodernity, and that the only refuge from Eurocentricity and racism is to be sought in philosophical and cultural relativism.[18] For all his Hegelian starting-points, Fukuyama's idea that recognition from one's exclusivist community is the only recognition worth having belongs squarely in the postmodernist world of relentless relativism, absolutisation of difference, and refusal to acknowledge that anything other than goods and services could define a horizon of universality or normative value.

Fukuyama thus shares many of the themes and convictions of philosophical postmodernity, especially the ones that are the most valued in postcolonial theory, as, for example, his conviction that the heterogenous is intrinsically superior to values of universality and equality; his wavering but eventual preference for self-referential communities over the integrative projects for creating a modern, democratic and secular state; the Nietzschean tenor of his conclusions about the Modern, etc. Even so, his sustained engagement with Hegel, though mediated through Kojève, still strikes me as being philosophically more arresting; and, in the political domain, he is quite evidently not much worse than the postmodern kinds of American pluralism and pragmatism as represented, for example, by Richard Rorty.[19] Meanwhile, there is something very honest and almost charming about Fukuyama's somewhat belated perception that what he took to be the outbreak of Liberty has produced a human condition fundamentally dehumanized and sordid, so that *his* declaration of the End of History, poised as it is against the narrative of the Fall of Man, appears to be far more ambivalent, bordering almost on the tragic, as compared to the celebratory tones in which Lyotard and his postcolonialist followers speak of the end of all metanarratives. But then, keeping with the temper of the times, Fukuyama's eclecticism quite matches that of the postmoderns; and, just as the typical postcolonial theorist routinely invokes contrary systems of thought to uphold a singular position in something of a philosophical pastiche, Fukuyama too finds it equally plausible to invoke, within a single line of argument, Hegel and Nietzsche together, not only in their generality but with reference precisely to those ideas about History and Reason in which the two are the most opposed.

This extended comment on Fukuyama has seemed necessary because the fact of so substantial a convergence between postmodernity, which purports to be a discourse of the Left, and Fukuyama, who confidently announces himself as a partisan of neo-liberal conservatism, should give us, I believe, some pause. Lyotard's posthistorical euphoria and Fukuyama's posthistorical melancholy are rooted in the shared conviction that the great projects for emancipatory historical change that have punctuated this century have ended in failure. When they speak of this failure, both have in mind, I think, the same three markers – anti-imperialist nationalism; leftwing social democracy; and communism – which Lyotard dismisses contemptuously as mere metanarratives of Reason and Progress, and Fukuyama regards as threats to Occidental civilization itself; what they do share is a sense of immense relief at the defeat. That the defeat of these three projects for positive historical change, these three ways of conceiving the universality of our common needs, has been decisive is, I think, beyond doubt. And, a charitable way of thinking about postmodernism and postcolonialism may well be that the prefix 'post' in these terms not only partakes of a generalised 'post-' condition but contains within it a sense of that ending, even if that sense of endings produces in most of them not a sense of loss but a feeling of euphoria.

What is striking about this euphoria, however, is that while the collapse of those three projects of universal emancipation is celebrated so very inordinately, postmodernity and its postcolonial offshoots hardly ever name that which has triumphed in consequence of those defeats. Even if we grant the word 'metanarrative', it is, I believe, necessary to state that only the metanarratives of Emancipation have met with defeat; the most meta- of all metanarratives of the past three centuries, the creeping annexation of the globe for the dominance of capital over labouring humanity, has met, during these same decades, with stunning success, in a very specific form, namely the form of neo-liberal conservatism. During precisely the period when the great struggles for redistribution of incomes downwards were defeated, the offensives for redistribution of incomes upwards did succeed – and succeeded spectacularly. The defeat of the so-called 'Metanarratives of Emancipation' produces among the postmoderns not mere incredulity towards them, as Lyotard puts it, but also great pleasure; indeed, what was lived as loss, tragedy and disorientation in the aesthetics of Modernity, is lived in the postmodern philosophy and aesthetics as pure pleasure, and perhaps even as a postmodern equivalent of the Kantian Sublime. By contrast, the triumph of the Metanarrative of Universal Subjugation produces in most of the postists no great disturbance. Fukuyama is superior on all counts: he *names* the victor, namely liberal capitalism; he *identifies* openly with that victory, camouflaging nothing; and yet, unlike the postists, he experiences this victory of his own side as if a handful of ashes had been thrust into his mouth. You can't really expect much more from a conservative, when so many radicals grant you so very little.

My main reason for so extended a comment on the basic formation of this 'Post Condition' can now be stated more directly: if philosophical postmodernity is by now at least one of the dominant if not *the* dominant form of Euro-American social and political thought, what is now called 'postcolonial theory' is itself one among many of the contemporary postmodern discursive forms – or, more accurately, a self-reflexive cultural *style* within philosophical postmodernity. Chronologically, of course, the term 'postcolonial' first arose much earlier, during the 1970s, in a wide-ranging political discussion, in which a number of people, from Hamza Alavi to John Saul, had participated, and to which I had myself contributed, in the 1980s, something of a footnote. Details of that discussion need not detain us at present. However, I did recapitulate the main contentions in a recent essay,[20] mainly to show how very different and how much more specific the meaning of this term had been before it was appropriated for literary and cultural studies and was then put to work as a cross-disciplinary postmodern hermeneutic. Participants in that debate had been concerned with, first, a specific temporal moment, namely the wave of decolonisations in the aftermath of the Second World War; second, a specific structure of power, namely the type of state that arose in the newly independent countries; and, third, the theoretical problem of re-conceptu-alising the Marxist theory of the capitalist state with reference not to the state of advanced capital but to the state that arose out of the histories of colonial capital, in the moment of decolonisation. The whole debate was centred, in other words, on a very specific problem of political theory, pertaining to a particular historical conjuncture.

The striking feature of the *culturalist* theory of postcoloniality as it arose more recently, after the Euro-American academy had been worked over by French Poststructuralism, is that it had none of the virtues of that debate but all its defects – and many more besides. The colonial/postcolonial binary is now used as a foundational category not just for certain states in particular countries but for trans-continental, trans-historical making of the world in general. The range of citations may be omitted for now. Suffice it to say simply that as one reads through a variety of postcolonial critics – Bill Ashcroft, Gareth Griffiths, Helen Tiffin, Vera Kutzinski, Sara Suleri Goodyear, Edward Said, Homi Bhabha, Ann McClintock, Gayatri Spivak, and others – the term gets applied to virtually the whole globe, including, notably, the USA, Australia, New Zealand, South Pacific Islands, the states arising out of the collapse of the Soviet Union and Yugoslavia, not to speak of the whole of Asia, Africa and Latin America. In some usages, the term applies to the historical period inaugu-rated, more or less, in 1492; in more outlandish writings, it applies to much older formations, such as the Incas and the China of Imperial dynasties. A number of the critics claim that any resistance to colonialism is always, already postcolonial, so that in these usages postcoloniality envelopes colonialism itself as well as all that comes after it, becoming something of a remorseless universality in which certainly the whole of the modern experience, sometimes the pre- and postmodern experiences as well, appear as some many variants of this universality.

When applied to the *world*, in other words, this remarkably elastic 'postcoloniality' seems to encompass virtually everything. When applied as a designation for theories and critics, however, the same term 'postcolonial' contracts very sharply, and refers to not all theoretical work done today, nor to all critics writing in these postcolonial times, but to a very small number of critics with recognisably shared points of theoretical departure. We thus have a telling discrepancy: immense globalisation of the object of analysis on the one hand, and, on the other, the constitution of a very small academic elite for deciphering that globalised object. This discrepancy leads then to a situation in which at the end of so huge a dispersal, 'postcolonialism' becomes, at least in one version, simply a hermeneutic of reading, a cultural style. As Helen Tiffin would have it:

> postcolonialism too might be characterized as having two archives. The first archive here constructs it as writing (more usually than architecture or painting) grounded in those societies whose subjectivity has been constituted in part by the subordinating power of European colonialism – that is, as writing from countries or regions which were formerly colonies of Europe. The second archive of postcolonialism is intimately related to the first, though not co-extensive with it. Here the postcolonial is conceived of as a set of discursive practices, prominent among which is resistance to colonialism . . .
> Very often it is not something intrinsic to a work of fiction which places it as postmodern or postcolonial, but the way in which the text is discussed.[21]

The way the two terms 'postmodern' and 'postcolonial' get conflated here as virtual synonyms, both constituted as such not by some quality intrinsic to the text but simply by the mode of discussion, is indicative of a much broader postcolonialist procedure. Then, there is the characteristic literary critical habit of construing postcolonialism itself as an 'archive' as well as the typical gesture of treating resistance to colonialism as a 'discursive practice' which is already 'postcolonial.' Gareth Griffith says something similar, in a similarly expansive tone:

> postcoloniality of a text depends not on any simple qualification of theme or subject matter, but on the degree to which it displays postcolonial discursive features. What these features may be is again open to interpretation as are those of any discourse which seeks to constitute itself as discrete, but I might suggest that such concerns as linguistic displacement, physical exile, cross-culturality and authenticity or inauthenticity of experience are among the features which one might identify as characteristically postcolonial.[22]

Now, it is not at all clear to me why the phenomenon of physical exile or the philosophical issue of *authentic experience*, which far exceed the historical experience of colonialism, should be regarded as 'characteristi-

cally postcolonial.' What is nevertheless striking about these later formulations by both Tiffin and Griffiths, who had earlier co-authored with
Ashcroft the founding text of Australian postcoloniality,[23] is that both
regard postcolonialism as a kind of textual hermeneutic. The entire field of
the application of this hermeneutic, regardless of subject matter, *becomes*
postcolonial by virtue of its being read in a certain way; and both Tiffin and
Griffiths regard postcolonialism itself as a specific discourse which nevertheless has neither a specific object nor definable set of non-discursive
features; it is, at any given point, what it *says* it is.

That postcolonial theory is a postmodern hermeneutic Homi Bhabha
has stated with uncharacteristic clarity: 'I have chosen to give poststructuralism a specifically postcolonial provenance.'[24] We may recall also that
the three most influential postcolonial critics – Edward Said, Gayatri
Spivak and Homi Bhabha – derive their respective inspirations, if not
wholesale methodologies, from three quite distinct but more or less equally
influential tendencies in French poststructuralism: Foucauldian Discourse
Analysis, Derridean deconstruction, and Lacanian psychoanalysis. Said of
course has become far more equivocal about Foucauldian invocations since
the writing of *Orientalism*; even so, the mark of their mutual difference,
not in just methodological preference but even in the texture of their
respective prose styles, is precisely that each subscribes to a different
tendency in the arrangements of the postmodern hermeneutic hagiography.

What, then, is postcolonial theory? As a starting-point I would suggest
that to the extent that it is a theory at all, postcolonial theory is marked not
by the specificity of its object, since its object is infinitely dispersed and
indeterminable, but by its hermeneutic procedure, above all as *style*. With
regard to *literary postcoloniality*, then, we could say that the emergence of
postcolonial theory since the late 1980s signifies the dissolution of certain
limited pedagogical objects – such as Third World Literature, Colonial
Discourse, *New* Literatures in English, even Comparative Literature in the
strict sense – and their reconstitution under the signs of cultural and philosophical postmodernities. This involves extending the meaning of
'postcolonialism' to include any and all structures of power and
domination, while, in another direction, also dissolving the difference
between procedures of literary study and methodologies of historical study,
so that Subaltern Studies, whose founder, Ranajit Guha, was quite aptly
described by Edward Said as a poststructuralist,[25] itself gets renamed as,
'Postcolonial Criticism' by one of the younger members of the Group,
Gyan Prakash, who directly invokes the authority of Lyotard, Derrida and
Spivak as he, and others, move to assimilate Subalternism to
Postmodernism and Postcoloniality. This postcolonialist dissolution of the
category difference between History and Literature, although in this case
philosophically much more naive, reminds one nevertheless of Habermas's

telling criticism of Derrida's similar dissolution of the category difference between Literature and Philosophy, which has the effect of expanding the sovereignty of rhetoric over the realm of the logical and greatly privileging the poetic function of language over other cognitive functions.

I just referred to the dissolution of such things as Third World Literature or Colonial Discourse Analysis, and their re-constitution under the sign of postcoloniality. How recent this process is can be gauged from the fact that, while Robert Young's very up-to-the-minute book of 1990 has separate chapters on Said, Spivak and Bhabha, it has no index entry for words like 'postcolonialism', 'postcolonial' etc, even though it does have twelve entries for the term 'third world' and twenty-two for the term 'colonial discourse'.[26] Within a couple of years, however, Arif Dirlik was noting in *Critical Inquiry* that '*Postcolonial* has been entering the lexicon of academic programs in recent years, and over the last two years there have been a number of conferences and symposia inspired by related vocabulary.' He also notes, again quite correctly, that intellectuals hailing from one country, namely India, 'have played a conspicuously prominent role' in the 'formulation and dissemination' of this vocabulary, pointing out that

> *Postcolonial* is the most recent entrant to achieve prominent visibility in the ranks of those 'post' marked words ... claim[ing] as its special provenance the terrain that in an earlier day used to go by the name of the Third World. It is intended, therefore, to achieve an authentic globalisation of cultural discourses by the extension globally of the intellectual concerns and orientations originating at the central sites of Euro-American cultural criticism ... The goal, indeed, is no less than to abolish all distinctions between center and periphery as well as all other 'binarisms' that are allegedly a legacy of colonial(ist) ways of thinking and to reveal societies globally in their complex heterogeneity and contingency.[27]

This formulation of Dirlik reinforces at least three points I have emphasized. That 'postcoloniality' is only the latest of the concepts arising within 'The Post Condition'. That the object is not to produce fresh knowledges about what was until recently called the Third World but to re-structure existing bodies of knowledge into the poststructuralist paradigms and to occupy sites of cultural production outside the Euro-American zones by globalizing concerns and orientations originating at the central sites of Euro-American cultural production. And, that the objective in much of this criticism, notably that of Homi Bhabha, is to dissolve all enduring questions of imperialism and anti-imperialism into an infinite play of heterogeneity and contingency.

This latest turn in cultural criticism is something of a point of culmination in a much longer process, starting in the mid-1970s, which I examined at very great length in my book, *In Theory*. I shall not try to recapitulate that argument here. Suffice it to say merely that my own book of course came much later, but a sense of menace – the sense that postmodernist appropriation of non-European histories and texts would be the inevitable result of postmodernist dominance within the Euro-American academe – had been there much earlier, virtually inscribed in the very making of that dominance, and one of the earliest to read the signs was the Indian feminist scholar, Kumkum Sangari, in her essay 'Politics of the Possible,' published in 1987 but first drafted, judging from the footnotes, three years earlier.[28] Toward the end of that essay, she speaks first of what she calls

> the academised procedures of a peculiarly Western, historically singular, postmodern epistemology that universalizes the self-conscious dissolution of the bourgeois subject, with its now famous characteristic stance of self-irony, across both space and time.

She then goes on:

> postmodernism does have a tendency to universalize its epistemological preoccupations – a tendency that appears even in the work of critics of radical political persuasion. On the one hand, the world contracts into the West; a Eurocentric perspective (for example, the post-Stalinist, anti-teleological, anti-master narrative dismay of Euro-American Marxism) is brought to bear upon 'Third World' cultural products; a 'specialized' scepticism is carried everywhere as cultural paraphernalia and epistemological apparatus, as a way of seeing; and the postmodern problematic becomes the frame through which the cultural products of the rest of the world are seen. On the other hand, the West expands into the World; late capitalism muffles the globe and homogenizes (or threatens to homogenize) all cultural production – but, for some reason, is one 'master narrative' that is seldom dismantled as it needs to be if the differential economic, class, and cultural formation of 'Third World' countries is to be taken into account. The writing that emerges from this position, however critical it may be of colonial discourses, gloomily disempowers the 'nation' as an enabling idea and relocates the impulses of change as everywhere and nowhere...
>
> Further, the crisis of legitimation (of meaning and knowledge systems) becomes a strangely vigorous 'master narrative' in its own right, since it sets out to rework or 'process' the knowledge systems of the world in its own image; the postmodern 'crisis' becomes authoritative because... it is deeply implicated in the structure of institutions. Indeed, it threatens to become just as imperious as bourgeois humanism, which was an ideological maneuver based on a series of affirmations, whereas postmodernism appears to be a maneuver based on a series of negations and self-negations through which the West reconstructs its identity ... Significantly, the disavowal of the objective and instrumental modalities of the social sciences occurs in the academies at a time when usable knowledge is gathered with growing certainty and control by Euro-America through advanced technologies of information retrieval from the rest of the world.

I have quoted at some length because a number of quite powerful ideas are summarised here, even though some phraseology (e.g., 'the West reconstructs its identity') indicates the Saidian moment of their composition. Kumkum Sangari was in any case possibly the first, certainly one of the first, to see how a late capitalist hermeneutic, developed in the metropolitan *zones*, would *necessarily* claim to be a *universal* hermeneutic, treating the whole world as its raw material. This goes, I think, to the very heart of the point I made earlier about the aggrandizements of postcolonial theory as it takes more and more historical epochs, more and more countries and conti-

nents, under its provenance, while it restricts the possibility of producing a
knowledge of this all-encompassing terrain to a prior acceptance of
postmodernist hermeneutic.

The work of Homi Bhabha is a particularly telling example of the way
this kind of hermeneutic tends to appropriate the whole world as its raw
material and yet effaces the issue of historically sedimented differences.
Indeed, the very structure of historical time is effaced in the empty play of
infinite heterogeneities on the one hand, and, on the other hand, the
relentless impulse to present historical conflicts in the terms of a
psychodrama. In the process, a series of slippages take place. The
categories of Freudian psychoanalysis which Lacan reworked on the
linguistic model were in any case intended to grapple with typologies of
psychic disorder on the individual and familial plane; it is doubtful that
they can be so easily transported to the plane of history without concepts
becoming mere metaphors. This problem Bhabha evaporates by offering a
large number of generalizations about two opposing singularities, virtually
manichean in their repetition as abstractions in conflict: the coloniser and
the colonised, each of which appears remarkably free of class, gender,
historical time, geographical location, indeed any historicisation or
individuation whatever. Both of these abstract universals appear as bearers
of identifiable psychic pressures and needs which remain remarkably the
same, everywhere. The colonizer, for example, is said to always be
unnerved by any of the colonised who has in any degree succeeded in
adopting the colonizer's culture. Translated into concrete language, it
would mean that colonizers were not afraid of mass movements resting on
the social basis of a populace very unlike themselves but by the upper
class, well educated intellectual elite that had imbibed European culture.

What historical evidence is there to show any of that? Bhabha is
sublimely indifferent to such questions of factity and historical proof
presumably because history in that mode is an invention of linear time
invented by rationalism, but more immediately because one allegedly
knows from psychoanalysis that the Self is not nearly as unnerved by
absolute Otherness as from that Otherness that has too much of oneself in
it. What is truly unnerving, in other words, is seeing oneself in mimicry
and caricature. That the hybridized colonial intellectual mimics the
coloniser and thereby produces in the coloniser a sense of paranoia is,
according to Bhabha, the central contradiction in the colonial encounter,
which he construes to be basically discursive and psychic in character. The
mimicry that Naipaul represents as a sign of a sense of inferiority on the
part of the colonised, becomes, in Bhabha's words, 'signs of spectacular
resistance.' The possibility that revolutionary anti-colonialism might have
unnerved the colonial power somewhat more than the colonial gentlemen
who had learned to mimic the Europeans, Bhabha shrugs off with

remarkable nonchalance: 'I do not consider the practices and discourses of revolutionary struggle as the other side of "colonial discourse." '[29]

Alongside this particular notion of 'mimicry' as 'spectacular resistance', the other idea that is central to Bhabha's discourse on postcoloniality is that of hybridity, which presents itself as a critique of essentialism, partakes of a carnivalesque collapse and play of identities, and comes under a great many names. In essence, though, it takes two forms: cultural hybridity, and what one might call philosophical and even political hybridity. The basic idea that informs the notion of cultural hybridity is in itself simple enough, namely that the traffic among modern cultures is now so brisk that one can hardly speak of discrete national cultures that are not fundamentally transformed by that traffic. In its generality this idea can only be treated as a truism, since a generalisation of that order cannot in any specific sense be *wrong*. The steps that follow this truism are more problematic, however. At two ends of this same argument, this condition of cultural hybridity is said to be (a) specific to the migrant, more pointedly the migrant *intellectual*, living and working in the Western metropolis; and, at the same time (b) a generalised condition of postmodernity into which all contemporary cultures are now irretrievably ushered. The figure of the migrant, especially the migrant (postcolonial) intellectual residing in the metropolis, comes to signify a universal condition of hybridity and is said to be the Subject of a Truth that individuals living within their national cultures do not possess. Edward Said's term for such Truth-Subjects of postcoloniality is 'cultural amphibians'; Salman Rushdie's treatment of migrancy ('floating upward from history, from memory, from time', as he characterizes it) is likewise invested in this idea of the migrant having a superior understanding of *both* cultures than what more sedentary individuals might understand of their own cultures.[30] By the time we get to Bhabha the celebration of cultural hybridity, as it is available to the migrant intellectual in the metropolis, is accented even further:

> America leads to Africa; the nations of Europe and Asia meet in Australia; the margins of the nation displace the centre ... The great Whitmanesque sensorium of America is exchanged for a Warhol blowup, a Kruger installation, or Mapplethorpe's naked bodies.[31]

In Bhabha's writing the postcolonial who has access to such monumental and global pleasures seems to have a taken-for-grantedness of a male, bourgeois onlooker, not only the lord of all he surveys but also enraptured by his own lordliness. Telling us that 'the truest eye may now belong to the migrant's double vision',[32] we are given also the ideological location from which this 'truest eye' operates: 'I want to take my stand on the shifting margins of cultural displacement – that confounds any profound or 'authentic' sense of a 'national' culture or 'organic' intellectual . . .'[33] Having thus dispensed with Antonio Gramsci – and more generally with the idea that a sense of place, of belonging, of some stable commitment to one's class or gender or nation may be useful for defining one's politics – Bhabha then spells out his own sense of politics:

> The language of critique is effective not because it keeps for ever separate the terms of the master and the slave, the mercantilist and the Marxist, but the extent to which it overcomes the given grounds of opposition and opens up a space of 'translation': a place of hybridity ... This is a sign that history is *happening*, in the pages of theory...[34]

Cultural hybridity ('truest eye') of the migrant intellectual, which is posited as the negation of the 'organic intellectual' as Gramsci conceived of it, is thus conjoined with a philosophical hybridity (Bhabha's own 'language of critique') which likewise confounds the distinction between 'the mercantilist and the Marxist' so that 'history' does indeed become a mere 'happening' – 'in the pages of theory' for the most part. These hybridities, cultural and philosophical, lead then to a certain conception of politics which Bhabha outlines in his essay 'The Postcolonial and the Postmodern: The Question of Agency' where we are again told that 'The individuation of the agent occurs in a moment of displacement'[35] because 'contemporary postcolonial discourses are rooted in specific histories of cultural displacement.'[36] This pairing of hybridity and agential displacement then calls forth a politics of 'contingency' while contingency is defined 'as the defining term of counter-hegemonic strategies'. This elaboration of hybrid, displaced, contingent forms of politics is accomplished with the aid of a great many writers including Ranajit Guha ('Guha's elaborations of rebel consciousness as contradiction are strongly suggestive of agency as the activity of the contingent')[37] and Veena Das. The latter reference should detain us somewhat, since it comes with a direct quotation from Das, greatly approved by Bhabha, which denies that there may be such a thing as an enduring caste consciousness to which one might refer in order to understand any particular caste conflict, of the kind that is so common in present-day India. I therefore quote both Bhabha and Das as she herself is quoted by Bhabha:

> In her excellent essay 'Subaltern as perspective' Das demands a historiography of the subaltern that displaces the paradigm of social action as defined by rational action. She seeks a form of discourse where affective and iterative writing develops its own language... This is the historical movement of hybridity as camouflage, as a contesting, antagonistic agency functioning in the time lag of sign/symbol, which is a space in-between the rules of engagement. It is this theoretical form of political agency I've tried to develop that Das beautifully fleshes out in a historical argument: 'It is the nature of the conflict in which a caste or tribe is locked which may provide the characteristics of the historical moment; to assume that we may know a priori the mentalities of castes and communities is to take an essentialist perspective which the evidence produced in the very volumes of *Subaltern Studies* would not support.'[38]

Setting aside the matter of the 'a priori' (no one has argued in favour of 'a priori' knowledges), the striking feature of Das' perspective is its advocacy that when it comes to caste conflicts each historical moment must be treated as *sui generis* and as carrying within itself its own explanation – unless one is willing to be accused of that dirty thing, 'essentialism'. That any understanding of a particular conflict must *include* an understanding of its particularity is so obvious as to be not worth repeating. What Das is advocating here is not just that obvious point but that the understanding of each conflict be *confined* to the characteristics of that conflict. What she denies radically is that caste mentalities may indeed have historical depth and enduring features *prior* to their eruption in the form of a particular conflict. What is denied, in other words, is that caste is a structural and not merely a contingent feature in the distribution of powers and privileges in Indian society, and that members of particular castes are actual bearers of those earlier histories of power and dispossession, so that the conflicts in which castes get 'locked' (to use Das's own telling word) are inseparable from those histories, no matter how much a particular expression of that enduring conflict may be studied in its uniqueness.

In terms of his own logic, though, Bhabha is right. Das's denial that there might be such a thing as a caste mentality and her assertion that all historical moments are *sui generis* is entirely consistent with Bhabha's own assertion that explanations for human action must be non-rational and that historical agents are constituted in displacement. Such premises preclude, I would argue, the very bases of political action. For, the idea of a collective human agent (e.g., organised groups of the exploited castes fighting for their rights against upper caste privilege) presumes both what Habermas calls communicative rationality as well as the possibility of rational action as such; it presumes, in other words, that agencies are constituted not in flux and displacement but in given historical locations.

However it may look from North America, and whatever 'the truest eye' of the migrant may choose to see, the fact of the matter is that History does not consist of perpetual migration, so that the universality of 'displacement' that Bhabha claims both as the general human condition and the desirable philosophical position is tenable neither as description of the world nor as generalised political possibility. He may wish to erase the distinction between commerce and revolution, between 'the mercantilist and the Marxist', and he is welcome to his preferences; but that hardly amounts to a 'theory' of something called postcoloniality. Most individuals are really not free to fashion themselves anew with each passing day, nor do communities arise out of and fade into the thin air of the infinitely contingent. Among the migrants themselves, only the privileged can live a life of constant mobility and surplus pleasure, between Whitman and Warhol as it were. Most migrants tend to be poor and experience displacement not as cultural plenitude but as torment; what they seek is not displacement but, precisely, a *place* from where they may begin anew, with some sense of a stable future.

This discussion of Bhabha came up in the context of my suggestion that the core of postcolonial theory, as it is enunciated by its principal architects, Bhabha and Spivak in particular, is a major instrument for establishing the hermeneutic authority of the postmodern over cultural materials retrieved from outside the advanced capitalist countries. The realignment of the subalternist paradigm, in the field of historical research, with the core of postcolonial theory, and the immense approval that the paradigm now receives in the United States, is a significant element in this particular globalisation of the postmodern. This I shall now want to illustrate with some observations about Gayatri Spivak's famous – possibly most famous – essay, 'Can the Subaltern Speak?'[39] It is a very long essay, and summarizing it is in any case not my intention. I simply want to trace a certain logic within Spivak's broader purpose.

Spivak begins with a long and spirited criticism of Foucault and Deleuze on the ground that their delineations of the structures of Power are fatally flawed because they treat Europe as a self-enclosed and self-generating entity, by neglecting the central role of imperialism in the very making of Europe, hence of the very structures of Power which are the objects of analyses for such as Foucault and Deleuze. The point is unexceptionable and Spivak argues it with much verve, though in justice it must be said that Said had made precisely that point about Europe a decade earlier, at great length, in *Orientalism*; and that by the time Spivak published her essay in 1988, Said had also criticized Foucault for neglecting the issue both of European imperialism and of the resistances to imperialist power outside Europe. Spivak was right but she was basically extending a well-known argument. The criticism of Foucault and Deleuze was then followed, in another section of the essay, by a considerable discussion of widow immolation, a discussion inspired by Lata Mani's earlier research on what she has called the Colonial Discourse on *Sati*.[40] There are of course several other digressions, on Marx, Freud, First and Third World feminisms, essentialism, Ranajit Guha and so on. It is only after reading over two-thirds of the essay that we begin to sense the real object of the writing – which is as follows.

It may be difficult now to recall that in the mid-80s, when this essay was written, the chief authority of French poststructuralism in the Anglophone countries was not Derrida but Foucault, and claims were often made about how much Foucault helped us understand history and politics. It appears from Spivak's quotations that this praise of Foucault was frequently coupled with some unfavourable reference to Derrida. She quotes Eagleton, Said and Perry Anderson as emphasizing Derrida's lack of engagement with politics. It now transpires that the whole object of

Spivak's own essay is to show that even though Foucault does talk about politics frequently he nevertheless presents arguments that are constitutively flawed, and that although Derrida is usually unconcerned with history or politics his deconstruction nevertheless provides a far superior way of reading into historical and political archives. The discussion of the British colonial ban on widow immolation in the early 19th century is organised, thus, to demonstrate the superiority of the Derridean hermeneutic over the Foucauldian.

The clinching argument comes in the last two pages of the essay, however, where Spivak summarises what little she knows about the suicide of an unmarried Bengali woman during the 1920s, about whom she has heard through, as she puts it, 'family connections.' The evidence is, in other words, non-archival and so little is known of the event that the motive behind the suicide must remain indeterminable; we only know that when she died she was menstruating, which shows that it was not as if she had had illicit sex and killed herself because of having become pregnant. This dead woman, whom Spivak calls 'the suicide text', becomes for her, in the first instance, the final proof of Derrida's insistence on the limits of textuality, on the undecidability of meaning, on how much readers need to be ironically aware of their own role in assignment of final meanings to any text at all. In the second instance, the woman, or rather 'the suicide text,' illustrates for Spivak how the real subaltern can never speak, so that any claims about subaltern consciousness are always a rationalization exceeding what can be known. In the third instance, however, and even though we have no access to the consciousness of this 'suicide text,' the fact that she was menstruating at the time of her suicide shows that she had with her own body inscribed herself as the very opposite of the immolated wife in rituals of *sati*, since menstruating wives are ritually forbidden from immolating themselves. We are then told in a more or less triumphal tone at the end of the essay that this acute understanding of the 'suicide-text' Derridean deconstruction makes possible in a way that Foucauldian discourse theory cannot.

Now, what I find most striking about this essay is the two-way operation of this postcolonialist hermeneutic: on the *one* hand, the deaths of unknown Bengali women who were unable to leave behind them any evidence about their own actions can nevertheless be staged in the language of high theory as evidence to settle a dispute which is internal to high theory, the dispute about the relative merits of Derrida and Foucault; on the *other* hand, the superiority of deconstruction can be established over the 'suicide text' by reading it both as absolute silence and as insurgent inscription. Equally striking, of course, is the fundamental thesis of the essay, namely that the true subaltern is the one who cannot speak for herself and whose history therefore cannot be written. This conclusion about the generalised condition of subalternity is certainly excessive in relation to the evidence produced in the essay, in the sense that most people would not want to draw so extreme a conclusion on the basis of some stray remarks about widow immolation and a brief resumé of a particular suicide. But the issue of the silence of the subaltern and the consequent impossibility of a history of the subaltern gets invoked among the subalternists frequently. So, it might be useful to ask who the subaltern is and how Spivak defines it. Indeed, since the term 'subaltern' comes into contemporary parlance from a Gramscian variety of Marxism and since Spivak identifies herself as a Derridean Marxist feminist, we may want to approach her definition of subalternity through a brief reference to her treatment of a theme familiar in Marxism.

'Imperialism,' Spivak says, 'establishes the universality of the mode of production narrative.'[41] Here we encounter, of course, the astonishing literary-critical habit of seeing all history as a contest between different kinds of narrative, so that imperialism itself gets described not in relation to the universalisation of the capitalist mode as such but in terms of the *narrative* of this mode. Implicit in the formulation, however, is the idea that to speak in terms of modes of production is to speak from within terms set by imperialism and what *it* considers normative. In the next step, then, Spivak would continue to insist on calling herself an 'old-fashioned Marxist' while also dismissing materialist and rationalist accounts of history, in the most contemptuous terms, as 'modes of production narratives'. This habit would also then become a regular feature of the 'subaltern perspective' as Spivak's gesture gets repeated in the writings of Gyan Parkash, Dipesh Chakrabarty and others.

This distancing from the so-called 'modes of production narrative' then means that even when capitalism or imperialism are recognised in the form of an international division of labour, any analysis of this division passes more or less casually over the fully differentiated classes of workers and peasants, and identifies as the truly subaltern only those whom Spivak calls 'the paradigmatic victims of that division, the women of the urban sub-proletariat and of unorganised peasant labour.'[42] It is worth saying, I think, that this resembles no variety of Marxism that one has known, Spivak's claims notwithstanding. For, there is surely no gainsaying the fact that such women of the sub-proletariat and the unorganised peasantry indeed bear much of the burden of the immiseration caused by capitalism and imperialism, but one would want to argue that 'the paradigmatic victims' are far more numerous and would also include, at least, the households of the proletariat and the organised peasantry. Aside from this definitional problem, at least three other moves that Spivak makes are equally significant. First, having defined essential subalternity in this way, she answers her own famous question – Can the Subaltern Speak? – with the proposition that there is no space from where the subaltern (sexed) subject can speak.[43] What it means of course is that women among the urban sub-proletariat and the unorganised peasantry do not assemble their own representations in the official archives and have no control over how they appear in such archives, if they do at all. It is in this sense that the *sati*, the immolated woman, becomes the emblematic figure of subaltern silence and of a self-destruction mandated by patriarchy and imperialism alike. As Spivak puts it: 'The case of *suttee [suti]* as exemplum of the woman-in-imperialism would . . . mark the place of 'disappearance' with something other than silence and non-existence, a violent aporia between subject and object status.'[44]

Now, it is not at all clear to me why the self-immolating woman needs to be regarded as the 'exemplum of the woman-in-imperialism' today any more than such self-immolating women should have been treated in the past by a great many colonialists – and not only colonialists – as representing the very essence of Indian womanhood. Why should the proletarianization of large numbers of poorer women, or the all-India productions of the *bhadramahila*, or the middle class nationalist woman, not be treated as perhaps being at least equally typical of what Spivak calls 'woman-in-imperialism?' Even so, the argument that the essence of female subalternity is that she cannot speak is itself very striking since in this formulation of the situation of the subaltern woman, the question of her subjectivity or her ability to determine her own history hinges crucially not on her ability to resist, or on her ability to make common cause with others in her situation and thus appear in history as collective subject, but on her *representation*, the terms of her appearance in archives, her inability to communicate authoritatively, on one-to-one basis with the research scholar, perhaps in the confines of a library. This is problematic enough. But, then, the implication is that anyone who *can* represent herself, anyone who *can* speak, individually or collectively, is by definition *not* a subaltern – is, within the binary schema of subalternist historiography, inevitably a part of the elite, or, if not already a part of the elite, on her way to getting there.[45] This is of course remarkably similar to the circular logic we find in Foucault, where there is nothing outside Power because whatever assembles a resistance to it is already constituting *itself* as a form of Power. But it also leaves the whole question of subaltern history very much in the lurch. If the hallmark of the true, the *paradigmatic* subaltern is that she cannot speak – that she must always remain an unspoken trace that simply cannot be retrieved in a counter-history – and if it is also true that to speak about her or *on her behalf* when she cannot speak for herself amounts to practising an 'epistemic violence', then how does one write the history of this permanently disappeared?

Spivak seems to offer four answers that run concurrently. First, there seems to be a rejection of narrative history in general, often expressed in the form of much contempt for what gets called empirical and positivist history, even though it remains unclear as to how one could write history without empirical verification; nor is it at all clear just how much of what we know as history is being rejected as 'positivist'; at times, certainly, all that is *not* deconstructionist seems to be categorised as positivist or some such. Second, in the same vein of emphasizing the impossibility of writing the history of the *real* subalterns, Spivak criticises those earlier projects of subalternism, including implicitly such writings of Ranajit Guha as his works on peasant insurgency[46], which sought to recapture or document patterns of subaltern consciousness even in their non-rationalist structures. She criticises such projects on the grounds, precisely, that any claim to have access to subaltern consciousness and to identify its structures is *prima facie* a rationalist claim that is inherently hegemonizing and imperialist. As she puts it, 'the subaltern is necessarily the absolute limit of the place where history is narrativised into logic,'[47] and 'there is no doubt that poststructuralism can really radicalize the old Marxist fetishisation of consciousness.' That scornful phrase, 'old Marxist fetishisation,' on the part of someone who often calls herself an 'old-fashioned Marxist' and whom Robert Young unjustly rebukes for taking too much from 'classical Marxism,' of course takes us back to the Derridean claim that deconstruction is a 'radicalisation' of Marxism and Bourdieu's retort to this Heideggerian 'second-degree strategy.'

Be that as it may. In terms of method, the previous formulation is of course the more arresting, so let me repeat it: 'the subaltern is necessarily the absolute limit of the place where history is narrativised into logic.' The programmatic move of theoretical anti-rationalism is stated here in methodic terms: while the statement appears to be merely anti-Hegelian, what it in effect rejects, in relation to subalternity, is the very possibility of narrative history, with its reliance on some sense of sequence and structure, some sense of cause and effect, some belief that the task of the historian is not simply to presume or speculate but to actually find and document the patterns of existing consciousness among the victims as they actually were, and a dogged belief, also, that no complete narrative shall ever be possible but the archive that the dominant social classes and groups in society have assembled for their own reasons *can* be prised open to assemble a counter-history, 'people's history', a 'history from below'. E. P. Thompson's great historical narratives on the Making of the English Working Class, on patterns of 18th Century English Culture, on the social consequence of industrial clock time for those who were subjected to it, come readily to mind in this context. I don't think it would serve Professor Spivak's purposes to dissociate herself from that tradition altogether, but the actual effect of her deconstructionist intervention in matters of writing the history of the wretched of this earth is to make radically impossible the writing of that kind of social history, whether with reference to the social classes of modern capitalism or in the field of literary analysis.

Such, then, are the burdens of the Post Condition, even for those who may recoil at the Fukuyamaist variant.

NOTES

1. This is the text of a lecture delivered at York University, Toronto, on 27 November 1996. Footnotes and some clarifications have been added for publication.
2. Lutz Niethammer, *Posthistoire: Has History Come to an End?* (London, 1992) [German original, 1989].
3. Francis Fukuyama, 'The End of History?', *The National Interest*, Summer 1989; and F. Fukuyama, *The End of History and the Last Man* (London, 1992). Fukuyama's version is much tamer than Kojève's lectures of the 1930s on Hegel's *Phenomenology*, from which he draws the interpretation of the Master-Slave Dialectic. By the 1950s, Kojève too had come to view the postwar United States as the EndState of equality and liberty, as we shall see.
4. Niethammer is particularly good on this second category of the posthistorical intellectuals. Heidegger hardly ever uses the term but his enthusiastic participation in the Nazi project and subsequent withdrawal into what I have here called 'clericism of Being' is illustrative of the sociological shift from one category to the second. On ambiguities of this episode, Habermas's criticism has never been properly answered, even though the literature on the subject is vast. See his chapter on Heidegger in *The Philosophical Discourse of Modernity* (Cambridge, Mass., translation copyright 1987) and, especially, his later essay 'Work and Weltanschauung: The Heidegger Controversy from a German Perspective', in Jurgen Habermas, *The New Conservatism: Cultural Criticism and the Historians' Debate* (Cambridge, Mass., 1989). See also Pierre Bourdieu's *The Political Ontology of Martin Heidegger* (London, 1991; French original 1988) which deserves to be better known. Both authors are notable for engaging the question of the relationship between Heidegger's thought and his Nazi affiliation in a manner that neither denies nor absolutizes the autonomy of philosophical thought. It needs also to be said that there is hardly anything in Heidegger's later and much overrated writings on the question of technology which is not already prefigured in Spengler's *Man and Technics*, first published in 1931, roughly at the time when Heidegger was strengthening his association with such other conservative thinkers of fascist political orientation as Carl Schmitt and the Junger brothers.
5. See Bourdieu, *op. cit.*, pp. viii, 49, 96.
6. Allan Bloom, Fukuyama's teacher, was an intimate of Leo Strauss and the English editor of Kojève's work on Hegel. See, *Introduction to the Reading of Hegel*, trans. James H. Nicholls Jr. (ed.), Allan Bloom, Ithaca, N.Y. 1969. Strauss, in turn, had been a friend of Kojève's since the 1930s (the two sharing an early admiration for Heidegger) as well as of Carl Schmitt, legal theorist and one-time fascist. When Strauss published his famous work on Tyranny, Kojève responded, on his friend's invitation, with his essay, 'Tyranny and Wisdom' to which too Strauss then replied. For relevant texts of this interlocution, see the edition of *On Tyranny* prepared by Victor Gourevich and Michael Roth (New York, 1991). Kojève declares in that essay that 'of all possible statesmen, it is the tyrant who is incontestably the most apt to receive and apply the advice of the philosopher.' The observation unwittingly offers a curious commentary on the fact that Kojève spent roughly the last two decades of his life as an official of the French government and that Fukuyama, the self-declared disciple of Kojève, works for the Rand Corporation and the U.S. State Department.
7. Derrida reasserts this status of deconstruction as a 'radicalization' of Marxism in his

recent *Spectres of Marx* (London and New York, 1994). But the claim goes back to Heidegger himself. As Bourdieu remarks: 'Of all the manipulative devices in *Letter on Humanism* none could touch the 'distinguished' marxists as effectively as the second-degree strategy consisting in ... talking the language of a 'productive dialogue' with Marxism, the typically Heideggerian strategy of an (artificial) *overcoming through radicalization*' (Bourdieu, *op. cit.*, p. 94; italics and parentheses in the original). For my own brief comment on Derrida's use of this Heideggerian device, see my 'Reconciling Derrida: "Spectres of Marx" and Deconstructive Politics', in *New Left Review*, no. 208, November-December 1994; reprinted in Aijaz Ahmad, *Lineages of the Present* (New Delhi, 1996).

8. Cited in Habermas, *The New Conservatism, op. cit.*, p. 142, from a report that Jaspers submitted in 1945 to the denazification committee established at the University of Freiburg, where Heidegger had served as a rector under the Nazis.

9. After the War, however, a commission of the French Communist Party was to indict Kojève's philosophy for a 'fascistic tendency.'

10. For Kojève's influence on Lacan, see Anthony Wilden, *Language of the Self* (Baltimore, 1968). As Wilden aptly remarks: 'Lacan's early use of the Hegelian notion of desire repeats Kojévian formulas. There are in fact few contemporary readings of Hegel which do not owe a considerable debt to Kojève's commentary, and he himself owes an equal debt to Heidegger ... Although it is sometimes difficult to tell whether it is Kojève, Heidegger or Hegel who is speaking. Lacan's works seem often to allude directly to Kojève' (pp. 193-4). See also the brief excursus on Kojève in Elisabeth Roudinesco, *Jacques Lacan & Co., A History of Psychoanalysis in France 1925-1985* (London, 1990). Remarking on the fact that Kojève's reading of Hegel was so 'original' that it often bore little resemblance with what Hegel had actually written, Roudinesco goes on to say: 'It was not by chance that Lacan discovered in Kojève's discourse the wherewithal to effect a new interpretation of an original body of thought. At Kojève's side he learned how to make Freud's text say what it does not say.' (p. 138)

11. Niethammer refers to Kojève's account of the structures of the modern world as 'blood-thirsty' (p. 91) and Descombes speaks of his 'terrorist conception of history.' See Vincent Descombes, *Modern French Philosophy*, Cambridge, 1980 (French original 1979); p 14.

12. Michael S. Roth, *Knowing and History: The Resurgence of French Hegelianism from the 1930s through the Postwar Period* (Princeton, 1988), p. 102.

13. Cited in Niethammer, p. 67.

14. *Introduction to the Reading of Hegel, op. cit.*, p. 160n, (italics and parentheses in the original).

15. Daniel Singer, 'Be Realistic: Ask for the Impossible.' *Nation* (31 May 1993).

16. The jubilation is itself is in fact characteristically postmodern. Nietzsche himself had a much more grim and ironic sense of it all. As he put it in *Thus Spake Zarathustra*, in the section from which Fukuyama takes part of his title:
'One has one's little pleasures for the day and one's little pleasures for the night: but one has a regard for health.
"We have invented happiness," say the last men, and they blink.'

17. See, for instance, Partha Chatterjee, 'Secularism and Toleration,' *Economic and Political Weekly*, vol. XXIX, no. 28, 9 July 1994. For a critique of a whole range of narrow communitarianisms prevailing in India today, see KumKum Sangari, 'Politics of Diversity: Religious Communities and Multiple Patriarchies,' *Economic and Political Weekly*, Volume XXX, nos 51 & 52, 30 December 1995.

18. Gyan Prakash, 'Postcolonial Criticism and Indian Historiography,' *Social Text*, no 31/32, 1992.

19. For a discussion of the convergence between pragmatism and postmodernity, see Sabina Lovibond, 'Feminism and Postmodernism', *New Left Review*, no. 178 (November-December 1989) and 'Feminism and Pragmatism: A Reply to Richard Rorty', *New Left*

AIJAZ AHMAD 381

Review, no. 193 (May-June 1992).

20. Aijaz Ahmad, 'Postcolonialism: What's In a Name?' in Roman de la Campa, E. Ann Kaplan & Michael Sprinker (eds.), *Late Imperial Culture* (London, 1995).
21. Helen Tiffin, in Ian Adam and Helen Tiffin (eds.), *Past the Last Post* (Calgary, 1990), p. vii.
22. Gareth Griffiths, 'Being there, being There, Kosinsky and Malouf,' in Adam & Tiffin, *ibid.*, p. 154.
23. Bill Ashcroft, Gareth Griffiths and Helen Tiffin, *The Empire Writes Back: Theory and Practice of Postcolonial Literatures* (London, 1989).
24. Homi K. Bhabha, *The Location of Culture* (London, 1994), p. 64.
25. Edward Said, *Culture and Imperialism* (London, 1993), p. 296. In an extraordinary pair of hindsights within a single sentence, Said first describes Guha's book of 1963 as 'archeological and deconstructive,' thus taking in both Foucault and Derrida quite nicely, and then goes on to specify 1826 as the year when the Act of Permanent Settlement was passed.
26. Robert Young, *White Mythologies: Writing History and the West* (London, 1990).
27. Arif Dirlik, 'The Postcolonial Aura: Third World Criticism in the Age of Global Capitalism', *Critical Inquiry*, Winter 1994, p. 329.
28. Kumkum Sangari, 'The Politics of the Possible', *Cultural Critique*, no. 7, Fall 1987.
29. The argument on the next few pages follows closely a section of my essay 'The Politics of Literary Postcoloniality' in *Race & Class*, vol. 36, no. 3, 1995.
30. The quoted phrases here are from Said's essay 'Third World Intellectuals and Metropolitan Culture,' in *Raritan*, Winter 1990; and from Salman Rushdie, *Shame* (New York, Vintage edition, 1984), p. 91.
31. Homi K. Bhabha (ed.), *Nation and Narration* (London, Routledge, 1990), p. 6.
32. Homi Bhabha, *The Location of Culture* (London, Routledge, 1994), p. 5.
33. *Location*, p. 21.
34. *Ibid.*, p. 25.
35. *Ibid.*, p.185.
36. *Ibid.*, p.172.
37. *Ibid.*, p.187.
38. *Ibid.*, pp. 192-3. Das is quoted from R. Guha (ed.), *Subaltern Studies VI* (Delhi, Oxford University Press, 1989).
39. Gayatri Chakravorty Spivak, 'Can the Subaltern Speak?', in Cary Nelson and Lawrence Goldberg (eds.), *Marxism and the Interpretation of Culture* (Chicago, 1988).
40. One among many published versions of this material may be found in *Cultural Critique*, no. 7, Fall 1987.
41. 'Can the Subaltern Speak?', *op. cit.*, p. 298.
42. Gayatri Spivak, 'The Rani of Sirmur,' in Francis Barker *et al* (eds.), *Europe and its Others* (Colchester, 1985).
43. 'Can the Subaltern Speak?', *op. cit.*, p. 308.
44. *Ibid.*, p. 306.
45. As she puts it elsewhere, 'If the subaltern can speak then, thank God, the subaltern is not a subaltern any more.' See Sarah Harasym (ed.), Gayatri Chakravorty Spivak, *The Postcolonial Critic: Interviews, Strategies, Dialogues* (London & New York, 1990); p. 158.
46. Ranajit Guha, *Elementary Aspects of Peasant Insurgency in Colonial India* (Delhi, 1983).
47. Gayatri Charavorty Spivak, *In Other Worlds: Essays in Cultural Politics* (New York & London, 1988), p. 207.